D1256158

German-Jewish History
in Modern Times

VOLUME 3
Integration in Dispute
1871—1918

German-Jewish History in Modern Times

VOLUME 1

Tradition and Enlightenment
1600—1780

VOLUME 2

Emancipation and Acculturation
1780—1871

VOLUME 3

Integration in Dispute
1871—1918

VOLUME 4

Renewal and Destruction
1918—1945

German-Jewish History in Modern Times

Edited by Michael A. Meyer

MICHAEL BRENNER, ASSISTANT EDITOR

VOLUME 3
Integration in Dispute
1871—1918

STEVEN M. LOWENSTEIN

PAUL MENDES-FLOHR

PETER PULZER

MONIKA RICHARZ

A Project of the Leo Baeck Institute

Columbia University Press

NEW YORK

Columbia University Press
Publishers Since 1893
New York   Chichester, West Sussex
Copyright © 1997 Leo Baeck Institute
All rights reserved

The chapters by Monika Richarz were translated from
the German by Carol A. Devore.

Library of Congress Cataloging-in-Publication Data

Deutsch-jüdische Geschichte in der Neuzeit. English.
   German-Jewish history in modern times / edited by Michael A. Meyer and
Michael Brenner, assistant editor.
   p.   cm.
   "A project of the Leo Baeck Institute."
   Includes bibliographical references and index.
   Contents: v. 3, Integration in Dispute: 1871–1918 /
Mordechai Breuer, Michael Graetz; translated by William Templer.
   ISBN 0-231-07476-x
   1. Jews—Germany—History. 2. Judaism—Germany—History. 3. Haskalah—
Germany—History. 4. Germany—Ethnic relations.
   I. Meyer, Michael A. II. Brenner, Michael. III. Breuer, Mordechai, 1918–   . IV.
Graetz, Michael. V. Title.
DS135.G32B48   1996   96-13900
943.'004924—dc20   CIP

Printed in the United States of America
c 10 9 8 7 6 5 4 3 2 1
p 10 9 8 7 6 5 4 3 2 1

Contents

Introduction   Peter Pulzer   1

Chapter 1   Demographic Developments
          Monika Richarz   7
    1. The Jews: A Dwindling Minority?   7
    2. Absorption Through Mixed Marriage and Baptism   13
    3. Foreign-Born Jews in Germany   17
    4. Mobility and Urbanization   23

Chapter 2   Occupational Distribution and Social Structure
          Monika Richarz   35
    1. Occupational Distribution   35
    2. In Commerce and Industry   43
    3. The Educated Elite   54
    4. Social Stratification   60

Chapter 3   Jewish Women in the Family and Public Sphere
          Monika Richarz   68
    1. Family and the Attainment of Middle-Class Status   68
    2. Family and Tradition   78
    3. Women's Education and Employment   85
    4. The Women's Movement   95

Chapter 4   Religious Life
   Steven M. Lowenstein   103
  1. The Landscape of the Jewish Religion in Germany 103
  2. Institutions and Style of the Religious Factions 108
  3. Orthodox Reactions to Minority Status:
    The Secession Controversy   114
  4. Renewed Strife and Strivings Among the
    Religious Parties   117
  5. Trends in Jewish Scholarship   121
  6. The Religious Influence of German Jewry Abroad 123

Chapter 5   The Community
   Steven M. Lowenstein   125
  1. Challenges of Urbanization   127
  2. The Jewish Press   130
  3. The Modernization of Charitable Activity 131
  4. Education   134
  5. The Rise of Nationwide Jewish Organizations 138
  6. Student and Youth Organizations 145
  7. International Ties   150

Chapter 6   Legal Equality and Public Life
   Peter Pulzer   153
  1. State Service: The Half-Open Door 154
  2. Jews and German Nationality   162
  3. Jews and Nationality in the Habsburg Monarchy 168
  4. Jewish Politicians in the Liberal Era 174
  5. Jews as Policy Makers   188
  6. Public and Private Jews   193

Chapter 7   The Return of Old Hatreds
   Peter Pulzer   196
  1. The Impact of 1848 and 1870   197
  2. The Beginnings of a Movement 204

3.   The Habsburg Monarchy   209
4.   The Initial Response   216
5.   The Changing Agenda of Antisemitism   220
6.   The German Antisemitic Parties after 1890   221
7.   Austria: The Triumph of Karl Lueger   225
8.   Jews and Slavs   231
9.   The Domestication of Political Antisemitism   234
10. Antisemitism as an Ideology   237
11. Race in Doctrine and Organization   242
12. Prophets of Race   245

Chapter 8   The Response to Antisemitism
              Peter Pulzer   252
1.   The Counterattack   252
2.   Achievements and Frustrations   263
3.   The New Style of Jewish Politics   267
4.   Escape Routes from Discrimination:
     Capitalism and Socialism   271

Chapter 9   Ideology and Identity
              Steven M. Lowenstein   281
1.   Reorientation of the Mainstream: The Centralverein   282
2.   Self-Rejection and Self-Hatred   287
3.   Zionism: The Jewish National Alternative   290
4.   Zionism and Centralverein: From Peaceful Coexistence
     to Confrontation   299

Chapter 10   Jewish Participation in German Culture
               Steven M. Lowenstein   305
1.   Chronology   308
2.   Cultural Centers: Vienna, Prague, Berlin   311
3.   Literature and Literary Criticism   314
4.   Music and the Visual Arts   322
5.   The Sciences and the Humanities   327

6. Jews as Patrons of Culture   330
7. Explaining Jewish Cultural Creativity   331

Chapter 11   New Trends in Jewish Thought
             Paul Mendes-Flohr   336
      1. The Essence of Judaism Debate   338
      2. Jewish Religiosity Redefined   348
      3. Deutschtum and Judentum   355

Chapter 12   The First World War
             Peter Pulzer   360
      1. The Civic Truce   361
      2. Jews and German War Aims Policy   366
      3. The Crumbling of the Civic Truce   370
      4. The Control of Immigration   378
      5. Toward the Revolution   381

Conclusion Monika Richarz   385

List of Abbreviations   389
Notes   391
Bibliographical Essay   407
Chronology   423
Sources of Illustrations   427
Index   429

Integration in Dispute
1871–1918

Introduction

This volume deals with the situation of the Jews of German-speaking Central Europe under conditions of legal equality. The principle of legal equality was enshrined in a law passed by the Reichstag of the North German Confederation on July 3, 1869, which in a single paragraph declared, "All remaining restrictions in civil and political rights based on differences of religion are hereby abolished." It was not new. The Basic Rights of the German People, adopted by the Frankfurt parliament in 1848, had included a similar declaration in almost identical wording. But with the defeat of the revolutions of 1848 the Basic Rights became a dead letter and similar provisions in the constitutions of the individual German states were widely evaded. Indeed the political institutions of the individual states continued to be important in determining the rights of citizens. The ambiguities of the Prussian constitution, which remained in force unamended until 1918, illustrate this; while article 12 repeated the words of the Frankfurt Basic Rights, article 14 guaranteed the privileged status of the Christian religion "in those state institutions that are connected with the practice of religion." This meant that the practical implementation of civic equality remained a matter of dispute.

The law of 1869 was the culmination of a long drawn-out movement. Several states had already granted complete equal rights, including Hamburg (1860), Baden (1862), and Württemberg (1864). When the German Empire was created in 1871, a federal law extended the 1869 law to the whole of the new *Kaiserreich*. A similar process was under way in the Habsburg Monarchy, which, after the dissolution of the German *Bund* in 1866, lost all formal links with the rest of Germany. The new Austrian Constitution of December 1867 echoed the words of the Basic Rights, as did a Hungarian constitutional law of the same year.

The final acts of emancipation coincided with the transformation of the political landscape of Central Europe. In the Habsburg Monarchy, defeated at the battle of Königgrätz, a Compromise (*Ausgleich*) in 1867 gave Hungary virtual self-government in internal matters, leaving the remaining crownlands as a de facto separate state west of the River Leitha, hence Cisleithania. The German Empire of 1871, which incorporated all German states except Austria, was not a unitary state but an "eternal alliance" of rulers. The imperial government had limited competences; the twenty-five constituent states continued to control all levels of education and most of the judicial system, and therefore employment in the relevant professions. This was of considerable importance to the career prospects of the increasing number of highly qualified Jews. Since the states also controlled religious matters, the legal status of Jewish communities differed considerably. Varying constitutional provisions also affected the opportunities open to Jews in political life. Since Jews, particularly in urban areas, now belonged to the higher income groups, and the municipal franchise favored higher taxpayers, they tended to become more prominent in local than in national politics.

None of these momentous legal and political changes, which revolutionized the situation of the Jewish population of a large part of Europe, happened in a vacuum. The German Empire was Europe's most dynamic economy, but the dynamism had begun before 1871; indeed it was one of the factors that fueled the movement toward national unity. From 1871 to 1910 the population of the empire rose from 41 to 65 million and the proportions living in cities of over one hundred thousand inhabitants doubled. Between 1882 and 1907 the percentage employed in industry and services rose from 50 to 65 at the expense of agriculture. From the foundation of the empire to the outbreak of the First World War real per capita incomes almost doubled. In the Habsburg Monarchy industrialization proceeded more unevenly. Though some crownlands, for example, Bohemia and Lower Austria (which included Vienna), were heavily developed, the majority of the population was still engaged in agriculture in 1900.

It is in this context that changes in the Jewish social structure should be seen. At the time that the German Empire was founded the great transformation of the Jewish population, as recounted in volume 2, was nearing its completion. Germany's Jews had left their marginal status behind; they were now predominantly middle-class, educated, and relatively secularized. Only a few were really rich and there remained pockets of deprivation, mainly in Southern and Eastern Germany. Jewish families became smaller. But for greater life expectancy and immigration from the East, the Jewish population of Germany would have declined absolutely as well as relatively. Nothing illustrated the changed economic status of Jews better than the high levels of taxation at which they were assessed and the steep decline in the rate of emigration. By the end of our period they were not merely an urban but a metropolitan group, over half of them living in cities of more than one hundred thousand inhabitants. Having established themselves economically, Germany's Jews sought increasingly to pursue careers in the liberal professions and intellectual life. In the Western crownlands of Cisleithan Austria, in Bohemia, Moravia, and Vienna, the trends were similar to those in Germany. Further east, in Galicia, where two-thirds of Cisleithan Jews lived, more traditional conditions prevailed. Emigration from Galicia remained a major escape route from great and increasing poverty.

Jewish religious life restabilized itself after the upheavals of the earlier decades of the nineteenth century. In the prosperous and acculturated communities of Central Europe adaptation to modernity became standard. The Orthodox were now a minority of no more than 20 percent, divided into those who seceded from established communities and those who remained inside them. But much of the heat had gone out of the conflicts between modernizers and traditionalists, and by the turn of the century most German-Jewish communities had accommodated themselves to a compromise in liturgical and constitutional matters. In Austria, on the other hand, Orthodoxy retained a stronger hold on the Jewish community, not only in Galicia. Modernization affected the secular activities of communal life, too, particularly in the more rational and bureaucratic organization of welfare, whether for native Jews, immigrants, or the impoverished masses of Eastern Europe. Moreover, all established groupings had to face a new challenge at the beginning of the twentieth century, that of the incipient Zionist movement. The growing integration of Jews into general society meant that religion was increasingly relegated to the private sphere. That in turn meant, in contrast with earlier times, moral and religious instruction and cultivation of the Jewish heritage became, to a larger degree, the province of the wife and mother. But the situation of

Jewish women, at least in the middle class, also yielded to the pressures of modernity as they sought to enter higher education and to qualify for professional work. The rival claims of career ambition and conventionally expected domestic duties contained the potential for severe conflicts. One symptom of these developments was the growth of the Jewish feminist movement.

There was a darker side to this general story of progress and betterment. Discrimination continued in both social and public life. Above all, antisemitism, far from disappearing, as Liberal optimists had expected, revived in both empires and became at times a considerable political force. The need to oppose this development, and to defend civil rights, brought about a resolidarization of Jewish life. A number of organizations, of which the Centralverein deutscher Staatsbürger jüdischen Glaubens (Central Association of German Citizens of the Jewish Faith) was the most influential, institutionalized this trend. As the prospect of total assimilation receded, interest in Jewish history and culture revived, and by the end of our period Jewish society showed an unprecedented organizational density.

Yet Jews did not withdraw from the public sphere. For Jewish scholars, scientists, writers, and artists the late imperial period was a golden age in which they earned worldwide reputations. In many cases their creativity was critical and innovative, which made their newly found prominence even more contested. Our period was also a golden age of specifically Jewish thought—in history, theology, and philosophy, associated with such names as Heinrich Graetz, Moritz Lazarus, Martin Buber, Leo Baeck, and Franz Rosenzweig. By 1914 Jewish life was more varied, and more fragmented ideologically, than it had been in 1870, with Zionism, Socialism, and a return to spiritual Judaism pointing the way to the tendencies of the 1920s. In the headlong rush to modernity that characterized both empires, Jews participated to an exceptional but not unique degree. They seized opportunities and in some crucial instances helped to create them, but they did so as part of a development that embraced the greater part of the German and Cisleithan-Austrian populations. What happened to the Jewish social structure, the Jewish family, and Jewish lifestyles did not go against the grain of general developments, but it did tend to go ahead of them.

The authors of this volume hope that by placing Jewish life in the context of the wider framework of late nineteenth-century Central Europe they have made it easier to understand both the great achievements and the great frustrations of the Jewish populations of that region—the successes and failures of legal emancipation, of social and economic integration, and of entry into the general culture. They hope that they have contributed to a better understanding of the pre-1914 world, an understanding without which the catastrophes of our own time would remain a closed book.

1 | Demographic Developments

1. The Jews: A Dwindling Minority?

Slightly more than a half million Jews lived in the German Empire of 1871. They were a tiny minority, less than 1 percent of the population in 1910. The development of this minority differed from that of the rest of the population in that it showed a greater regional and social mobility. Historically, Jews often had no choice but to become mobile in their search for rights, protection, education, and opportunities for making a living. Even after legal rights were obtained through the Imperial Constitution of 1871, Jews still retained a greater readiness to relocate. They were concerned not only with geographical but also with social mobility, with their further advancement to the status and security of middle-class life despite the confrontation with antisemitism. In the German Empire the majority of Jewish families moved away from rural areas and small towns into larger cities where they limited the number of their children, improving their education, and, along with their economic advancement, adopted the middle-class lifestyle in ever increasing numbers. By the eve of World War I Jews belonged overwhelmingly to the urban middle class, sharing many of its traits. Yet their religious customs and social behavior continued to be determined by Jewish traditions as well, so that they remained a clearly identifiable minority.

The first census conducted in Imperial Germany, in 1871, yielded approximately 41 million inhabitants, including a half million Jews. The following table shows later changes in the absolute and relative size of the Jewish minority:

TABLE 1.1

YEAR	GEN. POP. IN MILLIONS	JEWS	PERCENT
1871	41.06	512,153	1.25
1880	45.23	561,612	1.24
1890	49.42	567,884	1.15
1900	56.32	586,833	1.04
1910	64.92	615,021	0.95

Source: B. Blau, "Die Entwicklung der jüdischen Bevölkerung in Deutchland," 271. (unpublished manuscript at Leo Baeck Institute, New York)

Never were more Jews counted in Germany than in 1910. However, a comparison of percentages clearly shows how much more quickly the general population grew than the Jewish. Whereas the former climbed approximately 58 percent between 1871 and 1910, the Jewish population increased by only about 20 percent. Whereas the general population experienced its greatest natural increase during this period, the Jewish minority grew more on account of immigration. Although immigration had existed earlier and only its greater scope was new, the influx of Jews from the Habsburg Monarchy and czarist Russia increased rapidly after 1880. It was this immigration, mostly of poorer and unassimilated East European Jews, which prevented an even sharper decline in the Jewish population and changed the social profile of German Jewry. Almost 13 percent of all Jews in the German Empire in 1910 were citizens of foreign countries, most having emigrated from the Habsburg Monarchy or czarist Russia.

In the early twentieth century the generally negative Jewish demographic trend drew close attention from Jewish statisticians and sociologists. The Office of Jewish Statistics, founded in Berlin in 1905, published a *Zeitschrift für Demographie und Statistik der Juden* (Journal for Jewish Demographics and Statistics), which regularly analyzed the German censuses with an eye toward Jewish demographics. Arthur Ruppin and Felix Theilhaber published studies in which they portrayed the future situation of the Jewish population in Western Europe as threatened by dissolution and absorption. They regarded the number of mixed marriages, which had increased rapidly, as the most imminent danger. As a Zionist, Ruppin viewed the founding of a Jewish national state as the proper solution to this problem. Felix Theilhaber, in his work *Der Untergang der deutschen Juden* (The Decline of the German Jews), which appeared in 1911, advocated initiatives to raise the birthrate in the Jewish communities. He did not refrain from strong moral criticism of his fellow Jews and reproached them for egoism, a declining sense of family, and indifference toward Judaism.

The situation was different in Austria, where a much smaller number of Jews had attained middle-class status and where, from the time of their annexation as a result of the divisions of Poland, the Jews of Galicia constituted an inexhaustible population reserve. Not counting Hungary, there were over 1.3 million Jews in the Habsburg Monarchy in 1910, living mainly in the states of Lower Austria, Bohemia, Moravia, Silesia, Galicia, and Bukovina. Their distribution was very uneven, with two-thirds of the Austrian Jews still located in Galicia in 1910. The living conditions of many Galician Jews, who had only minimal opportunities for making a living, were characterized by hunger and extreme poverty. Thus they left Galicia in a steady stream, primarily emigrating overseas. But they also went to other parts of the Habsburg Monarchy, above all to Vienna, and some reached the German Empire. In the last decade of the nineteenth century alone more than one hundred thousand Jews left Galicia. An emigration movement also occurred in Bohemia and Moravia, where Jews had been suffering under an economic boycott. Since the population increase of the Galician Jews was extremely high, it could offset the emigration losses to Austria as a whole. The following table shows population trends in Austria and several of its states, among which Lower Austria reflects, above all, the strong growth of the Viennese Jewish population.

TABLE 1.2

YEAR	AUSTRIA	LOWER AUSTRIA	BOHEMIA	MORAVIA	GALICIA
1880	1,005,394	95,058	94,449	44,175	686,598
1890	1,143,305	128,729	94,479	45,324	772,213
1900	1,224,899	157,278	92,745	44,255	811,371
1910	1,313,698	184,779	85,826	41,158	871,906

Source: *Zeitschrift für Demographie und Statistik der Juden*, 10(1912):149.

According to these figures the Jewish population in the Austrian part of the Habsburg Monarchy grew from 1 million to 1.3 million within a span of thirty years. This growth almost corresponds to that of the general population since the percentage of the Jewish population decreased only slightly, from 4.8 to 4.6 percent of Austria's inhabitants. In 1910, in individual parts of the country, Jews comprised a much higher percentage of the population: in Bukovina it was almost 13 percent, in Galicia almost 11 percent of the inhabitants. The percentage of Jews in Austria in 1910 was more than four and one-half times greater than it was in the German Empire.

In Germany it was primarily the conspicuous decline in fertility that caused the relative decrease in the Jewish population. In Prussia, where almost two-thirds of all German Jews lived, Jewish families still had an average of 4.3 children at the beginning of the *Kaiserreich*, but by the first decade of the twentieth century the figure was down to 2.4 children per family. Within the German Empire the birthrate stood at 33 per 1,000 inhabitants in 1908, while among Jews it was only 17 per 1,000, or about half as many as in the general population. This rapid demographic transformation that came about through urbanization and the attainment of middle-class status was indeed quite alarming, but it was masked by a rising life expectancy. In the large cities the number of Jewish births decreased earlier and also more quickly. In Vienna during the first decade of the twentieth century, for example, the number of Jewish births fell by about 29 percent, while the number of all births dropped only about 22 percent. Only those Jews who had immigrated from the traditional milieu of Galicia still evidenced a high fertility rate. In Munich the East European Jewish families who had immigrated made up a third of the Jewish community in 1900 but produced 70 percent of all its children.

The direct cause for the declining urban fertility can be found mainly in the increased use of birth control, especially among middle-class urban Jews. In practice the religious commandment to bear children had been dispensed with in favor of the optimal rearing and education of only two or three children whose education and clothing required considerable expense. In 1911 Theilhaber writes the following about how common family planning was: "Today, the number of children a couple wants is determined almost before the marriage takes place. . . . The artificial manner of limiting the number of children is well known today in all circles whose members have a sense for the practical side of life, and not least among the Jews."[1]

The reduction in the number of marriages between Jews also contributed to the decrease in the number of children. Since expectations for the bride's dowry and for the bridegroom's occupational status had risen in the process of reaching the middle class, some marriages simply did not take place. The marital age remained unchanged: for women it was on the average 25 years, the same as in the Christian population; for men, it was, at 30 years, higher than among the majority. At the beginning of the century, there were 8.1 marriages per 1,000 inhabitants yearly in the German Empire, while only 6.5 new marriages took place among Jews. The increasingly high proportion of elderly German Jews also played a role here, of course, as well as the fact that more and more Jews, primarily men, were entering wedlock with a Christian partner, so that their marriage was not reflected in the Jewish statistics. The number of single people increased, among women in particular, since marriage was no longer viewed as an absolute requirement on religious grounds; and, beginning at the turn of the century, more occupational opportunities were open to women, enabling them to earn their own living.

Because of the greater social control in an endogamous minority and because most Jews belonged to the middle class, the proportion of illegitimate births among Jews was considerably lower than in the general population, although it did show a definite increase during the Kaiserreich. For example, in Frankfurt am Main during the period of 1880–1889 the proportion was 2.2 percent (10.6 percent among Christians), but during the period 1900–1913 it had already reached 5.3 percent (as opposed to 13.5 percent for Christians). This trend runs parallel to increasing urbanization and the growth of a lower social class that came about through the immigration of foreign Jews. In Prussia the percentage of illegitimate births for Jews during the period 1900–1915 stood at 5 percent, while a maximum of 10 percent was reached in Berlin. Measures for seeing to the welfare of these illegitimate children so that they, too, would remain Jewish began only very slowly.

Almost as great a threat to population growth as the decrease in live births was the rapid increase in mixed marriages, since most of the children from these marriages were lost to Judaism, as we shall see. In the first decade of this century approximately 10 percent of Jews were already marrying Christian partners, a trend that would increase considerably thereafter. Another contributing factor to the reduction of the Jewish population during the period of the German Empire was the emigration of at least seventy thousand to eighty thousand Jews. The emigrants were mainly young men who, in departing, lowered the potential birthrate and raised the average age of the Jewish minority.

Jewish immigration was the most important factor that offset the numerous negative influences. More than seventy-eight thousand non-

German Jews were counted in the Kaiserreich in 1910, so that we can assume the immigration more than compensated for the emigration. Along with this positive migration balance the higher Jewish life expectancy had a favorable effect on the population figures as well. Traditionally, Jews had an above-average life expectancy, largely because of a lower infant mortality rate and better medical care in the Jewish communities. When they attained middle-class status life expectancy rose even higher. At the beginning of the twentieth century in Prussia, for example, nineteen Christians per one thousand people died annually in comparison to only thirteen Jews. From the turn of the century onward, this lower Jewish mortality rate significantly raised the average Jewish age. The disproportionate number of elderly in the Jewish population, in turn, caused further decline in the birthrate, so that, after 1910, births no longer exceeded deaths. Corresponding to this trend was a change in the age distribution of the Jewish population: there were more and more elderly and fewer and fewer children. In the Grand Duchy of Hesse at the beginning of the twentieth century, for example, Jews had 22 percent fewer children under the age of fifteen than the general population. On the other hand, there were 32 percent more Jews who were over the age of fifty. For a Jewish population extremely influenced by social factors, such a population distribution could only lead to a negative demographic prognosis.

The fact that even after emancipation there was a fairly significant emigration of Jews overseas has long been ignored. If before the foundation of the German Empire emigration to America served simultaneously as an alternative to the lack of emancipation and as an expression of striving for economic and social advancement, the question remains as to why Jews continued to emigrate from the Kaiserreich even though their legal and economic situation had decisively improved. The emigration overseas of Germans in general reached its peak during the German Empire. In the period 1880–1893 alone more than 1.5 million Germans left the empire, mainly for the United States. However, the highest point in Jewish emigration had occurred prior to 1871 for the reasons indicated. It was now a matter of additional family members joining their families and of emigration from regions of the empire that presented unfavorable conditions for Jews. The more than one hundred thousand German Jews who had gone to America between 1840 and 1870 were now well enough established that they could help younger family members emigrate, bring parents to live with them, look for brides in their homeland, or make it possible for friends to join them as business partners. Those who emigrated under these circumstances did not face an uncertain future; instead, a secure family life and occupational opportunities awaited them. In the case of these emigrants, then, the dominant motive was more the expectation of a better life than the burden of their previous existence.

Yet the traditional motivation for emigration, flight from adverse living conditions in the former homeland, continued to exist as well. In the German Empire this factor applied primarily to Jews who left Alsace and the provinces of Posen and West Prussia. The annexation of Alsace by the German Empire had contributed greatly to emigration from the region, mainly to France and overseas. The mandatory three-year military service in the Prussian army was despised, and the fear of a new war over Alsace-Lorraine increased the desire to emigrate.

The province of Posen, where in the middle of the nineteenth century 40 percent of all Prussian Jews still lived, saw an even larger emigration. By 1871 this proportion had already shrunk to 19 percent and it dropped rapidly to just 7.5 percent by 1905. Of the more than forty thousand Jews who left the province by 1905, only a portion went to Berlin or the rest of the German Empire while many emigrated to England and the United States. The reason for leaving Posen was that their position between the German minority and the Polish majority put the Jews under extreme political and economic pressure, a situation reflected in the partial boycott of their shops. Also, more than half the Jewish population migrated from the predominantly agricultural province of West Prussia, some of them leaving the Kaiserreich entirely. Jews living in the provinces of Posen and West Prussia were relatively the poorest in the empire and so could only gain by emigrating. In economic terms their emigration also produced a positive result since it diminished competition among Jews, mainly in small businesses, and further reduced the size of the lower class.

2. Absorption Through Mixed Marriage and Baptism

Endogamy, or in-group marriage, had sustained and preserved Judaism over the centuries. For religious reasons Jews had always strictly refrained from marriages with partners who did not convert to Judaism. Endogamy was the strongest means of preserving Jewish identity and even during the nineteenth century served as the most important barrier to the dissolution of Judaism. Even many Jews who no longer defined themselves as religious avoided mixed marriages because they affirmed the preservation of the Jews as a sociocultural group connected by a long tradition. That Jews who were indifferent to religion still mainly married other Jews may also be an indication of the continuing social division between Jewish and Christian society.

The Christian churches had traditionally forbidden mixed marriages, and, with the exception of Hamburg, they were still illegal even after Jewish emancipation. Not until civil marriage had been established in the German Empire in 1875 did the situation change decisively, since marriages between Jews and Christians now became possible without religious conversion. During the first five years after civil marriage was introduced in Prussia almost twelve hundred Jews married non-Jewish partners. At the time of the First World War over one thousand Jews per year in Prussia entered into a mixed marriage. The following table shows the rapid increase in the number of mixed marriages and indicates the percentage of Prussian Jews who took non-Jews as marital partners:

TABLE 1.3

1876–1880	4.4 %
1886–1890	9.4 %
1896–1900	8.9 %
1906–1910	13.2 %
1916–1920	20.8 %

In Imperial Germany as a whole the percentage of marriages with non-Jews was not significantly lower and had reached 19 percent just before World War I. The period of time that showed the greatest increase in mixed marriages was thus before and during the war. However, the value of these statistics is limited since they do not include marriages in which a spouse had converted. It is possible that before 1900 more conversions took place for the purpose of marriage, whereas later such conversions were more often avoided. Between the years 1911 and 1915 22 percent of Jewish men and 14 percent of Jewish women entered into a mixed marriage. This difference between the sexes may likewise have been influenced by the fact that more women than men converted to the partner's religion before the marriage. In Austria, where marriages between Jews and Christians were still not permitted, the only possibilities were either conversion or one of the marital candidates dissociating themselves from their religious community.

The frequency of mixed marriages varied considerably from region to region. In the rural areas, where Jews lived more traditional lives and social control was stronger, far fewer marriages between Jews and Christians took place than in the cities. Also, the old social boundaries between Jews and peasants in the villages were more completely preserved than those between the Jewish and Christian middle classes in the cities, where the rate of mixed marriages was therefore at its highest. In Berlin, from 1911 through 1921, 22 percent of all Jews entered into marriages with Christians. That percentage was exceeded only in Hamburg where the rate of mixed marriages had already reached 24 percent and would climb to 39 percent by 1933. In the larger Jewish communities mixed marriage had become a common occurrence.

This rapidly growing phenomenon caused a great deal of concern in the Jewish public sphere because, in the long term, mixed marriages threatened the continuation of the Jewish community. The fertility of these marriages was considerably lower than in Jewish marriages, and fewer than 25 percent of the children born into them were raised as Jews. That meant the biological absorption of the Jewish minority by the dominant society had begun. The diminution of cultural and social barriers, increasing religious indifference, and the growing fear of an expanding antisemitism all contributed to this result.

The same direction is evident in the higher number of baptisms and withdrawals from the Jewish community. In Prussia it had been legally possible to withdraw from the organized community since 1873, even without conversion to Christianity. Beginning around the middle of the nineteenth century baptisms declined, but both withdrawals and baptisms increased markedly after 1880. Here the pressure exerted by antisemitism on those who were often religiously alienated from Judaism clearly played an important role. Even when Jewish parents did not themselves convert, it was not unusual for them to have their children baptized immediately after birth so that they would be spared "difficulties." The more Jews aspired to professions requiring a university degree, the greater the number of baptisms for the purpose of furthering careers that continued to be virtually inaccessible to Jews who refused them. Where the religious and social ties to Judaism had loosened, the temptation was great to abandon a group that was subject to discrimination.

It has been estimated that approximately 11,000 Jews underwent baptism in Germany between 1800 and 1870. During the following thirty years roughly the same number converted. Exact statistical information exists only for conversions to Protestantism in the Kaiserreich. According to those figures, 16,479 Jews converted to the Protestant Church between

1880 and 1919. Since generally less than a third of all converts chose Catholicism, it can be assumed that altogether about 25,000 Jews chose baptism. In a population of more than a half million Jews, this is a far less significant percentage than for mixed marriages. In addition to the Jews who converted to Christianity there was a growing number of dissidents, particularly in Berlin, who left Judaism but did not convert to another religion. Jewish Social Democrats usually chose this form as a way of severing ties with all religion.

In relation to the total number of Jews, the number who withdrew from Judaism cannot be seen as alarming. However, its increase can again be related to the rise of antisemitism. The willingness to renounce Jewish affiliation depended both on the individual's degree of assimilation and on the extent of political pressure, the latter particularly evident in certain occupational groups.

Those who left the Jewish community are specifically differentiable by occupation, gender, and age. In Berlin, three-quarters of those rejecting Judaism were males under the age of forty. Since women rarely pursued professional careers and left Judaism only in connection with a planned or existing marriage, they accounted for only a fourth of those who withdrew. Of the men in Berlin who left the community, 12 percent were doctors and 11 percent lawyers. Altogether, students and university graduates comprised 36 percent of those who left Judaism, while 43 percent were merchants. That meant that among the groups who left Judaism students and university graduates were overrepresented tenfold. The pressure for baptism was greatest among those university graduates who intended to pursue an academic career. Nowhere was there as high a proportion of baptized Jews as among the university lecturers and professors. In the German Empire it was extremely rare for a practicing Jew to receive appointment to a full professorship.

More Jews converted in Vienna than in any other European city, while in the other parts of Austria the number of baptisms remained quite low. Vienna was a city that attracted numerous Jews who had already assimilated to a high degree, especially those coming from Prague and Budapest. Others arrived to further their careers even at the price of baptism. The Austrian royal capital was home for a wealthy Jewish upper class and an extensive Jewish intelligentsia, many of them severely estranged from Judaism. At the same time, Vienna was becoming more and more the center of a militant and influential antisemitism, creating strong pressure on Jews and inducing a growing number, including many prominent personalities in the city's cultural life, to avoid the problem by choosing baptism. Yet precisely in Vienna it became evident early on that in the face of racial antisemitism conversion to Christianity had only the most limited social value. On account of their origins the converts continued to be perceived as Jewish by others around them and even by themselves. They continued to live in Jewish neighborhoods and mingled socially with Jews or with other converts. Social acceptance and absorption often proved impossible in a society in which antisemitism had become an integral element. In this atmosphere a few who had abandoned Judaism rediscovered it for themselves as possessing positive value.

In Vienna, too, it was predominantly young men who decided on baptism, mainly for the sake of their professional careers. Between 1870 and 1910 41 percent of them were university graduates and students, another 11 percent civil servants. The previously mentioned prohibition of mixed marriages in Austria increased the number of baptisms. Women who converted came mostly from the lower middle class and the bottom social rung, apparently undergoing baptism in conjunction with a planned marriage—which, of course, applied to some of the men as well. The number of baptisms rose sharply after the turn of the century, so that in Vienna there were now between five hundred and seven hundred conversions each year. These figures are approximately four times higher than for the contemporary Jewish community in Berlin, which was only slightly smaller. However, the number of those embracing Judaism also climbed in Vienna, up to two hundred individuals per year. To some degree this can be attributed to the conversion of Christian women before marrying a Jew but also in part to those who chose to return to Judaism.

The extent of baptisms in Austria, as in Germany, has generally been overestimated due to a disproportionate number of socially prominent persons who converted. Much higher was the proportion of Jews who, like Sigmund Freud, distanced themselves from Judaism as a religion but did not abandon it, either because they wanted to maintain solidarity with their group of origin or because they had formed a secular Jewish identity.

3. Foreign-Born Jews in Germany

The majority of European Jewry lived east of the German Empire in the territory of the Habsburg dual monarchy and in czarist Russia. Along with Prussia both states had participated in the division of Poland that resulted in the threefold division of the large mass of Polish Jewry. The

1 Members of the Bremen committee of the Hilfsverein der deutschen
Juden taste a meal prepared for East European Jewish transmigrants going
to America (1905)

immigration of Jews across the eastern border of Germany was neither a
new nor an uncommon occurrence. For centuries this incursion from the
East had been part of the history of the German Jews, repeatedly renew-
ing their community both biologically and intellectually. Those who came
were merchants, peddlers, beggars, rabbis, and students—thousands of
Jews who took flight from the pogroms and economic hardships, who were
looking for work, or who sought contact with Western culture. However,
never had as many of them crossed the eastern border of the empire as tra-
versed it during the mass exodus from Eastern Europe between 1880 and
World War I. About three million Jews left Eastern Europe in a flood of
refugees that was triggered and reinforced by the recurrent pogroms in
czarist Russia. Two and one-half million Jews set out from Russia; more
than four hundred thousand left other areas in Eastern Europe, primarily
Galicia and Romania, to a lesser extent also Bohemia, Moravia, and
Hungary. Most of these Jews were without resources and set all their
hopes for a better life on America. As they were often on their way to the
overseas ports of Hamburg and Bremen, their path took many of them
through the German Empire, where a few managed to remain.

    This large-scale migration met with resistance in Germany and with
antisemitic agitation directed against the *Ostjuden*, as these "Eastern

Jews" were called. The German Empire, however, could neither completely control its eastern border nor, on account of existing trade agreements, deny entrance to citizens of Russia and Austria. Moreover, it was in the interest of the German shipping industry not to refuse passage through Germany to some two million Jewish transmigrants. Most of the Jewish emigrants left Europe on ships belonging either to the Hamburg-based Hamburg-America Line (HAPAG) or to the North German Lloyd that was based in Bremen. Between 1904 and 1914 alone more than one hundred thousand Jews embarked annually from Hamburg. Although they mainly traveled in steerage, transporting them, along with the German emigrants, was a significant economic enterprise. Under its Jewish director, Albert Ballin, HAPAG became the biggest shipping line in Europe.

When cholera broke out in Hamburg in 1892 and claimed more than eight thousand lives in that port city, the Jewish emigrants were immediately blamed for introducing the epidemic. Controls were tightened on the emigrants so that they could cross Germany only in closed transports. At the eastern border, HAPAG and Lloyd built stations where emigrants had to show their tickets for ship's passage and where they were disinfected and quarantined. In Hamburg the Jewish emigrants were required to stay in specially built emigration halls located at the port where kosher food and a synagogue were available to them. Contact between those emigrants and the German populace ceased almost completely, while German Jews continued to play a relief role through railroad station committees and by taking care of religious needs in the ports of embarkation.

Antisemitic agitators exploited the transmigration of East European Jews to foment panic. They perceived Germany to be threatened by a flood of Ostjuden—by freeloaders, filth, and epidemics. In fact, the number of non-German Jews who remained in Germany was small when compared to the millions of transmigrants—in 1900 they only numbered forty-one thousand people. Most of these did not intend to remain long in Germany. Some stayed only a short time before continuing on to America or Western Europe; others came to study at German universities. For those who intended to stay indefinitely, achieving their goal was made as difficult as possible. They received only temporary work and housing permits, and they could be deported as "undesirable elements" as soon as the permits expired.

The majority of the foreign Jews came into Germany across the Prussian border, and many went directly to Berlin. As a result, the Prussian government pursued a deliberate policy of expulsion aimed at frightening off the immigrants. In Berlin, after the massive pogrom in Russia in 1881–1882 and again in 1905 after the Russian Revolution, a total of more than five thousand Russian Jews was expelled. The largest deportation of Jews from Prussia took place in 1885–1887, when, by order of the minister of the interior acting on behalf of the imperial chancellor, the government expelled approximately ten thousand Jews along with about twenty thousand Poles.

The only way for foreign-born Jews to live with some security in Germany was by attaining naturalization. In the empire the various constituent states made their own decisions on matters pertaining to German citizenship, which resulted in policies that varied but were usually restrictive. In Prussia naturalization became virtually impossible in 1880 when the Prussian minister of the interior began repeatedly warning his lower officials against naturalizing Russian, Polish, Romanian, and Galician Jews. Exceptions were made only when it was in the public interest. For the most part, even the children of foreign-born Jews, who were themselves born in Germany, could not become citizens at all or only with great difficulty. In 1910 the proportion of Jews in Berlin who were naturalized amounted to only 11 percent of the immigrants.

In spite of the insecure legal status and periodic expulsions, the number of foreign Jews increased in the empire, as indicated by data first collected in the census of 1890. The following table gives the number of foreign Jews who settled in the German Empire, in Prussia, and in Saxony in the period 1880–1910 (the numbers for 1880 are estimates) and their respective percentage of the total Jewish population:

TABLE 1.4

	1880	%	1890	%	1900	%	1910	%
Reich	15,000	2.7	22,000	3.9	41,113	7.0	78,746	12.8
Prussia	10,000	2.7	11,390	3.1	21,800	5.6	48,166	11.6
Saxony	1,000	15.3	2,800	29.9	5,637	54.5	10,378	59.0

Source: S. Adler-Rudel, *Ostjuden in Deutschland*, 164.

Thus, in 1910, foreign-born Jews made up almost 13 percent of all Jews living in Germany. At the beginning of World War I there were approximately 90,000 Jewish foreigners in the empire. Then, during the war, some 30,000 more Jews from the territories occupied by Germany were either recruited or forced to work in Germany while additional Jewish war refugees crossed the border. Although exact figures are not available, we can surmise that as the war neared its end there were some 150,000 foreign-born Jews living in the empire. Of these many later emigrated. Most of the foreign-born Jews lived in Prussia, Saxony, and Bavaria, which were all accessible directly across the empire's eastern border. In Saxony they even made up more than half of all Jewish inhabitants.

These new immigrants settled almost exclusively in the larger cities, since that was where they found not only the best economic opportunities but also relatives and others from their home communities who supported them. The following overview lists the ten cities with the highest number of foreign-born Jews in 1910 and also indicates their percentile share of the Jewish communities in that locality:

TABLE 1.5

Berlin	18,694	20.8 %	Dresden	1,948	52.2 %
Leipzig	6,406	64.8	Cologne	1,672	13.5
Munich	3,857	34.8	Breslau	1,455	7.2
Frankfurt a.M	3,541	13.5	Nuremberg	1,226	15.7
Hamburg	3,111	16.4	Königsberg	1,169	25.6

Source: J. Wertheimer, "Appendix," *Unwelcome Strangers*, table 2b.

In these cities, which had the largest Jewish communities in the empire, immigrants could hope to get help in case of need. It was just this combination of large cities and large Jewish communities that held the most promise for the immigrants. More Jews would surely have settled in the communities of Breslau and Königsberg, which were situated on the border where the trade with Eastern Europe played a large economic role, were it not that the politics of expulsion was implemented the most stringently in those cities.

The Jewish immigrants by no means formed a homogeneous group. They came from different countries, from various layers of society, from orthodox milieux (often hasidic), and from secular, frequently socialist ones. Among them, as well, were intellectuals with a highly Western orientation and artists from an education-conscious middle class who came to Germany from Prague, Vienna, Budapest, and St. Petersburg. There were also merchants who engaged in international business, common artisans, students, and the very poor petty traders. The majority of immigrants were hardly people of wealth, but it seems that those with no means whatsoever were more likely to emigrate overseas.

The majority of the Jewish foreigners in the empire came from the

Habsburg Monarchy, although more Jews, in general, emigrated from czarist Russia. Most of the Austrian Jews in Germany were from Galicia, but they came, as well, from Bohemia, Moravia, and Bukovina, and young Viennese Jews set out for Berlin to pursue careers. The following table provides an overview of the countries of origin of the most significant groups of Jewish immigrants:

TABLE 1.6

	FOREIGN BORN JEWS IN THE EMPIRE	FROM AUSTRIA	FROM RUSSIA	FROM HUNGARY	FROM RUMANIA
1890	22,000	8,803	9,897	1,688	—
1900	41,113	17,410	12,752	3,340	858
1910	78,746	41,512	21,644	5,475	1,509

Source: J. Wertheimer, "Appendix," *Unwelcome Strangers*, table 3b.

The above-mentioned recruitment and compulsory enlistment of Jewish workers from the occupied part of Russia during the world war very rapidly caused the Russian Jews in the Reich to outnumber those from Austria. This was particularly the case after the war began, when Austrian Jews were drafted into the army of the Austro-Hungarian Empire. The Russian and Galician immigrants remained socially apart, as we know from Berlin where the groups tended to settle separately from each other rather than together.

Like every immigrant population, the Jewish foreigners also differed from the German Jews demographically. On the average, immigrants were younger and predominantly men and bachelors, especially at first. The Russian immigrants tended to be young because they often left their country illegally when they reached draft age; others came with young families. All were striving to build a new life. Both the number of marriages and the number of children per family were considerably higher among foreign-born Jews. As we have seen, the birth rate of the German Jews had dropped sharply. The immigrants, however, came from areas in which fertility remained considerably higher. In Berlin in 1910, for example, German-Jewish women had 1.2 children under the age of 15 while the immigrant women had 2.9 children. Clear differences like these diminished, however, when the immigrants remained for a longer time in the country and very rapidly assimilated. Nonetheless, the immigrants had a rejuvenating and vitalizing influence on the German Jews.

Those foreign Jews who stayed clearly strove for acculturation and social advancement. They affirmed integration because they had brought along with them a very positive image of the superiority of German culture. They learned German quickly and sent their children to the best available schools. By the second generation, at the latest, they were absorbed into German Jewry, like so many Polish and Russian Jews before them. The stereotype of the East European Jew, which was very widespread among the German Jews, prevented their acceptance as a group, but, if they had attained middle-class status, they were accepted on an individual basis. The arrogance of many German Jews and their low opinion of the immigrants was linked to the fear of antisemitic attacks that would not differentiate between German and non-German Jews, thus threatening the middle-class life they had attained with so much effort. Immigration therefore contributed to a great deal of insecurity among German Jews. They may not have denied assistance to their coreligionists, but neither did they bid them welcome.

4. Mobility and Urbanization

Mobility has always been much greater among Jews than among the rest of the population. This was due less to their professional activities as merchants and traders than to their lack of legal domicile gained by birth. They could settle in a locality only if privileges were granted them by the ruling authority. There was always the danger of expulsion, and, along with it, forced relocation. Until the middle of the nineteenth century many towns had the right to deny settlement to all Jews. In Bavaria the so-called *Matrikelgesetz* (Registration Law) remained in force until 1861. It permitted only the eldest son in a family to take up residence in the same locality. Not until legal equality was obtained in the wake of emancipation were such restrictions on rights of residency lifted. Finally, with the establishment of the German Empire, legal differences between the individual states were eliminated and all citizens were guaranteed freedom of domicile.

Accustomed to mobility, the German Jews now made it the means to their social advancement. Until then, they had resided in villages, small towns, and the predominantly agricultural regions of Germany, places that had been unable to participate significantly in the modernization process. From at least the middle of the nineteenth century on, internal migration of Jews occurred on a larger scale, moving from east to west and from village or town to city. The general German population experienced the same migration, except that the process was much slower. Among the Jewish minority the tempo of urbanization accelerated during the Kaiserreich, so that before World War I more than half the Jews lived in cities with more than one hundred thousand inhabitants as opposed to only 20 percent of the general population. Jews, who at the beginning of the nineteenth century had, in large measure, still been forced to reside in rural regions, were transformed into typical city dwellers. This transformation was closely associated with the change in their occupational distribution and the ascent of most Jews into the middle class. Without rapid industrialization, the construction of railroads, and the growth of the commercial sector, such rapid changes would have been unthinkable. Their regional mobility enabled the Jews to play a role in the modernization of Germany unlike that of other groups. In the process they moved from the margins of society toward its center.

The rapid urbanization of Jews has obscured the fact that at the time of the founding of the empire the Jewish minority was still largely concentrated in rural areas. At that time 70 percent of Jews were living in villages and small rural towns with populations of under twenty thousand inhabitants. In 1910 there were still 32 percent who resided in a rural setting.

For historical reasons the distribution of this rural Jewish population within the empire varied greatly. Southern and western Germany— primarily Württemberg, Baden, Franconia, Hesse, and the Prussian provinces of the Rhineland and Westphalia—were typical areas for rural Jewish settlement. However, a substantial rural Jewish population was also to be found in recently annexed Alsace-Lorraine and in the Upper Silesian territory of Oppeln. Since the seventeenth century some imperial knights had admitted large numbers of Jews into their villages in the expectation that they would bring in substantial tax revenues. As a result, until the middle of the nineteenth century there were still many villages in these regions where most, or nearly half, of the population was Jewish. In Imperial Germany this had become exceptional, even a curiosity, as in the case of the village of Rhina in the Prussian province of Hesse-Nassau where in 1900 there were 297 Jews out of a total population of 569. In the villages of Rexingen and Buttenhausen in Württemberg and in Gailingen in Baden Jews at that time still comprised one-third of the village inhabitants. In Alsace, too, four villages still had over 30 percent Jewish inhabitants in 1875.

In these Jewish village communities there were hundreds of synagogues and schools served by Jewish teachers who also acted as cantors and kosher slaughterers. These teachers, although poorly paid, formed the intellectual elite of the rural Jewish communities, and their children, with some frequency, attended a university. The rural Jews continued to practice their traditional occupations; the majority were cattle dealers or engaged in the textile business, occupations that often gave them incomes exceeding those of the peasant farmers. The physician, Samuel Spiro, born as a teacher's son in a Hessian village in 1885, writes in his memoirs:

> The Jewish community of Schenklengsfeld was at that time—the last two decades of the previous century—one of the largest and most flourishing in the rabbinical district of Fulda. It numbered about fifty families whose leaders were almost exclusively cattle dealers and peddlers. The majority belonged to the so-called middle class, but there were also a few wealthy families and only very few that were truly poor.[2]

Thus, poverty was not, for the most part, the reason that Jews left the villages.

There were clear differences between the type of Jewish settlements in the southern German states and those in more heavily industrialized Prussia. Jewish population size in southern Germany stagnated and urbanization proceeded at a slower pace. In 1910 45 percent of the Jews in Hesse, 33 percent in Württemberg, and 30 percent in Bavaria were still living in villages with fewer than five thousand inhabitants. In Prussia, by contrast, except for the provinces that had been added in the nineteenth century, Jews had always been able to live in cities, and they now began to leave the smaller towns as well. This was especially true for Prussia's agricultural eastern territories and for the province of Posen, where at the beginning of the century Jews had often comprised half of the inhabitants in small towns. In 1910 only 27 percent of the Prussian Jews still lived in towns with fewer than twenty thousand inhabitants.

The migration of German Jews out of the rural areas generally occurred in stages, that is to say, the shift of domicile was carefully coordinated with occupational opportunities. Since over half the Jews were active in commerce, cities—as marketing and consumer centers—generally afforded them better opportunities. Rural merchants often moved first to a nearby provincial town before transferring their business, if it was doing well, to a large city. This pattern, however, did not apply to generational mobility, which played a major role. Jewish parents in rural areas, well informed about urban affairs because of their occupational mobility, almost always endeavored to give their children a good education. For many young people that meant leaving their parents' home relatively early in order to attend an academic high school in the city or begin an apprenticeship in a well-respected business. Thus accustomed from early on to mobility and urban life, this well-educated generation did not return to their home towns; their careers took them instead to large cities, even to Berlin. It was this combination of being prepared to relocate, having a commercial mind-set, striving for an education, and seeking advancement that led to the urbanization of the Jewish population.

The internal migration produced a rapid shrinking of the rural communities, where the Jewish population grew increasingly older. These communities often had difficulties continuing to hold religious services or paying for the religious education of the few children. The writer Sammy Gronemann, whose father served as rabbi for one such tiny community, gives us this description:

> They certainly had a difficult time, those small, rural Jewish communities. It was truly moving to see how, nonetheless, they preserved traditions and continued to exist as Jews. . . . They usually had a large Jewish cemetery, which attested to the fact that a larger community had once existed there. . . . The descendants of almost all the people who lay at rest under the weather-beaten headstones there had long ago gone to the big cities where they had better schools for their children and more abundant opportunities for making a living.[3]

We can illustrate the urbanization of the German Jews for all of the German Empire between 1871 and 1910 by taking note of the major change in percentage distribution among the variously sized localities in which they lived. For comparison, the following table also gives the corresponding proportion of the general population for each size of locality.

TABLE 1.7

MUNICIPALITY SIZE	1871		1910	
	Jews	General	Jews	General
under 20,000	70.4	87.7	31.8	65.3
20,000–50,000	6.2	3.5	8.0	7.9
50,000–100,000	8.8	4.0	7.0	5.5
over 100,000	14.6	4.8	53.2	21.3

Here, we can see just how far Jews outdistanced the general population in urbanizing and the speed at which this transpired. In only forty years the percentage of Jews who lived in villages and towns with under twenty thousand inhabitants shrank by 38 percent while the proportion of Jews who lived in big cities climbed in equal measure. Over half of all German Jews now lived in large cities where only about 20 percent of non-Jewish Germans resided.

Jewish mobility manifested itself not only by regional migration to the cities but also and at the same time by a general internal migration that proceeded from the agricultural to the industrialized regions. There were clearly apparent areas of emigration, others in which the Jewish population was growing, and still others where it remained stagnant. The following table provides an overview of the changes in the geographical distribution of the German Jews in Imperial Germany. Because of Prussia's geographical size figures for some of its provinces are also indicated.

TABLE 1.8

	1871	1910	% DIFF.
German Empire	512,153	615,021	+ 20.1
Prussia	325,587	415,867	+ 27.7
Greater Berlin	36,325	144,043	+ 296.5
Province of Posen	61,982	26,512	- 57.2
Province of West Prussia	26,632	13,954	- 47.6
Province of Westphalia	17,245	21,036	+ 22.0
Rhine Province	38,424	57,287	+ 49.1
Hesse-Nassau	36,390	51,781	+ 42.3
Bavaria	50,662	55,065	+ 8.7
Baden	25,703	25,896	+ 0.7
Grand Duchy of Hesse	25,373	24,036	- 5.3
Alsace-Lorraine	40,918	30,483	- 25.5
Saxony	3,357	17,587	+ 423.9

Source: B. Blau, *Entwicklung der jüdischen Bevölkerung*, 282.

Prussia—the most heavily industrialized state and the state with the most large cities—saw an increase of more than 25 percent in its Jewish population, despite the significant emigration from its eastern provinces. This emigration was offset by the immigration of foreign-born Jews and by the attractiveness of Berlin, the Ruhr area, and the Rhine-Main region to Jews from all parts of the empire. The internal immigration within Prussia is clearly apparent from the statistics. The eastern underdeveloped agricultural provinces of Posen, Pomerania, and West Prussia witnessed a sharp drop in their Jewish populations, a large portion of these Jews going to Berlin. Emigration from the province of Posen, which had already begun before 1871, continued at a more rapid pace once the situation of the Jews, caught between Germans and Poles, began to grow worse. Over half of the Jews left the province of Posen during the Kaiserreich with the result that the traditional form of Jewish life, which in this province had been able to maintain itself longer, declined more and more.

In their quest for education, advancement, and success more than one hundred thousand Jews moved to Berlin during the years of the German Empire, producing a fourfold increase in the Jewish population of the imperial capital and its suburbs between 1871 and 1910. Substantial increases were also recorded for the urban industrial areas in the West—on the Rhine and the Ruhr—as well as those in the region of Hesse-Nassau, north of Frankfurt am Main. Although Prussia's general population followed the same patterns of movement, there were significant differences: Jews were quicker to leave agricultural regions; the general population grew relatively more substantially over the long term in the urban areas on account of the availability of factory employment.

Almost two-thirds of German Jewry lived in Prussia at the end of the German Empire. Of the remaining states only the city-state of Hamburg and the Kingdom of Saxony recorded higher rates of increase in the number of their Jewish inhabitants than did Prussia. In Saxony, until the middle of the nineteenth century, only individual Jews had gained the right to settle in Leipzig and Dresden. However, once freedom of domicile was introduced, immigration began and foreign-born Jews, in particular, started to arrive. Soon they constituted the majority of Jews in Saxony, particularly in the city of Leipzig with its trade fair, and were heavily involved in commerce with Eastern Europe. In the southern German states of Baden, Württemberg, and Hesse, which were less industrialized than Prussia, the number of Jewish inhabitants did not grow. Bavaria was able to exhibit a modest increase in its Jewish population only on account of immigration to Munich, in which many foreign Jews took part. Alsace-Lorraine lost a fourth of its Jewish population, mainly to France, Switzerland, and overseas. In Switzerland, after abolition of the requirement that Jewish residence be limited to only two villages, the communities of Zurich and Basel grew to over five thousand and twenty-five hundred Jews respectively in 1910, particularly because of immigration from Alsace.

In Austria the trend in internal migration followed a similar course as in the German Empire, but the Austrian Jewish population continued to rise sharply because of the high birthrate in the most significant emigration state, Galicia. As we shall see, Vienna evidenced the highest rate of immigration, acting as a magnet for Jews from all the Dual Monarchy. In Bohemia and Moravia there was significant emigration because of the anti-Jewish boycotts that decimated the rural population in particular. On the other hand, in the industrial regions of Prague, Pilsen, and Teplitz the number of Jews increased. In 1910 nearly a third of the Bohemian Jews were already concentrated in the city of Prague and its suburbs. The exodus from rural areas by Moravian Jews took them primarily to Brünn and to the industrial region of Moravian Ostrau. In Galicia the Jewish population became denser in the city and district of Lemberg as well as in Cracow. Galician Jews, escaping from hunger, extreme poverty, and overpopulation, emigrated not only overseas and to the large European cities but also to other areas in the Habsburg Monarchy, especially Vienna. Finally, by 1910, Jews comprised a third of the inhabitants of Czernowitz, the capital of Bukovina, thus making it the city of densest Jewish settlement in Austria.

In looking at the growth of the urban Jewish population in the German Empire between 1871 and 1910, it appears that Jews emigrated predominantly from outlying areas to nearby cities. Hessian Jews went to Frankfurt, Franconian Jews went to Nuremberg, those living in the Province of the Rhine to Cologne and Düsseldorf, and those in Württemberg to Stuttgart. However, the larger the cities were the greater the likelihood that they would also attract Jews from further away or from outside the empire. In many cities a tripartite division emerged: old residents, those who had come from rural areas, and immigrants from the East. What is striking is that, despite their rapid urbanization, Jews did not constitute a rising percentage of the municipal population, as the table on the following page indicates. It gives an overview of the absolute and the relative growth of what were in 1910 the largest urban Jewish communities in Germany.

Although all these Jewish communities exhibited strong growth, their proportion relative to the urban population in general tended to drop slightly. The migration rate of the general population to the big cities proved to be even higher, which resulted primarily from the large number of industrial workers. The biggest Jewish community by far was in Berlin, where 23 percent of all Jews in Germany were already living in 1910.

TABLE 1.9

	1871		1910	
City	Jews	% of pop.	Jews	% of pop.
Greater Berlin	36,325	4.3	144,043	4.3
Frankfurt	10,009	7.1	26,228	6.3
Breslau	13,916	6.4	20,212	3.9
Hamburg	11,954	4.0	19,472	1.9
Cologne	3,172	2.4	12,393	2.0
Munich	2,884	1.8	11,083	1.9
Leipzig	1,739	1.1	9,434	1.6
Nuremberg	1,813	2.2	7,815	2.3
Dresden	1,276	0.7	7,334	0.6

Source: M. Richarz, ed., *Jüdisches Leben in Deutschland*, 2:21.

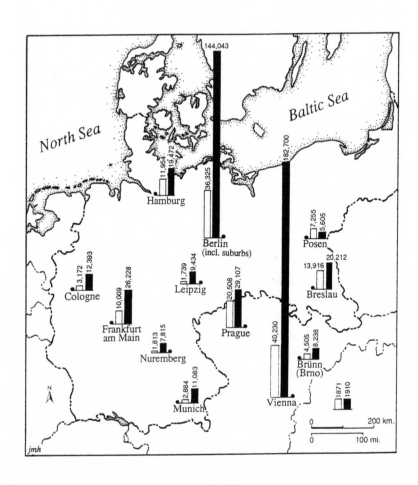

MAP 1 Jewish Population in Selected Central European Cities, 1871–1910

Berlin held the greatest attraction for Jewish immigrants, comparable in this respect only with the imperial city of Vienna. Drawn by the economic and cultural opportunities in both rapidly growing capital cities, hundreds of thousands streamed into these metropolises, full of hope for a better and freer life. Where did these people come from? For Berlin, data exist for 1910 regarding the origins of its Jewish inhabitants: only a third were born in Berlin, 46 percent came from Prussia, that is, from its eastern provinces; only 4 percent came from the rest of Germany and 17 percent were foreigners, mainly immigrants from east of the German Empire's border. Berlin had thus become the place of preference for Jews from eastern Germany and eastern Central Europe.

Berlin and Vienna were entirely comparable in the growth of their Jewish communities, even if the Berlin community did remain over 20 percent smaller. The following table presents the growth figures for both communities:

TABLE 1.10

GREATER BERLIN		% OF POP.	VIENNA		% OF POP.
1871	36,326	4.3	1869	40,230	6.6
1885	65,611	4.9	1880	73,222	10.1
1895	94,391	5.1	1890	118,495	8.7
1905	130,487	4.8	1900	146,926	8.8
1910	144,043	4.3	1910	175,318	8.6

Sources: G. Alexander, "Entwicklung der jüdischen Bevölkerung in Berlin," 289; M. Rozenblitt, *The Jews of Vienna*, 17.

Whereas the proportion of the Jewish population in Berlin in 1910 returned to the same percentage figure as in 1871, it was higher in Vienna and at 8.6 percent was twice as high as in Berlin. In 1880 barely a third of Viennese Jewry had been born in the city, 20 percent were from Bohemia and Moravia, 28 percent from Hungary, and 18 percent from Galicia and Bukovina. Immigration of the Galician Jews, many of whom came to the city as beggars or completely destitute, increased later. They remained the most difficult group to integrate since they were not only poor but also only minimally acculturated.

The distribution of the Jewish population according to residential areas of the cities in which they settled is of interest. In many cities, such as Berlin or Hamburg, one can clearly differentiate between an older residential area, located in the center of the city, and a newer one in the mid-

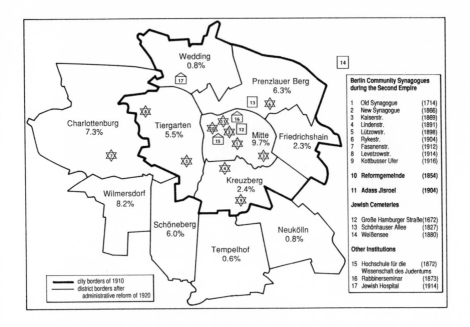

MAP 2 Percentage of Jews Within the Total Population of Berlin According to the
Later Districts and in Selected Suburbs, 1910

dle-class suburbs. In the wake of upward social mobility nearly all Jews
relocated, creating new areas of concentration within the middle-class
residential districts.

As long as Jews had remained orthodox, they had felt obligated to live
near a synagogue so they could walk there on the Sabbath, and, with this
in mind, they had always settled in close proximity. With the emergence
of Liberal Judaism and the increase in religious indifference, this consideration disintegrated for the majority of Jews. Yet Jews still tended to cluster within middle-class districts. Close social contacts and Jewish familial
networks persisted and prevented atomization. As earlier Jews had lived
in the vicinity of the synagogue, synagogues were now built as soon as a
new Jewish residential area came into existence.

In Hamburg, from the 1880s onward, a large portion of the Jewish
inhabitants left the Neustadt district and relocated to the recently established middle-class residential areas of Rothenbaum and Harvestehude,
which became the typical residential areas of Hamburg Jewry. If in
Hamburg Jews moved to the north, in Berlin middle-class non-Jews and
Jews alike preferred the western suburbs. The Jews who lived in

2   East European Jews in the Leopoldstadt district of Vienna (1915)

Charlottenburg, Schöneberg, and Wilmersdorf belonged to the organized Berlin Jewish community even though these suburbs were not at the time part of Berlin, belonging rather to what was classified as "Greater Berlin." In 1910 there were already twenty-two thousand Jews living in Charlottenburg and eleven thousand in Schöneberg. On some of the streets in the Hansa Quarter or near the Bavarian Square (Bayerischer Platz) they made up close to a quarter of the population. The Jewish upper class settled in the most expensive residential areas, Dahlem and Grunewald. The Central District (Berlin Mitte), still the location of Jewish institutions in Berlin, became the residential area for recent immigrants and the Jewish lower middle class.

In Vienna the Leopoldstadt, the district mostly thickly inhabited by Jews, became the Jewish Quarter. Poor and middle-class Jews lived here, where a third of the inhabitants was Jewish. Alsergrund, where Sigmund Freud resided, was preferred by Jews who were university graduates and white-collar workers. The poorest new immigrants from Galicia took up residency in Brigittenau; wealthy Jews lived in the First District (Innere Stadt) or in the villas in Döbling. Although many municipal neighbor-

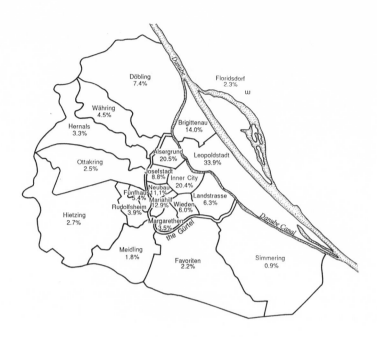

MAP 3 Division of the Jewish Population According to Municipal Districts in Vienna, 1910

hoods in Vienna were densely populated by Jews, Jews and Christians lived together in the same buildings, and, in the poorer quarters, even in the same apartments. As in Hamburg, the concentration of Jewish families was not a sign of imposed social segregation; rather, here too Jewish residence patterns revealed a striving for a middle-class lifestyle together with a desire for social contact with other Jews.

In sum, Jewish demographic trends in German-speaking Central Europe produced a highly urban and dominantly middle-class minority with an ever declining number of new births. Thus the Jewish minority, early on, exhibited the demographic characteristics of modernization: higher life expectancy, lower birthrate, and concentration in large cities— the common indicators of an advanced stage in the process of becoming middle-class.

2 | Occupational Distribution and Social Structure

1. Occupational Distribution

Just as the Jewish minority differed from the general population with respect to demographics, it also clearly diverged from it in occupational distribution, economic behavior, and social status. Jewish as well as Christian proponents of emancipation had expected that a gradual "normalization" of Jewish occupational distribution would take place as soon as restrictions compelling Jews to work only in commercial occupations were no longer in force. However, equal rights proved to have a limited effect on occupational redistribution and on realizing the expectations for a "more productive" Jewish minority. Before the revolution of 1848 state sanctions, aimed primarily at directing the poorest of the small-scale Jewish vendors toward farming and the practice of a trade, had likewise produced only a small number of permanent changes. When it came to choosing an occupation, Jewish behavior did not mesh with what the state had in mind but was instead based on whether or not Jews were accustomed to practicing a certain occupation, on economic trends, and on the degree of discrimination Jews might expect to encounter. There was a strong disinclination among Jews to change existing occupational patterns: over half the Jews in the German Empire continued to be concentrated in commerce, and the majority of all working Jews remained self-employed. However, adaptation to new economic and occupational opportunities was by no means ruled out. New trends became evident as Jews increasingly turned to professions such as law and medicine, industrial enterprises, and social work.

For centuries Jews in the German-speaking regions had been engaged almost exclusively in commerce and thus had both a long history and excellent experience in this sector of the economy. The business itself, the commercial knowledge gained, and the regular clientele were almost always passed down from father to son. There was little reason for breaking this traditional occupational chain in order to take up agriculture or ply a trade since, in an industrial age, assuming such occupations would result in a decline in social status. In general, even as agricultural production was on the rise the number of people engaged in agricultural work was, on account of mechanization, steadily declining. Because of growing industrial production, engaging in a craft likewise failed to offer good economic prospects. Jews who engaged in manual occupations in Germany had been mainly butchers and bakers. Even prior to emancipation they were allowed to practice these trades because of their need for kosher food. In Poland and in Prussia's former Polish territories, where Jews had been permitted to form their own guilds, the tailoring trade remained very important; many Jewish tailors who worked in the garment industry in Berlin and Vienna came mainly from the eastern Prussian provinces, Galicia, or Russia.

In contrast to agriculture and trades, the commercial sector in Germany had been undergoing constant expansion since the middle of the nineteenth century. Sales had risen sharply, and between 1867 and 1913 the number of people engaged in commerce climbed to over two million. Eleven percent of all those gainfully employed in Germany were now engaged in commerce. The majority, however, ran very small shops, as indicated by the fact that two-thirds of all retail businesses in 1907 managed without outside employees. The high level of economic activity within the commercial sphere was primarily due to a rapid increase in the production of consumer goods. Not only in the quickly growing big cities, but also in rural areas, people were increasingly giving up home-made goods and switching instead to factory-made products. At the same time, both the populace and its buying power increased markedly, so that the demand for commercial goods rose. Germany was also being integrated more and more into the world market, and, as a result, the export and import trade grew to an unprecedented degree. Thus the commercial sector offered the best occupational prospects, especially for experienced merchants who had commercial capital or credit at their disposal, were prepared to specialize, and were willing to innovate.

This growing industrial production afforded positive occupational prospects for German Jews as well. They became active mainly as entrepreneurs or white-collar employees, while foreign Jews, who had recently immigrated, went to work as industrial laborers. Being entrepreneurs was not something new for Jews; some had utilized commercial capital to establish factories as early as the eighteenth century. In Imperial Germany many Jewish industrialists had started in commerce and banking, but there were also Jewish artisans who first entered industrial production by way of decentralized production. Artisanship, commerce, and industry were sometimes intimately connected, as was the case to a large extent in the garment industry where Jews were strongly represented.

The enormous enthusiasm of German Jews for education and culture, their social ascent, and their adoption of middle-class values all led to large numbers of sons from merchant families boldly refusing to carry on the occupation of their fathers in order to pursue intellectual or artistic occupations instead. The painter Max Liebermann and the art historian Aby Warburg are examples of this structural shift. The opportunity available to many young Jews in Imperial Germany to study at universities and enter occupations that required a university education was in no small part due to the economic success of the older generation. Yet, on account of antisemitism, the chances for professional success in areas open to university graduates remained limited. It was exceedingly difficult for Jews to receive civil service appointments as teachers, professors, or judges. Thus most of the Jewish university graduates became either doctors, lawyers, or journalists—the so-called free professions in which, as a result, they were greatly overrepresented in the larger cities.

The following overview summarizes the extent to which Jewish occupational structure differed from that of the general population and gives the percentage distribution for persons drawing an income (excluding pensioners) in the occupational groups under discussion here:

TABLE 2.1

	1895		1907	
	Gen. Pop.	Jews	Gen. Pop	Jews
Agriculture	37.5	1.6	35.2	1.6
Trades and Industry	37.5	22.5	40.0	26.5
Commerce and Trade	10.6	65.2	12.4	61.4
Civil Service and Free Professions	6.4	7.1	6.2	7.9
Domestic Services	8.0	3.6	6.2	2.6

Source: U. Schmelz, *Die demographische Entwicklung der Juden in Deutschland*, 64.

While commerce remained by far the most important occupation for Jews, in the general population agriculture yielded to trades and industry as the main sector of employment. This took place during Germany's boom phase of industrialization when the society increasingly needed workers and merchants. Although 55 percent of all Jews were still employed in commerce, in 1907 they comprised only 6 percent of the total number of persons active in that sector. In the trades and in industry non-Jews were mainly employed as factory workers, while Jews were almost always tradesmen, white-collar workers, and entrepreneurs. By 1907 more than a quarter of all Jews were already working in the trades and industry sector (sixty-three thousand), while the proportion of those involved in commerce had slightly declined. The number of Jews as well as Christians engaged in domestic service decreased significantly. In the case of Jews this was due to their upward social mobility, while among Christians it was because they showed a preference for industrial work. Especially striking is the percentage increase of Jews in the category of civil service positions and the free professions. Whereas in 1907 only about 6 percent of all those gainfully employed worked in this sector of the economy, it was already almost 8 percent among Jews.

Deviating Jewish occupational distribution was especially marked by the greater number that were self-employed. Jews, who before emancipation had been almost exclusively self-employed merchants, were not prepared to abandon a long tradition of occupational independence. In 1895, for example, 60 percent of Jews involved in commerce and trade were self-employed, as opposed to only 36 percent of non-Jews. In the area of trades and industry the number of Jewish self-employed was double that of non-Jews. In showing a decisive preference for self-employment, Jews were swimming against the economic tide that ran to consolidation and to large-scale enterprises with an increasing number of white-collar employees. There has been speculation about whether or not this adherence to self-employment in small- and middle-scale business enterprises significantly restricted Jewish economic success as early as the imperial period. Certainly this behavior reflected Jewish social segregation. Self-employment made possible self-determination and independence from non-Jews and was thus an appropriate response to the social barriers that continued to exist between Jews and Christians. Fear of the possible effects of antisemitism in dependent work relationships was an important consideration, and it was therefore no coincidence that Jewish employees preferred to work in enterprises owned by Jews.

If we look at the proportion of people who had some form of employment in comparison to the unemployed population we see that in 1895, for example, only 34 percent of all Jews were gainfully employed as opposed to 40 percent of non-Jews. This contrast reflects the much higher representation of Jews in the middle-class; in keeping with middle-class values, fewer Jewish women pursued work outside the home. There were also more elderly people among Jews who could live from their savings and more young persons who were engaged in the long process of securing higher education.

The proportion of working women among Jews cannot be accurately determined because many of them were employed without wages in a family business. Moreover, women's work among the middle class was purposefully "hidden," since it was deemed inappropriate. The occupational census of 1907, which for the first time took into account "people helping in the family business," is therefore of only limited value. This last census conducted in Imperial Germany counted only forty-nine thousand employed Jewish women, of whom almost a fourth (twelve thousand) worked in family businesses. Thus only 20 percent of Jewish women were in the workforce in comparison with 30.4 percent of women in the population as a whole. Still, the difference in the employment rate was not as high as might have been expected given the difference in class status. Jewish women belonged only marginally to those social classes that furnished female farmers, industrial workers, and domestic help, the occupations engaged in by the majority of employed women.

Although most employed Jewish women were from the lower class of immigrant Jews and from the lower middle class, some bourgeois women also began to seek employment, at least until they married. Some received training in women's professions such as social work or teaching in a school or kindergarten. Most Jewish women worked as assisting or formally employed sales clerks and as secretaries and bookkeepers—the new office occupations for women. However, about a third of German-Jewish women in 1907 were self-employed in the commerce and trades sector where they ran their own shops or earned a living as milliners or tailors. Thus for women, too, the Jewish tradition of self-employment remained significant.

The employment distribution of Jewish women into individual occupational groups did not differ radically from that of Jewish men, if we exclude the agricultural and domestic service sectors in which men were only rarely still active. In 1907 a good half of all Jewish women worked in

3   Female employees in the women's clothing store of the brothers Katz in
Berlin (around 1910)

commerce and 28 percent in business and industry. The clothing industry
alone employed almost ten thousand Jewish women. The percentage who
worked as domestics fell to barely 9 percent, while 4 percent of Jewish
women continued to work in the agricultural sector. Rural Jewish women
mainly assisted in the work of the family, but, on the side, might also
engage in farming and animal husbandry while their husbands traded in
livestock. Almost 6 percent of the women had already started working in
public service occupations and in the free professions. They also sought
out occupations that required a university degree, but here their prospects
were usually limited to medicine.

    This overview of the occupational distribution of Jews in Germany
would not be complete without noting that for two Jewish groups in particular—rural Jews and foreign Jews—occupational distribution deviated
significantly from the norm. Rural Jews continued to live almost exclusively from financial transactions and trade in commodities, just as they
had in the period before the Emancipation. Their trade in agricultural
products like cattle, grain, hides, and hops facilitated the marketing of
farm products while their trade in general store items, textiles, and iron-
ware supplied the rural population with industrial goods. In addition to

4 The butcher Anselm Katz and the kosher slaughterer Sally Katz in Ostheim, near Hanau (1903)

merchants the rural areas had a few Jewish tradesmen, most of whom were butchers, as well as some teachers in those places that had Jewish elementary schools.

The foreign Jews living in Germany were younger and less well off than the average German Jew. Their employment rate was, therefore, considerably higher; in Berlin, for example, it ran to 61 percent in 1910. The occupational profile of foreign Jews likewise differed from that of German Jews especially on account of the larger proportion of craftsmen and of wage laborers who were prepared to work in industry. Most of the immigrants belonged to the lower social classes, yet among them were also members of the intelligentsia and the upper middle class.

Many foreign Jews ran small, low-capital retail businesses in which the entire family worked. Often they dealt in second-hand goods, sacks, eggs, hats, or cigarettes. In big cities like Berlin and Hamburg these small-scale shops, offering inexpensive merchandise, soon became a common feature of the urban scene. The foreign Jewish women worked in commerce, as maids, and, most frequently, as seamstresses in the clothing industry.

Many tradesmen among the immigrant Jews were employed as workers in the Berlin garment factories, in cigarette manufacture, or in the leather industry in Offenbach. A particularly large number of foreign Jews in Leipzig worked as furriers or fur dealers. The few Jewish wholesalers from Eastern Europe turned primarily to the export-import trade in furs, timber, and grain between Germany and czarist Russia.

The immigration of intellectuals and artists to Germany—primarily to Berlin—was proportionately very large. Jews from the Habsburg Monarchy, as well as those from czarist Russia, held German language and culture in high esteem. Musicians, writers, painters, actors, and journalists from these countries came to try their luck in the German capital. Another entirely different category of immigrants was made up of rabbis and cantors who were summoned from Eastern Europe to serve Jewish communities in Germany.

The beginning of World War I changed the situation of foreign Jews in Germany overnight. Austrian citizens were now conscripted into the army of their homeland while Russian Jews were frequently imprisoned as enemy aliens. But when, during the course of the war, Germany found itself in need of workers, approximately thirty thousand Jews from occupied Poland were recruited and brought to work in Germany, in some instances against their will. They were forced to perform hard physical labor in mining and industry under the worst of conditions. Then, in April of 1918, Prussia reversed its policy, blocking the border to Jewish workers from Poland, as had long been demanded by antisemitic agitators.

A comparison of Jewish occupational distribution in Germany with that in Austria indicates basic similarities as well as marked differences. The similarities result especially from similar occupational restrictions that existed for Jews in both countries before emancipation. The major differences are largely due to the presence in Austria of large numbers of extremely impoverished Jews from the Galician portion of the Habsburg Empire. For this reason Austrian Jews continued to have a lower social status, approximating that of foreign Jews in Germany. In Galicia Jews were more frequently agricultural workers, day laborers, and domestics than elsewhere in the country. Unlike the situation in Germany, it was not uncommon for Jews in Austria—primarily in Galicia and Bukovina—to be agricultural workers or to lease agricultural land. According to the Austrian census of 1910, there was a total of 1.3 million Jews, 509,000 of whom were gainfully employed. Of these, 11 percent worked in agriculture, some 26 percent in crafts and industry, 55 percent in commerce and trade, and 6.5 percent in civil service and the free professions. As was the case in Imperial Germany, the proportion of them working in trades and industry was below that of the general population. Also, most Jews who worked in the industrial sector, like their counterparts in Germany, were mainly in the clothing and food industries.

A further similarity was that in Austria, as well, half of all working Jews were self-employed. In contrast to Germany, however, only 11 percent were white-collar employees, while 39 percent were workers and day laborers. Among women, almost a quarter of whom were employed, self-employment predominated, just as it did for Jewish women in Germany, followed by work in the family business.

A comparison of the occupational situation of Jews in the national capitals, Berlin and Vienna, likewise shows more similarities than differences. Both metropolises had developed into industrial cities where, in 1890, some 15 percent of all gainfully employed inhabitants worked in the garment industry, in which Jews were especially involved. Not surprisingly, more Jews were employed in industry in these two cities than in any other locations. Finally, circumstances in Berlin and Vienna resembled each other also in the high representation of Jews in the artistic and intellectual occupations: 9 percent of all employed Jews in Vienna and almost 10 percent of those in Berlin were employed in the free professions or in public service. Each city, in short, was attractive to both the Jewish lower class and the Jewish intelligentsia.

2. In Commerce and Industry

Population growth, augmented income, expanding industrial production, and a larger export-import trade resulted in the number of commercial enterprises in Imperial Germany more than doubling between 1895 and 1907. As a consequence, by 1907 Jews comprised only some 8 percent of those employed in commerce. This figure, however, inadequately reflects their economic significance, since Jews were wholesalers and bankers as well as owners of retail businesses, traveling salesmen, sales clerks, and peddlers. The sales figures for businesses are not reflected in the statistics; only in a few instances do we know anything about a company's volume and then mainly for just the larger operations. As a result, it is almost impossible to quantify the economic role that Jews played in commerce.

The Jews' particular economic patterns—which continued to characterize them even after emancipation—were largely due to their having
lived for centuries under repressive restrictions. The past also affected the
highly unequal distribution of Jewish entrepreneurs within commerce
and industry, depending on whether they had been restricted or privileged in particular fields. Jews were highly represented in a few sectors
and barely at all in others. Their considerable participation in grain and
cattle trading resulted from Jews having been scattered to rural areas,
while their concentration in the iron trade emerged from earlier scrap
iron operations, and the strong Jewish presence in the food industry and
textile industries came from dealing in agricultural products and practicing the trades of butcher, baker, and tailor. The oldest tradition by far was
in monetary transactions and in banking. The prohibition against owning
land having relegated Jews to capital enterprises, they had become profi-
cient at converting money gained from commercial ventures into finance
capital and they possessed the requisite expertise for engaging in monetary transactions.

The main features that characterized the Jews' acquired economic
behavior were, above all, the courage to take risks, the readiness to be
innovative, and the ability to attract customers. They were also able to
facilitate their commercial endeavors through a network of contacts with
other Jewish enterprises both inside and outside Germany that made possible business partnerships and loans as well as the securing of apprenticeships and advantageous marital connections. Such economic behavior
had originated as a minority's survival strategy under the financial pressure of the German princes. Once the Jews were granted economic freedom, and with the emergence of commercial capitalism, their entrepreneurial orientation then gave them a decisive head start on modern
methods and on requisite flexibility. They were well acquainted with commercial initiatives based on analyses of market potential and adjustments
to market demand. Jewish entrepreneurs accommodated themselves
much more rapidly to the needs of the market; they were the first to use
advertising, to initiate new forms of business such as mail orders, to install
telephones, to adopt the foreign concept of the department store, and to
travel regularly to international trade fairs and world exhibitions in order
to familiarize themselves with new wares and new methods of production. In conjunction with the modernization of commerce, they opened
discount stores for the working class as well as luxury shops for the middle class, and those emporia of consumption—the department stores—for

all social levels. Their readiness to relocate permitted Jewish merchants to go wherever there was a need for goods or where one could be created. Their familial connections and social contacts outside Germany furthered their successes in the export-import trade, in which they engaged to a high degree. Additionally, Jews frequently combined manufacture and sales within a single family enterprise. This was especially true in the clothing sector, for example in ready-to-wear garments and textiles, as well as in the manufacture and sale of shoes, the fur business, and the trade in tobacco products.

Of those Jews in the "commerce and transport/travel" sector, 95 percent were active in the commerce portion, the rest in insurance and transportation as well as the restaurant and hotel business. There were still Jewish tavern keepers, primarily in eastern Prussia, who leased taverns on manorial estates and in villages, in keeping with the practice that had prevailed in Poland. Very different from these establishments were the modern restaurants that Jews now opened. The most elegant was the Kempinski Wine Restaurant on Leipziger Strasse in Berlin, which could accommodate up to twenty-five hundred guests in its luxurious rooms and was even visited by the emperor. New also were the Jewish hotel owners, who formed their own professional association. Their establishments were primarily kosher hotels and guest houses at spas and vacation sites. They catered to Jewish guests from Eastern Europe as well as to German Jews who, as antisemitism increased, were often turned away by prejudiced hotel keepers.

Since the transport of goods had originally been part of the service rendered by commercial entrepreneurs, Jewish teamsters had a long tradition in the transportation business. The number of shipping agents, teamsters, and coachmen continued to increase even after railways were built, since people and goods still needed transport to points beyond the railway terminals. Between 1895 and 1907 the number of Jews involved in transportation doubled. They were also innovative as ship owners, a capital-intensive sector in which a few Jews rose to prominence as large-scale entrepreneurs. Among them was Wilhelm Kunstmann (1844–1934), who in 1870 founded what became the largest shipping company on the Baltic Sea. The coal magnate and patron of the arts Eduard Arnhold (1849–1925) maintained a fleet of coal barges on the Oder River that supplied coal from Upper Silesia to the receptive Berlin market. Germany's leading shipping magnate was Albert Ballin (1857–1918), the son of an emigration agent of modest means. Ballin, who had early joined the Hamburg-

America Line (HAPAG), became its director in 1899. His vision and competence enabled him to build it into the most important transatlantic shipping line, which dominated in the transport of emigrants. The emigration
agencies and the HAPAG ships enabled millions of emigrants to cross the
Atlantic, among them hundreds of thousands of Russian Jews. Albert
Ballin's motto was "My domain is the world," and it was he who put the
port of Hamburg on the international map. As one of the economic advisers to William II, he was among the so-called *Kaiserjuden*, the Jews who
advised the emperor. Most of the Jews in the commercial sector concentrated on commodities and agricultural produce, a few acting as brokers
and wholesalers, while the most prominent group consisted of bankers
and financiers. A good half of the 137,000 Jews who were active in commerce in 1907 were self-employed, but the number of workers in family
enterprises, young salaried employees, and sales representatives was on
the increase—an indication of the expansion of Jewish commercial enterprises, since most Jews preferred to work together with their coreligionists. Traveling sales representatives made up a new category. They moved
about by train, carrying their sample cases and taking orders from their
customers.

Jews ran their small retail stores predominantly as family businesses.
With the growth of the consumer goods industry, such shops opened in
increasing numbers in provincial cities and villages where they sold
mainly textiles, shoes, hardware, foodstuffs, and spirits. Cattle dealing
continued to play an important role in villages and in local markets. In
Franconia, Hesse, Westphalia, and other regions of southern and western
Germany more than three-quarters of the cattle trade was in Jewish
hands. Because it demanded considerable capital, often gained through
bank credits, the trade in horses was held in high regard. Of similar significance in the rural areas was the trade in agricultural products, which
consisted primarily of animal feed, fertilizer, grain, tobacco, and hops. The
trade in agricultural products, however, suffered increasingly from the
competition of cooperatives that independently organized their own buying and selling, thus bypassing the middlemen. Whenever possible Jewish
traders in the rural areas tried to live in localities with rail connections,
since this allowed them to expand the perimeter of their businesses considerably. Visiting national markets was becoming ever more important
for cattle and grain dealers since their business shifted increasingly from
the rural areas to the urban centers of consumption.

Trade in agricultural products was not without its problems. In the

1880s and 1890s Germany was beset by an ongoing agricultural crisis. Grain prices fell under the impact of the world market, which, in turn, led to a growing indebtedness on the part of farmers. Despite the presence of credit associations, many farmers preferred to continue the practice of borrowing from Jewish merchants. If the farmers went bankrupt, they could then blame the Jews for being "usurers." Trade in agricultural products, therefore, always played a large role in antisemitic agitation. The antisemite Otto Böckel even created "Jew-free cattle markets," which, however, turned out to be a colossal failure.

Relatively more favorable was the situation of Jewish retailers in industrialized regions and in the big cities. These commercial enterprises were modernized to a greater degree; their attraction grew on account of greater specialization, wider selection of goods, the introduction of fixed prices, and better furnishings. The cities were also characterized by innovations such as mail-order businesses, enterprises with multiple branches, and department stores.

In the cities, too, Jews were predominantly concentrated in the textile industry where they sold fabrics, linens, women's apparel, men's clothing, hats, stockings, and coats, items that they often manufactured themselves. One example is the Grünfeld linen firm in Silesia, which transferred its main center of operations from its factory location in Landeshut to Berlin where it opened a textile department store on Leipziger Strasse. Grünfeld placed large advertisements, containing price lists, in hundreds of newspapers and offered mail-order service, which was often used to purchase goods for bridal trousseaus. In 1912 the company reached annual sales of 8.7 million marks with two thousand employees engaged in production and sales. On a smaller scale, the women's outer apparel company, Hirschfeld Brothers, in Hamburg, employed five hundred workers in manufacture and merchandising and reached an annual turnover of 2.4 million marks. Both of these large companies were run by three brothers as family businesses. Like many other successful enterprises, they too opened branch stores in other cities.

In addition to the textile trade, Jewish retailers were also very successful dealers in leather and shoes, leather having always been part of the traditional Jewish trade in agricultural products. The Salamander Company began as the shoe factory J. Sigle and Company in Kornwestheim, and Wilhelm Krojanker created Tack and Company in Berlin. Both shoe companies combined manufacture and merchandising and developed into businesses with a network of branches.

Jews possessed a significant share in the sale of foods, alcohol, and tobacco; they had long been engaged in the sale of wine and spirits. The well-run Meyer spirits company in Berlin, with its catchy motto, "Keine Feier ohne Meyer" (Without Meyer, no celebration is complete), sold their own products exclusively in some five hundred chain stores. Much the same could be said about the Berlin cigar company of Loeser and Wolff, which had its factories in East Prussia and operated innumerable cigar shops in Berlin. In the food industry there were many small Jewish businesses, like those selling eggs or vegetables, that were often run by immigrants. This was likewise the case for many coal distributors and second-hand stores. Jews were also heavily involved in book and art dealerships and antique stores—all of which required professional knowledge.

The department store, clearly an innovation, did not take hold in Germany until the 1890s. Jewish families introduced this method of merchandising goods, which had already been explored in the United States, France, and England, into Germany. In 1896 Hermann Tietz opened his first department store in Gera, where he had previously run a small linens shop. Wide selection, low prices, and sumptuous furnishings were some of the operational principles that characterized the department stores. Hermann and Leonhard Tietz each built up his own department store chain, the Wertheim Brothers opened four department stores in Berlin, Salman Schocken founded the first of his department stores in Zwickau, and in 1907 Adolf Jandorf opened the Department Store of the West (Kaufhaus des Westens, Kadewe) in Berlin, the largest and most elegant department store in Germany at that time.

In wholesaling as well as in the export-import trade Jews were represented in the same sectors as at the retail level. They held the strongest positions in textiles, in the international fur trade, in metals, coal, cattle, grain, and hops. Since Berlin had the largest market for beef cattle, it became the new hub of the cattle business. Many Jewish grain dealers found market outlets for their products in Breslau and Mannheim, and Jews were very prominent in the Nuremberg hops exchange. The center of the trade in fur was Brühl Strasse in Leipzig where Jews from Eastern Europe dominated both the trading and the processing of furs, making Leipzig an international center of the fur business. In 1913 70 percent of all companies that dealt in metals and almost half of all companies dealing in iron and scrap metal were owned and operated by Jews. Two of the most important businesses in this area were the Frankfurt Metal

5   Interior of the Tietz department store in Berlin

Company and the Aron Hirsch Company based in Halberstadt, which built up an international conglomerate of copper, brass, and steel works. The Hirsch family, which was Orthodox, had a synagogue built on the premises of their brassworks in Eberswald, and they also financed the Orthodox rabbinical seminary of Esriel Hildesheimer in Berlin. Eduard Arnhold and Fritz von Friedländer-Fuld played important roles in the wholesale trade in coal because it was their companies that delivered the coal from Upper Silesia to Berlin. Both of these mining industrialists numbered among the wealthiest men in Prussia and, following his baptism, Friedländer-Fuld was raised to the nobility in 1906. The leading wholesale business in cotton fabrics was Simon Brothers. James Simon, one of the co-owners of the company, was chairman of the Hilfsverein der deutschen Juden, the aid society of the German Jews, and an important patron of Berlin museums. The Berlin ready-to-wear clothing industry also conducted a substantial wholesale and export trade in Europe and overseas. Well-known Jewish ready-made clothing companies, such as Hermann Gerson's Fashion House and the Mannheimer Brothers and Nathan Israel companies, held prominent positions in this wholesale trade. In 1894 the Gerson company was the largest business in this area, with an annual turnover of 30 million marks.

The importance of Jews in banking declined because finance shifted increasingly from private firms to the newly established corporate banks, which, on account of their larger capitalization, were in a better position to serve the growing financial requirements of industry. The public, however, was less aware of this shift than of the fact that the large banking families with a Jewish heritage, such as Rothschild, Bleichröder, Warburg, Oppenheim, and Mendelssohn, were still among the wealthiest families in Germany. Gerson von Bleichröder, as banker to Bismarck and to the German Empire, continued to play a politically significant role. He was raised to the nobility in 1872 but socially remained an outsider. On the other hand, the younger banker Carl Fürstenberg proudly declined ennoblement. As director of a corporate bank, the Berliner Handelsgesellschaft, Fürstenberg became German industry's banker and financed, among other concerns, Emil Rathenau's General Electrical Works (Allgemeine Elektrizitätsgesellschaft, AEG). Jewish bankers and their capital greatly influenced several corporate banks during their early years, such as the Berliner Handelsgesellschaft and the Dresdener Bank, which put Jews on their board of directors. On the whole, though, the number of Jewish bank directors and bank owners was on the decline, amounting to only 38 percent in 1895, the majority being connected with small private banks. In the Imperial Loan Consortium approximately a third of the banks were owned by Jews.

The number of Jews engaged in trades and industry grew significantly in the *Kaiserreich* especially because many East European Jewish immigrants worked in this sector. Almost two-thirds of those active in it were artisans, with the tailoring trade, employing some fifteen thousand, being dominant. Most of the workers in this trade, largely foreign Jews and women, were employed in the ready-to-wear clothing industry. Second after tailoring clothes came butchering, an occupation in which only men engaged, followed by millinery, an occupation preferred by women. Other trades frequently represented were those of shoemaker, baker, and leather worker. Immigrant workers were also employed in factories, such as those of the Berlin cigarette industry. They made up a large portion of the Jewish lower class and, as mentioned above, also engaged in petty trade.

Increased industrialization brought more Jews into manufacturing. They entered it as craftsmen and as merchants for whom commercial capital smoothed their way. They tended to go into new and expanding branches of industry such as clothing, printing and publishing, chemicals, and electrical products. Jews took part in the economically important heavy industry of the Ruhr area only as bankers, although, as mentioned, a few Jewish entrepreneurs participated in the coal industry in Upper Silesia.

It can be assumed that Jewish companies in Imperial Germany produced more than half of Berlin's ready-made clothing. Often manufacture was distributed among several small producers and carried out by women who did the work at home, so that no expensive machinery was required. As indicated above, production and merchandising were usually combined and in small and large companies alike both were undertaken by a single family. Thus the clothing industry possessed a premodern structure, but one that meshed with the continuing Jewish concern for economic independence.

Berlin was also the center for Jewish printers and publishers. Since Jews had engaged in Hebrew printing for centuries, this enterprise, like the book trade in general, was hardly strange to them. In Imperial Germany, however, Jewish entrepreneurs moved increasingly from printing into publishing. The large Jewish publishers of books and newspapers, Rudolf Mosse and Leopold Ullstein, as well as the Societäts Publishing House of Leopold Sonnemann in Frankfurt am Main, brought out the most influential liberal newspapers. Among the literary publishing houses founded by Jews, the S. Fischer Verlag, established in 1886 by the Hungarian-born Samuel Fischer, attained the highest standing. The Jewish publishers were not only entrepreneurs, they also intentionally exercised a liberal influence on culture and politics.

In Germany the period between 1895 and the world war was characterized by a declining rural population, growing economic activity, and increasing prosperity. The onset of the advanced phase of industrialization raised productivity and at the same time increased the need for capital. The dominant industries of this period—mining, steel, electricity, and chemicals—were undergoing rapid expansion. Entrepreneurship now required not only more capital but also more technical and scientific expertise. Both as scientists and as entrepreneurs Jews were able to play an important role in the chemical industry. One example would be Heinrich Caro, the director of the indigo and soda factories in Baden (Badische Anilin- und Sodafabriken), who became chairman of the Association of German Chemists as well as chairman of the Association of German Engineers. Jewish industrialists also played a role in the rubber, potash, and dye industries and in the development of what later became the I. G. Farben conglomerate. Here, too, they were able to combine scientific research and development with entrepreneurial activity.

As a result of increasing industrial concentration and interconnection, the number of major enterprises grew. The largest founded by a Jew was the above-mentioned AEG, established by Emil Rathenau in 1887. As an engineer he had had the foresight to obtain rights to the Edison patents for Germany. He also knew how to win people over to the use of electricity and how to obtain—primarily from Jewish banks—the enormous credit necessary for developing electrical power. The AEG built the first massive power stations and was the leader in the production of steam turbines. At the time of Emil Rathenau's death in 1915 the AEG had seventy thousand salaried employees. His son Walther Rathenau, murdered in 1922 when he was serving as Germany's foreign minister, had joined the board of directors of the AEG in 1899 and often served as an adviser to the government on economic matters.

In Austria, where the Jewish population engaged in occupations similar to those practiced in the German Empire, its concentration in specific branches of commerce and industry also corresponded remarkably to the distribution in Germany. Bohemia and Moravia were the centers of industrialization while Vienna developed into an international financial and commercial center.

Jews occupied a powerful position in Vienna's banking industry, its stock market, and its credit business. Dozens of ennobled Jews attested to the success of the Jewish oligarchy as did their homes on the newly laid out Ringstrasse. The leading banks in Vienna were owned by the Rothschild and Königswarter families. Drawing upon their experience in finance, men of Jewish origins held almost half of all the directorial and governing positions in the Viennese banks. Many members of this upper class underwent baptism, but others, like Jonas Königswarter, served on the board of Vienna's Jewish community and endowed significant welfare institutions. To a great extent Jewish banks financed the industrialization of Austria and the construction of its railroads. A second area of concentration for Viennese large-scale entrepreneurs was the export trade, which was almost exclusively run by Jews and extended across the Balkans to the Middle East. Jews were also active as wholesalers dealing primarily in grain, wool, coal, and wine.

As in Berlin, clothing was the most significant economic sector for the Jews of Vienna. The ready-to-wear garment industry employed many of the poor Jewish immigrants from Galicia, producing for markets in

6   Thomas Edison with Emil Rathenau in the Berlin electrical works of the
AEG (1911)

Hungary, the Balkans, and the Ottoman Empire. Jews also ran most of the
retail shops that sold clothing. Although Jews held no monopoly on
department stores, the Jewish Gerngross firm established the leading one
of its kind in the city. There were also numerous very small retail businesses from which the poorest of the Jews tried to earn a living.

Although, except in the manufacture of clothing, the number of Jewish
industrialists in Austria was not as great as in Germany, they were
involved to a lesser degree in exactly the same branches of industry as
their counterparts across the border. Early on, Jews in Bohemia and
Moravia had founded textile factories, most of them cotton weaving mills.
The brewing industry provided the foundation for the Mauthner family
fortune, and other Jewish industrialists started up companies in the sugar,
spirits, and chemical industries, while still others manufactured shoes and
umbrellas. The Moravian coal wholesaler Wilhelm Gutmann supplied
coal to Vienna, Budapest, and Brünn and created an industrial conglomerate that included not only Bohemian coal mines, a plant for making
coke, and a steel works but also sugar factories and branches of his banking house in Vienna, Budapest, and Prague. The development of this conglomerate is reflective of the opportunities that the extensive market of

the Habsburg Monarchy afforded those industrialists who possessed unusual initiative.

During this period Jewish achievements in the area of commerce and industry were no doubt highly significant in both Germany and Austria. Yet Jewish entrepreneurs and merchants clearly focused on only a few traditional and several innovative branches of the economy. They played almost no role in Germany's leading industries at the time, coal and steel, and, of course, the same holds true for large-scale agricultural production. In an age of corporate banking and conglomerates Jewish adherence to family-run enterprises was structurally out of date. Jews had now reached the summit of their economic importance; soon thereafter they would begin their descent.

3. The Educated Elite

In Imperial Germany the number of Jews who were attracted to occupations requiring a university education grew in unparalleled fashion. Their enormous influx into the academic high schools, universities, and technical colleges cannot be explained solely on the basis of acculturation and their membership in the middle class. Jewish students were not only the sons of the urban middle and upper classes; there were also some from poorer families and from rural areas. Given the existing Jewish occupational profile, most of the Jewish pupils in *Gymnasien* and the students at universities, of course, came from merchant families. In Imperial Germany, however, merchants generally had relatively low social status since they were thought to be interested only in material things and were viewed as unproductive. Many of the sons who succeeded in gaining a good education were no longer satisfied to follow in their parents' footsteps, become merchants, and thus join the economic middle class. Instead, even at the price of a loss in income, they strove to be part of the educated middle class, that is, to positions requiring a university education. It was a matter of liberating oneself from commerce in order to join the humanistically educated elite. For centuries Jews had been forced to engage in commerce. Now, for the first time, after completion of the acculturation process, young Jewish men in larger numbers could abandon the occupations of their fathers in favor of intellectual ones that would better their social position and provide entry to the cultured class. The fact that Jews had attained middle-class status, along with their urbanization, obviously made such a decision easier and simplified its implementation.

Growing antisemitism also played a role in inducing Jewish parents to provide the highest possible level of education for their sons. With increasing secularization, the high regard in which rabbis were formerly held had declined, but the prestige of Jewish physicians and lawyers remained high. This prestige also guaranteed that marriages between the two groups would bind the new educated Jewish middle class with its older economic counterpart.

In 1906–1907 only 8 percent of all children in Prussia received more than an elementary school education; for Jewish children, by contrast, the proportion was 59 percent. Sixty-seven percent of Jewish children in Berlin, 86 percent in Frankfurt am Main, and as many as 96 percent in Hamburg went on to the secondary-school level. These figures present the clearest evidence of the Jewish population's extraordinary quest for education. The various secondary schools in Prussia together had 15,762 Jewish pupils in 1906 who made up 6.5 percent of all pupils attending Gymnasien, approximately six times the Jewish percentage in the general population. In Berlin the average proportion of Jewish pupils in Gymnasien amounted to 18 percent, and in Jewish residential areas it was even higher.

The proportions for Austria are comparable, differing only on account of the underdevelopment of some parts of the Habsburg Empire. Thus among Jews, as among Christians, relatively fewer children attended the Gymnasium. In 1903–1904 there were 15,880 Jewish pupils in Austria's humanistic and technical high schools—about as many as in Prussia—but here they made up about 14 percent of all pupils in these schools. Given the higher percentage of Jews in the general population, Jewish pupils in Austria were overrepresented by only three to one, half of the proportion in Prussia. In Vienna there were 5,605 Jewish pupils in various high schools in 1912, comprising 47 percent of all pupils. That meant Jewish high school pupils there were disproportionately represented by more than five to one. Between the years 1870 and 1910 a third of the Jewish Gymnasium pupils had been born outside Vienna, coming mainly from Bohemia, Moravia, and Silesia. The cosmopolitan cities of Vienna and Berlin attracted not only poor Jews but also, and above all, ambitious ones who sent their children to the best schools. Taken as a whole, the figures for Jewish Gymnasium attendance attest to a conscious effort by Jews to expand their numbers within the educated elite of Germany and Austria.

The situation with regard to universities and other institutions of advanced learning was similarly remarkable. In 1886–1887 the 1,134

Jewish students from within the imperial boundaries who attended Prussian institutions of advanced learning made up 9 percent of the students. This represented the peak proportion, which fell after 1887 as the general student population grew. Even though there were 1,356 Jewish students in Prussia in 1911–1912, they now made up only 5.6 percent. Nevertheless, still in 1911 five times as large a percentage of Jews as of non-Jews attended universities in Prussia. Similarly, in Austria, there were 4,272 Jewish students studying at institutions of higher learning in 1904, a figure that represented 18 percent of all students and a disproportion of four to one.

In both the Kaiserreich and in Austria Jewish students showed a preference for institutions located in the capital cities of Berlin and Vienna where the largest Jewish communities were also to be found. At the turn of the century more than half of all Jewish students in Austria were studying in Vienna, where they made up approximately a quarter of the students at the University of Vienna. The German university in Prague had a proportion of Jewish students as high as 27 percent, and at the small university at Czernowitz it was 41 percent. These figures attest to the fact that, in comparison to Germany, the Jewish educated elite in Austria occupied an even more important position. In Imperial Germany in 1886–1887 the highest proportion of Jews occurred at the Universities of Berlin and Breslau, with 17 percent in each instance. Both universities also attracted Jewish students from czarist Russia where there was a quota for Jewish students. Additional students came to the University of Breslau from the rabbinical seminary there because all rabbinical students were required to enroll in the university's school of philosophy.

In their choice of disciplines Jewish students in Germany and Austria clearly differed from their non-Jewish counterparts. This difference reflected the occupational restrictions that Jews anticipated would occur: the effects of antisemitism upon the employment of Jews in civil service positions. To be sure, equal access to such positions was constitutionally guaranteed, but there was a de facto understanding on the part of administrators to circumvent constitutional provisions, a practice more common in Imperial Germany than in Austria (see chapter 6). Only with difficulty and in exceptional cases could Jews get appointments as government officials, and, even then, they were rarely promoted. Thus, already as students, Jews saw their future limited to the free professions, knowing that, as we have noted earlier, if they sought positions as teachers, judges, or professors, they would face severe difficulties and experience considerable pressure to convert. The relatively high number of career-oriented baptisms among Jewish university graduates indicates that many students later gave in to the conversionary pressure. Most Jewish students, however, during their studies had already chosen a career in which they could be self-employed and hence avoid such coercion.

The result was that Jews gave preference to the study of medicine. The profession of physician had a long tradition among Jews and, because of their excellent reputations, Jewish doctors had usually treated Christian as well as Jewish patients. In 1886–1887 57 percent of all Jewish students in Prussia still chose to study medicine. As a result, 37 percent of all students in the medical school in Berlin and 34 percent of all the medical students in Breslau in those years were Jews. However, in the ensuing period the number of Jewish law students rose consistently and finally surpassed the number of those studying medicine. The reason for this increase was the liberation of the practice of law from state controls in 1879; until then practice had been conditional upon the receipt of state permission in Prussia, which was often denied to Jews. By the year 1905–1906 conditions had changed so much that 41 percent of the Jews in Prussia now studied law, 25 percent medicine, and 34 percent were enrolled in the sciences and humanities. The distribution of Jewish students into various disciplines was similar in Austria. There, in 1903–1904, 54 percent studied law, 21 percent medicine, and 25 percent were in the sciences and humanities. In both countries Jews still studied medicine more frequently than non-Jews, and they graduated less often in the sciences and humanities since those disciplines primarily served the training of teachers.

For the reasons mentioned, most of the Jewish graduates went on to set up private practices while a large portion of non-Jews obtained government positions. The unwritten restrictions affecting Jews were especially apparent in instances where they chose an academic career, with the result that they remained unsalaried lecturers (*Privatdozenten*). Rarely were they appointed to professorships, which were civil service positions. When they were, it was only after a lengthy period of waiting and then mostly to chairs in the natural sciences. From among the large number of highly qualified Jewish lecturers those who gained appointment as professors almost always paid the price of baptism. A Jewish university lecturer who was not also a physician or lawyer had to rely on funds obtained from his family or through his marriage. (On this subject see also chapter 6.)

Very few employment opportunities existed for Jewish teachers in the public school system since schools were assumed to be Christian and most of the educational institutions were religious schools. Only in nondenominational schools, like those found in Berlin and Baden, for example, did a few Jewish teachers find employment. Thus in Prussia in 1905 there were 290 Jewish teachers employed in the Jewish schools and only 48 in the public schools. Most of the Jewish teachers had no choice but the Jewish elementary schools, whose numbers were steadily decreasing with the growth of Jewish urbanization. In small Jewish communities many elementary school teachers also functioned as cantors and religious leaders since only larger Jewish communities were able to afford rabbis. As opposed to 1,100 cantors in Germany in 1905, there were only 217 rabbis. The latter were educated and trained at the rabbinical seminaries in Berlin and Breslau and almost always obtained a university doctorate as well. Most of the teachers had only attended a teachers college, but it was not unusual for university graduates to teach in urban Jewish schools as well.

A portion of those who graduated in the humanities turned to journalism. The expanding scope of the press made it possible for many Jewish university graduates to make a living as editors, freelance contributors, and critics. They worked not so much for the Jewish press, that is, for newspapers written by and for Jews, as they did for the liberal press of the Mosse and Ullstein publishing houses, for the recently established cultural periodicals, and also for the socialist press. Journalists such as Julius Bab, Alfred Kerr, Maximilian Harden, Ernst Feder, and Theodor Wolff gained significant reputations, but they were also attacked by conservatives and antisemites as representatives of the "Jewified press." Since the Jewish journalists were employed by the newspapers of the Liberal center, the left, and the cultural avant-garde, they easily attracted the intense dislike of right-wing conservatives.

Of those Jews holding degrees in law, the vast majority worked as lawyers rather than judges. In 1907 there were already 1,877 Jewish attorneys in the German Empire, 15 percent of all those in the profession. There were 526 Jewish lawyers in Berlin alone, representing over half the attorneys there. This high proportion indicates that the Jewish lawyers not only represented Jewish merchants but that their competence had also won them a sizable Christian clientele. Many of the attorneys were also employed as legal advisers for Jewish communities and for large Jewish organizations. This was particularly the case for the legal defense division of the Centralverein deutscher Staatsbürger jüdischen Glaubens

(Central Association of German Citizens of the Jewish Faith), created by Jewish lawyers. The constant need to defend Jewish civil rights against antisemitic attacks gave Jewish lawyers an additional sphere of legal work. Only with tremendous difficulty could Jews become judges, and even then they were subject to intense conversionary pressures if they sought promotion. In 1907 there were 155 Jewish judges (4.2 percent) in Prussia but an additional 108 who had converted out of Judaism. By 1914 the proportion of Jewish judges had fallen to 2.8 percent, an indication that Jewish students with a law degree almost always chose to practice as lawyers.

There is no doubt that Jewish doctors had the best occupational prospects since they worked overwhelmingly in private practice and their work was judged more by what they accomplished than by the fact that they were Jews. Jewish physicians did not find themselves in the center of political strife as often as Jewish professors, lawyers, judges, and journalists. Since, for the reasons already given, Jews continued to prefer the study of medicine into the 1890s, the medical profession among Jews in the Kaiserreich remained the most widespread of those requiring a university education. In 1907 there were 4,719 Jewish doctors and dentists in the German Empire, amounting to 6 percent. Like the attorneys, they were to be found primarily in the large cities where they practiced at municipal hospitals. In addition, there were also Jewish hospitals, for example in Berlin, Breslau, Hamburg, and Cologne, that afforded Jewish doctors additional opportunities for developing their medical skills. Numerous Jewish physicians gained reputations as important researchers —such as the Nobel prize winner for medicine Paul Ehrlich (1854–1918)—even if they did not get university chairs and, instead, ran specialized clinics or worked at research institutes.

The proportion of Jews in the professions who were self-employed continued to rise in Imperial Germany. By the time of the 1925 census Jews made up 26 percent of all lawyers and 15 percent of all doctors. Because of widespread urbanization the percentage of Jews in these professions increased to its highest level in the big cities. This was clearly the case for Berlin. Although there are no statistics available for Vienna, it is possible to draw a similar conclusion on the basis of occupations listed for the fathers of pupils in academic high schools. Between 1870 and 1910, for example, it appears on the basis of this evidence that Jewish attorneys, physicians, and journalists in Vienna comprised up to 40 percent of these occupational groups and that after the turn of the century they made up more than half. Such evidence is indicative of the large share of the Jewish minority within the Viennese intelligentsia.

The augmented entry of Jews into the professions coincided with a crisis in the job market for academically trained professionals. In the public debate over the saturation of this market and over extending the waiting period for those seeking positions as jurists and teachers, antisemitic agitators were quick to label Jews as the cause of this crisis, clearly expressing a fear of competition. The Jewish educated elite was, therefore, not only largely excluded from civil service positions, it was also repeatedly subjected to anti-Jewish hostility in the universities and the free professions.

4. Social Stratification

Just as Jews exhibited their own distinct occupational distribution, the social stratification of the Jewish minority was also distinguishable from that of the general population. Although the specifically Jewish class structure is difficult to document statistically, it is possible to make certain observations with regard to the social development of the Jewish minority and the relationship of the Jewish social structure to that of the population as a whole.

The increasing turn to occupations in trades and industry and to the professions had only a limited effect on the Jewish occupational structure in Imperial Germany. More significant transformations occurred with regard to positions held within a particular occupation. Although self-employment was still twice as high in the Jewish population as in the population as a whole, this gap began to narrow. In the short span from 1895 to 1907 the proportion of self-employed Jews fell from 58 to 50 percent, while that of salaried employees rose from 11 to 17 percent. This was a clear indication that, among Jews too, a new class of managers, administrators, and clerical personnel was emerging. The process of economic concentration necessitated a larger clerical and administrative apparatus in which an increasing number of female employees worked as well. Salespeople, consisting of sales assistants, family members who worked in the family business, and laborers, made up a third of the Jewish workforce. The laborers, defined as "support staff with no specific training," constituted only a very small portion of this group. Barely 3 percent of the Jewish workforce in 1907 fell into this category as opposed to 24 percent of the general working population, namely, the industrial and agricultural proletariat. Even when Jews were lower class, they were usually still self-employed, that is, as very small-scale vendors who operated without capital. However, as Jews valued vocational training highly and it was rare for a young man not to receive at least some training in business, few Jews joined the ranks of uneducated workers.

The various types of economic activity within a particular occupation do not in themselves reveal much about the income and class structure of the Jewish population. A self-employed person might be a large-scale entrepreneur or a peddler, and a salaried employee could enjoy a better income than many who were self-employed. Conclusions with regard to social stratification are therefore best made on the basis of income, education, and lifestyle. Precise data about the income and financial situation of German Jews are rare and rest only on a few tax records that, moreover, are difficult to interpret. We know even less about changes in the financial situation of Jews during the economic booms in Imperial Germany. From 1891–1895 and from 1911–1913 the Kaiserreich underwent intensive industrialization, and the real per capita income of the population rose on the average about 31 percent. It is difficult to know whether the Jewish population experienced the same rise or a disproportionately higher one. We can assume, however, that when compared to the general population Jews in the early years of the German Empire already formed a heavily middle-class minority with an income on the average higher than the rest of the working population. From a methodological perspective it thus makes more sense to compare their income with that of the middle class rather than the general population, which contained a large proportion of agricultural and industrial workers who were not at all typical among Jews. The divergence of the Jewish occupational structure necessarily entailed a divergent pattern of income.

In order to utilize tax records for the comparison of tax payments by Jews to those by the general population it is first important to note the proportion of working persons who were assessed income tax in the first place. In Prussia annual incomes under nine hundred marks remained untaxed, so that, for instance, 30 percent of Jews and 59 percent of the general population in Duisburg in 1899 did not have to pay any taxes at all. In Aachen in 1910, this rate was 24 percent for Jews and 51 percent for the total number employed. Thus it appears that the general population was assessed taxes only about half as often as were the Jews. These proportions certainly confirm the largely middle-class character of the Jewish minority, but they also reveal that a fourth of Jews in both of these cities belonged to the lower income groups.

Records from the city of Düsseldorf provide a rare opportunity to compare incomes on the basis of taxation categories. While two-thirds of the Jews who paid taxes there in 1902 were assessed in the lowest tax bracket (annual income between nine hundred and three thousand marks), 89 percent of all taxpayers fell into this category. Jews were overrepresented in the next five higher tax brackets, which again reflects the fact that they formed a higher proportion of the upper middle and upper levels of the middle class. However, among the seventy-one taxpayers in Düsseldorf in the highest tax bracket (annual income of over one hundred thousand marks), only four were Jews. This financial distribution in Düsseldorf, whose Jewish community was above average in terms of wealth, can perhaps be viewed as typical of the upwardly mobile Jewish communities in the industrial area of western Germany. Approximately a fourth of the Jews there belonged to the lower and lower middle classes, the middle and upper middle classes formed the broadest single stratum, while at the highest financial level Jews were scarcely represented. Seen as a whole, the distinguishing characteristics of this social structure are its middle-class nature and its great homogeneity. In comparison to the general population the payment of taxes by Jews in the industrial cities of western Germany was some three to four times higher, and it was still climbing after 1890 even as levels of payment were also rising for all taxpayers. If we look at the differentiation of Jewish incomes, a decrease in homogeneity is apparent beginning in 1885. On the one hand, this was due to the increase in incomes that occurred at the height of the boom phase, on the other, to a growing number of indigent Jewish refugees who had fled the pogroms in czarist Russia and come to the promising Ruhr area in search of work.

With regard to the larger Jewish communities, data relating to Jewish income and taxation are available for Breslau, Hamburg, and Frankfurt. Unlike the industrial cities of western Germany, these communities possessed long-established Jewish populations with greater representation in the highest income brackets. In Breslau, where the Prussian three-class voting system was in effect, voters registered according to three tax brackets. By 1874 15 percent of the Jews but only 2 percent of all taxpayers belonged to the highest tax classification, 49 percent to the intermediate as compared to 13 percent of the total, and only 36 percent of Jews, as against 85 percent of all those who had to pay taxes, to the lowest. This tax distribution gives us the image of a middle-class Jewish minority with a prominent upper class. It tells us nothing, however, about the classes at the bottom, who did not have to pay taxes.

More exact data are available for the incomes of Jews in Hamburg. As early as 1871 Jews there were a decidedly middle-class group with an above average income: 43 percent of Jews but only 26 percent of the entire population paid taxes on an annual income of between 1,200 and 3,600 marks; 27 percent of Jews had a higher income, while only 12 percent of all those paying taxes belonged to the higher income groups. In 1897, as a consequence of a general growth in income, the average income of tax-payers in Hamburg was 3,192 marks. Jews in Hamburg, however, had an average income of 4,052 marks, almost a fourth more. Three-quarters of all taxpayers, but only half of the Jews, belonged to the two lowest income brackets (800 to 2,000 marks), while 38 percent of Jews, in contrast to 17 percent of all taxpayers, were represented in the middle-income brackets (2,000 to 5,000 marks). Incomes of over 5,000 marks were earned by 17 percent of Jews but only 9 percent of all taxpayers.

This disproportionately favorable financial situation of the Jews in Hamburg was exceeded by the Jews of Frankfurt. In 1900 32 percent of the Jews there, as opposed to 16 percent of taxpayers in general, had an annual income of over six thousand marks, so that they were even better represented in the highest income bracket than were the Jews of Hamburg. But, as for Breslau, we have no information for either Hamburg or Frankfurt with regard to Jews who did not have to pay taxes—those with annual incomes of less than eight hundred marks for Hamburg or nine hundred marks for Frankfurt. Although the absence of such figures may make the Jews' economic situation appear somewhat too positive, it does not materially alter the picture of Jews in all three cities belonging mainly to the middle class, possessing income and wealth appropriate to that class, revealing a preference for middle-class residential areas, and striving for a higher level of education for their children.

The favorable income situation of the Jewish middle class in the big cities should not, however, be viewed as indicative of the situation of all Jews. First of all, we should recall the growing social differentiation based on income that characterized Berlin. The German capital was home to the most extensive Jewish upper class, consisting of a wealthy economic elite that included numerous millionaires. At the same time, many poorer immigrants from the eastern provinces of Prussia and from Eastern Europe lived there, some of them belonging to the lower class. The immigration movements that brought people from the economically underdeveloped regions to those that were modernizing ensured that, especially in the large cities, a lower class would always be present, people who were trying to better themselves and who, when they succeeded, attracted newcomers. Class distinctions had clearly developed among Berlin Jews, as well, but were moderated on account of the broad Jewish middle class and, not least, because of the well-organized Jewish social welfare arrangements.

The greatest differences in social class were to be found in Vienna, where a wealthy upper class of ennobled Jewish millionaires lived in splendid residences along the Ringstrasse. They stood in contrast to Jewish proletarians from Galicia, immigrants without any means or education, who lived in crowded conditions in the Leopoldstadt and Brigittenau districts. These immigrants came especially after the beginning of the century, fleeing economic boycott, antisemitism, and overpopulation. Before World War I Galicians accounted for at least a fourth of all Viennese Jews, although only very few of them appeared on the tax rolls. Definite social and cultural tensions existed between them and the other Jews of Vienna. But here, too, social polarization was lessened by the Jewish community's social welfare institutions.

Apart from the distinctive class structure of the Jewish communities in the big cities, there were also regional differences in income and wealth. Not only was there considerable differentiation between urban and rural communities but also between the more agricultural and the more industrialized regions. If during the mid-nineteenth century it was mainly the poor Jews from rural Jewish communities and agricultural regions who had emigrated overseas, by the end of the century it was many of their most affluent Jewish taxpayers, along with a large portion of the younger generation, who left for the cities. The result was a decrease in income in rural areas and an overage Jewish population. Yet if the rural Jews were now to be seen as lower middle class in comparison to urban Jewry, they still represented the middle class within the local village populations. The rural Jews also had their own small upper class of wealthy horse traders, brokers, and dealers in textile products, as well as a lower class of assistants who had no capital, and day laborers.

We know little about the social stratification of foreign Jews in Germany. It would be inaccurate to assume that they all belonged to the lower class. Among them were intellectuals, students, artists, people of private means, middle-class merchants, and well-to-do wholesalers. Nonetheless, most foreign Jews worked as tradesmen, small-scale retailers, and industrial workers and thus belonged predominantly to the lower and lower-middle classes. During World War I, as ever more Jews without financial means left the occupied territories and came to Germany as workers, an image of poverty came to be associated with East European Jews in general. Still, most of the foreign Jews in Germany were young and ambitious, and many succeeded in rising to the lower middle class.

Jewish criminal statistics were likewise stamped by class and occupational distribution. As a dominantly middle-class minority, Jews in general exhibited a lower rate of criminality than did the total population. Their participation in thefts, violent crimes, and murders was disproportionately low but relatively high for economic crimes. Thus in Prussia, for example, they were convicted four times as often as Christians for breaking laws governing trade and industry and for fraud, and twice as often for forgery.

If, on the whole, it can be said that Jews in Imperial Germany constituted a relatively homogeneous minority with approximately two-thirds of its members belonging to the middle class, it is clear that, nevertheless, they exhibited an internal class differentiation. At the top of the social hierarchy was a very small Jewish upper class, which, because of its wealth and economic importance, was highly visible and served as the main focus for antisemitic attacks. This uppermost group was principally concentrated in Berlin and consisted mainly of bankers and large-scale businessmen. Jews comprised half of the sixty wealthiest taxpayers in Berlin. A few members of this financial aristocracy, like Carl Fürstenberg, Emil Rathenau, and Fritz von Friedländer-Fuld, also had access to Emperor Wilhelm II, but they and their wives were denied formal presentation at court. Their ambiguous position in society in relation to the Christian upper class as well as to the Jewish community was a problem unique to this Jewish upper class. Highly acculturated and often readily willing to enter into a mixed marriage or be baptized, they frequently avoided appearing as Jews to the outside world. However, ever-present antisemitism prevented the Jewish upper class from ever gaining genuine social acceptance. They lived in villas in the Tiergarten and Grunewald sections of Berlin, maintained an appropriate lifestyle, and moved in their own circles as well as among artists, diplomats, and higher civil servants—much less frequently among the aristocracy. Several of them had turned down ennoblement although in Austria, under Emperor Francis Joseph, numerous members of the Viennese Jewish upper class accepted it. Antisemites attacked this class as the embodiment of capitalism and as dangerous social climbers, thus projecting the problems of an advanced capitalistic society onto a minority. Representatives of this Jewish upper class were found far less frequently outside Berlin. A few important families, like the Rothschilds in Frankfurt, the Oppenheims in Cologne, the Warburgs and Albert Ballin in Hamburg, belonged to it although they were not part of a local Jewish economic elite equivalent in size to those of Berlin and Vienna.

Just beneath the upper class in the social hierarchy came a rather broad upper middle class consisting of well-to-do merchants and manufacturers who increasingly counted lawyers and doctors among their family members and who often received the honorary title of *Kommerzienrat*. Members of this class served not only in chambers of commerce and city councils but also on the boards of directors of numerous Jewish organizations. In general, they expressed their Jewishness more openly than the members of the upper class. They lived comfortably in villas and in apartments in the best residential areas and mainly socialized within their own circle. A portion of this class was Orthodox and used its wealth generously to establish and maintain religious institutions.

The central layer of the Jewish middle class formed a broad and diverse stratum. It consisted of members of the middle-level income groups who were mainly independent entrepreneurs, merchants, and university graduates but also managers, bookkeepers, traveling sales representatives as well as some whose livelihoods were more lower middle class in nature. What they all had in common was a secure but limited income and the emphasis they placed on middle-class values and lifestyles. A striving for education and culture was a feature of this class as was higher education for their children and living in middle-class residential areas. Their political orientation was heavily Liberal and decidedly patriotic. Among most of its members religiosity had decreased, but there remained a wide range of Jewish identities running from Orthodoxy to Liberal Judaism to a secular Jewishness.

In its occupational distribution, family life, religion, and political orientation the Jewish middle class was clearly distinguishable. Despite acculturation, it remained to a large degree set apart, not fully integrated into the general middle class to which it felt that it belonged. Occupational discrimination continued to make its nonacceptance apparent. Even as antisemites attacked the Jewish financial aristocracy out of their displeasure with capitalism, they also stigmatized the Jewish middle class for its alleged capacity to destroy German culture. It was precisely the potential social convergence of the Jewish and the Christian middle classes on the basis of their common class identity that persuaded right-wing conservatives and antisemites that strong defensive measures were necessary to prevent it. Thus, although there were individual contacts between members of both classes, as a group the Jews failed to gain general acceptance.

In sum, then, the Jewish occupational structure in Imperial Germany underwent relatively little change even though an increased tendency for men to choose occupations that required a university education and for women to undertake remunerative employment became apparent. With the increasing production of consumer goods, the Jews' close connection with commerce, along with their moderately greater participation in business and industry, made it possible for them to experience unprecedented economic success. Such success was evident in their above average taxable income and in the fact that two-thirds of them belonged to the middle class. On the other hand, this relatively homogeneous middle-class social profile of German Jewry was diminished by the influx of poorer Jews from Eastern Europe, leading in turn to a more differentiated class structure.

3 | Jewish Women in the Family and Public Sphere

1. Family and the Attainment of Middle-Class Status

It is difficult to overestimate the significance of family life in the preservation of Judaism and the formation of Jewish identity. Certainly for observant Jews not only the Jewish community but also the Jewish family constitute an important sphere of religious activity. Keeping the dietary laws and the Sabbath and celebrating the holidays in the prescribed manner all characterize the traditional Jewish home. Here, well in advance of formal religious instruction, children acquire an emotional attachment to Judaism that they retain in the form of memories even if later in life they distance themselves from all religious practice. It is this close connection between family and religion that has played a large role in enabling Judaism to be passed down from generation to generation through the centuries.

A radical transformation in the German-Jewish family occurred during the nineteenth century. The emancipation of the Jews, their increasing acculturation, and the social ascent of most Jews into the middle class led to the Jewish family adopting the character and values of the middle-class family as its own. Social advancement entailed changes in its configuration and function. Jews now no longer lived exclusively in their own social and cultural milieu; rather, they strove for equal rights and integration into the larger society, while simultaneously retaining their specifically Jewish group identity. The family now assumed a dual function: it remained the most important means of preserving Jewish identity, while, at the same time, furthering the process of attaining middle-class status by adopting appropriate cultural norms and modes of behavior. It thus created a modern synthesis of Judaism and bourgeois values. The result was a distinctly Jewish middle class that differed from the German one and was never accepted as its equal.

By the middle of the nineteenth century the Jewish family was characterized by its oscillation between two poles: preservation of Jewish traditions and norms within the home and conformity to the patterns of family life that prevailed in the outside world, the latter usually accompanied by increasing secularization. Each family worked out its own individual solution. Even families that remained Orthodox adopted some middle-class values, while secularized families rarely gave up their Judaism entirely. The latter was most clearly illustrated by the widespread preservation of group cohesion and the practice of endogamy. Even after 1871 in-group marriage functioned to assure the continuity of Judaism and thus remained the strongest expression of Jewish identity and self-affirmation. Secular Jews, as well, often rejected marriage with non-Jews, justifying it as filial piety owed to their parents. Indeed, it was endogamy, primarily controlled and protected by the family, that was the most effective means for stemming the tide against absorption into the larger society.

The Jewish family in Imperial Germany was nearly always marked by a contrast between the lifestyles of the older and younger generations. In memoirs grandparents born before the middle of the century are usually depicted as living pious traditional lives, as opposed to children and grandchildren who have abandoned many traditions in response to rapid social and religious changes, especially in the urban centers. Some parents did not eat in their childrens' homes because the latter were no longer kosher. Instead, the extended family would often spend Friday evenings in a traditional manner, dining at the home of the grandparents. Within the younger generation individual families developed an astonishingly wide range of religious and cultural patterns of behavior. A single family might both celebrate Passover with the traditional festive family service around the table and Christmas with a Christmas tree. Religious and typically middle-class rituals could intermingle without those who took part in them perceiving any incompatibility.

Once middle-class status was attained the social gender roles of husband and wife underwent change. In traditional Judaism the husband, who alone is obligated to study Torah and Talmud, carries religious

7   Children of the Mosse family (from the album of Felicia
Mosse, wife of publisher Rudolf Mosse, 1903)

authority in the family. The study house, the synagogue, and the community had always been the domain of the husband, while the wife was
responsible mainly for the children and the home. However, before the
modern period Jewish commercial ventures had often been family enterprises in which the wife worked alongside her husband, especially when
business and living quarters were housed together. Then, in the course of
ascending to the middle class, the husband usually assumed sole responsibility for supporting the family as his increased income established the
prerequisites for a middle-class standard of living. In the process the wife
was relegated entirely to the home, the children, and the family. The
structure of the family thus remained patriarchal, and the polarization of

social gender traits came to approximate the typical pattern of the non-Jewish middle class.

As secularization advanced the husband's authority was based less and less on religious knowledge and far more on occupation, secular education, and wealth. Many married men no longer performed their religious functions within the family on Sabbaths and Jewish holidays, thereby relinquishing their religious authority. Their knowledge of Judaism had become meager and they often attended synagogue services only during the High Holidays, becoming so-called three-day-a-year Jews. In Orthodox families, by contrast, the husband's religious authority within the family did not decline. Likewise among lower middle-class rural Jews the religious way of life, and the traditional form of the family along with it, were maintained for a longer time. The same was true for most of the East European Jewish families that immigrated to Germany, although they also strove for middle-class status and after a time gave up the old way of life.

The Jewish head of the family represented his family's interests in the public sphere, joined associations and political parties, and held offices in Jewish and general organizations. Contact with non-Jews on an individual basis was largely the monopoly of the husband and took place outside the home. Since the arrangement of having home and business under one roof also became less common, the husband remained away from home for longer periods of time. This in turn tended to make the position of the Jewish wife even stronger within the family than it had been in the past. Like his middle-class counterparts, the Jewish husband increasingly viewed his family as a milieu for relaxation and recuperation from the stress of making a living. He is often portrayed in memoirs as absent from home, preoccupied, or secluded in his study, though rarely as a family tyrant incorporating the military lifestyle of the non-Jewish German man. The reason for the latter has to do with the Jewish husband's traditional respect for the home as his wife's domain and also perhaps with the fact that Jews could not join the higher ranks of the army and thus did not adopt the commanding tone associated with reserve officers. Above all, the Jewish husband saw it as his task to guarantee the family's status and respectability while leaving the family sphere itself mostly to his wife.

In the course of her social ascent the Jewish wife usually relinquished her role as her husband's business partner since it now seemed demeaning for her to be seen working. As was customary for the middle class, her visible idleness, as well as that of her daughters, was meant to demon-

8   The Meyers in Bardewisch (Oldenburg), a rural family at the end of the
nineteenth century

strate the prosperity and status of her family. In the household itself the
wife's duties likewise changed because she had fewer children to take care
of and had one or more servants to assist her. She devoted a larger portion
of her time now to those cultural and social obligations that would make
the family truly middle class. These were mainly four: attending to the
careful rearing and education of the children, raising the cultural level of
the home and the lifestyle of the family, arranging social gatherings
within the extended family and among friends, and, finally, the specifically Jewish task of preserving Jewish traditions in the home, with varying degrees of observance.

The wife's most important duty was teaching proper German values
and culture to her children. In the process of acculturation the greatest
accomplishment for the Jewish wife and mother was to have children who
were well brought up in terms of conformity to middle-class ideals. The
mother molded language and behavior, taste and manners. She selected
the children's clothing with care, supervised their educational progress,

provided them with music lessons, and joined them at piano practice. Jewish women took motherhood very seriously and felt solely responsible for the development of their children's personalities. Valuable information in this regard can be gleaned from the journal that was kept by the wife of a Berlin merchant on the progress of her six children. She watched over them both lovingly and critically, considering how she could best nurture their individual talents and, with the help of proper education, minimize their particular weaknesses. She mentions the father only once very briefly in this capacity. It is also clear from the journal that the likelihood of their being subjected to antisemitism was a weighty consideration in choosing a kindergarten and school for the children. Mothers preferred to send their children to kindergartens that were run according to the advanced educational theories of Friedrich Froebel since these institutions provided a nondenominational education.

In addition to her role as mother, the wife was responsible, to a considerable degree, for the lifestyle and culture of the family. She chose a residence in the proper neighborhood and picked out tasteful furnishings to go into it. Aside from music, she took charge of a number of other important activities that took place in the home, such as reading classical works of literature with the children, reading aloud the various roles in a play, memorizing poems, and composing occasional poetry for birthdays and weddings. The most recent novels were also read in the home, as were the newspapers preferred by the Jewish middle class, such as the *Israelitisches Familienblatt* and the liberal *Berliner Tageblatt*. Season tickets to the theater and attendance at concerts exposed the children to European culture.

It was the wife's task to make arrangements for social gatherings with relatives and Jewish friends. She had the table decorated in a festive manner, chose the menu, and organized dinners, home concerts, and balls. The extended family often assembled weekly on Friday evenings and on the Jewish holidays. Since the number of children in the parents' and grandparents' generations was still large, there were always numerous uncles, aunts, and cousins in the same locality or in other big cities. In addition, the wife was in charge of keeping in touch with relatives who lived further away through visits, correspondence, and summer trips taken together. Social gatherings were often useful for discreetly introducing potential marriage partners. Many a daughter became acquainted with her future spouse at an aunt's house or a cousin's wedding. If the family was more well-to-do, the summer vacation trip was a regular part of the year's activities. Mothers made extensive preparations for such vacations.

9   The Warburg family in Hamburg (1884)

Taking care of older relatives was also the wife's domain, and widowed parents were frequently absorbed into the nuclear family.

Education and culture were enormously important for Jewish families in Imperial Germany. *Bildung* was not only an end in itself, as had been the case even before 1871, but also the means to social advancement and integration. Education and culture were, however, entirely different for men and for women, for sons and for daughters. In Jewish middle-class families, as in non-Jewish ones, the education of sons and daughters was determined by the appropriate social gender roles. It was expected that sons would, if at all possible, graduate from an academic high school while daughters were sent to an appropriate girls' school from which they graduated at the age of sixteen. The advanced formal education of sons stood in contrast to the less professional training of daughters, who, as was generally the case in the middle class, did not receive preparation for a working life but for their later duties as wives and mothers.

Nonetheless, on the whole, Jewish girls received a better education than other daughters of the middle class. By the turn of the century the percentage of Jewish girls in the advanced girls' schools in Berlin and

Vienna was five times the percentage of Jews in the population. However, the girls' schools imparted only superficial knowledge, mainly in subjects considered to be "feminine" such as literature, music, French, and needlework. Daughters from wealthy families were sometimes sent away for an additional year to board at a girls' finishing school. After completing their schooling, girls began a long period of waiting at home. While their brothers attended *Gymnasium* (the academic high school) and university or served a commercial apprenticeship, the girls, as "refined daughters," customarily had to wait passively, sometimes for years, until a proper marriage would come along. During this interval the parents busied themselves looking for suitable partners for their daughters and pondered ways of raising a dowry. These years of waiting were viewed as wasted time, especially by those few women who later prepared for a profession. The Social Democrat Hedwig Wachenheim wrote in retrospect: "After finishing school my life consisted mainly of doing needlework, visiting my grandmothers, coffee get-togethers, attending theater and balls, ice skating, and going on six-week-long summer vacations."[1] In only a few middle-class families, Christian or Jewish, was professional training even considered for daughters. Such training, it was feared, might give the impression of financial difficulty and thus lower the daughter's prospects for marriage.

Jewish parents made every effort to send their sons to an academic high school. If the family lived in the country, sons would often be sent to board with a Jewish family in a nearby city to attend the Gymnasium there. Parents urged their sons to study hard because they saw successful completion of an academic high school as the prerequisite for a middle-class career. This was true not only for university-educated families but also for families that made their living through commerce. The result was that Jewish boys in the middle-class neighborhoods of big cities attended the Gymnasium in large numbers. In Berlin in 1905 a fourth of all pupils attending academic high schools came from Jewish families, although barely 5 percent of all boys in Berlin were Jewish.

Antisemitic incidents were not unusual in the high schools, although their frequency varied according to region. Parents reacted by sending their sons, if at all possible, to a Gymnasium that had a reputation for being liberal, but, for the most part, they were unable to spare their sons some bitter experiences. It was precisely because of antisemitism that Jewish families were so concerned to give their sons a solid foundation for making a living. Since the educationally oriented Jewish middle-class milieu created ideal conditions for success in school, the achievements of Jewish pupils generally exceeded the average.

It was important for the self-image of bourgeois Jewish families that they have at their disposal not only possessions but also Bildung. Indeed, it was through their educational and cultural attainments that they hoped to gain respect and acceptance within the German middle class. Culture was to become the medium for social integration. In Imperial Germany, however, the more idealistic, enlightened idea of Bildung, which German Jews had long taken as their model, was becoming obsolete. By this time the German educated middle class had absorbed nationalistic and antisemitic elements into its ideology and, using racist arguments, increasingly denied Jews the right to be bearers of German culture. As Liberal voices grew weaker, Jews encountered stricter limits on their social integration.

Not all German Jews seized the opportunity to become middle class in the manner portrayed here, although the majority did. In the lower middle class, in rural areas, and within the Eastern European Jewish proletariat the material circumstances of families were more modest, even if the bourgeois model, for the most part, was operative here as well. In the Jewish upper class lifestyles approaching those of the aristocracy prevailed, while the poorer immigrant population from Eastern Europe retained some elements of traditional Jewish family life. In the lower middle class and in the lower class women and girls often held jobs or worked in the family business. As a result, they had less leisure time for cultivating the family as a showpiece of middle-class life. There were few servants in these families; the mother ran the household herself, by necessity adhering to the virtue of frugality. Sons mainly served apprenticeships in their father's business, while daughters became teachers, nannies, or seamstresses.

The Jewish class structure could easily be detected in contrasting familial lifestyles. Even within the Jewish middle class there was a clear social hierarchy that reached from the urban upper middle class down to the families of village teachers. Wealthier mothers, to a large extent, turned over the upbringing of their children to a governess because they were deeply absorbed in displaying the representative lifestyle and fulfilling the social obligations of the family. One daughter wrote: "She was a mother whose hand we were allowed to kiss now and again and, after knocking on her door, could observe sitting in a dressing gown at her writing desk, book in hand. Meanwhile, upstairs, the maid was waiting to get us ready for bed."[2] In the countryside it was above all the families of teachers, living very modestly, who perceived themselves as cultured in

10   Mother, nanny, and children (Leipzig, 1901)

contrast to the Jewish traders in the village. Their wives had none but the children to call on for assistance in running their households. Only when it came time for the Sabbath meal on Friday evening did they get some rest from their exhausting labors and proudly survey their children. "Huge tears of joy roll down her face. This is mother's military review. Here she is general, a proud victor. Valiantly she has fought the battles of work, mended the baskets full of laundry, made all the clothing for her children, managed to feed them at little expense, and raised all eight. She has every right to be satisfied, and she is."[3] This family blesses the children on the eve of the Sabbath, the father recites the blessing over the wine and bread, and, after the meal, they play games and read together. Preserving the religious authority of the father and the division of religious gender roles, this rural family lived a significantly more traditional Jewish life.

2. Family and Tradition

The Jewish family's attainment of middle-class status during the *Kaiserreich* is easily documented and hard to overlook. But how Jewish did the family remain? How did continuity or change in Jewish tradition manifest itself in the face of middle-class status and secularization? These questions are far more difficult to answer because, apart from the Orthodox milieu and among rural Jews, religious themes usually receive scant treatment in autobiographical sources. That makes it hard to draw conclusions about the significance of religious traditions in daily life. The families proudly displayed their middle-class status and their Bildung to the outside world, but, apart from sporadic attendance at synagogue, exhibited their Jewishness only in the intimate family circle. It is not just a question of how extensively the family still observed the religious commandments, such as resting on the Sabbath and keeping the dietary laws. Cultural values, attitudes, and patterns of behavior, which had been observed and handed down for generations, were also part and parcel of the Jewish heritage. Examples are Hebrew and Jewish expressions in the family's colloquial speech, traditional Jewish foods, the high value placed on learning and on charity, the forms of matchmaking, and close family ties stretching across great distances.

When the German Empire was founded no more than two generations had passed since the time when the vast majority of German Jews still led fully observant lives, largely isolated, both socially and culturally, from the larger society. Thus the prevailing values and modes of behavior of the grandparents' generation were bound to leave traces in the lives of Jewish families in the Kaiserreich even if they were no longer present in their totality. Every Jewish family, regardless of how secularized it might be, was familiar with Jewish traditions, whether it preserved, disregarded, or made fun of them. However fragmentary, the heritage was still there, and, to varying degrees, played a role in Jewish family life. Much has been written about assimilation in the sense of social adaptation and abandonment of Jewish culture, much less on the continuity and change of Jewish traditions and the forms in which they continued to exist. It was within the family that both processes, simultaneously and intensively, took place.

As in the attainment of middle-class status, the key role in the preservation of Jewish tradition within the family fell to the women. They guided this cultural process primarily through their own example and through education. The transmission of Judaism, originally a task shared by husband and wife within the family, increasingly became the responsibility of the wife, who often possessed only a limited religious education. Husbands were more frequently absent and more rapidly secularized. In Orthodox as well as Liberal Judaism the realization arose that the religious significance of women had increased and that therefore it was necessary for them to receive an improved religious education in childhood as preparation for religious tasks in the family later on. The expectations focused on Jewish wives that were discussed in the Jewish press, primarily by men, were extremely high and followed by criticism if they were not met. In 1911 one author wrote in the *Israelitisches Familienblatt*:

> Alas, the sweet poetry of Judaism increasingly departs from the Jewish family and so on the inside we grow ever more impoverished from day to day. . . . We must provide Jewish life with new warmth, and for this task women can render us best service. . . . The Jewish woman should once more become the priestess of the home, even if her garb now differs.[4]

Something seemed lacking, and the Jewish woman was asked to make up for it. As public religion declined, for many Jews the family became its substitute, even as it had earlier been its principal support. The family now became the chief guarantor of Jewish continuity.

It appears that within the family the wife held on to Jewish traditions or their residue longer than her husband. On the one hand, this can be explained by the close connection in traditional Judaism between the wife's religious duties and the preparation of meals. Keeping a kosher kitchen and preparing for the Sabbath and Jewish holidays were tasks that wives relinquished only slowly or continued in a secularized form. On the other hand, the wife, who because of her duties at home had always attended synagogue less frequently than her husband, was used to praying at home out of a woman's prayer book. *Stunden der Andacht* (Hours of Devotion), the prayer book published by Fanny Neuda for the first time in Prague in 1855, went through sixteen printings in the years 1874–1916 alone. Such devotional books likewise sought to impress on wives their important role in the preservation of the Jewish religion. It is difficult to estimate the extent to which these books were not only received as gifts but also used by younger women. However, statistics show that Jewish women in this period opted for baptism and entered into interfaith marriages less frequently than did men. The difference is, of course, in large measure due to the fact that women, unlike men, did not undergo baptism in order to further a career. Moreover, parents played a larger role in the choice of their husbands. Thus their more conservative attitudes were no doubt influenced by the more protected environment in which they grew up within the family and their fear of hurting parents' feelings if they entered into a mixed marriage or underwent baptism.

In the memoirs of German Jews the question whether the family or the author preserved Jewish traditions was sometimes addressed directly. Certain basic criteria by which traditionalism versus secularization are measured occur repeatedly: the attitude toward the dietary laws, observance of the Sabbath and holidays, fasting on Yom Kippur—and the celebration of Christmas. If the authors of the memoirs grew up in a family that kept the Sabbath as a day of rest and celebrated the holidays in a festive manner, the memories remained with them their entire lives. Often, they later looked back fondly on these childhood experiences; family and religion remained indissolubly linked. The seder table at Passover with its prescribed foods and the ritual questions asked by the youngest child, the construction and decoration of the sukkah (reminiscent of the booths built by the Israelites in the desert) at Sukkot, and the costumes on Purim as well as the games played during Hanukah were all happy experiences for the children and the whole family. The writer Manfred Sturmann acknowledged in memoirs of his childhood: "The Jewish year, with its great variety of feasts and symbols, always exercised a tremendous attraction for me—to the same extent that the dead knowledge embedded in books remained alien."[5] The sensory experience of religious practices within the family circle strengthened both religiosity and family cohesiveness and, on account of its repetitive character, became deeply ingrained.

Yet religious forms could lose their intrinsic meaning and become routine, void of all devotion. They were retained longer in the countryside and in smaller towns where familial piety toward one's ancestors and social control were greater, yet even here they were threatened by petri-faction. One woman wrote about her family in Worms around 1880:

Lacking is what really gives life to these things as necessities: true belief and genuine piety. Fasting on designated days, preparing certain dishes, and attending synagogue were things that had always been there. They still maintained their outward appearance, like a building that has had almost all its supports removed but just manages to retain its old shape, as long as nothing disturbs it. If a gust of wind comes up, if one is cut off from one's old companions, it topples.[6]

The dietary laws focused attention on food and cooking and increased the wife's importance. The kitchen became an index of a family's piety. Traditional recipes and ways of preparing them were so intimately tied to the dietary laws that they served to sustain them. Judging from cookbooks, however, we can conclude that the transition from kosher to nonkosher cooking was a fluid one, corresponding to the generally slow change in eating habits. It seems that by the turn of the century most families no longer kept a kosher kitchen but instead combined elements of middle-class cooking with traditional Jewish recipes. They mixed meat and milk dishes at meals, cooked on the Sabbath, and no longer used only meat from ritually slaughtered animals. The prohibition against eating pork was the strongest food taboo and was retained the longest; it marked the boundary line of complete abandonment of the dietary laws.

Men and women distanced themselves from strict adherence to the religious laws at a different pace. In Imperial Germany only a few older women still wore a wig (*sheitel*) to cover their own hair and women who regularly visited the ritual bath (mikveh) were becoming rare. Disregard for more important laws, such as not working on the Sabbath, occurred first among men, since merchants often began to keep their stores open on Saturdays. On the other hand, even men who had completely removed themselves from religion continued to stand for election to offices in the organized Jewish community. The son of a shoe dealer in Chemnitz wrote of his father: "No matter how attached he remained to his Jewish heritage, under the sway of contemporary free thought he had renounced all religious activity. It pleased him when he was elected to the council of the organized community and he attended the meetings regularly, but he never went to religious services."[7] Here there is clear evidence of the formation of a secular Jewish identity that accepts membership in the historical and cultural group but refrains from religious practice. More and more, Jews took on this form of Jewish identity.

It has been estimated that only 15 percent of German-Jewish families at the most lived fully observant lives in 1918. The vast majority identified with Liberal Judaism or else gave up religion, assuming a secular Jewish identity instead. Judaism now meant something different for almost every Jew, which often led to conflicts within families. Influenced by the desire for socially appropriate marriages, unions took place in which one partner was religious and the other secular. When Sigmund Freud became engaged to the granddaughter of Hamburg's chief rabbi, Isaac Bernays, who had been raised Orthodox, Freud prophesied to her that she would join him in becoming a "good heathen," and he later forbade her even to light the Sabbath candles, a tradition she had wanted to preserve. Not every husband, however, conducted himself in so authoritarian a manner; some agnostics kept a kosher kitchen even though they could find no religious value in it.

It is hardly surprising that fully or partially secularized families also absorbed traditional elements from the surrounding culture. One of these was the bourgeois manner of celebrating Christmas, which, to a certain extent, was a German national holiday. The son of a middle-class Jewish family from a western neighborhood of Berlin described the widespread custom in that milieu of putting up a Christmas tree and exchanging presents:

> We celebrated Christmas, that went without saying. And, even if our parents offered the usual middle-class Jewish excuse that they did it for the maid's sake, they could not have believed it fully. Did the head of the house spend the better part of the morning on Christmas Eve climbing up and down on a ladder so he could decorate a Christmas tree that reaches to the ceiling just for the servants? And, how he decorated it! These trees were works of art, and they possessed one thing in the extreme: they seemed romantic![8]

The Jewish middle-class of Vienna also had its Christmas trees. After Theodor Herzl finished writing the manuscript of his famous Zionist work *Der Judenstaat* (The Jewish State) in 1895, he invited the chief rabbi of Vienna over to discuss it with him in the presence of the Christmas tree in his home. It would be an error, however, to interpret these Christmas trees in Jewish homes as religious symbols. Rather they served Christians as well as Jews as symptoms of their secularization. The tree was a requirement of the secular middle class that brought a festive atmosphere into the family while the religious occasion of the festivities receded further and further into the background. As the example of Herzl indicates, a Christmas tree in no way ruled out Jewishness.

An important topic, and one difficult to shed light on, is the extent to which Jewish families mingled socially with Christian friends. The important agents of socialization—school, university, and army—early on awakened in Jewish young people the realization that they were second-class citizens. Thus antisemitism was an ever-present silent guest in the Jewish family. At times confrontations with antisemitism characterized family life in Imperial Germany more strongly than did the continuation of Jewish traditions. The family was the one sphere that offered a haven from antisemitism and the place where defensive strategies against it were worked out. At the same time, the Jewish home remained, in reality or in memory, the place where religion was practiced. Both functions made this intimate family space ill suited for receiving non-Jewish guests. The Jewish home was a place where Jews could freely be themselves with other Jews. From memoirs, it is clear that visits by Christians to a Jewish home were the exception. Social gatherings were prompted mainly by the Sabbath or holidays, which provided an occasion for inviting extended family and Jewish friends. Gershom Scholem remarked in his memoirs of Berlin that Christian visitors never came to his parents' home, and this surely held true for many Jewish families. That did not rule out individual friendships between Jews and Christians, such as between former school mates or university friends, especially in the big cities. However, these friendships were mostly cultivated outside the home, with gentlemen attending male gatherings and ladies belonging to coffee circles. Evidence for entire families associating with one another in private homes is extant only for the upper class. In the countryside Jewish and Christian families got together in the gardens of inns where observant Jews could bring along their own meals. The aversion to mixed company in private circles may also have been influenced by the fear of promoting interfaith marriages.

Marriage remained the touchstone of how far Jewish families were ready to go in their acculturation and desire for social integration in the face of a society that continued to reject them. Most families wanted to take no risks in the case of their daughters and sought a Jewish marriage partner for them, while allowing their sons greater freedom of choice. A dowry was obligatory for Jewish as well as for Christian daughters of the middle class, and the size of it determined the social status to which they could aspire. Since Jewish men, in greater numbers, emigrated, underwent baptism, or entered interfaith marriages, fewer of them were available for potential Jewish brides. Thus a portion of the daughters would necessarily have to remain unmarried—which made marriage brokerage and the dowry that much more important.

The gradation of dowry amounts was common knowledge. A Jewish university graduate in Berlin around 1900 could expect, for example, about seventy-five thousand marks as a dowry from the bride's family— clearly a fortune. A woman with only a small dowry had to make compromises: she might find a suitor in the country or marry a widower with children. In families tied to commerce the wife's dowry together with the wealth of the husband made up the initial capital for their family business, providing the young couple with its livelihood. When the marriage was to a university graduate, capital was no longer the main consideration, the dowry rather serving as a guarantee that from the outset the couple would be able to afford an appropriate lifestyle. During the period of the Kaiserreich the size of the dowries demanded increased sharply as Jews became more affluent—which, in turn, led to critical discussions in the Jewish press and sharp denunciation by antisemites.

Marriage brokerage had a long tradition among Jews, prompted by the frequent necessity of having to bridge great distances if no suitable partner turned up in the home community. In Imperial Germany matchmakers were less often professional marriage brokers and more likely relatives, friends, teachers, or business partners. An increasing number of advertisements for marriage partners appeared in the Jewish press as well. In accordance with general middle-class practice marriages were now arranged far more discreetly. Parents would set up a nonbinding meeting, for instance at a spa, where daughters could get to know potential candidates. If through these "chance" encounters they found a partner, the engagement and marriage usually followed soon thereafter. These procedures assured not only a Jewish marriage but also an economically suitable one. Not coercion, but custom, social pressure, and the family's powers of persuasion convinced many girls, even as late as the Kaiserreich, to marry almost total strangers whom the family had pronounced appropriate. Families chose with great care because what was involved was not just an individual decision but rather the union of two families. Not the dowry alone but also the education, reputation, and, in the case of Orthodox families, the religiosity of the family were important considerations in making the choice.

Alongside marriage brokerage, marriages based on the personal choice of the partners began to gain significance. This trend can be seen, for example, in the growing number of interfaith marriages, which were probably rarely the product of matchmaking, although material considerations were sometimes a factor. One of the first female Jewish physicians, who in 1905 had chosen to marry an Orthodox childhood friend, wrote in her memoirs about the changing manner in which Jewish marriages were occurring at that time:

> My best friend, Fanni, had had a traditional engagement. Her father had chosen the young man and he had come to view the bride. Two days later the engagement took place. . . . Although I saw that Fanni was satisfied, deep inside I could not come to terms with it. . . . We had been told a hundred times that this form of finding a marriage partner was the proper one, submitting to the clear views of one's parents and not following our own hearts. I never did believe it.[9]

The heart was perceived as a poor adviser in questions of marriage. Moreover, even in the so-called marriages for love the heart did not react blindly because young people moved in the "proper circles" and their social conditioning steered them toward partners who came from similar Jewish environments. The prevalence of in-group marriage thus remained the strongest single expression of the families' desire to preserve Jewish tradition.

3. Women's Education and Employment

In general, women's education and employment experienced fundamental change in Imperial Germany. Jewish women in traditional Judaism had received less formal education than had boys since, as noted earlier, girls were not obligated to study the Torah and Talmud. With the adoption of middle-class norms, beginning earlier in the century, the education of Jewish girls improved, but it remained circumscribed by the narrow definition of female gender roles. In the Kaiserreich, however, the restricted scope of female education underwent decisive expansion. As early as the founding of the Allgemeiner Deutscher Frauenverein (General German Women's Association) in 1865 an intensive debate had begun with regard to the improvement of female education. It focused on furthering the employment of middle-class unmarried women as well as on permitting girls to attend an academic high school and university. Associations for the education and employment of women came into existence and discussed the so-called women question. Numerous Jewish women now took an active part in advancing the cause of the middle-class women's movement because they themselves largely belonged to the middle class and regarded their own education in the girls' school as quite inadequate in the educationally conscious milieu of the Jewish family. In Germany Jews had learned by experience that acculturation was a precondition for emancipation, and, perhaps analogously, Jewish women were now striving to use education to bring about a second emancipation—this time for women.

It was during this period that both Christian and Jewish women were finally successful in their fight for the right to an education and for admission to the Gymnasium and the university. As these institutions increasingly opened their doors to women after the turn of the century, Jewish girls and women everywhere were among the first to take advantage of the new opportunities with particular zeal.

The first institution devoted to women's higher education was the Victoria Lyceum, founded in Berlin in 1869. There professors gave regular courses and lectures intended for "ladies." Among the first students was Anna Ettlinger, the daughter of a Karlsruhe attorney, who later successfully taught courses in literature for women in Baden. She was unmarried, as were both her sisters who worked as translators. They were among the few Jewish women able to earn their own living in an intellectual profession, even before universities were opened to them.

In 1893 Gymnasium courses for girls were finally set up for the first time in Karlsruhe. They could study humanistic subjects and could obtain a certificate qualifying them for university study. In 1899 Rahel Goitein, daughter of the rabbi in Karlsruhe who later became the physician Rahel Straus, gave the festive address at the first graduation ceremonies. Not surprisingly, her talk drew upon Lessing's drama *Nathan the Wise*. She noted the similarities between the ideas of universal tolerance and women's education as two radically modern concepts that each met with opposition before they could prevail. She attempted to explain the motivation of the female pupils enrolled in the Gymnasium: "We wanted to learn how to learn, how knowledge gives people independence and inner freedom. . . . The second, and stronger reason, however, was the thought: we want to have a vocation, we want to occupy a place in life."[10] Education and knowledge are here understood to be the prerequisites for the self-emancipation of women.

11   A Jewish girls' school in Hamburg

In the Habsburg Monarchy, as well, women were permitted to take special Gymnasium courses on an individual basis, beginning in Prague in 1890 and in Vienna in 1892. Here it was Dr. Eugenie Schwarzwald (1872–1940), one of the first Jewish women to become a university graduate in the Dual Monarchy, who as an independent elementary school reformer pushed through the idea of high school education for girls on a larger scale. A Galician by birth, Eugenie Schwarzwald, along with many Russian Jews, had studied at the University of Zurich, which admitted women early on. She took over administration of a girls' high school in Vienna in 1901 and, after lengthy battles, was finally able to set up the first modern secondary school for girls. Students entered it immediately upon completion of the four-grade elementary school and graduated with a certificate that qualified them for university study. This Gymnasium was considered to be the "elite school of the Jewish bourgeoisie," and, at the time it was founded, was attended by 168 Jewish girls who comprised about half of the total number of pupils. The school was indebted to reform pedagogy and bore the stamp of Eugenie Schwarzwald's extraordinary personality. She was able to attract creative personalities like Arnold Schoenberg, Adolf Loos, and the young Oskar Kokoschka, all of whom taught for a time at the school.

After the turn of the century girls' academic high schools were established in the German Empire along with the gradual admission of women to the universities. From the outset Jewish girls were greatly overrepresented in these new educational institutions. In 1911 they were nearly 12 percent of the female academic high school graduates in Germany in a Jewish population that made up only 1 percent of the general population. In large cities such as Berlin and Frankfurt sometimes over a third of the female pupils taking an academic curriculum were Jewish girls. Although most of them immediately went on to university studies, only a minority then undertook a career. For daughters of the Jewish liberal middle class, successful completion of the academic high school became primarily a symbol of education and culture, class status, and modernity. After 1918, however, it enabled some women, who had not anticipated the necessity in Imperial Germany, to have an independent means of support.

The admission of women to university study did not take place simultaneously at all German universities but rather occurred piecemeal during the period from 1899 to 1908. In the first decade of women's studies, there was, in addition to completion of the Gymnasium, a second educational path that was of considerable importance for women seeking to enter the university. Jewish women who used their teacher training as a form of further education after the ten-year school for girls and were able to pass the certification examination at a teachers' college could proceed on to university study in the humanities without having completed an academic high school. In Vienna, for example, 273 Jewish women attended a teachers' college during the academic year 1881–1882, and in Czernowitz, in 1888, Jewish girls comprised almost half of all the female students in the college there. The teaching profession was one of the few women's occupations that met with middle-class approval, even in very conservative families. Most of those who passed the qualifying exam, however, never did get to practice their profession because in the predominantly denominational German school system, whose teachers were extremely antisemitic, their chances for employment were most limited. In Germany in 1907 there were 1,128 Jewish women who were certified teachers, but of these most were not working in their profession, and, of those that were, many served as private tutors or governesses. In Prussian schools, where denominationalism reigned, only 131 Jewish women were actually teaching in 1911, a figure that represented less than half of 1 percent of the total number of female teachers. Not only did they face discrimination in the public school system, on account of their gender they also encountered problems in the Jewish schools. Most of the latter were in the countryside where the small Jewish communities preferred to hire men who could simultaneously serve as the synagogue's prayer leader.

In view of this situation it is not surprising that many Jewish women teachers, who did not have to work for a living, went on to university studies with the approval of their families. Moreover, a course of study in the humanities—which was always terminated if a woman got married—was easier to reconcile with the traditional view of women than the study of law or medicine. Helene Nathan presents a typical example. She attended the college for women teachers in Breslau, registered at the university there in 1904, after completing her degree entered librarianship (a newly created women's profession), and ultimately became the director of the municipal library in Berlin-Neukölln during the Weimar Republic. Like her, most of the Jewish women who embarked on a professional career were unmarried.

Although many Jewish women took their courses in the humanities, they were more highly represented among female medical students. Medicine, a traditional Jewish profession, still offered the best occupational prospects and attracted many East European Jewish women who were studying in Central Europe. In 1910–1911 Jewish women students in the arts and sciences made up 8.6 percent of all women students in that area, but they accounted for 28 percent of women students in the school of medicine. In Vienna in 1913–1914 the corresponding proportions were as high as 38 (school of arts and sciences) and 58 percent (school of medicine). Almost half the Jewish women medical students in Vienna came from Galicia. Even before the First World War Jewish women, such as Rahel Straus and Käte Frankenthal, were practicing as physicians. Rahel Hirsch, granddaughter of the Orthodox rabbi, Samson Raphael Hirsch, finished her medical studies in 1904 and, on account of her work in research, in 1913 became the first woman in Germany to receive the title of professor.

The University of Vienna had begun admitting women to the school of arts and sciences in 1897 and to the school of medicine in 1900. By the winter semester of 1913–1914 307 Jewish women from all parts of Austria were studying there. They made up 38 percent of all women students and were, in comparison with the Jewish percentage in the population, overrepresented approximately eightfold.

By 1914 there were already over four thousand women, from all reli-

12   Rahel Hirsch, the first woman in Germany to gain the title of
professor, at her desk in 1913

gions, studying in the German Empire, where they comprised 6 percent
of the student population. Among them Jewish women were highly overrepresented—11.2 percent in comparison with a Jewish population percentage of 1 percent and a much higher proportion than that represented
by the male Jewish students, which stood at 5.6 percent of the male student body. This high percentage of Jewish women students—most of
whom did not go on to careers—demonstrates once more that advanced
education meant something different to Jewish women than it did to
Jewish men: in many cases they were simply seeking the attainment of a
high level of culture and personal emancipation.

Even if the first Jewish women students made up a kind of avant-garde
among Jewish women, their absolute number remained small. Most middle-class Jewish girls continued to stay at home in the family environment, awaiting marriage. The situation was different for Jewish girls in
the lower middle class, in rural areas, or in the East European Jewish lower
class. In most cases they could only attend elementary school and rarely
received formal career training, although they usually had to count on
earning a living. Many such girls acquired skills by helping out in the
family business and then going on to work as sales clerks or bookkeepers.

Others became domestic servants or seamstresses on the basis of experience they had gained working in the family. After marriage they of course worked in their husband's business.

Thanks especially to the German women's movement, an increasing number of institutions were established during the Kaiserreich that offered a vocational education to girls who did not come from the ranks of the middle class. Bertha Pappenheim, the founder of the Jüdischer Frauenbund (League of Jewish Women) made the case for women entering service professions and called upon Jewish parents to give their daughters as well as their sons a practically oriented education. Women's associations in the large Jewish communities saw to the occupational training of girls from less well-to-do families. In Hamburg, for example, they made it possible for over one hundred girls to learn the tailoring and beautician trades. Even domestic service became an occupation that required training, and for younger women the new social occupations of kindergarten teacher and social worker exercised a special attraction.

As much as the Jewish middle-class parents advocated education and even occupational training for their daughters, they remained critical of the actual employment of young women since having to earn an income undermined their idea of the family and their understanding of the wife's role within it. Of course, women of the lower social classes, those who lived in the country, and housewives and mothers, in general, had always worked. But that work was considered to be "natural" because it was work done for the family and in the family business and because it was unpaid. What was disconcerting now was that young women, in their urge to be independent or out of material necessity, wanted to earn money. The middle-class family saw in this trend a threat to its reputation and its status; it was, after all, based on a division of labor along gender lines, where the husband alone worked for income. A middle-class woman who received a salary jeopardized the reputation, and perhaps also the credit worthiness, of her family, which appeared unable to provide for her. What is more, she endangered her own future as well. Who would want to marry a young woman who was apparently working on her own because she had no chance of receiving a proper trousseau?

These gender role constraints came to be questioned more and more as defiant daughters deviated from the norm and because of the necessity to provide for unmarried women. They were still holding their own only to a limited degree when World War I and its aftermath deprived the mid-

13   Martha Kästner, an emancipated Jewish woman (1899)

dle-class family as well of the financial security to which it had earlier
grown accustomed. Beginning at the turn of the century it had become
increasingly acceptable to Jewish families that their daughters learn a
trade or occupation appropriate to their class and that they actually practice it before their marriage. On the other hand, gainful employment
while married remained a taboo for Jewish middle-class families that very
few women—mostly university graduates—were ready to break. Among
them was the above-mentioned Rahel Straus, who married a lawyer after
completing her medical studies. She opened a practice in Munich in 1908
and became the mother of four children. Straus was one of the first
women from the middle class to take on a "double load." In her memoirs

she reflects back on the difficulties she had combining her profession and motherhood:

> Numerous preconditions are involved. In the first place, the husband must see in his wife a companion who has full equality, whose first priority is not to be there for him, but who has the right to her own life and her own development. Second, there needs to be a financial foundation that enables the wife to have a paid staff of workers in the house and in the kitchen to take care of the children and to run the entire household. Without this financial base, a married woman cannot even get a start without feeling overwhelmed from the double workload. First and foremost, however, what is required are excellent health and a huge capacity for work.[11]

It was most exceptional for middle-class women in Imperial Germany to deal so directly with such basic gender issues, issues that remained relevant even generations later.

The increase in the employment of Jewish women was a sign of social change that not only concerned families but also conservative Jewish critics of contemporary culture. The leading Jewish statistician, Jacob Segall, wrote in 1911:

> The pace at which this entry into economic life is occurring, the rapid development of Jewish women taking part in the workforce, is disconcerting, arouses our concern. . . . This phenomenon is most alarming and deserves at least as much serious attention as the decline in the number of births—which is, in fact, intimately related to it. In our opinion, we need to initiate a healing process here if the modern Jewish condition is to begin a process of recovery.[12]

Segall regards the employment of women as the symptom of an illness, believes the wife and family are being destroyed by material pursuits, and sees in women who work the sacrifice made by a Jewish society that is overly concerned with its own prosperity. Segall was not alone in such conservative cultural criticism, which aimed directly at the Jewish wife, as it also did when it blamed her for the decline in religiosity. In his analysis, he gave little weight to all nonmaterial causes of the social transformation, such as women's desire to gain greater self-sufficiency, independence, and the improvement of their status. He also underestimated the growing array of jobs for women in the modern industrial society.

In addition to the Jewish women who were employed outside the home, there continued to be women, especially in rural areas and in the lower middle class, who worked together with their husbands. It is doubtful whether all of these women were counted in the census figures, which, from 1907 on, were supposed to include family members who helped out in the family business as well. Their work was viewed by men as part of the familial activities, as we find in the memoirs of a large-scale entrepreneur from Hamburg. He recalls his mother running the village tavern and second-hand goods store in West Prussia while his father distilled spirits and peddled them: "Mother took care of the children, the household, the cattle, and, in addition, the guests and the business. Father was away most of the time."[13]

Memoirs, in particular, enable us to see that up to and including the middle class the availability of a wife to assist her husband was such an obvious expectation that her work was not perceived as such. One Jewish wife in Berlin, for example, conducted all the commercial correspondence for her husband, who was a traveling salesman, took over the mail-order part of the business, and, on top of that, gave piano lessons. In a small town in Württemberg the wife was a salesclerk in the family's manufactured goods business and enjoyed the particular trust of the overwhelmingly female clientele. In a jewelry shop in Cologne the wife likewise took care of sales while her husband took care of the goldsmithing. Gershom Scholem, whose father owned a printing house in Berlin and had four sons, writes of his mother:

> She went to the business about nine o'clock in the morning, after I was already sitting in class, and only came home for lunch and a short rest afterward. Then, three or four times a week, she went back for two additional hours in the afternoon, so that we saw her very little during the day. Nonetheless she was a powerful presence.[14]

Betty Scholem (1866–1946) was the bookkeeper for the printing house, had power of attorney, and ran the business when her husband was away at the health spa. Her example illustrates how middle-class wives, too, took part in the family's business and could even run it. On the one hand, this was in accordance with the Jewish tradition, while, on the other, it was still less of an infraction of middle-class norms than employment in a nonfamily firm. Nevertheless, in her son's estimation this was a less-than-ideal situation for Betty Scholem who, like many women in Imperial Germany, had been unable to pursue her real calling: "She was a born journalist, who could express herself nimbly and to the point. Thus, at a time when women were not yet allowed into such professions, she definitely missed her true calling. She would have been splendidly suited for a position on the editorial staff of one of Ullstein's newspapers."[15]

4. The Women's Movement

To a great extent Jewish middle-class women devoted themselves to charitable work. Not only was that one of the main elements of traditional Jewish life, it also provided one of the few opportunities for these women to leave the home in order to engage in public activity. Volunteer work was considered respectable and in compliance with middle-class norms. The Jewish community's official relief for the poor was under the exclusive control of men, but during the course of the nineteenth century separate women's organizations were formed in all communities, which directed their efforts above all to aiding children and women. They collected food, clothing, and money for the poor and looked after unmarried mothers. These women's organizations too were partly under the direction of men.

In the Kaiserreich the work of the women's organizations was modernized. They had more funds at their disposal and they established larger, permanent institutions, such as convalescent homes, kindergartens, housekeeping schools, homes for wayward girls, and employment agencies. The organizations now also provided occupational training for girls and looked after unmarried working women and unwed mothers. This relief work gave experience and self-confidence to the volunteer workers, who soon cooperated with other Jewish institutions. In accordance with the contemporary middle-class view of women, the volunteers saw in this work an expression of the motherliness common to all women. The paradigms were, of course, marriage and family. These women's organizations created the basis for the Jewish women's movement, a movement both middle-class and moderate.

Women were especially active in the Jewish communities of Frankfurt and Hamburg, where their activity eventually led to a national amalgamation of Jewish women's organizations. In Frankfurt Bertha Pappenheim (1859–1936), who came from an Orthodox family in Vienna and had had only the usual education at a high school for girls, directed a Jewish orphanage. After the death of her father she was struck with a severe mental illness that was treated by the Viennese psychiatrist Joseph Breuer. Upon her recovery Pappenheim, who remained unmarried, moved to

14   Bertha Pappenheim, the leading Jewish fighter for
women's rights

Frankfurt and, in 1895, took over the directorship of the orphanage for
girls. In 1902, together with Henriette Fürth (1861–1938), she founded
the organization Weibliche Fürsorge (Women's Relief) in Frankfurt.
Fürth, an observant Jew and the mother of eight children, had, through
running an office for the legal protection of women in Frankfurt, gained
insight into the many problems of female employment. In the Women's

Relief the two founders, along with numerous Jewish women volunteers, developed modern forms of women's social work, conducted case studies, collected data, and set up job counseling and employment agencies for women.

In Hamburg, upon the initiative of the local B'nai B'rith lodge, the Israelitisch-Humanitärer Frauenverein (Jewish Humanitarian Women's Association) was founded in 1893. It remained under the guidance of the lodge president until 1909 when the Hamburg teacher, Sidonie Werner (1860–1933), became its director and men could no longer be elected to the executive committee. In 1912 this association had 750 women as members and operated a housekeeping school, a children's convalescent home, and a home for wayward girls. It defined its task to include not only social work but also moral education in Judaism and humanitarianism. Working closely with the lodge, it turned attention to the international Jewish white slave trade, which was in part conducted through the port at Hamburg and ran from Russia, Romania, and Galicia primarily to Latin America. The first German conference on this subject took place in 1902 in Hamburg. That same year, at a similar international conference in London, Bertha Pappenheim, Henriette Fürth, and Sidonie Werner met and discussed a plan to found an organization that would prevent the white slave trade by providing social relief work for women threatened by poverty. Since the issue of the Jewish white slave trade was seized upon by antisemitic agitators, it was not simply an evil in and of itself but presented a general danger for all Jews.

When the International Council of Women met in Berlin in 1904, Bertha Pappenheim, together with other Jewish conference participants, was able to use the occasion to found the Jüdischer Frauenbund (League of Jewish Women). She herself was the first to direct it, while Sidonie Werner became her deputy and, in 1915, was elected her successor. Pappenheim put her distinct stamp on the goals and work of the league, advocating ideas that were often more feminist than those of the women who made up its membership. Most of the local Jewish women's organizations merged with the league, so that by 1917 it comprised two hundred member associations that fully retained their independence. It was also possible for individuals to join the league. By 1917 it was one of the major Jewish organizations, with a total of approximately forty-four thousand members.

The Jüdischer Frauenbund was more than just an association of and for women who made social work and education their primary tasks and

sought to improve the status of Jewish women. It was also a decidedly
Jewish association and, as such, was part of that centripetal movement in
the Kaiserreich which, prompted by the rise of militant antisemitism, led
to the formation of more and more Jewish organizations on the national
level that would represent Jewish interests and promote Jewish self-
awareness. As a religion-based women's organization, it was also comparable in many respects to Christian counterparts that were organized at
the turn of the century in response to the increasing public influence of
the women's movement. A Protestant women's association was founded
in 1899, a Catholic one in 1903. Their religiously committed members
worked to improve the status of women in their churches and in society
at large. In so doing they drew upon conservative Christian models but at
the same time also pursued their emancipatory goals, thus giving their
organizations an ambiguous character. Similarly, the Frauenbund, in the
face of antisemitism, always directed its feelings of solidarity primarily
toward the Jewish community although that community allocated to
women no more than a subordinate role in Jewish life. Adapting parts of
its program from the German women's movement, the league sought to
combine these with the religious convictions and problems specific to
Jewish women.

Often there were clear differences between the politics of the league's
leadership elite and the mundane work accomplished in the independent
local groups. Probably the most radical demand of the league, and one by
no means advocated by all members, was for voting and election rights for
women in the elections of the organized Jewish communities. More
broadly supported were efforts to reach goals that had by now become
more acceptable, such as the improvement of women's education and
occupational training and aid for working women. However, Jewish communities viewed less favorably the league's commitment to illegitimate
children and their mothers and its fight against prostitution and the
Jewish white slave trade, since until that time Jews had customarily managed to suppress awareness of these social problems.

Like other middle-class women's associations, the league used the role
of the mother and the idealization of motherhood as strategies to gain
more influence for women in society. Social work, defined as "organized
motherliness," was laid out as a morally requisite element of Jewish life
with the intent that it would, in the long run, improve the legal position
of women in the Jewish community. The Frauenbund excluded particular
political or religious ideologies within the Jewish community in order to

reach as many Jewish women as possible. Nonetheless, as the representative of mostly middle-class women, it was closely allied with the Central Association of German Citizens of the Jewish Faith (see chapter 5). In religious terms, its homes and institutions were run in accordance with Jewish law, a necessity for gaining general acceptance. Bertha Pappenheim herself always lived the life of an Orthodox Jew and believed that it was an important function of the Frauenbund to convey to every woman the need to regard herself as both a teacher of Judaism and a bearer of Jewish culture.

The League of Jewish Women perceived itself as part of the general German women's movement, and several of its members, such as Henriette Fürth, were deeply involved in both. The newsletter of the league reported not only on the work of its own organization but also on the international women's movement. The Frauenbund was a member of the League of German Women's Associations, founded in 1894, which elected Bertha Pappenheim to its executive committee. In this position she insisted on full parity for the Jüdischer Frauenbund, but tensions often arose when the Jewish organization felt it was being ignored and excluded.

Although it succeeded in only some of its goals, the Frauenbund did strengthen the solidarity of Jewish women and raised their awareness of the need for reforms. Above all, it performed extensive social and educational work on behalf of Jewish women and girls, many of whom had immigrated from Eastern Europe. It was also able to bring about the entry of at least a few women into the executive committees of Jewish organizations. Voting rights in the organized Jewish community itself, however, continued to be denied women, a denial that was perpetuated in some places even during the Weimar Republic and is indicative of the opposition with which the Frauenbund had to cope.

Since it gave Jewish women experience in performing responsible work within the Jewish communities as well as in the larger German society, the league was able to produce prominent personalities who gave the Jewish women's movement respectability and importance in Jewish and non-Jewish circles alike. As the most significant among them one must once again mention Bertha Pappenheim, who, in her life-long work for the Jüdischer Frauenbund, made her top priority the battle against the white slave trade and efforts on behalf of single mothers. She was a passionate fighter and tireless worker who demanded much from herself and others. Beginning in 1903, she made a total of five trips to Eastern Europe to investigate the social causes of the Jewish white slave trade, made her findings public, and introduced measures to improve the situation. Her favorite project was the league's home for unwed mothers in Neu-Isenburg, which she directed out of a deep emotional commitment. In addition to her work for the Frauenbund, Pappenheim was also a writer of stories and poems, and translated *Tsenah ure'enah,* the so-called Jewish women's Bible, as well as the memoirs of Glückel of Hameln from the original Yiddish.

Three other prominent women from the leadership of the league like-wise deserve attention. Like Bertha Pappenheim, they combined devotion to Judaism with a commitment to women's rights. Sidonie Werner, the teacher from Hamburg mentioned earlier, was a close associate of Pappenheim and succeeded her as head of the Jüdischer Frauenbund in 1915. She founded two children's convalescent homes in Schleswig-Holstein, took part in the fight against the white slave trade, and spoke out loudly for the right of women to vote in Jewish community elections. Henriette May (1862–1928), also a teacher, founded an association of Jewish women teachers in Berlin, which became part of the Frauenbund. She was a life-long member of the league's executive committee. In 1917 both Sidonie Werner and Henriette May took part in the foundation of the Zentralwohlfahrtsstelle der deutschen Juden (Central Welfare Office of German Jewry), the organization that would coordinate all Jewish social work. In Breslau Paula Ollendorf (1860–1938) founded the local chapter of the league in 1908, sat on its national executive committee beginning in 1910, and at the same time played a role in the Centralverein and the national association that supported Liberal Judaism. All three of these women were active in Jewish communities in large cities, led local women's groups, and combined these activities with their work for the Frauenbund and other nationwide Jewish organizations.

Some Jewish women preferred to involve themselves exclusively in the general German women's movement, leaving the Jewish sphere behind and seeking contact with their Christian counterparts. Although their numbers were smaller, they played a qualitatively important role in the general women's movement.

Especially striking is the extraordinarily strong interest that Jewish women, from the very beginning, showed in the pedagogy of Friedrich Froebel (1782–1852), who had earlier established the kindergarten in Germany. His educational doctrine had as its goal the active guidance of children in their personality development and the disregard of social contrasts so that neither class nor religious differences would play a role among small children. This integrative concept was especially attractive to Jewish parents. They rallied to the support of the Froebel associations and kindergartens that sprang up in many localities. The most effective advocate of Froebel's pedagogy was Henriette Goldschmidt (1825–1920), the wife of the Liberal rabbi in Leipzig, Abraham Goldschmidt. In 1865 she took part in the establishment of the General German Women's Association and served on its executive committee for forty years. She argued fervently for Froebel's educational theories since she believed them ideal for inculcating respect for all humanity in very young children. In 1871 she also founded an association devoted to family and adult education that created numerous kindergartens in Leipzig, a school for kindergarten teachers, a high school for young ladies, and, in 1911, the Leipzig College for Women, which trained women lecturers for instruction in teaching and social work. According to the association's calculations, it trained 1,200 kindergarten teachers and approximately 150,000 children attended its kindergartens between the years 1871 and 1911. Both Jewish and Christian members of the organization, especially Leipzig fur dealers, financed its extensive work. In this way Henriette Goldschmidt not only succeeded in helping children but also advanced the cooperative efforts of the Jewish and Christian educated middle class in attaining a positive political and pedagogical objective. In so doing she was able to use Froebel's integrative pedagogy to further Jewish social integration.

Like Henriette Goldschmidt, Lina Morgenstern (1830–1909) in Berlin was an advocate of Froebel's educational theories and chaired the local organization that worked on their behalf. Herself a mother of five children, she published a Froebel textbook that had been reprinted seven times by 1905. But she was better known for the public soup kitchens she established, which daily offered thousands of poor people an inexpensive meal. Here, too, Liberal Jews and Christians worked together in the association that ran the kitchens. Yet, despite the support of the empress herself, the association came under virulent antisemitic attack in the early 1880s. One charge, among others, was that relief efforts by Jews were only a way to gain entrance to the higher circles of society.

The younger generation of Jewish women were critical of such relief efforts as soup kitchens. In accordance with Jewish social ethics, Jeanette Schwerin (1852–1899) emphasized the rights of the poor to social justice. In Berlin in 1893 she organized groups of girls and women who received systematic training in social work. She was also one of the women who

founded the League of German Women's Associations and devoted herself especially to the protection of working mothers and mothers of new-
born infants, the fight against child labor, and the introduction of legal
assistance for juvenile offenders. After her untimely death, her
coworker, Alice Salomon (1872–1948), took over her leadership of the
girls' and women's groups. Alice Salomon's most significant achievement was the Women's School of Social Work, founded by her in Berlin
in 1908, which trained generations of social workers. Approximately a
fourth of the pupils were Jewish girls. Alice Salomon, who converted to
Christianity in 1914, rose to become vice-chair of the League of German
Women's Associations, but the top position was denied her on account of
her origins.

In contrast to Salomon, the previously mentioned Henriette Fürth in
Frankfurt was committed both to women's rights and to Jewish self-assertion within an antisemitic society. Hence she became active in both the
general and the Jewish women's movement. In 1911, urging Jewish
women to join the Centralverein, she wrote: "We are not just women, we
are Jewish women. And as long as this adjective still carries a derogatory
meaning intended to set us apart, we may not give up the battle."[16] Fürth
published more than two dozen books, mainly on questions of women's
employment; she supported the right of every woman to a job and her
own income since only with these would she possess independence. As a
woman oriented to social reform, she later joined the Social Democrats.
She was also involved in the Jüdischer Frauenbund, the Centralverein,
and the Jewish relief agency. Indeed her broad range of social engagement
was unequaled by any other Jewish feminist.

With the beginning of World War I Jewish women patriotically made
themselves available in large numbers for social welfare tasks and were
active in the National Women's Service, which organized women's volunteer work during the war. Henriette Fürth opened a *Kriegsküche* (a
wartime kitchen) for the needy. Alice Salomon, a resolute internationalist, organized women's service in the occupied territories under the auspices of the War Office. However, such work—so readily undertaken for
the fatherland—did not result in the hoped-for greater integration. Once
Germany began to lose the war, antisemitism broadly and unexpectedly
reappeared in force. In the long run the German women's movement too
was unable to eliminate antisemitic tensions from within its own ranks.

4 | Religious Life

1. The Landscape of the Jewish Religion in Germany

In the Jewish religious sphere, as in the general political arena, the unification of Germany marked a transition from a period of struggle and conflict to one of consolidation. By the beginning of the 1870s the forces of Reform and Orthodoxy, which had collided for a generation, were reaching a state of equilibrium. Reform Judaism (now generally referred to as Liberal Judaism) was no longer an insurgent movement trying to change an overwhelmingly traditional German Jewry. By gaining control of virtually every major urban Jewish community in Germany, it was becoming the new establishment in German-Jewish life. (The term *Reform Judaism* was now generally reserved for the radical and atypical Berlin *Reformgemeinde*.)

By the 1870s the chief strength of Liberal Judaism was in the major cities, while the countryside was comparatively more traditional. With few exceptions the Jewish communities in large cities had at least one synagogue (usually the main one) with a Liberal service, complete with organ. In many cases the urban communities also contained more conservative groups, often with their own Orthodox synagogues and other traditional institutions. Small-town communities could not afford ideological splintering. Generally, they possessed only one of the two movements or a compromise between the two; they were by no means always Orthodox. There was also considerable regional variation; in some areas Orthodoxy remained strong in the countryside, while in others even the small-town Jews were greatly influenced by Liberal Judaism.

The decline in Orthodoxy and rise of Liberal Judaism, which had been very rapid in the period from 1850 to 1870, became less marked thereafter. Orthodoxy regained its bearings and slowed or stopped its losses, especially in the urban communities. Still, the steady migration from the countryside to large cities meant an overall weakening of the forces of tradition. By the turn of the century Orthodox strength was estimated at only 10 to 20 percent of the German-Jewish population. Compared to Germany the percentage of Orthodox adherents was probably higher (about 20 percent) in Vienna, where most traditionalists were migrants from Hungary or Galicia. By contrast, Orthodoxy was considerably weaker in Bohemia than in Germany; in neighboring Moravia Orthodoxy was not quite as powerless, but it represented only a small minority.

The geographic distribution of Orthodoxy and Liberalism in Germany was complex, with both Orthodox and Liberal strongholds scattered in various parts of the country (see map on following page). Traditional Judaism tended to be strongest in areas near the Main River (especially Hesse, the Lower Franconia region of Bavaria, and parts of Northern Baden and Württemberg) as well as in the eastern province of Posen. Liberal strongholds were found in the western, north central, and some eastern parts of Germany. Even rural sections of Westphalia, the Rhine Palatinate, and Pomerania were bastions of Liberal Judaism. Enclaves of strength of one party often adjoined strongholds of the other. In relatively traditional Hesse and Bavaria the Rhenish sections (Palatinate and Rhine Hesse) were conspicuous Liberal exceptions. In the Liberal central part of Germany Halberstadt stood out as an island of Orthodoxy. In the southwestern states of Baden and Württemberg the moderate reforms imposed by the official supreme councils (*Oberrat* and *Oberkirchenbehörde*) dominated many communities, but some towns continued to follow the unchanged traditional rites.

For the most part, Orthodoxy was strongest in areas that were relatively backward economically (for instance Upper Hesse, Lower Franconia, East Friesland, Posen), but there were some underindustrialized areas with strong Liberal Jewish traditions, such as Pomerania and northeast Westphalia. Orthodoxy seemed stronger in Catholic areas, while Liberal Judaism dominated in Protestant regions, but there were exceptions (Orthodoxy in Protestant East Friesland and parts of Hesse, Liberal Judaism in the Catholic Rhineland and Catholic regions of Westphalia). There seems also to be some parallel between the level of

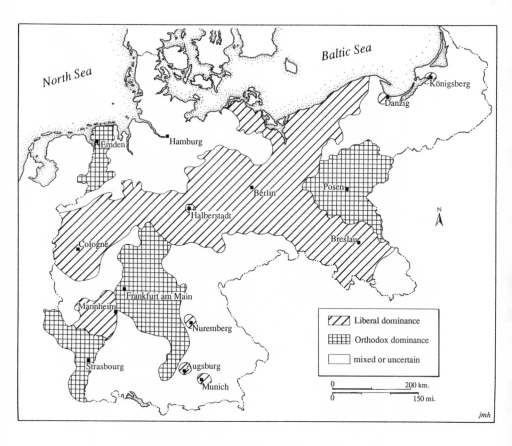

MAP 4 Approximate Geographical Division of Orthodox and Liberal Predominance in Jewish Communities During the German Empire

churchgoing among Christians and the degree of Jewish traditionalism, although again with important exceptions (for instance, East Friesland where Jewish traditionalism was high and Christian churchgoing low).

The declining small-town communities were the core of the phenomenon that Leo Baeck later called *Milieufrömmigkeit* (atmospheric piety). Such communities varied in religious observance from region to region but at least in the more traditional areas preserved rich elements of Jewish folk religion. The rhythms of the Jewish calendar, traditional customs, and life cycle events left a strong imprint on the lives of the members of such communities. Almost all memoirs of rural Jews describe in detail and with nostalgia the celebration of the Sabbath and holidays:

Friday evening was one of the high points of Jewish family life. On

15 Street scene in the Jewish quarter of Nikolsburg in Moravia around the
turn of the century

the table covered with a snow-white linen tablecloth were two
burning candles in silver candlesticks. At the father's place at the
table were two loaves of a special white bread, called *challot* or
barches, veiled with a covering embroidered just for this purpose.
Next to them was a silver cup filled with wine. After both parents
blessed the children individually, the father said the kiddush, the
Sabbath sanctification over the wine. . . . The meal followed, broken
up by Sabbath songs between the courses. The (partially) sung grace
after meals ended the domestic Friday evening celebration. . . .
When the Sabbath candles burned low the house became quiet and
all went to bed. The following morning the wife usually accompanied her husband to services. In order to give their mother a rest,
the grown daughters did those chores permitted on the Sabbath and
prepared the midday meal.[1]

16   View across the Spree river in Berlin to the kosher hotel Cassel on the
Burgstrasse (around 1888)

Such traditional practices remained characteristic of many small-town
communities up to their destruction by the Nazis.

Even in areas of Liberal predominance like Westphalia, Jewish life in
small towns and villages was quite different from that in the metropo-
lis. Small-town synagogues in such areas frequently had organs and
reformed liturgies, but attendance at services and participation in communal affairs were much greater than among urban Liberal Jews. Here
too Sabbaths and holidays were regularly observed, many followed the
dietary laws, and their homes retained a markedly religious atmosphere.

In the cities the Jewish population was divided between a minority that
evinced a keen interest in Jewish religious life and a majority that took little or no notice of it. Among those who displayed concern for religious
life, traditionalists played a role disproportionate to their percentage of
the Jewish population, although many Liberal Jews were also active. In
Hamburg, one of the few cities for which there are statistics, the mem-

bership of the voluntary Orthodox Synagogue Association ranged between 1,120 and 1,220 during the Empire period, as compared to 450 to 650 for the equally voluntary Liberal Temple Association. However, both groups together included barely a third of all families registered as Jews in Hamburg.

The Hamburg figures seem to indicate that most Jews in urban communities were neither Orthodox nor committed Liberals. Large numbers in the big cities were apathetic about religious matters yet continued to retain formal membership in the Jewish community and to pay their communal assessments as required by law. For such "three-day-a-year Jews" attendance at services was often restricted to the Jewish New Year, the Day of Atonement (Yom Kippur), and perhaps the anniversary of a parent's death. Some nominal members of the Jewish community (no one can be sure how many) were in fact totally secular in their outlook. Others subscribed to a vague religiosity more grounded in Goethe's poetry than in Jewish texts. Many were tied to Judaism by filial devotion (*Pietät*) rather than by religious piety (*Frömmigkeit*). Typical is this reminiscence:

> My parents were not really religious. All that remained of the earlier piety, rituals, and religious feelings with which our ancestors were so intimately bound up were some surviving forms and customs. Among these were the observance of the High Holy Days with their various requirements, fasting on the Day of Atonement (Yom Kippur), and attendance at services. However, all this was no longer done out of inner conviction but merely out of custom and habit.[2]

Thus religious attitudes in urban Jewish communities during the late nineteenth century ranged across a broad spectrum from atheism and minimalism through a committed Liberal Judaism and on to the strictest of Orthodoxy, with multiple personal variations in between.

2. Institutions and Style of the Religious Factions

In the course of becoming the dominant religious force in German Jewry Liberal Judaism lost much of its revolutionary impact. Despite the radical implications of the ideology and rhetoric of its earlier rabbinical leadership, the actual changes in communal practice made by the Liberals in their conquest of the German-Jewish communities were relatively moderate. In German Liberal synagogues most prayers were recited in

Hebrew, men and women were seated separately, and men wore hats during the services. Although Liberal prayerbooks made substantial ideologically motivated changes in certain prayer texts, they retained the general form of the traditional service. Even more moderate than the Liberal religious movement in Germany was its counterpart in Vienna and Bohemia-Moravia. Whereas a majority of German Liberal communities had introduced organs by the 1870s and eliminated prayers for restoration of the Jerusalem Temple and return to Zion, the Viennese community rejected the organ and turned the prayers for Zion into silent meditations (rather than abolish them) in 1871. Synagogues in Bohemia and Moravia generally used the Viennese Liberal liturgy, but many of them introduced organ music as well.

In the *Kaiserreich* most large German cities had magnificent Liberal synagogues in which the service was conducted with utmost pomp and to exacting aesthetic standards. Thus in Berlin:

> The Fasanenstrasse synagogue played a decisive role in the Jewish life of the capital. It was, so to speak, a symbol of "how far" German-Jewish emancipation could go. . . . In it the tradition created a generation earlier was upheld: modern forms but with the old contents. . . . Here Head Cantor Magnus Davidsohn, a former opera singer . . . with the looks of a Wagnerian tenor, officiated for decades. . . . He would always arrive at the front of the sanctuary—his stage—only after the organ prelude. A glittering gilded door opened. With his hymnbook, alias siddur, under his arm, a star-shaped biretta on his head, wearing a clerical robe, and with his prayer shawl folded like a stole over his shoulders, he strode, head erect, to the cantor's pulpit.[3]

Even in urban Orthodox synagogues robes for rabbis and decorum had become the rule. The music of Louis Lewandowski (1821–1894), though written for the mixed choir and organ accompaniment of the Liberal synagogue in Berlin, was used by numerous Orthodox synagogues with suitable arrangement for unaccompanied male choir. The official composer of Frankfurt separatist Orthodoxy, Israel Meyer Japhet (1818–1892), wrote music at least as westernized as that of Lewandowski or his equally Liberal counterpart, the Viennese Salomon Sulzer (1804–1890). The widespread use of Lewandowski's music was an indication of how much all religious trends in Germany shared a similar cultural and aesthetic style despite ideological differences.

17   The synagogue in Essen, built in 1913

However, this common aesthetic style did not usually appeal to the growing number of East European immigrants who flocked to the larger German cities after 1880. The newcomers, insofar as they remained traditional, tended to found their own small prayer houses that continued the more informal style of their homelands. In Vienna and a few German communities larger East European synagogues were also built, a phenomenon that was to become more common after World War I.

The 1870s and 1880s were a transitional time between the creation of new religious positions and the era when the various views hardened into institutionalized religious parties. Many of the original protagonists of the Reform-Orthodox conflict (such as the Liberals Abraham Geiger and

Ludwig Philippson, the more conservative Zacharias Frankel, and the Orthodox Samson Raphael Hirsch) were still active but now near the end of their careers. The last representatives of old Orthodoxy, whose traditional learning far outstripped their secular knowledge (rabbis like Jakob Mecklenburg, Elijah Guttmacher, and Zevi Hirsch Kalischer) passed from the scene in the 1860s and 1870s. From then on all the leaders of German Orthodoxy tried to bridge the gap between traditional practices and modern German culture. Although some of the later leaders of both Liberal Judaism and Orthodoxy who began to come to prominence in the 1870s and 1880s were productive and energetic leaders, none of them had the pioneering stature of the earlier generation. The movements now depended more on shared ideology and growing institutional cohesion than on charismatic leaders expounding new religious doctrines.

Though transitional in passing religious leadership from the founder generation to younger men, the first decades of Imperial Germany did not otherwise represent a sharp break from earlier trends. Change was gradual and often only noticeable in retrospect. The institutionalization of the religious movements proceeded slowly and unevenly, with local interests and customs sometimes countering trends toward national coordination.

Although just before the establishment of the Kaiserreich the Reform movement had made a renewed attempt at coordination by convening two synods, the first held in Leipzig in 1869, the second in Augsburg in 1871 (see volume 2), the development of Liberal Judaism had already been for some time occurring mainly on the local level. The 1850s and 1860s had produced a proliferation of Liberal prayerbooks in the various communities, most of them relatively conservative in nature and reflective of local customs. This productivity continued well into the following period.

More indicative of the trend toward national religious institutions was the creation of "denominational" rabbinical seminaries in the 1870s. Until then the only institution for the training of modern rabbis in Germany had been the Jewish Theological Seminary, headed by Zacharias Frankel since 1854. The Breslau seminary was a theologically conservative institution emphasizing Talmud and legal codes but with a modern critical approach to the sacred texts. Although opposed by the strictly Orthodox, it produced rabbis for all other trends during its early years. Even as it tended to exert a conservative influence on the Reform movement in Germany, diverting it from the progressive trend exemplified by Rabbi Abraham Geiger, it graduated men who ranged across a broad ide-

ological spectrum from those in sympathy with Orthodoxy to determined reformers like Caesar Seligmann (1860–1950) and Heinemann
Vogelstein (1841–1911).

Ideological dissatisfaction with the Breslau seminary from both the
left and the right resulted in the founding of two new seminaries almost
simultaneously in Berlin. The Hochschule (from 1883 to 1922, and again
after 1934: Lehranstalt) für die Wissenschaft des Judentums was founded
in 1870 and opened its doors in May 1872 under the leadership of
Abraham Geiger and Moritz Lazarus. Although formally a scholarly
institute for all branches of Judaism, the Hochschule was actually a
seminary for training rabbis of a thoroughgoing progressive type. Its
founders felt that the atmosphere in Breslau was not sufficiently free of
theological restraints, and they wished to train rabbis in a spirit of
untrammeled scholarly inquiry.

The Orthodox rabbinical seminary (Rabbinerseminar) in Berlin was
the brainchild of Rabbi Esriel Hildesheimer (1820–1899), who had arrived
in Berlin from Eisenstadt in 1869 to become rabbi of the separatist
Orthodox community. Like the Breslau school, the "Hildesheimer Seminary," which opened in the fall of 1873, emphasized Talmud and Jewish
legal codes and expected its students to have a university education.
Unlike Breslau, it insisted on acceptance of the Orthodox interpretation
of the divine origins of the Torah. The Orthodox seminary did use the
scholarly methods of Wissenschaft des Judentums, but only insofar as
they did not contradict traditional beliefs. David Hoffmann (1843–1921),
the later director of the seminary, and some of his colleagues availed
themselves of such modern methods especially to defend traditional dogmas against biblical criticism.

The Rabbinerseminar supplied the bulk of the candidates for Orthodox
synagogues in undivided communities and for independent Orthodox
congregations. Yet, although it declared that any graduate who served in
a synagogue with an organ would forfeit his ordination, the seminary's
espousal of Wissenschaft des Judentums aroused misgivings on the part
of Samson Raphael Hirsch and some of his South German Orthodox colleagues. Separatist communities sometimes preferred rabbis without
modern seminary training, often importing them from Hungary. The
founding of a yeshiva in Frankfurt by Solomon Breuer in 1890 recreated
a less modern model of higher Jewish education in Germany itself,
although its students generally did not seek rabbinical posts.

The founding of the Landesrabbinerschule in Budapest in 1877 was a

18   The Orthodox rabbi Esriel Hildesheimer

sign of the growing intellectual independence of Hungarian Jewry, despite the similarities between that institution and the Breslau seminary. Similarly, the creation of the Israelitisch-Theologische Lehranstalt in Vienna in 1893 freed the German-speaking provinces of the Austro-Hungarian Empire from their dependence on Breslau and other German seminaries.

The ideological divisions between the various religious factions did not always closely correspond to institutional groupings. Although the deepest ideological divisions were between Orthodox and non-Orthodox, institutional demarcations were much more complex. Whereas the rabbinical seminaries were split between the Orthodox Rabbinerseminar, the conservative or moderately Liberal Jüdisch-Theologisches Seminar, and the thoroughly Liberal Hochschule, the rabbinical organizations were divided into the Union of Liberal Rabbis, grouping both Breslau and Hochschule graduates, and two rival Orthodox rabbinical groups. The institutional split within Orthodoxy between the separatist and communal trends was mainly the result of sharply differing views on secession from the general Jewish community that arose in the late 1870s. This point of division, as well as certain other differences of approach, often embittered relations between the two Orthodox subgroups.

3. Orthodox Reactions to Minority Status: The Secession Controversy

Orthodoxy in the 1870s faced a very different situation than it had a generation earlier. Now, with few exceptions, Orthodox Jews were a minority in the large Jewish communities. The authority of the community, which had formerly been used to prevent the rise of non-Orthodox movements, was now in the hands of the Liberals. In many cities the latter had made thoroughgoing changes in the communal synagogue and left few institutions under Orthodox control. In such communities Orthodox Jews were forced to found private traditional synagogues or make use of existing private prayer houses. Generally, they were still required by law to be members of the Liberal-controlled organized community and pay taxes to it in addition to their dues to the private Orthodox associations.

The rabbinical leadership of Orthodoxy, most notably Samson Raphael Hirsch, considered this situation intolerable. Even though Orthodox Jews were free to worship and care for their other religious needs in their private associations, Hirsch felt that being forced to pay for the upkeep of "heretical" religious institutions interfered with freedom of conscience. As a small minority in most urban communities, the Orthodox despaired of ever regaining control of the communal apparatus and therefore began to look to complete separation from the general community as the only solution to their dilemma.

The decision to take practical steps toward legal secession from the Liberal-dominated Gemeinden seems to have been encouraged by two "outside" events. First, in the late 1860s Hungarian Jewry underwent a schism between the Orthodox and non-Orthodox communities. Second, during the Kulturkampf of the 1870s the Prussian government in 1873 tried to weaken the Catholic Church through a law that made withdrawal from religious bodies easier. This law permitted Jews to leave Judaism without embracing Christianity. The Orthodox, however, now sought the right to secede from the main local community and establish their own separate Orthodox Jewish communities. The secession law, which followed, was spearheaded by Eduard Lasker, a Jewish political leader of the National Liberal party, and finally passed the Prussian legislature in July 1876. Not only Orthodox leaders lobbied on its behalf; it was also supported by assimilationists and a few extreme religious Liberals for reasons having to do with liberty of conscience. The bulk of the German-Jewish communal leadership, however, opposed the proposal, arguing that voluntary membership would fatally weaken the Jewish community. They claimed that not only the Orthodox but also many wealthy contributors would use the law as an excuse to evade their community obligations.

After 1876 secessionist Orthodox communities were legal in Prussia and a few other German states such as Hesse, though Bavaria and Saxony, among others, continued to prohibit more than one community in each locality. Because secession was not legal in Bavaria, Orthodox minority congregations in Munich and Nuremberg, which, to a degree, resembled the Frankfurt separatists in outlook and social makeup, were unable to secede from the community. A similar situation existed in Vienna where the "Schiffschul" congregation, made up mainly of Orthodox Jews from Hungary, would have liked to quit the Viennese Gemeinde but was prevented by law from doing so. Galician Jews, who made up the majority of Orthodox Jews in the city, disagreed with the Hungarians and generally opposed secession.

In Frankfurt the successful passage of the secession law led to controversy of a new kind. While Rabbi Hirsch declared secession to be a fundamental religious duty of every loyal Jew, many of his congregants hesitated to make a break with the main community to which they felt attached by history and family ties. Some members of the congregation opened negotiations with the main community and procured major concessions. These included the offer to build a ritual bath, to exempt the Orthodox from that portion of their taxes that would have supported the Liberal service and school, and to provide Orthodox administration of kosher meat supervision, the communal hospital, and the cemetery.

For his part, Hirsch rejected every concession, declaring any recognition of "heretical" Reform Judaism an outrage. Yet most members of his congregation refused to resign from the main community. When the leading Talmudic authority, Rabbi Seligmann Baer Bamberger of Würzburg, was asked for his opinion, he reversed his former position and declared it religiously permissible to remain in the main community as long as that community provided for Orthodox religious needs. Bamberger and others of his party supported the secession law as a means of forcing concessions to the Orthodox but in the end did not believe that secession itself was a matter of principle. His decision led Hirsch to break off personal relations with him. Eventually all German Orthodoxy split between secessionist Orthodoxy and community Orthodoxy, the latter sometimes also referred to as "conservative."

Meanwhile, the main Frankfurt community built a large new synagogue on the Börneplatz and hired the Hungarian-born Talmudic scholar Marcus Horovitz (1844–1910) as its Orthodox rabbi despite Hirsch's attempt to dissuade traditionalists from accepting the post. Although the appointment of an Orthodox communal rabbi was a compromise by the Liberal-dominated Frankfurt community, it sealed the division between Orthodox supporters and opponents of secession. Frankfurt would now have three kinds of synagogues—Liberal, communal Orthodox, and separatist Orthodox.

In the last two decades of the nineteenth century separate institutional arrangements deepened the split within Orthodoxy. In 1885 Hirsch founded the Freie Vereinigung für die Interessen des Orthodoxen Judentums (Free Association for the Interests of Orthodox Judaism), a militant organization dedicated to fighting Reform. On the other hand, in 1896 nonseparatist Orthodox rabbis joined with Liberal colleagues to found the Allgemeiner Rabbinerverband (General Association of Rabbis). Among the leaders of this organization for the advancement of the rabbinical profession were Marcus Horovitz and other Orthodox rabbis. Though religious matters were specifically excluded from its agenda, the separatists opposed all such cooperation with Liberal Jews. Eventually separatists and nonseparatists even founded their own rabbinical associations (though some individuals belonged to both). Alongside the Verband traditionell-gesetzestreuer Rabbiner (Association of Traditionally Observant Rabbis), founded in 1897 with a communal Orthodox orientation, there was the Verband orthodoxer Rabbiner (Association of Orthodox Rabbis, founded in 1906), which automatically excluded from membership all who belonged to the General Association.

Frequently the leaders of the communal Orthodox groups were just as strictly Orthodox as the separatists. In some cases, however, Orthodox-trained rabbis who served in the main conservative synagogue of undivided communities had to make concessions. In Cologne, for instance, the conservative synagogue on the Glockengasse had no organ, but its liturgy did omit some medieval poetry as well as the *kol nidre* prayer on the Day of Atonement because the latter was thought to be politically problematic. Although otherwise similar in religious practice, the separatists in the Israelitische Religionsgesellschaft (Israelite Religious

Association) of Frankfurt did not accept the eruv (Sabbath boundary) used by their communal Orthodox neighbors to permit carrying items on the Sabbath. The two groups tended to form separate social circles even when living side by side.

Besides causing an institutional split in Orthodoxy, the secession law inhibited radicalism within Liberal Judaism. Fearing potential withdrawal by Orthodox elements, Liberal majorities were more reluctant than previously to make innovations like introducing the organ or giving women a larger role in the synagogue. In a number of communities the playing of the organ on the Sabbath was eliminated where it had formerly been instituted.

4. Renewed Strife and Strivings Among the Religious Parties

Toward the end of the century most German Jews, except for the adherents of militant separatism, had come to accept the existence of permanent religious parties that would have to live with each other. The new factor now was the entrance of Zionism onto the scene of community politics, with the result that Orthodox and Liberals occasionally formed coalitions against the seemingly more threatening Zionist advance and religious issues became mixed with questions of religious versus national Jewish identity. To a large extent the Zionism issue came to overshadow strictly religious questions. On the Liberal side the need to change traditions formerly regarded as stifling or backward looking was no longer regarded as pressing. Indeed, many lay people in Liberal Jewish communities were only dimly aware that such traditions still existed. Liberal rabbis now had to deal mainly with problems of widespread indifference and religious apathy. Their innovations were frequently intended to revive flagging religious interest. Nonetheless, Liberal proposals still clashed with halakhic norms and therefore provoked attack by Orthodox spokesmen.

Liturgical questions continued as before to be a source of many of the most conspicuous religious disputes. Two controversies—in Westphalia and in Baden—aroused widespread attention. In the Liberal stronghold of Westphalia, in 1892, the union of Jewish communities of the province commissioned the leading Liberal rabbi Heinemann Vogelstein of Stettin to prepare a new liturgy. In fact, the communities in the Westphalian union were already following Liberal liturgies when Vogelstein's prayerbook, which differed little from other prayerbooks of the progressive wing of German Liberal Judaism, appeared in 1894. Nevertheless, Orthodox leaders, led by the Freie Vereinigung, attacked it as "a sacrilege committed against all Israel."[4] The organization issued a book of fifty German-language responsa attacking the new prayerbook. Most of these came from rabbis in Germany, almost none of them residing in Westphalia. The union of congregations replied with its own collection of sixteen rabbinic opinions defending the new liturgy.

Although the Orthodox were unable to prevent the adoption of the Westphalian prayerbook, they soon set about organizing the Orthodox minority in Westphalia. In 1896 they established the Society for the Protection of the Religious Interests of Judaism in Westphalia, which hired its own rabbi. At its height the society had affiliates in some thirty-nine communities (out of a total of over one hundred in Westphalia); some of these communities were in villages, while others were generally small, separatist, Orthodox congregations in the large cities. Similar organizations were established in other areas of Liberal predominance such as the Rhineland (1902) and Baden (1903).

A decade after the Westphalian conflict a controversy broke out over a proposed prayerbook in Baden. There the government-sponsored Jewish Oberrat had followed a policy of moderate innovation for decades. The prayerbook, which it had authorized as early as 1895 and appeared as a draft in 1903, was much more traditional than the Westphalian liturgy, though still definitely not Orthodox. In Baden, unlike in Westphalia, Zionists joined Orthodox separatists in the attack. They opposed the prayerbook's elimination of references to the return to Zion and its universalization of nationalist passages. Different also from the earlier dispute was the role of a broader electorate. Every four years Baden Jews elected a Jewish synod that held the final decision-making power in liturgical matters. In the 1908 election a Zionist and Orthodox campaign was sufficiently successful to secure the election of fifteen opponents of the new prayerbook as against eleven supporters. As a result, introduction of the new liturgy was indefinitely postponed.

Other proposed Liberal innovations likewise divided communities. In Cologne, where a compromise liturgy had been in place for several decades, the communal board debated and finally accepted (in 1906) the introduction of an organ in the Roonstrasse synagogue, which had been built seven years earlier. This issue was the major point of division in communal elections of 1900 and 1903 and the main reason why the

Orthodox faction seceded from the community in 1906. In Berlin a proposal by some Liberal Jews to create a supplemental Sunday service for those whose businesses prevented them from attending on the Sabbath became a major source of contention. Although several thousand petitioners supported the new service, the issue was one cause for the defeat of the Liberals in the communal election of 1901. They were careful not to revive the proposal even after they subsequently regained power.

In Cologne, Baden, and Berlin the Zionists played an important role in the opposition to Liberal liturgical innovation. Unlike the separatist Orthodox, they did not propose a reversion to religious tradition. Rather, they saw the removal of references to the return to Zion or the use of German rather than Hebrew in the liturgy as a denationalization of Judaism and viewed the organ and Sunday services as a surrender of Jewish distinctiveness. Most Zionists active in the campaign against liturgical innovations were themselves not religious; some were even declared atheists, a fact eagerly noted by Liberal detractors.

In the period after 1890 traditionalist forces made efforts to regain positions previously lost to the Liberals. Occasionally, sometimes allied with Zionists and East European immigrants, they attained a measure of success. Such renewed support for tradition did not presage a return to Orthodox dominance, but it did show that the Liberal establishment could not take its hegemony for granted.

Faced with the challenges of strengthened Orthodox and Zionist opposition and of indifference in their own ranks, prominent Liberal rabbis worked to revive interest and commitment among Liberal Jews. Ten years after the creation of a Liberal rabbinical association, Rabbis Heinemann Vogelstein and Caesar Seligmann in 1908 helped to establish a lay organization intended to expand Liberal activities. With its own youth organization and its periodical *Liberales Judentum*, the Vereinigung für das liberale Judentum (Union for Liberal Judaism) aroused much initial enthusiasm. Its purpose was to promote Liberal Judaism not merely as a reaction to tradition but as a living faith designed to meet the spiritual needs of its adherents. In the words of the opening article of its journal: "Today Liberal Judaism wishes to awaken to new life. The will to Judaism has become strong among thousands who once stood on the sidelines. A new yearning for a renewal of Judaism in a spirit of freedom is sweeping through the German lands."[5]

In 1910 the union began work on its ideological platform, Guidelines Toward a Program for Liberal Judaism. The guidelines were concerned both with setting forth Liberal theology based on the idea of ethical monotheism and encouraging a Liberal form of religious observance. Their basic intent was not to criticize tradition but to fight indifference and to build a positive Liberal program:

> The Union of German Liberal Rabbis is filled with the holy conviction that in this way alone can it reconcile our religious traditions with the thinking, feelings, and opportunities of the life of our day. It will apply the uplifting basic truths and ethical ideals of our religion in creed and in life. It will keep vital the understanding that Judaism has a necessary role in the present and an irreplaceable significance for the future. In this way it will overcome religious apathy and alienation from Judaism and pass the loyalty to Judaism, preserved through millennia, on to coming generations.[6]

The original version of the guidelines also declared certain basic observances indispensable—such as circumcision, celebration of the Sabbath (though not necessarily according to traditional rules), and recitation of the *kaddish* prayer for the deceased. Although the Liberal rabbinate approved the draft overwhelmingly, the lay-dominated assembly of the Union for Liberal Judaism in October 1912 rejected the idea of required practices and instead left religious observance to the conscience of each individual. This weakened the guidelines but seems not to have dampened the initial enthusiasm for them in Liberal circles. From the other side, the reaction of German Orthodox rabbis, and some traditionalist non-Orthodox ones as well (especially in the small towns), was to protest the guidelines as unconscionable heresy.

After the appearance of the guidelines, Liberal Judaism once again became quiescent. Although Liberal rabbis continued their work to revive the "will to Judaism" among laypeople, most of the latter were too secularized to wax enthusiastic about religion. The Liberal movement was characterized by a small core of rabbis moving back toward a more traditional ideology and greater appreciation for Jewish peoplehood and a laity that was satisfied with a vaguely Jewish universalism.

In Orthodoxy, too, the early twentieth century was a time of renewed activity, especially among the separatists. In 1912 German Orthodox leaders, together with colleagues in Eastern Europe, founded the Agudat Israel, an international organization to further Orthodox aims. It declared vehement ideological opposition to both Liberal Judaism and Zionism. Similarly militant in character were the early writings of Samson

Raphael Hirsch's grandson Isaac Breuer (1883–1946), who argued that East European Orthodoxy was healthier than Western Orthodoxy. Defining himself as a national Jew (*Nationaljude*), Breuer was nonetheless a strong anti-Zionist who stressed the absolute authority of divine law and the importance of the principle of secession. Although heavily influenced by German philosophers, especially Kant, Breuer challenged the assumptions of an easy synthesis between Jewish and Western thought. Yet despite Breuer's strong criticism, most of German Orthodoxy continued in the now well accustomed paths of the Hirschian synthesis of Torah and Western culture.

Concentrating on the periodic battles between Orthodox and Liberal forces, however, would yield a one-sided picture of the relationship between the two movements during the Kaiserreich. Since members of both groups had become aware that neither would disappear, they were persuaded of the importance of coexistence. Except for the separatist Orthodox, who were generally a minority even among the traditionalists, German Jews of different religious orientations managed to work together in the official Jewish community. The value of living in a unified community, an *Einheitsgemeinde*, was appreciated by the community's Orthodox and Liberals alike. Frequently their rabbis acted jointly, in harmony, and with mutual respect. Orthodox leaders within the main community, like Marcus Horovitz and later Nehemiah Nobel in Frankfurt, often enjoyed the esteem of non-Orthodox Jews.

5. Trends in Jewish Scholarship

Throughout the empire period Wissenschaft des Judentums, begun in the early nineteenth century, continued to flourish, although its pioneers gradually passed from the scene. It was now generally freer of religious party interests, even if the issues that divided Orthodox and Liberal Jews never disappeared entirely. Communal rabbis, and now increasingly also professors at the rabbinical seminaries along a wide ideological spectrum, were the most active among the scholars, pursuing Jewish scholarship as an important part of their professional lives. For many of them the philological, historical, or literary analysis of Jewish texts became a sanctified task, as traditional Torah study had been earlier. Because German governments and universities generally refused to recognize Jewish studies as a legitimate scholarly field, only a few Wissenschaft des Judentums scholars were associated with universities as professors or lower ranking *Privatdozenten*, and these were hired in fields other than Judaica.

The main areas of scholarly interest in the late nineteenth century, as in the earlier period, continued to be the history, literature, and thought of the Second Temple, Mishnaic, and Talmudic periods, as well as medieval Jewish philosophy and poetry. To this the Kaiserreich period added a growing number of studies on local Jewish communities in Germany during medieval and modern times. In general, scholars concentrated on intellectual history, emphasizing philological and philosophical precision and the careful collection and evaluation of source materials. Sometimes their work was highly abstruse and, unlike Heinrich Graetz's popular and passionate *Geschichte der Juden* (History of the Jews) of a generation earlier, not easily accessible to a larger readership. The monographs and articles published in such long-running scholarly journals as the *Monatsschrift für Geschichte und Wissenschaft des Judentums* (see volume 2) were read mostly by other scholars rather than by the general Jewish public.

In the early twentieth century, as ideas of Jewish nationalism began to make headway, newer fields emphasizing Jewish peoplehood, such as the study of Jewish folklore, demography, and statistics, began to develop. Some of the new scholars were ardent Zionists whose ideology influenced their way of thinking. Arthur Ruppin (1876–1943), one of the pioneers of Jewish sociology, for example, tried to demonstrate in the 1911 edition of his *Die Juden der Gegenwart* (The Jews of Today) that the process of modernization threatened the survival of Judaism. Only a Jewish state could cope with this potentially destructive assimilatory process. Felix Theilhaber's pessimistic sociological treatises, including his *Der Untergang der deutschen Juden* (The Decline of German Jewry, 1911) shared commonly held views of his day about the dangers of modernity and urbanization for demographic growth and national vitality.

The expansion of Jewish scholarship was aided by the creation of new organizations such as the Society to Further Jewish Scholarship (1902), the Bureau for Jewish Statistics (1904), and the General Archives of German Jewry (1905). The society was one of the first efforts to make Jewish scholarship independent of denominational and communal organizations. It published important scholarly work and launched collective projects that no single researcher could undertake alone, such as *Germania Judaica*, intended to collect documentation on all early Jewish settlements in Germany. The General Archives and Bureau for Jewish

Statistics helped collect communal records and compile statistical information that could put the history and sociology of German Jewry on a firmer factual basis.

6. The Religious Influence of German Jewry Abroad

By the period of Imperial Germany its religious character distinguished German Jewry clearly from other Jewish communities. Although circles of traditional life and stringent modern Orthodoxy continued to flourish, the typical German Jew had long forsaken strict adherence to tradition. This abandonment of halakhic practice differentiated the majority of German Jews from their coreligionists in Eastern Europe and the Middle East who remained observant of most traditions. Even the minority of East European Jews who rejected Jewish law differed greatly from their German Jewish counterparts. Most East European Jews who left Orthodoxy turned to secular ideologies like Zionism, socialism, and diaspora nationalism. The middle-class style of German-Jewish religious Liberalism had scant appeal to modernizing Jews in Galicia, Poland, Russia, or Romania. Liberal Judaism, to which the majority of German Jews at least gave lip service, made little headway in Eastern Europe.

In Hungary the religious influence of German Jewry was more noticeable but declined in the later nineteenth century as native forces and the Hungarian language asserted themselves. Although the bulk of Hungarian Orthodoxy, unlike the traditionalists in Western Europe, rejected the acculturated model of German Orthodoxy, Liberal Judaism (called *Neolog* in Hungary) made extensive inroads, especially in the central portions of the country. Services often followed the German pattern, and for a time preachers used the German language in sermons. German Wissenschaft des Judentums also found some of its most distinguished practitioners among Hungarian Jews.

In England and France the bulk of the Jews, excluding recent immigrants, ignored much of traditional Jewish ritual (as in Germany) but showed relatively little interest in German-style Liberal Judaism. Only as a model of decorum and as a source of professional religious leadership and liturgical music did German Jewry influence religious life in the West European countries.

The impact of German Judaism was greater in the United States where the Reform movement became dominant in the third quarter of the nineteenth century. Although the rise of American Reform Judaism was also in large measure due to domestic factors, it imported both religious ideas and leading rabbinical figures from Germany. Reaching its peak shortly after midcentury, this influence waned a generation later as the English language replaced German and prospective Reform rabbis could avoid journeying to Germany by attending the Hebrew Union College, founded in Cincinnati in 1875.

By the end of the century the division of German Jewry into fairly stable groups of secular, Liberal, Orthodox, and rural traditionalist Jews with loose boundaries between them had become characteristic. Although there were gradual shifts in relative numbers, such as an increase among the secularists and a decrease among the rural traditionalists, all the groups showed signs of durability. German-Jewish communities were now far more likely to be split over Zionism versus anti-Zionism than over religious issues. The degree of heat generated by the new debate over Jewish nationalism made the continuing religious controversies seem mild by comparison.

5 | The Community

The basic unit of Jewish communal organization in nineteenth-century Germany was the local community (*Kultusgemeinde* or kehillah). In most of Germany all Jews residing in a locality were required by the state to be members of the community and pay for its upkeep. Local communities were controlled by an elected board of laymen who supervised financial matters, hired communal employees, and made communal regulations. In some states, like Bavaria, rabbis had considerable influence in communal affairs, while in others, notably Prussia, they were virtually excluded from decision-making power.

Premodern Jewish communities normally combined functions carried out by Christian denominations (worship, education, charity) with others usually associated with governments (tax collection and judicial matters). Though changes in Jewish status in the early nineteenth-century abolished most "political" functions of the Jewish community, it continued to perform a range of tasks that went beyond the purely confessional. Despite the opening of the general school and welfare systems to Jews, they continued to feel the need for specifically Jewish institutions. If anything, the system of Jewish charities and welfare institutions became even more ramified and well developed. In the educational field, despite the declining role of separate elementary schools, Jewish communities still played an active role in ensuring religious instruction.

The degree of coordination between local communities varied widely

19   A meeting of the Jewish community leadership of Vienna chaired by
its president, Heinrich Klinger. Watercolor by Emil Ranzenhofer, 1902

among the German states. Three main systems prevailed. A few medium-
sized states (Baden, Württemberg, Mecklenburg-Schwerin) centralized
Jewish communal life under a supreme council (*Oberrat* or *Oberkirchenbehörde*) that supervised all local communities. In Bavaria, Hesse,
and some areas incorporated into Prussia in 1866 district rabbinates covered many small communities. Some of the smallest states even had chief
rabbis, and in parts of Hesse there were parallel Orthodox and Liberal district rabbinates. By contrast the basic law of 1847 in Prussia—the largest
German state—provided no official link among communities. Each community was left totally independent of all others, though state law prescribed guidelines for the governing structure of the Gemeinde.

Although the basic structure of local communities changed little, the
overall organizational nature of German Jewry changed a great deal during the *Kaiserreich* period. As German Jewry became progressively more
urbanized the traditional kehillah, designed for relatively small communities, underwent strain. Decreasing membership in rural localities often
left communities unable to support their now too large array of institutions. The burgeoning urban communities had the opposite problem; the
traditional system was too rudimentary and new institutional frame-
works were needed to deal with memberships of many thousands.

Meanwhile, new political, social, and religious challenges prompted the growth of national organizations to accomplish what local communities were unable to do.

1. Challenges of Urbanization

At the time of German unification the bulk of German Jews still lived in small cities and villages. The total number of communities in Germany was very large (2,359 as late as 1899) and declined only slightly before World War I. However, the median size of the communities shrank greatly in the Kaiserreich period. On the eve of the war about half of the rural Jewish communities in Germany contained fewer than fifty individuals, including children.

Having lost their chief taxpayers, small-town Jewish communities frequently had to simplify their communal structure and to increase communal taxes until they far exceeded those imposed by the government. In some villages the synagogue became too large for a community that could barely muster a prayer quorum; many (though not all) district rabbis relocated from villages to the nearest city. Shrinking rural communities frequently had to make do with a single religious functionary who served as teacher, cantor, ritual slaughterer (shohet), and unofficial head of the community. Sometimes several communities had to share such a teacher who split his time among them. These teachers were the main source of Jewish knowledge for the tiny rural communities. Though frequently underpaid, their local influence was often immense—far greater than that of the rabbi who appeared once or twice a year.

Migration to the cities created even greater challenges for urban communities than for declining rural ones. In the early nineteenth century only the cities of Hamburg in Germany and Prague in the Austrian Empire had more than five thousand Jews. But by the eve of World War I Vienna and Greater Berlin each had well over one hundred thousand Jewish inhabitants and more than a dozen others numbered at least five thousand. In such large communities few members knew their leaders personally; relationships between members and leaders were by their nature bureaucratized and politicized.

Before the mid-nineteenth century a single main synagogue sufficed for most urban communities, perhaps supplemented by smaller private prayer halls. The religious conflict between Reform and Orthodoxy sometimes led to the founding of separate Liberal and Orthodox commu-

20   Procession of the Jewish community of Memmingen on the occasion of
the dedication of its new synagogue in 1909

nal synagogues, though many smaller and midsized communities were
able to agree on a compromise liturgy for their one town synagogue. By
the late nineteenth century the largest communities needed a multiplicity of houses of worship. At the time of the outbreak of World War I the
number of communal synagogues in Berlin had increased to eight, not
counting the numerous mainly Orthodox private synagogues that
banded together to form a Union of Synagogue Associations in Berlin.
Many, but not all the synagogue associations were founded by recent
immigrants from Eastern Europe. Twentieth-century Berlin also had a
multiplicity of rabbis who served the community as a whole rather than
specific synagogues; they sometimes preached in succession at different
locations, making a personal tie between rabbi and congregant difficult. In
large cities other than Berlin the number of communal synagogues was
smaller, but the pattern of more than one communal rabbi and synagogue
also became common.

The separation between individual member and communal leadership went far deeper than the fact that synagogue and community were
no longer identical. Communal elections, too, became far less personal.
Jewish community notables, who ran the affairs of the community, had
always been known to their fellow members for their wealth, status,

education, and charitable activities. Although most members of the executive boards and community councils in the Kaiserreich period had backgrounds similar to those of earlier notables, their election was now determined by inclusion on "party" lists rather than by personal reputation.

Although there had been some ideological elections based on disputes over religious reform even early in the nineteenth century, the organization of ideological parties in the communities first became common in the 1890s. After decades of relative quiet, with the Liberals controlling most large communities, the rise of Zionism and revival of religious controversy reawakened factionalism between 1890 and 1914. At times the Zionists made common cause with the traditionalists against the Liberals; at other times Liberals and traditionalists joined together against Zionism.

While controversial elections increased communal interest, the results of the voting did not necessarily reflect the distribution of opinion. Like so much else in Imperial Germany, communal elections were far from fully democratic. Not only were women excluded everywhere from the vote, but so were male adults who were not financially independent or did not pay a set minimum tax. In some places these restrictions of the franchise were exacerbated by curia voting based on wealth. In Cologne, for instance, each of the three curias (containing respectively 39, 194, and 1,998 voters) elected an equal number of representatives.

The unequal voting system usually favored the Liberals against their traditionalist and Zionist opponents—a reflection of the fact that the Liberals had become the urban Jewish establishment. This paralleled the position of late nineteenth-century Liberal political parties, especially in Austria where Liberal opposition groups campaigning for increased liberty had become in-groups defending their privileges. The Zionist and Orthodox opposition had little success before World War I in their occasional campaigns for lowered property qualifications, secret ballots, proportional representation, and abolition of curia voting. To counter such moves the Liberal establishment sometimes tried, though hardly more successfully, to take away the vote of foreign (mostly East European) Jews in communities where they were eligible to vote. In some communities Liberals had relatively greater success trying to ensure their continued hold on power by increasing property qualifications or giving especially wealthy voters a double vote.

Even among the eligible voters, the turnout was often small; in even the fiercest contests fewer than half those eligible actually voted. In Berlin the highest turnout in a communal election before World War I was a mere ninety-five hundred voters, less than 10 percent of the Berlin Jewish population. In Vienna, where property qualifications were even stricter, the percentage of eligible and actual voters was only about one-half what it was in Berlin. Large numbers of urban Jews saw little connection between themselves and the elected Gemeinde leadership. Among those who did participate, however, activity was often lively, with much discussion in the press and public meetings punctuated by heated debate.

2. The Jewish Press

Unlike other aspects of Jewish institutional life, characterized by local organizations preceding national ones, the national Jewish press was older than its local equivalents. Almost all the older nationwide newspapers, created during the struggle over religious reform, closed down before 1870 and were replaced by new ones. The one exception was the influential *Allgemeine Zeitung des Judentums* (published 1837–1921), founded as a moderately pro-Reform newspaper by Ludwig Philippson. The mouthpiece of separatist Orthodoxy was *Der Israelit* (founded by Markus Lehmann in 1860), which followed a militantly Orthodox and anti-Zionist line. More moderate and more favorable to Jewish nationalism was the *Jüdische Presse*, associated with the Hildesheimer rabbinical family of Berlin. A third Orthodox newspaper, variously titled *Die Laubhütte* and *Deutsche Israelitische Zeitung*, was published in Regensburg and directed mainly to rural Jews. Though traditionalist circles were a minority, they were more likely than Liberal Jews to read national Jewish newspapers. In 1901 *Der Israelit* claimed to have more subscribers than the *Allgemeine Zeitung des Judentums*. The *Israelitische Familienblatt*, a commercial enterprise with a wide circulation and a "neutral" religious viewpoint founded in 1898 and headquartered in Hamburg, gave considerable competition to the more ideological newspapers.

Two leading new Jewish periodicals established around the turn of the century—*Im deutschen Reich*, organ of the Centralverein deutscher Staatsbürger jüdischen Glaubens (Central Association of German Citizens of the Jewish Faith, cv) founded in 1895, and the Zionist *Jüdische Rundschau*, which originated as the *Israelitische Rundschau* in 1896—were symptomatic of the turn of Jewish attention to political issues. Competing with the *Jüdische Rundschau*, the newspaper of the German Zionist organization, was *Die Welt*, the mouthpiece of world Zionism. In

Austria the *Österreichische Wochenschrift*, founded by Rabbi Joseph Bloch, was similar to *Im deutschen Reich* in its non-Zionist defense of Jewish political equality.

Alongside the weekly or monthly press, with its mass circulation, were other Jewish periodicals that possessed a more cultural bent. During this period German Jewry published a number of scholarly journals with small circulations devoted to Wissenschaft des Judentums in general, to the history of the Jews in Germany in particular, and to Jewish demography and statistics. Culturally influential, despite relatively small readerships, were *Ost und West*, founded by the German branch of the Alliance Israélite Universelle in 1901, *Der Jude*, created in 1916 by Martin Buber, and *Selbstwehr*, the Prague Zionist publication founded in 1907. Community newspapers (*Gemeindeblätter*), an important medium during the Weimar Republic, were just beginning to come into existence during the first years of the twentieth century. The Berlin *Gemeindeblatt*, for instance, was not founded until 1910, although the bulletin of the Baden Oberrat dated back as far as 1884.

3. The Modernization of Charitable Activity

Methods of Jewish assistance to the needy underwent a steady and very gradual transformation throughout the nineteenth and early twentieth centuries, an evolution that was part of a Europe-wide trend toward the rationalization of philanthropy. Traditional personalized charity was gradually converted into a carefully planned and impersonal system of institutions designed to solve social ills. This change in attitude had many causes. In part it was a reflection of modern capitalist ideas prevalent throughout Western Europe, which distinguished between the "deserving" and "undeserving" poor and held that charity encouraged idleness. A specifically Jewish factor was the growing social distance between the bulk of German-speaking Jewry, now generally prosperous, and the Jewish poor, mostly (but not all) East European migrants stereotyped by Jew and non-Jew alike as beggars (*Schnorrer*). Additionally, the growth of social insurance, new social services, and the social work profession in Central European society created fresh models for dealing with social problems not only with money but also with advice, services, and retraining.

The traditional Jewish charity system had been far more extensive than its equivalent among non-Jewish Germans. Providing aid for wandering beggars (including free meals and lodging), care for the sick, and burial of the dead were considered religious obligations. Charitable societies (hevrahs) made up of unpaid volunteers dated back to the Middle Ages but continued to function until the 1930s. In small towns their role was especially large, but volunteer burial societies and other hevrahs persisted even in many urban communities. In the nineteenth century voluntary societies of women began to play a larger role in traditional Jewish charity alongside older exclusively male charitable organizations.

Each new stage in the transformation of Jewish welfare work supplemented rather than replaced earlier ones. First came the shift from unplanned charity toward rational planning, then the transformation from volunteer to professional welfare staffs. The slow process of change, beginning in Imperial Germany, was not completed until the 1920s at the earliest.

One symptom of changed attitudes was growing opposition to door-to-door solicitation of alms. The abolition of itinerant begging was one of the aims of the association of Jewish communities, the Deutsch-Israelitischer Gemeindebund. In addition, many local communities fought itinerancy by having members sign statements that they would not give to beggars at the door, sending them instead to a central aid office. Abolition of the visible side of the poverty problem, many felt, would help prevent embarrassment at having non-Jewish Germans see their outlandish and poor kinsmen, many of them from Eastern Europe, begging in public. A central office for aid to the migrant poor, created in 1910, struggled, with only limited success, to deal with the Jewish itinerants on a centralized basis. Other organizations helped transmigrants from Eastern Europe to America, in part so as to ensure that they did not become permanent residents in Germany.

The move from "outdoor" to "indoor" relief was reflected not only in opposition to begging but also in the creation of permanent institutions designed to provide services rather than money alone. Certain service institutions, notably Jewish hospitals and orphanages, had already existed before the unification of Germany, but now their number increased and their facilities were fully modernized. Most large communities built at least one Jewish hospital equipped with up-to-date operating rooms and other state-of-the-art facilities in the nineteenth century. The Berlin Jewish hospital, founded in 1703, was expanded and relocated several times (1753, 1821, 1861, 1910–1914). The last prewar facility had 230 beds (later even more) in several buildings. Although the building had a Jewish chapel and made kosher food available, it became an institution that served a wider clientele. Indeed, most of the patients were not Jewish. Besides a Jewish hospital, larger communities had a whole network of healthcare facilities. In Frankfurt, for instance, alongside the main 200-bed Jewish hospital, built in 1914, were a convalescent home, children's hospitals, and a tuberculosis sanitarium outside the city. In some cities the separatist Orthodox had their own independent hospital.

Besides healthcare facilities underwritten by major communities a number of independently funded sanitoria and convalescent homes were established in the presumably healthier country towns and at spas. One of the oldest such establishments was the Jewish sanatorium in Kolberg founded in 1872 with over one hundred beds. Modern homes for the aged, sponsored by individual Jewish communities or national organizations, became common. Homes for retarded children, the blind, the deaf-mute, and the insane were founded both in Germany and Austria (including the German-speaking sections of Bohemia and Moravia). The B'nai B'rith was especially active in social welfare, sponsoring summer vacation homes for children, training programs for Jewish nurses, and settlement houses for the urban poor. By the end of the nineteenth century local Jewish charities gave most of their donations to institutional recipients rather than to individual poor people applying in person.

Besides the many facilities for healthcare, Jewish organizations began to deal with poverty through institutions for sheltering or retraining the indigent. Some of these establishments placed as much emphasis on teaching the poor cleanliness and proper manners as on helping them with their economic needs. This mixture of help and condescension extended by middle-class German Jews to their mainly East European clients was characteristic of the social attitudes of middle-class welfare of the period. Still, there were some important differences. Unlike many of their non-Jewish counterparts who saw the poor as a potential revolutionary threat, middle-class German Jews viewed foreign wandering Jewish beggars largely as an embarrassment that called into question their own rooted-ness in Germany. Unlike the general policy of "keeping the poor in their place," Jewish organizations wanted their needy to follow in their foot-steps, enter the middle class, and thereby cease being noticeable.

The total amount of Jewish charitable and welfare activity was remark-able. One estimate counts five thousand Jewish organizations devoted mainly to welfare (though also including educational and self-defense groups) in Germany in 1906. Another survey shows that some twenty

thousand Berlin Jews belonged to at least one Jewish charitable organization and that thousands belonged to more than one. A number of extremely
wealthy German Jews participated actively in a multiplicity of Jewish welfare organizations. All this does not include the contributions of Jewish
philanthropists to nonsectarian causes of various types.

The new institutions for healthcare and care of the handicapped or
aged required professional staffs of doctors, nurses, caregivers, and
administrators. Nonetheless, a host of organizations continued to be
administered by volunteers—many of them female—and undertook
modern social welfare projects with unpaid staffs. Volunteers met immigrants at trains and directed them to sheltering organizations, subsidized
vocational training, maintained clubs for immigrant women and girls, ran
soup kitchens for the poor, and distributed milk to infants.

Along with this volunteer work went Jewish activity in applying general social work techniques within the Jewish community. The introduction of professional methods and staffs seems to have occurred first in
nondenominational charities, but by 1897 professionalization of Jewish
charitable work had proceeded far enough to require the founding of a
Federation for Jewish Welfare Work in Berlin. National centralization
came in 1917 with the establishment of a Central Welfare Office of
German Jewry. In the post-World-War-I period social workers were to
play an ever greater role in communal affairs.

4. Education

Unlike the expanding Jewish social welfare network, Jewish educational
institutions receded before the growing attraction of education under
non-Jewish auspices. Separate Jewish elementary and secondary schools
continued to exist in various German states but in declining numbers.
Since the vast majority of Jewish young people attended non-Jewish
schools, Jewish leaders focused increasingly on supplemental Jewish
instruction. The Jewish community was divided on the education issue—
some favored separate Jewish schools—but the majority endorsed nondenominational schools along with supplemental Jewish religious
instruction.

The legal position of Jewish elementary education differed from state
to state. Some regional governments forbade separate Jewish schools
while others encouraged them. In Baden all schools were interdenomina-
tional (*Simultanschulen*), while in neighboring Württemberg all schools

were divided according to religious denomination. Jewish educational institutions received both government recognition and subsidies in some states but in others had to make do without either.

Before the unification of Germany Jewish elementary schools were to be found in urban and rural, Orthodox and Liberal communities alike. But after 1871 their constituencies became increasingly restricted to rural or Orthodox Jews. Migration from villages to cities and changes in religious attitude from Orthodox to Liberal caused Jewish elementary schools to decline. In Prussia the percentage of Jewish children in Jewish schools fell steadily from almost 50 percent in 1864 to 38 percent in 1886, 32 percent in 1902, and only about 20 percent in 1906. The number of Jewish schools in Germany fell rapidly from 492 as late as 1898 to 247 by 1913. Of these the bulk, especially in such areas as Hesse-Nassau and Bavaria, were one-room schoolhouses with a single teacher. Migration to the cities frequently left these schools with such tiny enrollments that attempts by governments to set minimum enrollment standards could endanger their continued existence. In 1904 only 30 of 244 Jewish elementary schools in Prussia had more than 30 pupils.

The situation was different in the cities in that urban Jewish schools were much more substantial than the village schoolhouses and were often directed toward secondary rather than primary education. However, by the time of German unification most of the famous Jewish schools founded under Liberal auspices (like the Samsonschule in Wolfenbüttel and the Jacobsonschule in Seesen) accepted Christian pupils. Soon most of these ceased to have a Jewish character altogether. The Israelitische Freischule (Jewish Free School) in Hamburg, for instance, already had 305 Christians among its 577 pupils in 1871. By 1907 Jewish enrollment there had decreased to only 10.5 percent of all students, the school had changed its name to Foundation School of 1815, and it held regular classes on Saturday. The only Liberal Jewish secondary school still under communal auspices in 1914 was the Philanthropin in Frankfurt.

As schools under Liberal auspices declined the surviving urban Jewish schools catered almost exclusively to Orthodox students or to the children of recent immigrants. Two of the most successful Orthodox schools were the Hirsch-Realschule in Frankfurt, with over six hundred students by 1912, and the Talmud-Thoraschule in Hamburg of about the same size. Other Orthodox Jewish secondary schools existed in Fürth (founded 1862) and Leipzig (founded 1912). More such schools were established after World War I. In some cities there were separate schools for the

21   A class of the Talmud-Torah school in Hamburg around 1900

native Orthodox and for recent immigrants from Galicia and Russia (for instance, the Israelitische Volksschule in Frankfurt). Native-born German Jewish families, even Orthodox ones, avoided immigrant schools, which they considered schools for the poor.

Even privately funded Jewish schools faced close government supervision, which sometimes interfered with their freedom. Official inspectors stymied Samson Raphael Hirsch's desire to give equal time to Jewish and secular instruction, forcing his school to restrict the Jewish subjects to a mere one-fourth of the class time. They were especially hostile to extensive instruction in the Hebrew language and permitted the upper classes at the Hirschschule to offer only six hours of Bible and four of Talmud weekly. An even more extreme example of government interference occurred in Würzburg where, only with great difficulty, was the Bavarian government dissuaded from forcing the Orthodox teachers' seminary to train its students in playing the organ!

Since most German-Jewish children attended schools under non-Jewish auspices, the question of providing religious instruction for them became acute. Jewish communities could either set up supplemental religious schools before or after the "regular" school time or arrangements could be made for religious instruction within the framework of the non-

Jewish school itself. Under the latter arrangement a Jewish teacher could instruct pupils of his denomination during the time that the Protestant and Catholic children had their religion lessons. Although legislation differed from state to state, most governments refused to make Jewish religious instruction compulsory or to subsidize it. This refusal to recognize the Jewish denomination as equal to the Lutheran and Catholic was especially galling to the leaders of national Jewish organizations. Most Jewish parents availed themselves of the "freedom" not to send their children to Jewish religious instruction in the non-Jewish schools. Yet almost 10 percent of Jewish children in secondary schools attended classes on the Christian religion! Many communities, both small and large, had their own religious schools, which met either before or after the regular school. Such schools likewise reached only a minority of Jewish children. Some rural communities were too poor to afford a teacher, and many urban Jews did not avail themselves of the schools in their communities.

Even where supplemental religious instruction was available memoirs indicate that most students found such instruction uninspiring or even counterproductive. One wrote:

> Our Jewish religious instruction consisted of two unconnected halves: a moralizing religious doctrine that was too stupid for the most stupid among us and a practicum in Semitic philology that would have given a hard time to many a learned Orientalist. Over the years we, who had long come to feel that we were Jewish Germans or German Jews, accustomed ourselves to participating in these lessons as infrequently as possible.

And another recalled of her religion teacher: "But for me he wasn't the teacher I needed. He taught academic religious studies where I wanted religion and provided ideas and knowledge where I needed feelings. So I was dreadfully bored."[1]

The preparation of teachers for Jewish schools and supplemental education was usually provided by Jewish teacher training facilities, most of them under the auspices of one of the two opposing religious trends. As the Orthodox share in full-day Jewish education increased, so did the importance of their seminaries in comparison to the older Liberal-sponsored ones. There were Liberal institutes for teacher training in Kassel (more for the general than the Jewish subjects), Hanover (traditional but not Orthodox), and Münster (the Marks-Hainsdorf Foundation). The Münster institution had its own building and prepared teachers for both

Jewish and secular subjects; it served kosher food to its students, who attended services in the town's Liberal synagogue.

The two chief Orthodox teacher training institutes were located in Würzburg (founded in 1864) and the Rhineland (at first Düsseldorf, later Cologne, founded in 1867). The Würzburg seminary, led for many years by members of the Bamberger rabbinical family, had a four-year preparatory program in Bavarian villages followed by a three-year course at Würzburg. Despite the modest size of its annual enrollment (thirty-four in 1884), the Würzburg school had tremendous influence on Jewish instruction in Bavaria and all over southern Germany. By 1904 it had over four hundred alumni. The Cologne school, with a faculty of nine, mainly Gentile instructors, was neither as rigorous nor as influential. Its student body fell to a low of fifteen in 1905 but rose again to thirty-eight by 1911.

The question of Jewish schooling was, like much else, a subject of controversy between the Liberal majority and the Orthodox minority. National Jewish umbrella organizations actively lobbied the governments in favor of both the officially nondenominational although sometimes still residually Christian Simultanschule and compulsory Jewish religious education. The Orthodox opposed them on both issues. They favored the retention of separate Jewish elementary schools while objecting to compulsory religious education in government schools lest their children attending them have to submit to instruction by Liberal rabbis and teachers.

5. The Rise of Nationwide Jewish Organizations

National and regional Jewish organizations proliferated during the Kaiserreich period to deal with the many political, social, and communal challenges that could not be handled on the level of the local Kultusgemeinde. Religious issues played a smaller role in the new associations than did political matters, especially the challenge of antisemitism. Although occasional attempts to create a single Jewish organization representing all German Jewry were uniformly unsuccessful, a host of new and sometimes competing nationwide organizations did coordinate Jewish activities to an extent previously unknown.

The first major Jewish umbrella organization came into existence just before the founding of the German Empire. Unlike most of the later national organizations, the Deutsch-Israelitischer Gemeindebund (German-Jewish Communities Alliance, DIGB) remained basically a federation of local communities. The Gemeinden joined together to aid financially struggling small communities, fight against itinerant beggary, and negotiate with the government on matters of social welfare and communal administration. Later in its history the DIGB sponsored or cosponsored pensions for Jewish teachers, a historical commission, and a central archives of German Jewry.

The fact that the DIGB was founded at a meeting held simultaneously with the synod of Liberal Jews at Leipzig in June 1869 made Orthodox Jews suspicious of the new organization. The pamphlet by Emil Lehmann entitled *Höre Israel* (Hear O Israel) proposing the new organization bristled with suggestions for radical religious reforms. Only in the 1890s did some Orthodox leaders, notably members of the Hildesheimer family, participate in DIGB activities. Besides their specific misgivings, Orthodox Jews, now a minority in the Jewish community, came to suspect all proposals for nationwide Jewish organizations out of fear that they would suffer domination by the Liberal majority. Government officials, in turn, were able to use the objections of the Orthodox minority as a pretext for rejecting some of the proposals made by national Jewish organizations.

In the beginning the DIGB grew very slowly, gathering the 100 communities required in its bylaws only in 1872. Until 1875 it included Austrian communities but later limited itself to the borders of the German Empire. After moving its headquarters from relatively isolated Leipzig to the German capital in 1882, the DIGB began to grow more rapidly, reaching 183 communities in 1882, 350 in 1888, 652 in 1898 and 1,012—more than one in every three Jewish communities in Germany—in 1911.

Organizations dedicated to the fight against antisemitism (see chapter 8) had even more impact than the DIGB. In the 1880s attempts to counter antisemitism took place mainly behind the scenes or through groups of notables like the "Committee of December 1 [1880]" organized by Moritz Lazarus. A change in attitude by many German Jews in the last decade of the century led them to turn to a more militant and public approach. Following trends in German society as a whole, where mass politics was replacing the role of notables, Jews, too, began to organize on a nationwide basis and openly pursue political goals instead of only religious and charitable ones. Issues of legislation affecting Jews, government administrative policies, and even the proper attitude to take in political campaigns became integral to the activities of the new Jewish organizations. Economic interest groups such as the Bund der Landwirte (Agrarian League) and religious and national minorities like the Catholics and the Poles served as models for such activities even though they often pursued goals opposing those of the Jewish community.

The chief Jewish organizations combating antisemitism in Austria and Germany had remarkably parallel histories. Both the Austrian Öster-reichisch-Israelitische Union (founded 1886) and the Centralverein deutscher Staatsbürger jüdischen Glaubens (cv, founded 1893) started out as militant groups that felt the reaction of the official Jewish community to hatred was too timid. Both tried to combine loyalty to the state with defense of the rights and dignity of Jewish citizens. Both ended up eventually as establishment organizations supporting the Liberal point of view against Zionist and other challenges.

The creation of the cv (on which see also chapters 8 and 9) was only the first of a number of attempts to organize a centralized representation of German Jewry to the government. Even Liberal Jewish leaders, turning away from an earlier policy of minimizing Jewish distinctiveness, increasingly looked to the Catholic minority as a model for their relationship to public institutions. In 1900 Martin Philippson and Bernhard Breslauer, leading Liberal leaders of the DIGB and cv, proposed a *Judentag*, a Jewish version of the *Katholikentag*, the annual meeting of German Catholics. However, when the Zionists came out in favor of a democratically chosen Judentag in 1901 most Liberal leaders abandoned the idea of a mass organization. Occasional suggestions (or accusations) that a Jewish equivalent of the Catholic Center Party be created were rendered impractical by the small Jewish population in Germany. Similarly unproductive were attempts to create a central organization for all Jews in the huge state of Prussia between 1905 and 1909.

Although such ambitious plans for a nationwide Jewish representation were unsuccessful, a more modest national organization—the Verband der deutschen Juden (Association of German Jews, vdj)—representing communities and organizations rather than individual members was created in 1904. Both the cv and DIGB were well represented at its assemblies, along with the Zionists, the Jüdischer Frauenbund, representing Jewish women, and B'nai B'rith.

The vdj was supposed to deal with the government on behalf of the Jews of Germany concerning discrimination and legislation of Jewish interest. Despite all the high hopes at its founding, however, the vddj had relatively little success. Not only did it face constant opposition from the separatist Orthodox Freie Vereinigung (Free Association); even organizations represented in the vdj often acted independently. It lasted less than twenty years, fading out of existence shortly after World War I, in 1922.

The DIGB, CV, and vdj all claimed to represent German Jewry as a whole on a nationwide basis. In order to establish this position they proclaimed their neutrality with regard to both German party politics and internal Jewish divisions. The very idea of an all-inclusive neutrality with no official stand on religious conflicts or on the Zionist controversy was an innovation of the period. The new organizational leadership stressed a united front, implying that what bound Jews together was stronger than any ideology or religious viewpoint. Despite the nationwide organizations' claims of neutrality, however, many German Jews viewed them as representing the Liberal acculturated majority. Though they had some Orthodox, and even Zionist, representation, most of their leadership and members were recruited from among Liberal or nonpracticing Jews, a matter arousing suspicion among Zionists and Orthodox.

Other nationwide Jewish organizations also proclaimed their ideological neutrality, though without claiming to represent all of German Jewry. Two of the most influential of these organizations were the Independent Order of B'nai B'rith (Unabhängige Orden Bne Briss, UOBB) and the Jüdischer Frauenbund (discussed in detail in chapter 3).

The B'nai B'rith was founded in 1843 by German Jewish immigrants in the United States, where its international headquarters remained. The rise of German antisemitism and the growing exclusion of Jews from German Free Masonry and Odd Fellows lodges led to the founding of the first German B'nai B'rith lodge in Berlin in 1882. The German *Grossloge* was incorporated in 1885 with 12 lodges composed of 1,150 members and grew by 1912 to 79 lodges with 8,610 members. This made the German B'nai B'rith the second largest national group, after the Americans, in the international organization. Originally strongest in eastern Germany, the lodges eventually spread to all parts of the empire. Although women were excluded from membership in the lodges themselves, a number of "sisterhoods" (*Schwesternschaften*) were created as early as 1886.

The influence of B'nai B'rith went far beyond the size of its membership. It often included the leading men of the various Jewish communities, in part because of its success (after overcoming its original anti-Zionism) in maintaining neutrality among the various parties within Judaism. Members were screened before admission for both their moral character and their social respectability and were expected to take an active part in lodge activities. The UOBB was an influential force in the development of the modern network of Jewish social welfare in Germany, sponsoring settlement houses (the Toynbee Hallen), homes for the disabled, labor exchanges, and youth organizations. Partly because of its secrecy and partly because of its successes, B'nai B'rith was often attacked by antisemites as an international secret society with nefarious aims.

All the previously mentioned national Jewish organizations except the Frauenbund could be considered part of the Jewish establishment. The same could not be said for the Zionist organizations that came into existence in the late 1890s. Although there had been proto-Zionist organizations in Germany and Austria even before Theodor Herzl launched the Zionist movement in 1896, these had been relatively small and scattered. Thereafter the Zionist movement organized on three levels—international, national, and local.

The World Zionist Organization (WZO) was closely associated with German-speaking Jewry in the years before World War I. The official language of Zionist Congresses before the war and even thereafter was German (sometimes in the Yiddishized form colloquially known as *Congressdeutsch*). Until Herzl's death in 1904 WZO headquarters were in Vienna, after which they were moved to Cologne, the home of its second president, David Wolffsohn, and then when Otto Warburg became president, in 1911, to Berlin. German dominance came to an end with the outbreak of World War I, when the WZO moved to neutral Copenhagen, never to return to Germany.

The Zionistische Vereinigung für Deutschland (Zionist Union for Germany, ZVFD) was founded in July 1897 and, despite internal ideological disputes, was one of the few national Zionist organizations to remain united. The regional organization for Austria covered the entire non-Hungarian part of the empire and was divided into seven districts. In 1907 it split into three subregional organizations covering Galicia, Western Austria ("Inner Austria," Bohemia and Moravia), and Bukovina. In Germany there were noticeable differences in the makeup and functions of the WZO and the ZVFD, even though for some years they were headquartered in the same building. Most of the leaders of the WZO in Germany were Russian Jews who had settled in Germany temporarily, while the ZVFD leadership was made up almost entirely of German citizens.

Within the international Zionist movement the German Zionists played an important role as financial contributors, generally ranking third among national organizations in donations but a much smaller role in membership because of their small numbers. Measured by the number of *shekel* payers (contributors of at least one mark annually), the highest number of zvfd members before World War I was a mere 9,800 in 1914. Probably no more than one in three of these shekel payers were active members in the organization. Compared to the membership of the Centralverein, this Zionist affiliation was tiny. In Western Austria, too, affiliated Zionists were not numerous: in 1909 there were 1,401 shekel payers in Inner Austria, 2,216 in Bohemia, and 1,800 in Moravia-Silesia. In communal elections, sometimes in alliance with religious traditionalists, the Zionists showed considerably greater strength than in membership figures, although they rarely gained majorities. East European immigrants and their children made up a disproportionately large number of their rank and file.

Much of the growth in Jewish organizational life was related to Jewish reactions to antisemitism, even when the connection is not immediately apparent. The issue of occupational retraining, which would seem to be purely an economic matter, is a good example. Organizations for Jewish occupational redistribution were first founded in the early nineteenth century to meet the conditions for Emancipation. The 1880s witnessed a lively renewal of interest in the subject. The founders of new organizations devoted to the cause now hoped that generating an occupational distribution closer to that of non-Jews would counter antisemitic claims of Jewish domination in commerce and the professions. Among the major organizations to encourage occupational redistribution were associations to further the spread of handicrafts and agriculture among the German Jews. The Jewish horticultural school (Israelitische Gartenbauschule) in Ahlem near Hanover was dedicated to training Jews for an occupation not common among them. Founded in 1893 by Moritz Simon and funded by both organizations and private individuals, it served an average of seventy-five to eighty pupils and apprentices during its first years.

Jewish gymnastic societies and sports clubs followed the models of the German *Turnvereine* and the Czech and Polish *Sokol* societies. Like them, they were centers of nationalist activity. Aside from finding a place for Jewish youth excluded from the general gymnastic societies by "Aryan paragraphs" in their bylaws, Jewish associations, mostly founded by Zionists, intended to increase Jewish pride and national identity. Specific to the Jewish societies was the desire to refute the antisemitic stereotype of the Jewish bookworm by creating a new generation of *Muskeljuden* (muscular Jews). The first Jewish gymnastic society was established in Berlin in 1898, in 1900 a periodical, the *Jüdische Turnzeitung*, was founded, and by 1904 there were twelve Jewish Turnvereine. The rise of separate Jewish sports clubs and teams aroused dismay among many non-Zionist Jews as well as within the Jewish defense organization, the Verein zur Abwehr des Antisemitismus. These felt that separate Jewish sports groups only reinforced Jewish segregation and that they both copied and aided antisemitic exclusion based on ethnic origin. The journal of the Abwehrverein on one occasion derided Jewish sports clubs by titling an article "Jewish Exclusion Games."

Like the sports groups, new Jewish cultural organizations combined freshly awakened feelings of pride in the Jewish heritage with attempts to fight antisemitism. Hostility from the outside induced acculturated Jews to find out more about their heritage, both to refute anti-Jewish slurs and to clarify their own sense of identity. The Federation of Societies for Jewish History and Literature (Verband der Vereine für jüdische Geschichte und Literatur), founded in 1893, grew within ten years to 180 branches with 15,000 members. Through popular lectures on Jewish topics and the publication of a yearbook, it proposed to raise Jewish self-esteem and fight antisemitism. (Characteristically, the separatist Orthodox created their own Jewish Literary Society in 1902 with its own rival publication.) Another indication of the growing interest among some Jews in Jewish culture was the founding of Jewish libraries and museums in several Jewish communities around the turn of the century.

The growth of Jewish national organizations was simultaneously a sign of a turn inward toward greater Jewish involvement and a copying of patterns in the larger German society. Late-nineteenth-century Germany was characterized by a dense and growing network of clubs, societies, and interest groups. Such associations not only united society but divided it as well. The Catholics, the Socialists, and the Poles, for example, created their own institutional worlds that helped give their members a clearer sense of who they were. The parallel growth of new Jewish institutions in the same period followed much the same pattern. For many German Jews during the period of the Kaiserreich organizational activity became their principal mode of Jewish identification. Facing social or cultural rejection, some of the acculturated among them turned back to the Jewish community, though in a secular fashion. Expressing their Jewishness by fighting for Jewish rights, helping their coreligionists, or socializing with fellow

22   The Jewish athletic association Bar Kochba in Berlin (1902)

Jews functioned, for many, as a replacement for a Jewish life centered on the synagogue.

6. Student and Youth Organizations

Another fundamental change in Jewish organizational life, likewise influenced by broader changes in German society, was the increasing role of youth-oriented activities. This development stood in sharp contrast to the period before 1880 when almost all Jewish organizations consisted exclusively of adults. The impulse for this transformation was a mixture of outside hostility and a new cultural orientation stressing the special qualities of youth, often in contrast to the self-satisfied adult society. Yet, although the Jewish youth stressed their differences from the older generation, they could not escape a parallel fragmentation along ideological lines. Especially conspicuous was the division between Zionist and "German-Jewish" youth organizations. Often the alumni of the student groups played a disproportionate role in the leadership of the adult movements.

University students faced with growing antisemitism were the first to found Jewish youth organizations. Jews were increasingly excluded from fraternities and other university societies. Many of the remaining "inclusive" student groups ended up de facto as mostly Jewish in their membership. These nominally nonsectarian organizations did not satisfy all Jewish students. Some wanted a specifically Jewish response to the new exclusionary movements. In Germany Jewish fraternities favoring integration came first, with Zionist ones only later; in Austria the order was reversed. In both countries the ideological student groups actually preceded the adult ideological organizations.

In 1886 a group of Jews at Breslau University founded the Viadrina as a Jewish dueling fraternity dedicated to fighting antisemitism. Like the later CV, the Viadrina tried to combine Germanism with self-defense and initially aroused opposition from most Jewish leaders. In 1896 four Jewish fraternities united to form the Kartell Convent deutscher Studenten jüdischen Glaubens (Syndicate of German Students of the Jewish Faith, KC) Following the practice of non-Jewish fraternities, KC members wore colored caps and sashes, participated in ritualized drinking, singing, and fencing, and fought antisemitic students in duels. Their name and their ideological orientation resembled those of the CV:

> The ideology of the fraternities in the KC is based on German patriotic convictions. Their purpose is the fight against antisemitism among German university students and to educate their members as self-aware Jews, cognizant of the fact that the German Jews are an inseparable part of the German people, tied to the fatherland by history, common culture, and law. Thus they will always be ready and able to stand up for the political and social equality of the Jews.[2]

Zionist-oriented students found the KC fraternities unsatisfactory and gradually created a counternetwork of Jewish nationalist fraternities. In Germany the Zionist network developed slowly. Among the large number of Russian Jews studying in Germany a group of Jewish nationalists broke away from the socialist Russian Students Association to form the Russian-Jewish Scholarly Association (Russisch-jüdischer wissenschaftliche Verein) in 1889. This group, which eventually had hundreds of members, was the first proto-Zionist student organization in Germany. Meetings were often held in the Russian language. Later organizations tried to bring together native and foreign-born Jewish students sympathetic to Zionism. A Zionist-oriented coalition of Jewish fraternities—the Kartell Jüdischer Verbindungen (Syndicate of Jewish Fraternities, KJV)—was finally founded in 1914 as the result of successive mergers of smaller organizations, including that of the Russian Zionists. Like the KC, the KJV fraternities engaged in drinking, singing, and dueling, though they identified more with Jewish rather than German history and culture. By 1914 the KJV had some one thousand members, many of them from assimilated backgrounds, but it remained smaller than the KC.

The Zionist fraternities in the German-speaking parts of the Austrian Empire came into existence much earlier and were more intellectually oriented than those in Germany. The proto-Zionist Kadima was founded by Viennese university students led by Nathan Birnbaum as early as 1882. The Bar Kochba student association in Prague (1893) became a major cultural institution and was deemed the most intellectually significant Zionist organization in Austria-Hungary. Its members included intellectuals of the caliber of Robert Weltsch, Hugo Bergmann, Hans Kohn, and Max Brod, with Franz Kafka as an interested sympathizer. Consciously rejecting the fraternity traditions of colors and dueling, the Bar Kochba engaged in discussions, lectures, and a program of publications. The guest lectures of Martin Buber to the Bar Kochba in 1909 and 1910 (see chapter 11) were an important milestone in the development of Jewish cultural nationalism. In Prague Bar Kochba had to compete with two rival Zionist fraternities, the German-speaking dueling fraternity Barissia and the Czech-speaking Theodor Herzl Society.

University fraternities were one model for the new Jewish youth organizations; the German youth movement, which began to develop at the beginning of the twentieth century, was another. The youth movement, generally led by young people themselves rather than by adults, was a form of elite youth culture with a mystique all its own. Members of the

youth movement were generally well-educated young people in rebellion
against the bourgeois values of parents and official society. Though frequently vague, the ideology of the youth movement tended to value the
spontaneous and instinctual over the intellectual, rational, and material-
istic. It was strongly influenced by neo-Romantic *völkisch* ideas extolling
the countryside over the city and stressing blood ties, racial characteristics, and the *Führerprinzip* (leadership principle). The Wandervogel (hikers), the best-known organization of the youth movement, began a trend
throughout the youth movement of roaming the German countryside,
communing with nature and history, and singing folk songs around
campfires. Some, but not all, of the organizations in the youth movement
were strongly antisemitic in the racial sense.

Jewish organizations on the pattern of the German youth movement
were still in their infancy before World War I. The only important group
was the Jüdischer Wanderbund Blau-Weiss (Jewish Hikers Association
Blue and White) founded in 1912. Combining German back-to-nature
ideology with a strong Jewish national bent, the Blau-Weiss stressed
Jewish authenticity and criticized the ostentation and intellectuality of
city life. Although, on occasion, its publications denied that it was a
Zionist organization, the Blau-Weiss's orientation clearly subscribed to
cultural Zionism in a fairly radical mode:

> For us being Jewish is an ideal to which we aspire, not a memory we
> want to overcome. As Jews, we do not hike on the Sabbath, we cook
> kosher food over our campfires, and we greet each other and out-
> siders with the Hebrew greeting "Shalom." We celebrate our holi-
> days—Pesach, Purim, and Hanukah—openly and joyously. . . . We
> are not Zionistic, as others label us. We have nothing to do with par-
> ties and party politics. . . . What we are, we say proudly, is Jewish!
> Because we are Jewish, we aren't afraid to learn Hebrew, to cultivate
> Jewish songs along with German ones, and to think about Palestine
> and our brethren in the East.[3]

The Blau-Weiss, whose members, both male and female, were often
younger than university age, tried to connect such typical youth movement trappings as hiking in the German countryside with a focus on life
in Palestine.

Blau-Weiss members felt that their organization would create a true
sense of community, though some, notably Gershom Scholem, were
extremely critical of the group's youth movement trappings. Because of

23   The Zionist Gustav Krojanker in the uniform of his student
fraternity around 1910

its emphasis on spontaneity, the Blau-Weiss was a much more iconoclastic element on the Zionist scene than was the KJV.

Most Jewish youth organizations during the first years of the twentieth century were much more conventional than the Blau-Weiss and were
often sponsored by adult groups. Among the Orthodox there was a pro-

liferation of new organizations for the young, including a union of Jewish university graduates formed in 1903 and a union of Orthodox youth groups established in 1907.

The largest Jewish youth organization in prewar Germany was the neutral Verband der jüdischen Jugendvereine Deutschlands (Federation of Jewish Youth Associations in Germany) founded in 1909 with the support of B'nai B'rith, the cv, and the DIGB. By 1913 it had 14,500 members, both male and female. Although it had Zionist members, it leaned toward the Liberal point of view. Most of the Verband's members were between eighteen and twenty-five years of age and were often commercial apprentices or commercial employees rather than students. The program of the affiliated organizations was largely social, designed to bring together young Jewish men and women, especially recent migrants from the countryside. Social activities were supplemented by lectures designed to educate the membership on Judaism. The leadership of the Verband was generally more intellectual than its membership and often came from a more socially prestigious professional background.

7. International Ties

The relationship of organized German Jewry to Jews outside Germany was a paradoxical one. Although all but a small Zionist minority constantly stressed that their loyalty was to Germany alone, wide sections of German Jewry continued to have a keen interest in the fate of Jews all over the world. The creation of organizations to assist world Jewry was characterized by a curious mixture of German patriotism and Jewish solidarity. Organizations to aid Jews abroad had their greatest appeal precisely in those circles most likely to deny the existence of a worldwide Jewish people.

The oldest Jewish organization to aid Jews around the world was the Alliance Israélite Universelle (AIU), founded in Paris in 1859. Its main sphere of activity was in the Muslim countries but it also engaged in work in Eastern Europe. Spreading beyond its original national framework, the AIU by 1870 had gained more members in Germany than in France. Despite its ongoing activity, many German Jews eyed the alliance with some suspicion both because of its association with France, the political enemy of Germany, and because they feared the accusation of an international Jewish conspiracy.

An attempt in 1872 to create a separate German version of the AIU was not successful. Its equivalent in Austria, the Israelitische Allianz (1873), which operated mainly in Romania, Serbia, and the Austro-Hungarian Empire, had somewhat better success because it was supported by such notables as Joseph von Wertheimer and Baron Maurice de Hirsch. Similar nationally based organizations to aid Jews around the world were founded in other Western countries, notably Britain and the United States.

Fabulously wealthy individuals played as great a role in international Jewish philanthropy as did organizations. The Rothschilds, established in many cities of Europe including German-speaking Frankfurt and Vienna, supported numerous Jewish charities on a private basis. Baron Maurice de Hirsch, who was born in Bavaria and later became an Austrian citizen although he lived most of his life in Paris, was another benefactor on a huge scale. However, he preferred to give his philanthropic work a more organized form. Hirsch's largest project, the Jewish Colonization Association, founded in 1891, had as its main function settling large numbers of Russian Jewish emigrants in agricultural colonies, especially in Argentina. The Baron Hirsch Foundation, established 1888 and based in Austria, was active in the eastern provinces of the empire, especially Galicia, in creating a system of modern schools.

The emphasis by West European Jewish organizations on educational activities for their coreligionists in the eastern countries displayed a mixture of genuine caring with subtle or not so subtle attempts to wean the "native" Jews from their "backward" traditional culture. To replace this culture each organization fostered the culture of its own Western country, leading to considerable competition between German, English, French, and later also American Jewish philanthropies.

The Hilfsverein der deutschen Juden (Aid Society of German Jews), founded in 1901 to help the suffering Jews of the Middle East and Eastern Europe, was a consciously German organization whose purpose, in part, was to outflank the French cultural influence of the Alliance Israélite. The organization was closely associated with two leading German-Jewish philanthropists—James Simon and Paul Nathan—both strong German patriots. Simon was part of the small circle of *Kaiserjuden,* Jews who were on friendly terms with Emperor William II. As early as 1898 Nathan had proposed a German school association for the Jews of the East (Deutscher Schulverein für die Juden des Orients), requesting the official sponsorship of the German government. When this idea was not accepted in its original form, it was restructured as the Hilfsverein.

The Hilfsverein grew rapidly, enjoying support from a broad section of German Jewry. It organized the transmigration of large numbers of East European Jews to America via German ports and provided for their needs along the way. It intervened with East European governments, attempting to improve the legal position of Jews there and providing material aid in the wake of natural disasters and pogroms.

Aside from competing with the AIU in establishing schools in Palestine, the Hilfsverein also created a network of modern Jewish schools in Eastern Europe. Since Hilfsverein schools helped to spread German language and culture there, the imperial German government looked upon them with favor. For a time the Hilfsverein worked together with the Zionists, but, as elaborated in chapter 9, a vehement and divisive conflict with them over the language of instruction at its technical school in Haifa brought such cooperation to an end.

For the development of German-Jewish communal structures the years 1870 to 1918 do not constitute a clearly delineated period. Some of the processes leading to a more modern and complex network of institutions were in motion before the unification of Germany and persisted in the period after World War I. Although the locally based Gemeinde remained the basic Jewish institution, nationwide umbrella organizations were gaining influence in many areas of Jewish life. Social work and bureaucratic procedures slowly supplanted volunteer activity and personalized charity; ideological differences within German Jewry found their expression in competing organizations on the local and national level; youth work and independent youth and student organizations played an increasing role in the life of the community.

The challenges of outside hostility, internal indifference, and assimilation were met by a strong, modernizing, and constantly changing Jewish institutional network. Jewish activities on the organizational level were far from slackening. Quite the contrary, the growth of national Jewish institutions indicates an ongoing Jewish activism.

6 | Legal Equality and Public Life

"At long last," wrote the aged Jewish politician Raphael Kosch (1803–1872) just before his death, Jews had "reached safe harbor."[1] The safe harbor was the guarantee of equality before the law, enshrined in the law of July 3, 1869, which, in a single paragraph, declared the rights and duties of the citizen to be "independent of religious denomination."[2] It had been passed by the parliament of the North German Confederation, that embryonic nation-state that spanned the interval between the defeat of Austria in 1866 and the proclamation of the German Empire in 1871. Once that had been achieved, the law applied to the whole of the empire. Article 14 of the new Austrian constitution of December 1867 proclaimed the same principle in almost identical words. Throughout German-speaking Central Europe legal discrimination seemed once and for all to be a thing of the past.

Yet how safe was this harbor, how secure a protection against the storms of prejudice and discrimination? Emancipation is a legal concept, but legal processes do not happen in a vacuum. Emancipation has a dual aim: not only to change the status of an unprivileged group but also to change society—to create a set of human relationships in which the dominance of inherited characteristics gives way to the criterion of individual worth and individual usefulness. Therefore, when it happens it is consequence as well as cause. Jewish second-class citizenship had fitted into a segmented society that discriminated not only between adherents of different religions but between members of different estates and ranks as

well—landowners, guildmasters, bureaucrats, laborers, and serfs. Only
when the distinctions between these began to break down could one con-
ceive of a society based on individual rights, the type of political program
first proclaimed by the Constitution of the United States (ratified 1788)
and the French Declaration of the Rights of Man and Citizen (1789).

For at least two decades before formal emancipation was enacted
Jewish participation in public life had become quite normal. Indeed, it
needed to be normal before the final equality before the law would be
acceptable. Legal enactment was the last stage, not the first, of a long evolutionary process. The presence of Jews in public life therefore did not
merely accelerate the completion of legal equality, it was a precondition
for it. But even that was merely a symptom of a still wider development.
Jews entered parliaments because they were sent there by predominantly
non-Jewish electorates. They had, in a limited but significant way, entered
general middle-class society. The great majority of the Jews active in public life were men of substance, in some cases considerable substance:
bankers, merchants, manufacturers, lawyers, doctors, teachers, publishers.
They had taken advantage of the opportunities offered by a more open
society. Their social and economic emancipation consisted of a series of
individual processes. Not all wanted it, not all who attempted it succeeded.
But without it the culture of the German-Jewish community and the
nature of Jewish-Gentile relations in Germany could not have evolved as
they did. The "civic betterment" of the Jews, which had been the universal aim of Gentile reformers since the 1780s, was now largely complete.

1. State Service: The Half-Open Door

Those who advocated civic equality in the middle decades of the nineteenth century emphasized the removal not only of external constraints
on Jews but of informal social barriers. Jews were to be not merely entitled to enter all trades and professions and local and national politics but
enabled to do so. Yet all these transformations were restricted to the realm
of civil society. The self-emancipation of the Jew through education and
enterprise was, in the end, encouraged by the governments of most
German states and even welcomed by them, on the unspoken assumption
that there was a line around the inner sanctum of the state itself that was
not to be crossed. Even at the height of the Liberal epoch the notion
remained of an autonomous state, exercising authority separately from
civil society. Large areas of the state service thus remained obstinately

closed to Jews and others were opened only partially, reluctantly, and conditionally.

There were technical as well as ideological explanations for this continuing discrimination. The first is that the newly created empire accounted for only a small proportion of public employment in Germany. The individual states, with Prussia at their head, continued to be responsible for the greater part of it. Police and law enforcement were matters for the individual states, as was education. Even the military was in times of peace de facto decentralized, with individual regiments largely autonomous in the recruitment of their officers. The careers that educated Jews most coveted, those in schools, academia, and the judiciary, were therefore controlled by the ministries of the twenty-five constituent states. They responded to the claims of Jewish applicants in accordance with different priorities, pressures, and prejudices, but also on the basis of different and frequently ambiguous constitutions. Although the 1869 law was supposed to override the discriminatory provisions of individual states, the state governments continued to act largely on the basis of their older provisions. A case in point was in the Prussian constitution of 1851, which remained in force until 1918. Article 4 guaranteed the citizen's equality before the law, article 12 the equality of rights and duties irrespective of religion. Article 14, however, stipulated the Christian character of "those institutions concerned with the exercise of religion." What these were remained a matter of endless, acrimonious, and inconclusive dispute. Up to 1867 the Prussian Ministry of Justice stuck to the position that the 1847 law regulating Jewish status prevented Jews from administering Christian oaths and therefore disqualified them from appointment as judges. It was only under the impact of the 1869 federal law, which clearly superseded the internal arrangements of the individual states, that the first four Jewish magistrates were nominated in 1870. By 1879 there were ninety-nine judges of the Jewish faith in Prussia or 3.8 percent of the total. Jewish court trainees (*Assessoren*) numbered 12.8 percent of the total; in three of the court districts they accounted for over a quarter of the total.

Elsewhere the situation varied. Hamburg had been the first German state to appoint a Jewish judge, when Gabriel Riesser became a member of the High Court in 1860. Baden and, belatedly, Bavaria appointed Jewish judicial officials liberally; Saxony, Württemberg, Brunswick, and the Grand Duchy of Hesse pursued rigorously discriminatory policies. By far the most important appointment in this period occurred at the imperial level, when Levin Goldschmidt (1829–1897), professor of commercial law at Heidelberg, was made a member of the newly created Supreme Commercial Court in Leipzig. He was influential not only as a scholar but as a policy maker, as will be seen below. Of more symbolic significance, but none the less important for that, were two elevations to the new Imperial Supreme Court. The first was that of the baptized Eduard von Simson (1810–1899), who acted as its president from 1879 to 1881 and whose public offices had included the professorship of Roman law at the University of Königsberg, the presidency of the Frankfurt parliament, the presidency of the Prussian parliament and, from 1867 to 1874, the presidency first of the North German parliament and then of the Reichstag. The second was that of Jakob Friedrich Behrend (1833–1907), the only professing Jew to serve on the Imperial Supreme Court, to which he belonged from 1887 to 1890. In Austria advancement came very slowly. Professing Jews could become notaries from 1863 onward, but none were appointed to judgeships during the Liberal administration of 1871 to 1879, in which the baptized Jew Julius Glaser was minister of justice. It was left to the Conservative Count Schönborn to appoint the first Jewish magistrates and the first Jewish high court judge—Dr. Sare in Cracow—in 1893.

The controversy around judicial appointments revived in 1901, when one of the Jewish Progressive members of the Prussian parliament, Martin Peltasohn (1849–1912), complained that Jewish lawyers had to wait more than twice as long as Christians to be appointed as public notaries. Later that year the leader of the peasant wing of the Bavarian Center (Zentrum) Party, Georg Heim, introduced a motion in the Bavarian parliament proposing that Jewish judges should be appointed only in proportion to the Jewish share of the whole population. This was passed by the Lower House but rejected by the Upper House. In the Grand Duchy of Hesse Jewish organizations petitioned against the continuing breach of the constitution by the nonappointment of Jews, even though there had already been a debate on this in the state parliament in 1894 and a court case against the *Frankfurter Zeitung*, which had made the same accusation in 1899.

The arguments in each of these debates were the same. Jewish complainants and their allies took their stand on the law and the constitution. Ministers denied that there was discrimination but also insisted that no particular individual had a right to an appointment and that local conditions and prejudices had to be taken into account: in particular, they felt obliged to respect a demand, "the justification for which could not be denied," that officials be of the same denomination as the citizen.[3] Ministers had to be careful in what they said; backbenchers and journalists did not. There was no public consensus in Imperial Germany that religious equality was to be respected. The Conservative *Kreuz-Zeitung*, while acknowledging that Jews should be free to enter the professions of their choice, drew the line "at appointments to public office": "Here academic qualifications are by no means sufficient. . . . Here there has to be a guarantee of the appointee's moral qualification. . . . Jewish and Christian morality are different from each other."[4] Occasionally—and perhaps not so occasionally—such sentiments were shared by highly placed public officials. "In our view the average Jew is not endowed with a sense of justice," the president of the Provincial Supreme Court of Silesia reported, and recommended "a significant curtailment in the utilization of Jewish judges."[5] In the end, pressures by Jewish organizations had some effect: more Jewish judges were appointed and more were promoted to higher positions, especially in Prussia. But the debate on what state positions it was proper for Jews to occupy—and in what numbers— remained unresolved until the end of the empire, and, indeed, until the end of the Weimar Republic.

Apart from the judicial service the discrimination that Jews most keenly resented occurred in public education. Up to 1847 an academic career in Prussia had been open only at the price of baptism, though in some of the smaller states Jews had been able to become nonstipendiary lecturers. Developments in Austria paralleled those in the German states: baptism opened doors, especially before 1848, that would otherwise have remained shut. After 1848 professing Jews were appointed first to associate professorships and then to full professorships. The first such appointments in the most prestigious institutions of the capital cities did not occur until after 1870. They went to Ludwig Traube (1818–1876) in medicine at Berlin and Max Büdinger (1828–1902) in history at Vienna, both in 1872.

That most of these appointments, especially in Germany, were in the natural sciences was not surprising. The more value-laden humanistic subjects, whether classical philology, German literature, history, or law, which touched on ideological issues close to the German national identity, remained, with rare exceptions, closed to the unbaptized at the level of full professorships. That Jewish fortunes were, in this as in so many other areas, closely linked with the fluctuating influence of Liberalism was shown by the policies of Adalbert Falk, the Liberal Prussian minister of education from 1872 to 1879. It was he who appointed Levin Goldschmidt to the chair of commercial law at Berlin and—an even more exceptional step—the Kantian scholar Hermann Cohen (1842–1918) to the chair of philosophy at Marburg. This last aroused the considerable hostility of conservative members of the faculty. With the end of the Liberal epoch in Prussia and the Habsburg Empire in 1878–1879 policies also became more restrictive. However, the rapid expansion of scientific research in Germany during this period compensated Jewish scholars to some extent for the continuing "closed shop" in the humanities. In the academic year 1874–1875 9.4 percent of German university teachers were of Jewish origin, in 1889–1890, 12 percent. Even if we take into account that over one-third of these were baptized, and that they were disproportionately concentrated in the lower academic ranks, this was an impressive cultural breakthrough. While the employment situation in the judiciary improved, especially after the turn of the century, the trend was in the opposite direction in higher education. Whereas in 1889 twenty-two professing Jews (or 2.8 percent of the total) held full professorships at German universities, in 1917 the number was thirteen, or 1.2 percent. There is no single satisfactory explanation for this unfavorable development. The growing nationalist conformism of German academic life, which need not include antisemitism but was consistent with it, was no doubt a major factor. Accident can also have played a part since appointments were in the hands of the governments in the nine states that had universities. Those distinguished Jewish academics who reached the top of their profession did so in places that were highly dispersed, as, for example, the constitutional lawyer Heinrich Rosin (1855–1927), who became rector of Freiburg, and the Nobel Prize-winning chemists Oscar Wallach (1847–1931) and Richard Willstätter (1872–1942), who held their chairs at Göttingen and Munich respectively. One factor that should not be ignored is that Jews were losing the pioneering role in the German bourgeoisie—especially the intellectual bourgeoisie—that they had acquired in the 1830s and 1840s. As first Protestants and then Catholics became more urbanized and entered middle-class occupations in greater numbers, the relative number of Jews in the student body fell—from 9 percent among German citizens at Prussian universities in 1887 to 5.6 percent in 1911. Educated Jews were therefore at a demographic as well as political disadvantage, one that was to become even greater during the Weimar Republic.

Among these fluctuations in professional opportunities for unbaptized Jews, there is one striking factor common to academia and the judiciary, namely, the premium on conversion. It is evident that at any rate during the imperial period discrimination arose out of the Jew's failure to conform to the demands of the Christian state rather than racial prejudice. Once he was baptized the Jew's case was more often than not treated on merit. Between 1875 and 1895 18 percent of judicial appointments were made in the two highest ranks, but 28 percent of baptized Jews reached these ranks. In the universities of the empire there were 25 professing Jews (2.5 percent) among full professors in the academic year 1909–1910, 44 baptized Jews (4.5 percent), and 922 Christians by birth (93 percent). These figures if anything probably underestimate the number of academics and judges of Jewish descent, since the figures for the baptized relate only to converts and ignore those baptized at birth and the children of mixed marriages. The disproportionate number of converts in the higher levels of these two professions is a striking reflection of the greater extent to which Jews were now members of the urban professional middle class and holders of academic qualifications.

In other walks of public life merit was even less easily recognized. The state bureaucracy and diplomatic service were both closer to the exercise of political power and socially more exclusive and it was even harder for Jews to enter them. In Prussia their numbers were negligible. Even in the most liberal states the promotion of Jews to high bureaucratic positions was the exception, as exemplified by David Hugo Mayer (1854–1931), who became personal assistant to the Baden minister of the interior in 1879 and ended his career as *Geheimer Oberregierungsrat*, and Leo Lippmann, who reached the rank of *Regierungsrat* in Hamburg and rose to the rank of *Staatsrat*, the highest in the bureaucratic hierarchy, during the Weimar Republic. The army was even more firmly closed to professing Jews. There were no Jewish officers in Prussia during the imperial period and, after 1885, no Jew was admitted to a reserve commission. In Bavaria, the only state that had autonomy in these matters, there was a handful of exceptions. More than any other institution the army reflected the preindustrial social norms of Prussia. It was the privilege of each regiment to select its own officers, so that, despite repeated debates in the Reichstag and repeated assurances by ministers of war that the government opposed all discrimination, no professing Jew became an officer or reserve officer in the last thirty years of peace. While a handful of converts did succeed in becoming reserve officers, the obstacles they faced were heavy. As Count Westarp, a later leader of the Conservative Party, affirmed, "Our fundamental opposition to Jewish officers was based not so much on religious as on racial considerations. Officers of the Jewish 'race' should and could not command German soldiers."[6]

The position of Jews in the public service of the Habsburg Monarchy was in sharp contrast to that in Germany. It illustrated above all that popular antisemitism was only a fairly minor influence on government policy and on the Jewish population's assessment of its political environment. While German antisemitism flared in short epidemics, but otherwise seemed containable, many of Germany's middle-class Jews were constantly reminded by their governments' policy that equality of opportunity was not yet a full reality. In Austria, on the contrary, the much more menacing proportions of the antisemitic movement were, in the eyes of many Jewish citizens, compensated by the more benign policies of the government. The Jewish population of the Habsburg lands was much bigger than that of Germany, in relative as well as absolute terms, but this was not the only explanation for the difference. It was equally significant that the Gentile middle class, outside the state service, was smaller and Jews were therefore even more likely than in Germany to represent the liberal bourgeoisie, whether in business, the professions, or artistic and intellectual life. It is difficult to name a single area of intellectual endeavor in Vienna, Budapest, or Prague in which Jews did not play a prominent or even dominant part. Jewish academics were certainly more numerous than in Germany; though, as in Germany, conversion helped promotion and was often contemplated—not least by Sigmund Freud—as a defense against anticipated discrimination. A large-scale Jewish presence in academic life occurred only from the 1880s onward, with the result that the bearers of many of the most celebrated names, such as the economists Ludwig von Mises (1881–1973) and Otto Neurath (1882–1945), the philosophers of the Vienna Circle, and the members of the Vienna psychoanalytic school, reached the peak of their fame only after the First World War. But in medicine, at least, Jews reached academic recognition even before 1914. The anatomist Emil Zuckerkandl (1849–1910), the neurologist Moritz Benedikt (1835–1920), and the internist Enoch Kisch (1841–1918) were the most eminent of those who held full professorships, the first two at Vienna, the last at Prague. The natural sciences, in any case, offered other openings beside university chairs. Many German-Jewish scientists gained high positions in the Kaiser-Wilhelm-Institut (now Max-Planck-Gesellschaft), where appointments were bestowed by the emperor. Paul Ehrlich (1854–1915) was among the first ten senators of the institute appointed by the emperor. Medical scientists held high office in prestigious hospitals, especially in Vienna and Berlin, or in municipal employment. Perhaps the most interesting case was that of Friedrich Jakob Behrend (1803–1889), who was chief medical officer of the Berlin morals police.

The greatest contrast between Germany and the Habsburg Monarchy was to be found in the army. Almost one in five of the Austro-Hungarian reserve officer corps was a professing Jew and nearly one thousand Jewish career officers saw service in the period of the Dual Monarchy. They were most numerous where their professional training qualified them, namely, in the medical and technical service corps. A significant number, especially those in the higher ranks, converted, but this was not a necessity: the highest-ranking Austrian Jewish officer, Major-General (*Feldmarschal-leutnant*) Eduard Ritter von Schweitzer (1844–1920), retained his ancestral religion. In the more technical branches of the army the presence of Jews no doubt once more reflected their level of education, but their overall presence reflected the political role of the Austro-Hungarian army. Like all old established armies, it was socially exclusive, though by the turn of the century the traditional aristocratic element had declined sharply. But the army was also an instrument of political integration— indeed, by 1914, virtually the only genuinely supranational institution in the empire, apart from the Catholic Church. It could perform this role only if its membership was roughly representative of the ethnic and religious composition of the empire.

It was some time before Jews and Jewish organizations in Germany and Austria reacted to the continuing and in some respects intensified discrimination. Jewish spokesmen, lay and religious, had certainly not been reticent in the struggles for legal equality, even though it had in the end been achieved through the general triumph of Liberalism rather than the victory of a particular principle. But from 1869 onward they were prepared to be patient. In most spheres of activity opportunities seemed to be improving and discrimination declining. On balance things were getting better rather than worse. And in those occupations where they seemed again to be deteriorating, as in the 1880s, there were still reasons for hoping that this marked a temporary setback, not a permanent reversal. Moreover, the general trend of employment patterns was favorable to the preferences of most of the Jewish population. As cities expanded and German industry and commerce grew to overtake first France and then

Britain, the Jews of Germany could continue to emancipate themselves without the support of the state, or in spite of the absence of this support. Scientific research in private industry offered one alternative opening. The growing demand for medical services made a profession that had always drawn Jewish practitioners even more attractive. Other professions were liberalized. Legal practice, admission to which had been regulated by the state in Prussia until 1879, was thrown open to all qualified comers in that year, in response to a long-standing Liberal demand. In Austria, too, law caught up with medicine as a favorite Jewish calling once restrictions were lifted. In 1869 Vienna had 275 Jewish doctors but only 33 Jewish lawyers. Twenty years later the gap between the two professions had largely disappeared. In all, therefore, the grounds for optimism still outnumbered those that might arouse disillusionment.

2. Jews and German Nationality

Eighteen forty-eight affected the political consciousness of Jews not only by demonstrating the convergence of their interests with those of Liberalism and parliamentarism, but by emphasizing their identification with German national aspirations. There were a number of reasons for this, and they differed in their importance in the various German states, especially in the Habsburg lands. The first, common to the whole of Europe, was that the modernization of Jewish life meant the adoption of the surrounding secular culture, whether French, Dutch, Italian, or German. Whatever else "assimilation" or "acculturation" might mean, it certainly entailed the abandonment of a separate language and a separate educational system. The second is that the classical humanism of German literature and philosophy had a particular attraction for the new generation of educated Jews. "Our pride and our comfort are that great treasury of humanists . . . Lessing and Schiller, Goethe and Alexander von Humboldt,"[7] wrote Heinrich Jacques (1831–1894), the Viennese lawyer and publicist, in his 1859 memorandum on the status of Jews in Austria. More than half a century later the Zionist Franz Oppenheimer could write, "I would find, were I to explore my inner feelings, 99 percent Kant and Goethe and only 1 percent Old Testament, and even that essentially through the mediation of Spinoza and Luther's Bible."[8] The third reason is that German nationalism was—or at any rate seemed to be—an emancipatory movement. Its enemy was the old political order of absolutism, clericalism, and class distinction. A German nation-state would turn subjects into citizens, an ambition not exclusive to Jews, but one in which they had a particularly intense interest.

There was an additional psychological factor in equating liberated Jewishness with Germandom, one that caused much heart-searching and recrimination in later years. Not only did the adoption of a secular culture symbolize emergence from the ghetto, not only did it mark the final step from tolerated subject to citizen: there was also an apologetic note in the embracing of German nationality. It was a signal to one's fellow Jews that they were now normal human beings; it was, even more important, a signal to the Gentiles. The emphasis on the new Jew's Germanness was, above all, designed as a defense against the suspicion of incomplete assimilation, of doubtful allegiance, of dual loyalty. It was in this context that the *Allgemeine Zeitung des Judentums* (AZJ) coined the formula "German citizen of the Jewish faith,"[9] a formula that was to be turned into a political program in the 1890s by the Centralverein deutscher Staatsbürger jüdischen Glaubens.

Until the creation of the empire the political equation of Jews with Germans remained an aspiration only. Once national unification was achieved, and achieved with the active participation of numerous Jewish politicians, the claim to German identity was made all the more emphatically. At the memorial service for Eduard Lasker, one of the leaders of the National Liberal Party in the 1860s and 1870s, his political companion Ludwig Bamberger saw "a piece of German patriotic history" being carried to its grave. "Not he, but the majority of the German nation, spoke for more than ten years through his mouth."[10] It is easy to see why this dual program of national unity and constitutional development should appeal to the majority of Germany's Jews. But then as later there was no political unanimity among them. At least some Orthodox Jews remained indifferent to, or suspicious of, the temptations of emancipation. Religion was the defining characteristic of their Jewish identity and the reigning nineteenth-century doctrine of nationalism was secular, if not outright pagan. Yet these misgivings did not act as a bar to allegiance to German culture. For the ultra-Orthodox *Israelit*, as for secular Liberals, "We German Jews are Germans and nothing else. . . . Germans by birth and conviction."[11]

A second group that remained suspicious of the Liberal message was the fraternity of the court bankers and old established industrialists who saw their interests linked to monarchy rather than constitutionalism and had taken a strongly antirevolutionary line in 1848. Above all, the Rothschilds remained true to their monarchical loyalism. Meyer Carl von

24   Baron Meyer Carl von Rothschild, the first Jewish member
of the Upper House of the Prussian parliament

Rothschild (1820–1886), grandson of the founder of the dynasty, was
elected to the two North German parliaments of 1867 and then served in
the Upper House of the Prussian parliament. He was close to the Free
Conservatives, who supported Bismarck without being Prussian particu-
larists, and was the only professing Jew in these legislatures not to belong
to one of the Liberal parties.

Merchants and industrialists were more varied in their political allegiances. One category was represented by Leonor Reichenheim (1814–
1868), a leading Silesian textile industrialist and strong supporter of laissez-faire economics, founder-member of both the Deutscher National-

verein and the Progressive Party, and, after the Liberal split, of the National Liberal Party, which he represented in the North German Reichstag; or by Wilhelm Herz (1823–1914), founder of the Schultheiss brewery in Berlin, an elder of the Berlin Merchant Corporation (*Kaufmannschaft*) by the time he was forty-three, who also switched from the Progressives to the National Liberals. That was good enough to gain him the coveted title of *Kommerzienrat*. Other Jewish businessmen who remained with the Progressives were made to wait for this honor.[12] Further to the left, a small number of idealistic entrepreneurs were followers of Ferdinand Lassalle, the founder of the German labor movement. They included the industrialist Ludwig Loewe (1837–1886), who switched to the Progressives in the mid-sixties and served as a Berlin city councillor for twenty-three years and a member of the Prussian parliament and the Reichstag.

In contrast with the Jews of the Habsburg Monarchy, those of the German Empire lived in a linguistically homogenenous state and most of them were therefore not faced with competing pressures for national allegiance. There were, however, two frontier regions, the province of Posen and the newly annexed *Reichsland* of Alsace-Lorraine, where Jews did have to choose. In Posen they lived among Poles and Germans and, as elsewhere, it was the events of 1848 that signaled where loyalties would lie. Though the Polish National Committee of that year proclaimed civil equality for Jews, most Jews distrusted the Polish masses and had more faith in the prospect of a democratic Germany held out by the Frankfurt parliament. The seeds of later Jewish-Polish antagonism were thus sown. The antagonism was exacerbated after 1871, when Bismarck pursued an aggressively anti-Polish policy in conjunction with the Kulturkampf. That put an end to Polish Liberalism, identified the Polish cause with Catholicism, and deepened the gulf between German Liberals—Gentile or Jewish—and Poles. In their everyday dealings, especially outside the bigger cities, Jews had to interact with both Germans and Poles and were in many cases bilingual. But the culture to which they assimilated was German and the politics in which they participated was German. Most Jews found it easier to associate with middle-class Protestant Germans than with Catholic Poles who were either aristocrats or peasants. This social cleavage helped to reinforce the stereotype, already prevalent among the Jews of both Germany and Austria, of Slavs as backward and congenitally antisemitic.

The development of antisemitism among both nationalities during the

1880s and 1890s exacerbated Jewish-Polish relations more than Jewish-German ones. From the 1890s onward a number of chauvinistic German organizations, particularly the Agrarian League and the Ostmarken-verein, engaged in a policy of Germanizing the province by fostering col-onization and the acquisition of Polish property. In the politics of Imperial Germany such attitudes were readily associated with all other forms of xenophobia, including antisemitism, and antisemitic agitators began invading the province. But both the government and established local politicians appreciated that such a move would be fatal to the German-Jewish alliance. Antisemitism was avoided, at least in public utterances, and the electoral alliance of German parties ranged from the Left Liberals, the political home of most Posen Jews, to the Conservatives. As a result Jewish politicans were elected with Conservative votes and the future leader of the Conservatives, Count Kuno von Westarp, assured his Jewish electors in 1908 that he would not support "any legal or other restriction . . . of the Jews' constitutional rights."[13]

While the German right practiced a pragmatic abstention from anti-semitism, the tone of Polish nationalism became increasingly hostile. This was due partly to the influence of Roman Dmowski's National Demo-cratic Party but also to the growth of a Polish middle class that found itself in direct competiton with hitherto German- and Jewish-dominated com-merce. In the 1890s Polish nationalists launched a boycott campaign under the slogan "to each his own" (swój do swego po swoje). Nor did the recycling by the Polish press of ritual murder tales at the time of the Beilis trial in Kiev in 1913 do anything to reconcile the two communities. Nothing happened in these years to break the vicious circle of Jewish identification with the German cause and of Polish antisemitism as a function of both anti-Germanism and Catholicism. In view of these dual pressures it is not surprising that here, as in Bohemia, Zionism made more headway than in the rest of Germany in the years before 1914. It was encouraged by Max Kollenscher, a leading German Zionist based in the city of Posen, who appealed to the Jews' sense of being "a third nation" in the borderland.

At the other end of the Kaiserreich, in Alsace-Lorraine, the situation was different. Alsace, the home of nearly half the Jewish population of France, was one of the few provinces where popular antisemitism sur-vived, as illustrated by the riots of 1848. Nevertheless, France was the motherland of emancipation; the Jews of Alsace had, over two genera-tions, learned to become French patriots and had no great faith in the recent and untried German legislation on equality. In the end the German law of 1869 was not extended to the annexed territories, so that the French emancipation legislation of 1791 continued to apply. For many Alsatian Jews German annexation was a deep shock, as indicated by the rate of emigration to France. Of the forty-seven thousand Jews who lived in the areas annexed by Germany, some six thousand had left by October 1, 1872, the deadline for legal "option" laid down by the Treaty of Frankfurt. Between 1871 and 1900 an estimated fifteen thousand Jews emigrated from the *Reichsland* to France. Those who "opted" in 1871–1872 were predominantly middle-class and urbanized, in contrast with the poorer rural Jews who dominated earlier waves of emigration. The optants included the grand rabbis of Metz and Colmar and, among industrialists, the parents of André Maurois and Alfred Dreyfus. For the most part they were drawn from highly assimilated strata, which suggests a preponderance of political over other motives.

Despite determined efforts to appease the sizeable Jewish population, the government's policy of Germanization was distinctly less successful than in Posen. In contrast with other parts of the Kaiserreich, Jewish leaders were invited to official functions and government officials regularly attended synagogue services. The authorities acted energetically against printed and spoken antisemitism, banning publications by August Rohling and Theodor Fritsch. The German administration was also more liberal in its appointments policy. Jews were appointed to judgeships from the beginning of the occupation, and in 1907 a Jew became a High Court judge, well before any such promotion had occurred in Prussia. When limited self-government was granted, the grand rabbi of Strasbourg, Adolph Uhry, was appointed to the Upper House of the regional assembly, though only in response to considerable pressure from the Jewish community.

Opposition to the German occupation did not begin to soften in the two provinces until the 1890s, as a new generation became resigned to the status quo and strove to make the best of it. This trend applied to the Jews as well, though there is no evidence that it applied more strongly to them, despite the strains that the Dreyfus Affair put on their French loyalties. In any case, the composition of the population slowly changed through Jewish immigration from the rest of Germany. In 1913 a branch of the Centralverein was founded, suggesting an increased readiness to act in politics on German terms. Nevertheless the loyalty of Alsatian Jews to the Kaiserreich remained suspect. Antisemites were inclined to see them as part of a Franco-Jewish plot against Germany.

3. Jews and Nationality in the Habsburg Monarchy

While the attractions of German nationality were obvious for most Jews who lived within the boundaries of the new German Empire, the age of nationalism presented the much more numerous Jewish population of the Habsburg lands with a dilemma. The Jewish masses, especially in Galicia and Eastern Hungary, spoke Yiddish; the more educated urban population, German. Given the close relationship between the two languages, it was not too difficult for Jews to switch from one to the other as they rose in the social scale. That caused no problems in purely German-speaking areas such as Vienna. But until the late 1860s few of the Habsburg Monarchy's Jews lived there. The majority found themselves in areas of linguistic conflict and forced to choose between rival pressures. Their story is therefore of two divergent developments—that of Jews becoming more strongly German and that of Jews ceasing to be German.

These pressures were greatest in the lands of the Bohemian crown, Bohemia and Moravia. There was no viable answer to the question, posed by *Der Orient*, "What are the Jews to do between Scylla and Charybdis?"[14] For much of the nineteenth century relations between Jews and the Czech-speaking population were tense on both the political and the socioeconomic level. Though most Jews of the two lands probably needed to be bilingual, German was their primary language. In part this was due to the identification with German culture that characterized the educated Jews of Central Europe generally. But it also reflected the status of German as the language of commerce and government in the Habsburg Monarchy. Moreover, since the reforms of Joseph II in the 1780s Jews had been obliged to attend German-language schools and to keep their business records in German. For two crucial generations, therefore, modernization meant Germanization. This identification with the existing distribution of ethnic power in the monarchy was one reason for Czech-Jewish tensions. The other was the socioeconomic distance between the two population groups. The Jews of the Czech lands had the same occupational profile as their coreligionists elsewhere in Central Europe. They were urban and self-employed in either commerce or the professions. They also provided a large proportion of the factory owners in the incipient industrialization of the region. The Czech-speaking population, on the other hand, was largely low status until well into the century. The linguistic polarity therefore overlay the social. Periodic anti-Jewish riots reinforced the image that many Jews had of the Slavs as "still wading in a medieval swamp."[15]

As elsewhere in Central Europe, it was the events of 1848 that spelled out the choices in the political allegiance of Jews. They could support national self-determination, that is, participate in the Frankfurt parliament on behalf of a Greater Germany or a reformed Habsburg Monarchy outside a unified Germany, as favored by the Czechs—or, indeed, an unreformed Habsburg Monarchy, which the Czech leaders were in the end prepared to accept after the defeat of the revolutions. This identification of the Slavs with "reaction"—despite the support for Jewish rights by the leader of the Czech Party, Ladislav Rieger—pushed the Jews further in the direction of an alliance with the Germans, though this alliance was never complete and certainly not permanent. One symptom of the evolving agenda was the changing ethnic character of Prague, which gave the city its first Czech mayor in 1860. It was this turning of the tide that led the German-speaking middle class to organize in order to defend its social and political interests. After 1848, and the more so after 1860, they thought of themselves less as Bohemians who spoke German and more as Germans who lived in Bohemia. German associational life was crowned by the creation in 1862 of an overarching body to defend the interests of the German minority, named the German Casino, the subscription to which was one hundred florins, thus underlining its exclusive character. The exclusion was not directed against Jewish businessmen and professionals within the German-speaking bourgeoisie. Friedrich Jodl, who moved from Munich to take up a chair of philosophy at the (German-language) Charles University in 1885 summarized the golden rule of Prague German Liberal politics: "Only two things are obligatory: no flirting with the Slavs and no hostility toward the Jews."[16]

The Casino certainly observed this obligation. In 1879 38 percent of the members were Jews, by 1907 it was 48 percent. Jews became prominent officeholders. Dr. Otto Forchheimer, an agricultural merchant, was its president from 1894 to 1914 and simultaneously president of the German Club, the Casino's political offshoot. By 1913 all the club's principal officers were also Jews. The textile manufacturer Siegmund Mauthner presided over the German Merchants' Club and was succeeded in this position by the insurance broker Philip Falkowicz. Though these men were fully acculturated, they did not cut their ties with Judaism. They held high office in Jewish organizations, whether communal or philanthropic, Dr. Ludwig Bendiener, vice president of the German Club, being also vice president of the Community Council.

These Jewish and Gentile notables, integrated in their associational life, became less and less representative of Bohemian politics as the century wore on. Industrialization and the attendant migration changed the economic and political balance and the urban Jews of Bohemia found themselves in an increasingly Slav environment. Moreover, outside Prague they lacked the resources that the German Liberal bourgeoisie had been able to summon in the capital. Increasingly they were obliged to reconsider their instinctive alliance with the German element and to abandon the sort of idealistic allegiance to a binational Bohemia described by the philologist Fritz Mauthner (1849–1923), that of being "a platonic German, without political needs . . . a German-speaking European."[17] While Mauthner decided to throw in his lot with the Germans, others, beginning in the 1870s, looked increasingly to a Czech identification. Led by Professor Alois Zucker, who taught law at the Charles University, a number of organizations arose to encourage Jews to learn and speak Czech, attend Czech schools, and identify with Czech political parties. From 1883 onward Jews running on Czech tickets gained election to the Bohemian diet and the Reichsrat. Jewish votes enabled Czechs to gain control of chambers of commerce, hitherto the strongholds of the German-speaking bourgeoisie. A similar tale is told by the decennial census figures, which asked all citizens to specify their language of daily use. By 1900 only a minority of Jews (43.7 percent) declared themselves to be German speakers; in the city of Prague the percentage was slightly higher (45.4 percent), having been 73.8 percent ten years earlier. In Moravia and Silesia German still held sway at 77.4 percent and 80.7 percent respectively. No doubt there was an element of opportunism in these census declarations; but there was not much future in being inopportunistic. A different index of Jewish cultural loyalties is the choice of educational institutions. Of the Jewish pupils who attended higher secondary schools in Bohemia (*Gymnasien* and *Realschulen*), 81 percent attended German-language schools in 1882; by 1912 the share still stood at 69 percent. In Prague the shares were higher still: 83 percent at higher secondary schools in 1910 and 89 percent at elementary schools. Universities told the same story. In 1882 the Charles University of Prague and the Prague Technical University were divided into German and Czech branches. In 1890 there were 506 Jewish students at the German university and 44 at the Czech; in 1906 367 and 92, a decline from 91 percent to 84 percent in preferences for German. At the Technical University the decline was from 94 percent to 89 percent.[18] Here, too, it is best not to seek simple explanations. There may well have been a widespread belief that academic standards were higher in the older established German-language schools and universities or, at any rate, that their qualifications enjoyed greater prestige. The Central European Jewish belief that the only culture worth having was German was hard to shift.

In the other lands of the Bohemian crown, Moravia and Silesia, the Czech cause made rather slower headway among Jews. In part this had to do with the lower temperature of the linguistic conflict, since Bohemia was the greater political prize. But the most important factor was the different legal status of the Jewish municipalities. In contrast with Bohemia, where only the Jews of Prague had this privilege, all the Jewish communities of Moravia had been self-governing, with German as the language of administration. To maintain German control of the Moravian diet the government established these communities as separate municipal units, attached to the urban voting curia. The result was that until the electoral reform of 1905 the Germans commanded a majority in the diet, although their share of the population (29 percent) was lower than in Bohemia. In their choice of educational institutions Jewish students in Moravia were even more inclined toward German than their coreligionists in Bohemia. At the German Technical University of Brünn (Brno) there were 166 Jewish students in 1905 (25.3 percent of the total), at the Czech branch there was 1.

The great majority of the Jews of the Habsburg Monarchy lived neither in Vienna nor in the Bohemian crownlands. Out of a total population of 1,643,708 in 1880, 638,314 (or 38.8 percent) lived in Hungary. Of those in the Austrian half of the monarchy, 686,696 (or 68.2 percent) lived in Galicia. Until the middle of the century the educated among them looked to German as the language of progress and enlightenment. But with the emergence of native nationalist movements in 1848 Jews fell under the suspicion, as in Bohemia, of being agents of German domination. Relations with the Poles of Galicia and the Magyars of Hungary were, however, different from the dilemma between Czech and German that the Jews of Bohemia faced. In both Galicia and Hungary there was a clearly dominant nationality that could both exert pressure and offer favors in return for collaboration. From the Compromise of 1867 onward, when Hungary had virtual self-government in domestic affairs, a fruitful partnership began between the Magyar rulers and the Jewish middle class, who soon acquired a dominant role in business and the professions, though not in government service. The Magyarization of Hungarian Jewry was rapid, if never complete. In 1880 the proportion of declared

Magyar to German speakers was 57.5 percent : 35.9 percent, in 1910 75.7 percent : 21.8 percent. In Budapest the proportions were 75.0 percent : 22.9 percent in 1880 and 90.3 percent : 7.2 percent in 1906.[19]

In Galicia, where, in contrast with Hungary, Jews had been settled for centuries, the link with Polish culture was in any case closer and the Polonization of Galician Jewry seemingly more effective than even Magyarization in Hungary. In 1900 the proportions of declared Polish and German were 76.6 percent : 17.1 percent, in 1910 92.7 percent : 2.9 percent. As in Bohemia, the Hungarian and Galician figures reflected political pressure as much as actual usage and failed to reflect the polyglot character of the Jewish population: in 1906 71 percent of Budapest Jews were bilingual and 19 percent spoke three or more languages. More than in Bohemia the figures disguised the fact that for the great majority of Galician Jews and a substantial proportion of Hungarian Jews the language of daily use continued to be Yiddish. Yiddish was not, however, a language recognized by article 19 of the Fundamental Law of December 21, 1867, and therefore could not feature in census returns. Some Jews in Cracow were fined when they insisted on declaring Yiddish to be their language of daily use to the 1910 census takers.

The local variations and the conflicts of interest that lay behind the official desire for legal uniformity were illustrated by the case of the city of Brody against the Ministry of Education before the Imperial Supreme Court in 1880. Brody in Eastern Galicia had the highest proportion of Jews of any town in the Habsburg Monarchy—76.3 percent. When the Galician provincial administration established two new elementary schools, it stipulated that instruction should be in Polish only. The municipality protested against this decision, demanding instruction in German instead, pointing out that the business of the town council and the Chamber of Commerce and the lessons of the high school were all in German. The court decided in their favor. Acknowledging that Jews were not recognized as a nationality (*Volksstamm*) under article 19 of the Austrian constitution and therefore had no claim to a language of their own—that, indeed, they were not a nationality because there was no language spoken by all of them—the German speakers among them had the right to adhere to the German nationality. In many ways this judgment symbolized the end of an era. Under the de facto autonomy that Galicia gained in 1868 German was displaced by Polish as the language of administration, which led to the rapid Polonization of Galician Jewry after 1880. The court's verdict was a last tribute to the midcentury equation of legal equality with assimilation, on the understanding that in the context of the Habsburg Monarchy assimilation meant Germanization.

There was one other region with a sizeable Jewish population, viz. the easternmost crownland, Bukovina. Here Jews were able both to pursue their preference for German-language status and to secure partial recognition as a separate nationality. The key to this development was the authorities' increasingly flexible interpretation of article 19 of the constitution. It was the Jews' lack of Volksstamm status that led to the competition for their linguistic allegiance in Galicia, the Czech lands, and Hungary. In Bukovina Jews were exempt from this competition. In the 1910 census 90 percent of Jews declared German to be their language of daily use. The urban bourgeoisie, especially in the capital Czernowitz, where they constituted a third of the population, were a mainstay of German culture. The German-language university, founded in 1875, and the state Gymnasien were heavily patronized by Jewish students. However, the everyday language of the majority of the Jews was, as in Galicia, Yiddish. This, and the growth of nationalist-autonomist sentiment, led to energetic litigation on behalf of separate national status for Jews. It was in Czernowitz that Nathan Birnbaum organized his international conference on Yiddish, and here that the Reichsrat deputy for Czernowitz, Dr. Benno Straucher, originally elected as a German Liberal, founded the Jewish National Party (Jüdische Nationalpartei). The pressure for official recognition of the Jewish nationality was intensified by the apparent success of the Moravian compromise of 1905 in which different language groups acquired separate electoral curiae. A proposal by the diet of Bukovina that the reorganization of electoral curiae on the Moravian model should allow for a separate Jewish one was vetoed by the government in Vienna. Jews were instead allocated to the German curia, but with important provisos that recognized their interests. Constituency boundaries were so drawn that Jewish majorities were created and the two representatives of the chambers of commerce were in any case likely to be Jewish. The German-Jewish deputies thus elected formed themselves into a separate grouping from that of the Gentile Germans. The verdicts of the *Reichsgericht* notwithstanding, some municipalities continued to record their proceedings in Yiddish as well as in recognized languages, and from 1912 students at Czernowitz University could register their nationality as "Jewish."

These unofficial concessions did not solve the general question of Jewish national identity or the particular one of the Jewish-German special relationship. Straucher's and Birnbaum's efforts met with strong opposition from Jews in Vienna. They saw in the possibility of a separate Jewish nationality a form of resegregation and a breach of article 14 of the Constitution, which made civil rights independent of religion. Antisemites, they feared, would use it as a pretext to demand legalized discrimination. The Jews of Bukovina were an exceptional community. They constituted a distant exclave of Central Europe in present-day Ukraine. They, or at least their educated middle class, continued to speak German when those to the north and west of them had converted to Polish or Magyar. But the growth of autonomist sentiment among them showed that they no longer adhered to the assimilationist consensus that still prevailed in Vienna and the Czech lands.

The story of Austria-Hungary's Jews outside the strictly German-speaking areas is therefore one of Jews ceasing to be Germans. But this embracing of the surrounding culture was never complete. Writers such as Franz Kafka and Joseph Roth continued to find German the more attractive language, as did many academics and publicists—Hungarians as different as Theodor Herzl and the literary critic György Lukács will serve as examples. But allegiance to German culture did not necessarily entail identification with German nationalist politics, as will be seen below.

4. Jewish Politicians in the Liberal Era

Jews were more numerous and more prominent in the politics of the two empires during the Liberal decades than ever before. Only with the rise of Social Democracy in the years before the First World War did the numbers again approach those of the 1860s and 1870s. Numbers, however, are not the same as influence. The legislatures of Germany and Austria-Hungary were forums for public debate, and their consent was needed for legislative proposals and budgets. But neither empire had responsible parliamentary government. Ministers were not drawn from parliament or appointed by it and they were not subject to parliamentary confidence or censure. Parliament belonged to the sphere of society, the executive to the sphere of the state, and it was much more difficult for Jews to enter the latter, even in the era of Liberalism. Indeed only one professing Jew reached cabinet rank between 1861 and 1917—Moritz Elstätter (1827–1905), minister of finance in Baden from 1868 to 1895 and, in this capacity, a delegate to the Federal House of the German Imperial Parliament (Bundesrat) from 1871. Several other men of Jewish descent held ministerial office during this period. Karl Rudolf Friedenthal (1827–1890) and Heinrich von Friedberg (1813–1895), both of them baptized Protestants, were heads of government departments in Prussia under Bismarck, having previously had distinguished careers in local government and the judicial service respectively. Friedenthal, who came from the financial-industrial patriciate of Breslau, entered politics in the 1860s. He was second vice president of the Prussian parliament in 1873–74 and Prussian minister of agriculture from 1874 to 1879; he declined offers to take over the Ministries of the Interior and Commerce. Friedberg's expertise lay in legal matters. He was one of the main drafters of the penal code of the North German Confederation, based on the Prussian code of 1855, became undersecretary of state (i.e., deputy head) of the newly created Reich Office of Justice in 1874 and its head in 1876. From 1879 to 1889 he was Prussian minister of justice. In both these offices he played a major role in drafting the Imperial Civil Code, a process that lasted two decades and is discussed below.

In Austria two converts held high ministerial office in the Liberal government of Prince Auersperg from 1871 to 1879: Josef Unger (1828–1913), who had been a student revolutionary in 1848, as minister without portfolio and Julius (Joshua) Glaser (1831–1884) as minister of justice. Even more than their German equivalents, Glaser and Unger, who developed a close personal friendship, reshaped their country's legal structure. Glaser, who had been appointed to a chair at the University of Vienna in 1860 and was a prolific author on legal procedures, was responsible for the complete reform of criminal procedure, introduced in 1874. After the fall of the Auersperg government he spent the remaining five years of his life as attorney general of the Supreme Criminal Court. Unger, who also taught at the University of Vienna, did for civil law what Glaser did for the criminal code. They were jointly responsible for the compilation of reports of the Supreme Court, a series that continued beyond their deaths. Unger's most fruitful period of activity spanned his presidency of the Reichsgericht from 1880 until his death in 1913 at the age of eighty-three. Between them these five ministers represented the political mainstream of their day. They were administrative reformers, concerned to modernize the departments of which they had been put in charge. Their aim was to consolidate the new political structures, which they welcomed, not to destabilize them with pressures for radical change. In party affiliation Elstätter was a National Liberal; Friedenthal was one of the founders of the Free Conservative Party, whose representatives in the Reichstag called themselves the Reichspartei, strong supporters of the Bismarckian course, though Friedenthal himself was keener on continued links with National Liberalism than many other members of his party; Friedberg belonged to no party, but his outlook was that of the National Liberals. So, too, Unger and Glaser, though without formal party affiliation, were close to the German Liberalism of the Verfassungspartei.

In their ideological predilections these ministers were fairly typical of the politically conscious Jewish population. Once the battle of Königgrätz had put an end to dreams of a democratic Greater Germany, Liberals among the victors and vanquished had two choices. Among the victors one could either accept a German nation-state under Prussian leadership and hope to make it as liberal as possible or reject the military and authoritarian domination of Prussia as inherently illiberal and a bar to further constitutional development. There were powerful arguments on grounds of foreign policy and military security to accept the first, a choice made easier by the relatively liberal institutions that characterized the North German Confederation and the empire—freedom of movement, liberalization of commerce and the professions, universal male suffrage (which by no means all Liberals welcomed), and, of course, Jewish emancipation. As a result the majority of voters and parliamentarians followed the compromise solution advocated by the National Liberals who outstripped the old-style Progressives in all six Reichstag elections between 1867 and 1878.

In this respect Jews did not differ from their fellow Germans. Of the seventeen professing Jews elected to the Reichstag in this period one was a Free Conservative (Meyer Carl von Rothschild), seven were National Liberals, six were Progressives (plus the radical Leopold Sonnemann), and two were Social Democrats. The National Liberals included such luminaries as Eduard Lasker (1829–1884), Ludwig Bamberger (1823–1899), Levin Goldschmidt, and Heinrich Bernhard Oppenheim (1819–1880). The baptized deputies of Jewish origin had a more conservative profile. They numbered one Conservative, one Free Conservative (Friedenthal), three National Liberals, and two Progressives. Again it was the National Liberals that provided the best-known names—among them Eduard von Simson, later president of the Imperial Supreme Court, and Friedrich Dernburg, editor in chief of the *National-Zeitung*. The thirty-nine Jewish members of the various Landtage in the same period had a similar party affiliation. Just as Conservative Jews were becoming the exception in this Liberal era, so were Socialist Jews. The first generation of revolutionaries with Jewish origins—Karl Marx, Stephan Born, Moses Hess, Ferdinand Lassalle—either lived abroad or were dead. The handful of Jewish Socialist deputies in the Reichstag were not men of the front rank, except for the radical Johann Jacoby (1805–1877), who joined the Social Democratic Party late in life and refused to take his seat when elected in 1874 to a parliament that he despised. The younger recruits, like Eduard Bernstein and Paul Singer, would not make their mark till later.

As it turned out, the Jewish-National Liberal axis was short-lived, for it depended in turn on an axis between the National Liberals and Bismarck. As long as Bismarck was prepared to extend—or, at least, not reverse—the scope of the liberal nation-state, with its individual liberties and careers open to talents, the majority of Jews were content to identify with it. They were conscious of its imperfections, above all the remaining barriers to entry into state service, but as long as these seemed to be diminishing their loyalty was not under excessive strain. Once the prospects of further progress receded, a reappraisal of the alliance became necessary. That is what happened at the end of the 1870s. Increasingly resistant to National Liberal pressures for further reforms, Bismarck turned to the Conservative parties and the Catholic Center for a parliamentary majority, abandoning the free-trade policies he had upheld for a decade or more and reintroducing tariffs on grain and iron. The move split the National Liberals, with the main body agreeing to remain loyal to Bismarck. But its left wing, which contained most of its Jewish members and above all its leading parliamentarians, Lasker and Bamberger, seceded in 1880 and joined with the Progressives in 1884 to form a new Left Liberal force, the Deutsch-Freisinnige Partei.

The significance of Bismarck's policy turn was not lost on its contemporaries. It was a defeat for those who helped to unify Germany and marked the reemergence of those conservative forces that had viewed the events of the previous fifteen years with distaste or skepticism. The AZJ was blunt in its verdict: "The thrust of these parties is not directed merely to gaining temporary power but to enabling the principles of the Middle Ages . . . to prevail once more."[20] Antisemitism played a subordinate role in these events, but it was undoubtedly there. Since Bismarck's change of partners coincided with the revival of popular and academic antisemitism (see chapter 7) and since these were handy weapons against Liberalism and, above all, free trade, the split in the National Liberal Party understandably exacerbated the tensions between the more nationalist and the more liberal factions. No Jewish candidate was elected on the National

25 Ludwig Bamberger, a leader of the National
Liberal Party

Liberal ticket in the 1879 elections to the Prussian parliament—Lasker
himself was defeated—and no Jew was nominated by the National
Liberals for the Reichstag elections of 1881. Jewish candidates for the
Liberal Union (Liberale Vereinigung), as the "Secession" now called itself,
or the Progressives who opposed National Liberals, had to suffer antisemitic innuendoes, though these did not prevent their success.

26   A caricature of the Jewish politician Eduard Lasker together with
Bismarck that appeared in the humor sheet *Kladderadatsch*

The political sea change of 1878–1879, often called "the second foundation of the empire," marked the end of Liberalism as a dominant force
in national politics. It also changed the political loyalty of the Jewish population for the long term. Until 1879 the Liberalism of most German Jews
was equated with German unification and an economy based on free
enterprise, as personified by Lasker and Bamberger. After 1879 it meant
the Liberalism of civil rights, antimilitarism, and constitutional reform, as
represented by the shifting kaleidoscope of the Liberal left—the "secessionist" Liberal Union, the old established Progressives, the post-1884
Progressives (*Freisinn*), and the small democratic Deutsche Volkspartei of
Frankfurt and the southwest.

The switch was decisive but not absolute. There had been Left Liberal
Jews before 1879, especially in Prussia, where memories of the constitu-

tional conflict of the 1860s were strong, and there were still Jewish supporters of National Liberalism in the 1880s. These included not only, as
one might have expected, the heads of leading private banks and merchant
houses, such as Carl Fürstenberg (1850–1933, Berliner Handelsgesellschaft), Ludwig Max Goldberger (1848–1913, Internationale Bank, later
merged with Berliner Handelsgesellschaft), Max Steinthal (1850–1940,
Deutsche Bank), and Carl Ladenburg (1827–1909), but also eminent academics and intellectuals, such as Levin Goldschmidt (1829–1897) and
Moritz Lazarus (1824–1903), and officials of representative Jewish organizations, like Jacob Nachod (1814–1882), the president of the German-
Jewish communities alliance, the Deutsch-Israelitischer Gemeindebund.
Party lines and party organization in newly unified Germany were still
fluid; in southwest Germany the National Liberal Party did not turn as far
to the right as further north, and Jews continued to serve as party officials
and members of regional parliaments in Hesse-Darmstadt (Otto
Wolfskehl) and Baden (Robert Goldschmidt, Emil Mayer, and Carl
Ladenburg, who was baptized) right up to the First World War. Indeed a
small number of businessmen were still either members or supporters of
the increasingly antisemitic Conservative Party, among them the clothing
manufacturer and supplier to the Imperial Court, Falk Valentin Grünfeld.
They counterbalanced the increasing number of Left Liberals among
manufacturers, such as the brothers Isidor and Ludwig Loewe. It was age
as much as status that determined political outlook. Those who had been
frightened by the revolutions of 1848 were inclined to put their trust in
the state rather than the people, though there were officials like Chief of
Police Bernuth of Berlin who thought that "sound political conviction"
was "notoriously rare among Jews."[21] Those who belonged to the unification generation found it much more difficult to adopt a critical attitude
toward the state they had helped to create or to separate their nationalist
enthusiasm of the 1860s from the cruder chauvinism of the 1880s.

A test for this group came in 1887, when Bismarck dissolved the
Reichstag on the issue of the military "septennate," that is, whether the
army budget should be fixed for three or seven years. National Liberals
and Conservatives, including antisemites, were ranged against Progressives and the Catholic Center. For Levin Goldschmidt the Progressives'
alliance with "ultramontanes, Guelphs, and Poles" was "treason to the
German Reich." As for the alleged antisemitism of some of the candidates
running on the government's ticket, this paled into insignificance "when
the battle is about quite different matters, namely, the most important

interests of state and Reich."[22] For Lazarus the election was an opportunity "to refute by a deed the assertion . . . that every Jew must, as a Jew, belong to the opposition."[23] Indeed, more than one rabbi urged his flock to cast a patriotic vote.

German Liberalism undoubtedly became less liberal in the 1880s. After the achievement of national unification the emancipatory message of nationalism was muted. With rapid economic transformation a market economy gave way to the rivalries of organized interests. Remarkably quickly the Liberal elites of Germany were able to assume many of the values of their previous Conservative opponents, including a rejection of equal rights for Jews. But German Liberalism was imperfect even in its heyday. Equality before the law applies not only to individuals but to groups, and two groups were subjected to deliberate discrimination during the 1870s, Catholics and Socialists. It was in this context that the so-called Kulturkampf took place, first in Prussia and then in the whole empire, which gave the state authority over the training of priests and over church schools, forbade political sermons, instituted civil marriage, and banned the Jesuit order from Germany.

The purely secularising measures won universal assent from the Liberal parties. Jewish politicians and publicists might well be expected to welcome this humbling of their ancient persecutor, the Catholic Church. Many vied with their Gentile fellow citizens in seeing the anticlerical campaign as the culmination of national unification. Bamberger saw in the Kulturkampf "the symbol of the empire"[24] and Levin Goldschmidt saw in the ultramontanes "the only dangerous enemies of our future."[25] Nor were these merely individual points of view. The AZJ acknowledged, "We Jews have a great interest in the so-called Kulturkampf in the German Reich, greater than we would wish. . . . The Syllabus [of Errors] does not merely condemn freedom of religion and conscience but the civic equality of the adherents of non-Catholic religions."[26] In language more usually associated with its opponents it proclaimed, "The Jesuit order and the ultramontane World League exist and make themselves felt everywhere."[27] To secularize the state was one thing, to single out one religious order, however symbolic it might be of popish intrigue, and to deprive it of the protection of the law, was another. The anti-Jesuit law passed the Reichstag, urged on by public enthusiasm, but Lasker and Bamberger, alone among National Liberals, opposed it and Friedenthal was the only member of the Reichspartei to oppose it. Discriminatory legislation was a red flag to Jews with long memories. As the Progressive Ludwig Loewe acknowledged in the 1881 Reichstag election campaign, the Kulturkampf had "contributed heavily to bringing religious hatred to the fore."[28]

If Jewish deputies turned away instinctively from discrimination against Jesuits, some of them yielded to the temptation of Bismarck's anti-Socialism. That those on the right of the National Liberal Party should have done so is not surprising. Levin Goldschmidt had no doubt that "a real and strong exceptional law" was needed.[29] Both the Orthodox and the Liberal Jewish press agreed. For the *Jüdische Presse* Social Democracy was "guilty of treason" and "a danger to the state."[30] The AZJ noted, "Socialism has declared open war on the state and the state must therefore turn its weapons against it. . . . Even though it is to be fought with legal regulations and their vigorous implementation—but these will not suffice."[31] The last point underlined the dilemma that faced Lasker and Bamberger. Bamberger's hatred of Socialism—somewhat in contrast with his revolutionary attitudes in 1848—was consistent with his general outlook in the 1870s. In proletarian collectivism he saw as great a threat to individual liberty as in Bismarck's authoritarianism and agrarian reaction. But he, like Lasker, as a Liberal also held that ideas were not to be suppressed with legislation. In the end he surrendered to self-deception and voted for the anti-Socialist law, believing he was supporting a less draconian measure than it turned out to be and no doubt conscious of the pressure on his party after an election campaign fought almost solely on this issue. Lasker, too, submitted after he had succeeded in softening the measure in committee. In retrospect Lasker confessed that it was the one action in his political life that he genuinely regretted and he voted against the law's renewal when this was due in 1880. Bamberger did not come to that view until 1884. Unlike the National Liberals all Progressives had voted against it in the first place, as had the Center Party. What Jewish politicians and publicists had in common in this period was that, with few exceptions, they were placed somewhere within the Liberal spectrum and reflected the gradations of that spectrum. On only three questions were they unanimous. They stood for a secular educational system. They opposed, or at least abstained on, the anti-Jesuit bill. And no Jewish member of the Reichstag—not even the *bien-pensant* Rothschild—voted in favor of the death penalty.

There was one further point on which they showed if not a consensus then at least a conspicuous deviation from the conventional wisdom of their day, namely, their dislike of war. That was all the more true if one includes in their ranks the leading bankers of the day who, even if they held no formal political office, certainly had views on policy and the opportunity to transmit these. Reporting to Lord Granville, the British foreign secretary, in 1881, the British ambassador in Berlin wrote of Gerson Bleichröder, Bismarck's financial confidant, that "as a Banker, [he] is a man of peace."[32] Indeed Bleichröder had earned the distrust of Prussia's militarists in 1871 when negotiating the indemnity that France was to pay after her defeat by Prussia, which was ultimately settled at 5 billion gold francs. Bleichröder thought this too high: if Germany asked for more than 3.75 billion "the blessings of peace will not be ours." His fellow banker Abraham Oppenheim thought 3 billion the maximum "if we want to have the gratitude of the neutral powers."[33] At the height of the Franco-Prussian war Moritz Ritter von Goldschmidt wrote Bleichröder despairingly from Vienna to ask "when the blessed shalom will come." Ten years later Goldschmidt deplored the billions "taken away from industry and from useful production" so that "the people's welfare is sacrificed for militarism."[34]

It is a moot point whether this financier's pacifism arose from self-interest or altruism. Those involved would no doubt answer that the distinction is false; that a vocation with beneficial results for humanity is a worthy vocation and that those who choose it are worthy individuals. At any rate it was a constant complaint of antisemites that Jewish love of money undermined patriotism and the primacy of martial virtues. It is, however, significant that Jewish Liberal politicians adopted attitudes very similar to those of the bankers on foreign policy questions. Bamberger was an ardent advocate of free trade, which he believed would "lead to progress, peace, and freedom"; he opposed colonial expansion and imperialism, arguing that a nation's prosperity was best achieved "through peaceful agreements with its neighbors"; he endorsed the American ideal of "trade and not dominion"[35]—an attitude rebuked by the *Preussische Jahrbücher* as that "of the haggling Jew."[36] Lasker became president of the German section of the London-based International Arbitration and Peace Association, in the hope that the inevitable differences of interest between nations would be settled "if possible, amicably."[37] The Austrian Liberal Adolf Fischhof, whom we shall meet below, published his disarmament proposal in 1875, *Zur Reduktion der kontinentalen Heere* (Toward Reduction of the Continental Armies).

The developments in Austrian Liberalism and their effects on Jewish politicians ran parallel to those in Germany. The political battles over language and nationality in the individual crownlands were a microcosm of larger battles in the Habsburg Monarchy. There, even more than in the remaining German states, the interconnection between emancipation and Liberalism and between Liberalism and German unification seemed self-evident. The experience of 1848 reinforced these connections. But the national question was only one of several overlapping circles in the Austrian political agenda. Jews had every reason to oppose the privileged status of the Catholic Church, enshrined in the Concordat of 1855, and to support the German Liberals who were committed to rescinding it. Jews had every reason to favor a centralized administration that would ensure the enactment and enforcement of equality before the law and allow as little discretion as possible to the individual crownlands. The German Liberal Party—officially known as the Constitutional Party (Verfassung-spartei)—not only promised, it delivered. It was the centralizing Liberal ministry of Prince Adolf Auersperg that revoked the Concordat and passed the basic laws guaranteeing equal rights. For these reasons the Jews of Vienna and the Bohemian crownlands feared the demands of the Slav leaders, supported by the German-speaking Conservatives, for "federalism," that is, a reversion of policy-making powers from the center, where the 1867 constitution had placed it, to the individual crownlands. "Before you have time to notice it, the federal state will once more pin the yellow patch on you," *Die Neuzeit* warned.[38]

It is therefore not surprising that initially almost all the Jewish members of the Reichsrat belonged to the German Liberal Party. In the first Reichsrat of 1867, which was still elected indirectly by the diets of the crownlands, there were four Jewish members, all Liberals. In the Reichsrat of 1873, the first to be directly elected, though by a restricted franchise, there were thirteen. All but one of these were Liberals. In the Reichsrat of 1879 there were again thirteen, but in that year the divergences in Jewish national allegiances became evident, with all but one of those elected in Galicia joining the Polish *Klub*, as these parliamentary groupings were known. One significant newcomer from that crownland was Rabbi Joseph Bloch, elected at a by-election in 1883, whom we shall meet again as a major figure in the organization of Habsburg Jewry.

In the 1885 Reichsrat the incipient political fragmentation of Habsburg Jewry was more in evidence. Not only did all but one of the Galicians join the Polish Klub, but two of the Jewish deputies from Bohemia, including Alois Zucker, joined the Czech Klub. Only a bare majority—eight out of fifteen—were now affiliated with Liberalism. More ominously for the Jews of Austria, German Liberalism itself was

now divided, the Deutscher Klub being more radically German nationalist and the Deutschösterrichischer Klub, to which the Jewish deputies
belonged, being less so. All but one of the Jewish deputies represented
urban constituencies; of the twenty-eight professing Jews who were
members of the Reichsrat between 1867 and 1891, twelve sat as representatives of the curia of the Chambers of Commerce. The Brody and
Czernowitz chambers had Jewish representatives continuously from 1873
to 1907, when universal male suffrage was introduced and the chambers
lost their special deputies.

Whether Jews supported German Liberalism or the local non-German
nationality depended to some extent on their social status. The Jewish
urban bourgeoisie had the greatest psychological stake in a German cultural identity and the greatest political stake in Liberal-dominated cen-
tralism. This was illustrated most clearly in Prague by their involvement
in the German Casino and the various associations that radiated from it,
including the Constitutional Union of Germans in Bohemia (Verfassungsverein der Deutschen in Böhmen), whose directors counted most of
the leading figures of Prague Jewish public life, including Dr. Otto
Forchheimer. Those Jews who represented the chambers of commerce in
linguistically mixed areas supported German Liberalism longer than
those in other curiae. In Galicia, too, there was a fear of Slav anti-
Liberalism, and, with the coming of direct elections in 1873, Jewish urban
notables formed a "central election committee of the Jews in Galicia" with
a program of "holding on to the constitution."[39] Five years later a delegation from Brody called on the governor of Galicia to urge measures
against "the dreadful blood-red Social Democrats" on the grounds of the
danger that this posed "to the Liberal Party . . . and, with it, to Jewry."[40]

This equation of Jewish interests with those of German Liberalism
declined in mixed-language areas not only because of Slav or Magyar
pressure but also because politics was no longer the preserve of the leaders of commerce and the professions. As the Jewish lower middle class
acquired political influence, the Germanophile elite was increasingly isolated. The pro-Polish attitudes of much of the Galician rabbinate was one
illustration of this. With the passage of time Jews of all classes showed
themselves flexible in accommodating to their linguistic environment.
The Jews of the German-speaking areas had no such choice. They were
tied to Liberalism—or thought they were. As long as the Liberal parties
of Germany and Austria guaranteed equal rights and welcomed assimilation, and were the main power in the state, the Jewish-Liberal alliance

cemented in 1848 was secure. For much of the 1860s and 1870s the portents were favorable. From the 1880s onward it began to look less as though the continuation of progress was inevitable. The Liberal administration of Prince Auersperg fell in 1879 and at the parliamentary election that followed the Liberals lost their majority in the Reichsrat to a Conservative-Slav majority and never regained power. The brief period of Liberal dominance was therefore coterminous with that in Germany. That change in the parliamentary balance initially made little difference to the political outlook of a significant section of Jewish opinion. The preacher Adolf Jellinek (1821–1893), who in 1848 had proclaimed, "The liberty of the Jews is at the same time the liberty of Germandom,"[41] reminded his coreligionists,

> The Jews of Austria . . . cannot forget that that central parliament, which represented the whole of Austria, voted for the Basic Rights. . . . It is a historical fact that the liberty of the Jews of Austria found its expression in the legislative body in which the whole of Austria is represented.[42]

While this was not explicit support for Austro-German hegemony, it was unconditional support for the existing constitution that had come into being under German Liberal dominance. In this he spoke for the majority of Viennese Jews and those of the Bohemian crownlands. But, as we have seen, he was also speaking in a period of increasing political fragmentation. Differences began to emerge, even among those who remained in the broadly defined German Liberal camp. As long as the Verfassungspartei was in power the conflict between liberal principles and nationalist demands could be reconciled. Habsburg Liberalism was at this stage predominantly German but not exclusively so; it retained the support of some non-German voters and some deputies for whom Liberalism was more valuable than tribalism. After the defeat of 1879 this minimal consensus disintegrated.

On the one hand, that wing of the German Liberals that valued ethnic interest more than constitutional principles asserted itself. It conducted a double campaign against the oligarchical leadership of the Verfassungspartei, accusing it both of neglecting the interests of the Germans of Austria and of being in league with high finance and big business. Thus the demands for political and economic reform went hand in hand and were doubly attractive to those who felt excluded from power and privilege, expecially when the franchise was extended in 1882. The more militant German nationalists within the Verfassungspartei had already formed an autonomous parliamentary grouping in 1873. The continuing divergence became clear when the party once more divided after the 1885 election into the more moderate Deutsch-österreichischer Klub of eighty-two members and the more radical Deutscher Klub of fifty members. The Deutscher Klub merely reflected the extraparliamentary initiatives of those who had drawn up the German nationalist, anticapitalist Linz Program of 1882. This group contained a number of Jews, including the historian and publicist Heinrich Friedjung (1850–1920), the future leader of Austrian Social Democracy Victor Adler (1852–1918) and his brother Siegmund, and the reformist politicians Julius Mandl and Serafin Bondy. The *Deutsche Wochenschrift*, edited by Friedjung, became the organ of the Deutscher Klub, to be followed in 1886 by the *Deutsche Zeitung*, when Friedjung became its editor. Friedjung, who had belonged to the Germania fraternity while a student at Prague, was in no doubt about the German character of Austria: "Let us not forget that until recently Austria was united with Germany. . . . A people does not forget its thousand-year history in ten years,"[43] he wrote in *Der Ausgleich mit Ungarn* (The Compromise with Hungary), a work so critical of the 1867 constitutional settlement that the government secured his dismissal from his teaching post at the Commercial Academy of Vienna. However, the German nationalist movement of the 1880s was soon riven by anti-semitism, which put an end to Jewish participation in it, as described in detail in chapter 7. If the 1879 elections showed how narrow the basis of Austro-German Liberalism was, the events of the 1880s showed how narrow was the base of the Jews within it.

One veteran Jewish politican who foresaw this development at an early stage was Adolf Fischhof (1816–1893), one of the leaders of the 1848 revolution in Vienna. His *Österreich und die Bürgschaften seines Bestandes* (Austria and the Guarantees for Its Endurance), published in 1869, argued that the unitary state envisaged by the 1867 constitution could not satisfy the multiple aspirations of Austria's subject peoples. Instead he held up Switzerland and the United States as examples of a consensus based on federalism and proposed universal suffrage with clauses for the protection of minorities as a solution. He tried to carry his ideas into effect in 1882 with the creation of a Deutsche Volkspartei, "a concentration of all the liberal forces in Austria on a supranational basis." He had some Jewish supporters, including the journalist Theodor Hertzka (1845–1924), the publisher of the *Wiener Allgemeine Zeitung* and later author of the utopian novel *Freiland* (Free Land), which had considerable influence on the social thought of Theodor Herzl. He also had some interesting non-Jewish supporters, including the antisemite Karl Lueger. But he had more numerous Jewish opponents: among those who broke up the opening meeting of the new party was Friedjung.

Fischhof's party got nowhere; Austrian Liberalism, decreasingly liberal, had broken up into its national components. After Fischhof's death one of the cofounders of the Deutsche Volkspartei, Ferdinand Kronawetter (1838–1913), reprimanded the Jews of Vienna for their indifference to his message:

> I have to say openly that the Deutsche Volkspartei has received no encouragement, especially not from Jews, and that we were attacked especially heavily from that side. . . . I think you will think differently today from the way you thought in 1882.[44]

5. Jews as Policy Makers

Though it was Jews in public, official positions who best illustrated the change in the legal position that the third quarter of the nineteenth century brought about, and the conspicuously moneyed Jew who corresponded most to the popular stereotype, it did not follow that those who belonged to either of these categories were the most influential. Since Jews in both empires continued to be excluded from the other main source of power, the state bureaucracy, it is best to attribute any influence that particular Jews might have had to their personal intellectual qualities rather than to any institutional affiliation.

There were two policy areas that were regarded as particularly suitable for the exercise of Jewish expertise: finance and law. No man was more instrumental in the creation of a unified German financial system than Ludwig Bamberger. He saw that the new empire had two needs, each to be satisfied quickly: a single currency based on gold, capable of competing on equal terms with sterling and the Latin Monetary Union of France, Belgium, Switzerland, and Italy, both of which were backed by gold, and a monopoly of the rights of issuance, to be held by the Kaiserreich. In the course of four years the imperial government produced three bills, one in 1871 to provide for the minting of gold coins, one in 1873 to establish the Reichsmark as a new currency, and one in 1874 to regulate the issuing of banknotes, but without mention of a central bank. Each of these bills

Bamberger regarded as defective. Through pamphlets, hour-long speeches, and tireless work in parliamentary committees he persuaded the government and the majority of the Reichstag to move most of the way toward his viewpoint. The outcome of these exertions was a central bank, which, though technically private, was under government supervision and responsible for the control of all currency circulation in the German Empire, and a Reichsmark tied to the price of raw gold. Bamberger could not have achieved these successes had he not been a member of the Reichstag, although he was no more than a backbencher within it. But the true measure of his success he owed to his close relationship with Bismarck and Rudolf von Delbrück, the president of the Chancellor's Office, and to his own incontrovertible expertise. Outside the Reichstag he showed this expertise through his role in the founding of the Deutsche Bank in 1872 as an institution for financing Germany's foreign trade. He was also instrumental in finding one of the bank's first codirectors, Hermann Wallich, of the Jewish banking family.

Austria did not embrace the gold standard until 1892, when the traditional florin was replaced by the crown. This, too, was the work of a statesman of Jewish descent, the convert Emil Steinbach (1846–1907), who was appointed minister of finance in 1891. Steinbach was a protégé of Julius Glaser, who brought him into the Ministry of Justice, where he rose to the rank of *Sektionschef*. Steinbach's other achievement as minister was the reform of the taxation system, which shifted the burden from the poor. This accorded with his well-developed social conscience, which had made him the author of the first Austrian compulsory insurance schemes while at the Ministry of Justice. His belief in sound money did not, as Bamberger's had done, lead to a rejection of all collectivism.

The role of Glaser and Unger in reforming the Austrian legal system has already been mentioned. The equivalent task in Germany was the elaboration of a new civil code (*Bürgerliches Gesetzbuch*). This spread over twenty years and was the work of many hands, but the contributions of both Eduard Lasker and Levin Goldschmidt may be singled out. Legal unity was of both practical and symbolic importance in the early years of the empire. The formal demand for it had first been formulated in 1867, the year of the debate on the constitution of the newly created North German Confederation, in a motion proposed by Eduard Lasker and his fellow National Liberal Johannes Miquel (1828–1901). This required that the confederation have legislative competence over the whole of civil law and the organization of the courts. The Lasker-Miquel motion was passed

five times by the Reichstag, though in the later instances without any reference to the courts, and was finally accepted by the Bundesrat in that
form in 1873. Lasker's colleague Levin Goldschmidt saw it as "no accident, that the irreconcilable enemies of the German Reich are to be found
among enemies of a German legislative institution."[45]

There was no consensus on whether legal unity demanded a single
code, a solution to which the governments of the southern states were
predictably opposed. The matter was therefore to be settled by a Preparatory Commission, presided over by Goldschmidt. Heinrich Friedberg,
then undersecretary of state at the Reich Justice Office, would probably
have preferred Goldschmidt to do the work single-handedly, but this was
unacceptable to the federalists, whose demands Goldschmidt's reports
partially reflected. Twenty-two years were to elapse before the code was
in place, and during that period the political balance and ideological epi-
center of the Kaiserreich shifted considerably—away from the National
Liberals' twin principles of legal uniformity and the primacy of nego-
tiable property. The only Jewish legislator associated with this final phase
was the Hamburg National Liberal Isaac Wolffson (1817–1895), who was
nominated by the Bundesrat for the committee that considered its second
reading. The final version made some significant moves away from
absolute freedom of contract and the strict Roman Law basis that
Goldschmidt would have preferred toward "social" obligations in the
legal system. The euphoria of national unification belonged to the early
years of the debate and it was then that the spirit of Lasker and
Goldschmidt most affected it. Though Goldschmidt's direct influence on
the Civil Code faded at an early stage, his contribution to German commercial law generally was profound and long-lasting. His *Handbuch des
Handelsrechts* (Manual of Commercial Law), first published in 1862,
went through three editions. He also founded and for many years edited
the *Zeitschrift für das gesamte Handelsrecht*.

Two areas in which Jews were widely held to exercise great power were
the press and banking. There were good reasons why both should be
attractive to Jews. They were innovative, closely related to the emergence
of a more urban economy and a more mobile and politicized society. There
were strong historical reasons for Jewish prominence in banking in
Central Europe. Jewish bankers, though they have a long history as individuals, emerged as a class in the eighteenth century to serve the absolute
rulers of Central Europe; their successors in the nineteenth provided
much of the capital for the new industries of Germany and Austria-

Hungary. Newspapers and periodicals had an obvious attraction for the growing number of educated Jews, with an increasingly literate public. They were an even more speculative and uncertain enterprise than banking, at least before 1848 when they were subject to censorship and other restrictions. Though some Jews had managed to make their mark in this profession before the revolutions, 1848 was the golden year of the Jewish journalist, more so in Vienna than anywhere else. It irrevocably created the stereotype of the radical Jewish publicist. Some of the survivors of the mainly ephemeral publications of that year emerged as the creators of the Liberal press that revived in the 1860s. Its most celebrated example was the *Neue Freie Presse*, founded in 1864. Under the editorship of Eduard Bacher and Moritz Benedikt (1841–1920), it became the leading political, financial, and literary organ of Central Europe, proclaiming German Liberal orthodoxy. Its contributors included the music critic Eduard Hanslick (Jewish on his mother's side) and Theodor Herzl. In 1867 Moritz Szeps (1834–1902) founded the *Neues Wiener Tagblatt*, which quickly identified itself with democratic Liberalism. In the 1880s it printed frequent anonymous contributions by Crown Prince Rudolf. In contrast with the *Neue Freie Presse* it was anti-German and pro-French. Equally associated with democratic Liberalism was the *Wiener Allgemeine Zeitung*, established in 1880 and edited by Theodor Hertzka.

Liberalism of various gradations was also a feature of the Jewish-owned and Jewish-edited press of Germany. The outstanding name here is that of the industrialist and banker Leopold Sonnemann (1831–1909), who founded the *Frankfurter Handelszeitung* in 1856. He turned this into the *Frankfurter Zeitung* in 1867 and remained its sole proprietor and editor until his death. It spoke for the anti-Prussian democratic Liberalism of the southwest, opposing the Kulturkampf, anti-Socialist legislation, protective tariffs, the growing militarization of the Kaiserreich, and the naval program of Tirpitz. It was a paper of great integrity and international renown. More in line with the mainline Liberalism of the empire were the Berlin papers belonging to Rudolf Mosse (1843–1920) and Leopold Ullstein (1826–1899). Mosse had made his money in another innovative venture, an advertising agency, and branched out into newspapers with the foundation of the *Berliner Tageblatt* in 1872, which quickly became the leading quality paper in Berlin and, thanks to its location in the new capital, acquired national importance. To these Mosse added the more popular *Berliner Volkszeitung* and *Berliner Morgenzeitung*, which soon acquired competitors in Ullstein's bid for the mass market with the *Berliner Morgenpost*—the paper with the highest circulation in the capital—the *B.Z. am Mittag* and the *Berliner Illustrierte Zeitung*. However, the Ullstein house did not enter the quality market until 1914, when it bought the *Vossische Zeitung*, the oldest newspaper in Berlin.

Another innovation in the mass media that was due to Jewish initiatives was the news agency, designed in the first place for the quick transmission of financial news. The pioneer in this field was Bernhard Wolff (1811–1879), already established as a financial journalist, who began using the Berlin-Aachen telegraph link for this purpose in 1851, taking the French Havas agency as his model. Two years later Israel Beer Josaphat (Paul Julius Reuter, 1816–1899) extended the line to London and eventually across the Atlantic. With Reuter established in Britain, Wolff retained a monopoly in Germany, but his independence did not last long. Subjected to a number of takeover crises in the 1860s, he sought the help of the North German Confederation. In return for financial aid for his board he was obliged to accept government vetting of political dispatches and to make his services available to German officials abroad on demand.

How much real political power these editors and press proprietors wielded is a disputed question. Their readership was, in the main, restricted to the middle and lower middle classes in urban and metropolitan areas. Elsewhere the population either read no papers or was restricted to a semiofficial local paper, generally conservative or ecclesiastical in tone. Only in Austria could the Liberal press be called a Jewish monopoly.

If the political influence of newspapermen is difficult to verify, that of bankers is even more so. The older generation of bankers was, as we have seen, inclined to conservatism, and the links that many of them had with heavy industry predisposed them to prefer protection over free trade. That was certainly true of the Oppenheim and Rothschild banks in the late 1870s, though neither of these can have been a decisive force in the government's turnaround. In the 1880s most of the major banks, whether Jewish-owned or not, favored colonial expansion, but here again it would be difficult to single out the Mendelssohns, Oppenheims, Schwabach, or Fürstenberg as forces that tipped the balance. One banker who enjoyed a special relationship with both the government and the crown was Gerson Bleichröder (1822–1893). His was a crucial role in financing the Prussian-Austrian war, in negotiating the French indemnity in 1871, in rescuing German investments in Romanian railways, and in issuing numerous

German and foreign government loans. His advice was freely sought and given, generally, as we have seen, on the side of caution and against speculation and more often in reaction to the approaches of others than his own initiative. On two notable occasions he intervened on behalf of his fellow Jews. The first was in 1878 at the Congress of Berlin at the end of the Russo-Turkish War, to ensure equal rights for Jews in the enlarged kingdom of Romania—a clause that remained for the most part a dead letter. The second was in response to the antisemitic campaign of the court preacher Adolf Stoecker, when he succeeded in eliciting a mild rebuke from Emperor William I.

In one respect Bleichröder set a precedent. He was the first unbaptized Prussian Jew with male descendants to be ennobled. Apart from him and Abraham Oppenheim (1804–1878) there were only 3 other bankers among the 419 ennoblements in the reign of William I. Oppenheim died without an heir, yet even his elevation was a triumph of sorts. In 1833 the governor of the Rhine Province advised against awarding him the title of *Kommerzienrat*, as "his adherence to the Israelite faith would occasion offense among the public."[46] In granting titles of nobility to professing Jews Prussia was well behind the Austrian practice, where ennoblements were almost wholesale—understandably so, given the permanent dependence of the state on Jewish fund-raisers. Between 1701 and 1918 some 450 Jews were ennobled in Austria; up to 1848 some three-quarters of those ennobled converted, thereafter continued allegiance to Judaism became more common. In addition, members of 346 Jewish families in Hungary were ennobled between 1800 and 1918, the great majority of them after the Compromise of 1867.

6. Public and Private Jews

What the many individuals described and discussed in this chapter had in common was that they were Jews or of Jewish descent. Most had two Jewish parents, some only one. Some converted, most remained formal members of their ancestral religion; of these, some were observant, in some cases Orthodox, others indifferent. Yet the degree of religious observance tells us little about their Jewish consciousness or perceived identity. Ludwig Bamberger, for instance, was certainly aware of his Jewish identity, as his letters, diaries, and memoirs testify, yet he recorded no religious affiliation in his Reichstag curriculum vitae. The doctrine of assimilation, prevalent in its simplest form during the Liberal decades, stressed the distinction between private religion and public citizenship. The effect of this was that the more involved an individual was in public life the further removed he was likely to be from Jewish religious or associational ties. That was certainly true of leading parliamentarians like Lasker, Bamberger, Reichenheim, Sonnemann, or Max Hirsch (1832–1905, cofounder of the Liberal Hirsch-Duncker trade unions). Others, like Levin Goldschmidt, steered clear of religious involvement but were active in philanthropic work or secular communal organizations, like the Deutsch-Israelitischer Gemeindebund, while Heinrich Bernhard Oppenheim involved himself in publicity on behalf of Romanian Jews. A third category combined parliamentary activity with membership or office in the Jewish community council (*Repräsentanten-Versammlung*) or community executive (*Gemeinde-Vorstand*). The industrialist Ludwig Loewe, for instance, served on the Berlin community council while he was a deputy in the Prussian Landtag and the Reichstag. A fourth category consisted of notables within their own cities, who occupied a multiplicity of political, communal, and professional offices. In Breslau the Progressive Wilhelm Salomon Freund (1834–1915) served on the city council for forty-four years and as its chairman for twenty-eight, belonged to the Prussian parliament from 1876 to 1879 and the Reichstag from 1879 to 1881, and was for thirty years chairman of the Chamber of Advocates of Silesia and president of the Breslau Jewish community council. In Hamburg the National Liberal Marcus Wolf Hinrichsen belonged to the City Council for thirty years and the North German Reichstag from 1868 to 1870, was president of the Chamber of Commerce for thirty years, and a member of the community executive. In Nuremberg the Progressive Wolf Frankenburger (1827–1889) belonged to the Bavarian parliament from 1869 until his death, to the Reichstag from 1874 until 1878, and was a member of the city council's executive and of the Jewish community executive. Examples could be multiplied. Links between professional and economic position, community activity, and municipal office were especially common in the eastern provinces of Prussia with large Jewish urban populations, particularly Posen and Silesia.

The same applied to Austria, where the links between communal and political life were in any case stronger—not only in Galicia, where one might expect it, but also in the secularized atmosphere of Vienna and Prague. Ignaz Kuranda found time, in addition to his parliamentary and journalistic activities, to serve as president of the Vienna Jewish community. Other prominent Liberals, like Adolf Fischhof and Heinrich Jacques, held no formal community office but were closely engaged in Jewish political concerns and civil liberties issues. There was no Austrian equivalent to the secular, indifferent public figures represented in Germany by Lasker, Bamberger, and Sonnemann. The first generation of emancipation did not produce a single type of Jewish public figure. Whether in parliament or the press or in academia a number of choices, not all of them easily resolved, were open. Conversion led in one direction, the combination of communal with public office in another. Some saw public activity as an extension of religious obligation, others saw the religious obligation as a routine, subordinate to the attractions of the new secular life.

7 | The Return of Old Hatreds

Just as the revolutions of 1848 set the agenda for Jewish emancipation in Central Europe, they also established the repertoire of antisemitism. And just as formal emancipation was not realized for another twenty years, so antisemitism as a viable political movement lay dormant for the best part of a generation. Yet everything that was common currency in the antisemitic campaigns of the 1880s and the 1890s had already been said in 1848–1849.

What was new in the 1880s was the word. It was launched, though not invented, in 1879 by the radical publicist and journalist Wilhelm Marr (1818–1904), cofounder of the Antisemiten-Liga (Antisemites' League), which came into being at a public meeting in Berlin on September 26, 1879. The date chosen was the Day of Atonement, to ensure the absence of Jews from this event, a stratagem that was not entirely successful. Marr had been involved in the revolutionary politics of Hamburg in 1848 and had published a pamphlet and a couple of anti-Jewish articles in the 1860s that had fallen flat. But by 1879 he had moved to Berlin and the political climate had changed, so that his *Der Sieg des Judenthums über das Germanenthum* (The Victory of Jewry Over Germandom) evoked a greater echo. He followed this success with further pamphlets, including *Wählt Keinen Juden!* (Elect No Jews!), timed for the elections to the Prussian parliament of the same year. What was the point of the word *antisemitism*? The clue may be found in the subtitle of *Der Sieg des Judenthums über das Germanenthum:* "considered from the nonconfessional point of view." This wording served two purposes. It was designed to contrast Jews with Germans, rather than Christians, and therefore to imply an antagonism that was ethnic and unbridgeable. Though Marr lost control of the league he founded, he retained the patent on the word.

Marr was important for launching a word but not for anything else he said. The message he publicized had been maturing for the better part of a century. Antisemitism, as we know it today, was a response to emancipation. Before that, for something like fifteen hundred years, Jews had occupied a subordinate but usually secure place in Christian Europe. The churches preached anti-Judaism, condemning the Jews for failing to accept Christ as the Messiah and indeed fastening the guilt for his crucifixion on them, but the moral and spiritual defects of the Jew could be rectified by conversion. All this was changed by the coming of emancipation. The Jewish demand now was for equality, not toleration. When the French Revolution in 1789–1791 abolished all distinctions based on religion, Jewish-Gentile relations were put on a new footing. Jews—and their well-wishers—hoped that as the ghetto walls came down tensions and misunderstandings would also disappear and mutual respect would take their place. But emancipation, like all revolutions, brought its reaction. Equality offered Jews what they had lacked before: access to power. Where they had previously inspired contempt, they now inspired fear. Where they had previously been accused of individual acts of wickedness, they now appeared collectively responsible for general public ills. Thus what had been a prejudice became an ideology, what had been a street cry became a policy platform. Preemancipation anti-Judaism was a set of attitudes that could remain dormant for long periods. Postemancipation antisemitism was a movement with a program.

1. The Impact of 1848 and 1870

Before 1848 German society was largely prepolitical. Antisemitic writings, and the replies to them, had a restricted audience among officials and the intelligentsia. The revolutions of 1848 changed all that. Like the French Revolution, they brought about a twofold, interconnected change in the public agenda. Politics became mass politics and Jewish emancipation became an inescapable issue. Though the debate about Jewish rights was much older, the politics of antisemitism began in 1848. The sudden outbreak of public politics—unprecedented in continental Europe outside France and Belgium—and the emergence of Jewish formulators of public demands reinforced the Conservatives' image of the post-1789 Jew: as an unwanted intruder, arrogant, skilled, and power hungry. The effect of 1848 on Germany was similar to that of 1789 in France: it raised the bogey of Jewish omnipotence. The immediate impact of the antiemancipatory writings was limited, but they established an agenda. At the height of the Liberal consensus of the 1860s antisemitism was at a discount. When Richard Wagner revealed in 1869 that he had been the anonymous author of *Das Judenthum in der Musik* (Judaism in Music), this confession evoked no fewer than 170 published protests and attacks.

Wagner's ill-timed incursion into these polemics, like that of the young Wilhelm Marr, served as a reminder of the tradition of social-radical or revolutionary antisemitism. There was also a quite notable antisemitic component, to be considered below, in the controversies within the emergent labor movement between the followers of Marx and those of Lassalle. None of this, however, belonged to the mainstream of German antisemitism in the second half of the nineteenth century. This antisemitism of the left, which was also anti-intellectual and anti-industrial, was more French than German and more common before 1848 than after, though it began to revive in a different form in the late 1880s. In our period antisemitism was predominantly conservative, opposed to the trend toward a more secular society, a more liberal state, and a more money-based economy. For some thirty years the dominant themes of antisemitic writings in both Germany and Austria were the Jewish assault on traditional forms of property, particularly agricultural and artisan business, the Jewish assault on traditional political structures, and the essential "otherness" of Jews, which made a mockery of all theories of emancipation and assimilation.

These themes, to which the revolutions of 1848 had given enhanced currency, acquired new salience through the legislative changes of the 1860s and 1870s, which favored unrestricted enterprise. This liberalization was accompanied by the speculative boom that culminated in the Viennese stock exchange crash of 1873, the effects of which quickly spread to Germany, and by the unsavory revelations concerning some of the participants in both the boom and the crash. These were the years of the *Gründerzeit*, the promoters' era, during which some valuable real assets were created but a great many fools parted with their money for the benefit of a small number of crooks. Of the promoters many were holders of ancient titles of nobility; others were the offspring of respectable Protestant and Catholic homes. But given the disproportionate presence

of Jews in commercial activity it was not surprising that Jews should feature prominently in these activities and that the least reputable among
them should reinforce a stereotype already well established. During the
1860s and 1870s a few Conservative publicists kept the antisemitic flame
alive against considerable public indifference. In Germany these included
a number of independent writers, some of them expert and scholarly in
their own field, who denounced Jews as part of their general attack on the
prevailing Liberal order—the economists Rudolf Mayer and Adolf
Wagner and the political theorist Constantin Frantz being the most
prominent. In Austria antisemitism was restricted to the Catholic opponents of Liberalism and constitutionalism, led by the *Wiener Kirchenzeitung* of Sebastian Brunner, who was succeeded as editor in 1866 by the
even more virulent Albert Wiesinger. They gained an ally in 1870 when
the North German convert from Protestantism Karl Freiherr von
Vogelsang (1818–1890) became editor of *Das Vaterland*, turning it into
one of the main European organs of conservative social reform.

One pamphleteer whose words summarized the anti-Liberal agenda of
those years was the Berlin magistrate C. Wilmanns. Like Wilhelm Marr
he is better known for the phrase that he launched—the "golden international"—than for the details of his arguments. *Die "goldene" Internationale* was a complaint against the "one-sided tendency of legislation," favoring speculative capital,[1] a call for "the emancipation of honest
employment from the domination of privileged money power" and a
demand to "liberate landed property from the shackles of Roman Law."
This was the standard plea on behalf of the losers in Germany's rapid
transformation into a mature capitalist economy. It could easily have been
made without mentioning Jews. But in the atmosphere of postcrash
Germany the temptation to link the bankruptcy to the scapegoat was irresistible: the golden international was, by definition, Jewish. The international's "focal points and bases are the stock exchanges and banks." As
everyone knows, exchanges and banks are dominated by the Jewish people.[2] This Jewish internationalism meant that "every attempt at national
fusion must necessarily fail."[3]

Wilmanns' pamphlet was the first to present the complete antisemitic,
anti-Liberal agenda, but the individual components of this were far from
new. The first component was root-and-branch opposition to the political
changes of the 1860s. Ultraconservatives did not care for the new German
Empire, with its liberal, centralizing tendencies, nor for the post-1867
Austrian constitution that shared these characteristics. For Constantin

Frantz, one of the most vigorous and persistent defenders of the old order, it became evident that it was "precisely those elements that form the stable basis of the nation that have no interest in a general uniform civil law" and that "nothing suits the Jewish point of view better than the idea of the so-called rule of law (*Rechtsstaat*)."[4] The themes of Austrian Catholic anti-Liberalism were identical. Vogelsang, by now the chief spokesman of this school, thundered against machines and against the system in which "the Jew destroys the artisan" and "speculating Jews ruin cobblers."[5] For all the traditionalism of these arguments and resentments, they contain a modern element without which they could not have hoped for any impact. While Jews still retained all the undesirable qualities of the ghetto, they now became wielders of power. They were no longer merely contemptible unbelievers; they were a menace and an enemy. "The weapons that Jewry uses to reach its sole object, domination of the Christian world, are its money, its commerce, and its newspapers," Vogelsang wrote.[6] There is scarcely an anti-Liberal publication of this period that does not speak of "Jewish domination" (*Judenherrschaft*). But there is one instrument of this domination that stands out above all others: the "bedouins of the press."[7]

After the crash of 1873 the victims of the new economic order became more numerous, the potential audience larger, and the charges more specific. There was a good deal more muck to be raked, even if much of the raking continued to be rather indiscriminate. The raking began with a series of articles in the popular Liberal weekly *Die Gartenlaube* at the end of 1874 by the journalist Otto Glagau that were republished in expanded form in two volumes in 1876 and 1877.[8] Glagau was followed in the middle of 1875 by the Conservative *Kreuz-Zeitung*, which printed a series of five articles attacking the Liberal regime under the title "The Bleichröder-Delbrück-Camphausen Era"; these, too, were reprinted as a pamphlet.[9] The Catholic press, in particular the main organ of the Catholic Center (Zentrum) Party, the *Germania*, took up the theme at more or less the same time, but since the Center was fighting a slightly different battle its campaign will be considered separately below.

There was little difference in content in this rising flood of print. The main theme was the rejection of the "Manchester doctrine"—shorthand for laissez-faire—and its association with Jews. "Judaism is the applied Manchester doctrine carried to its extreme,"[10] wrote Glagau. "Bank and stock exchange privileges are, as matters now stand, Jew privileges," Franz F. Perrot, the author of the *Kreuz-Zeitung* articles, echoed.[11] Hostility to the Liberal regime of the new empire also meant hostility to its head of government. For much of the 1870s Bismarck was a hate figure among the ultraconservatives. Was not Gerson Bleichröder his intimate adviser and the disburser of his slush funds? Were not Lasker and Bamberger the chief legislators in favor of the joint stock company and the gold standard? Had he not signed the act of emancipation? By the middle of the decade the ultras had come together in the Anti-Chancellor League (Anti-Kanzler-Liga), which managed to recruit the economist Rudolf Meyer, who had links with the respectable Verein für Sozialpolitik. Like others, Meyer came to antisemitism by stages; there was plenty in his anti-Gründer book: "As long as Prince Bismarck remains the all-powerful idol, the German nation will be sacrificed to the Reich, the Reich to the chancellor, and the chancellor—belongs to the Jews and promoters."[12]

In their hatred of the Bismarckian dispensation ultraconservative Protestants and Catholics were drawn together, not least because of common opposition to the Kulturkampf. "What a pleasure this Kulturkampf is for the Jews!" Constantin Frantz wrote;[13] the Kulturkampf in Germany and the revocation of the Concordat in Austria were only different aspects of the triumph of Liberalism that threatened everything the Catholic Church stood for. Between 1859 and 1871 the map of Europe was redrawn to the triple disadvantage of the Church. In place of a Central Europe dominated by Catholic Austria there arose a Protestant German Empire, a liberal Italian nation-state that swallowed the Papal States, and an Austria-Hungary both halves of which had anticlerical governments. That Jews should support the secularization of the state as a guarantee of civil rights was self-evident; that some of them should relish revenge for centuries of discrimination was understandable. In an age when most Jews were Liberals and Liberalism meant anticlericalism, it was only to be expected that Catholic anti-Liberalism should entail antisemitism. Since, moreover, Catholicism was the principal loser in the shift of the political balance, the theme of Jewish power was bound to feature strongly. It was not a new theme; the first issue of the *Historisch-Politische Blätter für das Katholische Deutschland* had warned that since "the power of money lies in the hands of the Jews . . . one can envisage the social preponderance that the Jews would attain [after emancipation]."[14] Bishop Ketteler of Mainz, one of the inspirers of German political Catholicism, blamed "insolent, Jewish-Masonic Liberalism, filled with hatred for Christianity" and the "heathenish-Jewish party" for the misfortunes of the Emperor Francis Joseph in 1866.[15]

It was, however, the real or apparent conjunction of the Kulturkampf and the Gründer speculation that fueled Catholic antisemitism in the 1870s. The main instrument was the Center Party's organ, *Germania*, which, in turn, gave the lead to large sections of the provincial Catholic press. It saw the Kulturkampf as a diversion from the "promoters' swindles" and declared that "the true Kulturkampf" was to be waged "against the Jewish spirit and Jewish money domination."[16] These arguments combined the secular elements with the religious; the traditional image of the Jew as the enemy of Christianity merged in the more modern image of the Jew as the economic enemy of the honest man and woman. Nowhere was this more clearly expressed than in an old established anti-Jewish genre that now enjoyed a remarkable revival, namely, revelations about the alleged contents of the Talmud. This, too, was a Catholic specialty, though Protestant writers were ready enough to accept the material thus provided. The figure most strongly associated with this was August Rohling, associate professor at the Catholic Academy at Münster and, from 1876, professor of biblical studies and Old Testament exegesis at Prague. In 1871 he published *Der Talmudjude* (The Talmud Jew), largely plagiarized from Andreas Eisenmenger's *Entdecktes Judenthum* (Judaism Unmasked) of 1710. Eisenmenger's tract was old-fashioned religious anti-Judaism; Rohling went further. He stressed the standard components of the anti-talmudic repertoire, in particular that the Jewish religion enforced no moral obligations toward non-Jews and that a Jew's oath was not binding. But in the context of emancipation these defects had a different significance. They demonstrated that Jews did not deserve civic equality, since they exercised the rights of civil society with the allegedly low morality of the ghetto. The modern meaning of this ancient repertoire lay in his charge that Jews aimed "to attain mastery over the universe."[17]

Rohling's pamphlet went through numerous editions; thirty-eight thousand copies of the sixth edition were distributed gratis by the Bonifatius-Verein of Paderborn. The short-term impact of these various publications was to underline the interest that most German Jews had in the new political order and the open society that it promised. If the enemies of the Jews were also the enemies of Bismarck and the new Germany, Jews would all the more firmly become, in the words of the AZJ, "to all intents and purposes allies of the great Liberal Party."[18] Moreover, as long as the loudest antisemites were those who were manifestly swimming against the tide of history, there was little to fear from them. If Jews took them seriously they would "demean the significance and greatness of our times in noting and attaching importance to the utterances of some uneducated and insignificant personality."[19] The threat to emancipation would, however, become more serious if this purely reactionary antisemitism became fused with more modern arguments, such as those of race, or if it were incorporated in an organized political movement. And the antitalmudic pamphlets became a matter of public scandal when orators could secure acquittals in courts of law by calling on Rohling's writings.

The argument of race was similar to that of the antitalmudic literature. It aimed to show that emancipation had done nothing, and could do nothing, to remove the Jews' moral inferiority. It was this proposition that was popularized by Wilhelm Marr, and this was the function of the newly minted term *antisemitism*. Earlier anti-Jewish propaganda had already stressed that Jews were a separate nation, or *Volk*, from Christian Germans or Europeans, and inferior to them, but had stopped short of implying that the gap could never be closed—whether by baptism or by a conscious renunciation of cultural separateness. In the course of the nineteenth century advances in anthropology, ethnology, and philology had given rise to a spate of writings, in France and Britain as well as Germany, attributing human abilities to racial characteristics. But the proposition that the differences between Jews and non-Jews were biologically determined and irremediable emerged in Germany. It was a precondition of successful political antisemitism that the distinction between traditional anti-Judaism and modern "scientific" beliefs be blurred and that the racial challenge be formulated in now-or-never terms. The tone of Marr's *Der Sieg des Judenthums über das Germanenthum* reflected the despair of those who were obsessed with the degree of Jewish power in the modern world: "Life and the future belong to Judaism, the past and death to Germandom."[20]

One more work dating from this time added significantly to the repertoire of racial antisemitism, Eugen Dühring's *Die Judenfrage als Racen-, Sitten- und Culturfrage* (The Jewish Question as a Question of Race, Morals, and Culture, 1881). Dühring (1833–1921) was an economist at the University of Berlin and proclaimed himself to be a Socialist. Though at odds with official Marxism, and denounced for his errors in Engels's *Anti-Dühring*, he was not without influence among some of the German left in the early 1870s and had even earned the approval of August Bebel and Eduard Bernstein. His antisemitic writings came after the anathema pronounced by Engels and therefore had little influence on the working-class movement. Nevertheless, his uncompromising rejection of any rapprochement with Jews, based as it was on an equally uncompromising rejection of Christianity, put him firmly in the tradition of the earlier radical antisemites. Indeed his "solution" of the Jewish Question contained thinly veiled genocidal threats: "What then remains aside from using other than spiritual means . . . to thoroughly redeem the world of everything Jewish?"[21] Dühring's impact was long-term; he was taken up by radical student antisemites, especially in Austria in the 1880s, and later feted by Nazis.

2. The Beginnings of a Movement

An antisemitic movement, as opposed to intermittent outbursts, emerged in 1879. What made the launching of a movement possible was a partly accidental conjunction of events. Marr's popularization of the concept of antisemitism made the impact it did because it coincided with the articles of Heinrich von Treitschke in the *Preussische Jahrbücher*, the oratorical debut of the court preacher Adolf Stoecker (1835–1909), and Bismarck's decision to yield to anti-Liberal pressures by abandoning free trade and breaking with the Liberal parties.

To Stoecker belongs the distinction of being the founder of the first antisemitic political party anywhere. Like most of his antisemitic contemporaries, he arrived at his political position by stages. He was in many ways a typical Conservative of the 1870s—monarchist, sympathetic to the preindustrial economic strata, suspicious of the new, secular, capitalist social order, of urbanization and its concomitant, irreligion. He saw Liberalism dominant among the middle classes and revolutionary Socialism threatening to take over the proletariat. Hence his decision to launch a Christian Social Workers' Party in Berlin at the beginning of 1878. As an attempt to wean the workers from the Social Democrats this was a failure; in any case the government had itself moved against the Socialist enemy with its anti-Socialist law. Stoecker therefore turned to a different constituency, the hard-pressed artisans and craftsmen. It was with them in mind that he launched his antisemitic manifesto in September 1879, "Our Demands of Modern Judaism": "Our first demand: a little more modesty. . . . Our second demand of the Jewish press: a little more tolerance."[22] It was not too great a step from that to his assertion that in Berlin "Jewish and Christian spirits were locked in a battle for dominance."[23]

The impact of Stoecker's speech and the large audiences that his later

Stöcker, der Schußheilige der Radaubrüder.

27   A caricature of Adolf Stoecker as "patron saint of the
rowdies" (1880)

utterances attracted were amplified by the historian Heinrich von
Treitschke's editorial in his intellectual fortnightly, *Preussische Jahrbücher*.
The topic was the sudden growth of antisemitism. Treitschke deplored the
vulgarity and coarseness of much that was said; he took it for granted that
legal equality could not be rescinded. But he had no doubt why there was
unease in the nation: there was, once again, "a German-Jewish question."
Its causes were to be found in Jewish arrogance: "In recent times a dangerous spirit of arrogance has arisen in Jewish circles. . . . The influence of
Judaism on our national life, which in former times achieved some good,
has more recently shown itself to be in many ways harmful"; in Jewish

dominance in the public media: "For ten years public opinion in many German cities was 'manufactured' by Jewish pens"; in Jewish immigration from the uncivilized East: "Year after year there pours over our eastern frontier from the inexhaustible Polish cradle a host of ambitious trouser-selling youths, whose children and children's children one day will dominate Germany's stock exchanges and newspapers." All this has resulted in a predictable reaction: "Far into the most educated circles, among men who would reject with disgust any thought of ecclesiastical intolerance or national pride, we can hear, as if from one mouth: 'The Jews are our misfortune.' "[24]

Treitschke was the most distinguished public figure yet to lend his voice to the unease about the effects of Liberalism on German culture and society. Once he had spoken, the "Jewish Question" could no longer be dismissed as a fringe phenomenon. It was back in the mainstream of political debate: "What *he* said was thereby made respectable," as his main antagonist, the classical historian Theodor Mommsen, put it.[25] A declaration signed by seventy-five Gentile notables, including Mommsen, the historian Heinrich von Sybel, the constitutional lawyer Rudolf von Gneist, the industrialist Werner von Siemens, and the mayor of Berlin, Max von Forckenbeck, warned:

> The revival of an ancient prejudice is threatening, like a contagious pestilence, to poison the relations that Christians and Jews have proclaimed on the basis of tolerance in state and parish, in society and the family. If at present envy and malice are preached by the leaders of this movement only in the abstract, the crowd will not delay in drawing the practical conclusion from such vague speech-making. . . . Already we hear the cry for discriminating legislation and the exclusion of Jews from this or that trade or profession, honor or position of confidence. How long will it be before the herd clamors for this, too?[26]

In contrast with previous antisemitic outbursts, eminent Jews were on this occasion moved to protest. There were articles and pamphlets from, among others, the historians Heinrich Graetz and Harry Bresslau and the philosopher Hermann Cohen. Among politicians Ludwig Bamberger and H. B. Oppenheim entered the debate. The "Declaration of the Notables" notwithstanding, Stoecker and Treitschke made their mark, and a petition was circulated throughout Germany demanding a number of restrictions on Jews that would, in effect, amount to revocation of emancipation. The organizers collected 265,000 signatures and presented their petition to the imperial government, which ignored it. Its attitude toward the renewed agitation was, however, at best neutral. Bismarck's deputy, Count Otto von Stolberg-Wernigerode, contented himself with declaring that "no change in the law was envisaged."[27] Though the petition itself failed in its objective, the agitation that accompanied it had two significant consequences for organized antisemitism in Germany. Of the 265,000 signatures, some 4,000 were provided by university students—amounting to almost one in five of the German student body. The organizers of the petition in the universities went on to found the Verein Deutscher Studenten (Association of German Students, vDSt) in 1881. Though many of the older student corporations, whether the aristocratic Corps or the more middle-class dueling Burschenschaften, may have shown a snobbish aversion to their Jewish fellow students, and some had from time to time excluded Jews from membership, antisemitism was not their primary objective. The vDSt differed sharply from these. Its sole purpose was to politicize a new generation of students with an exclusive, integralist nationalist message from which militant antisemitism was inseparable. There was no shortage of patronage for the fledgling student group. Treitschke refrained from public support for them, although he was unquestionably the hero of all nationalistically minded students and their role model. But they enjoyed the open support of Dühring and above all of Stoecker, who was originally scheduled to be the key speaker at their first national congress in Halle in July 1881. The second consequence of the Antisemitic Petition was that it produced new antisemitic cadres. Some of them, like Bernhard Förster, the initiator of the petition and later to be the (despised and resented) brother-in-law of Friedrich Nietzsche, soon faded from the scene. Others, including Stoecker, gained election to the Reichstag and the Prussian parliament. An antisemitic political leadership was in the making.

A twofold question remains: why did the tide turn when it did, and, why did it not turn sooner? The main explanation is to be found in the wider political environment. By the end of the 1870s Bismarck was anxious to rid himself of dependence on the two Liberal parties, which had now served their purpose in helping to create a Prussian-dominated Kaiserreich. His switch to a policy of protective tariffs, which caused the split in the National Liberal Party, brought the more conservative interests of agriculture and heavy industry into favor. Part of the answer, therefore, is that the antisemites benefited from Bismarck's agenda. The two agendas were not the same; nevertheless, his switch of partners signaled that the emancipatory phase of German politics, associated with Liberal dominance, was now over. Bismarck's own attitude toward Jews and antisemitism was ambivalent. He had close personal relations with his financial adviser, Bleichröder, and the lessees of the mill on his Pomeranian estate, the Behrend brothers. In private he was prepared to condemn antisemitism and to praise the patriotic services of Jews. According to his private secretary, Moritz Busch, he felt that Jews ought to be grateful to him, since he had secured their political rights "at any rate through my signature."[28] On the other hand, he was quick to react when Jewish politicians and Jewish-edited newspapers identified themselves with oppositional Liberalism, especially after the split in the National Liberal Party. He was probably speaking his mind when he distinguished between rich Jews "who do not mount the barricades" and "the ambitious, who have no property yet, especially in the press."[29]

Bismarck's timing also explains, at least in part, why the revival of organized antisemitism was so long delayed. The stock exchange crash of 1873 and the onset of agricultural depression in the middle of the decade might have been expected to trigger increased support, and in the long run they did. But the antisemites of the 1870s suffered from one fatal disadvantage: whether as Catholics or as opponents of the new Kaiserreich or as bankrupt speculators, they were a cartel of losers, out of touch with the euphoria that accompanied the coronation of the new emperor. Ten years later much of the euphoria had evaporated. But equally a new generation of political leaders had arisen who accepted the Reich, admired Bismarck, welcomed his break with Liberalism, and saw in antisemitism a weapon for perfecting the national spirit that the new state still seemed to lack. Treitschke or Stoecker or the leaders of the VDST were far removed from the negative resentments of the Anti-Chancellor League. Treitschke rejoiced that "the nation was reflecting on itself [and] mercilessly passing judgment on itself": "The instinct of the masses has indeed correctly identified a grave danger, a highly alarming defect in the life of the new Germany."[30] The new nationalism emerged most clearly from the students' manifesto, since most of them could scarcely remember the world as it had existed before Königgrätz: "Today it is not the external enemy that threatens; today we have to take sides for German character and German customs, for German loyalty and German faith."[31]

Once an antisemitic organization was established in Berlin, the provinces responded with the creation of "Reform Associations"

(Reformvereine). These, too, produced a new wave of publicists and organizers. The most important figure in the long run was the chairman of the Leipzig Reformverein, the milling engineer Theodor Fritsch. More radical than most, he opposed the strategy of forming political parties and fighting elections and was determined to concentrate on propaganda. For these purposes he founded a newspaper, the *Antisemitische Correspondenz*, in 1885 and became a tireless publicist throughout the imperial and Weimar periods, producing thirty-one editions of the *Handbuch der Judenfrage* (Manual on the Jewish Question). He lived long enough to become a Nazi member of the Reichstag.

A second Reformverein functionary to gain national significance was Otto Böckel, a young librarian at Marburg University. He was an expert in folktales and peasant traditions and one of the few antisemitic politicians with a doctorate. He sympathized with the Hessian peasants' dependence on credit provided by Jewish merchants but above all realized the opportunities provided by universal suffrage under the Reich constitution. He determined to mobilize the rural voters, campaigned in modern style, and secured election to the Reichstag for the Marburg constituency in 1887. He was the first antisemite to achieve a popular electoral success against the established parties and ensured in doing so that antisemitic politics in the 1890s would be very different from those a decade earlier. One further outcome of the Reformverein activities were the international Anti-Jewish Congresses. In their attempt to unite the disparate and quarrelsome antisemitic sects of Germany they failed. What was significant about them, however, was that antisemitism had ceased to be a German specialty. Delegates came from Russia, France, and Romania, but above all from Austria and Hungary. It is time therefore to turn to the antisemites of the Dual Monarchy.

3. The Habsburg Monarchy

In May 1879, a few months before Stoecker, Marr, and Treitschke were to launch their campaigns in Berlin, a correspondent was able to reassure the readers of the *Allgemeine Zeitung des Judentums* (AZJ) that "especially here in Vienna the *rischuss* [Jew-hatred], as it is still familiar in the major cities of Northern Germany, does not exist. So, too, in social circles there are no religious distinctions."[32] Peace was not to last much longer. True, Catholic anti-Liberal antisemitism, as preached by Vogelsang in *Das Vaterland*, abounded, but its impact was limited. Like its analogue in

Germany, it sounded too much like the lamentations of the losers. True as well, the 1873 crash had hit the Austrian economy more severely than the German, but it was some years before it was evident that the depression had come to stay. When popular antisemitism did revive in Austria in the 1880s it was more intense and more concentrated than in Germany. It was above all a Viennese phenomenon and from there spread to the Alpine provinces. It was quiescent in Bohemia and Moravia, whether among Germans or Czechs, as also in Galicia, though this was to change in all three crownlands in the 1890s. There was a brief outburst in Hungary, but of no great staying power.

The new wave of antisemitism had two separate starting points and it was some time before they were able to merge effectively. The first was in the parliamentary party groupings of German-Austrian Liberalism, the second in the municipal politics and artisan organizations of Vienna. They shared the widespread disillusionment with Austrian Liberalism that became a dominant theme of politics once the Verfassungspartei lost power in 1879. Austrian Liberalism suffered from two major weaknesses. It rested on a narrow social base and on a narrow national base. It owed its majorities in both the Reichsrat and the city council of Vienna to a restricted franchise and it spoke predominantly, even if initially not exclusively, for the German-language population. It was therefore doubly the vehicle for the maintenance of privilege. With the enactment of the Constitution of 1867 and the revocation of the Concordat in 1869 its leaders had more or less completed their program. Unlike their German confreres in the 1870s, whether National Liberal or Progressive, they had no agenda for further reform. The Liberal Party was therefore divided at an early stage into the satisfied and the frustrated, into factions that were on the one hand more conservative and authoritarian, on the other more radical and even antiparliamentary than was customary in nineteenth-century Liberalism elsewhere. That put it in a poor position to resist a reaction that both preached intolerance and claimed democratic credentials.

Within parliamentary Liberalism oppositional forces demanded on the one hand more vigorous defense of German-Austrian interests, on the other hand state intervention for the protection of farmers, artisans, and even workers. They were nationalist and anticapitalist. After the defeat of the Verfassungspartei in 1879, a younger generation set themselves up as an extraparliamentary radical pressure group. The only parliamentarian among them was Georg von Schönerer (1842–1921), the son of a railway engineer who owned a small estate to the northwest of Vienna, where he emerged as a spokesman for peasant grievances. The remainder were Viennese intellectuals and provincial schoolmasters and lawyers, including numerous Jews (see chapter 6). What united them was a desire to extend political rights. Schönerer, for instance, had presented a motion in favor of universal suffrage in the Reichsrat. Together they drew up the so-called Linz Program of 1882, which combined the constitutional proposals of Friedjung's *Der Ausgleich mit Ungarn* and the anticapitalist elements of Schönerer's 1879 election address.[33] The unanimity was not to last. Schönerer had shown earlier signs of antisemitism, but as long as this was a subordinate part of his program his colleagues shrugged it off. When, in 1885, he insisted on adding a twelfth point to the Linz Program, "The removal of Jewish influence from all areas of public life is indispensable for carrying out the reforms aimed at,"[34] most of his original colleagues parted company with him if they had not already done so. Racial pan-Germanism of the most dogmatic kind, to the exclusion of almost all other considerations, now became his obsession. This isolated him politically but ensured him a place as the intellectual patron of what was to become National Socialism in post-1918 Austria and Czechoslovakia.

One of the influences on Schönerer came through his student contacts. He was a sponsor of the student literary society, the Leseverein der deutschen Studenten Wiens, and was closely associated with a number of the Burschenschaften. The Leseverein combined an interest in aesthetics and social concerns with close links to the more radical-nationalist wing of the Verfassungspartei. Its leading members included those who were to draft the Linz Program and therefore a number of Jews. But the Leseverein also showed the way that Austrian-German nationalism was moving by welcoming the treatise on medical education published in 1873 by the eminent surgeon Theodor Billroth (1829–1894). Though his main argument, not always tactfully expressed, was directed against the influx of ill-qualified East European medical students, "mainly from Galicia and Hungary . . . mostly Israelites," his book was widely interpreted as an antisemitic tract, to Billroth's considerable distress.[35] The Burschenschaften were even more militantly nationalist than the Leseverein, representing as they did a generation that had experienced the exclusion of Austria from the German Empire, and was readier to identify with the dynamic state created by Bismarck than with the apparently stagnant, multiethnic Habsburg Monarchy. The Libertas of Vienna declared in 1878 that Jews were not be regarded as Germans, "even when they are baptized,"[36] and in 1881 refused dueling challenges from them. One by one the others followed suit until in 1896 a conference of all dueling corporations collectively resolved to deny duels to any Jew, "since he is totally devoid of honor according to our German concepts."[37] Austrian student corporations were well in advance of those in Germany in pursuing policies of racial exclusiveness, and it was through them that German ideologies of racialism, in particular those of Eugen Dühring, filtered into Austria and into the receptive ears of politicians like Schönerer.

More significant in the short term than parliamentary maneuverings or student rhetoric was the rise of the artisan movement in Vienna, for it was this that provided the mass base for the anti-Liberal counterrevolution. The politics of Vienna, like that of the Reichsrat, rested on a narrow and segmented franchise, with electors divided into three curiae according to the taxes they paid. From 1850 to the late 1880s city politics was dominated by a Liberal oligarchy, challenged in the third or lowest curia by oppositional Democrats. Some of them, notably Ferdinand Kronawetter (1838–1913), genuinely remained true to the principles of 1848; he was a joint proposer, with Schönerer, of the Reichsrat motion on universal suffrage and a supporter of Adolf Fischhof's multinational Deutsche Volkspartei. But most of the others had the more limited sectional aim of extending the existing political and economic privileges to their lower-middle-class clientele. Hence it is not surprising that the anti-semitic political leadership was to a considerable extent recruited from them. Their cause was helped when the new Conservative government in 1882 lowered the franchise from ten-florin to five-florin taxpayers, which more than doubled the electorate and specifically (and intentionally) strengthened the anti-Liberal constituency. It also benefited from organized discontent. Eighteen eighty and 1881 saw two large Artisan Congresses (Gewerbekongresse) in Vienna that demanded general protective legislation and, more specifically, protection against peddlers who were mainly Jewish and whose numbers had increased with the outbreak of the pogroms in Russia. Though these congresses were clearly a grass-roots phenomenon, two groups of politicians quickly tried to associate themselves with them: the Viennese Democrats, including younger opportunists like Karl Lueger, and Catholic social reformers like Vogelsang and Prince Alois Liechtenstein, who saw an opportunity to break out of their clerical-conservative ghetto. They gained reinforcements from two sources. The first was the Österreichischer Reformverein (Austrian

Reform Association), which sprang up in 1882 on the German model. Unlike the Artisan Congresses it was "directed more and more against the Semites . . . [being] a movement that is not a religious but a social one."[38] The second was a new generation of radical priests who spread their anti-Liberal gospel as much through journalism and public lectures as through sermons. The political coalition of Democrats, artisan activists, and anti-semites was unstable. Though it was able to unite on some promising issues, such as opposition to the renewal of the Rothschild bank's franchise of the Northern Railway in 1884, too many questions divided them. The movement therefore quickly fragmented, but the new constituency it had created,which had been reinforced by the franchise reform, remained. What it lost through the defection of the pan-Germans it gained through the increasing interest of Catholic-conservative social theorists and radical clergy. It became more Catholic, but no less antisemitic. In contrast with the 1870s it had shock troops and the beginnings of a viable organization. What it still lacked was a political leader. He emerged in the person of Karl Lueger.

Lueger (1844–1910) had always had a foot in more than one camp. He had tried to cooperate with Schönerer and had been a supporter of Fischhof's short-lived Deutsche Volkspartei. His interest in the reform of the artisan law had brought him into brief contact with Vogelsang and Count Taaffe, the prime minister under whose aegis the protectionist Small Business Law of 1883 had been passed. But his moves toward explicit antisemitism were cautious. True, he had supported Schönerer's Reichsrat motion in 1887 to limit Jewish immigration. He showed his cards more clearly in June 1887 when he described Liberal politics as "fit for the Talmud"[39] and more clearly still in September when he not only asserted that those who struggle against corruption "come up against the Jew at every step" but also returned to the assault on capitalism, which "wishes to do away with religion, fatherland, and nation."[40] Lueger, the supreme opportunist, had scented the antisemitic wind in his nostrils. He saw that those older Democrats who rejected antisemitism uncondition-ally, like Kronawetter, were on their way out; equally, that fanatical anti-semites were isolating themselves, as indeed proved to be the case in 1888, when Schönerer was imprisoned for leading a physical assault on the editorial staff of the *Neues Wiener Tagblatt*. Step by step he had served the apprenticeship of the successful demagogue—the insider pretending to be the outsider. He had discovered a constituency and was now cultivating it—a constituency that wanted to be rid of the existing elites, and inherit

their privileges, but desired no fundamental social change. For this purpose a rapprochement with the Christian Social associations was useful,
indeed essential; as was a similar convergence with the more moderate
German Nationalists who were bidding to become the dominant faction
in the disintegrating Liberal Party.

After the 1885 Reichsrat election the Liberals once more split, with the
more nationalist faction forming a separate Deutscher Klub. Two years
later this in turn split, having been divided on the question of Schönerer's
anti-immigration motion and on whether to continue accepting Friedjung
as editor of the *Deutsche Wochenschrift*. The new group, the Deutschnationale Vereinigung (German National Union), was led by Otto
Steinwender (1847–1921), a schoolmaster from Carinthia, whose antisemitic motion in the larger Deutscher Klub had met with resistance.
Friedjung had meanwhile solved the question of the party paper by
resigning from the editorship of the *Deutsche Zeitung*. The "Jewish
Question" was increasingly a weapon in the internal disputes of the
Liberal Party, especially as the German national movement struck root in
the provinces. The effect of these developments, reinforced as they were
by the franchise reform of 1882, was that German nationalists were on
occasion tempted to forget their anticlericalism and seek electoral allies
among Catholic antisemites. From 1887 onward such alliances brought
more than one victory and the new coalition became known as the
"United Christians." Though never very stable, it formed the basis of the
antisemitic victories of the 1890s and served as a machine for Lueger's
propulsion into national politics.

One reason often advanced for Lueger's antisemitic overture in
September 1887 is that it was a spontaneous attempt to match a preceding tirade by a visiting Hungarian, Dr. Ferenc Komlóssy. That should
serve to remind us of the role of Hungary in the development of antisemitism. The link between the Jewish community and the dominant
Liberal oligarchy was stronger and lasted longer in Hungary than in
either Austria or Germany. Resentment at this alliance, whether among
peasants or the non-Magyar population, was therefore all the more likely
to take an antisemitic turn. The first notable antisemite in post-*Ausgleich*
Hungary was a back-bench Liberal, Gyözö Istóczy. He made repeated
anti-Jewish speeches in parliament; one in which he proposed the wholesale deportation of Jews to Palestine persuaded Wilhelm Marr to advocate
the same policy. What propelled him and his colleagues to national and
international celebrity, however, was not their own journalistic or organi-

zational enterprises, nor the example of Stoecker and Marr, nor even infection from the Russian pogroms, but the disappearance of Eszter Solymosi, a fifteen-year-old servant girl of Tisza-Eszlár, on April 1, 1882, the Sabbath preceding Passover.

The rumor soon spread that she was the victim of a ritual murder. The yearlong investigation and trial of the Jewish suspects, at which August Rohling offered to give evidence, sparked anti-Jewish riots, as did the ultimate acquittal of the accused. Istóczy and a fellow antisemite, Geza Önody, were invited to the First International Anti-Jewish Congress in Chemnitz, where an idealized portrait of Solymosi decorated the rostrum. Önody made the keynote speech and Istóczy's "manifesto to the governments and peoples threatened by Judaism" was unanimously adopted. Tisza-Eszlár was the first "ritual murder" trial after the Central European emancipations and, as such, a source of great inspiration to all those who thought that Jews were irremediably wicked. Ernst Henrici, one of the new Berlin antisemites, proclaimed, "This little spot in Hungary has become a turning point. . . . It may be the end for Israel."[41] Fresh from their agitational triumphs, Istóczy and his followers founded the National Antisemitic Party, which gained seventeen seats in the 1884 parliamentary election. The party did not last long. The limited franchise worked against it and the government's considerable autocratic powers were mobilized against it.

By the end of the 1880s antisemitism had reached different stages of development in Austria, Hungary, and Germany. Something of the stigma of medieval obscurantism still attached to it, though less so than in the Liberal decades of the 1860s and 1870s. The financial upheavals of the 1870s and popular disillusionment with Liberal nostrums made the enunciation of anti-Liberal—including antisemitic—sentiments once more respectable. In part this was a generational phenomenon, with students, as exemplified by the Association of German Students and the Austrian Burschenschaften, in the vanguard of a resurgent illiberalism. The continued discrimination by all three governments against Jews in public employment also gave antisemites some moral encouragement. The inhibition of overt antisemitism by governments was greatest in Hungary. In Germany a mixture of collusion and disassociation kept the growth of public political antisemitism within limits, though the emergence of Otto Böckel as an uncontrolled popular force foreshadowed the antisemitic boom of the 1890s. It is in Austria that, despite a late start, organized antisemitism took the greatest steps forward, so that by the end of the decade it had become not only a viable but an almost irresistible movement. The Liberal Party, which in its 1885 election manifesto had still condemned antisemitism as "unworthy of a civilized country," decided at the 1891 election to keep silent on the matter.[42] At the fourth and last Anti-Jewish Congress in Bochum, in 1889, Schönerer was billed as the featured speaker.

4. The Initial Response

The survival and revival of antisemitism caused both dismay and confusion among Jews. Few had believed that the passage of the emancipation laws in Germany and Austria would end all prejudice and discrimination overnight, but many believed that the end of these burdens was in sight. Emil Lehmann, one of the founders of the Deutsch-Israelitischer Gemeindebund (DIGB), expressed this widespread optimism:

> Gone are the medieval times of the persecutions of Jews, of Jew ordinances, of Jew districts, and of all the hateful elements that characterize the age of religious romanticism. . . . For the civilized states of Europe and America the question whether religious belief is independent of civil and political rights is solved.[43]

When, therefore, some antisemitic agitation persisted through the 1870s, this did not cause great concern. Time would heal, and those who still tried to resist the onward march of equal rights would sooner or later acknowledge their defeat. It was not only Liberal community leaders and publicists who were anxious to play down such remnants of prejudice as remained. The Orthodox, who in any case had invested less in the Liberal idea of emancipation, were equally dismissive of the "old chronic sickness" of antisemitism.[44] As long as the Liberal parties maintained their majorities in German and Austrian parliaments, and their opponents seemed to be merely resenting the way history had passed them by, one could view these antics with indifference. Even the resurgence of antisemitism in Germany in 1879 evoked widely divergent responses. The poet and novelist Berthold Auerbach was close to despair. He felt that he had "lived and worked in vain! . . . The knowledge of what Germans can still harbor and can suddenly explode, that is indelible."[45] Bamberger was more resigned, and felt the air had been cleared: "It is better for Jews to know the feeling of rejection, which lies hidden behind the constraints of politeness."[46] The AZJ, which had not underestimated the political signif-

icance of Bismarck's turn to the right, remained philosophical on antisemitism: "What is to be done against this? Nothing, except to appeal to
the public conscience to the best of everyone's ability."[47]

But *how* was the public conscience to be aroused? On this there was no
consensus. Many Jews echoed one of the misgivings of the antisemites by
reminding their coreligionists of the implicit terms of the "emancipation
contract." The notion of a "reciprocal obligation" (*Gegenleistung*) went
back to the beginnings of the emancipation debate, as formulated by
Gabriel Riesser. Emil Lehmann, who had launched the term *Gegenleistung*,
went further and suggested not merely civic conscientiousness but total
cultural assimilation as the price Jews had to pay. Jews, he argued, should
abandon not only Sabbath observance but also circumcision.[48] Other Jews
stressed that the process of self-improvement, demanded from the beginning not only by the leaders of the Jewish Enlightenment, the Haskalah,
but by the Gentile pioneers of emancipation, like Dohm and Humboldt,
was by no means complete. "Do we not," the DIGB asked in 1880, "see in
the present movement that touches us so painfully a providential sign to
work even harder than before at our self-ennoblement?"[49]

But the question of internal reform was not a substitute for that of a
public reaction. On this, too, counsels were divided. Wherever and whenever antisemitism has arisen as a problem, Jewish communities have been
divided between a high-profile and a low-profile response. The case for
the high-profile response is that evil must be exposed and nipped in the
bud. The case for the low-profile response is that the lunatic fringe should
not be given free publicity. But there is a further, more complicated consideration. The aim of the antisemites was to demonstrate that Jews have
not fulfilled—or indeed cannot fulfil—their part of the emancipation
contract; that they remain a special segment of the population with particular interests. Should Jews seek to negate this accusation by adopting a
low profile? Or should they risk appearing to corroborate their enemies'
charge by mounting a high-publicity lobbying effort? In the early 1880s
indifference, or at least diffidence, won the day. This applied equally to
efforts from within the Jewish community and to those of Gentile well-
wishers. Certainly the Declaration of the Notables, directed mainly
against Treitschke's articles, was a boost to Jewish morale, as was
Mommsen's counterblast. But the Protestant theologian Franz Delitzsch,
who had gone to considerable trouble to rebut Rohling's antitalmudic
pamphlet,[50] complained that his efforts were unappreciated. The attempts
by Ludwig Philippson, the editor of the AZJ, to create a network of local

activists devoted to combating antisemitism, fell on deaf ears. The *Jüdisches Comité vom 1. Dezember 1880*, called into being by Lazarus, fared no better. It held one meeting, which served only to illustrate the divisions of opinion among Jewish community leaders.

There was, however, one aspect of antisemitic activity that called for a more determined response, however belated, namely, the "antitalmudic" writings. When Rohling's *Der Talmudjude* was first published, few Jews took much notice, even though the number of copies in circulation by the end of the 1870s was considerable. It was widely plagiarized and excerpts were serialized in a number of German and Austrian newspapers and periodicals. What gave the matter a more serious aspect in the 1880s is that courts of law began accepting Rohling's assertions, which antisemitic agitators cited as evidence in their defense when they stood trial for incitement to hatred. In 1880 a Dresden court not only rejected charges against Alexander Pinkert's pamphlet *Die Judenfrage*, but, referring to Rohling and Treitschke, stressed the need "to combat the teachings of the Talmud with the greatest determination."[51] Two years later Franz Holubek, a member of the Viennese Reformverein, secured acquittal on similar grounds. Rohling was by this time something of a celebrity and, as we have seen, hoped to star in the Tisza-Eszlár trial.

It was at this stage that an Orthodox rabbi from Galicia, newly arrived in Vienna, Joseph Bloch (1850–1923), decided to challenge Rohling, accusing him of ignorance and incompetence in a series of articles in Theodor Hertzka's *Wiener Allgemeine Zeitung* and the *Morgenpost* and challenging him to translate a randomly chosen passage from the Talmud in open court. Rohling sued, but the case ended in anticlimax: Rohling withdrew his suit in 1885 two weeks before the hearing was due to begin and retired from his chair at Prague four years later. *Der Talmudjude* continued to be reprinted, though it was now discredited in Catholic circles and the post-1918 editions bore the imprint of Theodor Fritsch's Hammer publishing house. Rabbi Bloch's political program went beyond discrediting Rohling. He wished to wean Austria's Jews from their allegiance to Austro-German Liberalism. He supported Fischhof's Deutsche Volkspartei, and Fischhof's influence showed in his own *Der nationale Zwist und die Juden in Österreich* (The National Discord and the Jews in Austria), in which he argued that Jews should stand aloof from the empire's nationalist hatreds and reserve their loyalty for the Habsburg dynasty. That this publication was subsidized by the Conservative Taaffe government did not endear him to all his potential audience. Bloch pointedly called his journal, launched in 1884, *Österreichische Wochenschrift* and the defense organization he founded in 1886 the Österreichisch-Israelitische Union. Though the union did not at first gain the unanimous support of the Viennese Jewish leadership, it soon became the most important Jewish political organization in Austria and played an influential role in the 1890s.

Bloch's was not the only reaction to those attacks on the Jewish religion that had a plainly political motive. Instigated by a number of prominent Viennese Jews, an international committee was set up in 1883, recruiting, among others, F. D. Mocatta and Philip Magnus from London, Grand Rabbi Zadoc-Kahn from Paris, and Moritz Lazarus and Ludwig Loewe from Berlin. It held two meetings and resolved to produce a learned work on Jewish ethical teachings and other apologetic and educational works.[52] However, nothing came of this. Lazarus's *Die Ethik des Judenthums* (The Ethics of Judaism), published fifteen years later, was an indirect outcome of these meetings, but by then the heat had gone out of this particular controversy.

Opponents of antisemitism, whether Jewish or Gentile, were reluctant to believe that the triumphs of the 1860s and 1870s were now irrevocably reversed. The public antisemitic rhetoric was offensive and the continued discrimination vexatious, but it was by no means clear whether they represented more than a temporary setback. Many hopes were invested in the German crown prince, widely believed to hold Liberal views, but he was terminally ill when he ascended the throne in 1888 and reigned for only ninety-nine days. In retrospect it is easier to see that the reasons for the change of mood were more than merely temporary and contingent. The disillusionment with Liberalism, whether in its political or in its economic form, ran deep. The new German Empire had a constitution that failed to satisfy the emotional needs of a nation awakening to a new position in the world; it provided a set of monarchical arrangements, not a sense of identity. After the easy victories of the 1860s many Germans sought, and failed to find, a new meaning in the state that they—or, more precisely, the Prussian army—had created. There were many scapegoats for this failure: Catholics, Socialists, and Bismarck as well as the Jews, but the Jews filled the need best. They had the fewest friends, they were the most recently integrated, and they were most manifestly associated with the Liberal order. Treitschke had a point when he identified cultural unease as the main cause of the German nation's farewell to the Liberal experiment. It was "as if the nation . . . were passing judgment on itself."[53] Predictably, the nation's verdict was that somebody else was to blame.

5. The Changing Agenda of Antisemitism

In the eight years between Stoecker's first antisemitic speech (1879) and Lueger's decision to follow in his footsteps (1887) antisemitism became part of the public agenda of the two empires. The growing popular appeal required favorable objective conditions—economic distress, rapid social upheaval, and disappointment at the undelivered promises of Liberalism. It also benefited from the programmatic eclecticism of the new gospel. There was, as we have seen, an antisemitism based on religion, which argued that the Jew as Jew had no claim to an equal place in the Christian state. There was economic antisemitism, which argued either that all those economic activities with which Jews were associated were harmful or that they had a harmful effect when exercised by Jews. There was the antisemitism of exclusive nationalism, which argued that Jews were not true Germans (or Hungarians or Czechs or Poles). Lastly there was racial antisemitism, derived from amateurish distortions of anthropology and biology, which preached that only the strictest segregation of incompatible ethnic groups could save one's own tribe from degeneration and destruction. To be a successful antisemitic agitator it was necessary to blend these elements. Those who restricted themselves to religion lost their audience in an increasingly secular age. Those who stressed only race, as did Dühring or Schönerer, were marginalized—at least in their lifetimes. The politics of resentment, which is what antisemitism was, required a polymorphous target, which depicted the Jew as a combination of alien exploiter, religious renegade, and conspirator.

Catholic and Protestant antisemites, who frequently made a point of disavowing racial arguments as being anti-Christian, nevertheless found it increasingly difficult to avoid using them. For the Catholic theologian Joseph Rebbert the Jew's "whole character" was incompatible with that of "the Germanic peoples": "The individual may well give up his religion but not the peculiarities of his race; even the humanistic Reform Jew is and remains a Jew."[54] Stoecker went further and moved closer and closer to the vocabulary of his atheist racialist rivals. "Modern Judaism," he argued, "is an alien drop of blood in our people"s organism."[55] Jewish participation in higher education led to a conflict of "race against race."[56] If Stoecker, the revivalist pastor, had no compunction in appealing to "Christian-German spirit" and "Christian-German national character,"[57] less sophisticated and more opportunistic politicians and pamphleteers would do so all the more readily. Ernst Schneider of the Austrian

Reformverein, who had split with Schönerer over the latter's anti-Catholic and anti-Habsburg stance, spoke of "halting . . . the subversion of Aryan society."[58] This blurring of distinctions between categories that were not only separate but, as in the case of race and religion, in contradiction with each other was essential to the success of the antisemitic appeal. It reflected the political reality of the 1880s or, at any rate, an important segment of it.

In Germany the empire created by Bismarck was now an accepted fact and an increasingly welcomed one. What lost its sheen was the political and economic Liberalism that had accompanied its foundation. Monarchical loyalism and respect for authority were to be the state's moral base from now on, and with these attitudes went increasing hostility toward nonconforming groups. That did not mean that there was a new consensus. Social Democrats, persecuted but not destroyed, were as much victims of the new orthodoxy as were Jews; the remaining left-wing Liberals, united after 1884 in the Deutsch-Freisinnige Partei, were equally opposed to it, many of the more conservative National Liberals found the polarizing political style of the antisemitic demagogues repellent and dangerous, and the Catholic minority, however little sympathy they might have with Jews, had little reason to welcome the new identification of patriotism with militant Protestantism. Not even all antisemites accepted the new orthodoxy. Some wanted something more uncompromising as a preparation for the coming race war. But such radicals became more important after the turn of the century. In Austria, by contrast, the imperial political structure became less accepted as time went on. The fusion of "Germanic" and "Christian" ideology, therefore, though it emerged later, proclaimed the exclusion of Jews from the political and social community more emphatically and ultimately more effectively. Its Socialist and Liberal opponents were weaker and the ultraradicals under Schönerer more challenging. But in the formative phase of the new movement in both empires the blurring of categories brought more benefits than drawbacks.

6. The German Antisemitic Parties After 1890

Although many of the new antisemitic party formations were short-lived, and almost all of them were characterized by division and bitter factional fighting, they retained an underlying sense of having a common enemy. Similarly, in Austria the German nationalists who had separated

from the main body of Liberalism, but continued to share its anticlericalism, were on occasions prepared to ally with radical Catholics against "Jew
Liberalism." In both empires the term *Christian* in a political context
came to have more and more of a national—even racial—connotation. An
explicitly anti-Christian antisemitism, of the sort associated with the
writings of Eugen Dühring or Adolf Wahrmund, made little public impact
at this stage. In both Germany and Austria the rivalries and interrela-
tionships of the various antisemitic factions determined the extent of the
very considerable successes they were to enjoy in the 1890s. In Germany
the election of Otto Böckel to the Reichstag in 1887 opened a new phase
in antisemitic agitation. Unlike Stoecker he had no sympathy with
Throne and Altar; he campaigned as much against the aristocratic
landowners of the East ("against Junker and Jews") as against the rural
moneylenders of Hesse. Unlike earlier racialist radicals he was able to
communicate with ordinary people and to build up a popular base. But his
victory did not merely affect the direction that antisemitism was to take,
giving it a barnstorming populist impetus it had hitherto lacked. It revi-
talized other antisemites of all stripes and in the next Reichstag election,
that of 1890, they won four more seats.

   This advance further encouraged both wings of the antisemitic movement. On the radical side it produced the pathetic demagogue and pamphleteer Hermann Ahlwardt. His first publication, *The Oath of a Jew*
(1890), which accused the banker Bleichröder of having committed per-
jury in a paternity suit, earned him a four-month prison sentence. His
second, *Jewish Rifles* (1892), accused the Jewish-owned Loewe firm of
supplying defective weapons to the Prussian army. He was saved from
serving a further five-month sentence by a fortuitous parliamentary
vacancy at Arnswalde-Friedeberg, a Conservative-held rural seat in
Pomerania. Ahlwardt decided to contest it and, in a campaign reminiscent
of Böckel's, capitalized on his notoriety and secured election. Ahlwardt's
election did not merely boost the morale of the radical antisemites, it also
threatened to split the Conservatives. Court Preacher Stoecker's ally,
Wilhelm Freiherr von Hammerstein, the editor of the *Kreuz-Zeitung*,
encouraged Ahlwardt, though he had little enough in common with genuine Conservatism, simply because his campaign demonstrated the effec-
tiveness of antisemitic slogans. Faced with this challenge, the Conservative leadership was divided. The more traditional leaders saw their
worst fears confirmed by Ahlwardt: this is what Stoecker's indiscipline
and demagogy led to. Others, in contrast, became convinced that there

was no political future for them unless they jumped on the antisemitic bandwagon. The Arnswalde by-election highlighted their dilemma. In the runoff Ahlwardt faced a Progressive, the Conservative candidate having been relegated to third place. The local Conservatives were in little doubt that this made him the lesser evil and their defeated candidate lent him full support.[59] His crushing victory, by eleven thousand votes to three thousand, occurred four days before the Conservatives were due to confer in the Tivoli Hall in Berlin. The Tivoli conference of 1892 was not particularly representative of Prussian Conservatism; this was not surprising, given that this aristocratically led party had only the most minimal organizational structure. Provincial supporters of Stoecker dominated the proceedings. The parliamentary leadership, hoping to stave off too radical an outcome, presented an ambiguous resolution, which pledged the party not only "to combat the widely obtruding and decomposing Jewish influence on our people's life" but also "to condemn the excesses of antisemitism." The second part of the resolution was defeated with only seven votes cast in its favor. The first part became an integral component of the Conservative program.

Antisemitism thereby entered the mainstream of German parliamentary politics. For a brief period antisemites flourished electorally. In the 1893 Reichstag election they won 3.4 per cent of the total vote and sixteen seats, in 1898 ten seats, and in 1903 eleven. The cometlike rise of German parliamentary antisemitism in the 1890s and its equally swift decline are easily explained. Its representatives did reflect some long-term developments in the political atmosphere of the empire; at the same time they were too much at the mercy of short-term political fluctuations. Stoecker's fate illustrated these as well as that of any of the antisemitic bit players. He had at various times been unquestionably useful to Bismarck, to the government generally, to the imperial house, and to the Conservative parties by mobilizing sections of the public against the Social Democrats and, more important, the Progressives. He and his supporters mistakenly assumed that the new emperor, William II, would be sympathetic to him. But William was too inexperienced and too intolerant of insubordination to play this role and obliged Stoecker to choose between his pastoral office and his political career. Stoecker decided to sacrifice the politics and did not contest his Reichstag seat in 1890 but, under pressure from the Church, also resigned his position as court preacher that same year. Nor was the triumph of his cause at the Tivoli conference of lasting effect. Many Conservatives shared his unfavorable view of the Jews, but the adoption of the antisemitic program also reflected the panic after Ahlwardt's election and the way the assembly had been packed. The Conservative Party undoubtedly needed a firmer organizational base, better resources, and a popular cry, but it acquired a more attractive and more useful one the following year. The 1890s saw the beginning of mass-based interest politics, frequently reinforced with an ideological message. The lobby closest to the Conservatives was the Agrarian League (Bund der Landwirte, BdL), founded in 1893. Its Junker leaders had every sympathy with antisemitism—indeed the BdL's statutes barred Jews from membership—but none with Stoecker's social message. In 1896 the former court preacher and his followers severed their links with the Conservatives, but even independence could not save the Christian Social Party. Too radical for the Conservatives, Stoecker was too conservative for the younger social reformers in the party. Led by Pastor Friedrich Naumann, they seceded to form the National Social Union (National-soziale Vereinigung), which soon disassociated itself from its antisemitic heritage and in 1903 merged with the Freisinnige Vereinigung, one of the left-wing Liberal parties.

A further factor that destabilized political antisemitism was the rapidly changing political environment. Antisemites, however radical their language, were not—at this stage—disloyal to the state. At most they claimed, in the language of Charles Maurras's famous distinction, to stand for "le pays réel" as opposed to "le pays légal," seeing in the emancipation law the most objectionable feature of le pays légal. Between 1890 and 1894 Bismarck's successor as chancellor, Count Leo Caprivi, pursued a number of liberal policies, unwelcome in particular to agriculture and artisans. A vote for antisemitic candidates was therefore also—and in some cases primarily—a vote against depressed prices and liberal trade policies. But when William II appointed his own uncle, Prince Chlodwig von Hohenlohe-Schillingfürst, as chancellor the threat to Conservative dominance in Prussia and the Kaiserreich was over. The fluctuating fortunes of electoral antisemitism between 1887 and 1898 showed that German antisemites did not constitute a homogeneous movement. Indeed, they fell into three broad categories: 1. ideologues for whom the reversal of emancipation was the main, and possibly the only, policy objective, 2. opponents of political and economic Liberalism, for whom antisemitism was an integral part of a wider political outlook or who calculated that antisemitic rhetoric would enable them to recruit followers for their cause, and 3. opponents of political and economic Liberalism, for whom antisemitism was a self-evident but strictly subordinate part of their general outlook.

Those in the first category undoubtedly had a long-term effect on German public consciousness, but in the period under review they were little more than a fringe group. Most of the active antisemitic politicians fell into the second category—Stoecker, Böckel, and their parliamentary colleagues, however much they might differ on other issues, were united in this. On the other hand, the more deranged participants in "the movement," such as Ahlwardt, are virtually impossible to classify. Most of the Conservative Party, which retained the antisemitic declaration in its Tivoli program without taking it very seriously, fell into the third category, as did politicians in some other parties, including the Catholic Center and the National Liberals. Electoral and parliamentary antisemitism in Imperial Germany was important because it was public and visible. It set an agenda and instigated a debate. It posed a challenge to the leaders of Germany's Jews, which they were eventually forced to take up, as we shall see in chapter 8. But in terms of practical measures it achieved nothing. Only one of its legislative proposals, the reintroduction of the denominational form of the judicial oath, was accepted, because it was also supported by the Conservatives and Catholic Center Party for reasons that had little to do with antisemitism. Its initiatives for limiting immigration from Eastern Europe, for banning kosher slaughtering, and for appointing commissions to examine the morality of Jewish religious texts all failed. In this respect the contrast with Austria-Hungary could not have been greater.

7. Austria: The Triumph of Karl Lueger

The uneasy alliance of Catholic social reformers and German nationalists, who had come together in 1887 under the name United Christians, had some disadvantages compared with their German colleagues but also some decisive advantages. Although they had aristocratic sympathizers, they did not, as did Stoecker, have friends at court; Emperor Francis Joseph lost no opportunity to express his disapproval of antisemitism. On the other hand, they had an organized political base in the revived artisan movement of Vienna and in the much stronger antisemitic presence in the student corporations, they faced a weaker and more demoralized Liberal party than in Germany and a Social Democratic movement that remained in disarray until 1890, and they benefited from the electoral system, since there was no universal male suffrage, as there was in Germany for the Reichstag, but many of their natural constituency were enfranchised by the reform of 1882. It was the last two of these factors that gave them a decisive advantage over the German antisemitic movement. By 1889 the United Christians had acquired a program that not only demanded the usual restrictions on commerce and financial operations but specified strict anti-Jewish measures. These included, apart from restrictions on immigration, the "de-Judaization" of the civil service, the judiciary, the officer corps and the professions, and barring Jews from teaching non-Jews and from the ownership of landed estates.[60] This emphasis on antisemitism was a necessity for tactical as well as strategic reasons. It undoubtedly appealed to an increasing proportion of lower-middle-class electors. Most important, it was all that the various factions of Christian Socials and German Nationalists had in common. With Schönerer temporarily out of the way, a broad antisemitic coalition became more viable; Lueger was more than ever the obvious leader of such a coalition.

One further reason the antisemites of Austria triumphed is that they set themselves a limited initial objective: the conquest of municipal power in Vienna, an objective made all the more tempting in 1890, when the government decided to incorporate a number of outer suburbs into the capital, thereby increasing its population by 40 percent. With one renewal after another of the city council the antisemites increased their strength, until in 1895 the council was deadlocked between them and the hitherto dominant Liberals. To achieve this the antisemites had had to broaden their social base. Having mobilized the artisans who voted in the third curia they set about organizing the school teachers, white-collar employees, and lower-rank state and municipal officials who voted in the second curia. By 1895 the antisemites of Vienna possessed what their German equivalents always lacked—a secure, broadly based social coalition—and were able to impose Lueger as deputy mayor. A further election designed to break the deadlock produced a clear majority for Lueger. The arrival of an avowed antisemite as civic head of a major European capital city caused a national and, in some respects, an international crisis. The government was concerned as much with Lueger's subversive demagogy generally as with his antisemitism; above all, with the potential that office in Vienna would give him for disruption in the Reichsrat, of which he was also a member. The emperor, in particular, inclined against confirmation. There were, however, further factors. Lueger's demagogy was directed not only against the Jews of Vienna but against the Hungarian government and the influence that Jews allegedly exercised over the "Judaeo-Magyar" elite. Since a renegotiation of the terms of the Austrian-Hungarian Compromise was about to begin, the Hungarian prime minister, Baron Bánffy, expressed the most vigorous objections to a ratification of Lueger's election.

The strongest card that the imperial government hoped to play, but which turned out to favor their enemy, was that of relations with the Holy See. Not the least contribution to Lueger's victory came from the parish clergy and from Jesuit preachers. Ever since the beginning of the Catholic social reform movement sections of the clergy had seen relations with the Holy See as a weapon against the hierarchy, which they regarded as passively subordinate to the state and its Liberal constitution. The bishops were therefore faced not only with an ideological heresy but with a disciplinary challenge. Before the 1891 Reichsrat elections they had denounced "pagan racial hatred" in a joint pastoral letter;[61] in 1895 they intended to issue one condemning the Christian Social Party and its antisemitism. A delegation sent to Rome to secure the approval of the Holy See returned emptyhanded. Pope Leo XIII, though less hostile to Jews than his predecessor, Pius IX, was deeply disturbed by the rise of revolutionary Socialism and Anarchism.[62] He was, moreover, impressed by the religious revival attributable to the missionary zeal of the reformist clergy, on which he received favorable reports from the nuncio in Vienna. The pope was therefore prepared to accept the assurance of Prelate Franz Schindler that "we do not countenance a certain radical antisemitism, which is directed against the Jewish people as such"[63] and to support Lueger against the wishes of the hierarchy. That "a certain radical antisemitism" was an integral part of the Christian Social campaign in this crucial period is, however, only too evident. The main exponent of this was Father Joseph Deckert of the suburban parish of Weinhaus who, following an old popular tradition, likened "Jewish domination" of Vienna to the threat from the Turks at the end of the seventeenth century. He revived the "blood libel," only to be successfully challenged, like Rohling before him, by Rabbi Bloch. This did not, however, diminish his rhetorical enthusiasm: "I acknowledge that I have an antipathy against the Jewish race, an antipathy that I share with all honest Aryans."[64] Thus protected, Lueger's machine was able to advance on its next objective, that of wresting control of the diet of the crownland of Lower Austria, which it succeeded in doing in November 1896. As in Vienna, the Christian Socials swept the board by mobilizing a vital inter-

28   Karl Lueger and Emperor Francis Joseph (1906)

est group, this time the peasants. They were organized in the Association of Lower Austrian Farmers, which in 1901 formally announced its support for the Christian Social party; in 1906 it became the Niederösterreichischer Bauernbund under the party's auspices and has survived in this form to the present day.

By April 20, 1897, the government surrendered: Lueger was sworn in as mayor, the emperor's veto having lapsed. Lueger had become all the more acceptable as the Badeni government had introduced an electoral reform that added a fifth curia of seventy-two seats, based on universal male suffrage, to the existing four. This quadrupled the electorate and gave the Social Democrats, who had already begun nibbling at the Christian Social vote, their first realistic opportunity to gain representation in the Reichsrat. They did indeed elect fourteen members, but none in Vienna and Lower Austria, where the Christian Socials made a clean sweep. Lueger had achieved a double triumph: having risen to power as the enemy of privilege, including that of the bishops, he now stood revealed as the defender of order against the threat of revolution. Lueger was the outstanding nineteenth-century example of a politician who, blending radicalism with respectability, was able to use antisemitism to build a lasting power base, an achievement acknowledged by his most important admirer in *Mein Kampf*.[65] In part this was attributable to his organizational ruthlessness, his campaigning skill, and his undeniable charisma. These qualities were independent of the message he preached and could, under slightly different conditions, have been used in the service of other causes. But in the context of the 1880s, when he embarked on his political career and first formulated his ambitions, antisemitism was the most useful formula for rallying lower middle-class discontent. This device divided the Democrats, and those among them who were either Jews (like Ignaz Mandl) or opposed to antisemitism (like Ferdinand Kronawetter) found themselves obliged to seek refuge with the Liberals. He also succeeded in detaching enough German Nationalists from Schönerer to broaden the basis of his following. Sufficiently Catholic by the end of the 1880s to be acceptable to the parish clergy and the social theorists around Vogelsang and Schindler, sufficiently "nonclerical" to be acceptable to a crucial section of public servants and professionals, he was careful to advance under such banners as the "United Christians" and "Antisemites." When the results of the 1891 city council elections made it clear that he needed to win over the solid citizens of the second curia, he moderated his language, stressed his Christianity rather than his Catholicism and discouraged rowdyism and hooliganism. He had, more and more, to seek refuge in high-sounding rhetoric against abstract enemies: "We do not fear freemasons and Jews, we fight for the freedoms of our Christian peoples, of our church, for German ways and customs," he told a public meeting after his election as deputy mayor. But he also felt under increasing pressure to emphasize his conservatism: "Why should I not be confirmed [as mayor]? Am I perhaps not a man who has been loyal to his emperor and his fatherland?"[66]

Of all the tendencies represented in the Reformverein of the 1880s, the Christian Socials—originally neither very numerous nor influential—became the chief beneficiaries of the discontent with the traditional political leadership of Austria. Outside Vienna and Lower Austria the Deutsche Volkspartei of Otto Steinwender increasingly absorbed the anticlerical and nationalist heritage of the once great Liberal Party, leaving it only a few strongholds in Bohemia and Moravia. The Deutsche Volkspartei, too, demanded "liberation from the harmful influences of Jewry,"[67] so that in the last two imperial parliaments elected under the old franchise the majority of deputies owed their seats to parties that were at least nominally committed to antisemitism. This was all the more true since in 1897 Schönerer returned to the Reichsrat—not, this time, as the tribune of the peasantry of Lower Austria but for a rural constituency in Northern Bohemia. That would have been an event of minor importance, had the Badeni government not presented him with the issue that came close to destroying the Habsburg Monarchy: a decree that placed the German and Czech languages on an equal footing for all official business in Bohemia. Expelled from Vienna and the Alpine crownlands by Lueger and by his own intransigence, he found a new constituency in the German-Slav borderlands. His program for the 1901 Reichsrat election called for the "destruction of the three internationals: international Jewry, international Catholicism, and the international house of Habsburg" and liberation from "every foreign influence—Jewish and Roman."[68] Schönerer's antisemitism had in no way abated, nor had that of the student corporations for whom he was once more a hero. But what gained him his votes was his stand against equal rights for the Czechs, and what gave his movement momentum was the "Break with Rome" initiative, launched in 1899 to persuade German-Austrians to convert to Protestantism.

What had happened in the 1890s was that antisemitism had become an integral part of the political attitudes of a large section—probably the majority— of German-Austrians. For a few it was an obsession, for others it gave coherence to what would otherwise have been a set of impracticable and contradictory demands, for others still a subordinate component of their economic resentments and political aspirations. Only the Social Democrats and what remained of Austrian Liberalism opposed antisemitism in principle, and even among them this opposition was sometimes honored more in the breach than in the observance. Antisemitic rhetoric operated at many levels. It was not always meant literally; Austrian public life had a strong theatrical element and Lueger was as likely to be admired for the skill of his performance as for the strict content of his words. Nor did the conquest of city hall by an antisemitic coalition necessarily disturb the normal professional and commercial relationships between Jews and non-Jews that were common enough in Vienna by the end of the nineteenth century. The policies of the new municipality were opportunistic—almost frivolously so. It sent a wreath for the funeral of the president of the Jewish community, Gustav Simon, in 1897. But it also bestowed its highest award, the Salvator Medal, on the antisemitic Father Joseph Deckert; it employed few Jews and discriminated in handing out contracts. When the Austrian government resolved not to confirm Lueger's election, he ordered a boycott of Jewish shops, which was apparently quite effective. In the heated atmosphere of the repeated city council elections acts of violence against individual Jews increased. Jewish merchants, fearing for their lives and property, desisted from moving their businesses to Budapest only when assured by the emperor that he would protect all his subjects impartially.

In the end Jews survived the political takeover both physically and economically. That takeover was nevertheless a symbol and a trauma. It signaled the end of an era of relative tolerance, of relative enlightenment, and of a narrowing of the distance between Jew and Gentile. Lueger's followers stood for provincialism, narrow-mindedness, and philistinism. They despised the cosmopolitan high culture that the educated Jewish middle class identified with. Antisemitism continued as part of the Christian Social Party's public rhetoric, even though it had lost much of its function as a weapon against a now irretrievably defeated Liberalism. The never ceasing calumnies and vulgarities uttered in parliament, the provincial diets, the city council, and the press may have been intended as little more than a safety valve or morale booster for party activists, but their effect was to poison the political atmosphere and to turn the articulation of hatred into a daily routine. Antisemitism became inseparable from Viennese public life. Some Jews adjusted stoically to the new circumstances, others engaged in apocalyptic visions. In June 1895 Theodor Herzl, then in Paris, received visitors from Vienna: "They moaned softly about antisemitism. . . . The husband awaits a new St. Bartholomew's Night. The wife believes conditions could hardly get any worse." He contrasted this with his life as a Jew in Paris, even as the Dreyfus Affair was moving to a climax: "In Austria or Germany I constantly had to fear that someone would call out 'hep hep!' after me. But here I pass through the crowd unrecognized."[69]

8. Jews and Slavs

It was only in German-speaking Austria that parties with explicit antisemitic programs arose on any scale; only in German-Austrian politics that antisemitism became an issue between parties. That does not, however, mean—as we have already seen—that this phenomenon was absent among other nationalities. In Hungary, after the flare-up occasioned by the Tisza-Eszlár ritual murder accusation, peace was restored between Magyars and Jews, largely thanks to the exclusion of the masses from effective politics. In Bohemia and Galicia, however, after a quiescent

1880s, the Jewish community found itself once more caught in the cross
fire of ethnic and economic antagonisms. In the Czech lands, as in German
Austria, the early 1890s saw the rise of a more radical populist nationalism. The most important of the new parties were the Young Czechs, who
had formally separated from the leadership of Palacky and Rieger in 1879
and had a virtual monopoly of Czech representation by 1891. They in
turn faced competition from a number of new formations, including a
National Socialist Party, which aimed at weaning Czech workers from
"international" Social Democracy, and a Christian Social Party. It is not
surprising that in these heightened conflicts between Czech and German
nationalists, and between the more moderate and the more militant Czech
factions, hopes of a Czech-Jewish symbiosis, as first articulated in the late
1870s, became more and more chimerical.

The 1890s began badly for the Jews of the Czech crownlands with
Czech-instigated campaigns to boycott German- and Jewish-owned shops
under the slogan of "Svuj k svému" ("to each his own"). In 1892–1893
there were no fewer than three rumors of ritual murder that led to anti-
Jewish riots. The more radical followers of the Young Czech movement
were clearly not satisfied with the moves Jews had made to identify with
Czech culture. The economic gap between the two communities, though
narrowing, remained, and Jews continued to prefer German-language
education, not least in the remaining Jewish denominational schools.
Though the Young Czechs' official program stressed a commitment to
religious equality, and that of the other parties was mostly silent on the
matter, many of their publicists did not hesitate to adopt anti-Jewish positions. Only the Radical Progressives, whose founders included Tomás G.
Masaryk's later collaborators, the Hajn brothers, explicitly opposed antisemitism. In 1897 the Young Czechs adopted the antisemite Václav
Breznovsky as their candidate for the Prague constituency in the newly
established fifth (universal suffrage) curia, where he was opposed by the
equally antisemitic Josef Simon, a Christian Social priest. Most Jews
resolved the dilemma by voting for the Social Democrat who, however,
lost heavily to Breznovsky. In the diet elections of 1901 the two Jewish
incumbents for the Josefóv district of Prague were not renominated.

All these slights, however, paled into insignificance compared with two
developments that deeply traumatized Czech Jewry—the reaction to the
Badeni language ordinances and the Polná ritual murder trial of 1899. The
failure of Badeni's reforms, which resulted in his resignation, led to serious Czech rioting, beginning in Prague and spreading to the rest of

Bohemia and Moravia. German and Jewish properties were attacked and several synagogues vandalized. The Polná trial, in which Leopold Hilsner, an itinerant cobbler of low intelligence, was accused of the murder of Anezka Hruzová, a nineteen-year-old seamstress, was even more critical for Czech-Jewish relations. As at Tisza-Eszlár, antisemitic politicians saw their opportunity. Karel Baxa, now a Progressive Party member of the Bohemian diet, became counsel for the Hruza family and insinuated that the motive was ritual. Hilsner was found guilty and sentenced to death, but a retrial was ordered, largely thanks to the intervention of Masaryk, at that time professor of philosophy at Prague, whose pamphlet, denouncing the ritual murder superstition,[70] provoked student disturbances at his lectures. The retrial confirmed the previous verdict, but the sentence was commuted and Hilsner was pardoned by Emperor Charles I in 1918. In 1969, shortly before his death, Jan Hruza confessed to the murder of his sister Anezka.

In Galicia, where the bulk of Habsburg Jews lived, social and economic tensions between them and the neighboring Polish and Ruthenian population were traditional, but overtly political antagonism played a smaller role. There were parallels and differences in the relations between Jews and the local aristocracy in Hungary and Galicia. In both areas Jews had abandoned their instinctive identification with German culture and transferred their allegiance to the locally dominant nationality. In contrast with Hungary the Polish nobility in Galicia were able to secure their position without the aid of a Jewish middle class and therefore owed their Jews less of an obligation. Though in the main free from the cruder forms of antisemitism themselves, they had less of an incentive to curb it when organizations advocating it did appear. The most important of these was the National Democratic Party (Endecja) of Roman Dmowski, whose strongly nationalist and increasingly antisemitic agitation was concentrated in Congress Poland, that is, the part of Poland under Russian rule. In Galicia the new politics was dominated by rival peasant parties; indeed the bloody disturbances of 1898 are attributable partly to the divisions between them. Victory eventually went to the more moderate and less antisemitic Polish Peasant Party of Jan Stapinski, but it was not itself free of the suspicion that Jews were disloyal in the national question. Its 1903 program advocated an independent Poland, with full equality for assimilated Jews, but recommended emigration to Palestine for "those who regard themselves as foreign to the [Polish] community, tending usually toward German culture."[71]

Antisemitism among the Slav peoples of Central Europe operated on three levels. It was directed against Jews as the real or alleged allies of the dominant ethnic group, whether the Germans in the lands of the Bohemian crown and Posen or the Russians in Congress Poland. It was directed against Jews as the real or alleged allies of the economically dominant group, which in Galicia meant the Polish landowning class. It was also a weapon in the intensifying competition between the newly emergent parties for the newly enfranchised electorate. Nothing was easier than to accuse a party that was insufficiently militant on nationalist issues of being in the pay of the Jews—a charge that could be directed on the one hand against the more conservative Polish aristocrats, on the other against the internationalist Social Democrats. The identification of the Jews with the enemy of the moment became an almost automatic reflex for the more extreme Czech nationalists. Most of the Czech press sided against Dreyfus because they saw the campaign for reopening his case as a German plot to discredit France. They opposed Masaryk's intervention in the Hilsner case because, in the words that were chalked on Masaryk's blackboard, "He wants to divide the whole nation for the sake of a Jew. . . . He plays into the hands of the aggressive Germans!"[72] Reality was more complicated. The German-language antisemitic press could not resist the temptation to side with the ritual murder accusers against Masaryk; Masaryk in turn was not without Czech support, especially from the Social Democrat *Právo lidu* and student journals. The fact that it was individual politicians rather than parties that were identified with antisemitism made this a less divisive issue in Czech politics. The effect on Czech-Jewish relations was, however, more profound. The attitudes of the majority of the Czech-language press on the one hand and of Masaryk on the other brought about a decisive reorientation of Czech-Jewish relations, to be discussed in chapter 8.

9. The Domestication of Political Antisemitism

From the 1890s onward antisemitism was both a movement and an ideology. As a movement with visible popular and electoral support it reached a climax in the mid-1890s in both Germany and Austria; after the turn of the century it declined as a movement but grew in influence as an ideology.

The reasons for the parliamentary decline in Germany lay in the poor quality of the antisemitic leaders and the changing terms of electoral competition. Once the antisemites had failed to maintain their momentum in the 1898 Reichstag election, it was evident that an anti-Jewish crusade through the ballot box had little prospect of success. Not enough Germans were interested in that question above all others. Once other parties or pressure groups, such as the Conservatives or the Agrarian League, had adopted antisemitic platforms, it was no longer evident that there was a place for specifically antisemitic parties or candidates. Beginning in the late 1890s the principal domestic issues were fiscal: for or against protective tariffs, for or against inheritance taxes, for or against a graduated income tax. The principal foreign issues rested on defense and imperialism: for or against colonial expansion, for or against a navy to equal that of Britain, for or against a bigger army. On these questions the antisemitic parties had no specific contribution to make. They represented no identifiable class interest, as did the Social Democrats, nor an identifiable ecclesiastical one, as did the Center Party, nor identifiable constitutional positions, as did the Conservatives or the various Liberal parties. In the 1907 Reichstag election the number of antisemitic deputies rose to seventeen, in 1912 it dropped to six, thus confirming the decline we have already noted. These fluctuations had less and less to do with the popularity of the antisemitic cause than with the changing terms of electoral politics. While the more radical antisemites had initially advocated democratic reforms and attacked the property of the rich, the rise of the Social Democratic Party (SPD) forced a revision of such tactics. More and more Reichstag elections were dominated by the imperative of containing the SPD, so that antisemites, opposed as they were to internationalism, class war, and the participation of Jews in politics, found themselves with rare exceptions in the anti-Socialist camp. They did well in 1907 because the right as a whole did well and badly in 1912 because that year saw a victory of the left.

Equally ominously for the antisemitic movement, there were few replacements for the pioneering generation. Böckel and Ahlwardt left the Reichstag in 1903; Wilhelm Marr died in 1904, Stoecker in 1909. New recruits did not inspire confidence. A ritual murder allegation in the West Prussian town of Konitz in 1900 launched the careers of Count Pückler and Pastor Karl Krösell. But Pückler was a deranged landowner who was prosecuted at the instigation of the CV and consigned to a mental hospital. Krösell was soon to be defrocked and was banned from speaking in schools by the Prussian minister of education. Such behavior ensured that partisan antisemites returned to the margins of politics, from which they had emerged in the 1880s. That many of the antisemitic orators were objects of scorn made it easy to underestimate the impact of their message. The most successful antisemitic politicians had their base not in their party organizations but in the better funded and more coherently run economic or ideological interest groups. They will be described below.

Given the continuing success that political parties with antisemitic programs had in Austria, it might be thought that their fate would contrast with that of Germany. Yet in Austria, too, antisemitic agitation peaked in intensity in the mid-1890s. In Austria, as in Germany, the political agenda changed and antisemitism was adapted, and in many cases subordinated, to newer campaigns. With Liberalism defeated, Austrian politics after 1900 was dominated by the nationalities conflict and, following the introduction of universal male franchise in 1906, the rise of Social Democracy. The exacerbation of the German-Czech struggle revived, as we have seen, the fortunes of Georg von Schönerer and his allies. Their advocacy of the German cause was expressed in strongly pan-German and racist terms, but their followers gave priority to the German-Slav dispute over the Aryan-Semitic one. This applied even more when Schönerer's lieutenant, Karl Hermann Wolf, led the majority of Schönerer's Reichsrat deputies and voters' caucuses into a rival Free Pan-German Party, later known as Deutschradikale. Wolf's primary concern was to be the most militant advocate of German-Austrian claims in the Habsburg Monarchy, not to bring about the monarchy's destruction, which remained Schönerer's ambition. But playing practical politics in Bohemia and above all in Moravia meant angling for Jewish votes where they were needed to win an election or keep control of a school board or a chamber of commerce. Wolf's newspapers were prepared to acknowledge "the joint effort of all parties" in Bohemia-Moravia and to concede that "it would be more than folly to fight against such 'influence.' "[73] A further symptom of Schönerer's inability to hold together a mass constituency was the formation of the German Workers' Party (DAP) in 1904 by leaders of German nationalist trade unions in Bohemia. In its ideology it was a reversion to the early, socially radical days of the Austrian pan-Germans, and its founders more than once referred to the writings of Eugen Dühring as an inspiration. They were bitterly opposed to the "internationalism of an alien race" in Social Democracy, which would "exploit the German worker for the temple of Jewish world domination," and equally so to the "Black [i.e., Catholic] International." The DAP secured a modest following in Bohemia and Austrian Silesia; it is of historical interest because in 1918 it turned itself into the Deutsche Nationalsozialistische Arbeiterpartei (DNSAP), thus becoming the direct ancestor of the Nazi parties of interwar Austria and Czechoslovakia.

The "Black International"'s incursion into working-class politics had taken place earlier, in direct response to the introduction of universal suffrage. Antisemitism played a more specific role in its program, especially in defining its relationship with the mainstream Christian Social movement. The Christian Social Workers' Party, led by Leopold Kunschak (1871–1953), was founded in 1896 and was at all times an integral part of Lueger's party. Once the Christian Social Party had turned into a defender of property and the established order, Kunschak turned to antisemitism to maintain his movement's anti-capitalist credentials. Indeed, along with Catholicism, antisemitism was a necessary distinguishing feature of the Christian workers' movement. As with the DAP, with which it otherwise had little in common, antisemitism is what separated it most from the Socialist movement. Antisemitic rhetoric continued as part of the Christian Social routine long after power had been gained and secured, and it probably played a role in maintaining the morale of minor functionaries. But, insofar as Jews were now identified with an enemy, that enemy was no longer the haute bourgeoisie or the Galician peddler but the Socialist movement. The rising agitation for unqualified universal suffrage, which climaxed in 1905–1906, led to threats of pogroms on the Russian model from Lueger:

> I warn the Jews in Vienna not to go as far as their coreligionists in Russia in getting mixed up with Social Democratic revolutionaries. . . . We in Vienna are antisemites, but we are certainly not made for murder or homicide. But if the Jews threaten our fatherland, then we, too, shall know no mercy.[74]

10. Antisemitism as an Ideology

As long as antisemitism, whether in Germany or the Habsburg Monarchy, was primarily anti-Liberal in its thrust, it risked the odium of extremism and intolerance, and this reinforced the Liberal impulse to take countermeasures. As the emphasis moved toward anti-Socialism, it was easier for antisemitism to enter the patriotic consensus. The principal vehicles for it in this later stage were no longer parties and electoral campaigns but interest groups and social organizations. Some of these were exclusively and aggressively antisemitic, others "also antisemitic," but the dividing line became increasingly blurred. Specifically antisemitic ideologies became more widespread in the two decades before the outbreak of the First World War, as racial theories in general gained a following. These ideologies in turn strengthened the antisemitism of interest groups and social organizations, for such bodies were rarely purely functional or politically neutral in either of the two empires. What characterized all such bodies that preached or tolerated discrimination during our period was fear. However aggressive their rhetoric or their attitudes might be, their essential character was defensive; they were there to fend off the influence of a threatening outsider. Though the ingredients of this threat varied in time and according to the propagandist, its perceived existence was there as a permanent factor.

One central feature of this perception was cultural unease, which saw in the emancipated Jew the symptom of an undesirable modernity. That did not necessarily involve an indiscriminate rejection of all modern developments; in the course of time most antisemites accepted—even embraced—such highly modern developments as the nation-state, imperialism, and industrial capitalism. Racialism, too, based as it is on the assumption that the findings of natural science can be applied to the organization of political life, is an ultramodern phenomenon. Nevertheless, cultural unease was common to conservatives out of tune with the developments of the nineteenth century and to preachers of racial purity and imperial expansion. Indeed the imperialists frequently derived the unease from the conservatives. Common to them all was a sense of threatened values in which the cohesion of established communities was undermined by rationalism, commercialism, democratic leveling, and cosmopolitanism. Initially, as might be expected, this message was broadcast by regretful conservatives, though even at this stage it was accompanied by threats. "The Semites will specifically have to atone for their totally unjustifiable interference in all sorts of affairs," Jakob Burckhardt wrote to his friend Friedrich von Preen in 1880, adding, "Even then . . . I do not believe that the present agitation will die down."[75] A more persistent critic of the cultural decline of Germany was the Göttingen theologian and orientalist Paul Bötticher (Paul de Lagarde), a contemporary and fellow spirit of Constantin Frantz. In what was intended as a reply to the Declaration of the Notables of 1880, he argued that the power of the Jews was not only a cause of Germany's degradation but a sign of its moral fee-

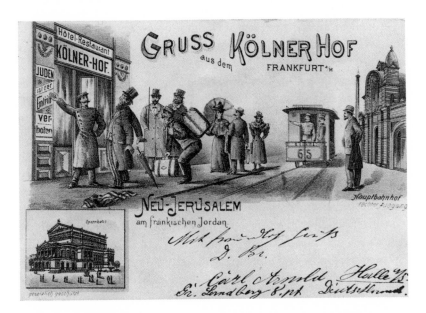

29   An antisemitic postcard used by the Kölner Hof hotel in Frankfurt
to advertise for guests around the turn of the century

bleness: "Every Jew who is objectionable to us is a severe reproach to the
genuineness and sincerity of our Germandom."[76]

As an academic, Lagarde was particularly concerned by what he saw as
the decline of standards in German education, which he attributed to its
"Judaization." This was a term he did much to popularize, though it had
actually been launched in 1850 by that other great Germanic cultural
critic, Richard Wagner, and reemphasized in Treitschke's fears about a
"German-Jewish mongrel culture."[77] Concern about the content of
German education and the status of those engaged in it was frequently
expressed in antisemitic terms. The Association of German Students, the
VDST, proclaimed its antisemitism and its general xenophobia as part of a
wider anxiety about the cultural identity of the new Germany. Its mission
was to exclude, or at least to marginalize, the position of the Jew in
German universities, and by 1902 it felt able to claim that it had achieved
"the social isolation of the Jewish student."[78] This claim was valid insofar
as all German student corporations, whether the middle-class Burschenschaften or the more aristocratic Corps, had by then decided on the
explicit or tacit exclusion of Jewish members. These bodies represented
only a minority of German students, especially in the more impersonal

metropolitan universities, such as Berlin. But their members went on to form the German administrative academic and ecclesiastical elite to a quite disproportionate extent; many of the civil servants, judges, professors, and Lutheran bishops of the Weimar Republic had been through this school. In so far as it was the intention of the VDSt to change the ideological composition of Germany's future leaders, they had a fair amount of success. Precisely because the VDSt steered clear of vulgar public agitation and violence and concentrated on converting mentalities, it was able to achieve a breakthrough where demagogues like Förster and Böckel had failed. That the educational system was the battleground for the maintenance of the cultural purity of Germany and German Austria was widely acknowledged. Even those who disavowed antisemitism, like the educationist Friedrich Paulsen, were disturbed by the presence of Jews in German academia: For "a people that only a hundred years ago was regarded as alien, and felt itself to be so, to conduct the business of the world, create public opinion, and fill colleges and universities is indeed a process that leads to abnormal conditions."[79] Equal opportunities for Jews in this field, as demanded by Liberals, would inevitably lead to "foreign domination."[80]

The same reluctance to accept Jews as fit persons to share in German culture was to be seen at the opposite end of the educational spectrum, in experimental rural boarding schools. While some of these, like Gustav Wyneken's Wickersdorf and Paul Geheeb's Odenwald school, remained true to their humanistic and democratic ideals, the founder of the boarding school movement, Hermann Lietz, turned increasingly toward *völkisch* ideas, though this did not prevent some Jewish parents from continuing to patronize his school, Haubinda. In his memoirs he recalled that "the half or entirely Semitic pupils generally showed little inclination, and even less ability, at practical work. They surpassed their fellow pupils, who often seemed dull and timid in comparison, in intellectual agility and quick-wittedness."[81] It is not clear which of these qualities was the more objectionable in Lietz's mind.

The rural schools were only one part of an increasingly widespread response to the cultural discontents of Imperial Germany, which had been expressed by figures as diverse, and in many cases mutually hostile, as Nietzsche, Wagner, and Dühring. Lagarde had been a major influence on Lietz, but by far the most effective prophet of idealistic revolt was Julius Langbehn, whose *Rembrandt als Erzieher* (Rembrandt as Educator), published anonymously in 1890, became a bestseller. It went through thirty-nine printings in its first two years and by the end of the Second World War had sold one hundred and fifty thousand copies. Langbehn, like others before him, denounced the aridity of German education, the pretensions and materialism of city life, and the destruction of the simple preindustrial community. Early editions of his work contained little about Jews, but he quickly appreciated that in his struggle against modernity Jews were an obvious obstacle and a convenient scapegoat. If "equality is death [and] hierarchy is life," then the "modern, i.e., plebeian Jews are a poison for us and will have to be treated as such. . . . They are democratically inclined, they prefer an affinity with the mob; everywhere they are in sympathy with decay."[82] It did not take him long to become associated with the German-Austrian antisemitic network. One commentator attributed the antisemitic gains in the 1893 Reichstag elections to his influence. Like many völkisch utopians he saw salvation in a superhuman hero who would lead his people to redemption: this "secret emperor," "a Caesaristic-artistic individual," would intervene in "the all-important Jewish Question . . . and separate the sheep from the goats."[83]

Langbehn's appeal was greatest among those whom he saw as his natural audience: youth. Less pedantic than Lagarde, less challenging than Nietzsche, he articulated the romantic yearnings of a discontented younger generation. The German youth movement emerged in the Berlin suburb of Steglitz in the late 1890s and was organized on a national level into the Wandervögel (Hikers) by a schoolmaster, Karl Fischer, who was directly inspired by Langbehn. As might be expected, the movement was eclectic in its beliefs. It was "nonpolitical" in the sense of being indifferent to party matters and practical policy questions, but it was certainly ideological. Hiking and camping were returns to nature, cultivation of folk songs and folk poems encouraged the revival of tradition, visits to German-speaking minorities elsewhere in Europe were acts of ethnic solidarity. All this implied a cultivation of cultural exclusiveness if not racial superiority. Some Wandervögel leaders did advocate the study of racist writers and the exclusion of Jews; some branches accepted Jewish members, while the majority made a point of excluding them. How easily the search for a communitarian ethic could lead to intolerance, however, is shown by one Wandervogel defense of discrimination: "Only those of a like mind could influence and educate one another. . . . These young people possibly had no idea what antisemites were, even if deep down they perceived that distinctive Jewish ways were totally alien to them."[84] Langbehn's slogan, "Youth against the Jews!"[85] had evoked a resonant echo.

A similar ideological ambiguity was to be found in the agricultural communes that sprang up in Germany during the same period. Their inspiration was diverse: it came from völkisch "Socialists" like Dühring and from numerous Jewish social reformers, such as Theodor Hertzka of the *Neues Wiener Tagblatt* and Franz Oppenheimer, both of whom in turn influenced Theodor Herzl, and the anarchists Gustav Landauer and Erich Mühsam. Some of the communes, like Neue Gemeinschaft in the select Berlin suburb of Schlachtensee, were left-wing in inspiration; its interdenominationalism reflected the ecumenism of the Berlin bohemian scene. Rather more typical of the commune movement was the Obstbau-Kolonie Eden north of Berlin. It was dedicated to organic agriculture, vegetarianism, homespun clothes, and abstention from alcohol and tobacco. Franz Oppenheimer was coauthor of its constitution and as late as 1920 he praised it as "an oasis in the midst of the capitalist desert."[86] But völkisch ideas gained ground and it increasingly emphasized its Aryan basis with the observance of Germanic customs and festivals. This trend was even more marked in communes founded by Eden members after 1918. One of these was Donnershag, whose applicants had to declare on oath that they were "free of Jewish or colored blood";[87] its journal, *Neues Leben*, was decorated with the swastika. It was only after the First World War that youth groups, rural schools, and communes with a specifically "Aryan" basis became common, but their ideological roots lay in the years before 1914. What is significant with regard to these formative years is that the "Jewish Question" was raised at all and that it was indeed central to the efforts of Haubinda, the Wandervögel, and Eden at working out their identities.

11. Race in Doctrine and Organization

The student corporations, the schools, the communes, and the youth groups were central to German intellectual history, though—with the exception of the student groups—they were fairly marginal to German society. But the same debate took place in the much larger professional and producers' interest organizations, which began proliferating in the Germany of the 1890s and few of which could avoid ideological commitments or disputes. Three are of particular interest for our purposes: the Agrarian League (Bund der Landwirte, BDL), the artisan and small business organizations, and the shop employees' trade union, the Deutschnationaler Handlungsgehilfen-Verband (DHV). In both the BDL and the

DHV hostility toward Jews played a central role. Both were founded in 1893 at a time when not only antisemitism but the drive to create mass membership political and economic organizations were at their height. Of the two the BdL fitted more clearly into the revolt against Chancellor Caprivi's liberal policy trend. Since the BdL was at all times primarily a lobby, it naturally sought and secured allies outside the Conservative Party, with which its ties were closest, for instance among the right wing of the National Liberals or the Center and among those party antisemites who abstained from anti-Junker demagogy. Membership of the BdL was from the start restricted to "adherents of a Christian faith,"[88] a condition that cannot be explained purely in terms of its interest-articulating function. Its antiurban bias, its antagonism toward democracy and Socialism, and its sense of social exclusiveness led quite automatically to antisemitism: "It is really in the nature of things that agriculture and Jewry have to engage in a life or death struggle until one of the combatants lies lifeless, or at least powerless, on the ground."[89] But as its apparatus grew and it acquired a predominantly middle-class and intellectual staff, a more radical and racist tone entered its propaganda. The BdL's chief publicist, Diederich Hahn, had been one of the founders of the Association of German Students.

The more radical and racist tone was there from the start in the DHV. Unlike the BdL, its founders lacked a base of traditional interest and established notables. The white-collar employees in the private sector were, at the end of the nineteenth century, a new stratum that Liberals and Social Democrats were beginning to unionize with some success. The DHV was therefore created from above and outside, with a specific ideological motivation. It was the creation of antisemitic politicians looking for a mass base. Whereas the BdL's antisemitism had been directed against finance and free-trading Liberals, that of the DHV was directed against the Social Democrats. The statutes of the union declared its purpose: "to fend off the penetration of Social Democracy into the commercial estate." The provision excluding Jews was strengthened in 1909 to exclude "Jews and members of other nations and races that adopt conscious antagonism toward Germandom."[90] The centrality of ideology in the union was shown by a change in its name from "German" to "German National" in 1895. Most of its officials were activists or legislators of antisemitic parties. The success of the DHV as a union made it a major force in antisemitic politics. By 1910 it had seventy-five thousand members, outstripping its Liberal, Social Democratic, and nonparty competitors. In accordance with its pan-

German ideology its organization spread to Austria, where it also became the biggest union of its kind.

Neither the BdL nor the DHV had a monopoly on representing the interests it claimed to speak for. A more heterogeneous stratum whose members were much more severely cross-pressured were the self-employed among artisans, shopkeepers, and the owners of small businesses generally. Conventionally considered the natural constituency of antisemites and the radical right—a role that they largely fulfilled in Austria—they were not so easily penetrated in Germany. Artisans and retailers did not necessarily have common interests; in their policy preferences they were divided into the advocates of self-help and state protection. The individualistic nature of their callings meant that their fragmented defense organizations defied all attempts at unification. Early antisemites made a point of appealing to the *Mittelstand*, the "estate" of small business. The first antisemitic speeches at congresses of the German General Association of Artisans were heard in 1892, eleven years after its foundation, when Stoecker addressed the delegates. A renewed attempt to mobilize artisans and retailers for the right came in 1909 in Saxony under the leadership of Theodor Fritsch. Out of this grew the Reichsdeutsche Mittelstandsvereinigung (RDMV), dedicated to fighting those twin enemies, "the one . . . the golden, the other the red international"[91] and "the subversive activities of an un-German people," in the form of the department stores.[92] After the turn of the century, as questions of graduated taxation and tariffs became central to domestic politics, Mittelstand organizations were more divided than ever, and some of them briefly favored collaboration with the Liberal-inclined pro-free trade Hansa-Bund. One factor that affected Mittelstand politics less than might have been expected was the relatively large number of Jewish tradesmen. At least one Jew, Hugo Lissauer, was an active organizer of retailers. His union of persons engaged in commerce and trades, concentrated in Berlin, was highly effective, with seventy-four hundred members in the capital.

In contrast with Austria German antisemites were never able to build a secure social base rooted in interest organizations. They were able to hold Liberalism in check, but not, as in the Habsburg realms, to virtually destroy it. The BdL and the DHV were two among many pressure groups. They won some battles and they lost some. At no stage could they seriously threaten the constitutional rights of Jews. What they could achieve was to keep the "Jewish Question" on the public agenda, to remind a population well beyond their own immediate membership that, whatever the law might say, Jews were not really Germans and to remind their Jewish fellow citizens that they might enter general society, but not without knocking. The same undertone questioning the Jew's claim to membership in the German nation occurred in the intellectual debates of the early twentieth century.

12. Prophets of Race

That most of the organizations we have met were not content with the defense of material interests but embraced nationalist and even racist ideologies, and at times gave priority to them, reveals much about Central European politics in this period. The growing interest in theories of evolution and heredity and in ethnography and anthropology gave rise to numerous attempts to explain history and politics in terms of biology. Theories of racial distinctiveness, with an increasing emphasis on an unalterable hierarchy of higher and lower races, were widespread in Britain, France, and the United States. But it is only in Germany and Austria that they became politically significant. In Austria that can be attributed without much difficulty to the increasingly intense battle between nationalities. Schönerer and the more extreme student fraternities had embraced racialism as early as the 1880s. In Germany it arose out of a more complicated set of insecurities about identity and geopolitics. Strategically vulnerable in the center of Europe, only recently and imperfectly unified and culturally still fragmented, the German Empire lacked the kind of consensual identification with the national territory and national past that could be taken for granted in established nation-states like France, Britain, or Sweden.

Some of the prophets of the new nationalism preached the need for an intense cultural homogeneity and conformity, others an inexorable law of racial segregation, but the line between them was often hard to draw, if only because of their predilection for cloudy language. Paul de Lagarde is as good an illustration as any of this definitional difficulty: like Langbehn he was more concerned with culture than biology and at an early stage he declared that Germandom was based "not on blood, but on the spirit."[93] But how far Jews could be admitted to this spirit was something he could never quite decide. Some Jews, he agreed, had successfully "amalgamated" with the German people "because the hosts made no secret of the fact that it was they who were giving and elevating."[94] This formulation, which enabled the exceptional Jew to escape the collective inferiority into which he had been born, was especially useful to the members of the Bayreuth circle, who needed to explain the phenomenon of Hermann Levi, the rabbi's son who had conducted the first performance of *Parsifal*. According to Wagner's son-in-law, Houston Stewart Chamberlain, Levi's intellectual capacity made possible "so intimate a contact with us Teutons, that we could count him as one of our own. . . . Levi's religion was an upward gaze toward German culture."[95] At other times both Lagarde and Langbehn used the kind of bacteriological discourse that suggested an irreconcileable gulf between races. "One does not negotiate with trichinae and bacilli. . . . They are crushed as quickly and as thoroughly as possible," Lagarde wrote of "this rampant vermin,"[96] while for Langbehn Jews were merely "a passing plague and cholera."[97] On the other hand, those for whom race was the key to the understanding of human affairs did not necessarily give the greatest priority to the denigration of Jews. Count Arthur de Gobineau's *Essai sur l'Inégalité des Races* (Essay on the Inequality of the Races) had little to say about Jews and that little was mainly complimentary. His ideas were popularized in Germany by Ludwig Schemann's translation and the Gobineau-Vereinigung that he founded in 1894. Jews were not excluded from membership, though only those belonging to the "excellent minority" applied to join, so that Schemann's experience of them was "highly favorable."[98]

The appeal of racial and völkisch ideas lay in the emotional cement that they provided. An antirace or a selection of antiraces offers additional reassurance of national unity, and Jews were conveniently available for this purpose. But quite often antisemitism was also a subordinate means to another end: the general assertion of a German or Aryan superiority. Friedrich Lange's Deutschbund, founded in the same year as the Gobineau-Vereinigung, aimed at creating a warriorlike master race (*Herrenvolk*), with the proviso that "antisemitism [can be] only one element and *by no means the most important* of a Weltanschauung that extends far wider and higher."[99]

No book expressed the mood and taste of the times better, and had a greater immediate impact on the political and educated public, than Houston Stewart Chamberlain's *The Foundations of the Nineteenth Century*, which appeared in 1899. Like Schemann, Chamberlain (1855–1927) had been introduced to Gobineau by the Wagners; like many others, he learned his antisemitism in Bayreuth. The key to understanding human civilization, he concluded, lay in race: "The whole of living nature shows us the fact of race as the foundation of all exceptional achievements

[and] of all the noblest cultural attainments," he told the emperor.[100] The positive component of his message concerned Germanic superiority. Some anthropologists had claimed that all races were equally gifted: "We have pointed at the book of history and answered: you are lying! . . . The Germanic peoples belong to that group of the most gifted that are commonly called Aryans."[101] Jews are inferior, but thanks to their remaining strengths, also a danger:

> One cannot understand Jewry and its power, as well as its indestructible tenacity . . . as long as one has not registered the demonic genius of its origins. It really is a case here of a struggle of One against All; the One has accepted every sacrifice, every disgrace in order one day, never mind when, to bring on the Messianic Empire in which it will wield sole power for the glory of Jahweh.[102]

Chamberlain offered no practical solution to this menace. Nevertheless, he became a public figure, unlike many of his contemporaries who went on muttering into their sectarian corners. By 1915 *The Foundations* had sold over one hundred thousand copies; its enthusiastic readers included William II. It became a classic völkisch text long before the Nazis officially elevated it to that status.

Though *The Foundations* was directed at a German audience, it was written in Vienna, where Chamberlain spent most of the 1890s. Vienna was not only dominated at this time by the antisemitic politics of Lueger and Schönerer and by the German-Czech language disputes, it was also the home of some of the most extreme of racial theories, associated with the names of Guido von List and Adolf Josef Lanz (who adopted the name of Jörg Lanz von Liebenfels). Although both were primarily literary figures, they had links with the world of politics. Both drew on apparently incompatible sources of inspiration: an interest in the occult and gnosticism (i.e., the existence of secret writings imparting universal knowledge) and the severely positivistic monism of the biologist Ernst Haeckel, who derived his doctrines of racial purity from his reading of Darwin. List's concern was with the origins of the Aryan race, which he sought to find in archaeology, place names, and above all symbols, including runes and various versions of the swastika. Even more removed from the world of reality was the ex-Cistercian novice Lanz, whose journal *Ostara* publicized his doctrine of theozoology. Influenced, like List, by both occultism and Haeckel, he painted a Manichaean world in which the forces of good and evil were represented by race types: "the blond heroic man, the beautiful, moral, aristocratic, idealistic and religious man of genius, the creator and preserver of all scholarship, art, and culture," as proclaimed on the title page of *Ostara*, and the "Sodom-apelings."[103] Lanz claimed a circulation of one hundred thousand for *Ostara*, which seems greatly exaggerated, but it is probable that Hitler was a reader, at least for as long as he lived in Vienna.

Even more than Chamberlain, List and Lanz would have counted for little had they not collected influential friends. The fifty founding members of the Guido von List Society included Lueger, numerous officials of German antisemitic parties and the DHV, as well as members of the Bayreuth circle, including Wagner's biographer, Conrad Friedrich Glasenapp. It is evident that these doctrines—and one can easily add to the list of their propagators—not only reflected the temper of the times but filled a political need. The ideologues and the political pressure groups of Wilhelminian Germany and late Imperial Austria complemented each other. In the Germany and Austria of that time (and of later periods too) interest and Weltanschauung were inseparable. The völkisch authors needed the lobbies to propagate their doctrines; the lobbies welcomed the doctrines as a way of recruiting and enthusing their members.

The most important lobby in this category, the Pan-German League (ADV), founded in 1893, pursued mainly foreign policy objectives, such as the promotion of imperialism and the defense of German-language interests in the Habsburg Monarchy. Jews were not excluded from membership until 1919, though some branches, including that of Berlin, did impose restrictions from the outset. But the tone and purpose of the league was compatible with antisemitism. Most antisemitic Reichstag deputies belonged to it, as did officials of the DHV. Its first chairman was Ernst Hasse, who, though supporting the liberal membership rules, also accepted the arguments of the racial thinkers of the time. "Our future lies in the blood!"[104] he proclaimed. Since even German-born Jews had retained their moral and spiritual qualities, Germanization was shown to be an impossibility.[105] It was under its second chairman, Heinrich Class, that the ADV took a decisive turn toward racialism. Class had been a member of the VDST, had come under the influence of Treitschke, and had campaigned for Böckel while a student at Giessen. He was the (originally pseudonymous) author of a book that came second only to Chamberlain's in its sales and public impact. *Wenn ich der Kaiser wär'* (If I Were the Emperor), published in 1912, was less speculative and more directly political than *The Foundations*. It not only demanded the revocation of emancipation but advocated the suspension of universal suffrage and the (limited) powers of the Reichstag as well. On the "Jewish Question" there was none of Chamberlain's ambivalence: Germany could be regenerated only "if Jewish influence is either excluded completely or driven back to an extent that makes it safe and tolerable."[106] The next year a prominent member of the ADV, General Konstantin von Gebsattel, sent a memorandum to the crown prince, who in turn passed it on to the emperor and to Chancellor Theobald von Bethmann-Hollweg, which, if anything, went further than Class's book, demanding that the constitution be suspended and that Jews be taxed at twice the rate of "Teutons."[107]

One factor drawing the ADV further in the direction of racism and antisemitism was its link with Austrian pan-Germans, but the ADV was only one of many organizations in which Austrian branches exercised a radicalizing influence. We have already seen that it was Austrian Burschenschaften that took the lead in excluding Jews. German organizations that sought to further German-speaking or Protestant interests elsewhere in Europe, such as the Allgemeiner Deutscher Schulverein (General German Schools Association) and the Gustav-Adolf-Verein, certainly tolerated antisemites in their midst, if only because their members included veterans of the VDSt, and there was a considerable overlap with more extreme bodies. The militantly Protestant Gustav-Adolf-Verein, for instance, subsidized Schönerer's Break with Rome enterprise. But in their official statements these bodies generally observed studied neutrality.

In Austria, by contrast, the "Jewish Question" divided the Deutscher Schulverein almost from the start. Jews were, as we have seen, among the most ardent supporters of German-language education in mixed-language areas and Jewish schools benefited from Schulverein subsidies. While Schönerer's attempt to found a racially pure Schulverein für Deutsche was unsuccessful, the main Schulverein was unable to resist the antisemitic tide and in 1899 it permitted individual branches to draw up their own membership rules and more than one branch to exist in one locality. In Germany the Schulverein managed to avoid decisions on this matter. There were similar pressures in the Deutsche Turnerschaft of 1861, the gymnasts' body that continued as a single organization even after the end of the German Confederation. When some Austrian branches excluded Jews from membership in 1887, the national parent body expelled them from the regional group (Kreis 15); however, by 1901 Kreis 15 was able to disaffiliate all its Jewish branches and Jewish members, who now formed their own Kreis. In 1904 Kreis 15 left the gymnastic society altogether, having offended the German parent body, which, like the ADV, preferred organizational unity to racial purity.

It is evident that between 1890 and 1914 the emphasis in antisemitic discourse changed. Electoral antisemitism climaxed in the 1890s. Thereafter it declined in Germany to negligible proportions by 1912 and even in Austria the Christian Social Party's losses in the 1911 Reichsrat election showed that its drawing power was not what it had been. After the turn of the century the emphasis shifted from economic reform to race, world power, cultural regeneration, an international struggle for survival, and a battle against the enemies of the German people—Slavs, Latins, international Socialism, and the Catholic Church. The new constituency of ideological antisemitism was the professional, intellectual, and white-collar middle class, with substantial support from the military and the landed upper class. Antisemitism had a secure place in this new Germanic ideology, though with differing degrees of emphasis, ranging from Ernst Hasse's doubts about the Jews' ability to assimilate to Lanz von Liebenfels's genocidal rantings. But all variants of this ideology were authoritarian, dogmatic, exclusive, and antipluralist. They were, consciously and explicitly, the antithesis of nineteenth-century Liberalism, that set of beliefs in which Jews had placed their hopes for real, not just legal, emancipation and through which two generations of Gentile Liberals had, in the words of the Declaration of the Notables, aimed at "the reconciliation of all differences that continue to operate within the German nation."[108] In the years before the First World War the taboo had been removed from antisemitism as an attitude, even if it still applied to street demagogy. To be a pan-German, a nationalist, an imperialist, or an opponent of democracy implied being an antisemite. Conversely, to be a committed Liberal or Socialist, an advocate of democracy, or at least no opponent of democratization, meant recognizing antisemitism as a weapon of the enemy that "has set our entire culture back by a hundred years," as Theodor Mommsen told Hermann Bahr.[109] Antisemitism had become, in the words of one modern historian, a "cultural code,"[110] rather more so in Austria than in Germany.

As antisemitism lost broad political appeal, though gaining in intellectual acceptance, its advocates became more desperate and more conspiratorial. This applied in particular after the electoral victories of the parties of the left in the Reichstag elections of January 1912. The immediate reaction to this was the formation of the initially secret League Against

Jewish Arrogance. The key figure in this development was Theodor Fritsch, whose Hammer-Gemeinden, based on his journal *Der Hammer*, became the Reichshammerbund in 1912. The League Against Jewish Arrogance overlapped with other "orders" also founded by Fritsch, the Guido von List Society and the established radical right, such as the Pan-German League and the DHV. In 1914 Alfred Roth of the DHV became president of the Reichshammerbund. In the context of 1914 these groups' self-importance seemed matched only by their insignificance. A year after their formation they numbered no more than a few hundred members. But their leading men, like those of the German Workers' Party in Austria, were not all negligible. They formed a direct link with post-1918 National Socialism and the Third Reich. Their organizations were weak, but the mentalities that they transmitted endured and ultimately triumphed.

8 | The Response to Antisemitism

1. The Counterattack

With organized antisemitism reaching its peak in the 1890s, Jews and their well-wishers at last overcame their reluctance to take coordinated action against both the advocacy and the practice of discrimination. The psychological obstacles to such a step were considerable. It was important for the defenders of emancipation to believe that they were swimming with the tide of history, away from an age of prejudice toward an age of reason. They were therefore at all times tempted to play down any evidence to the contrary, as their predecessors had done in the face of the anti-Jewish propaganda after the Napoleonic wars or the anti-Jewish violence in the early phases of the 1848 revolutions. As late as 1892, at the time of the Xanten ritual murder trial and only a few months before the election of Ahlwardt and the Conservatives' Tivoli conference, the *Allgemeine Zeitung des Judentums* (AZJ) reaffirmed, "In spite of everything we put our trust in humanity's spirit of progress. Our optimism is as indestructible as our religious existence."[1]

By the early 1890s that was ceasing to be a representative view. There were, however, good reasons why Jewish organizations had been discouraged from engaging in public action against rising antisemitism. One was the indifference of the authorities. As early as the 1870s the association of Jewish communities, the Deutsch-Israelitischer Gemeindebund (DIGB) had experienced these frustrations. Its revised statutes of 1877 specified "all common matters in relation to the legal and social situation of those professing the Jewish religion, and defense against attacks on these"[2] as the DIGB's task. Of the prosecutions it instituted, only one was successful, that against the Paderborn Domvikar Schröder, author of an antitalmudic tract, who was sentenced to three months' imprisonment. It may be that at the height of the Kulturkampf the courts were more inclined to convict a Catholic offender. All later litigation by the DIGB was of no avail; even Wilhelm Marr's monthly *Deutsche Wacht* was not prosecuted, since it did not attack the Jews as a religious community. In addition to its legal activities the DIGB also subsidized and distributed "defense literature," including Franz Delitzsch's refutation of the ritual murder accusation and Josef Schrattenholz's *Antisemiten-Hammer*. But all attempts to organize systematic resistance to antisemitism at this stage failed for lack of support. In many ways it was easier for the younger generation to recognize that the ideological wind had changed direction. Max Weber, a student at Berlin University in the early 1880s, noted with disapproval the "frenetic cheers" that Treitschke's remarks received during lectures as well as the antisemitic graffiti "of varying degrees of coarseness."[3] Jewish students, who were in the front line against the new militant antisemitism, were even better placed to gauge the new atmosphere. In their 1886 manifesto the founders of the Viadrina fraternity at Breslau warned,

> The young people at the universities are looked upon as the leaders of the nation who will influence the life of the nation to a very great extent. . . . If that is so, no end to this movement can be foreseen. Racial hatred will become a tradition and will increase from one generation to the next. The tension accumulated in this way may one day explode over our heads with elemental force.[4]

In the 1880s these were isolated voices. By the early 1890s not only had the situation changed but so had the personnel. A new generation of Jewish activists and Gentile politicians took up an altogether more combative stance. The first public initiative was taken by a number of Gentile notables. At the end of 1890, following the antisemitic successes in the Reichstag election, the Left Liberal politician Heinrich Rickert published an article in Theodor Barth's *Die Nation*, calling for a counterattack "against this agitation that offends against the constitution and culture."[5] It was the first significant public utterance that implied Germans, whether Gentile or Jewish, could no longer rely on the passage of time and the progress of civilization for an end to prejudice and discrimination. Rickert's article was followed by an appeal signed by some five hundred

The Response to Antisemitism

Gentile notables, drawn from business, politics, the professions, and academia and by the formation, in March 1891, of the League to Combat Antisemitism (Verein zur Abwehr des Antisemitismus, better known as the Abwehr-Verein). Every effort was made to present the new organization as a Christian one, in order to demonstrate that opposition to antisemitism was a general German interest, not merely a specifically Jewish one, and because of the residual Jewish preference for seeking Gentile patrons to lend respectability to their cause. In fact Jews were quite heavily involved in the formation of the Abwehr-Verein, including Paul Nathan (1857–1927), the deputy editor of *Die Nation*, and above all the Frankfurt banker Charles Hallgarten (1838–1908), who was not only a major fund-raiser for it but a tireless publicist of its work within the Jewish community. The result was that from an early stage a sizeable proportion of the Verein's membership was Jewish and the greater part of its income came from Jewish sources.

The Abwehr-Verein engaged in three main activities. The first was publicity, contained above all in its weekly (and, from 1911 onward, biweekly) journal, the *Mitteilungen aus dem Verein zur Abwehr des Antisemitismus*, and its reference work, the *Antisemiten-Spiegel*. The *Mitteilungen* covered the activities (and misdemeanors) of all prominent antisemitic politicians and journalists, refutations of their accusations, and informative articles about Jewish life and religion. The *Mitteilungen* did not reach a broad public but served as a guide and a source of moral support to those on whom the Verein depended for carrying on its battles. The second activity consisted of encouraging interventions in the Reichstag and in state parliaments to protest not only against antisemitic agitation but against discriminatory practices in the public services. The third, which in the course of time became the most important, was electoral intervention, designed to prevent any antisemitic candidate, whether to the Reichstag, a state parliament, or a municipality, from gaining election and to urge voters to support whoever was the antisemite's best-placed opponent.

The style of the Abwehr-Verein's work, and the priorities it set itself, illustrated its strength as well as its limitations. It spoke with the voice of Liberal Germany. It was Protestant, middle-class, and patriotic. Its starting point was the defense of equal rights for all citizens; it saw the antisemitic assault on this principle as not merely a specific evil but a threat to Liberal institutions and Liberal values generally. For Theodor Barth, president from 1903 to 1909, "the political maturity of a people" was signified "by the zeal with which it reacts to infractions of equality before the law."[6]

That meant, however, that it adhered to the Liberal orthodoxy of the full acculturation of German Jews, as it had been preached from the beginning of the Enlightenment to the foundation of the German Empire by Christian Wilhelm Dohm, Wilhelm von Humboldt, and Theodor Mommsen. Thus the Abwehr-Verein rejected not merely the incipient Zionist movement but any other symptoms of "separatism," such as Jewish student corporations. The general thrust of its philosophy was non-pluralistic and hostile to a continuing Jewish identity within German society. The commitment to Liberalism also determined the party affiliation of the Abwehr-Verein's leadership. The names of those who signed Rickert's manifesto included many of those who had signed the Declaration of the Notables ten years earlier, including Theodor Mommsen himself. This indicated the obvious link with the Left Liberal parties and, to a lesser extent, the left wing of the National Liberal Party. The first president of the Abwehr-Verein was the celebrated constitutional lawyer Rudolf von Gneist, a National Liberal; on his death in 1895 he was succeeded by the Left Liberal Heinrich Rickert, with the National Liberal Georg Winter as his deputy. In 1903 Theodor Barth, the editor of *Die Nation* became president and in 1909 George Gothein. Rickert and Barth both belonged to the Freisinnige Vereinigung, one of the parties into which the Deutsch-Freisinnige Partei had split in 1893. Gothein came from the more radical Freisinnige Volkspartei and joined the Fortschrittliche Volkspartei when the forces of Left Liberalism merged again in 1910. Unlike his predecessors, Gothein was of Jewish descent, a fact that he preferred to keep quiet. Though nominally nonpartisan in its constitution, the Abwehr-Verein initially saw political possibilities only in collaboration with the various Liberal parties and rejected any collaboration with either Social Democracy or the Center Party. This was to cause difficulties after the turn of the century, as will be seen later in this chapter.

Much as the foundation of the Abwehr-Verein was welcomed by German Jews it was evident that it could not act as a representative of specific Jewish interests. Yet the need for such representation became more, not less, evident at precisely the time that the Abwehr-Verein began its activities. The intensity of antisemitic activity continued to increase. The ritual murder accusation against a Jewish butcher in Xanten in 1891, in the Catholic Rhineland, though resulting in an acquittal, emphasized how much under siege a nominally emancipated minority could be. Nor did the political strategy adopted by the Abwehr-Verein seem all that promising. The split in the Deutsch-Freisinnige Partei, though on an issue that had nothing to do with Jewish matters, and the losses suffered by the two successor parties in the 1893 Reichstag election further weakened the public support that the cause of civil rights might expect. When the increasingly disillusioned Ludwig Bamberger retired from active politics in that year, there were no further unbaptized Jews in the delegations of any of the Liberal parties either in the Reichstag or in the Prussian parliament. This became a matter of growing concern among the newly emerging Jewish political leadership.

Another factor that encouraged a new Jewish activism was a gradual change in the style of German politics. The Abwehr-Verein, with its appeal to reason and its reliance on distinguished notables, represented an older, predemocratic approach. But from the beginning of the 1890s mass politics, based on interest groups and parties with large-scale memberships, became more and more the rule. On the left this applied to the Social Democratic Party, the membership of which escalated once the anti-Socialist laws lapsed in 1890, reaching over one million in 1914. It was, however, on the right that these organizations proliferated most conspicuously. Both the Agrarian League and the DHV achieved six-figure memberships within twenty years of their foundation. It was not merely the anti-Liberal populism of these groupings that posed a challenge to German Jews but the development in the form of political activity that they represented. To compete effectively in the politics of influence it became increasingly necessary to have the backbone of a mass membership, a professionally edited press, and a properly funded head office staff.

It was this need that the Centralverein deutscher Staatsbürger jüdischen Glaubens (Central Association of German Citizens of the Jewish Faith, CV) aimed to meet at its first public appearance on March 26, 1893. Like all such bodies, it had a prehistory of trial and error. The first attempt at Jewish self-organization came from two prominent members of the Abwehr-Verein, Paul Nathan and Edmund Friedemann, in the form of the Committee for Defense Against Antisemitic Attacks of June 1892. But it was quickly superseded by a more comprehensive initiative, launched by two hundred leading Jewish citizens, in a letter to the AZJ, calling for "a serious and dignified defense" of the Jewish community's rights.[7] A move in this direction had been reinforced by two publications, *Wehrt Euch!!* (Defend Yourselves!!), by an "F. Simon," and an anonymous pamphlet, published at the beginning of 1893, with the title *Schutzjuden oder Staatsbürger?* (Protected Jews or Citizens?), the principal message of which was that it was time for Jews to embark on their own defense of their rights. Its author was soon revealed as the theatrical pioneer and translator of Tolstoy, Raphael Loewenfeld (1854–1910). The founding fathers of the CV were drawn from the two hundred signatories of the February 1893 appeal. They included members of the abortive committee, like the industrialist James Simon and Julius Isaac, at whose home the founding meeting had taken place; they also included leading figures of the DIGB, among them its chairman, Samuel Kristeller.

Though the CV had begun life, like the Abwehr-Verein and the committee, as a creation of notables, it soon developed a solid membership base: it numbered forty thousand individual members by the outbreak of the First World War and the circulation of its monthly journal, *Im Deutschen Reich*, was almost as great. It was the most ambitious and the most successful attempt yet at a political union of Germany's Jews. But like all such attempts it was also divisive. Those who launched the CV belonged to the assimilated intelligentsia, were predominantly based in Berlin, and, like the founders of the Abwehr-Verein, associated with the parties of the Liberal left. In this last respect at least they were representative of the majority of their urban coreligionists. In religious questions they belonged to Liberal Judaism; some, like Raphael Loewenfeld, a member of the Ethical Culture Movement, held only a very diluted form of religious belief. Loewenfeld's rhetorical question whether "we educated Jews are closer to the fanatic of talmudic wisdom than to the enlightened Protestant"[8] earned him a reproof even from the middle-of-the-road AZJ. It is therefore not surprising that the CV failed in its ambition to speak for the "totality of German Jews without exception."[9] Many Orthodox Jews were rebuffed not only by Loewenfeld's tactless rejection of their stance but by the CV's analysis of the causes of antisemitism and of the cure for it. The CV's initial program was derived from the notion of the "emancipation contract." Prejudice, discrimination, and hostile propaganda were to be fought ruthlessly, but on the basis of total loyalty to the German Empire and nation. In words closely derived from Loewenfeld's pamphlet it proclaimed, "We German citizens of the Jewish faith rest firmly on the ground of German nationality. . . . As citizens we joyfully fulfill our duty and hold fast to our constitutional rights."[10] This affirmation was repeated countless times. Not all of the Orthodox rejected this appeal: for instance, Hirsch Hildesheimer, editor of the *Jüdische Presse*, was active in the CV. The followers of Samson Raphael Hirsch, on the other hand, saw the strategy of the CV as profoundly mistaken. They were no less disturbed by the survival and revival of antisemitism, but to them it demonstrated the bankruptcy of assimilationism. It was the secularized Jew, they argued, seeking full absorption in German society, whom the antisemites rejected.

Thus though the CV could never claim to speak for all German Jews—its relationship with Zionism became as problematic as its relationship with Orthodoxy—it nevertheless mounted an increasingly effective defense of Jewish political rights. Whereas little was achieved to diminish discrimination in public service, there were moderate successes (detailed below) in persuading nonsocialist parties to nominate professing Jews as candidates for political elections. Where it undoubtedly secured a breakthrough was in the use of the criminal law. Following the DIGB's failure in this regard in the 1870s and 1880s there was some hesitation in resorting to this weapon. But since the entire raison d'être of the CV was a new political self-assertion, its credibility required a strategy of legal action. Moreover, the CV had at its disposal a great deal of legal expertise. The clauses of the German criminal code most frequently used by the CV's Legal Defense Commission were art. 130 (incitement to class hatred) and art. 166 (defamation of a religious community). It faced, and continued to face, two major obstacles: the reluctance of public prosecutors to take up cases where Jews were the offended party and the excessive leniency of the courts when the offending parties were found guilty. Gradually the CV succeeded in making a modest breakthrough. In 1899 it instigated the prosecution of the agitator Count Pückler, in the course of which the court recognized that Jews were entitled to protection under art. 130, and this facilitated later prosecutions. A more important victory occurred as the result of a ritual murder accusation at Konitz in West Prussia in 1900, when the publisher of a postcard illustrating the alleged murder was sentenced to six months' imprisonment under art. 166. Starting at the turn of the century the CV's legal department dealt with an average of over a hundred cases per year, admittedly with mixed results. One cannot change a climate of opinion by litigation; the CV's victories, such as they were, were symbolic. State prosecutors and the courts were obliged to take art. 130 and art. 166 more seriously, and agitators had to choose their words more carefully. The electoral decline of the antisemitic parties after 1900 owed little to the efforts of the CV. The toning down of the more offensive forms of public agitation, in particular the decline in ritual murder accusations, may have been due to the combined work of the CV and the Abwehr-Verein. What the CV achieved more than anything else was to raise the morale of the Jewish community. The days when the most offensive charges could be made with impunity were over.

Within a few weeks of the foundation of the German Abwehr-Verein an Austrian equivalent came into being. Indeed the two organizations were almost a joint creation. The inspiration in Austria came from the pacifist leaders Baron Arthur Gundaccar von Suttner and his wife Bertha (1843–1914), the daughter of Field Marshal Franz Joseph Count Kinsky and winner of the 1905 Nobel Peace Prize. Gundaccar von Suttner had been among the signatories of Rickert's German manifesto; Bertha contributed a preface to F. Simon's *Wehrt Euch!!* The Austrian Abwehr-Verein held its first public meeting on July 2, 1891, supported by a list of eminent persons almost as distinguished as that of its German partner: academics like the geologist Eduard Suess, the physiologist Hermann Nothnagel and the psychiatrist Richard von Krafft-Ebbing, writers including Peter Rosegger and Marie von Ebner-Eschenbach, and—most celebrated of all—Johann Strauss the Younger. It was an even more Gentile group than the German—only Suess and Strauss had any Jewish ancestors. The link with pacifism was also common to both countries. "I fight the antisemites just as I fight against war—after all, they represent the same spirit,"[11] Bertha von Suttner wrote.

The Austrian Anti-Verein (as it came to be known) started well enough. Its weekly newspaper, *Das freie Blatt*, secured an interview given by the emperor to Eduard Suess, in which he denounced antisemitism as "a disgrace and a scandal."[12] But the success did not last; by 1900 the Anti-Verein could no longer afford the rent for its office. There were a number of reasons for its failure. Herzl was probably right when he argued that it had come "ten or twelve years too late."[13] By the time it appeared on the scene Lueger was on the brink of his victory. The liberal-minded middle and upper class who were its founding group were even more isolated and more on the defensive, and had an even weaker parliamentary base, than in Germany. A political message that was cosmopolitan, pacifist, anticlerical, and antinationalist had very little appeal in the Austria of the 1890s. But perhaps the most significant factor was that, in contrast with Germany, Austrian Jews had set up their own defense organization some years before the Anti-Verein or the cv in the shape of the Österreichisch-Israelitische Union (Austrian-Jewish Union, öiu).

The öiu was the brainchild of the tireless Rabbi Joseph Bloch and was, like his other creations, not free from controversy. His first bid to become a representative public Jewish figure came in 1884, in the midst of his involvement in the Rohling case, with the foundation of the weekly *Österreichische Wochenschrift*. Its columns first proposed and reported

30   Torch of enlightenment in hand, Rabbi Joseph Bloch drives
off the antisemite August Rohling

the creation of a Jewish Citizens' Union (Jüdischer Bürgerverein), out of which there emerged the ÖIU, launched in April 1886. Bloch had had three aims in mind, which he regarded as interconnected. The first was to revive Jewish "ethnic consciousness"—not in a Zionist or national autonomist sense but in contrast with what he saw as the passive, unconditional devotion to assimilation. That meant, among other things, fighting the established leadership of the Vienna Organized Jewish Community (Israelitische Kultusgemeinde, IKG), drawn in the main from a wealthy, Viennese-born elite. The second, as outlined in his pamphlet, *Der nationale Zwist und die Juden* (The National Discord and the Jews), was to extract the Jews of Austria from siding in the nationalist rivalries of the empire and turn them into "Austrians *sans phrase.*"[14] The third was to fight antisemitism. The ÖIU as finally constituted fulfilled only some of these aims. In its statutes political objectives got only indirect mention in "combating all attempts at aggravating denominational and racial differences."[15] It is thus not surprising that Bloch declined to serve on the executive of the ÖIU and preferred to conduct his campaign against antisemitism in the columns of his increasingly influential *Österreichische Wochenschrift.* In its early years the ÖIU's membership did not exceed 250 and it was more concerned with intra-Jewish politics than with public activity. It existed mainly to mobilize middle-class and lower-middle-class non-native Viennese Jews. With the election of one of its members, the university lecturer Dr. Josef Grünfeld, as president of the IKG in 1888 one of its missions was accomplished; relative peace could be established between the IKG oligarchy and its challengers and their combined forces could be utilized against the external enemy.

Since it was in the electoral arena that the antisemites mounted their main assault in the early 1890s, it is there that the ÖIU had to concentrate its resistance. In doing so, it could count on a number of advantages. The first was its mere existence. The second was that Vienna had a much larger concentration of Jews than Berlin or any other German city, who were a potential electoral resource of some size. A third—though this was a more doubtful asset—were the close links between the leadership of the Jewish community and at least some of the Viennese Liberal politicians. But in the end the odds that the ÖIU faced were too great. Jewish voters *were* mobilized, though not always very effectively, given the legitimate political differences among them. Liberal candidates for the city council, the provincial diet, and the Reichsrat were encouraged to oppose antisemitism more firmly and explicitly, and the ÖIU was involved in the cre-

ation of a new reformist party, the Sozialpolitische Partei, designed to give
Liberalism a more popular base. Lueger's steamroller flattened them all.
For the remainder of its life span the ÖIU therefore concentrated on propaganda and legal activity, seeing the climate of opinion rather than the
composition of elected bodies as its target. Unlike parliamentary speeches,
which were covered by privilege, public speeches, ordinary newspaper
articles, slanders against individual persons, and incitements to boycotts
were actionable. To meet this need the ÖIU followed the example of the CV
by setting up a Legal Defense Committee in 1895, which expanded into a
permanently staffed Legal Aid and Defense Bureau two years later. These
activities had a number of beneficial effects on the ÖIU. They increased the
importance of its journal, *Mitteilungen der Österreichisch-Israelitischen
Union*, founded in 1889, which in 1901 became the main medium for
publicizing the ÖIU's legal action program. They also gave the union an
incentive to spread its activities and organization beyond Vienna, so that
by 1910 it numbered seven thousand members. But it never became
either as large or as rich as the CV.

   In part the change of emphasis was a response to the course of events.
Once Lueger had been confirmed as mayor of Vienna, the focus of violent
antisemitism shifted to the Slav areas—the rioting in Bohemia in the
wake of the failure of Badeni language decrees, the pogroms that accompanied the rival peasant parties' campaign in Galicia, and above all the
Polná ritual murder case, in the last of which the defense bureau was
extremely active, both by providing defense counsel and by monitoring
tendentious publications. Between 1897 and 1910 the defense bureau
claimed to have taken up over five thousand cases. Only a minority of
these resulted in formal action and the success rate was mixed. Where the
legal situation was clear-cut, and where the ÖIU's case coincided with government policy, the outcomes were favorable—for instance, in preventing
the Lueger administration in Vienna from segregating school pupils by
religion or banning kosher slaughtering or in taking action against the
forced conversion of children, which was especially prevalent in Galicia.
Given the more patrimonial system of government in Austria, direct
approaches to highly placed officeholders, including ministers and even
prime ministers—steps that would have been unthinkable in Germany—
could be highly effective. Such *démarches*, however, risked putting the
petitioners in a false position, emphasising their de facto status as "protected Jews" rather than citizens with equal rights. As in Germany, the
union particularly monitored ritual murder allegations—thirty-five

major cases between 1897 and 1910—and forced retractions and apologies by antisemitic newspapers. As the incidence of both these categories declined after the turn of the century, some credit for this may be due to the ÖIU. Like the CV, the ÖIU's main function was to turn the tables on the accusers and to reassure its own members and followers. Both scored some notable victories, but they could not single-handedly slay the dragon.

2. Achievements and Frustrations

The contradictory experiences of the 1870s and 1880s in both the German and the Austro-Hungarian Empires had left many Jews confused and some, as we have seen, embittered. Within the realm of civil society Jews continued the advances they had begun making in the earlier decades of the nineteenth century. To an increasing degree they filled the liberal professions of law, medicine, and journalism; they retained their strong position in trade and finance and were dominant as industrial entrepreneurs in at least some sectors and some regions. Those antisemites who complained of Jewish domination in these callings frequently exaggerated the incidence of Jewish membership and certainly exaggerated the influence and power that this upward mobility carried with it. But there was no denying that the mobility was there: it was a source of pride to many Jews, but also of growing concern.

The concern was twofold. The first rested on the nagging question of whether it would last. The political hegemony that Liberalism exercised in both empires from the early 1860s to the late 1870s seemed to be in tune with developments throughout Europe. The imperfections of Liberalism in Germany and Austria were therefore regrettable rather than fatal: there was a reasonable prospect that time would remedy them. If the Liberal loss of power merely represented the swing of the political pendulum, then patience might still be rewarded. But if the Liberal phase was no more than an interlude, the outlook was bleaker. The second source of concern related to the social acceptability and national identity of its members. For the Orthodox minority, and certainly for the members of the secessionist congregations, this was less of a problem. Anxious though they were to be German citizens with full rights, they were too strongly committed to their Judaism to exchange it for a secular national allegiance. Indeed, they had an ill-disguised and often explicit contempt for the integrationist aspirations of their more liberal coreligionists.

Self-criticism was not, however, restricted to the Orthodox or to those who were skeptical toward the cultural ideal of German-Jewish symbiosis. The rich blamed each other for the ostentatiousness that bred envy and resentment. Meyer Carl Rothschild told Bleichröder that the "arrogance, vanity, and unspeakable insolence" of the Jews were a cause of antisemitism;[16] Meyer Carl's Parisian relative Guy thought that Bleichröder himself, grown arrogant through his close links with the government, was "one of the causes of the Jewish persecution."[17] Middle-class Jews, if anything, felt the defects of their coreligionists even more deeply. Berthold Auerbach conceded to the Gentile Liberal Friedrich Kapp in America that "there is much fault to be found with the Jews on both sides of the ocean."[18] In light of these assessments it is not surprising that all Jewish initiatives to resist and combat antisemitism contained an appeal to self-improvement. The manifesto of May 1893 that led to the foundation of the cv called on Jews to collaborate on "improvement internally and externally."

More than in any other European state the Jews of Germany felt under pressure to emphasize and reemphasize that they had a full commitment to German culture and no loyalty other than to Germany. A major reason for this was the insecurity that Gentile Germans felt about their nationality in the light of the long history of German territorial fragmentation and the recent and by no means unanimously accepted process of unification. There had been a tendency ever since the first modern "national experience," the wars against Napoleon, to define what is German in restrictive and exclusive terms, by stressing the criteria of what was *not* German as well as what *was* German. This definition contrasted with the French voluntaristic, inclusive notion of nationality, a notion summarized by Ernest Renan as "un plébiscite de tous les jours."[19] Since Jews were frequently the object of this German exclusive definition, they could react in one or both of two ways. Some, like Moritz Lazarus, who may well have influenced Renan, saw salvation in his inclusive definition. The great majority reacted by affirming their Germanness in the manner of the Player Queen in *Hamlet*, by "protesting too much." Almost in despair, the AZJ editorialized: "In vain the Jews have demonstrated that apart from their religious observances and some charitable institutions they have no common interests or concerns, that they belong to the people wholeheartedly and with their entire fortune."[20] Again and again Jewish spokesmen echoed the phrase of Heymann Steinthal, Lazarus's close colleague, that "we . . . can be good Jews only if we are good Germans but can be good Germans only if we are good Jews."[21] It was this particular combination of religious and national identity that the name of the Centralverein deutscher Staatsbürger jüdischen Glaubens was intended to convey. The cv's often-cited commitment to the "unqualified cultivation of German convictions" was incorporated into its revised statutes in 1909.

One way in which Jews could emphasize their loyalty to the peoples among whom they lived was by demonstrating their allegiance to the dynasties that ruled their empires. This was easiest in the Habsburg Monarchy, where the Emperor Francis Joseph ruled as father of his varied peoples from 1848 to 1916. While many Jews, beginning with the 1840s, debated which of the empire's nationalities they were to identify with, almost none of them wanted to see an end to the empire and its dynasty. Though Francis Joseph, as a conventionally Conservative Catholic, was probably out of sympathy with the political aspirations of many of his Jewish subjects, he never disguised his disapproval of antisemitism. His instructions to Prime Minister Count Taaffe in the 1880s were typical of his attitude, "I tolerate no agitation against the Jews in my empire. Every antisemitic movement must be nipped in the bud at once. . . . The Jews are brave and patriotic and joyfully risk their lives for emperor and fatherland."[22] So was his guarantee of safety to the Jews of Vienna after Lueger's election in 1895. In Germany the situation was more complicated. William I, the first monarch of the new empire, was privately unhappy about the extent of Jewish rights and voiced no public disapproval of antisemitism. However, one reason many Germans remained confident that this coolness might be only temporary lay in the hopes they had invested in William's son Frederick and his English wife, Victoria. The princely couple did not conceal where their sympathies lay. Following the outbreak of the Treitschke and Stoecker campaigns Frederick attended a synagogue service in field marshal's uniform; his comment to Geheimer Kommerzienrat Meyer Magnus that antisemitism was the "disgrace of the century," though only indirectly corroborated, is certainly consistent with his other pronouncements on the subject.[23] His accession on the death of William in 1888 was greeted with alarm in Conservative court circles. Field Marshal Alfred von Waldersee, a confidant of the new Crown Prince William, particularly feared the new empress's "predilection for the Progressive-Jewish clique." In fact, no professing Jews were ennobled during Frederick's ninety-nine-day reign, though the converts Heinrich Friedberg and Eduard Simson were so honored, as were notable opponents of antisemitism like the mayor of Berlin, Max Forckenbeck, and the physiologist Rudolf Virchow. When Frederick died and William II ascended the throne, Waldersee gloated: "The Progressive gentlemen and their Jewish appendage are . . . hard hit. . . . They see their hopes of a golden age evaporate and fear Prince William."[24]

The first of these sentiments was certainly shared by many Jews. What they were to make of the new emperor was an altogether more complicated question. On Jewish matters, as on almost every other topic, he gave conflicting signals. He did not share his father's Liberalism. He had close relations with the circle around Stoecker; he identified with the military, with an aggressive foreign and imperial policy and with the increasingly popular pan-German ideology. He was an admirer of Houston Stewart Chamberlain, with whom he conducted a voluminous correspondence. His numerous antisemitic comments, both before and after his accession, were made in private, but it is difficult to believe that Jews remained totally ignorant of them. At the same time his social contacts with selected prominent Jews were wide, so much so that the somewhat heterogeneous group around him later became known as the *Kaiserjuden*. They included bankers like Max Warburg and Carl Fürstenberg, industrialists like Walther Rathenau, James Simon, and the director general of the HAPAG shipping line of Hamburg, Albert Ballin. As we know today, William did not reciprocate their friendship. "Serves him quite right," he commented on hearing of the murder of Rathenau in 1922. He also claimed to have been unaware that Ballin was a Jew.[25] The Kaiserjuden flattered the emperor with gifts of works of art and sometimes very large donations (in two cases one million Reichsmarks) to his favorite charities. Jewish philanthropists also supported the Kaiser Wilhelm Institut, the emperor's foundation for the support of scientific research. William reciprocated with honors and ennoblements—eight ennoblements up to the outbreak of the First World War. While moneyed men of intellect and taste frequented the court, the Kaiserjuden included no intellectuals or academics and certainly no journalists. William's hatred of "press Jews" dated from before his accession, when Berlin papers criticized his public association with Stoecker. It merely escalated in 1907 when Maximilian Harden's *Die Zukunft* exposed the decadence of William's court flatterers and a year later when a constitutional crisis erupted over his ill-advised interview to the London *Daily Telegraph*, at that time owned by the Levy-Lawson family. None of this deterred Jewish opinion leaders from the most deferential expressions of loyalty: "It is a strong support for a weak minority, which is unable to help itself, that the country is ruled by a king who tolerates no injustice," the AZJ wrote on the emperor's thirty-ninth birthday.[26]

3. The New Style of Jewish Politics

Nowhere was the dependence of Jewish fortunes on the strength of Liberalism more clearly illustrated than in parliamentary politics. With the defeat of Liberal majorities in Prussia and the Kaiserreich in 1879, the prominent role that Jews had played in German legislatures came to an end, and when the last Jewish legislator of the founders' generation, Ludwig Bamberger, retired in 1893 the Reichstag contained no Jew outside the ranks of the Social Democratic Party until 1912. In the Prussian parliament there were no professing Jews for over a decade after 1886. Jews reacted to this exclusion in different ways. On the one hand, the moral cowardice, not to mention the occasional covert antisemitism, of the Liberal parties was painful; on the other hand, there was some opposition to token or "ghetto" candidacies. In the end the argument in favor of having Jewish spokesmen to air Jewish grievances won out, on the grounds that "where there is a plaintiff, there must be counsel for the defense."[27] The terms on which Jews were to play a part in politics had evidently changed. Their claims to participation still rested on equal citizenship, but the Jewish legislator was also to be there to speak for the minority from which he stemmed.

However, the limited opportunities that the Reichstag offered resulted in changed priorities. There were general complaints that its members were mediocre and that its debates lacked interest and achieved minimal effect. Its membership was now dominated by lawyers, civil servants, and professional lobbyists. In contrast with the 1870s, it contained few men prominent in business or intellectual life. The Jewish demand for representation was therefore symbolic as much as instrumentally motivated. Practical influence could be achieved away from the formal institutions of the Kaiserreich, at the level of state and municipal government and in interest groups. It is here that Jewish political efforts were concentrated from the 1890s onward. Beginning in 1898 Jews were again elected to the Prussian parliament, first for the Left Liberals and finally for the National Liberals also. In part this may have been a response to the pressure of the CV, but it also reflected the decline of overt antisemitic agitation, so that there seemed to be fewer risks attached to nominating a Jew. Nevertheless, Jewish political participation was now more localized and the typical Jewish politician was more likely than before to be a notable within his community. The Jewish deputies in the Prussian parliament came overwhelmingly from either Greater Berlin or the province of Posen, in

Baden they came from Mannheim or Karlsruhe, in the Grand Duchy of Hesse from Darmstadt. The greatest concentration of local politicians was to be found, as before, in the traditional areas of Jewish settlement, especially Posen and Silesia, and here the links between communal, professional, and party activity were especially strong. All five of the Jewish members of the Prussian parliament for Posen were officeholders in the Jewish community executive or representative council; they also either held high municipal office, or were prominent in the Chamber of Advocates or the Chamber of Commerce. The banker Louis Aronsohn of Bromberg (1850–1928) was a typical example of these Posen notables. He was at various times president of the community executive, a city alderman, a member of the provincial diet, a member of the Prussian parliament, and president of the Chamber of Commerce. Similar patterns could be found in other medium-sized towns in the eastern provinces, such as Posen and Hohensalza or Beuthen and Kattowitz in Upper Silesia. In Berlin and other large cities links were more likely to be with the newer, secular Jewish organizations, such as the CV, the B'nai B'rith, or the charitable organization of the German Jews, the Hilfsverein der deutschen Juden. Increasingly these bodies became a career ladder for politically ambitious Jews to whom other openings were not available. But they also played an integrative role for Jews who retained an ethnic identity without deep religious feeling. Very quickly the CV advanced from being a defense organization and a lobby to being an instrument for the "internalization of Judaism,"[28] so that activity in a wider political arena became a logical step from a commitment to the new Jewish politics.

A further reason for the restricted Jewish access to national politics was the changing party constellation. The Conservative Party, though not officially antisemitic until 1892, was always hostile to Jews and their political aspirations. Its ally, the Reichspartei, was not officially antisemitic but was prepared to collaborate with politicians that were. The National Liberals were, after the split of 1880, largely inhospitable to Jews, except in certain areas such as Baden and the Rhineland. The Center, as a Christian and overwhelmingly Catholic party, was of little interest to Liberal Jews. For almost the whole of the period from 1879 onward governmental majorities in the Reichstag included the two Conservative parties, either in a "black-blue" coalition with the Center Party or in combination with the National Liberals. Opportunities for a politician of the caliber of Lasker or Bamberger to influence policy at the national level were therefore negligible. During these years most Jews identified with one or the other of the Left Liberal parties, but as their voting strength diminished, so did the opportunities they could offer. Only where the franchise was biased in favor of the well-to-do, as for most of the state parliaments and, even more, for the municipalities, could Liberalism and Jewish participation in it survive.

Some Jews undoubtedly continued to vote for the right-of-center parties. Especially among the older generation and in the banking and industrial upper middle class there was a residual loyalty to the National Liberals. A few intellectuals, including the Zionist Gustav Witkowsky, hoped for a home for their ideological conservatism, but the Reichspartei was the furthest they were willing to move to the right. The Center had rather more appeal for certain sections of German Jewry. Though some of its orators and newspapers engaged in antisemitic demagogy, the party always resisted calls for any reversal of emancipation; it was therefore a bulwark against the practical implementation of antisemitism, even if not against the dissemination of its rhetoric. Between the greater part of the Jewish and Catholic populations of Germany there was a considerable cultural gulf. The one was predominantly urban, even metropolitan, cosmopolitan, and open to avant-garde ideas; the other predominantly rural or small-town and conservative in its values. But Orthodox rural Jews, especially in Southern Germany, did not share the assimilationist ambitions of their Reform-minded coreligionists. Above all, they were suspicious of the Liberals' aim of nondenominational—or, as the Orthodox saw it, Godless—education. While majority Jewish opinion opposed denominational schools—"We do not want to segregate ourselves, that is what our opponents want"[29]—the secessionist Orthodox in particular supported the Center's advocacy of religious education during the debate on the Prussian Schools Bill of 1905, especially since the bill as passed provided some modest subsidies for Jewish schools. Moreover, Center Party politicians could always be relied on to defend "the integrity of the sacred objects of our religion,"[30] especially when antisemites wished to ban kosher slaughtering.

Though Jews were well represented in municipal politics and regained a foothold in state politics after the turn of the century, they did not advance to positions of national leadership. The only Jew in the executive of the Left Liberal Fortschrittliche Volkspartei was Oskar Cassel (1849–1923), who also served as deputy chairman of the Berlin city council and from 1917 onward was chairman of the Verband der deutschen Juden (Association of German Jews). The National Liberals' reluctance to nominate Jews as parliamentary candidates was not, in the main, racially motivated. Baptized Jews played a more prominent part in its affairs than among the Progressives. The most eminent of these were Robert Friedberg (1851–1920), who became party leader and de facto prime minister of Prussia in 1917, and Eugen Schiffer (1860–1954), who also held a ministerial post during the First World War and a number of high offices after 1918. In peace time, however, even a person of immediate Jewish descent was virtually barred from ministerial office. The only exception to this was the banker Bernhard Dernburg (1861–1937), appointed to direct the newly created Imperial Colonial Department in 1906. Though descended from a family of Lutheran pastors on his mother's side, he was widely regarded, and attacked, as a Jew. His appointment by Chancellor Bülow was part of a short-lived experiment (the "Bülow Bloc") to mobilize middle-class liberal support for the government's foreign and imperial policy, one that came to an end with Bülow's resignation in 1909. This Liberal coalition with the Conservatives was a further illustration of the unsteady posture of German Liberalism and of the uncertain support that the cause of civil rights could expect from that quarter.

While Liberal forces in Germany managed to maintain a coherent, even if weakened, minority status, those in Austria had all but ceased to exist by 1914. They had retreated before a triumphant Catholic anti-Liberalism and the growth of chauvinism and racism in their own ranks. For the Jews of the Habsburg Monarchy these developments posed a multiple dilemma. Within the relics of German-speaking Liberalism they were increasingly treated as alien; attempts to revive genuinely Liberal movements were generally too heavily dependent on Jewish support to be successful. In areas of mixed nationality they were under pressure to identify with rival chauvinistic movements; their pledges of allegiance, often embarked on opportunistically, were rarely reciprocated. Universal male suffrage, introduced in 1906, was the death knell of Liberalism as an independent force.

Concern about the weakness of Liberalism in Vienna dated back to the 1880s, as was shown by the foundation of the Österreichisch-Israelitische Union, and was reinforced by Lueger's victory in the 1890s. The attempt to found a Gentile-led Abwehr-Verein led nowhere, as we have seen. A more promising initiative arose out of the Wiener Fabier Gesellschaft, founded in 1893 on the model of the British Fabian Society. Many of its members were veterans of earlier reformist groups; what was significant was that its composition crossed the boundaries that were beginning to divide the rest of Austrian society. It brought together prominent Gentiles, like the economist Eugen von Philippovich and the social philosophers Michael Hainisch and Tomás G. Masaryk, respectively the first presidents of post-1918 Austria and Czechoslovakia, and leading Jews, including Heinrich Friedjung, Josef Redlich, and the future Socialist leader, Victor Adler. Many of these were in turn instrumental in founding the Sozialpolitische Partei, designed to reinvigorate Viennese Liberalism by advocating social reform, a democratic suffrage, women's rights, and strict opposition to antisemitism. Its electoral committee included the Jewish social reformer Dr. Julius Ofner, who was also one of its parliamentary candidates, the vice chairman of the ÖIU, Sigmund Mayer, and the chief rabbi of Vienna, Moritz Güdemann. The Sozialpolitiker got no more votes than the Liberals before them, nor did they get the wholehearted support of the capital's Jews. For many middle-class Jews their program was too radical. The dilemma of the Liberal Jew in an illiberal society remained unresolved.

4. Escape Routes from Discrimination: Capitalism and Socialism

The rhetoric of the antisemitic politicians and journalists was at all times offensive and on occasion physically threatening—as, for instance, in the final phases of Lueger's mayoral campaign or at the time of ritual murder charges. But the limited electoral success of the antisemites, at any rate in Germany, the personal discredit of many of their spokesmen, and the modest triumphs that the defense organizations managed to achieve through litigation reassured many Jews. Here was a prejudice, they felt, that could be contained, even if not defeated. It was, in the words of the Zionist leader, Richard Lichtheim, "irksome . . . but by no means dangerous."[31] That verdict seemed particularly valid to anyone successful in his business or profession, as most Jews were during the long economic expansion from the 1860s to 1914. The material condition of the Jews of Central Europe was undoubtedly better in 1871 than it had been in 1815 and undoubtedly better in 1914 than in 1871. What hurt many Jews and what convinced them that they had still, in Walther Rathenau's phrase, "entered the world as second-class citizens,"[32] was continuing discrimination in public life. In the light of restricted opportunities in conventional politics and public service careers, it is not surprising that most German and Austrian Jews sought openings for themselves in the professions or in business and, if in politics, then increasingly in unconventional politics. Not that even professional or business life was entirely free from discrimination. Many Gentile medical or legal practitioners specified non-Jewish applicants when advertising for partners. Jewish journalists were unlikely to find employment outside the metropolitan Liberal press or Social Democratic party publications. These exceptions notwithstanding, the segregation of Jew from Gentile mattered less in civil society than in the realm of the state. In the years of Germany's great economic leap forward Jews ceased to be a caste with a peculiar economic function and became an increasingly integrated part of the business community.

Nothing illustrated this better than the number of honorific positions held by Jews. The baptized Franz (von) Mendelssohn was president of the Berlin Merchant Corporation (Kaufmannschaft) in the 1880s, to be succeeded by the unbaptized Wilhelm Herz. When the Berlin Chamber of Commerce was created in 1902, Herz became its first president and was succeeded on his death by Franz von Mendelssohn's son. Throughout this period between one-third and one-half of the elders of the Berlin Kaufmannschaft were Jews or of Jewish descent. Similar patterns of office holding can be seen in almost all the major cities of Germany—Hamburg and Breslau, Danzig and Königsberg, Mannheim and Cologne. Jewish businessmen and industrialists gained recognition not only from their peers; it also came from on high. Between 1879 and 1900 16 percent of those who received the title of Kommerzienrat and 19 percent of those honored by the higher distinction of Geheimer Kommerzienrat in Prussia were Jews. To some extent such honors were substitutes for denial of public office or empty concessions to snobbery. But in a status-conscious society they also conferred status and the status thus acquired was not without commercial advantage.

Another public opening for the Jewish businessmen was the policy lobby and the trade association. From the 1870s onward important sectors of the German economy were organized in interest groups designed to influence government policy. The pro-tariff Central Association of German Industrialists (1876), representing heavy industry, and the Agrarian League (1893) were unattractive to Jews, most of whom were instinctively suspicious of this anti-Liberal "alliance of iron and rye." Even the more liberal League of Industrialists (1895), which represented manufacturing and exporting, had few Jewish members. What Jewish businessmen were interested in, both as businessmen and Jews, was the policy debate between protective tariffs and free trade, agriculture and industry, and rural versus urban interests, which also became in the German context a contest between the advocates of a closed and an open society. In an organized form this contest came into the open when Chancellor Bülow proposed replacing Germany's existing relatively tariff-free trade treaties at the turn of the century with higher tariffs. The Association for Trade Treaties of 1900, founded to argue for freer trade, failed in this objective and was succeeded in 1909 by a much more broadly based middle-class alliance in the form of the Hansa-Bund. Wilhelm Herz of the Berlin Chamber of Commerce became the second chairman of the Association for Trade Treaties; the Hansa-Bund's president was Jakob Riesser, the baptized nephew of Gabriel Riesser, a former director of the Darmstädter Bank and vice president of the Berlin Chamber of Commerce. Those who founded these two bodies and belonged to their executives included a virtual who's who of Jewish-descended millionaires—bankers, such as Carl Fürstenberg, Franz von Mendelssohn, Paul von Schwabach, and Max Warburg, industrialists, such as Franz Oppenheim, James Simon, and Emil Rathenau, and Albert Ballin to represent shipping. Both bodies were promptly denounced as "Judaized." Yet, for once, Jewish spokesmen did not resent this attribution and welcomed the Hansa-Bund's support for equal opportunity: "The Hansa-Bund inscribes justice on its banner. That, too, is what we German Jews desire, justice that regulates the reciprocal obligations of the citizen and the state."[33] At a more modest economic level Jews played leading roles in trade organizations. Oskar Tietz was not only the cofounder of the Tietz chain of department stores but also chairman of the Association of German Department Stores; Heinrich Grünfeld, owner of the famous linen shop that served Berlin's elite, was chairman of the Association of Berlin Specialist Shops; Hermann Bamberg of Gebrüder Mannheimer, Germany's largest ready-to-wear firm, was chairman of the Association of Ladies' and Girls' Coat Manufacturers. Such positions, too, offered both status and influence, even if not at the level of the grand banking dynasties.

One idealistic cause that did appeal to a significant number of Jews, as it had to the contemporaries of Bleichröder, was an aversion to war. The chief force behind the German Peace Society, founded in 1892, was the Viennese-born journalist and publicist Alfred Fried (1854–1921). Although he soon quarreled with the organization he had helped to found, he remained influential and was rewarded with the Nobel Peace Prize in 1911. Other Jews closely involved in its foundation were the Left

Liberal politicians Max Hirsch and Adolf Heilberg; those who at one time or another gave it active support included the newspaper publishers Leopold Sonnemann, Hans Ullstein, and Rudolf Mosse, and, among academics, Moritz Lazarus and Theodor Lessing. But though the society also had the active support of distinguished Gentiles it could never escape the accusation that it represented yet another aspect of unpatriotic Jewish cosmopolitanism. Even Bertha von Suttner felt obliged to warn Fried, "The way things are, the initiative must not emerge from too many Jews."[34] More characteristic of the activities of Liberal Jews in this field was the advocacy of international reconciliation and arbitration, as exemplified by the Association for International Conciliation of 1911, which attracted the support of Hermann Cohen, Eduard Cassirer, and Hugo Preuss, the Franco-German interparliamentary meetings of 1913 and 1914, whose participants included the Progressive Reichstag deputy Ludwig Haas as well as the Social Democrats Hugo Haase and Eduard Bernstein, and the numerous attempts of Albert Ballin to avert a breach with Britain over naval policy in the years before 1914.

Those Jews who sought outlets for their political ambitions in a business environment were certainly aware of the constitutional defects of the German Empire but were not in systematic opposition to the established order. The last twenty years before the outbreak of the war did, however, see a revival in Germany, and even more in Austria, of a figure reminiscent of the first half of the nineteenth-century, namely, the radical or revolutionary Jew. By 1912, at the time of the last prewar Reichstag election, an estimated one in five Jewish electors supported the SPD; in Austria, at any rate outside Galicia and Bukovina, where Jewish politics followed its own rules, the proportion was probably higher. There were several reasons for these developments. As the Social Democratic parties of both empires became larger and more moderate, in practice even if not in their official programs, liberally inclined middle-class Jews had fewer compunctions in voting for them. The Social Democratic parties had always stood for equality before the law and had opposed discrimination. But as long as they threatened the rights of property, and acted like revolutionaries, few Jews sympathized with them. Official Jewish organs were eager to dissociate Jews from the politics of subversion: as late as 1891, after the anti-Socialist laws had lapsed, the AZJ insisted "in the whole of God's wide world there cannot be two more severe antagonisms [sic] than that between Judaism and Social Democracy."[35] From then on, and especially after the turn of the century, Jewish organizations and publications increasingly acknowledged the role of Social Democracy as a bulwark against antisemitism. Yet, when patriotic sentiment was high, as in the 1907 Reichstag elections fought by Chancellor Bülow in alliance with the Liberal parties on a pro-colonial platform, older instincts reverted. Defending the "necessary fight against Social Democracy," Hermann Cohn of Dessau, a leading member of the cv, acknowledged that "many considered the antisemitic danger as the lesser and more remote compared with the Social Democratic."[36]

Social Democracy became all the more attractive to Jewish voters as disillusionment with Liberalism grew. Above all, the composition and outlook of the German-speaking Jewish population was changing. By 1914 its members were overwhelmingly urban, even metropolitan; uprooted from their traditional environment, they were secularized, with a sense of Jewish identity that was more political, cultural, and social than religious. The new generation, especially those who had run the antisemitic gauntlet of university studies, did not necessarily share the liberal optimism of their parents or their often complacent faith in progress. An increasing number had to make their way as wage earners in a difficult labor market, mainly in the growing white-collar sector, where many Gentile employers were disinclined to hire them, many Jewish employers were reluctant to favor them, and many of their fellow employees were antisemitic. For such men and, increasingly, women, Social Democracy was a powerful magnet.

But it was not only the growth in the generally passive electoral support for the Social Democratic movements that was significant in the years before the First World War. Equally remarkable was the emergence of a whole generation of politicians and publicists, without whose participation and leadership Central European Social Democracy would have had a very different character. In the formative years of the spp, during the 1870s and 1880s, Jews had played a minor role. The revolutionaries of 1848 were dead, scattered, or disillusioned; the next generation was absorbed by the enthusiasm of Liberal state building and, as we have seen, an antirevolutionary consensus. From the 1890s onward this picture changed. In the last six Reichstage of the German Empire some 10 percent of the spp delegation consisted of Jews. Their importance, moreover, was greater than their numbers. What Jews contributed to the labor movement was educational and professional qualification. In the Reichstag of 1912 eleven of the twelve Jewish spp deputies were university graduates, compared with eight of the ninety-eight non-Jews. Jews also rose to high

leadership positions. From 1890 onward Paul Singer (1844–1911), a former Liberal and co-owner of a successful ladies' garment firm, became
cochairman of the party. After Singer's death in 1911 Hugo Haase
(1863–1919), a lawyer from a Königsberg Jewish family, succeeded him
and from 1912 onward combined that post with leadership of the SPD
party group in the Reichstag. In 1913, following the death of the venerable party leader, August Bebel, Haase became party chairman jointly with
Friedrich Ebert, who was to become the first president of the Weimar
Republic. Haase's chairmanship became a source of agony for him when
the outbreak of the world war challenged his pacifist leanings, as we shall
see in chapter 12.

The greatest professional service that Jews rendered the SPD was in
journalism, whether in the party's popular press or its more specialist and
academic journals. The party's official daily newspaper, the Berlin
Vorwärts, nominally edited by Wilhelm Liebknecht until his death in
1900, was edited de facto by Kurt Eisner (1867–1919), better known as the
head of 1918 revolutionary government of Bavaria. Eisner, who at that
time was on the right of the party, was one of the losers in the great ideological battle over control of the party press in 1905 and moved to
Bavaria, working first on the *Fränkische Tagespost* of Nuremberg and
then on the *Münchener Post*. The second-largest daily circulation was
that of the *Leipziger Volkszeitung*, founded in 1894 by Bruno Schoenlank
(1859–1901), who was succeeded as editor on his death by Friedrich
Stampfer (1874–1957), both Jews. As editor of *Vorwärts* from 1915
Stampfer became one of the party's leading journalists during the First
World War and the Weimar Republic. Jews were equally active in the
SPD's intellectually more ambitious publications. Heinrich Braun (1854–
1927), the brother-in-law of Victor Adler, was cofounder with Karl
Kautsky (1854–1938) of the party's main theoretical journal, *Neue Zeit*;
from 1902 onward Emanuel Wurm (1857–1920), also a Jew, was
Kautsky's chief collaborator.

In Austria the Social Democratic Party emerged later; for that reason
and because of the greater role of Jews in Austrian intellectual life, Jews
were from the start dominant in its organization, to an extent that created
considerable problems from time to time. Its creator and first chairman
from the time of the founding congress at the end of 1889 was Victor Adler,
whom we have already met in the context of Left Liberal reformist circles
in the 1880s and who had converted to Protestantism at the age of sixteen.
Other Jewish founding fathers included his close contemporaries Wilhelm

Ellenbogen (1863–1951) and Friedrich Austerlitz (1862–1931), who became editor of the party newspaper, the *Arbeiter-Zeitung;* a younger generation included Adler's son Friedrich (1879–1960) and Otto Bauer (1881–1938), who succeeded to the leadership on Adler's death in 1918.

Given their predominantly intellectual bent, Jews were heavily involved in the doctrinal disputes of the Socialist movement, but not particularly with any one tendency. What attracted Jews to Socialism was idealism and utopianism: the search for a society in which inherited or arbitrary distinctions, whether of class or ascription, would disappear. It marked a desire to escape from antisemitism but also, in many cases, to escape from Judaism. Hence, while some of the idealism was reformist and democratic, amounting to little more than an attempt to realize the ideals on which the existing society claimed to be based, some of it was revolutionary, preaching that only the overthrow of the existing order would bring justice. The members of the second group, which included such celebrated theorists of revolution as Rosa Luxemburg (1870–1919), Leo Jogiches (1867–1919), Alexander Israel Helphand ("Parvus," 1867–1923) and Karl Radek (1885–1939), helped to perpetuate the stereotype of the revolutionary Jew. The fact that most of them were immigrants from the czarist or Habsburg empires made them seem doubly dangerous and contributed to their isolation not only within German intellectual life but even within the SPD. They undoubtedly represented a recognizable type of radical Jewish intellectual but they were not typical of Jews, or even Jewish theoreticians, in the SPD. At least as important, and more immediately influential, were the theoreticians of the SPD's right. The most prominent of these was Eduard Bernstein, whose "revisionist" manifesto, *Evolutionary Socialism,* disputed Marx's forecast of the inevitable collapse of capitalism. While his views were disavowed by party conference votes, the SPD's practice, as opposed to the claims of its manifestos, was not far from Bernstein's positions. Bernstein's moderate humanitarianism also made him a near-pacifist; others on the right of the party drew different conclusions. The circle around the periodical *Sozialistische Monatshefte,* founded by Joseph Bloch (1871–1936), advocated support for German expansionism and imperialism, on the grounds that in a competitive world the German working class would be the loser if it opposed such policies. One consequence of the greater support that the *Sozialistische Monatshefte* showed for nationalism in general was a sympathy toward Zionism that was otherwise taboo in the SPD.

Within the Austrian Social Democratic Party the intellectual contribution of the Jewish members developed more slowly. That was due partly to its later foundation, partly to the tendency of some of its best brains to move to Germany, whether Jews like Rudolf Hilferding and Heinrich Braun or non-Jews like Karl Kautsky. Otto Bauer did, however, make his mark in 1907 with *Die Nationalitätenfrage und die Sozial-demokratie* (The Nationalities Question and Social Democracy), a choice of topic that revealed the different doctrinal agendas of the two parties. While the SPD was torn by the disputes of the revisionists and the radicals, the Austrian party was largely indifferent to that issue. What the Austrian party had to come to terms with were the Habsburg Empire's nationality disputes—in the end unsuccessfully, as its Czech wing, the second strongest in the party, broke away.

Jews dominated neither the left nor the right of their Social Democratic parties, whatever popular stereotyping might say. They did dominate the parties' media, whether of the left or of the right, and played a leading, if not dominant, role in its doctrinal disputes. One question on which they tended to have a common view, much like their Liberal coreligionists, was a commitment to international understanding. It was this that bound together men of the SPD's right, like Eduard Bernstein and Ludwig Frank (1874–1914), with those of the left, like Hugo Haase. Frank's experience highlighted the dilemmas of the patriotic internationalist. Coming from Baden, a state known for its tolerant and conciliatory politics, he took it for granted that one worked for the realization of one's aims within the existing order. He was a leading advocate of Franco-German reconciliation, but he recognized earlier than most that if war came the SPD would have to vote the necessary credits. At the end of July 1914 he collected the signatures of those Reichstag deputies who would support those credits, whatever the party's collective decision. Frank was the only member of the Reichstag to fall in the war.

The aims and motives of those Jews who joined the Socialist movement were varied and in some cases contradictory; so, too, were the responses of the German and Austrian parties to their Jewish supporters and to antisemitism. Although antisemitism had not been uncommon in the European left earlier in the nineteenth century, as time went on Socialist parties came to recognize it as a weapon of the right. Even those German Social Democrats who had once been quite free with their anti-Jewish remarks, like Friedrich Engels, came to acknowledge the role of Jews in the movement. Some residue of older resentments survived in the party: it was based on anti-intellectualism and on suspicion of the motives of the mainly middle-class Jews who flocked to the party; it was also sometimes a weapon in doctrinal disputes. The radicals of East European origin were most frequently the objects of antisemitic innuendo, largely for their heavily didactic manner. Bernstein, Haase, or Frank never suffered in this way.

More important, official Social Democracy was hostile to the perpetuation of any Jewish ethnic or national identity. Jewish minority characteristics were seen as the result of persecution and premodern economic conditions. First capitalism and then socialism would eliminate any differences between Jews and non-Jews, and it was the duty of the working-class movement to encourage and accelerate the assimilation of Jews in general society. Though Otto Bauer had defined nations as "communities of character" and "communities of fate," he excluded Jews from both these categories. The Austrian party's Brünn program of 1899, which had tried to institutionalize national autonomy, had similarly excluded Jews. Hence the strong opposition not only to Zionism but to any form of Jewish national movement. This ideological orthodoxy had a number of consequences. It meant that Jews in the Social Democratic parties could not constitute a separate interest: the struggle for civil rights and against discrimination was that of the whole party and not the province of particular individuals within it. In practice, however, some exceptions were made. There was little pressure on Jewish legislators to leave the Jewish faith, compared with the quite intense pressure on Catholics and Protestants to do so. Those who did leave the Jewish faith did so voluntarily, a step that some, like Eduard Bernstein, afterward regretted. Those that remained were often religiously indifferent: their motive was "solidarity with Jews reduced to second-class citizenship."[37] One other respect in which the SPD treated Jews as a group generously was in the nomination of parliamentary candidates, even though in some areas or run-off elections that might have deterred potential voters. Indeed Paul Singer was nominated first for the Berlin city council and then for the Reichstag at the height of Stoecker's campaign as a deliberate (and successful) challenge to antisemitism. The Austrian party was initially reluctant to adopt such a course, feeling itself vulnerable both in the large number of its Jewish leaders and the greater strength of antisemitism, but relented once universal male suffrage arrived. A convention, however, arose that the Austrian party executive should always have a non-Jewish majority.

These often confused attitudes toward Jews led, in turn, to confusion about antisemitism. The rationalist optimism of most Socialists made it difficult for them to take antisemitism seriously as a political phenome-

non with long-term prospects. In 1901 Bebel assured Victor Adler that
even in Vienna "the days of its dominance are numbered."[38] The political
attraction of antisemitism was explained on the one hand as a cry of
despair by declining elements—"the disgruntlement of certain bourgeois
strata, which feel themselves oppressed by the development of capitalism"—on the other hand as a diversionary tactic by the ruling class to
manipulate social discontent—"hence the support that antisemitism
derives from Junker and priests."[39] Compared with the conflict between
capital and labor, Socialists regarded the dispute about antisemitism as a
secondary phenomenon, especially since much of the Liberal opposition
to antisemitism seemed to Socialists to be a defense of capitalism or of
Jewish special interests. The Social Democratic parties therefore adopted
an uneasy neutrality between antisemitism and what they regarded as
"philosemitism," especially in Austria, where the prominence of Jews in
the capitalist class and the often anti-Socialist tone of Jewish-owned
newspapers diminished any sense of solidarity there might be between
Jews and the working-class movement. "Social Democracy has never
been a 'guard for the protection of Jews,' " Otto Bauer declared.[40]

The ambivalence of the Social Democrats' attitude toward Jews and
antisemitism underlined the political dilemmas of the German and
German-Austrian Jews as the world war approached. Jews were what they
had always been, a recognizable minority. The nature and structure of this
minority changed; it was certainly very different from what it had been a
century before. But just as the pattern of Jewish economic activity was a
product of minority status, so were Jewish political reflexes. The overwhelmingly middle-class Jews of German-speaking Central Europe were
Liberal not merely because this coincided with their material interests but
because their collective memory persuaded them to side with their enemies' enemies. More strongly than their fellow citizens, they favored
careers open to talents, constitutional evolution, and a peaceful world
order. Though capable of patriotic fervor, they were more skeptical than
their Gentile colleagues of navies, colonies, and—especially in Austria—
the clash of nationalities. Insofar as the Socialist movements also offered
fulfillment of these aspirations, Jewish support for them grew. But as long
as the Social Democratic parties remained hostile not only to property
and religion but to any form of Jewish communal life, and as long as some
of their anticapitalist rhetoric bore disturbing resemblances to that of the
antisemites, many Jews remained stranded between a dying Liberalism
and a not yet mature Socialism.

9 | Ideology and Identity

At the turn of the century a profound change in orientation took place among certain sections of German-speaking Jewry. In the early and middle nineteenth century debate among German Jews focused on how best to integrate into German society. The main division then lay between Orthodoxy and an emerging Liberal Judaism. Acceptance as full citizens and acquisition of German culture were goals most German Jews shared. Except for extreme traditionalists, they agreed that Judaism was primarily a religion rather than a nationality and that the national elements in Judaism should be toned down if not eliminated altogether. Despite vehement disagreement on issues of ritual and liturgical change, they shared a self-definition as Germans of the Jewish faith.

Three developments during the last third of the nineteenth century challenged the conventional definition of Judaism in denominational terms. Most dramatic was the rise of political and cultural antisemitism, analyzed in chapter 7, with its denial that Jews were part of the German nation. A less dramatic reason making self-definition as a German of the Jewish faith more problematic in 1900 than it had been in 1850 was that many Jews no longer affirmed any elements of the traditional faith of their ancestors. Though some secularized Jews continued to pay lip service to the redefined Jewish creed of Liberal Judaism, others no longer accepted the theistic beliefs inherent in it. Here the challenge was not to the "German" part of the equation but to the "Jewish faith" portion.

Some secularized Jews responded to their loss of belief in Judaism by cutting their ties with the Jewish community, while others struggled for new communal definitions based on criteria other than religion.

There was a third element, less of a challenge to assumptions than the example of an alternative path, that induced questioning of the national identity of German Jews—the growing impact of East European Jewry. The *Ostjuden* (the term itself came into vogue only after World War I) were a double challenge. In their native lands East European Jews had retained their cultural and national separateness and had not integrated into the culture of their non-Jewish neighbors as had their German-speaking coreligionists. The waves of migration beginning in the 1880s, which sent large numbers of Jews from Russia, Romania, and Galicia westward, forced German Jews to confront in person the growing contrast between the East European and German Jewish roads to modernity. Eastern immigration, though seen by some analysts as causing "dissimilation" in German Jewry, actually worked, much like the influence of antisemitism, in two antithetical ways. For some it led to a deepening of Jewish identity based on the inspiration of an unspoiled Jewish community. For others, probably most, it was a source of repulsion impelling them to distance themselves ever more from their embarrassing kin.

The new challenges shifted debate within German Jewry from liturgical and theological issues to questions of national and cultural identity. The spectrum of views on issues of *Deutschtum und Judentum* (Germanness and Jewishness) ranged from Jewish self-rejection, through assertions of the compatibility of dual forms of identification, to Zionist proclamations of a national identity other than Germanness. Even the majority of German Jews who believed it was still possible to reconcile German nationality and Jewish identity were won over to the need for more active confrontation with antisemitism. The "political" issue of the right of Jews to be Germans began to affect both Jewish organizational life and the self-understanding of many German Jews. Even those who still upheld the slogan of "German citizens of the Jewish faith" began to allow overtones of ethnicity and "community of fate" into their "religious" definition of Judaism.

1. Reorientation of the Mainstream: The Centralverein

The vast majority of German Jews continued to espouse some kind of synthesis between their Germanness and their Jewishness. Aside from agreement that they were both Germans and Jews, members of this mainstream varied widely in their opinions on how to deal with antisemitism. While some thought that prejudice was best ignored as a last gasp of the Middle Ages, others reacted with anger and wished to take action in word and deed. Still others felt that Jews should redouble their efforts to integrate into Germany. Without totally rejecting their fellow Jews, they accepted some of the criticisms of Jewish behavior, traditions, or social structure and called for Jewish self-improvement. Many, however, felt that solidarity required them to defend even aspects of Jewishness that they did not personally believe in. Often individuals combined diverse approaches to the question of Jewish identity without trying to reconcile their contradictions.

The founding of the Österreichisch-Israelitische Union, German-oriented fraternities, and the Centralverein deutscher Staatsbürger jüdischen Glaubens (CV, see chapters 5 and 8) marked an important turning point in Jewish attitudes toward championing their own interests. Previously the Jewish establishment had tried to avoid controversy, deal with problems quietly behind the scenes, and abstain from speaking in terms of specific Jewish needs. Now pride, self-respect, and "manly honor"—virtues much praised in fin-de-siècle Germany—would not allow Jews to remain silent or let others do their fighting for them:

> But can it be acceptable for us, can it even conform to our self-respect and dignity to allow ourselves to be defended by others without joining in ourselves? . . . It goes without saying that we will never ever work in opposition to the [Gentile-led] Verein zur Abwehr des Antisemitismus; but what differentiates us from them, though it does not divide us, is the principle of self-help: that it is the duty of all decent persons to defend themselves.[1]

This new attitude expressed itself not only in the increased willingness to go to court or answer antisemitic pamphlets. At the universities it was communicated by the readiness of Jewish students to fight duels against antisemites. The participation by the Kartell Convent fraternities (and even by some Zionist ones) in what to later generations looked like antiquated rituals of drinking, carrying colors, and fencing were in part ways to express pride and defend the honor of the Jews according to the chivalrous code of the fraternities. The unwillingness of antisemites to "give satisfaction" to Jewish challenges to duel were taken as a deep insult, while the readiness of Jews to provoke fights with their enemies was a source of pride.

Outside the rarified atmosphere of student life, the cv urged its members to show self-respect by openly "acknowledging" their Jewishness rather than trying to hide it:

> When the Jews will see that a large number of their own (and not the worst among them) repeatedly assert in public: "Yes, we are Jews, and what we want is not to plead for protection but to claim our rights," then broader circles among us, who at present don't even dare raise their heads in their hostile surroundings—as if they had committed a sin by being Jews!—will gradually reach the point where they will declare . . . as openly as we do: "Yes, we are of the Jewish faith, and we are just as good or as bad as any other German citizen."[2]

Coupled with this increased willingness to proclaim one's own Jewishness was the cv's stress on self-defense "in the public eye." Behind the scenes activity would not help raise self-esteem in the way that public action could. Despite having abandoned some of Judaism's traditional beliefs, many members of the fraternities and cv felt it a point of honor not to abandon a people under siege. This, and other military images, were frequently used by secularized Jews in denouncing converts to Christianity. Often those actively pursuing Jewish defense were defending not a specific Jewish concept or way of life but rather their own self-respect. Some called this attitude *Trotzjudentum* (Judaism to spite the enemy).

The forthrightness with which the new defense organizations engaged in the fight against antisemitism encountered bitter initial opposition from established community leaders as a break from former policy. Yet the basic aim and self-conception of the defense groups was little different from that of the Liberal leaders who preceded them. Their dearest desire was to be accepted as Germans or Austrians, not to break away from the land of their birth and culture. Even as they asserted pride in who they were, they claimed to fight only for what was due them as citizens, not for any special status. Deutschtum and Judentum were not in conflict, they believed; Jews were acting exactly like other Germans in standing up for their interests and in so doing would in fact become better Germans. Thus, despite the cv's repeated proclamation of Jewish self-respect, its basic tendency was to play down Jewish difference:

> We are not German Jews but German citizens of the Jewish faith. As citizens we need and demand no other protection than our con-

stitutional rights. As Jews we do not belong to any particular political party. Political opinions, like religious ones, are a matter for the
individual. Our beliefs are firmly based on German nationality. We
have no more connection with Jews in other countries than German
Catholics or Protestants have with Catholics and Protestants in
other lands. Our morality does not differ from that of our fellow citizens of other faiths. We condemn the unethical actions of individuals regardless of their faith. We reject any responsibility for the
actions of individual Jews and protest against the generalization . . .
that makes the collectivity of Jewish citizens responsible for the
actions of individual Jews.[3]

The self-definition as "Germans of the Jewish faith" involved certain
conceptual problems. Many of those active in defense of Jewish rights
were themselves highly secularized. Although the very title of the organization defined the Jews as a "faith," the cv declared its neutrality on all
internal Jewish debates on the nature of religion. Its members were free
to believe and practice whatever they desired or to refrain from belief and
practice altogether. Some cv leaders insisted that "the expression 'of the
Jewish faith,' used in the name, was chosen because it is the governmental category into which Jews in Germany are placed; it is a term based on
government policy, not religion."[4] This definition of "Jewish faith," which
avoids reference to religious content, seems—ironically—to indicate an
understanding of Judaism as something other than merely a confession.

For some of those turning from a purely confessional definition of
Judaism the religious element of Judaism was not distinctive, since all
religions had the same principles. They looked instead to a shared history
of Jewish suffering. This idea, later formulated in terms of a community
of fate, was already emerging before the founding of the cv:

And here lies the answer to the question of the duties of Germans
of Jewish ancestry. They should not form a separate ancestral group
[*Stamm*], for they are Germans, nor an isolated and exclusive religious community, for their God and moral doctrines are the God of
all humanity, the morality of all moral people. They should, however, remain mindful of their history of suffering. . . . And may this
community of suffering [*Leidensgenossenschaft*]—the principle
that "Judaeus sum, nil Judaici a me alienum puto" (I am a Jew and I
am not indifferent to anything that affects Jews)—inspire their
feelings of duty, honor, and empathy.[5]

The formulation "Germans of Jewish ancestry" is a reflection of the growing role played by the idea of ancestry and race in late-nineteenth-century German thinking. Some defenders of the Jewish claim to full Germanness did take into account, at least in part, the different ancestry, original geographical roots, and even physical appearance of German Jews and non-Jews. Non-Zionists who accepted the idea of Jewish ethnic characteristics generally spoke in terms of ancestry rather than nation or race. Some compared the Jewish ancestry to the Bavarians or Saxons who had their own regional character, linguistic patterns, and habits, but were still part of the mosaic of the German nation.

Antisemitic attacks on Jewish religious texts and practices placed secularized leaders of Jewish defense in the uncomfortable position of having to defend what they did not personally believe in. Some spokesmen for self-defense felt that the Jewish religion itself was an obstacle to integration. Occasionally a forthright attack on antisemitism, such as the pamphlet by Raphael Loewenfeld that helped launch the cv, contained a call for radical religious reforms along with harsh criticism of Orthodoxy. Yet such anti-Orthodox views did not become the official position of the defense organizations. In the case of kosher slaughter, for instance, Jewish activists came to the defense of a practice they personally did not observe for the sake of freedom of conscience. Some Jews replied to attacks on the Talmud by stating that traditional religious texts no longer possessed authority for modern Jews, but all the while they defended the Talmud in print and in the courts.

The attitude of the Liberal majority to criticism of East European Jewish immigrants resembled their approach to defense of religious practice. In private at least, many German Jews shared their non-Jewish neighbors' negative opinions about the honesty, cleanliness, and level of culture of East European Jews. Some thought the Easterners were the real target of Gentile hatred, or at least that their presence was an important factor in exacerbating it. Despite such widespread feelings, Jewish organizations generally defended the rights of Jewish immigrants and transmigrants, sometimes protested against attempts at deportation, and almost always organized philanthropic aid for them, in part to speed the Ostjuden on their way and prevent their remaining in Germany. The defense of the rights of Jewish immigrants was a defense of the legal equality of the Jews. Even German Jews who had little personal appreciation of the immigrants saw the danger posed to all Jewry by antisemitic calls for closing the borders.

Many German Jews rejected the generalized nature of antisemitic reproaches but felt that fighting prejudice should go hand in hand with self-improvement, which would remove some of the causes of prejudice. This approach was evident in the reactivation of Jewish groups to encourage agriculture and crafts, in repeated pleas to Jewish women to dress less conspicuously, and in efforts to remove traces of Jewish intonation and vocabulary from Jewish speech. Such actions point to the incorporation of antisemitic value judgments even among those Jews who fought antisemitism. An opponent of the main speaker at a Zionist meeting, for instance, stated:

> I defended the point of view that we can make no progress if we are always looking for the shortcomings of others instead of our own. The emancipation of the Jews is recent enough for large circles still to carry much more of the ghetto around inside of them than they are willing to admit to themselves. What we need, first of all, is self-improvement in the areas of modest behavior and better understanding of German culture.[6]

The revival of Jewish self-assertiveness in defense organizations thus had its limits. It meant insistence upon the right of Jews to be included in the definition of who is a German but not upon an identity that set one apart from other Germans. Jewishness was something to be proud of, but it was not an identity that would separate the Jew from the culture or the nationality of the majority.

2. Self-Rejection and Self-Hatred

In contrast to the majority of German Jews who reacted to Jew hatred by asserting Jewish rights, there was a small group, mainly known through the writings of a few intellectuals, who appropriated a highly negative view of Jewishness. At times their images of the Jews differed little from those of the antisemites. Thinking of this type has often been called "Jewish self-hatred," a phrase made popular in 1930 by the philosopher Theodor Lessing (1872–1933) for those individuals who profoundly loathed the community from which they stemmed.

The application of criticism to the Jewish community was not limited to persons who rejected their Jewish selves; many of those campaigning for Jewish rights were likewise frank about Jewish failings. Even Theodor Herzl sometimes used terminology borrowed from the antisemites (like

31   "Something Darwinian," a caricature against assimilation from the
Zionist satirical journal *Schlemiel*

"Mauschel") when criticizing the shortcomings of Diaspora life. What
made self-rejecters distinctive was the global nature of their disapproval
of Jewishness. Although even the most extreme Jewish "self-haters"
rejected racial antisemitism of the crudest type, several subjected the Jews
to evaluations that were almost totally negative. Among them were
Walther Rathenau, Karl Kraus, and Otto Weininger, who represent three
very different types of Jewish rejection of Jews.

In his early essay, "Höre Israel" (Hear O Israel, 1897), which he later
repudiated, Walther Rathenau (1877–1922) criticizes the Jews for their
alienness: "A strange vision! In the middle of German life an isolated,
alien tribe, with hot-blooded, lively gestures, decked out in glittering and
conspicuous finery. An Asian horde on the sands of Brandenburg."[7]
Rathenau wished to eliminate typically Jewish characteristics from himself and other Jews and to substitute their opposites. In common with
völkisch thinkers he preferred the "soul" over the intellect. He criticized
Jews who fought antisemitism by calling for "defense rather than self-
examination."[8] Despite these negative views about Jewishness, Rathenau
rejected conversion as unworthy and supported equality for the Jews.
Although he persisted in his low opinion of many aspects of Jewishness
and saw himself as one of a small group of aristocratic Jews free of his
coreligionists' personality traits, unlike more extreme critics he later
developed a more positive view of his fellow Jews.

Karl Kraus (1874–1936), the sharp-tongued Viennese critic who had
converted to Catholicism in 1898, held similarly negative views on the
Jews but expressed them more often and more consistently than did
Rathenau. Although he rejected racial antisemitism, he sometimes borrowed the vocabulary of the racial antisemites. His mockery of his coreligionists expressed itself in satirical remarks about Jewish profiteers, back-

ward Galicians, Zionism, and Jewish literary figures. Often he employed Yiddish expressions as a device for derision. Like the antisemites, Kraus was a strong anti-Dreyfusard and an opponent of the liberal and Jewish-owned *Neue Freie Presse*. Still, there were occasions on which he attacked antisemitic excesses or championed certain Jewish writers, notably Peter Altenberg and Else Lasker-Schüler.

Kraus's 1913 essay "Er is doch e Jud" (He's a Jew After All) is a good example of his highly ambivalent attitude toward his origins. Answering an antisemite who asked him if he believed he could "leave his race," he denied that he had any Jewish traits, claiming:

> I go along with the development of Judaism up to the Exodus but I won't participate in the dance around the Golden Calf. . . . I really don't know what Jewish characteristics are nowadays. If there is one trait in particular—greed for power and possessions—that blocks out all the better ones, then that trait, as I see it, is equally distributed among all the peoples of the West.[9]

Kraus distanced himself from both antisemites and Jews by denouncing the bad characteristics of both. In addition, he attacked Zionism in a blistering satire, *Eine Krone für Zion* (A Crown for Zion, 1898), which considered the new movement "Jewish antisemitism" because it agreed with the antisemites that Jews did not belong in their countries of residence.

Anti-Jewish utterances, while common enough, do not play the central role in the work of Rathenau and Kraus that they do in the writings of the tragic Viennese figure Otto Weininger (1880–1903). Unlike the others, Weininger spoke not so much in terms of specific Jewish traits as of Judaism as an "ideal Platonic type":

> I am not here concerned about a race nor about a people, even less about a legally recognized religious denomination. One should think of Judaism only as a tendency of the spirit . . . that is a *possibility* in *all* human beings, and has only found its most grandiose *realization* in historical Judaism.[10]

Weininger's description of the Jews, influenced by the antisemite Houston Stewart Chamberlain, tends to be highly abstract. While denying that he favored persecuting them, he described the essence of the Jews in extremely negative terms paralleling, though differing from, his negative portrayal of women. Jews were said to lack personality, honor, self-worth, depth, the possibility of greatness, and a sense of the individual.

They were irreligion personified. In Weininger's ascetic and antisexual value system, the Jews were inferior because they lacked the ability to transcend the material realm and because they championed sexual union and the family. Weininger's writings were the product of a tortured soul who committed suicide at the age of twenty-three shortly after his conversion to Protestantism and the publication of his book *Sex and Character*. Many of his statements, often quoted out of context, were eagerly used in antisemitic works with intellectual pretentions, as were the comments of Walther Rathenau in "Höre Israel."

Although extreme rejection of Judaism is most evident in the published works of intellectuals, it was also to be found among scattered individuals throughout the Jewish community. Antisemitism had a negative effect on the psyche of some German Jews, just as it had a mobilizing effect on others. Even among those who did not overtly reflect an anti-Jewish viewpoint, there were quite a few who reacted to hatred by turning away from Judaism through conversion, secession from the Jewish community, changing their name, or breaking all social ties to other Jews. Behavior of this type was far more common than the anti-Jewish writings of intellectuals.

3. Zionism: The Jewish National Alternative

At the opposite end of the spectrum from Jewish self-rejection was the Zionist revival of Jewish nationalism. Like the defense organizations, the Zionists found an important initial constituency among young people, especially at the universities. But they also had a strong following among East European immigrants—a group barred from membership in the cv, which was restricted to German citizens. Unlike the cv, the Austrian Union, and other defense groups, the Zionists did not win over the Jewish establishment but rather remained an oppositional minority throughout the *Kaiserreich* period. The Jewish nationalist militancy of some Zionists made the activism of the cv appear tame. In the eyes of militant Zionists the members of the defense organizations, like the German Jewish establishment they eventually joined, were assimilationists who did not understand the true nature of the Jewish situation.

The precursors of Zionism had emerged before the founding of the organizations to fight antisemitism. Although the proto-Zionist works of Zevi Hirsch Kalischer and Moses Hess in the early 1860s (see volume 2) found little resonance, the rise of political antisemitism and especially the

Russian pogroms of 1881 had led to the emergence of a pre-Herzlian Zionist movement. This proto-Zionist movement, known as Ḥibat Tsiyon (Love of Zion), came to the fore with the publication in 1882 of a German-language pamphlet, *Auto-Emancipation*, by the Russian-Jewish writer Leo Pinsker (1821–1891). In Pinsker's analysis, antisemitism was a pathological condition not subject to cure by reasonable arguments and caused by the ghostly existence of the Jews as a nation without a homeland. Western Jewry had a role to play in helping to organize the rescue of East European Jews from it.

Although Ḥibat Tsiyon was centered in Eastern Europe, it found some bases of support in German-speaking Jewry. Among these were the previously mentioned Viennese university students who founded the Jewish nationalist society Kadima in 1882, Russian-Jewish students at German universities, Orthodox circles around Rabbi Esriel Hildesheimer in Berlin, and scattered rabbis, intellectuals, and community activists. Early leaders included Nathan Birnbaum (1864–1937), a militant young Viennese intellectual, Isaac Rülf (1834–1902), the rabbi of Memel, long active in rescuing East European Jews, and Willy Bambus (1862–1904) of Berlin, who gave inspiration to the Esra fund-raising organization for Jewish agricultural colonies. Some important leaders of later German Zionism, among them Max Bodenheimer and David Wolffssohn, both of Cologne, were already engaged in Ḥibat Tsiyon activities in the early 1890s.

There was little coordination between the different groups involved in proto-Zionist activities. The international conference of Ḥibat Tsiyon in the Upper Silesian city of Kattowitz in 1884, though an early indication of strength, was unable to create a strong central focus for the movement. Proto-Zionism remained a loose federation of groups dedicated mainly to philanthropic aid for Jewish colonization in Palestine intended to rescue Russian Jewry. It had little in the way of nationalist ideology and was not much of a force in Central Europe. All of this changed with the sudden appearance of Theodor Herzl (1860–1904) and the political movement he created. Herzl seems to have had little awareness of the existence of Ḥibat Tsiyon and developed his revolutionary ideas independently. Like many of his later followers in the German-speaking countries, Herzl was deeply acculturated and initially accepted the liberal Jewish worldview from which he was later estranged. After arriving in Vienna from his native Budapest, Herzl joined a German nationalist dueling fraternity from which he resigned in 1883 when it expressed support for antisemitism. As

32   Theodor Herzl on his way to Jaffa

an author of popular plays and a correspondent for the *Neue Freie Presse*, he was a well-known figure on the Viennese cultural scene.

Herzl's break from the conventional optimistic liberal view of Jewish integration was brought about by his experiences with antisemitism. He himself later emphasized the effect that the Dreyfus Affair and its attendant hatred of Jews had on him when he was a correspondent in Paris in 1894. However, recent scholars ascribe a greater role to Viennese antisemitism, especially the 1895 electoral successes of Karl Lueger, later mayor of Vienna.

Before he conceived a Zionist solution for antisemitism, Herzl toyed with other "solutions": a ceremonious mass conversion at the Vienna cathedral or a heroic reaction like that of the main character in his 1894 play *Das Neue Ghetto* (The New Ghetto), who dies in a duel with an antisemite. By January 1896, however, in an article in the London *Jewish Chronicle*, and one month later in his book, *Der Judenstaat* (The Jewish State), Herzl proclaimed that he had found his answer to the Jewish Question.

The appearance of Herzl's book created a sensation and aroused both great enthusiasm and violent opposition. On the one hand, the book quickly led to the emergence of a full-fledged international Zionist movement. The combination of Herzl's charismatic personality with the prac-

33   Advertising booth for "products of Jewish villages in Palestine" at the
world's fair in Berlin in 1896

tical organizational proposals he set forth made it possible to proceed
rapidly to the creation of local and national Zionist groups, the organization of fund-raising for the new enterprise, and the calling of a Zionist
congress, which met in August 1897 in Basel.

While arousing much enthusiasm among the East European masses
and among some (mainly young) Western Jews, Herzl's movement provoked opposition to a greater degree, especially in the West. Even some of
the original adherents of Ḥibat Tsiyon were ambivalent or opposed to
Herzlian Zionism. Rabbi Moritz Güdemann of Vienna attacked Herzl and
his ideas sharply in his book *Nationaljudentum* (National Judaism, 1897).
Indeed, rabbinical opposition to Zionism was initially almost universal in
German-speaking lands. The newly founded Allgemeiner Rabbinerverband (General Union of Rabbis), representing both Orthodox and
Liberal German rabbis, issued a formal protest against Zionist plans to
hold the first Zionist congress in Munich. The rabbis declared Judaism to
be a universal religion, not a nationality. Herzl replied by derisively label-
ing his opponents *Protestrabbiner.*

Other elements of organized German Jewry also opposed Zionism, although, at first, they did not consider it a serious threat. Eugen Fuchs, a leading spokesman of the CV, could state benignly in 1897 that he saw Zionism as "an excess of religious loyalty," which, like antisemitism, had the value that its adherents "shake up indifference . . . that they give the Jew back his self-assurance and pride" but that both antisemitism and Zionism "will be overcome."[11]

The controversy aroused by Zionism focused less on its ultimate plan of recreating a Jewish homeland in Palestine than on the implication of the new movement for Jewish identity in Europe. Two principal views were held by Western Zionists. According to one, Zionism was essentially a philanthropic enterprise designed to create a haven for Eastern Jews suffering persecution in their lands of residence. According to a second, the movement required an awareness that Jewishness was a separate nationality and that even untroubled Western Jews had to see themselves as potential emigrants to the Jewish homeland. The more radical Zionists declared themselves members of the Jewish nation, not the German one, and called for an uprooting of the sense of cultural Germanness. This strictly nationalist definition of Zionism, with its implication that Jews could never be at home in the Diaspora, aroused tremendous opposition even among those who had no objection to philanthropically motivated colonization efforts in Palestine.

Much of the debate about national identity was highly theoretical and subtle. Positions advocating emigration to Palestine were hardly ever implemented in the lives of individual Zionists. The gap between the objectively German cultural lifestyle of German Zionists and their subjective identification with the Jewish nation and culture is striking. Even radicals who called for learning Hebrew did not represent an existing population of active non-German speakers in the way that Polish nationalist leaders in Germany did. Creating a Jewish national culture and identity required intensive effort for those West European Jews who desired it. Some Western Zionists envied the Jews of Eastern Europe for whom Jewish culture did not have to be artificially created as in the West.

Those Zionists who stressed the national culture aspect of the movement inverted the conventional German-Jewish image of East European Jews. Most German Jews felt a sense of estrangement from their coreligionists in the East—an estrangement not ameliorated by contact with Jewish immigrants and transmigrants. The "ghetto novels" of Karl Emil Franzos (1848–1904) and others helped perpetuate a picture of Eastern

34 Scene from E. M. Lilien's *Songs of the Ghetto*

Europe as a backward, dirty "Semi-Asia." The Jews of the East, whose cultural level was seen as deplorable, required Western culture. Even many Zionists and Orthodox Jews shared the negative views of much of the Liberal establishment about the East European immigrants, despite the fact that the newcomers were valuable reinforcements as Orthodox worshipers, Zionist members, and anti-Liberal voters in community elections.

But supporters of cultural Zionism, especially in the younger generation, often replaced such negative stereotypes of Ostjuden with idealization. Some considered East European Jews an example of the authentic Jewish Volk, absent in Germany, that could serve as a model for the Jewish nation in the making. Unlike Zionists in Eastern Europe who often deplored the wretched economic conditions and backward "ghetto" culture of their lands of birth, Martin Buber, Berthold Feiwel, and other young German-speaking cultural Zionists praised the pious, joyous Hasidim and admired Yiddish literature alongside Hebrew as a vital part of Jewish national culture. Such publications as *Ost und West*, initially a journal sponsored by the non-Zionist Alliance Israélite, the *Jüdischer Almanach* (Jewish Almanac), published by the Zionist Jüdischer Verlag, and the Prague Bar Kochba society's 1913 essay collection *Vom Judentum* (On Judaism) interpreted East European Jewish culture to Western Jews in a favorable light.

There were even small numbers of Western Jewish intellectuals who felt that Zionism was too lukewarm in its recognition of East European Jewish culture. Nathan Birnbaum, one of the leaders of pre-Herzlian Zionism, moved from Zionism to Diaspora Jewish nationalism and helped initiate the Czernowitz Yiddish language conference in 1908. Eventually, he went even further, turning from support of autonomous East European culture to Orthodoxy as one of the world leaders of Agudat Israel. The essayist Fritz Mordechai Kaufmann (1888–1921) likewise adopted a non-Zionist—though, in his case secular—appreciation of East European Jews. His journal *Die Freistatt* (The Sanctuary) was dedicated to East European Jewish life and proclaimed a "pan-Jewish" view based on the East European model in contrast to both Zionism and assimilationism. Equally extreme was Franz Kafka's friend, the poet Jiři (Georg) Langer (1894–1943) of Prague, who adopted the hasidic lifestyle after a visit to Galicia in 1913.

The early leaders of German Zionism such as Franz Oppenheimer (1864–1943), Adolf Friedemann (1871–1932), and the founding president Max Bodenheimer (1865–1945) were moderates who saw their mission as a humanitarian endeavor to save the suffering Jews of Eastern Europe. They supported Herzl's political Zionism, emphasizing the securing of international recognition for a Jewish homeland over cultural goals, and played down the nationalist element without rejecting it:

> Bound together by common ancestry and history, the Jews of all countries make up a national community. This conviction in no way lessens the ability of Jews, especially German Jews, to espouse patriotic attitudes and to fulfill their duties as citizens for their German fatherland.[12]

A younger generation of Zionists, led by Kurt Blumenfeld (1883–1963) and Richard Lichtheim (1885–1963), rejected the earlier leaders' moderation. Often coming from totally assimilated families and experiencing a sense of "conversion" to Zionism, they defined the movement as "postassimilationist Judaism." In their eyes Zionism was not merely a colonization scheme to aid suffering Ostjuden. It was "a movement intended to shake up the spirit and revive the powers of Judaism."[13]

In the years before World War I the younger generation of Zionists, led by Blumenfeld, gained control of the Zionistische Vereinigung für Deutschland (Zionist Union for Germany, zvfD). Blumenfeld was appointed to the new post of party secretary in 1909 and the following year Arthur Hantke (1874–1956) replaced Bodenheimer as president of the zvfᴅ. Not only did the new leaders bring about greatly increased interest and membership, they also endeavored to make their viewpoint the official doctrine of the movement. Their radicalism expressed itself less in musings about Jewish national character than as a commitment to cut themselves loose from German society. At the convention of the zvfᴅ in Posen in May 1912 a resolution was passed declaring:

> Because of the surpassing importance of the Palestine work for the liberation of the individual personality as well as for the achievement of our final goal, the convention declares it to be the duty of every Zionist—and especially of those who are economically independent—to include migration to Palestine in the plan for their lives.[14]

Once they became aware of what a radical step this resolution represented, the moderates counterattacked, but they were outvoted at the 1914 convention. On that occasion the renowned economist Franz Oppenheimer explained how the moderate view differed:

> I am not an assimilationist, but I am assimilated. I am a German and am proud to be a Jew. . . . But I am just as proud to have grown up in the land of Walther von der Vogelweide and Wolfram von Eschenbach, of Goethe, Kant, and Fichte and to have absorbed their culture within myself.[15]

Jews in Germany, according to this view, were *Kulturdeutsche* (cultural Germans) and could not be *Kulturjuden* (cultural Jews).

The 1912 Posen resolution was unique in the international Zionist movement. Even though the members of the Russian and Galician Zionist organizations had far deeper roots in Jewish culture and much more Jewish knowledge than the German branch, they never adopted an equally radical statement. Zionism outside of Germany experienced all manner of deep divisions—between religious Jews and secularists, socialists and nonsocialists, advocates of political and of cultural Zionism. As a result some of the Zionist national organizations split along ideological lines, something that did not occur at this time in German Zionism, where controversy raged instead over the implications of the Zionist commitment for the individual.

Despite the vehement controversy among German Zionists over whether Zionism entailed a break with German culture and German nationality, there was considerable common ground in the day-to-day work of the movement. German Zionism devoted a great deal of its energy to fund-raising, using such trappings of older Jewish charitable appeals as collection boxes, stamps, and certificates, both to raise money and to create a sense of Jewish peoplehood. Such solicitations remained purposely vague about any need for a personal commitment to migrate to Palestine and appealed to charitable feelings for oppressed Jews instead. The payment of the shekel and the blue and white Jewish National Fund box were, for many of the rank and file, their chief means of Zionist identification.

While declaring their alienation from Germany and its culture, the radicals too were deeply influenced by German intellectual currents, especially by the völkisch ideas common in the youth movement. Their speeches and articles were just as likely to be filled with quotations from German poets and philosophers as were those of the moderates. However, cultural Zionists like Martin Buber and Berthold Feiwel emphasized the importance of their essential subjective Jewish "uniqueness" (*Eigenart*) over the merely external cultural traits they had absorbed from their surroundings. Against the moderates' stress on the objective fact that even radicals were heavily influenced by German culture and knew little about Jewish tradition, cultural Zionists called for the expression of a "will to Judaism." They urged Jews to make a deliberate effort to become nationally conscious and accused the moderates of self-satisfied acceptance of the status quo.

In trying to find what exactly it was that made them essentially Jewish, when their overt cultural traits were so much influenced by the German environment, cultural Zionists looked for an unconscious and ineffable Jewish identity buried deep within the soul. Expressed in the language of poetic metaphor rather than rationalist analysis, this idea often borrowed völkisch language. Racially tinged vocabulary such as "common blood" and even "racial influence" were used to express rootedness in a common ancestry and a common fate. However, in contrast to "Aryan" völkisch thinking, most Zionist versions did not claim racial superiority or deny the possibility that hereditary characteristics could be modified by the environment. They saw Jewish specificity as part of a world in which each nation had its own legitimate character and individuality. The Zionist sociologist Arthur Ruppin (1876–1943) gave the following formulation:

Just as it would be foolish to destroy the multiplicity of varieties of fruits in favor of a single species, so it would be foolish to wish to blot out national differences. The goal toward which humanity strives today is not sameness but rather the utilization of the distinctive features of various peoples for the sake of the collective culture.[16]

In this theoretical framework hereditary difference became an argument for cultural pluralism.

Unlike its German counterpart, Austrian Zionism was divided not by different views of Jewish nationalism but by the issue whether or not to become involved in Austrian politics. In 1906 advocates of involvement were victorious and the Austrian Zionists supported rights for the Jews as an autonomous Jewish minority within the empire; they asked for recognition of Jewish nationality and language in the census. In the same year Zionists joined with autonomists to form a Jewish National Party (Jüdische Volkspartei) that won seats in the Austrian parliament.

In Austria, too, the degree of identification with German nationality was not as great as in Germany. Even the founder of the non-Zionist Österreichisch-Israelitische Union, Rabbi Bloch, had favored a generalized Austrian rather than a German identification. Jewish nationalism was stronger in Austria, in part because so many Viennese Jews were born in Eastern Europe. In 1910–1911 one-third of the Jewish students at the University of Vienna registered their nationality as Jewish.

4. Zionism and Centralverein: From Peaceful Coexistence to Confrontation

From its inception Zionism was a force outside the Jewish establishment in Germany. Often the public meetings called by the Zionists aroused vehement opposition from the communal leadership. Sharp language and rhetorical outbursts by speakers on both sides made for lively interest and filled meeting halls but sometimes created bitter feelings. During the period of moderate control of the Zionistische Vereinigung, despite the frequent heated debates between Liberal and Zionist spokesmen, hostility between the Zionists and the established national organizations remained muted. The umbrella organizations tried to maintain their neutrality until sharp antagonism began to flare up in the wake of gains by radicals within the Zionist movement. Before that time the most vehement attacks on the Zionists came from religious circles, especially from the Liberals but also from some Orthodox groups.

Liberal religious opposition to Zionism, expressed by the Berlin Reform Congregation and, after its founding in 1908, by the Union for Liberal Judaism, was based both on communal politics and on basic religious principle. Liberal leaders resented Zionist opposition in Jewish communal elections, their occasional coalitions with the Orthodox, support for more Hebrew in the service, and attacks on the organ and liturgical reform. But deeper than this was recognition of the Zionist challenge to some of Liberal Judaism's most cherished tenets—the idea that the Jews had progressed from the national to the universal stage of religious consciousness, that the Jewish state belonged to a past age, and that Judaism was only a set of religious beliefs. The vast majority of Liberal religious leaders in Germany (and elsewhere) were outspoken in their anti-Zionism. The editor and historian Ludwig Geiger (son of the Liberal leader Abraham Geiger) went so far as to declare that those Zionists who claimed membership in a Jewish nationality should lose their German citizenship. When in the late fall of 1912, following passage of the Posen resolution, an Anti-Zionist Committee was founded by Hermann Veit-Simon, its headquarters were located in the same building as those of the Union for Liberal Judaism.

The small number of Liberal rabbis who supported Zionism, like Isaac Rülf of Memel, were the exception to the rule. Students at the Liberal seminary in Berlin who founded a Jewish nationalist association were forced to disband it in 1901. When a young Liberal rabbi employed as a preacher and teacher in Berlin publicly expressed Zionist views, it stirred a bitter confrontation that deepened the gap between Liberals and Zionists. Rabbi Emil Cohn (1881–1948) had been appointed on the condition that he not use his position to spread Zionism. When it was discovered that Cohn had expressed strongly Zionist beliefs to a Christian high school director, the community suspended him from his position in 1907. The communal president allegedly told Cohn: "You are our paid employee. You are required to represent our views."[17] The Zionists publicized the case through mass meetings and editorials, proclaiming the community's action a violation of free thought. None of this helped Rabbi Cohn, whose suspension became permanent dismissal. Instead it strengthened Liberal opposition to Zionism and even led to a coalition between Liberals and traditionalists against Zionism in the subsequent Berlin communal election.

In the secular Jewish nationwide organizations opposition to Zionism was at first restrained. Although Zionist ideology did not mesh with the

Centralverein's emphasis on German identity, the cv did not dwell on this point. Along with the Hilfsverein der deutschen Juden and the Verband der deutschen Juden, the cv proclaimed neutrality in internal Jewish controversies in order to assert its right to speak for the whole community. As late as February 1912 one of its leaders could maintain:

> We may be of different opinions as to whether the Jews are still a people, nation, race, or just a social and religious grouping . . . whether it is true that the Jewish spirit today is homeless and will only find a home when a real homeland exists for the people. The Zionists hope for it, the non-Zionists don't believe in it. But these differences of opinion must not . . . divide us, not cause us to abandon the banner raised by the Centralverein.[18]

However, the rise of the radical new generation within the Zionist movement led to a worsening of relations between Zionism and the mainstream umbrella organizations. Besides the Emil Cohn affair and the Posen resolution, a series of other controversies served to aggravate relations. One centered upon the writings on Judaism by the leading non-Jewish economist and sociologist Werner Sombart whom many Zionists saw as an ally for their cause when he declared the Jews a distinct nationality, which deserved full equality but should display the "tact" not to assume positions of social and cultural influence that should not be held by outsiders. Such views seemed to undermine the Centralverein's accustomed tactic of contesting any attempt to exclude the Jews from German life. Liberal attempts to disenfranchise East European voters in Jewish communal elections in Duisburg and other cities likewise kindled fires of dispute, as did the failure of the cv to prevent the nomination of an apostate Jew, Otto Mugdan, for the Reichstag. Zionist rhetoric in the latter two controversies was caustic. Headlines in the Zionist press spoke of "the shame of Duisburg" and referred to the Mugdan case as "the bankruptcy of the Centralverein."

In reaction to the new Zionist militancy, voices within the Centralverein called for a more openly anti-Zionist stance. The relatively moderate Eugen Fuchs had the cv pass a resolution in March 1913 that distinguished between radical Zionists who could have no place within the Centralverein and moderates who were still welcome:

> Insofar as a German Zionist strives to create a secure homeland for the oppressed Jews of the East or to raise the pride of the Jews in their

history and religion, he is welcome to be our member. But we must separate ourselves from *that kind* of Zionist who rejects German national feelings ... and considers his nationality to be *only* Jewish.[19]

The CV did not adopt more radical action, like official support for the Anti-Zionist Committee or condemnation of the Basel Program, calling for an internationally recognized Jewish homeland. But its distinction between radicals and moderates did nothing to prevent a break. In fact, it infuriated the Zionists, who saw it as a tactic to split their movement. In May 1913 they called upon their members to resign from the Centralverein and even tried, without success, to create a rival defense organization against antisemitism, the Reichsverein der deutschen Juden (Association of German Jews in the Reich).

Shortly after these incidents the relationship between the Zionists and another establishment Jewish organization, the Hilfsverein, likewise deteriorated. Originally the Zionists and the Hilfsverein had cooperated on a number of projects, especially schools in Palestine. The breach between them came in a dispute concerning the Hilfsverein's decision to limit the use of Hebrew and favor the use of German at the Technikum (now Technion) that it had founded in Haifa. When the Hebrew teachers of Palestine went on strike in 1913 against this decision, the German Zionists supported the strike and resigned from the Hilfsverein board. In retaliation the two principal leaders of the latter organization, James Simon and Paul Nathan, joined the Anti-Zionist Committee in 1914.

The radicalization of Zionism in the immediate prewar period thus led to a permanent break between the Zionists and the mainstream organizations. During and after World War I even moderates in the CV reiterated their anti-Zionist views. For their part, Zionists, on frequent occasions, made statements indicating that they thought the CV's fight against antisemitism was a hopeless waste of energy. The distinction between Centralverein adherent and Zionist became a staple of the post-1912 German-Jewish scene.

Yet one should not exaggerate the depth of the split between the two groups. Even radical Zionists still made a distinction between their Jewish nationality and the civic duties they continued to acknowledge as German citizens. Some even used the phrase "Deutsche Staatsbürger jüdischer Nation" (German citizens of the Jewish nation). During the world war Zionists felt no conflict between patriotic duties and Jewish nationalist feelings.

Moreover, despite its rejection of Jewish nationalism, the Central-verein increasingly shared with the Zionists their negative evaluation of assimilation and apostasy. *Assimilation,* formerly a neutral or positive term, was now used as a pejorative by both groups. In Eugen Fuchs's words: "Fortunately, the intellectual current has changed. The slogans 'assimilation,' 'amalgamation,' and 'unreserved total absorption' have lost their attraction. Conversion and baptism are once again stigmatized as desertion and lack of loyalty."[20] Naturally, assimilation did not mean the same thing for the cv as for the Zionists. The former resented Zionist attacks on them as assimilationists and German chauvinists. They denied that rejection of Jewish nationalism meant assimilation: "We too want inner revitalization, a renascence of Judaism, not one-sided assimilation."[21]

The cv eagerly welcomed the emperor's call to all Germans to preserve their distinctiveness, which made it easier for them to assert their own religious and ancestral identity even as they rejected the idea of a Jewish nation. Once more it was Fuchs who expressed the dominant sentiment:

> We want to belong to the German fatherland and we will belong to it. At the same time we can and must remain true to our religious community and our ancestral history. "Proud of their individuality and loyal," our king recently said about the various German regional cultures [*Stämme*]. We can apply this expression to our ancestral group [*Stamm*] as well. National amalgamation can coexist with social groupings; our distinctiveness is hardly greater than that of other German groups, regional cultures, and classes [*Stände*], and, even if it were, it would make no difference.[22]

On the eve of the First World War both the mainstream "Germans of the Jewish faith" and the Zionists reflected a change in attitude from the low-profile Jewish leadership of the pre-1890s era. Their defense of Jewish difference, rejection of complete assimilation, and open espousal of Jewish interests indicated a strengthening of Jewish self-consciousness. But the emergence of radical Zionism, although a further step on the same course on which the Centralverein itself had embarked two decades earlier, went far beyond what the cv could accept and produced a deep schism. While still claiming neutrality on the subject of Zionism, the cv found itself the main advocate for the Liberal conception of Jewish identity, which defined itself largely in opposition to Zionist views. What had started out in the 1890s as a rebellion against the passivity of the notables then leading the Jewish community now became the voice of the establishment directed against a more radical and youthful form of Jewish expression. To Zionist challengers the cv's defense of Judaism appeared only marginally more militant than that of its predecessors and its rejection of Jewish national identity as too great an accommodation to the non-Jewish majority.

The more encompassing definitions of Jewishness in Wilhelminian Germany, as well as the growth of the Jewish organizational network, has been seen by scholars as a sign of Jewish revival. Yet there is a curious paradox here: the same community that was expressing an unprecedented pride in its individuality was also a community more acculturated than ever before. Measured by levels of secular education, decline in traditional religious practice, and increased intermarriage, the Jews of German-speaking Europe were integrated as never before. It was largely the rise of antisemitism that prodded them to reassert their identity in new ways. In a situation where cultural differences between educated Jews and non-Jews were smaller than ever before but hostility to Jewish aspirations remained prevalent, large numbers of German Jews, in one fashion or another, continued to assert their difference.

10 | Jewish Participation in German Culture

U nderstanding the impressive role of persons of Jewish origin in German culture and scholarship between 1871 and 1918 requires an exploration both of its magnitude and its distinctiveness. How widespread was Jewish cultural activity? How was it distributed among the various time periods, creative fields, and schools of thought? What were the areas where Jews did, and where they did not, exercise a vital influence? Having once ascertained the overall profile of the Jewish cultural role, we can then deal with a second issue: was Jewish participation in German culture and science different from that of non-Jews, and, if so, what was the reason for the difference?

During the *Kaiserreich* the increasing role of Jews in German culture became conspicuous and, therefore, a matter of controversy. Many non-Jewish observers looked upon the growing prominence of Germans of Jewish origin in literature, the arts, the universities, and culture in general with anxiety or even alarm. The fear that Jews were disproportionately dominant was to be found not only in overtly antisemitic circles crying out against *Verjudung* (Jewification), but even among more "neutral" observers such as Werner Sombart. In the eyes of many non-Jewish cultural critics the extensive participation of Jews in German culture represented the rise of a foreign influence, the impetus to establish a "mixed culture" instead of a purely German one.

However, it is possible to view Jewish participation in German culture from a perspective diametrically opposed to that of the anti-Jewish critics.

Freitag Abend.

35 "Friday Evening," an antisemitic caricature from 1879

Rather than representing the degree to which Jewish elements were influencing (or dominating) German culture, it can be noted as a sign of how Germanized the German-speaking Jews had become. Not only had they learned the German language and its cultural forms, but they were able to create within these forms in ways that appealed to predominantly non-Jewish audiences. In fact, the degree to which participants in German culture of Jewish origin represented specifically Jewish values is subject to debate. The personal biographies of most Jews famous for taking part in German civilization indicate little education in Jewish traditions and often little conscious sense of Jewish identity.

The conceptualization of the Jewish cultural role in Germany is therefore a problematic one. The usual terminology of Jewish "contributions" to German culture is unsatisfactory, since it implies a collective enterprise of the Jewish community in giving a gift to the non-Jewish majority. In fact, Jewish "contributions" were individual rather than collective. Moreover, many of the "contributions" had no Jewish content; they can be considered Jewish only by artificially separating them from those of others. As a phenomenon, Jewish "contributions" tell us more about the Jewish community, its degree of acculturation, its inclusion in and exclusion from German society, than they do about the Jewish "element" in

German culture. For the history of the Jews in Germany and Austria, the historical importance lies most in the light Jewish cultural participation sheds on their peculiar position as part of, yet separate from, German society.

Whereas significant cultural creativity was individual and limited to the few, the growth of a culturally receptive Jewish public was a much broader phenomenon, beginning late in the eighteenth century and steadily accelerating thereafter. Ever larger circles of German Jews acquired the formal education and the social skills necessary to become part of the *Bildungsbürgertum*, the educated middle class.

In Jewish family and communal life cultural activities played an important role. During the first half of the nineteenth century, acquiring *Bildung* had been both a means to achieving political emancipation and cultural acceptance and a goal in itself. In their efforts to acquire the knowledge, tastes, and manners of the educated middle class for them-selves and their children, Jewish parents worked hard to eliminate distinctively Jewish habits of speech, gesture, and emotional expressiveness. They inculcated admiration for the German classics (Goethe, Schiller, and, for most Jews, Heine as well), musical high culture, and liberal intellectual and political values. Though some Jews acquired these trappings of refinement only to make a proper bourgeois impression, others became genuinely devoted to the values of high culture.

Even among rural Jews or recent immigrants from Eastern Europe the interest in fine art, music, and literature, while less widespread, was by no means absent. They, too, often read the German classics, subscribed to urban newspapers, and played musical instruments. Orthodox Jews were as likely to attend cultural events and read current literature as their less traditional coreligionists. Women played a large role in spreading high culture in the Jewish family, more than among non-Jewish families of the same status (see chapter 3).

Infrequent among the partisans of conservative writers, painters, and political commentators favored by William II's court circles, Jews were overrepresented among the supporters of innovative cultural trends. In disproportionately large numbers Jews attended theater performances and concerts, showing special sympathy for cultural experimentation and progressive cultural attitudes. They were noticeable among the devotees of the works of Gerhart Hauptmann and of Wagnerian opera—despite Wagner's unconcealed antisemitism. In a well-known humorous poem the novelist Theodor Fontane commented on the large percentage of

Jewish names among those congratulating him on his seventy-fifth birthday in 1894:

> Names ending in "berg" and "heim" cannot be numbered,
> In huge masses they storm right in,
> Meyers come in battalions,
> Also Pollacks and those who live still further east;
> Abram, Isack, Israel,
> All the patriarchs are at their posts
> They kindly place me at their head . . .
> I've been someone for each one,
> Reading me they all have done,
> To them all I've long been known,
> And that's the main thing . . . come on in, Cohn."[1]

1. Chronology

The growth of the Jewish share in German culture was by no means a uniform steadily ascending curve. Except in the fields of medicine, politics, and journalism, the 1870s and 1880s were marked by a lull in important Jewish cultural productivity. Then the last two and a half decades of Imperial Germany displayed a powerful upsurge in Jewish cultural activity far overshadowing Jewish contributions to German culture in the previous quarter century. In many fields, especially in literature and the arts, but also in psychology, the emergence of a leading Jewish presence was sudden and in sharp contrast with what had come before. In fact, there was a sharper boundary between the earlier Kaiserreich period and the 1890s than between the last decades of the empire and the Weimar years—in spite of the much greater political changes. In some of the sciences the participation of Jews does show a steady increase. Jews and persons of partially Jewish background played important roles in medicine, biology, and chemistry throughout the second half of the nineteenth century. Their participation began earliest in medical-related fields such as bacteriology, physiology, and pathology, then spread to chemistry, and finally became weighty in physics in the early twentieth century. In the 1870s and 1880s persons of partially Jewish ancestry were much more prominent in the sciences than Jews who had remained within the community. Best known of these were the organic chemist Adolf von Baeyer (1835–1917, Nobel prize 1905) and the physicist Heinrich Hertz (1857–

1894). In the decade immediately preceding World War I the sciences show a sharp increase in the number of important Jewish figures, this time including many who remained unbaptized. This increase was especially apparent in theoretical physics and chemistry with the appearance of such towering figures as Albert Einstein, Paul Ehrlich, Fritz Haber, and Richard Willstätter.

The Jewish role in journalism and cultural criticism was not adversely affected by the sharp decline in Liberal political influence with which it was often linked. Although not increasing as in the sciences, it remained significant after 1880. The leading Liberal newspapers owned by Jews, like the *Frankfurter Zeitung*, the *Neue Freie Presse* in Vienna, and the *Berliner Tageblatt*, continued to have a considerable political and cultural impact throughout the prewar period despite the general decline in political liberalism. Besides these wide-circulation newspapers a number of small but influential journals edited by persons of Jewish birth emerged, especially after 1890, among them Maximilian Harden's *Zukunft* (The Future, 1892) and Karl Kraus's *Die Fackel* (The Torch, 1899). Even the more conservative intellectual journal *Deutsche Rundschau* was edited by a Jew, Julius Rodenberg (1831–1914).

In contrast to patterns in politics (a peak in the 1860s and 1870s) and in the sciences (a steady increase rising more prominently after 1900), Jewish distinction in the literary and fine arts was marked by a sudden and remarkable upswing in the 1890s after a lull of half a century. The fields of literature and music were exceptional because they had produced a few very influential writers and composers of Jewish origin early in the nineteenth century: Heinrich Heine and Ludwig Börne, Giacomo Meyerbeer and Felix Mendelssohn. Their eminence, however, was not equaled in the next generation. In the middle of the century and in the 1870s and 1880s Jewish participation in literature and the arts did not produce figures of classical stature. Men like Berthold Auerbach (1812–1882) and Karl Emil Franzos (1848–1904) in literature or musicians like Karl Goldmark (1830–1915) and Joseph Joachim (1831–1907) were famous in their day but were not on the level of the men that preceded or followed them.

With the exception of the few great names of the pre-1850 period the emergence of Jewish eminence in the arts was delayed longer than in the sciences. That the fields of literature, music, and visual arts require a particularly thoroughgoing acquaintance with the subtleties of general culture—something less necessary for a scientist—may have been a factor that caused some of the delay. In any case, when Jews again come to the fore in literature and music (less so in the visual arts) beginning in the mid-1890s, the numbers involved are much greater than they had been in the early nineteenth century, even if none of the new leading Jewish figures in literature—like the playwright Arthur Schnitzler, the poet Else Lasker-Schüler, and the novelist Jakob Wassermann—equaled the genius of a Heinrich Heine. In music, on the other hand, composers such as the baptized Gustav Mahler and Arnold Schoenberg overshadow the earlier figures. The rise of musical productivity also began about a decade earlier than in literature (with the creative work of Mahler in the mid-1880s).

The chronology of scholarship in the humanities resembles the pattern of the sciences more than that of the arts. Participation here increased slowly rather than suddenly. Throughout the second half of the nineteenth century Jews played a role in various scholarly fields, including history, philology, law, and philosophy, but not as disproportionately as in the sciences. Restrictive practices of the governments made it difficult for Jews to acquire university positions, forcing those in the humanities, especially, to choose between remaining independent (and therefore underpaid) scholars or converting to Christianity in order to receive professorships.

Philosophy had a greater attraction for Jews than most other humanities. Their presence among leading philosophers, already notable in the third quarter of the nineteenth century, is exemplified by the ethical theorists Heymann Steinthal (1823–1899) and Moritz Lazarus (1824–1903) as well as the neo-Kantian Hermann Cohen, who continued to produce important derivative and original works from the 1870s until the end of his life in 1918. Other important philosophers of Jewish origin, such as Fritz Mauthner (1849–1923) and Edmund Husserl (1859–1938), wrote their first influential works around 1900, but unlike Steinthal, Lazarus, and Cohen, showed no interest in Jewish thought.

By the fin-de-siècle and immediately pre-World-War-I periods there were no longer merely a few outstanding creative Jewish thinkers, artists, and scholars but rather a multitude of important figures. Although the antisemitic claims that Jews dominated German culture were wildly exaggerated, it was certainly true that the work of persons of Jewish origin was now quantitatively much greater and of larger collective import than in earlier periods. The cultural efflorescence that took place in the Weimar Republic was produced in large measure by Jewish intellectuals who had already made prominent contributions under the empire.

2. Cultural Centers: Vienna, Prague, Berlin

Within the German Empire avant-garde culture was not yet as developed or as concentrated in Berlin as it would be during the Weimar period when the public mind often associated the "Berlin Jewish spirit" with cultural experimentation. Some have even argued that the role of Jews in the Kaiserreich was neither particularly distinctive nor daring. But none have said the same about contemporary Vienna. Indeed, before World War I no city was more associated with culturally pioneering Jews.

Fin-de-siècle Vienna has exercised a fascination on later observers, both scholarly and popular. Displaying seemingly contradictory combinations of outward gaiety and inward decay, cosmopolitanism and narrow-minded prejudice, anti-intellectualism and pioneering intellectual breakthroughs, Vienna seems the birthplace of much that is typical of intellectual modernism. The uncertainties and confusions of Viennese life are often cited as prototypes of the unease that characterizes twentieth-century life and thought.

Viennese culture at the end of the nineteenth century, and the Jewish contribution to it as well, are marked by a curious dichotomy between challenges to rational endeavor in some fields and the triumph of rationalism in others. On the one hand, persons of Jewish background were very prominent on the Viennese literary scene, especially among the playwrights, poets, columnists, and coffeehouse literati of the "Young Vienna" movement. Though certainly not a uniform school, Jung Wien writers leaned towards subtlety of nuance, intuitive insight and aestheticism while tending to avoid the straightforward and sometimes brutally analytic naturalism popular among some writers of their day. On the other hand, Jews were also conspicuous among the scientists and rationalist philosophers of Vienna. In some fields, notably psychology and music, persons of Jewish origin broke with the traditions of their fields and established new models considered shocking to many. Freudian psychology, closely associated with Viennese Jews, combined a devotion to rationalist scientific method with a doctrine teaching that human motivation—far from being rational—was instead largely determined by subconscious urges.

A brief listing of the most prominent Viennese of Jewish origin in the city's intellectual life does not do justice to the great variety of their contributions but does give an idea of the magnitude of their influence. In literature Arthur Schnitzler (1862–1931), Richard Beer-Hofmann (1866–

1945), Felix Salten (1869–1945), Alfred Polgar (1873–1955), Egon Friedell (1878–1938), and Peter Altenberg (Richard Engländer, 1859–1919) reached various degrees of prominence. In the preceding chapter we have already mentioned the critic Karl Kraus who, though born a Jew himself, was a vehement opponent of the heavily Jewish Young Vienna. Much of the psychoanalytic movement in Vienna was made up of Jews—not only Freud (1856–1939) but also Alfred Adler (1870–1935), who later rejected "orthodox" Freudianism. Likewise many of the members of the (post-World-War-I) Vienna circle of logical positivists were Jewish, as were leading Austro-Marxist intellectuals such as Otto Bauer (1882–1938) and Max Adler (1873–1937). The composers Gustav Mahler (1860–1911) and Arnold Schoenberg (1874–1951) helped create twentieth-century musical modernism.

Many of the Jews who contributed richly to Viennese culture possessed only the most marginal of Jewish identities, though the Jewishness of such prominent figures as Schnitzler, Freud, and Beer-Hofmann was clear and unapologetic. There were numerous conversions to Christianity, including Mahler, Schoenberg (later reversed), Karl Kraus, and the psychologist Alfred Adler. Persons of partially Jewish descent, among them the writer Hugo von Hofmannsthal (1874–1929) and the philosopher Ludwig Wittgenstein (1889–1951), are often counted as prominent Viennese Jews even though they themselves hardly ever consciously acknowledged any personal relationship to the Jewish community or Judaism.

The disproportionately large role of Viennese Jews as pioneers of modern culture was due to a number of factors. To begin with, by 1880 the Jewish population of Vienna had reached a higher percentage of the general population than in any major German city. This large and concentrated mass of Jews was highly educated, with Jews making up about one-third of the students in Vienna academic high schools. The collision of Western education with remnants of Jewish belief and traditions could create the stimulus to new modes of thought and expression.

Also significant for cultural innovation among Jews was Vienna's ethnic diversity. The German-speaking capital was a mecca for migrants from all over a polyglot empire representing subservient nationalities, like the Czechs and the Poles, who were in the process of asserting their cultural autonomy. Even ethnic Germans in Vienna were caught between their specific Germanness and identification with the Habsburg Empire as a whole. For Jews ethnic identity in this milieu was less clear and more complex than in Germany. Indeed, the Germanness of Viennese Jews, who had for the most part arrived recently in the city, often from non-German speaking areas, was even more beset with ambiguity—and hence with creative potential—than that of Viennese Christians.

And finally, there was the pervasive Viennese antisemitism, the underside of the appeal of Viennese German culture, which was associated with pan-Germanism and made Jews feel they were outsiders no matter how well they had assimilated the German language and conventional culture. Such antisemitism was one among the factors that affected the work of Sigmund Freud, even as it helped motivate his strong identification with fellow Jews. In two of the major works of Arthur Schnitzler, his novel *Der Weg ins Freie* (The Road into the Open, 1908) and his play *Professor Bernhardi* (1912), antisemitism became an important theme.

The Jewish role in the culture of Prague was quite dissimilar from what it was in Vienna. The German-speaking minority there was too vulnerable to the onslaught of the rising Czech majority to support virulent antisemitism. Prague Jews were among the mainstays of German culture in the city, but they began to reconsider their identification as German influence declined. Some identified with the Czechs, while a notable minority of creative young people flirted with Zionism as an alternative to choosing sides. This Zionist subgroup produced many leading Jewish writers and thinkers including the novelist Max Brod (1884–1968), the Zionist editor Robert Weltsch (1891–1982), and the philosopher Hugo Bergmann (1883–1975). A sympathetic outsider to Zionist circles was Franz Kafka, clearly the most important modernist writer of the city (see below).

In Imperial Germany no city as yet had the cultural predominance that Vienna possessed in Austria and Prague in Bohemia. Writers, artists, and thinkers were to be found in Hamburg, Dresden, Munich, and smaller university towns like Göttingen, Heidelberg, and Marburg as well as in Berlin. For Jewish intellectuals this was a period of migration to the German capital. Numerous Jewish scientists were attracted to the Kaiser Wilhelm Institute founded in Berlin just before the First World War. Jewish journalists and visual artists also flocked to the city. By the early years of the twentieth century Berlin had begun to acquire the image of a center of cultural innovation and daring that would characterize it after the war.

Those Jews who played a role in the cultural life of pre-World-War-I Berlin, despite their growing numbers, did not form as clearly marked a group nor did they as yet exert as pioneering an influence as their Viennese counterparts. The fields of Jewish prominence in Vienna and Berlin were also quite different. In Vienna Jews were important as composers, writers of fiction, psychologists, and positivist philosophers. In Berlin there were important Jewish painters (a relatively unimportant field of endeavor for Viennese Jews), physicists, and chemists. In both cities Jews were active as journalists and literary critics.

3. Literature and Literary Criticism

Within the various literary trends Jewish participation differed greatly both in degree and in type of involvement. Jews were most associated with the neo-Romantic (sometimes called impressionistic) trend, especially in the abovementioned Young Vienna, where they predominated. In the naturalist movement, whose straightforward description of sometimes sordid social conditions opposed the more subtly psychological Young Vienna approach, Jews were less prominent as authors. As literary critics and theater directors—and as audiences—however, they played a major role in helping advance the cause of naturalism. Jews also played a surprisingly large role in the aristocratic neoclassicist Stefan George circle and were active, though not predominant, among Expressionist poets.

Within the literary movements individual Jewish writers differed from one another in literary style as well as in attitude toward Jewishness. This is best illustrated by the most "Jewish" of all the literary schools, Young Vienna. The lyrical language of Richard Beer-Hofmann was entirely different from the psychological analysis and experiments with stream of consciousness that characterized Schnitzler. Beer-Hofmann, who sympathized with the Zionist movement, gave powerful expression to his sense of Jewish identity in several of his works. In his reflective *Schlaflied für Mirjam* (Lullaby for Miriam, 1899), written for his young daughter, he asserted a sense of identification with an inherent Jewishness reminiscent in some ways of the early thought of Martin Buber:

> We are but riverbanks, and deep within us runs
> Blood of those who came before, rolling toward those to be,
> Blood of our fathers, full of restlessness and pride.[2]

Beer-Hofmann's later biblical plays, beginning with *Jaákobs Traum* (Jacob's Dream, 1918), meditate on the nature of Jewish fate in elevated and poetic language. Such assertions of Jewishness dismayed Hugo von

Hofmannsthal despite his own partially Jewish background. Schnitzler's literary production, which found a wider audience than that of Beer-Hofmann, shared neither this elevated style nor this vision of Jewishness. His work was notorious for its frank exploration of the psychology of sexuality in Viennese society, a fact that led Sigmund Freud to see Schnitzler as a kindred spirit. His play *Reigen* (Round Dance, first published in 1903), depicting ten interlinked sexual encounters, most of them marked by hypocrisy and the absence of honest love, was initially considered too shocking to be performed. Conservative and antisemitic circles attacked Schnitzler as an indecent writer obsessed with sex, preferring to ignore his implicit criticism of the state of mind behind the casual encounters between men of the upper classes and the "sweet girls" whom they often victimized. Similarly critical of Austrian mores was Schnitzler's monologue *Leutnant Gustl* (Lieutenant Gustl, 1901), a pioneering work of stream of consciousness writing that satirized the irrationality of the Austrian military's code of honor and practice of frequent dueling.

The problem of societal hostility to the Jews was the chief Jewish motif that entered Schnitzler's literary work. Unlike Beer-Hofmann's proud Zionism, his view of Jewishness was more detached and less ideological. Although he explored Jewish nationalism and other possible Jewish "solutions to the problem of antisemitism" in *Der Weg ins Freie*, he remained unconvinced that any movement could provide an adequate solution. His residual identification with Jews and contempt for antisemitism did not lead him to any religious or ideological commitments.

The very popular novelist Jakob Wassermann (1873–1934), who was born in Franconia and retained a close association with the region of his birth even after he moved to Vienna, did not share the aestheticism of Young Vienna. He wrote in a much more direct style and with more interest in depicting common social situations and moral dilemmas. Although Wassermann identified himself strongly with the plight of Jews suffering from antisemitism, those of his novels that include Jewish characters often emphasize their unpleasant attributes, to the point that contemporary Jewish readers complained about such negative portrayals. In fact they reflect an ambivalence about Jewishness expressed most clearly in Wassermann's autobiography *Mein Weg als Deutscher und Jude* (My Path as German and Jew, 1921) but already evident in his first novel, *Die Juden von Zirndorf* (The Jews of Zirndorf), which appeared in 1897. Its prologue, entitled "Sabbatai Zewi," in recollection of the seventeenth-century false messiah, emphasizes the mysterious and superstitious side

36   The playwright Arthur Schnitzler

of Judaism, dwelling in sensationalist detail on the orgiastic practices of the followers of this "messiah." The body of the novel portrays many (though not all) of its Jewish characters as money-grubbing gougers or cowards. Its Jewish hero Agathon Geyer rejects both Judaism and Christianity in favor of a superhuman activism reminiscent of the ideas of Nietzsche. Wassermann's later novels, which do not deal with Jewish themes quite as intensively, but in which Jewish characters and their fate play noticeable, if mostly secondary roles, retain some of this same ambivalence.

Unlike Wassermann, the Elberfeld-born expressionist poet Else

37 The novelist Jakob Wassermann by Suzanne Carvallo-
Schülein

Lasker-Schüler (1869–1945) experimented with bold images, frank eroti-
cism, and unorthodox use of language. She purposely projected an eccen-
tric "Middle Eastern" image of herself and was known among some of her
literary friends as "the black swan of Israel." Both her love poetry and her
writings on Jewish themes were totally idiosyncratic and personal.
Unconventional sentiments are widespread throughout her poetry, as for
example:

> Threads I'd like to draw around me–
> Ending chaos!

38   Self-portrait of the poet Else Lasker-Schüler

    Confusing,
      Bewildering you,
        So as to escape
          Toward myself![3]

or

    Your diamond dreams
    Slice open my veins.[4]

Her Jewish images are equally unconventional. The retelling of Bible stories in her *Hebräische Balladen* (Hebrew Ballads) often has little in common with the original. Her inclusion of Mary and Jesus in her religious poetry is certainly far from normative Judaism. So, too, are her daringly anthropomorphic images of God:

> God, I love you in your dress of roses . . .
> So come then,
> You sweet God,
> You playmate God,
> The gold of your gate melts at my desire.[5]

But what is clear is that Lasker-Schüler did the opposite of hiding her Jewishness; she turned it into a mystique, refusing to have her poems translated into Hebrew because, she insisted, "they are written in Hebrew." She even provided a pseudo-Hebrew version of two of her poems in a mixture of nonsense syllables with a few authentic Hebrew words:

> Abba ta Marjam
> Abba min Salihï
> Gad mâra aleijâ
> Assâma anadir . . .[6]

The mixture of strong Jewish identification with an unconventional and critical view of the Jewish people is evident in her poem "Mein Volk" (My People), with its picture of Jewish decay:

> And always, always still the echo
> In me,
> When frighteningly toward the east
> The crumbling skeleton of stone,
> My people,
> Cries out to God.[7]

A number of Jewish writers were also active in the Stefan George circle. George's aristocratic and elitist views, and his cult of male beauty and male friendship, would not seem likely to attract either Jewish or female followers. Yet Jewish men like the poet Karl Wolfskehl (1869–1948) and the critic Friedrich Gundolf (originally Gundelfinger, 1880–1931) and, to a lesser extent, Jewish women like the poet Margarete Susman (1874–1966) and the philosophical writer Edith Landmann (1877–1951) played important roles in the group.

Even though most of his greatest works were not published until after the war, the titanic literary figure of Franz Kafka (1883–1924) belongs in part to this period. The strong tone of despair, the seemingly irrational and uncontrollable nature of daily life, the surrealistic combination of impossible basic premises with minute description of details were to a degree reflections of his life in Prague during the last days of the Habsburg Empire. Kafka was among the radicals who, in the decade before World War I challenged much of what earlier generations had considered true and beautiful. His impact, however, would not be felt fully until after his death in 1924.

While Kafka was creating works of depth and permanence, other Jewish writers, like the biographer Emil Ludwig (Emil Ludwig Cohn, 1881–1948), for example, wrote immensely successful books for a mass audience. Certain writers found resonance among Jewish readers but had less influence outside Jewish circles. One such literary figure was Georg Hermann (Georg Hermann Borchardt, 1871–1944), whose novels of Berlin Jewish family life, *Jettchen Gebert* (1906) and *Henriette Jacoby* (1908), were extremely popular among German Jews. Hermann combined a lovingly detailed description of the milieu of earlier middle-class Jewish life with an advocacy of acculturation and a disdain for the supposedly vulgar *Ostjuden*.

Literary critics of Jewish origin were generally more controversial than Jewish poets and novelists. Antisemites accused them of controlling German culture and of touting fellow Jews at the expense of worthy Aryans. They insisted that such critics played an especially large part in the "disintegrative" influence Jews supposedly exercised over German culture. Such accusations, aside from their unfairness, ignored the vast differences between the major critics of Jewish origin.

Of all the prewar Jewish critics Karl Kraus is the one who today receives the most attention. He was a maverick among his colleagues, opposed not only to many of the popular cultural and literary trends of his day but also to the journalistic practices of his contemporaries. Kraus saw himself as a guardian of the purity of the German language against writers, official spokesmen, and journalists other than himself who allegedly abused it. As noted earlier, he had a special hatred for the *Neue Freie Presse*, the respected Viennese liberal newspaper, which he considered culturally corrupt.

Among Kraus's many enemies was the Berlin theater critic Alfred Kerr (originally Kempner, 1867–1948). Although far from being an observant Jew, Kerr wrote about Jewish matters with much less of the mordant negativism that characterized Kraus. He shared neither his Viennese con-

39   The literary critic Karl Kraus (1908)

temporary's earnest moralism nor his linguistic purism. In fact Kerr's language was quite idiosyncratic, full of puns, humorous turns of phrase, and an unusual aphoristic style. He believed that criticism was the fourth genre of literature, alongside the epic, the lyric, and drama. What Kerr shared with Kraus was a biting wit in attacking his opponents, a sense of his own cultural importance, and a love of controversy. He diverged from the Viennese critic by being an aesthete who believed in art for art's sake, an idea anathema to Kraus.

Maximilian Harden (born Felix Ernst Witkowski, 1861–1927) was as colorful a personality as Kraus and Kerr, and at times an enemy of both. Unlike the other two, his interests were as much political as cultural and literary. Harden started out as a supporter of Bismarck and, despite his sarcastic barbs against the personality of William II, long defended the institution of monarchy while advocating a strong and aggressive Germany. However, during the First World War he became a radical opponent of the war, thereby earning the undying hatred of the right.

Criticism by Jews focused in large measure upon the theater, where they were especially numerous among directors and producers and also well represented among actors and actresses. Otto Brahm (born Abrahamsohn, 1856–1912) was both a critic and a leading theater director. The Freie Bühne (Free Stage, founded in 1889), in which he played a leading role, was instrumental in supporting playwrights of the naturalistic school, especially Gerhart Hauptmann, as well as promoting the performance of Ibsen's dramas in Germany. The younger and much more flamboyant Max Reinhardt (born Goldmann,1873–1943) was originally an actor in Brahm's theater and in 1905 succeeded him as the director of the Deutsches Theater. Reinhardt became known for his showmanship, innovative staging techniques, and support of Expressionist theatrical styles.

4. Music and the Visual Arts

During the years between 1890 and 1914 composers of Jewish origin were controversial figures in the forefront of musical modernism. Gustav Mahler began as a conductor and composer in the Romantic tradition but stretched its limits by experimenting with immense orchestras, incorporating folk melodies of various origins, combining symphonic and choral elements, and drawing literary inspiration from the most diverse sources. He experimented with five-movement symphonies and devised unusual harmonies. Despite his Jewish birth, many of his works are filled with Catholic piety; others are inspired by German folktales or Chinese poetry. Although Mahler's work was often vilified during his lifetime as an iconoclastic distortion of native traditions, some of it resembles the grandiose works of Anton Bruckner, the pious Catholic Austrian composer with whom, ironically, he was sometimes contrasted by antisemitic enemies. Mahler was often accused of sneaking Jewish themes into his music, and some later critics have claimed to hear hasidic motifs in it. Most, however, identify the purportedly Jewish motifs as themes from Bohemian folk music.

The music of Mahler's countryman Arnold Schoenberg broke with the traditions of classical music in a much more radical way. His early works, such as the *Gurrelieder* and *Verklärte Nacht* (Transfigured Night) were

40 The composer Gustav Mahler. Charcoal drawing
by Emil Orlik, 1902

large-scale Romantic compositions with more than a trace of Wagnerian influence. But between 1908 and 1918 he broke sharply with musical tradition. The compositions of those years, such as *Erwartung* (Expectation, 1909) and *Pierrot Lunaire* (1912), ignored all the accepted rules of tonality. His vocal works, with their strange high-pitched recitative, seemed shockingly dissonant to their listeners and certainly not in line with conventional ideas of beauty. In the post-World-War-I era Schoenberg then created a new twelve-tone system to replace the old tonalities he had rejected. The music of the Austrian Jew Schoenberg, like that of his non-Jewish Russian contemporary Stravinsky, stood in the forefront of the avant-garde "modern music" of the twentieth century. Their revolution can be compared to the radical break with tradition made by French Cubist painters in the same decade before World War I. Though Schoenberg's early music and writing, like Mahler's, show little overt Jewishness, his compositions after the world war often deal with Jewish themes—for instance the cantata *Die Jakobsleiter* (Jacob's Ladder, begun 1915) and the 1932 opera *Moses und Aron*—and his writings were increasingly marked by support for Zionism. In 1933 he formally renounced his conversion and returned to Judaism.

In painting there was little participation by German-speaking Jews either in the "Cubist revolution" or, with a few notable exceptions, even in the Expressionist movement in visual art (which, unlike Cubism, was largely based in Germany and Austria). Max Liebermann (1847–1935), the most prominent Jewish painter, was initially controversial because of his championing of Impressionism. As the founder of the Berlin Secession (1898), which rejected the conservative style of painting favored by official circles, he gained some notoriety, but in his later years became respectable enough to serve as president of the Prussian Academy of the Arts, a remarkable accomplishment for a non-baptized Jew. Liebermann saw no contradiction between his strong sense of Germanness and his loose identification with the Jewish faith. "After all, I'm only a painter," he protested on one occasion, "and what does painting have to do with Judaism?"[8] Although Jewish themes are noticeable in a few of his works, particularly his "The Young Jesus in the Temple" in which the ancient priests and elders look much like bearded Jews in a European synagogue, this was the exception rather than the rule. Lesser Ury (1861–1931), whose reputation has risen to some extent at the expense of Liebermann's, was likewise a leading German Impressionist. French Impressionism was mediated to the German public largely by the influential Jewish art dealer Paul Cassirer (1871–1926). His art gallery was the first to exhibit the works of Manet, Monet, and van Gogh and his publishing house helped to promote new developments in contemporary art—often against initial resistance by the German art establishment. On the eve of the world war Ludwig Meidner (1884–1966) gained lasting fame with a series of apocalyptic landscapes that pictured a frightening urban environment. He was one of the few Jews prominent in German Expressionist art.

41   The painter Max Liebermann having his picture taken

42   Ludwig Meidner's "The Prophet" (1915)

In the graphic arts Hermann Struck (1876–1944) and Ephraim Moses Lilien (1874–1925) devoted numerous etchings and (in the case of Lilien) woodcuts to Jewish themes. Whereas Struck was influenced mainly by the Impressionists, Lilien worked under the influence of the decorative Jugendstil and of the British Pre-Raphaelites. The work of both artists figured prominently in the publications, public appeals, and imagery of the Zionist movement, with which they sympathized. Lilien, born in Galicia and much influenced by East European life, was one of the founders of the Zionist Jüdischer Verlag, which published essays and books on Jewish artists. Struck, born in Germany, was one of the few contributors to German culture who was an Orthodox Jew.

5. The Sciences and Humanities

The participation of German-speaking Jews in the sciences during the years between 1890 and World War I was at least as substantial as their participation in the arts. In Germany and Austria a disproportionately large number of Jews stood at the forefront of physics, chemistry, biology, and psychology. They had been early attracted to medicine-related sciences, in part no doubt because of the long tradition of Jewish physicians. Within medicine they gravitated to newer specialties like microbiology and dermatology, which, unlike surgery, were less under the control of the medical establishment and thus less likely to be closed to them.

In physics, especially theoretical physics and atomic theory, persons of Jewish origin played a prominent role. Although many names could be mentioned, no single individual has had the towering influence of Albert Einstein (1879–1955). His theory of relativity, first published in 1905, revolutionized scientific views of the universe. Such new ideas as the convertibility of mass into energy, the role of time as a fourth dimension, the curvilinear nature of space, and the changes in time and mass as objects approached the speed of light fundamentally modified Newtonian physics.

Only slightly less important was the role of Jewish scientists in chemistry and biochemistry. Fritz Haber (1868–1934) was best known for his discovery of the fixation of nitrogen from the air to make ammonia, a process of great importance to the German war effort in World War I. Richard Willstätter (1872–1942) worked on the structure of chlorophyll and other pigments. Both men won Nobel prizes in chemistry. Paul Ehrlich (1854–1915), one of the pioneers of chemotherapy, won a Nobel prize in medicine for his discovery of Salvarsan as a treatment for syphilis. Although Jews in the sciences were found in a wide variety of subfields and specialties, they seem to have been especially numerous and influential in those areas with a more theoretical than experimental bent.

The Jewish commitments of these scientists varied greatly. Haber converted to Protestantism because he found no religious meaning in Judaism. Willstätter, his close personal friend, remained proud of his Judaism, though he kept no Jewish religious practices and rejected Zionism. His militancy against antisemitism found its most public expression in his resignation from the University of Munich in 1924 because it indiscriminately rejected Jewish candidates for academic positions. Einstein, whose religious ideas were certainly far from conventional Judaism, was an active Zionist and a public supporter of the establishment of the Hebrew University in Jerusalem.

Despite some friendships between individuals, the German-speaking Jews who contributed to the physical sciences did not constitute a unified social or intellectual group. In this they differed from Jews in the psychoanalytic movement. Not only Freud, its founder and central figure, but virtually all the early leaders of the movement were Jewish. Despite his strong reservations about latent elements of Christian mysticism in Carl Jung's thought, Freud was gratified when this non-Jew joined his circle because it would prevent antisemites from seeing psychoanalysis as a Jewish science and hence resisting its influence. It was a severe blow for Freud when Jung defected from his following in 1911.

Although Freud was a thoroughgoing atheist, he maintained personal and organizational ties to the Jewish community. Deeply embittered by antisemitism, he felt a subconscious affinity to other Jews that he attributed to the "familiarity of similar mental structures." The Jewishness of Freud, which has been sharply debated by scholars, was manifested, in particular, through his active association with the B'nai B'rith (where he first presented his views on dreams and on the psychopathology of everyday life) and in some of his writings, notably his work on jokes and his controversial last book, *Moses and Monotheism* (1939). Although Jews were often to be found in other branches of psychology than psychoanalysis, for instance Gestalt psychology, they played a far smaller role in them than in Freudianism and its offshoots. Thanks largely to Jewish efforts, Freudianism was able to enter the cultural vocabulary of Europe and the West, especially after the First World War.

In the new field of sociology Jews were important pioneers, especially Georg Simmel (1858–1918), who, though baptized at birth by a father who had converted much earlier, suffered considerable opposition on account of the allegedly Jewish nature of his thinking. Whereas in the historiography of modern Germany, so closely associated with German national pride, Jews could make few inroads before World War I, in classical studies and ancient history they were more successful. Certain fields seem to have attracted Jews because of their proximity to Judaism, notably Islamic and Semitic studies. Ignaz Goldziher (1850–1921), who wrote in German though he lived in Hungary, was one of the world's leading Islamicists. Jews were also to be found among prominent literary historians, mathematicians, legal scholars, and economists. The numerous Jewish socialist theoreticians stood on the border between politics and intellectual life. They were present in all wings of Marxism from radicals like Rosa Luxemburg, through Austro-Marxists like Otto Bauer, to Revisionists like Eduard Bernstein, who criticized many aspects of Marx's theory.

In philosophy Jews were especially prominent in the neo-Kantian school associated with the names of Hermann Cohen (1842–1918) and Ernst Cassirer (1874–1945). Its combination of rationalism, systematic thinking, and strong ethical interest seems to have made it especially attractive to Jews. However, they played important roles in other schools as well. Phenomenology was founded by Edmund Husserl (1859–1938) and had numerous other Jewish adherents. Jews were frequently to be found in fields dealing with epistemological questions and with the adequacy of language to represent reality. These issues were of central importance not only to Husserl but also to such thinkers of Jewish origin as Fritz Mauthner and (later) Ludwig Wittgenstein.

This brief survey of Jewish participation in the sciences and the humanities reveals the massive and wide-ranging role of Jews, but may, at the same time, create a false impression. With a few exceptions—psychoanalysis is probably the best example—Jews in scholarly fields did not work in isolation from non-Jews. Needless to say, whatever contributions they made to their fields were intimately connected with advances made by scholars of non-Jewish background. It would be impossible, for example, to separate the role of such non-Jews as Max Planck, Werner Heisenberg, and Erwin Schrödinger from those of Jews like Einstein, Max Born, and James Franck in the creation of quantum mechanics between 1900 and 1930. In the "hard" sciences, at least, intellectual discussion advanced with little regard to the personal background of the participants. And, even in the arts, relationships between Jews and non-Jews played crucial roles in the work of individual artists and artistic movements. The relationships between Gerhart Hauptmann and Otto Brahm, between Stefan George and his Jewish followers, or between Else Lasker-Schüler and her non-Jewish friends and lovers are cases in point. To understand the role of Jews in German culture and science requires both an assessment of the special nature of Jewish participation and an awareness of the larger milieu, which, in most instances, provided the context for their creativity.

6. Jews as Patrons of Culture

German Jews were not only significant as consumers and producers of culture, they were also active as patrons and sponsors. Although exact comparisons are difficult, it seems that wealthy Jews were much more likely to contribute financially to cultural causes than their non-Jewish counterparts of equal wealth. Moreover, Jewish philanthropists, like German Jews in general, were prone to support progressive or even avant-garde cultural activities to a much greater extent than non-Jews, who often showed more interest in conservative and "patriotic" culture. The role of the German Jew as Maecenas is especially notable in the visual arts, in science, and in the creation of the University of Frankfurt.

In the visual arts Jews played a more prominent role as patrons, art dealers, and collectors than as artists. The very dissimilar figures of Aby Warburg and James Simon illustrate the wide range of activity of upper-class Jews in the German art world. Aby Warburg (1866–1929) turned away from his family's major banking business in Hamburg to pursue a life devoted to the visual arts. Having written his doctoral dissertation on Botticelli, he established a collection containing thousands of volumes on classical culture and on the Renaissance, which after World War I became the basis for an important research institute devoted, like his many writings, to elaborating the place of art within general culture.

Like Warburg, another German Jewish patron of the arts, James Simon (1851–1832), was fascinated by Renaissance art, of which he possessed a rich collection. He became one of the most generous contributors to museums in Berlin, donating important Renaissance works to the Kaiser-Friedrich-Museum in 1904 and 1920 and contributing richly to the German folklore museum. He was also one of the founders of the German Oriental Society, devoted to archeological expeditions in the Middle East. Whereas Warburg turned his back on his early intense Jewish upbringing, Simon was active in Jewish causes, especially the Hilfsverein of which he was a cofounder. He was often able to use his personal acquaintance with Emperor William II to further both general philanthropic and also specifically Jewish causes.

Jewish philanthropists often devoted themselves especially to furthering the culture of their native towns. Although hundreds of such cases in communities large and small could be cited, nowhere was the contribution as massive as it was in Frankfurt am Main. The best example of this role among Frankfurt Jews (some of them baptized) is in the founding of the University of Frankfurt in 1914. This institution of higher learning was unique both because it was under local rather than state control and because its bylaws forbade religious discrimination in faculty appointments. Wilhelm Merton (1848–1916), who was initially motivated by Jewish traditions of tithing for worthy causes but eventually turned away from Judaism and converted, was the spearhead of the drive to create the university. Having gained wealth as a metal trader, Merton believed strongly in the social responsibility of the wealthy toward the poor and in the importance of rational planning in social assistance. In 1890 he created an Institute for Public Welfare (Institut für Gemeinwohl), which was followed by numerous other social institutions.

The largest monetary contributors to what came to be the University of Frankfurt were the Georg and Franziska Speyer Educational Foundation and the Gans family, which were especially interested in the natural sciences, complementing Merton's focus on the social sciences. Many other Frankfurt Jews set aside smaller but still substantial amounts. In fact, according to conservative estimates, persons of Jewish background gave almost 80 percent of the 8 million marks donated toward establishing the university; other calculations place the total Jewish contribution considerably higher.

Another important scholarly institution benefiting greatly from the attention of Jewish philanthropists was the Kaiser Wilhelm Institute for the Sciences founded in Berlin-Dahlem in 1912. At least twenty-five of the eighty-nine founding members of the Kaiser Wilhelm Gesellschaft (which helped establish the institute) were of Jewish background. Indeed, large-scale Jewish benefactions may have been one of the reasons so many leading scientists of Jewish origin were able to find places at the institute.

7. Explaining Jewish Cultural Creativity

Even as the sheer magnitude and quality of participation by persons of Jewish identity or Jewish origin point to the great importance of the Jewish role in German culture, the wide variety of fields of activity and the diversity of approach among Jews within these fields raise the difficulty of specifying that role. To be sure, Jews tended to cluster in distinctive patterns within their respective fields, but so many exceptions exist that one is reluctant to argue for the influence of any "Jewish traits." Although, for example, Jewish intellectuals tended to be concentrated on the theoretical, the rationalistic, and the progressive or radical side of a given spectrum, there are generally also abundant examples of thinkers who were empirical, antirationalist, or conservative.

Questions regarding the origins and nature of Jewish prominence in German-speaking culture after 1890 remain the subject of intense debate among scholars. Why were so many Jews active in cultural and scholarly activities? Were the contributions of Jews different from those of their non-Jewish counterparts? Specifically, were Jews particularly to be found among cultural innovators and the avant-garde? If their contributions were different from those of their neighbors, was that the result of specific traditional Jewish characteristics and values carried over into the modern world, or merely the product of the marginal position of educated Jews in Western society, or even nothing other than an illusion or a chance occurrence?

The most extreme positions on opposite sides of this issue either claim to find elements in the works of modern German-speaking Jews borrowed directly from Jewish tradition or deny any specifically Jewish element in them altogether. Attempts by some observers to discern biblical, talmudic, or kabbalistic themes in the thinking of writers like Karl Marx, Sigmund Freud, or Franz Kafka have rarely uncovered much specific evidence. Some, including many antisemites and a few Jewish scholars, have resorted to hypotheses about inborn Jewish modes of thinking or collective memory. On the opposite side of the spectrum is the attempt to deemphasize the distinctiveness of Jews involved in German culture. Certainly if one defines Jewishness in conventional religious terms, it is easy to show that few prominent Jewish thinkers in Germany incorporated elements of the Jewish religion in their work. In Imperial Germany (though not in Vienna) one can also make a case against the common notion that Jews were in the forefront of modernism.

However, there is no need to go to the extremes of total denial of Jewishness or comprehensive ascription of Jewish origin to the cultural works of Jews in German-speaking Europe. There was indeed something distinctive about Jewish participation in cultural life, but it was brought about mainly by the Jewish position in German-speaking society (and Western society in general), not by the introduction of specifically Jewish themes.

Many have explained the Jewish penchant for Western education and cultural activities as a secularization of the traditional Jewish value placed on study of the Torah. According to this line of argument, Jewish tradition had always valued book learning and, unlike many other cultures, did not look down on purely theoretical discussions. When they were admitted into the secular school system, Jews simply transferred these preexisting cultural values to new fields. Although this supposition has much to recommend it, it is subject to the objection that the representatives of Jewish traditional culture, who encouraged intellectual pursuits through love of Torah study, were, at least initially, strongly opposed to secular learning. Conversely, those Jews most productive in secular culture were generally the ones furthest removed from practice and even awareness of the traditional attitudes they were supposedly carrying over into Western culture. They were rebels against the content of Jewish tradition even as they seem to have shared its veneration for intellectual pursuits.

Although the hypothesis of the secularization of traditional Jewish learning may have some value in accounting for the immensity of Jewish cultural contributions in the modern world, it can scarcely explain the iconoclastic nature of so many of them. To shed some light on this complex issue, it is necessary to take into account the special relationship between modernization and secularization for Jews, as well as the impact of marginality on cultural creativity.

Modern culture had a different impact on members of the Jewish minority than it did on the Christian majority. Especially in the early stages of Emancipation, Jewish young people interested in Western culture had had to turn away from a Jewish tradition that frowned on such pursuits. Simply taking the step of acquiring a secular education meant moving away from the security of Jewish tradition. Once at a university, Jewish students, unlike their Christian counterparts, could not look forward to positions in a civil service that tended to support cultural conservatism. Unless they converted to Christianity, there was little opportunity for Jews to function as guardians of majority traditions, traditions that, in any case, generally implied their cultural exclusion. Thus they were commonly limited to choices at the center or left of the cultural and political spectrum. If they favored a secularized rather than religious society, it was because they feared a Christian one would exclude them. Leery of too strong a Christian influence in society, they allied themselves with "progressive" opponents of a church-state union. The combined need to turn away from their own traditional culture in order to gain European education together with fear of Christian dominance as an exclusionary factor thus made educated Jews more secularist and progressive than their non-Jewish counterparts.

Jewish social marginality had a somewhat more subtle influence on the nature of Jewish cultural creativity. The marginality argument posits that Jews were especially creative because of their double alienation from the society in which they lived: they had abandoned Jewish tradition and could not return to it while at the same time they could not simply become complacent members of the majority society. Their different background made them see things differently and, moreover, the majority often refused to admit them to its ranks. Because of their double sense of exclusion, Jewish intellectuals were inclined to see the traditions both of Judaism and of the majority culture as artificial barriers standing in the way of progress and human development. This led them to create innovative intellectual constructs in which customary barriers became irrelevant. The theory of marginality would thus explain why it was precisely the "non-Jewish Jew" (to use a phrase coined by Isaac Deutscher) who was the most creative and iconoclastic contributor to human civilization, while Jews more loyal to their own traditions made far more modest contributions. Some analysts claim that the works of marginal Jews share certain precise characteristics, such as internationalism, determinism, and rationalism. But it seems more reasonable to see marginality as a state of mind that could lead to the most varied intellectual and political conclusions.

The argument that exclusion from the inner circle of German traditional culture made Jewish participation so fruitful gains additional force from the chronology of Jewish creativity. Jewish participation in German culture became the most significant precisely at a time of increased antisemitic cultural rejection of the Jews in the years after 1890; by contrast, it was much more modest during the earlier, more liberal period. The extraordinary amount of creative work by Jews converted to Christianity gives further evidence for the marginality hypothesis. An even larger percentage of converted Jews than of identifying Jews was to be found among the leading thinkers. Although many sought baptism to escape discrimination, they sometimes found themselves yet more on the boundary than Jews who remained in the fold. Racial antisemites still denied them the status of Germans though they now lacked any formal tie to Judaism.

If one searches not merely for Jewish origins in an author or artist but also looks for some Jewish content in their work, one rarely finds it present in any obvious way. Jewish factors in personal biography generally remain separate from creativity. Rather the work of Jewish writers, musicians, artists, and intellectuals is, with certain exceptions to be sure, much more reflective of German, European, or worldwide cultural currents than of the Jewish background of the individuals who created it. It is more generally the case that Jewish creativity simultaneously communicates the extent to which Jews had adopted the culture of their surroundings and the extent to which such creativity was considered by others to be "peculiarly Jewish." Its skewed distribution, reflecting the variation in levels of opportunity open to Jews, is a further indication of how external rather than internal factors were predominant in determining the curve of Jewish creativity. The patterns of exclusion were, in turn, reflected in the patterns of Jewish cultural participation and in intellectual attitudes.

Ironically, the disproportion and uneven distribution of Jewish participation in German culture, itself a product of exclusion motivated by anti-semitism, magnified the tendency to view Jews as dangerous to German society. In response, some Jewish intellectuals and artists tried to prove through their works just how German or European they were, while others, not hopeful or not desirous of achieving that objective—like the Jewish thinkers discussed in the next chapter—chose to dwell upon the Jewish elements in their worldview and turned toward the creation of a culture that was specifically Jewish.

11 | New Trends in Jewish Thought

Jewish thought in the last two decades of Wilhelminian Germany is bracketed by two decisive events: the founding in 1897 of the World Zionist Organization, whose initial leadership came principally from German-speaking Jews, and the trauma of World War I. Although still a numerically small movement within Germany in these years, Zionism had a palpable impact on German Jewry. Even when it was rejected, the movement's national and secular conception of the Jewish people and culture influenced the discourse and self-definition of German and Central European Jewry. Hence, non-Zionists, such as the young Walter Benjamin, would begin to speak of themselves as "national Jews" (*Nationaljuden*), as did the Orthodox philosopher and staunch opponent of Zionism, Isaac Breuer, whose views were discussed in chapter 4.

The subtle change in consciousness indicated by this adoption of Zionist vocabulary is perhaps most dramatically registered by Hermann Cohen. Toward the end of his life, the venerable philosopher and passionate proponent of Jewish integration into German culture and society acknowledged in a polemic against Zionism that the Jews were a "nationality," although he was careful to point out that this fact had no political significance; for a nationality is to be distinguished from a nation, which, given its historical and political character, is deserving of statehood. Jews are, Cohen argued, but a nationality, the nation to which they belong varying in accordance with the state in which they might be citizens. As a nationality, the Jews were the "anthropological means" to promote the idea of Judaism. Nonetheless, as a nationality they were a distinct community of shared cultural and social interests that went beyond the circumscribed sphere of the synagogue, and even beyond the borders of Germany. Indeed, during the world war Cohen undertook a highly publicized trip to Eastern Europe to express his solidarity with the plight of the Jewish communities there.

Increasingly, German Jews regarded the *Ostjuden* not only as distressed brethren but also as a source of vital and creative Jewish culture seemingly lost by Western assimilated Jewry. Efforts to appropriate aspects of East European Jewish culture, particularly its folklore, became a central element of the Jewish renewal that began in this period and fully blossomed in the years immediately following the world war. Indicatively, this "Jewish renaissance"—the term dates back to a programmatic essay by Martin Buber in 1901—focused not only on sentimental, idealized images of the ghetto but also sought to find its own voice, especially in areas not cultivated by Jews until modern times, namely, belles lettres and the arts. Thus we read in the preface to the *Jüdischer Almanach* of 1902, published by the Jüdischer Verlag, the Jewish publishing house founded earlier that same year in Berlin:

> We wanted to produce—and even more, help to mediate—a piece of Jewish culture by creating a center for the promotion of Jewish literature, art, and scholarship. It is our intent to establish a Jewish aesthetic realm alongside the Jewish moral ideal, which is restoring to the Jewish person unity and strength, national and personal self-esteem.[1]

A variety of publishing houses, journals, and other forums were founded around the turn of the century to promote the renewal of Jewish life in Germany. Although these efforts were largely secular, they did not necessarily preclude religious concern. On the contrary, they often allowed for the exploration of new perspectives on the spiritual heritage of Israel and the possibilities of religious renewal.

Jewish solidarity was thus no longer confined to the synagogue, delineated by the denominational affiliations that crystallized in the nineteenth century, or to efforts to combat antisemitism. What emerges is a pattern of dissimilation: having in many instances reached the brink of total assimilation, some German Jews now halted and sought to reaffirm and revitalize their Judaism. Significantly, this process of dissimilation was not simply a defiant expression of pride in the face of antisemitism—what was called *Trotzjudentum*—but an unapologetic assertion of Jewish cultural and spiritual distinctiveness.

The debate on the "essence of Judaism" that took place in the first decade of the twentieth century illustrates this development. It marks a transition from the apologetic posture of the previous century—and the recurrent efforts to accommodate Judaism to the prevailing intellectual and aesthetic criteria of the *Bildungsbürgertum*—to a reaffirmation of the unique nature of Israel's faith.

The quest, especially on the part of the younger generation, to find a postassimilatory understanding of Judaism is illustrated by the enthusiastic reception accorded Martin Buber's celebration of a primal Jewish religiosity or metaphysical sensibility that somehow endures in the soul of every Jew, despite the encrustations of alien cultures. An eagerness to identify fundamental Jewish religious attitudes and sensibilities—as distinct from the formal institutional doctrines and practices of Jewish religion—set the tone for much of Jewish religious self-reflection in this period. Franz Rosenzweig would take special pride in the fact that in his *Stern der Erlösung* (Star of Redemption, 1921), which was drafted in the trenches of the world war and recorded the results of his quest for a spiritually compelling Judaism, he did not once use the word *religion*.

During the war Rosenzweig's mentor, Hermann Cohen, reasserted the vision of a union between Judaism and German culture but also subtly redefined its terms. In two seminal essays, which we will discuss in detail, he no longer presented *Deutschtum* and *Judentum* as simply compatible; he now proudly emphasized their parity and complementarity. Cohen's confidence in the eventual triumph of this vision was not universally shared, however. The younger generation of Jews, especially, had festering doubts about the place of Jews in German culture.

1. The Essence of Judaism Debate

In the winter semester of 1899–1900 the eminent church historian Adolf von Harnack (1851–1930) delivered a series of sixteen lectures on the liberal conception of Christianity to a class of some six hundred enthralled students drawn from virtually every faculty of the University of Berlin. Published a few months later under the title *Das Wesen des Christentums* (The Essence of Christianity), these lectures provided an eloquent presentation of the Christian faith shorn of what its author regarded as the unfortunate accretions of dogma, sacraments, and ecclesiastical power. The response was unprecedented. Harnack would proudly report that when the book was first published the main railroad station of Leipzig, one of the largest in the world, was clogged with freight cars carrying copies of the book to all parts of Europe and beyond. Indeed, by 1927 Harnack's book had undergone fifteen printings, was translated into fourteen languages, and had exercised a profound influence on the educated public in the first decades of the twentieth century. The editor of the prestigious periodical, the *Preussische Jahrbücher*, hailed Harnack's book as a signal achievement of its era and attributed its significance to its articulation of a conception of Christianity that appealed to the modern individual while providing definitive religious answers to the excessive claims of science, materialism, and skepticism.

In crisp, compelling prose Harnack summarized the contributions of modern historical scholarship regarding the birth of Christianity. On the basis of this scholarly identification of the original Christian faith, or *Urchristentum*, unsullied by later historical accretions and doctrines, he called upon liberal Protestantism to free itself from the last remnants of paganism and idolatry introduced by Roman Catholicism, which even Luther's Reformation had failed to remove entirely, and return to the original source of Christianity, namely, Jesus the man, his exemplary life and pristine message. Jesus, he argued, embodied the "essence" or the enduring ethical and spiritual core of Christianity that remained firm despite the vicissitudes of history and the intrusion of alien values and principles. The essence of Christianity was to be found in the religion *of* Jesus as opposed to the religion *about* Jesus with its increasingly untenable metaphysical claims. It is to this essence that the liberal Protestant remains beholden and that, Harnack held, still remains urgently relevant to the modern world. Focusing on the synoptic gospels as the authentic repository of Jesus's teachings and the "essence" of the Christian faith, Harnack sought to underscore the originality of those teachings by isolating them both from their allegedly distorted expressions in the Church and from what he derisively characterized as the Pharisaic, spiritually jejune Judaism of Jesus's contemporaries. Not surprisingly, Catholics and Jews took affront at Harnack's thesis.

Liberal Jews in particular could not remain indifferent to the negative portrayal of Judaism in an enormously popular book speaking in the name of the liberal ethos. Ever since the Emancipation Jews had regarded liberal Protestants as their allies, sharing with them the common vision of a social order guided by the Enlightenment with its optimistic trust in the efficacy of universal education, science, and civic equality. Accordingly, Jews were sensitive to the opinions that Liberal Protestants had of them as well as to the conclusions Protestant scholars drew with regard to Judaism. Moreover, as Rabbi Joseph Eschelbacher perspicaciously noted, many modern Jews were so profoundly estranged from the sources of Judaism that they had little recourse but to arrive at a self-definition through such books as Harnack's.

Rabbi Eschelbacher (1848–1916), who served in Berlin, penned two learned responses to Harnack: *Das Judentum und das Wesen des Christentums* (Judaism and the Essence of Christianity, 1905) and *Das Judentum im Urteile der modernen protestantischen Theologie* (Judaism in the Judgment of Modern Protestant Theology, 1907). He was joined by other leading members of the Jewish community who endeavored through lectures, conferences, and essays to correct Harnack's representation of Judaism; in the years 1901 through 1907 at least a dozen monographs devoted to this end were published by Jewish scholars. They objected to Harnack's practice of contrasting the "essence" of Christianity, grounded in the exalted moral teachings of Jesus, with the alleged ritualism and legalism of the Pharisees, an approach that in ignoring the ethical teachings of the Rabbis, perforce cast Judaism in a negative light. No less invidious was Harnack's depiction of Pharisaic theology: "They imagined God as a despot who stands watch over the ceremonial tasks of His household. . . . They saw him only in His law, which they had made into a labyrinth of gullies, erroneous paths, and secret exits."[2]

Eschelbacher and his colleagues also objected to Harnack's—as well as other Liberal Protestant scholars'—practice of employing scholarship to justify the Christian theological prejudice of viewing Judaism as an anachronism whose divinely appointed vocation was assumed by Christianity. Indeed, Harnack explicitly claimed that Jesus was the authentic spiritual heir of Israel and the "stubborn" survival of the Jews had no other legitimation except as a living testimony to the manifest truth of the Christian faith, evidenced by their two thousand years of suffering. But, he continued, the emancipation and the alleviation of the Jews' agony rendered even this negative function superfluous. Hence, contemporary Judaism was utterly bereft of any compelling raison d'être. Harnack, who regarded himself a Liberal and an opponent of political antisemitism, even suggested that the continued and obstinate survival of the Jews in the modern liberal state, which had offered them equal rights and the opportunity to integrate into the life of the dominant Christian society, was an expression of arrant ingratitude.

One of the most trenchant Jewish assessments of Harnack was written by a twenty-seven-year-old Liberal rabbi from Oppeln (Silesia), Leo Baeck (1873–1956). At the time unknown, Baeck published a review of *Das Wesen des Christentums* in the September 1901 issue of the premier journal of Jewish studies in Germany, the *Monatsschrift für Geschichte und Wissenschaft des Judentums*; the following year he put out an expanded version of the same essay as a separate pamphlet. He then elaborated his critique of Harnack in a book that appeared in 1905 as *Das Wesen des Judentums* (The Essence of Judaism), a work that was to go through further revision and editions and many printings and that speedily brought him to the attention of the German-Jewish community at large. Two years later he was called to serve as a rabbi in Düsseldorf, and five years thereafter was invited to Berlin to assume a dual position as a communal rabbi and an instructor in midrash and homiletics at that city's Lehranstalt für die Wissenschaft des Judentums, an institution for training Liberal rabbis and modern scholars of Judaica.

The young Baeck unhesitatingly faults the venerable Harnack on methodological and factual grounds. Baeck notes that in his eagerness to highlight the transhistorical, perduring significance of Jesus, Harnack detaches him from the historical context that nurtured his thought and spiritual sensibility. Hence Harnack permits himself observations that reflect either an abysmal ignorance or a tendentiousness unbefitting a scholar of his stature. One such error of judgment cited by Baeck is Harnack's remark that "it is highly improbable that [Jesus] was educated in the schools of the Rabbis; nowhere does he speak like someone who has adopted their technical theology and artfulness of learned exegesis."[3] Regarding this statement, which is meant to underscore that Jesus had nothing in common with the "Pharisees," Baeck comments that Harnack either simply does not understand Judaism or is unaware that in addition to law (Halacha), the rabbis developed a rich and spiritually nuanced homiletic tradition (Agada):

> Mr. H. would be right in his assertion if it were true that there existed no religious thinkers and poets among the Rabbis. But whoever knows anything about them immediately recognizes that Jesus's words are spirit of their spirit. Every one of his sayings, every one of his parables, every one of his words of consolation

43   Leo Baeck as a young rabbi

reveal him as a disciple of the Rabbis. . . . Whoever judges the way
Mr. H. does knows nothing about a large domain of Jewish spiritual
life at that time—or is forcing himself not to see it.[4]

Willfully or not, Baeck concluded, Harnack ignored the Jewish background of Jesus's life and thus failed to appreciate the Jewish inflections
of his teachings.

Indeed, Baeck argued, Jesus can only be properly understood in his
Jewish context. So understood:

Most biographers of Jesus neglect to call attention to the fact that in every one of his traits Jesus is thoroughly a *genuinely Jewish character*, that a man like him could only have arisen from the soil of Judaism—only there and nowhere else. Jesus is a genuine Jewish personality; his strivings and actions, his sufferings and feelings, his speech and his silence—all bear the stamp of Jewish idealism, the best that there was in Judaism . . . at that time. He was a Jew among Jews. . . . In no other people would he have found apostles who believed in him. Harnack has chosen to ignore this mother soil of Jesus's personality.[5]

It has been observed that not until Martin Buber would later acclaim Jesus as his brother did a Jew speak so warmly of him. For Baeck Jesus was a fellow Jew not only by virtue of his evident skill in agadic discourse but preeminently because of his moral passion—the ethical idealism that he shared with the Pharisaic sages. Here, too, Baeck pointed out, Harnack (like many other Protestant scholars) misrepresented the Rabbis. For Jesus as for the Rabbis, he explained, the ethical act was the fulcrum of religious life.

It was this latter point that Baeck developed in *Das Wesen des Judentums*, the title indicating his continuing confrontation with Harnack. But rather than being only another critique of the great scholar's portrayal of the Pharisees, Baeck's book was a systematic work in its own right. Although the editions differed substantially, one of his close associates, Fritz Bamberger (1902–1984), noted, "In a certain sense it remained the only book that Baeck ever wrote. . . . A single idea makes up its foundation stone: the God of Judaism is a commanding God. The ethical commandment, the 'You shall' and the 'You shall not,' are the sole rule of Judaism. . . . The categorical character of the ethical demand is never called into question."[6] The ethical deed enjoined by God is the ground of Jewish spirituality. In contradistinction to religions that place importance on the inner experience of faith: "In Judaism religion is not to be *experienced* but *lived*." And Baeck adds, "Whoever does not attain awareness of God through good, noble deeds will likewise always fail to truly experience God's essence through any inner feelings." Baeck concluded that, with regard to Judaism, "it is ethics that comprises its principle, its essence."[7]

Baeck thus identifies the "essence of Judaism" with what became known in the nineteenth century as "ethical monotheism." According to this concept, the "radical innovation" of biblical faith, particularly of the prophets, was that the belief in the one God entailed an inescapable responsibility to serve as God's coworker in the establishment of a just and compassionate world order. This conception of the founding impulse of Judaism particularly appealed to those who were sensitive to the Kantian critique of Judaism, which branded it a heteronomous religion of law and thus but a pseudoreligion. Eager to counter this charge, thinkers from Reform to neo-Orthodox were quick to adopt the notion of ethical monotheism and focus on the universal, ethical (that is, metahalachic) aspects of Judaism. It is not by chance that this conception of Judaism found its major exponents in two leading Kantian scholars, Moritz Lazarus (1824–1903) and Hermann Cohen (1842–1918).

An adjunct professor at the University of Berlin from 1873 until 1896, and a prominent lay leader of Liberal Judaism in Germany, Lazarus devoted numerous essays and a two-volume study, *Die Ethik des Judenthums* (The Ethics of Judaism, 1898–1911), to a systematic presentation of Judaism's inherent compatibility with Kant's conception of morality and true religion. In developing this thesis, he drew upon the principles of *Völkerpsychologie*, the comparative psychology of peoples, a discipline he founded together with his brother-in-law Heymann Steinthal (1823–1899). Accordingly, he contended that this approach would best illuminate the governing values and ethos of the Jewish people. For an empirical resource he turned to the classical literary sources of Judaism, which to his mind most accurately recorded Jewish convictions, purposes, and the Jewish way of life. Lazarus thus abjured all speculative constructions of Judaism, which had until then characterized modern Jewish thought. In consonance with his empiricism, he introduced Kantian categories not as speculative propositions but merely as heuristic principles to elucidate the "empirical" structure of Judaism and help illuminate the objective unity of its "ethical cosmos."

Lazarus maintained that such a study demonstrates Judaism to be a system of autonomous ethics; specifically, the teachings, rites, and values of Judaism foster the development of what Kant celebrated as the moral consciousness. The ethical piety engendered by Judaism is best characterized as "holiness"—a quality of life that bespeaks neither a numinous nor a transcendent reality but rather the firm conviction that a moral life provides the ultimate meaning and purpose of existence.

Lazarus's work would serve Liberal Judaism in this period as a kind of theoretical platform. Nonetheless, it was subject to severe criticism by Hermann Cohen, also a Liberal Jew and widely regarded as the foremost

Kantian philosopher of his day. Cohen faulted Lazarus for locating the sources of Judaism's ethical teachings in the folk-soul of the Jews. To Cohen such a concept, grounded as it is in psychology and history, undermined the reliability and certitude required of a genuine ethical system. Ethics must derive their validity from rational universal concepts. What renders Jewish ethics interesting, Cohen contends, is its distinctive dependence on the idea of a universal unique God—understood not merely as an intuitive construction of the Jewish folk-soul but as a rationally defensible concept.

Cohen was the founder of the neo-Kantian school of philosophy at the University of Marburg, where he taught for some forty years before his retirement in 1912. He sought to maintain a rigorous separation between his philosophical writings and those on Jewish affairs—at least until his posthumously published work *Religion der Vernunft aus den Quellen des Judentums* (Religion of Reason from the Sources of Judaism, 1919), which revealed how intimately connected his philosophical and Jewish interests truly were. His overriding philosophical concern was to preserve philosophy as a universal rational discourse and free it from the irrational clutches of Romanticism and Hegelianism, which since the death of Kant in 1804 had seized the helm of academic philosophy in Germany. Joining those who had gathered under the banner of "back to Kant," Cohen developed his own distinct approach to reviving the project initiated by the sage of Königsberg. In a series of exegetical and original monographs, he endeavored to refine Kant's transcendental or idealistic method of determining a priori rational concepts to guide both theoretical and practical (i.e., moral) life. Following Kant, Cohen did not regard religion as constituting a separate discipline but as complementary to rational ethics. Allied, religion and ethics are charged with the task of leading humanity to moral perfection. Cohen took the vague belief in progress that had inspired liberal society since the Enlightenment and placed that belief in the firm grip of reason. His rational confidence in progress lent his philosophical system a uniquely twofold idealistic character: while promoting the epistemological idealism of transcendental logic, it sponsored the moral idealism of an exalted vision of the good.

In his earliest writings on Judaism Cohen spoke of a fundamental affinity between Liberal Protestantism and Judaism based on a common realization that no longer God per se but rather ethics had become the focus of religion. The liberal expressions of Protestantism and Judaism, he contended, share a refined conception of the biblical God that grounds

genuine religious consciousness in the cultivation of the moral sensibility. Philosophically, he presented God as a "concept"—a construct of reason—that allows one to postulate the unity of the natural world (which
construed from the perspective of the natural sciences alone is finite) and
the moral order of existence (which according to the precepts of practical
reason requires an infinite journey toward perfection); as such, God is a
rationally necessary concept providing the logical conditions for the progressive ethical development of humankind. Cohen argued that this conception of God as the transcendental ground of both the natural order and
the ethical task was also inherent in biblical monotheism, especially as
articulated by the prophets. The oneness of God, Cohen explained, was
understood in the Bible to imply God's uniqueness and thus utter tran-
scendence, which the prophets identified with the moral imperative
instructing Israel that the messianic future—in which the oneness of God
will be complemented by the moral oneness of humanity and the reign of
universal peace—was not only a divine promise but an ethical responsibility and task to be realized through human deeds.

In elaborating the philosophical implications of biblical faith, Cohen
further claimed that ethical monotheism foreshadowed the ethical idealism of Germany's finest spirits, especially Immanuel Kant (who, Cohen
acknowledged, was sadly ill-informed about the true spirit of Judaism).
This proud assertion is said to have done much to strengthen the self-
esteem of German Jewry. As Robert Weltsch observed, "not all German
Jews, of course, had an accurate idea of Kant, nor, for that matter, had all
Germans. . . . What more could be desired than [Cohen's] message of a
sort of identity of the Jewish spirit with the doctrine of Germany's greatest philosophical genius!"[8]

Cohen's intention was unabashedly apologetic. Indeed, throughout his
life he vigorously sought to guard the honor of his fellow Jews as they
strove to gain acceptance in a Germany presumably beholden to liberal
values. But Cohen did not confine his political activity to soliciting the
well-being of his Jewish brethren. For him, the prophetic heritage of Israel
commanded a committed concern for the poor and disinherited members
of the general society within every political entity:

> The messianic God, however, does not simply represent the image
> of the future for world history. Rather, by force of the moral ideas
> that come together within Him, He requires political activity, stead-
> fast, persistent participation in the concrete tasks of the state. *It is*

the task of the Jew to act within the state that is his homeland to bring about the messianic age.[9]

Cohen's moral-religious commitment led him to endorse socialism, observing that the politics of the prophets "are nothing other than what we today call socialism."[10]

It was Cohen's ethical socialism, which with learned detail he explicated on the basis of the teachings of the prophets and the Rabbis, that appealed to many of his contemporaries. Some of his disciples would find their way into revolutionary politics, most would follow a more moderate path of political and social engagement such as Cohen himself pursued. Not all his socialist disciples were, of course, Jewish; moreover, there is no evidence that those who were read him as a fellow Jew whose message was addressed to their Jewish loyalties. On the other hand, many Liberal Jews such as Baeck did. Indeed, they regarded Cohen's thought as "the culmination and representation in systematic form of the ideas that had become the common coin of the Reform movement in the nineteenth century."[11] Cohen's formulation of the doctrine of ethical monotheism palpably inspired Baeck's *Das Wesen des Judentums*, which speaks of the one God "whose essence is the moral law, who is the guarantee for morality, the surety for its eternal reality." Accordingly, it was incumbent on Judaism "to preserve the pure faith in the one God as the destined goal of the religious development of humanity."[12]

In subsequent editions of his book—reflecting his enthusiastic reading of Rudolf Otto's classic of 1919, *Das Heilige* (The Idea of the Holy)—Baeck departed somewhat from his rigorous adherence to a rational conception of faith and spoke of the "mystery" (*Geheimnis*) of God's presence manifest in the commandments. In heeding the ethical commandment, one encounters not only the will of God but also the *mysterium tremendum*, the numinous reality it bears. The ineffable "mystery" of God—who is no longer a mere idea for Baeck—thus intersects with the rational certainty of the commandment; the inscrutable, infinite presence of God hovers above the commandment, where infinite and finite meet. To live with both mystery and commandment is the sublime paradox of Jewish existence. Baeck had, in effect, thus shifted the focus of his theology from the essence of Judaism to the existence of the Jewish people. Nonetheless, ethical monotheism remained the overarching theme of Baeck's conception of Judaism; the meaning of Jewish existence was expressed in the Jews' abiding moral responsibility to be "a light to the nations."

2. Jewish Religiosity Redefined

Not all Jews eager to affirm their Jewishness were receptive to Baeck's—
or similar—teachings, however. Those in search of a more existentially
meaningful Judaism could hold with Franz Rosenzweig that God gave
Israel the Torah, not monotheism. Already at the turn of the century
Jewish intellectuals sharing the general malaise of the period—and especially the youth—were disenchanted with the Enlightenment and modern civilization and detected in liberal conceptions of Judaism an unwar-
ranted "bourgeois" optimism, a misguided faith in reason and history
that neglected the more existential and personal aspects of religion. They
found talk of ethical monotheism and Israel's mission spiritually and
intellectually dissatisfying.

In the midst of their spiritual crisis those given to what has been characterized as a romantic discontent with modernity followed the lead of
their non-Jewish peers and increasingly turned their attention to the irrational dimensions of culture and faith: peoplehood (in the form of Zionism
and its new sense of Jewish community), myth, and mysticism. They
found in Martin Buber (1878–1965) a unique blend of these new vistas of
Jewish experience—new at least for assimilated youth of Central Europe.

Buber was born in Vienna but raised by his grandparents in Lemberg
(Lviv), administrative center of Galicia, an eastern province of the
Habsburg Empire with a mixed Polish and Ukrainian population as well
as a large minority of mostly traditional Jews. He attended Polish secular
schools and at the same time, with the aid of private tutors including his
grandfather, Solomon Buber (1827–1906), a renowned scholar of
midrash, received a solid traditional Jewish education. From his grandparents he also imbibed a passionate attachment to German literature and
culture. Later he would study and settle in Germany. While still in his
twenties he was in the forefront of the literary effort, known as the New
Romanticism, to recover lost texts of myth and mysticism. He published
translations of Celtic, Chinese, Finnish, Flemish, German, and Jewish
myths and mystical testimonies.

Parallel to his literary activity, Buber was a Zionist, who, after a brief
period of cooperation with the founder of the world Zionist movement,
Theodor Herzl (1860–1904), joined those who opposed his strictly political conception of the movement's objectives. Buber preferred to see
Zionism as a framework for the cultural renewal of Judaism, a conception
of Zionist priorities associated with the Russian Hebrew writer Ahad

Ha'Am (Asher Ginsberg, 1856–1927). But whereas Ahad Ha'Am argued for the secularization of select traditional Jewish values and the rendering of Judaism as a "national culture" to enable the modern secular Jew to live creatively as a Jew, Buber sought the renewal of Jewish religiosity, albeit in radically new forms that would scandalize the adherents of Jewish tradition. He located the sources of this renewal in myth and mysticism, features of the Jewish spiritual legacy often, he held, suppressed by "official" Judaism (by which youth of the period understood, as Buber undoubtedly intended: the "bourgeois establishment"). These features, he contended, are the truly creative forces of Judaism, as opposed to rabbinic law and learning. The soul of Judaism is not in its laws and institutions—in its "official" expressions—but in the subterranean world of its rich and vibrant mystical and mythic tradition. It is this world that must be tapped anew if Judaism is to renew its soul. The first Jewish myths Buber presented were in two collections—*Die Geschichten des Rabbi Nachman* (The Tales of Rabbi Nachman, 1906) and *Die Legende des Baalschem* (The Legend of the Baal-Shem, 1908). Here he "retold" the tales of Hasidism, the Jewish mystical movement founded in eighteenth-century Poland and Ukraine. He employed the hermeneutics of recovery that he had learned from his teacher at the University of Berlin, Wilhelm Dilthey. He would seek to recover the spirit, animating lost voices of the past by reliving the original experience embodied in those voices. Buber's emergence as a leader with a wide following, however, was occasioned by a series of lectures that he delivered before the Bar Kochba Jewish Student Association of Prague.

The letter inviting Buber to Prague explained that a colloquium was to be held that would address "the broad assimilated [Jewish] public" of the city and that another speaker would deal with "urban Jewish society's lack of values and roots." But the organizers of the colloquium were eager to complement the discussion on the negative aspects of assimilation with Buber's reflections on the abiding qualities of Jewish existence: "How can the remnant of Jewishness be transformed into one's own, even among the Jews of the West? How can this particular element provide the Jewish writer with his own sense of cultural value?" Buber's correspondent further observed that "naturally this holds for the Jews of Eastern Europe to a signficantly greater extent. But this time it might be appropriate to demonstrate it, in particular, for the West European Jews." The letter concluded with a plea to help stem the tide of assimilation among the Jews of Prague, who precisely because of their fervent attachment to high

German culture required someone as sophisticated as Buber to inform them about Judaism. "In the entire West, in fact everywhere, we have today no more sensitive interpreter of Jewish existence than you."[13] Buber accepted the invitation with alacrity and came to Prague in January 1909 to deliver a lecture entitled "The Meaning of Judaism." As the writer (and future executor of Kafka's literary estate) Max Brod (1884–1968), who had hitherto been indifferent to Judaism, reported, the lecture deeply touched him and converted him to a passionate Zionism; others were similarly moved. Among the latter were individuals who were to become some of the most prominent personalities in European Jewish life— Robert Weltsch (1891–1982), the courageous editor of the Zionist *Jüdische Rundschau* before and during the Third Reich, his cousin Felix Weltsch (1884–1964), a philosopher and editor of the Prague Zionist weekly, *Selbstwehr*, Hans Kohn (1891–1971), who after a short but intense period in Palestine emigrated in the early 1930s to the United States, where he gained renown as a scholar of modern European and German history, and the philosopher Hugo Bergmann (1883–1975), who settled in Palestine in 1921 where he was one of the founding members of the faculty of the Hebrew University. Franz Kafka, who was a marginal member of the Bar Kochba, also attended Buber's lectures—which left him cold, although he found Buber personally engaging.

Under the auspices of the Bar Kochba Association Buber would return to Prague often. The product of his first three visits was his *Drei Reden über das Judentum* (Three Addresses on Judaism, 1911), which became the vade mecum of Central European Jewish youth for more than a decade. Fifty years later Gershom Scholem would recall with regard to Buber's *Drei Reden*: "At that time a signficant magic went forth from these words. In those years I could name no book on Judaism that even remotely had the same effect—not just on scholars, who scarcely read these addresses—but on young people, who were being called here to a new awakening, one that many of them took seriously."[14]

In the *Drei Reden* (and other addresses he was subsequently to deliver to the Bar Kochba Association), Buber systematically elaborated on themes he had already adumbrated in his earlier volumes on Hasidism. There he had evoked the mystical strain and spiritual nobility of these representatives of East European Jewry who had hitherto been ridiculed and vilified in the West—an attitude that many Central and Western European Jews had unquestioningly adopted. In Buber's gracefully written and elegantly presented books (he insisted that the lettering and jacket design be executed by the leading Jugendstil artists of the day), the hasid, for so long the emblem of the putatively backward, uncouth Ostjude, was no longer a source of embarrassment. Behind the strange exterior of these residents of what the Austrian Jewish writer Karl Emil Franzos (1848–1904), derisively called "Semi-Asia," Buber disclosed a remarkable spiritual universe of mystical profundity. He rendered Hasidism respectable, as it were, by integrating this most distinctive manifestation of East European Jewish culture into the general discourse and idiom of the New Romanticism (and, later, Expressionism). By virtue of Buber's inspired presentation, Hasidism—and the millennial Jewish mystical tradition, the Kabbalah—was now deemed relevant to the concerns of the educated individual.

In a manner today considered methodologically questionable by some scholars, Buber presented Hasidism in these lectures in terms of its legends and myths: the pre-Enlightenment folk wisdom that the publisher Eugen Diederichs, the Maecenas of the New Romanticism, celebrated as capturing an intuitive and therefore genuine metaphysical experience of the world's primal unity, which had been obstructed by the instrumental rationality and divisive ambitions that dominate modern urban civilization. Further, Buber related Hasidism to the other mystical and mythic traditions honored by the New Romanticism and compellingly indicated how its insights bore on what were considered to be most urgent questions of the mystical quest: how to apply the metaphysical unity (beyond space and time) to restore unity in the real world of space and time, specifically, to regenerate the life of *Gemeinschaft*, the organic community of human solidarity forged by bonds of mutual trust and care, brutally displaced by the fragmenting bustle of modern society. Thus in his legendary tale of the founder of Hasidism he had noted that hasidic spirituality was dialectically upheld by two poles: *hitlahavut* (ecstasy) and *avodah* (worship): "Hitlahavut is the embrace of God devoid of time and space. Avodah is the service of God in time and space."[15] This dialectic of hasidic piety, as Buber explained in the second of his addresses to the Bar Kochba Association, reflected the most fundamental experience of the Jew: a striving for unity. It was this striving within the personal, political, and metaphysical spheres, Buber told his enthralled audience in Prague, "that makes Judaism into a universal phenomenon, the 'Jewish Question' into a human question."[16]

In a later speech in Prague, "Der Geist des Orients und das Judentum" (The Spirit of the Orient and Judaism, 1912), Buber argued that this striving for unity was what distinguished the Jew, and not just the hasidim. Despite the ravages of assimilation, the Jew had remained a Jew, at least in terms of fundamental sensibility. Borne by that abiding awareness, he averred, the Jew understands the unity of the world to be an overarching demand for its redemption. The deracinated Jew of the West might be estranged from the Law and from rabbinic learning, but he had not thereby necessarily vitiated his Judaism, for Judaism (and undoubtedly this was Buber's most intriguing message to the Jews of Prague) was ultimately not a matter of formal articles of faith and prescribed ritual practices but rather of a specific spiritual orientation. Indeed, Buber contraposed this sensibility, articulated most forcefully in Israel's mystical tradition, to the "official" Judaism of the Rabbis. The former, the truly creative element of Judaism, had been repeatedly suppressed by the Rabbis, and as a result been forced to lead a largely "subterranean" existence. At critical moments in history, however, this authentic but submerged spirituality of the Jew asserted itself publicly to renew Judaism, as "in the great religious upheaval of Hasidism." To be sure, the creative spirit that animated Hasidism had been checked and eventually stifled by the custodians of official Judaism, but the possibility for the renewal of the spirit continued to exist, hidden within the very depths of the Jew. The foundation for the renewal of Judaism, Buber reassuringly told the assimilated youth of Prague, "is the soul of the Jew itself."[17]

With Nietzschean inflections, Buber thus called for the liberation of the Jewish soul from the shackles of assimilation and the pretensions of institutional religion. In yet another lecture in Prague in 1913 he declared that

the renewal of Judaism means the renewal of Jewish religiosity. I am saying, and I mean, religiosity. . . . Religiosity is the creative principle, religion the organizing one; religiosity begins anew with every young person who is shattered by the mystery, religion wants to inject that mystery forcibly and for all times into its stabilized system; religiosity means activity—an elemental setting oneself into relationship with the Absolute, religion means passivity—taking upon oneself the law that has been handed down; religiosity only has its goal, religion has purposes; on account of religiosity sons rise up against fathers in order to find their own God, on account of religion fathers condemn sons because they refuse to accept their God; religion means preservation, religiosity means renewal.[18]

It was a stirring message and one that exercised an immense appeal for

Jewish youth longing to reaffirm their Jewish identity as an access to a spiritually engaging life but who found the established form of Jewish religious life—liberal and traditional alike—uninspiring. Yet, as Buber himself realized, beyond its dramatic and incandescent imagery, the vision was ill-defined and vague. Although he would never abandon his religious anarchism (a term he used to describe his position), he sought to move beyond his early ideas of Jewish religiosity and renewal. After a long and at times troubled gestation, the principle of dialogue was born, which Buber introduced after the war in his small but magisterial volume of 1923, *Ich und Du* (I and Thou).

I and Thou, along with Franz Rosenzweig's *Star of Redemption,* marks a radical, existential turn in Jewish religious thought. These two works, conceived in the midst of the world war, would become the focus of a veritable renaissance of Jewish religious concern in the Weimar Republic. Yet both Buber and Rosenzweig point to Hermann Cohen's *Religion of Reason,* published during the chaotic period immediately following the collapse of the Kaiserreich, as anticipating many of the central existential and dialogical elements of what Rosenzweig called the "new thinking."

During his last years Cohen increasingly devoted himself to clarifying his understanding of religion. According to his most mature conception, religion finds its distinctive expression precisely in ritual and liturgy, which Kant had dismissed as ultimately irrelevant to true service of God. Cohen now understands religion, in contradistinction to ethics, as addressing the individual as such and not merely as a representative of rational humanity. Religion pertains to the individual, especially through the notion of "sin," which Cohen defines as the individual's anguished realization of moral failings. This consciousness of sin, Cohen observes, bears the danger that the individual will despair of his own moral worth and abandon all subsequent moral effort. The self-estrangement attendant upon sin requires the concept of a forbearing God who by the act of forgiveness serves to reintegrate the atoning individual into an ethically committed humanity. The atonement of sin, however, is not effected by God's grace but by individuals who, acknowledging God's forgiveness, dedicate themselves anew to the moral task.

Religion is thus preeminently a series of acts of atonement—rites and prayers expressing remorse and repentance focused on the belief in a merciful, forgiving God. To Cohen this reconciliation between God and human being in turn requires that God be conceived not as an idea but as a being who relates to the finite, ever-changing world of becoming, of

44 Hermann Cohen with students in Marburg in 1912.
Drawing by Leonid Pasternak

which the individual is a part. Despite the fundamental ontological distinction separating them, being and becoming are thus interrelated
through what Cohen calls "correlation." God and person are correlated to
each other when individuals cognizant of God's mercy—love and concern—dedicate themselves to emulating in their actions these divine
qualities. Cohen understands correlation as a shared holiness in which
God and human beings engage together in the work of creation.

The first edition of Cohen's *Religion of Reason*, in which he
expounded these ideas, contains a slight but crucial error in the title. The
editors of the volume inadvertently added the definite article "the" (*die*)
before religion, erroneously suggesting that for Cohen Judaism was *the*

religion of reason. What Cohen sought to argue is that a religion of reason can be constructed, as the subtitle of the work tells us, "from the sources of Judaism." He wanted to present a deductive and logical construction, not a historical exposition. Hence Cohen constructs a "religion of reason" on the basis of a selective exegesis—guided by a priori principles—of the sources of classical Judaism: the Bible, midrash, and the traditional liturgy. As he interprets them, these classical expressions of Jewish piety are made to exemplify the most refined conception of religion. While the resulting portrait of Judaism as a faith of deep personal significance suggested to some the anticipation of an existentialist theology, with its emphasis on the dialogic relation of the individual with a living, personal God, other commentators have pointed out that Cohen continues to speak of a "religion of reason" and that his God remains the rational God of ethics. Moral reason is still for Cohen the heart of religion, and thus it is not surprising that when he speaks of divine revelation he grounds it in reason: "Revelation is the creation of reason."[19] Accordingly, although in striking contrast to Kant he ascribes intrinsic significance to religion qua prayer and ritual, Cohen still does not regard religion as a fully independent reality enjoying a unique ontological and epistemological status. While not entirely absorbed into ethics, the "religion of reason" for Cohen ultimately remains ancillary to ethics. Religion, and Judaism in particular, is conceived as an instrument for enhancing moral consciousness—that is, moral reason—and commitment. It facilitates the individual's acceptance of "the yoke of the Kingdom of God" and the ongoing ethical task incumbent upon rational humanity.

3. Deutschtum and Judentum

In his last years, beginning with his retirement from the University of Marburg and his move to Berlin, Cohen devoted himself to more than the clarification of his understanding of religion and Judaism. He also addressed a variety of practical issues facing the Jewish people, in particular the vexatious question of the relationship of Judaism to Deutschtum, that is, to German culture and identity. Ever since his exchange with Heinrich von Treitschke in 1880—in which he vigorously defended the right of Jews to consider themselves Germans spiritually and culturally, and not merely in a formal political sense—Cohen had come to "symbolize more than anyone else the union of Jewish faith and German culture."[20]

During the world war Cohen published two essays identically entitled "Deutschtum und Judentum." With demonstrative pride, he clearly proclaimed in the second of these the compatibility and complementarity of Judaism and German culture:

> With regard to our own spiritual lives, we [German Jews] have become aware of the very close religious association that exists in the correspondence between Jewish messianism and German humanism. For that reason our German sentiments toward state and people are, as it were, transfigured and confirmed by our religion; our soul flourishes equally and harmoniously both in our German patriotism and in our religious consciousness, which has its root and its pinnacle in the unique God of humanity.[21]

It would be mistaken to read such pronouncements, which abound in Cohen's writings, as a mere exercise in apologetics, as a naive and benighted protestation of Jewish loyalty to Deutschtum. Cohen was, after all, a Kantian and should be read through the prism of his idealistic, that is, regulative categories. Read as such, there is a great deal of irony—and anguish—between the lines.

As a Kantian, Cohen was fiercely anti-Hegelian, and deemed it as both philosophically inane and politically dangerous to view, as Hegel had, the real, empirical world as rational. "Here the vast difference between Hegel and Kant becomes apparent," Cohen averred, "for Kant would say: what is rational is not real; rather it must become real."[22] What Cohen offered in his political writings was, accordingly, but an ideal construct meant to disclose the shortcomings of the present reality. Holding up the ideal as a mirror, he sought ever so gently to rebuke contemporary Germany and prod it to honor its humanistic heritage. Speaking of the ideal Germany, he indirectly criticized its empirical counterpart. Earlier, in 1907, he had acknowledged en passant in the preface to a philosophical treatise on ethics that his views differed from the modern "sort of Deutschtum." He added, however, that he took heart from knowledge of the existence of an alternative tradition that informs "German spiritual existence" and that, graced by its "primordial power," will ultimately prevail over its "degenerate ephemeral form."[23]

In the conclusion of the second of his "Deutschtum und Judentum" essays, Cohen offers a vision:

> There has never been a lack of German people who were fond of

their German Jews and trusted them. Perhaps—who can gauge the course of world history—it will one day be accounted not the least of the German people's crowns that they not only bestowed protection and civil rights upon their Jews but also gave them a share in the German spirit, in German science and art, in German creativity in all realms, that they sincerely encouraged the Jews' religion—for the sake of the entire world: that they have uniquely prepared the way, in a manner perhaps unparalleled in its depth among all modern nations, for a harmonization between these two folk-spirits, a harmonization that, to be sure, casts the chief obligation of gratitude upon the Jew.[24]

There is in this vision a tone of wistfulness—"who can gauge the course of world history?"—rather than prophetic certainty. It is a vision, not a description of the empirical Germany; it expresses a guarded hope that the Jews' embrace of German culture will no longer be a cause of contempt but of a pride evoking fraternal feelings between Jews and Germans.

Cohen's vision was challenged not only by subsequent events but by his fellow Jews. Two years before his death he engaged Buber in a debate over Zionism. The polemical exchange was provoked by Buber, who had published an open letter to Cohen protesting his refusal to view the Jews as a nation with their own distinct historical destiny. To Buber, the Zionist, the realization of this destiny did not need to conflict with Israel's ethical mission and messianic task:

> What Zionism is fighting against is not the messianic idea but its disfigurement and distortion, as one finds it in a considerable portion of the literature of Liberal anti-Zionist Jews. Such disfigurement and distortion makes use of messianism to glorify the dispersion, the abasement, the homelessness of the Jewish people as something of absolute value and beneficence, as something that must be maintained because it prepares the way for a messianic humanity.[25]

In response, Cohen defended the Liberal Jewish position, while not denying the ambiguity of modernity, which undoubtedly prompted some Jews to abandon Judaism and others to opt for Zionism. As for Buber's objection to placing value on the continuing "homelessness" of the Jew, Cohen affirms that "this messianic faith cannot be compromised through any historical reality, any distress, or even through the good fortune of civil equality." Jewish destiny lies in exile, or rather dispersion, for as the prophet Micah declares, "And the remnant of Jacob shall be in the midst of many nations like dew from the Eternal One" (5:6). Cohen comments, "We are proudly conscious of living on as divine dew in the midst of the nations, remaining fruitful among them and for their sake."[26]

In the years immediately prior to and during the world war, this conviction, which had been shared by the vast majority of German Jewry, was increasingly questioned by Jew and non-Jew alike. Doubts regarding the place of Jews in German culture had, of course, been voiced all along. The cultural and intellectual attainment of Jews frequently begot resentment and suspicion. But by and large in liberal circles such feelings were regarded as a bias not properly broached in public. Certainly Jews wedded to the liberal ethos preferred to ignore the issue. This silence was unceremoniously broken in March 1912 with a bold, indeed brash, article, "Deutsch-jüdischer Parnass" (German-Jewish Parnassus), published in the prestigious cultural review, *Der Kunstwart*. This article, in the words of Gershom Scholem, "broke a taboo that otherwise had only been violated by antisemites."[27]

Written by a young Jewish student of German literature, Moritz Goldstein (1880–1977), the article provoked a ramified debate that reverberated for several years throughout the German press. Goldstein obviously touched a raw nerve when he asserted, "We Jews are administering the spiritual possessions of a people that denies us the right and capacity to do so." He continued to explain:

> We Jews, among ourselves, may have the impression that we are speaking as Germans to Germans—we do *have* that impression. But however fully German we may feel ourselves to be, *the others feel that we are fully un-German*. We may be called Max Reinhardt and have raised the theater to unprecedented heights, or as Hugo von Hofmannsthal have replaced Schiller's outdated metaphorical language with a new poetic style, or as Max Liebermann be in the vanguard of modern painting. We may call all that German, but the others call it Jewish; they detect the "Asiatic" in it, they miss the "teutonic soul." And when they have no choice but to acknowledge the achievement (with reservations, of course), *they express the wish that we would achieve less*.[28]

Goldstein addressed these remarks to his fellow "Jewish literati" (*Literaturjuden*). He conceded that by raising the issue as he did in the general press he would doubtless tap anti-Jewish sentiments. But he felt he had no other forum. Indeed, he turned to the periodical *Der Kunstwart*, dedicated to conservative views and edited by a nephew of Richard Wagner, Ferdinand Avenarius, only after having his article rejected three times by liberal organs that found it inappropriate. Borne by a sense of urgency, he sought to awaken his Jewish colleagues from what he believed to be a dangerous complacency and even a studied indifference to what he deemed "the intolerable and undignified ambiguity"[29] of being both a German and a Jew. At the conclusion of the article he admitted confusion. Although drawn to Zionism, he knew he could not turn his back on Germany and German culture:

> The German spring is our spring as well, as the German winter was our winter. . . . Didn't we grow up with German fairytales? Didn't we play Little Red Riding Hood and Sleeping Beauty? Weren't we saddened for Snow White and cheerful with the Seven Dwarfs? Doesn't the German forest exist for us too? May not we too catch a glimpse of its elves and gnomes? Don't we too understand the rushing of the brook and the song of the birds?[30]

To deny being German would, then, be both ludicrous and impossible.

Offering no solace, Goldstein makes do with calling upon his fellow educated Jews simply to acknowledge their dilemma. "Our worse enemies," he exclaims, are not the antisemites but rather "the Jews who don't notice a thing, who incessantly produce German culture, who act as if it were otherwise and convince themselves that they are not being identified as Jews. These are our true enemies."[31] The questions raised by Goldstein and the debate that followed in its wake would accompany the Jews into the Weimar Republic.

12 | The First World War

The outbreak of the world war brought about a dramatic change in the relationships between Jews and their governments in both the German and the Austro-Hungarian Empires. The course of the war and the ultimate military defeat of both empires resulted in even greater changes, the nature and extent of which none of the participants anticipated in 1914. In Germany there had been in the immediate prewar period a perceptible element of mutual suspicion between the imperial government and the Jewish community. The systematic discrimination practiced by the majority of public authorities constantly reminded even the most prosperous and professionally successful Jews that legal equality was a matter more of theory than of fact. Well-established organizations like the previously mentioned Central-verein deutscher Staatsbürger jüdischen Glaubens (cv) and Verband der deutschen Juden (vdj) were able to chalk up periodic successes in the struggle against these inequalities; that they were needed at all showed how wide was the gulf between reality and what the law promised. In their pursuit of genuine equality the leaders of Jewish organizations found their allies and well-wishers—who could, at times, be quite effective—among the Liberal left and to some extent in the spd and the Catholic Center. But this was a mixed blessing, for it helped to typecast Jews as oppositional, unreliable, or subversive. In the Western crownlands of Austria the situation was reversed. At the political level the reliable opponents of antisemitism were almost nonexistent, given the weakness of Liberal forces and the reluctance of Social Democracy to get involved. In the increasingly bitter conflicts between the nationalities, Jews were caught in the cross fire. Pragmatic alliances or even alliances of principle could be formed, as, for instance, between Bohemian-Moravian Jews and Masaryk's "Realist" Party, but there was never a guarantee that these would last or, if lasting, that they would be effective. What protected the Jews of Austria was the imperial government, partly because of the personal integrity of Emperor Francis Joseph, partly because Jews were an integrative, centripetal force at a time when the thrust of politics was almost entirely in the opposite direction, but also because they played a role in the empire's economy that verged on the indispensable. Even this security was threatened by the known reactionary and antisemitic sympathies of the heir to the throne, Archduke Francis Ferdinand. His assassination on June 28, 1914, removed that particular threat but unleashed the far bigger one of the war.

1. The Civic Truce

Initially war improved the situation of the Jews of both empires. The declaration of the "civic truce" (*Burgfrieden*) in Germany raised Jewish morale more than any event since the enactment of legal equality in 1869. The emperor's words, "I know no parties any more, I know only Germans," constituted an olive branch that, even if not directed at Jews, evoked in them "enthusiastic rejoicing."[1] For Jews of virtually all political persuasions and religious denominations the war offered the hope that the unity of the German nation would at last embrace them too and the opportunity to demonstrate beyond all doubt their loyalty and devotion to the German cause. This reaction was easiest for the mainstream of German-Jewish opinion, as represented by the CV. In their joint appeal the CV and the vdj called on their coreligionists "to devote your resources to the fatherland beyond the call of duty."[2] The Orthodox minority was equally filled with patriotism; few among them questioned whether wartime military service would interfere with their religious obligations or whether duty to the emperor overrode these. Among most Zionists, too, Arthur Hantke's prewar rejection of "every doubt about our patriotic convictions" found an echo.[3] In words almost identical with those of the CV and the vdj, the Zionist Organization (zvfD) and the Reichsverein der deutschen Juden (Association of German Jews in the Reich) declared, "We shall as German citizens gladly fulfill all demands on our possessions, on

45 Grasping for announcements of the outbreak of war in front of the
Mosse publishing house in Berlin

46 German-Jewish soldiers worship together on the Day of Atonement in
Brussels in 1915

life and blood."[4] Even in the middle of the war, the Prague Zionist weekly,
Selbstwehr (Self-Defense), was still urging "unlimited sacrifices for the
great aims of the war."[5]

In 1914 the patriotic consensus among German Jews differed little
from that among their Gentile compatriots. The "Manifesto of the
Ninety-Three," in which leading German academics and artists tried to
proclaim the justice of Germany's cause to the world, contained the signatures of several eminent Jews, including the painter Max Liebermann,
the stage director Max Reinhardt, and the Nobel laureate Paul Ehrlich.
Ehrlich and Liebermann were among those who returned their British
honors and decorations. Some went even further: Ernst Lissauer composed his *Hassgesang gegen England* (Song of Hate Against England), a
literary achievement rewarded by the Prussian Order of the Red Eagle.
Other Jews helped the war effort in a more material way. The baptized
Fritz Haber, a future Nobel laureate, pioneered the development of poison
gas, and even Albert Einstein, despite his pacifist leanings and Swiss citizenship, remained in the employment of the Kaiser Wilhelm Institut.
Austrian Jewish writers were, if anything, more consistently enthusiastic

for the war effort—not only Felix Salten (1869–1945) and Siegfried Trebitsch (1869–1956) but the former and later pacifist Stefan Zweig (1881–1942) and the former and later anarchist Stefan Grossmann (1875–1935). Unlike its German analogues, to be discussed below, the leading liberal newspaper of Vienna, edited by Jews, the *Neue Freie Presse*, maintained an uncritical posture throughout the war. The only notable exceptions to this consensus were Arthur Schnitzler (1862–1931) and Karl Kraus (1874–1936), whose *Die Fackel* kept up a constant campaign against the hypocrisy of war propaganda. Of Austrian Jewish academics the most notable critic of the war was Sigmund Freud, who found that "never [had] an event destroyed so much that was precious in the common property of mankind, confused so many of the most lucid minds, so thoroughly debased the elevated."[6]

There was an obvious reason for this predominantly bellicose reaction, apart from the no doubt genuine surge of patriotic fervor and the hope of reciprocity from the authorities and from fellow citizens: the war was being waged against the archenemy of all Jews, czarist Russia. For any Jews who might otherwise have had doubts about the German cause, "the struggle against Muscovy" was conclusive.[7] At this early stage of the war few Jews had doubts. Albert Einstein was one, though even he developed into fully fledged pacifism only as the war went on. Among the Social Democratic left the most notable opponents of the war from its very beginning were Hugo Haase, the joint chairman of the party, and Rosa Luxemburg; outside the party there was the Socialist anarchist Gustav Landauer (1870–1919). Among the Orthodox, isolated voices, like that of Isaac Breuer (1883–1946), hoped that good might come out of evil: "We Germans are at war, so that we can finally get significantly closer to our ideal of world peace. Our victory is at the same time the victory of world peace."[8] Some prominent Zionists also deviated from the mainstream, though not necessarily out of principled opposition to war. The young Gershom Scholem (1897–1982), calculated on the basis of realpolitik that an Anglo-French victory was more likely to further Zionist aims than a German one. But in the summer of 1914 the hesitation of some Zionists was counterbalanced by Martin Buber's bellicose enthusiasm: "In the tempest of the events the Jew has discovered with elementary violence the meaning of community."[9] "Incipit vita nova," he wrote to the Prague Zionist Hans Kohn (1891–1971).[10]

If the civic truce in Germany promised to suspend the battles between the parties, the hope in Austria was that it would suspend the battle between the nationalities. That was certainly in the interest of the Jewish population, for whom the war was an opportunity to reinforce their loyalty to the dynasty and the Empire. In this aim they were soon doubly disappointed. The nationalist struggles aborted only briefly; long before the war began to go badly for the Central Powers the leaders of the Czech, Italian, or Romanian minorities explored Russian and Western support for greater autonomy and ultimately independence. As the war situation deteriorated that applied even to Hungarians and Poles. The pro-Russian attitudes of many of the Czech nationalist leaders tied the Jews of Bohemia and Moravia even more strongly to the supranational monarchy, a loyalty that many Czechs mistook for devotion to the German-Austrian cause: watching Jews marching through the center of Prague in August 1914, Jan Herben, the editor of Masaryk's *Cas*, expressed his disgust at "this most warlike of the Austrian tribes."[11]

In the German-Austrian crownlands, in contrast, a civic truce prevailed initially. Bloch's *Österreichische Wochenschrift* thanked the (antisemitic) municipality of Vienna for its aid to refugees from Galicia and the German-Radical Karl Iro, a former follower of Schönerer, conceded that any Jew who had served at the front "has secured his right to be one of us."[12] In the eastern crownlands there was an immediate military threat to Jews, since the war zone ran through the areas of densest Jewish settlement in Galicia and Ukraine. The Jewish population was distrusted by both sides, suspected of disloyalty and espionage, and accused of smuggling and black marketeering. On the Russian side up to half a million Jews were deported, on the Austrian side a stream of refugees fled westward to Bohemia and Vienna without doing much to improve their situation.

However, in their relations with the governments of the empires Jews undoubtedly benefited initially. There were a number of reasons for this. The German government desired the civic truce. It needed national unity, and that meant making concessions to Jews and repressing antisemitism. It also needed Jewish resources in finance and brainpower if it was to prosecute the war effectively. Most important, it needed the goodwill of Jews outside the territories of the Central Powers, even if in pursuit of this aim the two allied governments exaggerated both the cohesiveness and the influence of "world Jewry." Jews responded immediately to their leaders' appeal for "donating money and property in the service of the fatherland"[13] by subscribing to war loans and war charities. Jewish notables were recruited to preside over philanthropic committees in a way that would have been unthinkable before the war. Almost revolutionary in

47   Army chaplain Dr. Samuel Link conducts a patriotic celebration for
Austrian-Jewish reserve officers

terms of German political conventions was the appointment of Jews to
administrative positions that virtually oversaw the economic manage-
ment of the war effort. Walther Rathenau became head of the raw materials procurement agency, Albert Ballin of the central purchasing agency,
and the economist Julius Hirsch (1882–1961) was put in charge of price
regulation. Given the prominence of Jews among professional and business talent and the personal connections of men like Rathenau and Ballin,
it was not surprising that other Jews, including Carl Melchior (1871–
1933) of the Warburg Bank, were active on the staffs of these bodies—a
fact that did not go unnoticed among antisemites.

2. Jews and German War Aims Policy

Even more revolutionary than the new appointments policy was the role
that the governments assigned to Jews in pursuit of their diplomacy and
war aims. Unprecedentedly, Jews now became participants in policy, not
merely its objects. The first step in this direction was the attempt to secure
the allegiance of the Jews of Russian Poland. A proclamation by the
German and Austro-Hungarian military command promised, "We come

48 A conference of Jewish army chaplains on the Eastern Front, held
in Riga during February 1918. (From *left* to *right*: Rabbis Hanover, Tänzer,
Arthur Levy, Baeck, Sali Levy, Rosenack, Sonderling)

to you as friends and liberators. Our banners bring you justice and freedom." It also urged them not to forget the Beilis trial and "the despicable
lying accusation of ritual murder" that was raised there,[14] quite ignoring
that similar developments had not been unknown in the lands of the self-
appointed liberators. This proclamation was not only aimed at the czar's
subjects. There was an even more important audience in the neutral
United States, where there were over two million Jews of East European
origin. Both German diplomats and German-Jewish intellectuals were
drawn in to foster the image of Germany as the friend of the Jews. The
German ambassador to Washington, Count Bernstorff, assured the *New
Yorker Staatszeitung*, "After the war Jew hatred will disappear" thanks to
the wartime camaraderie of Gentile and Jewish Germans. Hermann
Cohen begged American Jews not to favor Russia over a Germany in
which every Jew was "in full legal possession of his share in the power of
the state" and with which "the Jews of the Occident . . . [have] an intellectual and spiritual link."[15]

Jews quickly responded to the changed political environment and to
what they saw as their improved bargaining position vis-à-vis their governments. A number of organizations emerged, sometimes in competi-

tion with each other, either to further their programs for the Jews of
Eastern Europe or to establish themselves as legitimate spokespersons for
Jewish interests in the eyes of the government or both. The German
Committee for the Liberation of Russian Jews, founded in August 1914
on the initiative of Max Bodenheimer and Franz Oppenheimer, was too
Zionist in its direction to gain general credibility. A similar committee in
Austria, founded by Martin Buber and Nathan Birnbaum, with the goal
of winning Russian Jews for the Austrian-German cause was also short-
lived. The German Committee was succeeded in November by the more
broadly based Komitee für den Osten (Committee for the East), which
brought together leading figures of the CV, the VdJ, the DIGB, the ZVfD, and
B'nai B'rith. It was, however, easier to reach consensus within such an
organization on humanitarian work than on a political program of
national and cultural autonomy for the Jewish populations of Eastern
Europe. Finally in November 1915 the even more comprehensive German
Association for the Interests of East European Jews was founded. It
boasted a distinguished membership, including Albert Ballin, Max
Warburg, and Paul Nathan as well as the leading officeholders of representative Jewish organizations, and largely downgraded the Committee
for the East. The German authorities responded at least indirectly to these
Jewish initiatives by setting up a "Jewish Section" within the military
government of occupied Poland, headed by the Progressive Reichstag
deputy Ludwig Haas. However, the German and Austrian governments,
while content to exploit Jewish discontents, were in no hurry to choose
between the various solutions to the "Eastern Jewish Question" on offer.
There was as yet no certainty what the postwar map of Eastern Europe
would look like. Both governments were at least as anxious to secure the
support of Polish nationalists who were most unfavorable to any Jewish
claims to separate status.

Despite this German ambivalence, or because of it, Jewish organiza-
tions and individuals were eager to make the most of the convergence of
German and Jewish interests, whether in Eastern Europe or in the Middle
East. In both cases Jews were presented as the natural beneficiaries of
German dominance and the natural agents of German culture. One
Zionist writer, Adolf Friedemann (1871–1932), a close collaborator of
Theodor Herzl, claimed that the six million Jews of the Russian Empire
"can be pioneers of German supremacy in the East, carry German cultural
values into distant parts and render invaluable services to German
trade."[16] Moreover, the better the Jews of Poland and Russia were treated

by the German authorities the less they would be tempted to migrate to Germany. Once Turkey had entered the war on the German side, Zionists increased their pressure on the German government to support Jewish settlement in Palestine, then part of the Ottoman Empire. Kurt Blumenfeld argued that "with the aid of the old Oriental people of the Jews, German linguistic and educational influence could advance to first place in Turkey and German economic influence could be strengthened in all sectors."[17] All these arguments rested on multiple wishful thinking. The first illusion was that the governments of the Central Powers, however anxious they might be to secure the goodwill of Jews, would sacrifice other interests to this objective. In Poland, as we have seen, the appeasement of Polish nationalism was bound to have priority. Nor was the government of Turkey interested in fostering Jewish immigration to Palestine; this presented an immovable obstacle to any preferences the German government might have had in this matter. The second illusion was that Jews worldwide could be persuaded to identify with the German cause. The educated classes among East European Jews were no doubt admirers of German culture, but there is no evidence that a significant number among them translated this into political sympathy. Equally, political preferences among American Jews, whether of German or of East European origin, were at best divided. The American financial community, whether Jewish or Gentile, was more Anglophile than pro-German, if the direction in which loans raised in the American market went is anything to go by. Nor could it be assumed that Jewish settlers in Palestine, even if they owed their good fortune to German influence, would Germanize the *yishuv* (the Jewish settlement in the land of Israel). After a major dispute in 1913, the language of instruction ultimately chosen for the new Haifa Technion was Hebrew, not German, in spite of the wishes of the founding German-Jewish philanthropists.

The final illusion shared by the advocates of a German-Jewish harmony of interests was that the Central Powers would win the war or would at least be able to influence the terms of the peace. The end of the czrist regime in Russia in March 1917, though attributable to German military prowess, was a mixed blessing politically. Fear and hatred of czarist tyranny had been a cement for German and German-Austrian public opinion well beyond its Jewish component and had been at least a factor in neutral America. The establishment of a liberal provisional government in Petrograd further undermined the crumbling civic truce. American entry into the war a month later was an additional blow to

German, and especially Liberal German, calculations. With America now allied with the enemies of Germany and Turkey, the time was opportune for the Western powers to announce their qualified support for Zionist aims in Palestine, expressed in the British government's Balfour Declaration of November 2, 1917. True, German Zionists used the occasion to press the German government even harder to compete with an offer of its own; true, at the turn of the year they received vague words of encouragement from the Turkish grand vizier and vague words of support from the German Foreign Office. But the main card that German Zionists could play, namely, the offer to mobilize the support of the world's Jews to the German cause, had been rendered worthless. The race to become the diplomatic patron of Zionism had been won by the other side.

3. The Crumbling of the Civic Truce

The civic truce was a fair-weather construction. If the war had brought a quick German victory, by Christmas 1914 or the spring of 1915, before the British Empire, let alone the United States, could bring its weight to bear to rescue France and Russia, the patriotic euphoria of August 1914 might have had a lasting effect. The fortunes of war dictated otherwise. As the war dragged on and as a successful conclusion of it seemed more and more remote, the prewar fault lines of German and Austrian politics reappeared, this time fatally so.

The hard core of the radical right saw, correctly from its point of view, that the terms of the civic truce ran counter to its own agenda. As before the war, this went well beyond antisemitism and comprised the abolition of universal suffrage, restrictions on Social Democracy, a military dictatorship, and an expansionist foreign policy. If the emperor and the chancellor really meant what they said, then the government was moving in the opposite direction. The civic truce meant conciliation toward the "internationalist" (and therefore unpatriotic) Social Democrats, toward the "ultramontane" (and therefore unpatriotic) Center Party, and toward the "cosmopolitan" (and therefore unpatriotic) Jews. It implied cautious steps toward greater powers for the Reichstag and a reform of the plutocratic electoral system in Prussia, though promises along these lines did not come until 1917 and related to the postwar period. While Chancellor Bethmann-Hollweg was no enemy of territorial expansion, he drew the line at the military's demands for unrestricted submarine warfare and would have preferred a peace by negotiation to waiting for an increasingly elusive final victory. For all these reasons they saw him as no more than the ally of "the Golden and Red International"[18] who would lead "the essence of our people into the Jewish-democratic abyss."[19] The government therefore had every incentive, quite apart from any desire to appease Jewish opinion, to inhibit the activities of the radical right. Their newspapers regularly fell foul of the censorship and their orators were barred from morale-raising visits to the troops. Nor was such self-restraint restricted to official circles. A small but significant change was that the mildly antisemitic caricatures of Germany's leading satirical weekly, *Simplicissimus*, ceased abruptly.

If the war had gone according to the government's plans, the radical right would have stayed on the fringes of politics. The more critical the war situation became, the more these men, and their opinions, moved into the center stage. Three episodes in particular illustrated the decline and end of the civic truce: the Jewish military census of 1916, the constitutional crisis of 1917, embracing the departure of Bethmann-Hollweg and the Reichstag's Peace Resolution, and the closing of the eastern frontier to Jewish immigrants in 1918. The first and third primarily concerned relations between the Jewish community and the government, while the 1917 crisis had a greater impact on the German political structure generally. But all three symbolized the polarization between the reformist and the antireformist forces in Germany, a polarization already evident before 1914 but now present in an enhanced form.

The Jewish military census of 1916 was the most explicit sign of the way the "spirit of 1914" had evaporated and of the extent to which the ideas of the radical right had penetrated the military command. From the very beginning of the war *völkisch* antisemites had been on the lookout for any advantages Jews might gain from the new atmosphere. As early as August 1914 the Reichshammerbund began collecting "war reports" about the military and civilian activities of Jews. In contrast with the prewar years, Jews gained commissions in the armed forces as well as high appointments in government service. Antisemites feared that once these openings were accepted, it would be impossible to reverse them when the war was over. They therefore needed to discredit the entire wartime role of Jews. As long as the patriotic consensus was dominant, Jews fared relatively well in the army: many reported on the friendly and comradely treatment they experienced, though this sometimes took peculiar forms: "Now you see, this has made up for the stigma of your ancestry," the wounded volunteer Ernst Toller (1893–1939) was told on receiving his Iron Cross.[20]

Two years into the war the mounting casualties, the shortages of food and fuel, and the receding prospect of decisive victory led to a sharp deterioration of group relations. The most open sign came from the Center Party deputy Matthias Erzberger, a politician not normally in the vanguard of antisemitic agitation but sensitive to the changing public mood. In October 1916 he demanded in the Reichstag finance committee a survey of those employed in the wartime corporations by age, sex, salary, and religion. The government declined, committed as it was to what was left of the civic truce, but Erzberger achieved his public relations success and the message he sent out was not lost on Jews in the public service. Melchior resigned from the Central Purchasing Agency; the ultrasensitive Rathenau had already left the Raw Materials Procurement Agency the previous year. Earlier than most prominent Jews he foresaw the effects of the war: "Hatred will double and triple."[21]

While the government was able to resist discriminatory pressures in the departments it directly controlled, it failed to do so in the army, which was by now largely a law unto itself. A few days before Erzberger's intervention, the Prussian War Ministry ordered an inquiry on the positions held by Jews in the army. The official justification for this initiative lay in the increasing number of complaints that Jews were evading active service and the need "to examine these and if necessary refute them."[22] Few believed this explanation. The High Command had been discussing some form of Jewish census for several months and the pressures became greater as the older and more traditionally minded generals retired and the pan-Germans around Quartermaster-General Erich Ludendorff became more influential. Whatever the true motivation, the effect on the Jewish population was disastrous. No single wartime act of the regime did more to alienate them or remind them of their status as stepchildren. "I feel as if I had received a terrible box on the ears," Georg Meyer reflected two months before he was killed in action.[23] His comrade-in-arms Julius Marx was surprised "that troops did not refuse to obey orders issued by an " 'object of the census.' "[24] Many government officials were well aware of the offense caused. The police president of Frankfurt am Main, a man possibly in closer contact with members of the Jewish elite than most other German bureaucrats, reported that the local Jews were "now alienated and adopting a very reserved attitude toward my efforts on behalf of the war collection."[25] But such warnings counted for nothing against the decisions of the military.

Representative Liberal Jewish figures were also in a dilemma. They were one and all indignant, but divided on how to express their indignation. On the one hand, they were put under pressure to defend Jewish honor, especially by serving soldiers and their families. They had also to fear increasingly militant defense rhetoric from Zionists. On the other hand, they saw the government of Bethmann Hollweg, for all its weaknesses and defects, as a barrier against völkisch and militarist forces and felt compelled not to embarrass him. They also calculated that this was not the moment to depart from the unconditional patriotism to which they had committed themselves. In their private communications to ministers they were more outspoken, but even then more in sorrow than in anger. In public Eugen Fuchs, the chairman of the cv, claimed, as late as 1917, that "the government has become more and more open-minded" and his colleague Felix Goldmann reaffirmed the cv's "innermost link with Germandom, its hope for the victory of justice."[26] Beyond causing bad blood, the army census achieved nothing. Its results were never published and the records perished during the Second World War.

The constitutional crisis of 1917 involved Jews only indirectly but the effect on Jewish-Gentile relations was profound. The fall of czarism, the entry of America into the war, the stalemate on the Western front, and the growing material privations at home intensified the political polarization. Bethmann Hollweg became convinced that morale could be maintained only by concrete promises of political reform, especially of the plutocratic franchise for the Prussian parliament, and these the chancellor undertook in the spring and early summer of 1917. Such measures were, however, too much for the military leadership of Hindenburg and Ludendorff, who threatened to resign if Bethmann Hollweg stayed. The result was that William surrendered to his generals' blackmail and obliged his chancellor to resign on July 13. Six days later the Reichstag passed a resolution in favor of "a peace based on compromise." The majority supporting this "Peace Resolution" consisted of the winners of the 1912 Reichstag election—the Social Democrats and the Left Liberals—and the Center, spurred on by the leader of its left wing, Erzberger. The old pre-1914 antagonisms were thus fully restored: with the departure of Bethmann Hollweg and the passing of the Peace Resolution the civic truce was finally buried.

In this repolarization Jews were part actors, part victims. Jewish participation in the bellicose consensus of the summer of 1914 did not last long. After the academic declarations of 1914 came the petition of July 1915, organized by the Protestant theologian Reinhold Seeberg, which

49 Emperor William II presents a medal to Sergeant Karl Neuhof from
Friedberg (1915)

demanded widespread annexations. It got no Jewish support. A much
smaller counterpetition, initiated by the economist Lujo Brentano and the
historian Hans Delbrück, also attracted leading Protestants and Catholics,
but what distinguished it from Seeberg's petition was the addition of
Jewish names. Indeed the codrafter of the counterpetition was the editor
of the *Berliner Tageblatt*, Theodor Wolff (1868–1943), who thereby
became the chief coordinator of the intellectual opposition to expansionist war aims and of the intellectual advocacy of domestic reforms. His
newspaper, the circulation of which swelled considerably in the course of
the war, opposed annexations and unrestricted submarine warfare,

warned against antagonizing America, and above all consistently exposed the increasingly dictatorial character of the imperial regime. This editorial line earned it several suspensions by the wartime censors. Wolff and the *Berliner Tageblatt* thus symbolized the "Jewish-democratic cosmopolitanism" on which the pan-German right ultimately blamed Germany's defeat.

The other newspapers normally stigmatized as "Jew-liberal" played a rather smaller role in influencing antiwar opinion. The *Frankfurter Zeitung*, which enjoyed only one-third the circulation of the *Berliner Tageblatt*, was slower to recover from its initially patriotic line and its support of the submarine offensive but was equally enthusiastic in favoring the Peace Resolution and democratization. It was more emphatic than the *Berliner Tageblatt* in 1918 in urging peace and demanding the abdication of the emperor. Thus in the last year of the war it became, if anything, more hated than its Berlin sibling. It was able to sue Houston Stewart Chamberlain successfully for having asserted that it stood "in the service of Anglo-American finance capital."[27] In contrast to the *Berliner Tageblatt* and the *Frankfurter Zeitung*, the *Vossische Zeitung*, edited by Georg Bernhard (1875–1944), remained pro-expansionist well into 1917. Unlike the greater part of German Liberal opinion it was consistently anti-British and anti-American and hoped for a separate peace, first with Russia and then with France, in pursuit of these aims. Equally significant for the swing of opinion among the Jewish journalistic intelligentsia from ultrapatriotism to near pacifism was Harden's *Die Zukunft*. Its circulation was much smaller than that of the Liberal newspapers but thanks to Harden's contacts with Bethmann Hollweg, ex-Chancellor Bülow, and Albert Ballin it was able to reflect the policy debate within the government better than the "outsiders" of the daily press.

The Liberal press was the principal disseminator of these heretical ideas, but it was not the only one. From 1916 onward an increasing number of informal groups met to discuss policy options and to advocate a postwar order based on international conciliation. The main pacifist salon was that of the department store owner Oskar Tietz (1858–1923), the main coordinator of these various activities the banker Eugen Landau (1852–1935), who had the distinction of being the first Prussian staff officer of the Jewish faith. Other Jewish entrepreneurs, including Carl Fürstenberg and Paul von Schwabach, were involved in these initiatives, as were many Gentiles. In any case, there was no unanimity among Jews on war aims, but there was, as there had been in prewar politics, a recognizable tendency. Jews were overwhelmingly patriotic; they did not want Germany to lose the war. They merely appreciated earlier than the majority of Germany's policy makers and opinion leaders that the pursuit of unlimited expansionism was bound to be counterproductive. Yet even Rathenau and Warburg, who had urged moderation at many stages during the war, opposed an armistice in October 1918, when defeatism had gripped even the most militaristic minds. Nor were leading Jewish entrepreneurs opposed in principle to extending German economic dominance in the wake of conquest. In a world of competing imperialisms it seemed legitimate to them to seize any advantage that presented itself. But thanks to their international links and their more cosmopolitan open-mindedness they had a better notion of the costs attached to the benefits. What distinguished them from a substantial number of their Gentile compatriots was a civilian rather than a military perspective on politics, a distrust of pan-German rhetoric and a preference for not antagonizing too many adversaries at once. Their imperialism was one of commerce, not conquest. They had no objections to the profits of war, but no desire to go to war or to continue the war for the sake of profits. The issue that most clearly divided the rational from the irrational patriots was that of unrestricted submarine warfare, which was designed, in Grand Admiral Tirpitz's words, "to force England to its knees" but also risked bringing America into the war. With the exception of Albert Ballin, who initially supported the submarine campaign, virtually all Jews prominent in commerce and industry joined the many Gentile Liberals who saw its folly. The attitude of Jews toward the submarine campaign, the role of Theodor Wolff as the orchestrator of proposals for a compromise peace, and the key role of the Social Democratic and Left Liberal parties in passing the Peace Resolution all reinforced the determination of the radical right to stigmatize as a "Jew peace" any peace proposal short of outright victory.

The military stalemate did not merely affect the shift of Liberal opinion on war aims from affirmation to doubt. It equally affected Social Democracy, and this, too, had a Jewish dimension. Most Social Democrats, like most Jews, had welcomed the civic truce and were prepared to abide by it loyally. Only 14 of the 110-member SPD delegation in the Reichstag opposed a vote in favor of war credits in August 1914; of the 12 Jewish SPD deputies only 2, Joseph Herzfeld and the party's cochairman, Hugo Haase, were in the opposing minority. Many of those who later became leading advocates of a compromise peace, like Eduard Bernstein and Kurt Eisner, were at this stage convinced that Germany was fighting a just war of defense against czarism. Ludwig Frank, an ardent prewar advocate of Franco-German reconciliation, even volunteered for military service at the age of 40 and was killed in action in September 1914. In the course of 1915 the mood changed. In June of that year Bernstein of the party's right wing joined Haase of the left and Karl Kautsky of the orthodox center in publishing a call for a peace of reconciliation. This article, "Das Gebot der Stunde" (The Demands of the Hour), largely drafted by Bernstein, marked the beginning of a realignment in the party. In December 1915 42 SPD deputies either abstained or voted against further war credits in a Reichstag vote, including 7 of the remaining 11 Jews. The final rupture came in the spring of 1917 when the antiwar dissidents formed themselves into a separate Independent Social Democratic Party (USPD), which 6 of the Jewish SPD deputies joined. Outside the Reichstag, and only barely within the USPD left, were the revolutionaries who had been outright opponents of the war from the first: Karl Liebknecht (1871–1919; not a Jew, though frequently categorized as such by his enemies), Rosa Luxemburg, and a young lawyer, Paul Levi (1883–1930), who had been defense counsel at Luxemburg's trial in 1914. Luxemburg's *Spartacus Letters* were the rallying point for this group. Though hampered organizationally by imprisonment and by Levi's exile in Switzerland, they formed the Spartakusbund, the forerunner of the German Communist Party, as the war drew to a close. In Austria, where parliamentary life was suspended for most of the war, Social Democratic activity, whether in support of or in opposition to the war effort, was marginalized. The most spectacular act of dissent by a member of the party's left was the assassination of the prime minister, Count Stürgkh, by Victor Adler's son Friedrich in 1916.

One notable development among Jews in the Socialist movements of both empires was a growing recognition of Jewish identity, something that had been taboo before 1914. In part this was due to greater contact with the Jews of the East, in part also to the way the war challenged all existing allegiances. Eduard Bernstein wrote of the Jews' mission "to act as mediators between the nations,"[28] a view that was coming to be shared by a number of Jews outside the Socialist movements, such as the writers Arnold Zweig (1887–1968) and Georg Hermann (1871–1943). The shift of opinion among Jews within the Social Democratic parties was by no means complete. Leading members of the SPD executive like Otto Landsberg and Georg Gradnauer continued to be loyal to majority party policy; the Berlin *Vorwärts*, edited by Friedrich Stampfer (1874–1957), and the Viennese *Arbeiter-Zeitung*, edited by Friedrich Austerlitz (1862–1931), maintained the same attitude. Joseph Bloch's *Sozialistische Monatshefte* predictably remained true to its prewar pro-imperialist line and Bloch's collaborator Max Cohen-Reuss even supported the submarine campaign.

This variety of views among Jews did little to neutralize the stereotype of the Jew as defeatist, a stereotype that was accepted even by some Social Democrats of the right. But while antisemitism within the Socialist movement was a sign of the nervous tensions of the times, on the right it was an indispensable component of the militarist-annexationist ideology. A number of völkisch periodicals that gained the peak of their influence after 1918 were founded during these crisis years. The dormant League Against Jewish Arrogance (Verband gegen die Überhebung des Judentums) sprang to life with the journal *Auf Vorposten*, which in 1919 was responsible for the first German publication of the Protocols of the Elders of Zion, the Munich publisher J. F. Lehmann launched *Deutschlands Erneuerung*, and the pan-German League took control of the right-wing *Deutsche Zeitung* in 1917. In the context of the Peace Resolution debate this newspaper now contrasted "pan-German" with "pan-Jewish."[29] The main organized response to the challenge of the Peace Resolution came in the form of a new mass-membership political party of the nationalist right, the Deutsche Vaterlandspartei, founded in September 1917. While the party's statutes made no mention of antisemitism, the leadership tolerated its private expression by individual members. In response to a complaint by the cv, the Vaterlandspartei's chairman, Grand Admiral von Tirpitz, replied that "if nevertheless some members of the Vaterlandspartei express antisemitic views, they may do so only in a private capacity."[30]

4. The Control of Immigration

Up to 1917 the German government had aimed at diminishing discrimination against Jews and discouraging and even repressing antisemitic propaganda. Since there were various states within the state, of which the most important was the army, and since for most of the time the government had higher priorities, some of which were in potential conflict with the repression of antisemitism, this policy was not always pursued with great energy or success. Nevertheless for the first three years of the war it represented the government's true intentions. As Ludendorff's star rose and the departure of Bethmann Hollweg symbolized the end of any effective civilian control over the government, that policy, too, came to an end. The final act of policy reversal, of which the army census had been the curtain-raiser, was the ban on Jewish immigration from the East.

This ban had complex antecedents. There was nothing new about Jewish migration from East to West. It had gone on continuously for the better part of a century, accelerated by the pogroms in Russia, the growing impoverishment of Galician Jewry, and the attractions of a prosperous Western Europe. As a consequence, the agitation for a ban of Jewish immigration had become a common theme for antisemites in both Germany and Austria well before 1914. Since most of the "Eastern Jewish" migrants in Austria came from Galicia and therefore from inside the empire, intensified frontier control would have achieved little. In Germany, too, twice as many immigrants came from Galicia as from the Russian Empire and there were diplomatic considerations that weighed against the formal exclusion of Austrian citizens. The German authorities therefore relied on administrative measures to limit numbers: frontier controls, the withholding of residence permits or of naturalization, and expulsion.

The war, by pushing the area of Austro-German control further east, but also by devastating the areas of some of the densest Jewish population in Europe, gave this migration a further impetus. It also led to the breakdown of the prewar control mechanisms, so that from 1914 to 1918 the number of "Eastern Jews" in Germany nearly doubled. To the 90,000 foreign Jews already in Germany at the outbreak of the war there came 35,000 war workers, many of them forcibly recruited, and another 35,000 prisoners of war and civilian internees. In Austria the situation was much more acute; the number of war refugees, mostly Jewish, from the eastern provinces of the monarchy was estimated at 350,000 in 1915, and even in 1918 there were 100,000 destitute Jewish refugees in Vienna and Bohemia-Moravia. From the beginning of the war pan-Germans and antisemites demanded a rigid ban on Jewish immigration into Germany. But the needs of the war economy and the constraints of the civic truce led the government to reject these demands. The unfavorable public relations effect of an outright prohibition in neutral countries was a further consideration. As the war progressed the pressures for a ban intensified. In the main these merely reflected the changing ideological balance within the government and the growing influence of pan-German and völkisch lobbies. But the authorities also counted, wrongly as it turned out, on the complaisance of German-Jewish organizations.

The influx of Jews into Germany and Western Austria, as well as the contacts that Jewish soldiers and civilian administrators made with the Russian-Polish population, were a moral and cultural challenge to the assimilated communities of Central Europe. While some experienced a fraternal sympathy with coreligionists who had kept their beliefs and traditions intact, the majority were to a greater or lesser extent embarrassed by the squalor and backwardness that they found or that the immigrants brought with them. "No sensible person [can] maintain that they are our brothers," the Czech-Jewish journal *Rozvoj* wrote of the Galicians who had arrived in Prague.[31] Similar sentiments were common among German Jews, whether assimilationist or Zionist. The Eastern immigrant was blamed for undermining the integration of the existing Jewish population and for reintroducing "the air of the ghetto" into the enlightened German-Jewish culture.[32] The Zionist Max Bodenheimer argued that no one had "any interest in or benefit from a . . . mass emigration of Jews from the occupied territories."[33] It did not follow from this, however, that Jews could be won for an openly discriminatory policy of exclusion. When Kurt Alexander of the cv urged restrictions on immigration, he was careful to include all East European "elements on this cultural level without consideration of religious affiliation."[34]

When therefore the Prussian Ministry of the Interior unilaterally closed the frontier to Jewish migrants in April 1918, representative Jewish bodies were unanimous in their protests, though with different degrees of emphasis. The motivation for the closure was explicitly antisemitic. Polish-Jewish laborers, according to the decree, were "work-shy, unclean, morally unreliable . . . to a great extent infested with lice . . . especially apt carriers and spreaders of typhus and other infectious diseases."[35] Although the text of the decree was never made public and news of its existence emerged only with some delay, it soon became obvious that an important branch of the government had reverted to the preemancipation principle of "Jew laws."[36] While Zionists were the first and most insistent in their reaction, no Jewish organization, whatever its reservations about Eastern Jews, could accept a measure of explicit discrimination. Once the principle of discrimination was conceded, it could easily be extended to all Jews, which is certainly what some of the advocates of frontier closure intended. Moreover it was increasingly obvious that pejorative statements about Eastern Jews were merely coded attacks on all Jews.

50   The surgeon Professor James Israel with his assistants in a
hospital train

Accordingly, in July the Union of German-Jewish Organizations for
Protecting the Rights of the Jews of the East, which had been formed at
the beginning of the year, lodged a formal protest with the chancellor,
Count Hertling. However, in the dying days of the war the opinions and
sensitivities of even the most patriotic Jews were no longer of any importance. It took the government three and a half months to reply that the
measures taken "had to do with medical controls" only. It was significant
that the Foreign Ministry, which might have been concerned with the
effect of the decree on foreign opinion, was neither consulted nor
informed. Priorities had turned full circle since the government's assumption in 1914 that Jews, inside or outside Germany, represented an interest
to be treated with respect and conciliation. Having briefly been the participants in policy, Jews were now once more its objects.

5. Toward the Revolution

The war years had a sobering effect on the Jews of both Germany and
Austria. The doubts and disappointments they had experienced in the last
decades of the peace had been temporarily set aside by the "spirit of

1914." For many Jews this provided an occasion for reaffirming their Germanness or their Habsburg loyalism; but even a reinforcement of Jewish identity was consistent with enthusiasm for the German and Austrian causes: "So it came about that we went off to the war because we were Zionists, not in spite of being Jews."[37] Under these circumstances the temptation to discount survivals or revivals of prejudice and discrimination was great. The calls of patriotism and of a crusade against czarism made such concerns seem petty. Only the experience of the later war years exhausted this diffidence.

As in previous phases of antisemitism, the concerns of Jews inside and outside Germany were motivated at least as much by consideration for Germany's reputation as by self-interest. In October 1914 the German-born New York banker Jacob Schiff (1847–1920) pointed out to the German government that Jews born in America did not share their parents' pro-German sympathies "because this younger generation, conscious of its human dignity, cannot forget that Germany was the breeding ground of antisemitism." To counteract such views a new spirit was needed, "for which the government must as a matter of course take the initiative."[38] Two years later, after the army census decree, the Hamburg banker Max Warburg made a similar point to the undersecretary at the Reich Chancellery, Arnold von Wahnschaffe:

> We are often surprised that the Germans are so unpopular and wrongly condemned as brutal wielders of power: hardly any circumstance has favored this misunderstanding as much as antisemitism, which at any rate first acquired a long-term "scientific" rationalization in Germany.[39]

It was easier for eminent citizens like Schiff and Warburg to speak candidly in private than for Jewish functionaries to do so in public. Indeed, it was easier for Gentile opponents of antisemitism to do so. It was the Abwehr-Verein that noted in March 1916 how Jews "had become severely disappointed by the revival of the old, embittering conflict that poisons our whole political and social life."[40] By 1918 few Jews, whether Orthodox, Liberal, or Zionist, could conceal from themselves which way the wind was blowing. "The cup is almost full and will overflow," the cv declared. The time had come to abandon moderation and "to go over to the attack."[41] The journal *Ost und West*, which was close to the Zionists, concluded "that we have to be prepared for a Jewish war after the war."[42] That was indeed the case. Pan-Germans and antisemites did not need to

wait for the armistice, the abdication of the emperor, and the proclamation of the German Republic in November 1918 to know whom to blame
for the disaster. With the appointment of Prince Max of Baden as chancellor on October 5 a parliamentary regime had been established. The
Germany that the antisemites believed in and that they had hoped to preserve by means of the war had ceased to exist. The time had come to proclaim the "collective guilt" of the Jews. As we have seen, the ammunition
for this enterprise had been amassed since the first day of the war.

What applied to Germany applied in a more complex way to Austria.
As early as December 1916, a month after the death of Emperor Francis
Joseph, the Liberal Reichsrat deputy Stefan von Licht (1860–1932)
warned the president of the Jewish Community Council of Vienna: "In
Christian Social, German Nationalist, and other nationalist circles a
movement is being prepared, which is to break forth once 'normal circumstances' have returned." Even liberal-minded politicians were being
urged not "to attach themselves to any 'Jewish protective guard.' "[43]
Evidence for Licht's warning was not lacking. In the last two years of the
war the Christian Social and pan-German press shed the inhibitions that
the civic truce had imposed and the government lost the will to enforce
the censorship.

The military defeat of Germany and Austria-Hungary led to popular
uprisings. In Germany the contest was between the advocates of a parliamentary democracy (Left Liberals and Social Democrats) or government
by revolutionary councils and violent overthrow of the existing order
(Spartacus League), with the armed gangs of the radical right on the sidelines. In Austria the German pattern was repeated in Vienna, except that
the Social Democratic Party had managed to preserve its unity. In
Hungary, the Czech lands, and the South Slav lands new sovereign nation-
states were proclaimed. In Germany, Austria, and Hungary an unprecedented number of Jews emerged as political leaders, whether among
Liberals, Social Democrats, or Communists. To the antisemites this was a
gift, though one they did not really need: they had already decided to
blame the Jews for the disastrous outcome of the war before the names of
the revolutionary leaders became known. The Pan-German League had
established its "Committee on the Jews" as early as September 1918.
Though the Jews of Germany viewed the new developments with sentiments that ranged from enthusiasm to mistrust, the majority soon concluded that there was little point in mourning a monarchy that had failed
them in essential respects. Martin Buber's periodical *Der Jude* probably

spoke for the majority in anticipating that the new order would bring "full and comprehensive legal equality."[44] In Austria the collapse of the protecting Habsburg umbrella affected the Jews rather differently. Those who had sheltered under it could only regard the triumph of the competing nationalisms with dismay. "Who will shield us now?" an elderly Jew cried out as he saw the Habsburg emblems being removed from the buildings of Prague.[45] And so in the winter of 1918–1919 the Jews of the defeated empires trod the path from the old to the new, not knowing whether to fear or to hope. The ambiguities of democracy were about to be tested.

Conclusion

It is generally assumed that the Jews in Imperial Germany experienced the most secure, the most successful, and the most prosperous period in German-Jewish history. By 1871 they had already made impressive gains in their social status. Their education and possessions now made them preponderantly members of the urban middle class; their scientific and artistic accomplishments reached a remarkably high level. However, these successes should not cause us to overlook the negative aspects of being Jewish in this era. The emergence of modern antisemitism in the last two decades of the nineteenth century cast a perpetual shadow on the daily existence of Jews at school, at work, and in society. It turned out that equal legal rights, guaranteed by the Imperial Constitution of 1871, offered no protection against social and occupational discrimination and that education and wealth were no guarantee of admission to the middle class. Antisemitism posed the question of Jewish identity in a new way and for many Jews who had become indifferent to their religion brought on a crisis in self-perception. Maintaining a dual existence as both German and Jew proved to be a balancing act that had to be performed day after day and to appear as if it were being done with ease.

The history of the Jews in the *Kaiserreich* reveals more continuities than ruptures. Jews continued to modernize much more rapidly during their rise to middle-class status than did the population at large. Jewish life expectancy continued to increase, while the number of children per family dropped to about half the German average. Only the immigration of East European Jews prevented a decline in the Jewish population. Urbanization increased sharply, raising the Jews' visibility. By the end of the period more than half of all Jews in the German Empire lived in large cities, a quarter of them in Berlin alone. In the Habsburg monarchy Jews immigrated in large numbers to Vienna, relocating there from Bohemia, Moravia, Hungary, and, above all, Galicia.

Continuities are even more apparent in occupational and economic developments. Contrary to the expectations of reformers at the beginning of the nineteenth century, more than half the Jews remained active in commerce, even after they obtained legal equality. Contributing factors to this persistence were a traditional preference for certain occupations and the need for independence as a way to protect against discrimination. However, more than anything else, industrialization, by increasing consumer goods, caused an extraordinary expansion in the commercial sector, of which Jews were able to take advantage. The share of Jews in industry also grew, while the trades and agriculture, caught as they were in a recession, were not at all attractive. Since, for the most part, Jews remained de facto excluded from civil service positions, an increasing number of Jewish university graduates went into self-employed professions. The strong representation of Jews among lawyers and doctors in the large cities, as well as among the journalists of the liberal press, became especially apparent in Berlin and Vienna.

Shifts and changes took place in the Jewish class structure. The immigration of East European Jews seeking to escape the pogroms in czarist Russia produced a Jewish lower class that grew when East European Jewish workers were recruited and conscripted during World War I. By the beginning of the Weimar Republic approximately one in every five Jews living in Germany had immigrated from outside the country and did not hold German citizenship. In Berlin, primarily, and in a few other big cities, a Jewish lower class came into being that worked in factories or even in mines or peddled their wares. A portion of the immigrants came to Germany from Galicia, although these, for the most part, extremely poor Jews more frequently migrated to Vienna. Class tensions were considerably more pronounced among Jews in Austria than they were in Germany.

Jewish organizations everywhere responded to the plight of the refugees by providing assistance. In so doing, they also attempted to lessen the negative reaction that these culturally "more Jewish" immigrants provoked in the antisemitic milieu. The German Jews often felt estranged from their coreligionists, who were not acculturated and to whom they felt superior. These sociocultural differences, much sharper than they had been earlier, led to tensions within the Jewish population.

This trend did not alter the fact that the German Jews now belonged predominantly to the middle class and had adopted its values, mediated especially by the women as educators of the young children. Nevertheless, the Jewish middle class remained separate from its non-Jewish counterpart. Although acculturation had led to the adoption of German culture, Jewish traditions were by no means given up entirely. Even families that were not religious often preserved some form of Jewish identity and expected their children to marry Jewish partners. In political orientation the Jewish middle class was mainly left-wing liberal. It did not share the militarized masculine ideal that was common in Wilhelminian society, it provided its children with a considerably above average schooling, and it supported the education of girls, some of whom then became active in the women's movement. Social intercourse remained limited to the extended family and to Jewish friends, mainly because antisemitism was increasingly becoming part of the German nationalistic self-perception, especially in the educated middle class. The more that class assumed an antiliberal and chauvinistic stance, the less was it prepared to accept Jews who sought to preserve elements of their own culture.

In the religious realm secularization increased significantly. By the end of World War I the majority was either indifferent to religion or had become "three-day-a-year Jews" who exercised their Judaism only during the High Holidays. Conflicts between Liberal and Orthodox Jews had lessened considerably once both branches became firmly established. Among the minority of Jews who regarded themselves as Orthodox the traditional way of life continued to hold sway mainly among rural Jews and East European Jewish immigrants, who maintained their own prayer houses. Thus, although the religious spectrum had broadened, religion had lost its primary significance for most Jews. Yet for a small number, especially among the young, the latter portion of the period was marked by a reversal of this trend, manifesting itself in a renewal of religious thought in the writings of Hermann Cohen, Leo Baeck, and Martin Buber.

Given the general decline of interest in the Jewish religion, a variety of new secular forms of Jewish identity emerged in the struggle against antisemitism. Zionism, which had a small but resolute following primarily among young people at the beginning of the century, triggered the most intense conflicts within Jewry. Propagation of Jewish nationhood and plans for a Jewish state aroused fear in many Jews that these might endanger their hard-won emancipation. The vast majority of German Jews attempted to continue along the path of integration. In 1893, for the purpose of combating antisemitism, they organized the Centralverein deutscher Staatsbürger jüdischen Glaubens (Central Association of German Citizens of the Jewish Faith), which became the largest Jewish organization in Germany. It claimed an identity for Jews as "Germans of Jewish heritage" and employed political and legal means to protect their equality. Standing up for Jewish rights, playing a role in various newly established social and cultural Jewish organizations, and performing Jewish social work—these enabled many secularized Jews to perceive themselves as Jewish despite their lack of religiosity. Although no fully representative structure came into existence, the network of Jewish organizations, old and new, reached into even the smallest localities, connecting their members to the Jewish community.

The prominence of Jews in the cultural and political life of the German Empire and the Habsburg monarchy was definitely a new phenomenon, occurring primarily in Berlin, Vienna, and Prague. However, as antisemitism supplanted liberalism in the educated middle class Jews were forced into an opposition role in politics and culture, a precarious position for a minority. Since the larger society was not prepared to accept Jews as shapers of German culture, their notable scientific and artistic achievements, ironically, led to claims that the Jews were corrupters of that culture.

In 1914 almost all Jews greeted the First World War and the so-called civic truce with patriotic enthusiasm. They supported the struggle against a czarist Russia that they detested because of its persecution of Jews. From the war they hoped to gain nothing less than the final realization of their long-sought social integration. About twelve thousand German Jews died in combat during the war. But as the wartime economic crisis worsened Jews increasingly came under attack by the antisemitic right for being goldbrickers and profiteers. These accusations prompted the Prussian minister of war to order a Jewish military census, with the result that the German Jews once again saw themselves singled out as objects of discrimination. As the period of the Kaiserreich came to an end, it was apparent that full social integration without the loss of Jewish identity had remained an unfulfilled hope.

Abbreviations

AZJ	*Allgemeine Zeitung des Judentums*
BA	Bundesarchiv
BLBI	*Bulletin des Leo Baeck Instituts*
BrLA	Brandenburgisches Landesarchiv
CAHJP	Central Archives for the History of the Jewish People
CEH	*Central European History*
CV	Centralverein deutscher Staatsbürger jüdischen Glaubens
DIGB	Deutsch-Israelitischer Gemeindebund
GStD	Geheimes Staatsarchiv Preussischer Kulturbesitz Dahlem
GStM	Geheimes Staatsarchiv Preussischer Kulturbesitz Merseburg
HPB	*Historisch-Politische Blätter für das Katholische Deutschland*
HUCA	*Hebrew Union College Annual*
IdR	*Im deutschen Reich*
JIDG	*Jahrbuch des Instituts für Deutsche Geschichte*
JR	*Jüdische Rundschau*
Kfdo	Komitee für den Osten
KZ	*Kreuz-Zeitung*
LBIYB	*Leo Baeck Institute Year Book*
MGWJ	*Monatsschrift für Geschichte und Wissenschaft des Judentums*
MM	*Militärgeschichtliche Mitteilungen*
MÖIU	*Mitteilungen der Österreichisch-Israelitischen Union*
Mosse	Werner E. Mosse, ed., with the assistance of Arnold Paucker, *Juden im Wilhelminischen Deutschland 1890–1914* (Tübingen, 1976)
Mosse/ Paucker	Werner E. Mosse, ed., with the assistance of Arnold Paucker, *Deutsches Judentum in Krieg und Revolution 1916–1923* (Tübingen, 1971)

MVA	*Mitteilungen des Vereins zur Abwehr des Antisemitismus*
NJM	*Neue Jüdische Monatshefte*
ODR	*Ostdeutsche Rundschau*
ÖstH	Österreichisches Haus-, Hof- und Staatsarchiv
ÖV	*Österreichischer Volksfreund*
PJ	*Preussische Jahrbücher*
Richarz	Monika Richarz, ed., *Jüdisches Leben in Deutschland. Selbstzeunisse zur Sozialgeschichte im Kaiserreich* (Stuttgart 1979)
SPD	Sozialdemokratische Partei Deutschlands
StBR	*Stenographische Berichte über die Verhandlungen des deutschen Reichstages*
StBPrA	*Stenographische Berichte des Preussischen Abgeordnetenhauses*
UDW	*Unverfälscht Deutsche Worte*
VdJ	Verband der deutschen Juden
ZDSJ	*Zeitschrift für Demographie und Statistik der Juden*
ZVfD	Zionistische Vereinigung für Deutschland

Notes

1. Demographic Developments

1. Felix Theilhaber, *Der Untergang der deutschen Juden* (Berlin, 1911), 151, 153.
2. Richarz, 139.
3. Ibid., 395–96.

3. Jewish Women in the Family and Public Sphere

1. Hedwig Wachenheim, *Vom Grossbürgertum zur Sozialdemokratie. Memoiren einer Reformistin* (Berlin, 1973), 20.
2. Julie Kaden, "Der erste Akt meines Lebens," in Richarz, 333–34.
3. Johanna Harris-Brandes, "Fröhliche Kindheit im Dorf," ibid., 159.
4. Fabius Schach, "Die Frau im Judentum," *Hamburger Israelitisches Familienblatt*, December 29, 1911, 9.
5. Manfred Sturmann, "Grossvaters Haus," in Richarz, 209.
6. Philippine Landau, "Kindheitserinnerungen," ibid., 343.
7. Paul Mühsam, "Ich bin ein Mensch gewesen," ibid, 360.
8. Julius Posener, *Fast so alt wie das Jahrhundert* (Berlin, 1990), 64.
9. Rahel Straus, *Wir lebten in Deutschland. Erinnerungen einer deutschen Jüdin* (Stuttgart, 1961), 104.
10. Rahel Goitein, "Abiturrede" (delivered in Karlsruhe in 1899), Stadtarchiv, Karlsruhe, Ak8-STS 13–344. My thanks to Dr. Susanne Asche for bringing this address to my attention.
11. Rahel Straus, *Wir lebten in Deutschland*, 141.
12. Jacob Segall, "Die wirtschaftliche und soziale Lage der Juden in Deutschland," zDsj 7(July/August 1911):102.
13. Isidor Hirschfeld, "Tagebuch," in Richarz, 244.

14. Gershom Scholem, *Von Berlin nach Jerusalem: Jugenderinnerungen* (Frankfurt am Main, 1977), 28.

15. Ibid., 29.

16. Henriette Fürth, "Ein offener Brief," IDR 17(1911):405.

4. Religious Life

1. Willi Wertheimer, "Erinnerungen," in Richarz, 183–84.

2. Philippine Landau, "Kindheitserinnerungen," ibid., 343.

3. Conrad Rosenstein, "Der Brunnen. Eine Familienchronik," ibid., 66–67.

4. Abraham Berliner, *Das Gebetbuch des Dr. Vogelstein beurtheilt* (Berlin, 1894), 1.

5. "Zur Einführung," *Liberales Judentum* 1(1908):1.

6. "Richtlinien zu einem Programm für das liberale Judentum," *Liberales Judentum* 4(1912):214–15.

5. The Community

1. Fritz Mauthner, *Erinnerungen. Prager Jugendjahre*, quoted in Wilma Abeles Iggers, *The Jews of Bohemia and Moravia: A Historical Reader* (Detroit, 1992), 209; Julie Kaden, "Der erste Akt meines Lebens," in Richarz, 335.

2. This statement appeared beneath the title of every issue of the monthly *K.C.-Blätter* during World War I.

3. Georg Todtmann, "Was wir wollen," *Blau-Weiss Blätter. Eine Flugschrift* (c. 1916), 2–3.

6. Legal Equality and Public Life

1. Quoted by Jacob Toury, *Die politischen Orientierungen der Juden in Deutschland. Von Jena bis Weimar* (Tübingen, 1966), 139.

2. Law Concerning the Equality of Religions in Civil and Civic Matters of July 3, 1869; Ismar Freund, *Die Emanzipation der Juden in Preussen unter besonderer Berücksichtigung des Gesetzes vom 11. März 1812. Ein Beitrag zur Rechtsgeschichte der Juden in Preussen* (Berlin, 1912), 2:22.

3. StBPrA, January 30, 1901, 930.

4. "Das Judenthum und die gelehrten Berufsarten," KZ, April 22, 1885, p. 1.

5. GStD, Rep. 84a, 2941:187–89.

6. Kuno Graf von Westarp, *Konservative Politik im letzten Jahrzehnt des Kaiserreiches* (Berlin, 1935), 1:298–99.

7. Heinrich Jaques, *Denkschrift über die Stellung der Juden in Österreich* (Vienna, 1859), xcvi.

8. Franz Oppenheimer, *Erlebtes, Erstrebtes, Erreichtes. Erinnerungen*, 2d ed. (Düsseldorf, 1964), 216.

9. AZJ, September 18, 1866, p. 595.

10. Ludwig Bamberger, *Eduard Lasker. Gedenkrede gehalten am 28. January 1884* (Leipzig, 1884), 9, 14.

11. *Der Israelit*, 1870, p. 597; 1881, p. 826.

12. "Verleihung des Titels 'Commerzienrath' und 'Geheimer Commerzienrath,' " GStD, Rep. 90, 2002; "Verleihung von Commerzienrath-Titeln," GStM, Rep. 120A, 4:5, 11:59–61.

13. "Die 'Judenfrage' und die Konservativen," AZJ, December 11, 1908, pp. 593–94.

14. *Der Orient*, February 6, 1844, p. 200.

15. *Der Orient*, July 2, 1847, p. 213.

16. Margarete Jodl, *Friedrich Jodl. Sein Leben und Werk* (Stuttgart, 1920), 117–18.

17. Fritz Mauthner, *Erinnerungen. Prager Jugendjahre* (Frankfurt am Main, 1969), 520.

18. Hillel Kieval, *The Making of Czech Jewry: National Conflict and Jewish Society in Bohemia, 1870–1918* (New York, 1988), 56; Gary B. Cohen, "Jews in German Society: Prague, 1860–1914," CEH 10/1(1977):38. ÖStH, 11:56–57, 64–65; 26:70–71.

19. *Statistisches Jahrbuch der Haupt- und Residenzstadt Budapest* 10:23; "Die Budapester Juden nach ihrer Nationalität," ZDSJ 5/9(September 1909):143; Wolfdieter Bihl, "Die Juden," in A. Wandruszka and P. Urbanitsch, eds., *Die Habsburgermonarchie 1848–1918* (Vienna, 1980), 3/2:907.

20. "Zur Situation in Deutschland," AZJ, June 17, 1879, pp. 385–86.

21. Quoted by W. E. Mosse, *Jews in the German Economy: The German-Jewish Economic Elite, 1820–1935* (Oxford, 1987), 81, n. 35.

22. Levin Goldschmidt, *Zur Reichstagswahl vom 21. 2. und 2. 3. 1887* (Berlin, 1887), 25, 27.

23. Moritz Lazarus, *An die deutschen Juden* (Berlin, 1887), 7.

24. Stanley Zucker, *Ludwig Bamberger: German Liberal Politician and Social Critic, 1823–1899* (Pittsburgh, 1975), 95.

25. Goldschmidt to Professor Stobbe, April 23, 1871. A. Goldschmidt, ed., *Levin Goldschmidt. Ein Lebensbild in Briefen* (Berlin, 1898), 347. See also ibid., pp. 304, 374, 376.

26. "Der ultramontane Bau," AZJ, July 24, 1877, p. 469.

27. "Die ultramontane Weltliga," AZJ, August 21, 1877, p. 534.

28. Reichstag election speech, October 4, 1881. BfLA, Pr. BR. Rep. 30, Berlin C, Pol. PrSs., Tit. 95, Sect. 5, Lit W, 2/32:569.

29. Goldschmidt to Professor Stobbe. Goldschmidt, *Levin Goldschmidt*, 410.

30. *Jüdische Presse*, 1879, p. 192.

31. "Der Classenkampf in Deutschland-II," AZJ, June 18, 1878, p. 386; ditto-III, AZJ, June 25, 1878, p. 403.

32. Fritz Stern, *Gold and Iron: Bismarck, Bleichröder, and the Building of the*

German Empire (New York, 1977), 308.

33. Ibid., 151, 152.

34. Ibid., 142, 308.

35. Zucker, *Ludwig Bamberger*, 183, 189; stBR 76(June 26, 1884):1066.

36. "Dampfersubvention," pj 54(1884):97.

37. James F. Harris, *A Study in the Theory and Practice of German Liberalism: Eduard Lasker, 1829–1884* (Lanham, Md., 1984), 31–32.

38. *Die Neuzeit*, June 3, 1870, pp. 245–46.

39. Saul Raphael Landau, *Der Polenklub und seine Hausjuden* (Vienna, 1907), 6–7.

40. azj, August 13, 1878, p. 525.

41. Adolf Jellinek, "Die Juden in Österreich," *Der Orient*, May 13, 1848, p. 154.

42. "Jüdisch österreichisch," *Die Neuzeit*, June 15, 1883, p. 225.

43. Heinrich Friedjung, *Der Ausgleich mit Ungarn. Politische Studie über das Verhältniss Osterreichs zu Ungarn und Deutschland* (Leipzig, 1877), 27–28.

44. Address on April 9, 1898, "Adolf Fischhof und die Verfassungskämpfe der Gegenwart," möiu 10(April 1898):15.

45. Levin Goldschmidt, *Die Nothwendigkeit eines deutschen Civilgesetzbuches* (Berlin, 1872), 18.

46. gstm, Rep. 120, A IV 13, pp. 65–66.

7. The Return of Old Hatreds

1. C. Wilmanns, *Die "goldene" Internationale und die Nothwendigkeit einer socialen Reformpartei* (Berlin, 1876), 1, 58.

2. Ibid., 58.

3. Ibid., 61.

4. Constantin Frantz, *Der Nationalliberalismus und die Judenherrschaft* (Munich, 1874), 34–35, 21.

5. Wiard Klopp, *Die sozialen Lehren des Freiherrn Karl von Vogelsang* (St. Pölten, 1894), 436.

6. *Das Vaterland*, December 20, 1871.

7. Robert von Mohl, *Staatsrecht, Völkerrecht und Politik* (Tübingen, 1860–1869), 3:679.

8. Otto Glagau, *Der Börsen- und Gründungsschwindel in Berlin* (Leipzig, 1876); *Der Börsen- und Gründungsschwindel in Deutschland* (Leipzig, 1877).

9. [Franz F. Perrot], *Die Ära Bleichröder-Delbrück-Camphausen. Separat-Abdruck der 5 Aera-Artikel aus der Kreuz-Zeitung nebst Literatur darüber und ein Vor- und Nachwort des Verfassers* (Berlin, 1876).

10. Otto Glagau, *Der Bankerott des Nationalliberalismus und die "Reaction"* (Berlin, 1878), 71.

11. kz, June 19, 1875; Glagau, *Der Börsen- und Gründungsschwindel in Berlin*, xxiv.

12. Rudolf Meyer, *Politische Gründer und die Corruption in Deutschland* (Berlin, 1877), 204.

13. Frantz, *Der Nationalliberalismus und die Judenherrschaft*, 22.

14. "Die jüdische Frage," HPB 1/2(1838):390.

15. Wilhelm Emmanuel Freiherr von Ketteler, letter to Francis Joseph, August 18, 1866, in Wilhelm Emmanuel Freiherr von Ketteler, *Sämtliche Werke und Briefe*, ed. Erwin Iserloh (Mainz, 1971–), sec. 1, 4:72, n. 5; Wilhelm Emmanuel Freiherr von Ketteler, "Der Culturkampf gegen die katholische Kirche und die neuen Kirchengesetzentwürfe für Hessen" (1874), in Wilhelm Emmanuel Freiherr von Ketteler, *Sämtliche Werke und Briefe*, sec. 1, 4:438–39.

16. *Germania*, August 9, 1879, p. 1.

17. August Rohling, *Der Talmudjude. Zur Beherzigung für Juden und Christen aller Stände dargestellt*, 3d ed. (Münster, 1872), 59.

18. "Der Liberalismus und das Judenthum," AZJ, June 4, 1872, p. 441.

19. AZJ, February 1, 1876, p. 70.

20. Wilhelm Marr, *Der Sieg des Judenthums über das Germanenthum. Vom nicht konfessionellen Standpunkt aus betrachtet* (Bern, 1879), 38.

21. Eugen Dühring, *Die Judenfrage als Racen-, Sitten- und Culturfrage. Mit einer weltgeschichtlichen Antwort* (Karlsruhe-Leipzig, 1881), 113.

22. Adolf Stoecker, "Unsere Forderungen an das moderne Judentum," in Adolf Stoecker, *Christlich-Sozial. Reden und Aufsätze* (Berlin, 1885), 146.

23. Letter to William I, September 23, 1880, cited in Walter Frank, *Hofprediger Adolf Stoecker und die christlichsoziale Bewegung*, 2d ed. (Hamburg, 1935), 89.

24. Heinrich von Treitschke, "Unsere Aussichten," PJ 44(November 15, 1879):572–76; see also Walter Boehlich, ed., *Der Berliner Antisemitismusstreit* (Frankfurt am Main, 1965), 7–14.

25. Theodor Mommsen, *Auch ein Wort über unser Judenthum* (Berlin, 1880); also in Boehlich, *Der Berliner Antisemitismusstreit*, 221.

26. Boehlich, *Der Berliner Antisemitismusstreit*, 240–41. A full list of signatories may be found in Hans Liebeschütz, *Das Judentum im deutschen Geschichtsbild von Hegel bis Max Weber* (Tübingen, 1967), 341–42; the English translation of the text of the declaration is in Peter Pulzer, *The Rise of Political Anti-Semitism in Germany and Austria*, rev. ed. (London, 1988), 326–27.

27. STBPrA, November 20, 1880, p. 232.

28. Moritz Busch, *Tagebuchblätter* (Leipzig, 1889), 3:44–45.

29. Ibid., 12–13.

30. Treitschke, "Unsere Aussichten," 572–73; Boehlich, *Der Berliner Antisemitismusstreit*, 7, 9.

31. Norbert Kampe, *Studenten und "Judenfrage" im Deutschen Kaiserreich. Die Entstehung einer akademischen Trägerschaft des Antisemitismus* (Göttingen, 1988), 44.

32. AZJ, May 20, 1879, p. 328.

33. See chapter 6, n. 43. For the text of the Linz program, see Pulzer, *The Rise of Political Anti-Semitism*, 145.

34. Eduard Pichl, *Georg Schönerer und die Entwicklung des Alldeutschtums in der Ostmark* (Oldenburg, 1938), 1:122, 275.

35. Theodor Billroth, *Über das Lehren und Lernen der medicinischen Wissenschaften an den Universitäten der deutschen Nation* (Vienna, 1873), 148; *Prof. Dr. Th. Billroths Antwort an die Adresse des Lesevereins der deutschen Studenten Wien's* (Vienna, 1875), 8.

36. Paul Molisch, *Die politische Geschichte der deutschen Hochschulen in Österreich von 1848 bis 1918* (Vienna, 1939), 121.

37. UDW, April 1, 1896.

38. "Der Antisemitismus und die Staatsgrundsätze," *Patriotische Flugblätter* 1(December 5, 1881):3, CAHJP, Israelitische Kultusgemeinde Wien, AW 316.

39. *Das Vaterland*, June 15, 1887, pp. 4–5.

40. ÖV, October 2, 1887, pp. 6–7.

41. Paul Nathan, *Der Prozess von Tisza-Eszlár. Ein antisemitisches Kulturbild* (Berlin, 1892), 21.

42. Pulzer, *The Rise of Political Anti-Semitism*, 151.

43. Emil Lehmann, "Höre Israel! Aufruf an die deutschen Glaubensgenossen," in Emil Lehmann, *Gesammelte Schriften* (Dresden, 1899), 291, 293.

44. *Der Israelit* 17(1876):1, cited in Mordechai Breuer, *Modernity Within Tradition: The Social History of Orthodox Jewry in Imperial Germany* (New York, 1992), 339.

45. Berthold Auerbach, *Briefe an seinen Freund Jakob Auerbach. Ein biographisches Denkmal* (Frankfurt am Main, 1884), 2:442.

46. Ludwig Bamberger, *Deutschtum und Judentum* (Leipzig, 1880), 35.

47. "Das judenfeindliche Treiben in der Gegenwart," AZJ, October 28, 1879, p. 691.

48. Lehmann, "Höre Israel!" 316.

49. 'An unsere Glaubensgenossen!' CAHJP, DIGB M1/15.

50. Franz Delitzsch, *Rohling's Talmudjude beleuchtet*, 1st–6th eds. (Leipzig, 1881).

51. "Die Staatsanwaltschaft beim Landesgericht Dresden, 7. Dezember 1880," CAHJP, DIGB M1/15.

52. CAHJP, Israelitische Kultusgemeinde Wien, A/W 317.

53. See note 30 above.

54. Joseph Rebbert, *Blicke in's talmudische Judenthum. Nach den Forschungen von Dr. Konrad Martin, Bischof von Paderborn, dem christlichen Volke enthüllt. Nebst einer Beleuchtung der neuesten Judenvertheidigung* (Paderborn, 1876), 81.

55. Adolf Stoecker, "Die Selbstverteidigung des modernen Judentums in dem Geisteskampf der Gegenwart," in Adolf Stoecker, *Christlich-Sozial. Reden und Aufsätze* (Berlin, 1890), 186.

56. "Notwehr gegen das moderne Judentum," ibid., 167.

57. "Wie haben Deutsche und Christen sich gegen die jüdischen Mitbürger zu verhalten?" cited in Dietrich von Oertzen, *Adolf Stoecker, Lebensbild und Zeitgeschichte* (Berlin, 1910), 2:248; "Das Judentum im öffentlichen Leben. Eine Gefahr für das deutsche Reich," in Adolf Stoecker, *Christlich-Sozial*, 211.

58. öv, March 30, 1884, p. 2.

59. Aufruf des Landrates, Geheimer Regierungs-Rat v. Bornstedt, GSTD, Rep. 90, 306.

60. "Programm der Vereinigten Christen," *Deutsches Volksblatt*, February 20, 1889.

61. Erika Weinzierl, "Katholizismus in Österreich," in K. H. Rengstorf and S. von Kortzfleisch, eds., *Kirche und Synagoge. Handbuch zur Geschichte von Christen und Juden* (Stuttgart, 1970), 2:515.

62. Rudolf Lill, "Der heilige Stuhl und die Juden," ibid., 2:368, n. 17.

63. Friedrich Funder, *Vom Gestern ins Heute. Aus dem Kaiserreich in die Republik* (Vienna, 1952), 145–46.

64. Joseph Deckert, *Türkennot und Judenherrschaft. Drei Conferenzreden* (Vienna, 1893); Joseph Deckert, *Ein Ritualmord. Aktenmässig nachgewiesen* (Dresden, 1893); Joseph Deckert, "*Der wahre Israelit*" vor den Wiener Geschworenen (Vienna, 1896), 81, 94.

65. Adolf Hitler, *Mein Kampf*, trans. Ralph Manheim (London, 1969), 51, 64.

66. Rudolf Kuppe, *Karl Lueger und seine Zeit* (Vienna, 1933), 335–36.

67. "Das Programm der Deutschen Volkspartei," in Klaus Berchtold, ed., *Österreichische Parteiprogramme 1868–1966* (Munich, 1967), 205.

68. Andrew G. Whiteside, *The Socialism of Fools: Georg Ritter von Schönerer and Austrian Pan-Germanism* (Berkeley-Los Angeles, 1975), 215.

69. Theodor Herzl, *Tagebücher. Gesammelte Zionistische Werke* (Tel Aviv, 1934), 2:52, 56.

70. Tomás G. Masaryk, *Die Notwendigkeit der Revision des Polnaer Processes* (Vienna, 1899).

71. Peter Brock, "The Early Years of the Polish Peasant Party, 1895–1907," *Journal of Central European Affairs* 14/3(1954):232.

72. Z. A. B. Zeman, *The Masaryks: The Making of Czechoslovakia* (London, 1976), 52.

73. ODR, August 24, 1909; *Deutsches Nordmährerblatt*, September 1912.

74. "Bürgermeister Dr. Lueger über die aktuellen Fragen," *Volksblatt für Stadt und Land*, December 8, 1905.

75. *Jakob Burckhardts Briefe an seinen Freund Friedrich von Preen, 1864–1893* (Stuttgart-Berlin, 1922), 137 (January 2, 1880).

76. Paul de Lagarde, "Die graue Internationale," *Schriften für das deutsche Volk* (Munich, 1934), 1:358, 370.

77. Treitschke, "Unsere Aussichten," 573; Boehlich, *Der Berliner Antisemitismusstreit*, 8.

78. Kampe, *Studenten und "Judenfrage" im Deutschen Kaiserreich*, 140.

79. Friedrich Paulsen, *System der Ethik, mit einem Umriss der Staats- und Gesellschaftslehre*, 6th ed. (Berlin, 1903), 554.

80. Friedrich Paulsen, *Die deutschen Universitäten und das Universitätsstudium* (Berlin, 1902), 200.

81. Hermann Lietz, *Lebenserinnerungen*, ed. Alfred Andreesen (Weimar, 1935), 114–15.

82. Julius Langbehn, *Rembrandt als Erzieher*, 38th ed. (Leipzig, 1892), 159, 292.

83. Ibid., 276, 293.

84. Dr. Memmendorf, "Wandervogel und Judentum," *Der Kunstwart*, 26/1b (June 1914):298.

85. Langbehn, *Rembrandt als Erzieher*, 351.

86. Franz Oppenheimer, *Erlebtes, Erstrebtes, Erreichtes. Erinnerungen*, 2d ed. (Düsseldorf, 1964), 162.

87. U. Linse, ed., *Zurück o Mensch zur Mutter Erde. Landkommunen in Deutschland 1890–1933* (Munich, 1983), 193.

88. Hans-Jürgen Puhle, *Agrarische Interessenpolitik und preussischer Konservatismus im wilhelminischen Reich (1893–1914)*, (Hanover, 1966), 35.

89. *Bund der Landwirte*, June 6, 1895, cited in Puhle, *Agrarische Interessenpolitik*, 130.

90. Iris Hamel, *Völkischer Verband und nationale Gewerkschaft. Der Deutschnationale Handlungsgehilfen-Verband 1893–1933* (Frankfurt am Main, 1967), 53, 83.

91. Richard Gellately, *The Politics of Economic Despair: Shopkeepers and German Politics, 1890–1914* (London, 1974), 179.

92. Heinrich August Winkler, "Der rückversicherte Mittelstand: Die Interessenverbände von Handwerk und Kleinhandel im deutschen Kaiserreich," in Heinrich August Winkler, *Zwischen Marx und Monopolen. Der deutsche Mittelstand vom Kaiserreich zur Bundesrepublik Deutschland* (Frankfurt am Main, 1991), 29.

93. Paul de Lagarde, "Über die gegenwärtigen Aufgaben der deutschen Politik," *Schriften für das deutsche Volk*, 1:30.

94. Idem, "Juden und Indogermanen," *Mittheilungen* (Göttingen, 1884–1891), 2:331.

95. Houston Stewart Chamberlain, "Richard Wagners Briefe an Hermann Levi," *Bayreuther Blätter*, 1901, pp. 15–16.

96. Paul de Lagarde, "Juden und Indogermanen," *Mittheilungen*, 2:339.

97. Benedikt Momme Nissen, *Der Rembrandtdeutsche Julius Langbehn. Von seinem Freunde* (Freiburg, 1927), 184.

98. Ludwig Schemann, *25 Jahre Gobineau-Vereinigung,1894–1919. Ein Rückblick* (Strasbourg-Berlin, 1919), 48.

99. Friedrich Lange, *Reines Deutschtum, Grundzüge einer nationalen Weltanschauung* (Berlin, 1904), 109.

100. Paul Pretzsch, ed., *Houston Stewart Chamberlains Briefe 1882–1924 und Briefwechsel mit Kaiser Wilhelm II* (Munich, 1928), 2:151.

101. Houston Stewart Chamberlain, *The Foundations of the Nineteenth Century*, trans. John Lees (London, 1911), 1:542.

102. Ibid., 1:488.

103. Cited in Jost Hermand, *Der alte Traum vom neuen Reich. Völkische Utopien und Nationalsozialismus* (Frankfurt am Main, 1988), 83.

104. Ernst Hasse, *Deutsche Politik*, vol. 4: *Die Zukunft des deutschen Volkstums* (Munich, 1907), 46.

105. Ibid., 68.

106. Daniel Frymann [Heinrich Class], *Wenn ich der Kaiser wär'. Politische Wahrheiten und Notwendigkeiten* (Leipzig, 1912), 74.

107. "Gedanken über einen notwendigen Fortschritt in der inneren Entwicklung Deutschlands," Hartmut Pogge von Strandmann and Immanuel Geiss, *Die Erforderlichkeit des Unmöglichen. Deutschland am Vorabend des ersten Weltkrieges* (Frankfurt am Main, 1965), 16–17.

108. Boehlich, *Der Berliner Antisemitismusstreit*, 205.

109. Hermann Bahr, *Der Antisemitismus. Ein internationales Interview*, ed. Hermann Greive (Königstein/Taunus, 1979), 27.

110. Shulamit Volkov, "Antisemitism as a Cultural Code: Reflections on the History and Historiography of Antisemitism in Imperial Germany," LBIYB 23(1978):25–46.

8. The Response to Antisemitism

1. "Die Blutlüge vor Gericht," AZJ, July 15, 1892, p. 337.

2. *Revidirte Statuten des Deutsch-Israelitischen Gemeindebundes angenommen durch den ausserordentlichen Gemeindetag zu Leipzig am 19. September 1877*, 1. CAHJP, DIGB M1/1.

3. To Hermann Baumgarten, July 14, 1885, in M. Weber, ed., *Jugendbriefe* (Tübingen, 1936), 174.

4. Adolph Asch and Johanna Philippson, "Self-Defence at the Turn of the Century: The Emergence of the K.C.," LBIYB 3(1958):122.

5. Heinrich Rickert, "Die Judenverfolgung in Deutschland am Ende des neunzehnten Jahrhunderts," *Die Nation*, August 9. 1890, pp. 667–69.

6. Theodor Barth, "Das Gespenst der Rechtsgleichheit," *Die Nation*, September 5, 1906, p. 67.

7. "Zur Abwehr," AZJ, March 24, 1893, p. 135.

8. [Raphael Loewenfeld], *Schutzjuden oder Staatsbürger? Von einem jüdischen Staatsbürger* (Berlin, 1893), 11.

9. "Ein Wort der Einführung," IDR 1/1(July 1895):3.

10. Paul Rieger, *Ein Vierteljahrhundert im Kampf um das Recht und die*

Zukunft der deutschen Juden. Rückblick auf die Geschichte des Centralvereins deutscher Staatsbürger jüdischen Glaubens in den Jahren 1893–1918 (Berlin, 1918), 21.

11. To Alfred Fried, January 22, 1893, cited in Brigitte Hamann, *Bertha von Suttner. A Life for Peace* (*Syracuse, 1996*) 121.

12. *Das freie Blatt*, October 9, 1892.

13. Hamann, *Bertha von Suttner*, 117.

14. Joseph S. Bloch, *Der nationale Zwist und die Juden in Österreich* (Vienna, 1886), 41.

15. Jacob Toury, "Troubled Beginnings: The Emergence of the Österreichisch-Israelitische Union," LBIYB 30(1985):467.

16. Letter of September 16, 1875, cited in Fritz Stern, *Gold and Iron: Bismarck, Bleichröder, and the Building of the German Empire* (New York, 1977), 520, n.

17. To Disraeli, November 22, 1880, cited in Stern, *Gold and Iron*, 520.

18. To Friedrich Kapp, July 19, 1877; Anton Bettelheim, *Berthold Auerbach. Der Mann, sein Werk, sein Nachlass* (Stuttgart-Berlin, 1907), 375.

19. Ernest Renan, "Qu'est-ce qu'une Nation?" *Oeuvres Complètes*, ed. Henriette Psichari (Paris, 1947–1962), 1:904.

20. "Der Classenkampf in Deutschland—I," AZJ, June 11, 1878, p. 371.

21. Heymann Steinthal, "Das auserwählte Volk, oder Juden und Deutsche,"in *Über Juden und Judenthum* (Berlin, 1925), 15.

22. Adolf Kessler, "Die Juden in Österreich unter Kaiser Franz Josef I," Ph.D. diss. (Vienna, 1932), 125.

23. Quoted by Richard Eickhoff, STBR March 23, 1905.

24. Heinrich Otto Meisner, ed., *Denkwürkigkeiten des Generalfeldmarschall Alfred Grafen von Waldersee* (Stuttgart, 1923), 1:402, 405.

25. Harry Graf Kessler, *Tagebücher 1918–1937* (Frankfurt am Main, 1961), 386.

26. "Vaterlandsliebe (Zum Kaisergeburtstag)," AZJ, January 21, 1898, p. 26.

27. "Jüdische Sonderkandidaturen," AZJ, February 11, 1898, p. 61.

28. Maximilian Horwitz, "Die Ziele und Bestrebungen des Central-Vereins," IDR 3/2(February 1897):118.

29. M. Spanier, "Jüdische Volksschulen oder nicht?" IDR 7/6–7(June-July 1901):329.

30. *Der Israelit* 53(1912/1913):2.

31. Richard Lichtheim, *Die Geschichte des deutschen Zionismus* (Jerusalem, 1954), 143.

32. Walther Rathenau, "Staat und Judentum. Eine Polemik," in Walther Rathenau, *Gesammelte Schriften* (Berlin, 1925), 1:189.

33. "Neue Fronten," AZJ, August 20, 1909, pp. 5–6.

34. September 10, 1892. Cited in Hamann, *Bertha von Suttner*, 132.

35. "Judenthum und Sozialdemokratie," AZJ, April 3, 1891, p. 157.

36. Dr. [Hermann] Cohn, "Die deutschen Juden und die Reichstagswahl," AZJ, April 5, 1907, pp. 161, 163.

37. Georg Davidsohn, "Die jüdischen Reichstagsabgeordneten," AZJ, April 5, 1912, p. 160.

38. Bebel to Adler, July 8, 1901. Friedrich Adler, ed., *Victor Adler. Briefwechsel mit August Bebel und Karl Kautsky* (Vienna, 1954), 359.

39. *Protokoll über die Verhandlungen des Parteitages der sozialdemokratischen Partei Deutschlands, abgehalten zu Köln am Rhein* (Berlin, 1893), 223–24.

40. "Sozialismus und Antisemitismus," *Der Kampf* 4(1910–1911):94.

9. Ideology and Identity

1. M. Mendelssohn, *Die Pflicht der Selbstvertheidigung* (Berlin, 1894), 7.

2. Ibid., 20–21.

3. Ibid., 13–14.

4. Paul Rieger, *Ein Vierteljahrhundert im Kampf um das Recht und die Zukunft der deutschen Juden* (Berlin, 1918), 19.

5. Emil Lehmann, "Die Aufgaben der Deutschen jüdischer Herkunft" (1891), in Emil Lehmann, *Gesammelte Schriften* (Berlin, 1899), 366.

6. Hans Schäfer, "Erschautes. Erlebtes, Erdachtes, Erstrebtes," in Richarz, 275.

7. Originally published in *Die Zukunft*, March 6, 1897, reprinted in Walther Rathenau, *Schriften*, ed. Arnold Hartung et al. (Berlin, 1965), 89.

8. Ibid., 90.

9. Reprinted in Karl Kraus, *Untergang der Welt durch schwarze Magie* (Munich, 1960), 333.

10. Otto Weininger, *Geschlecht und Charakter. Eine prinzipielle Untersuchung*, 3d. ed. (Vienna and Leipzig, 1904), 412.

11. Eugen Fuchs, "Enquete über den Zionismus" (1897), in *Um Deutschtum und Judentum. Gesammelte Reden und Aufsätze*, ed. Leo Hirschfeld (Frankfurt am Main, 1919), 228–29.

12. "Thesen der national-jüdischen Vereinigung Köln," in Jehuda Reinharz, ed., *Dokumente zur Geschichte des deutschen Zionismus 1882–1933* (Tübingen, 1981), 37.

13. Richard Lichtheim, cited by Yehuda Eloni, "Die umkämpfte nationaljüdische Idee," in Mosse, 685.

14. Reinharz, *Dokumente*, 106.

15. From Oppenheimer's speech at the 1914 Delegiertentag, reprinted in Reinharz, *Dokumente*, 141.

16. Arthur Ruppin, *Die Juden der Gegenwart* (Berlin, 1911), 192.

17. JR 17(April 26, 1907), quoted in Jehuda Reinharz, *Fatherland or Promised Land: The Dilemma of the German Jew, 1893–1907* (Ann Arbor, 1975), 178.

18. "Zur Jahrhundertwende des Emanzipationsedikts" (1912), in Fuchs, *Um Deutschtum und Judentum*, 120.

19. Fuchs, "Referat über die Stellung des Centralvereins zum Zionismus in der Delegierten-Versammlung vom 30. März, 1913," ibid., 245–46.

20. "Zur Jahrhundertwende des Emanzipationsedikts" (1912), ibid., 118.
21. Fuchs, "Erstrebtes und Erreichtes" (1918), ibid., 329.
22. Fuchs, "Sombart und die Zukunft der Juden" (1912), ibid., 132–33.

10. Jewish Participation in German Culture

1. "Als ich 75 wurde. An meinem 75ten," in J. Krueger and A. Golz, eds., Theodor Fontane, *Gedichte* (Berlin-Weimar, 1989), 2:494. Quoted by Peter Gay, "Begegnung mit der Moderne," in Mosse, 257.
2. Richard Beer-Hofmann, *Schlaflied für Mirjam* (1898) (Berlin, 1921), 2.
3. From the poem "Weltflucht," first published in the collection *Styx* in 1902 and included in Else Lasker-Schüler, *Sämtliche Gedichte* (Munich, 1966), 12.
4. From the poem "Dem Barbaren," ibid., 130.
5. From the poem "Zebaoth," first published in *Hebräische Balladen* in 1913, ibid., 181.
6. Ibid., 326.
7. First published in *Hebräische Balladen*, ibid., 172.
8. Quoted by Gay, "Begegnung mit der Moderne," 249.

11. New Trends in Jewish Thought

1. Berthold Feiwel, "Geleitwort zur ersten Ausgabe" (1902), *Jüdischer Almanach* (Berlin, 1904), 16.
2. *Das Wesen des Christentums*, 4th ed. (Leipzig, 1901), 33.
3. Ibid., 20–21.
4. "Harnack's Vorlesungen über das Wesen des Christentums," MGWJ 45(1901):110.
5. Ibid., 118.
6. Fritz Bamberger, "Leo Baeck, der Mensch und die Idee," in Eva G. Reichmann, ed., *Worte des Gedenkens für Leo Baeck* (Heidelberg, 1959), 79.
7. Leo Baeck, *Das Wesen des Judentums* (Berlin, 1905), 36, 39.
8. Robert Weltsch, "Introduction," LBIYB 13(1968):viii.
9. "Religiöse Postulate," in Hermann Cohen, *Jüdische Schriften* (Berlin, 1924), 1:9.
10. Hermann Cohen, *Ethik des reinen Willens* (Berlin, 1904), 528–29.
11. Michael A. Meyer, *Response to Modernity: A History of the Reform Movement in Judaism* (New York, 1988), 206.
12. Baeck, *Das Wesen des Judentums*, 59, 149.
13. Leo Hermann to Buber, November 14, 1908, in Buber, *Briefwechsel aus sieben Jahrzehnten*, ed. Grete Schaeder (Heidelberg, 1972–1975), 1:268–69.
14. "Martin Bubers Auffassung des Judentums," in Gerschom Scholem, *Judaica* (Frankfurt am Main, 1977), 2:149.

15. Martin Buber, *Die Legende des Baalschem* (Frankfurt am Main, 1920), 10.

16. Martin Buber, *Drei Reden über das Judentum* (Frankfurt am Main, 1911), 41–42.

17. Martin Buber, *Vom Geist des Judentums* (Leipzig, 1916), 41–42.

18. Ibid., 50–52.

19. Hermann Cohen, *Religion der Vernunft aus den Quellen des Judentums*, 2d ed. (Leipzig, 1929), 84.

20. Leo Strauss, preface to *Spinoza's Critique of Religion* (New York, 1965), 15.

21. Hermann Cohen, *Jüdische Schriften* (Berlin, 1924), 2:316.

22. Cohen, *Ethik des reinen Willens*, 314.

23. Hermann Cohen, preface, ibid. (1907 ed.), x.

24. Cohen, *Jüdische Schriften*, 2:317–18.

25. *Der Jude* 1(1916/1917):286–87.

26. Cohen, *Jüdische Schriften*, 2:335.

27. Gershom Scholem, "On the Social Psychology of the Jews in Germany: 1900–1933," in David Bronsen, ed., *Jews and Germans from 1860 to 1933: The Problematic Symbiosis* (Heidelberg, 1979), 30.

28. Moritz Goldstein, "Deutsch-jüdischer Parnass," *Der Kunstwart*, 25(1912):283, 286.

29. Moritz Goldstein, "German Jewry's Dilemma: The Story of a Provocative Essay," LBIYB 2(1957):245.

30. Goldstein, "Deutsch-jüdischer Parnass," 291.

31. Ibid., 294.

12. The First World War

1. Ludwig Holländer, "Krieg und Centralverein," IDR 20/10–12(October–December 1914):370.

2. "An die deutschen Juden," IDR, 20/9(September 1914):339.

3. JR, June 19, 1914, p. 273.

4. "Aufruf des Reichsvereins der deutschen Juden und der zionistischen Vereinigung für Deutschland," JR, August 7, 1914, p. 343.

5. *Selbstwehr*, April 17, 1916.

6. Sigmund Freud, "Zeitgemässes über Krieg und Tod," in Sigmund Freud, *Gesammelte Werke* (Frankfurt am Main, 1963), 10:324.

7. "Unter den Waffen," IDR 20/9(September 1914):342.

8. Isaac Breuer, "Der Friedenskrieg," *Jüdische Monatshefte* 1/10(October 1914):347.

9. Martin Buber, "Die Losung," *Der Jude* 1/1(April 1916):1.

10. September 30, 1914. Martin Buber, *Briefwechsel aus sieben Jahrzehnten*, ed. Grete Schaeder (Heidelberg, 1972–75), 1:371.

11. Cited in Christoph Stölzl, *Kafkas böses Böhmen. Zur Sozialgeschichte eines Prager Juden* (Frankfurt am Main, 1989), 92.

12. Munin [Karl Iro], *Österreich nach dem Krieg. Forderungen eines aktiven österreichischen Politikers* (Jena, 1915), 25.

13. IdR, 20/9(September 1914):339.

14. S. Adler-Rudel, *Ostjuden in Deutschland. Zugleich eine Geschichte der Organisationen, die sie betreuten* (Tübingen, 1959), 156–57.

15. Hermann Cohen, "Du sollst nicht einhergehen als ein Verleumder. Ein Appell an die Juden Amerikas," *Jüdische Schriften*, ed. Bruno Strauss (Berlin, 1924), 2:232–33.

16. Adolf Friedemann, "Die Bedeutung der Ostjuden für Deutschland," *Süddeutsche Monatshefte*, 13/5(February 1916):680.

17. Kurt Blumenfeld, "Der Zionismus," PJ, 161/1(July 1915):110.

18. J. F. Lehmann to Prof. Hans Freiherr von Liebig, April 16, 1916. BA Potsdam, 1416, 235.

19. Albrecht von Graefe to Count Westarp, January 28, 1916. Kuno Graf von Westarp, *Konservative Politik im letzten Jahrzehnt des Kaiserreiches* (Berlin, 1935), 2:326.

20. Walter von Molo, *So wunderbar ist das Leben—Erinnerungen und Begegnungen* (Stuttgart, 1957), 217.

21. Walther Rathenau to Wilhelm Schwaner, August 4, 1916, cited in Werner Jochmann, "Die Ausbreitung des Antisemitismus," Mosse/Paucker, 427.

22. Erlass des preussischen Kriegsministers Wild von Hohenborn zwecks Nachweisung aller beim Heere befindlichen wehrpflichtigen Juden, October 11, 1916, in Werner T. Angress, "Das deutsche Militär und die Juden im ersten Weltkrieg," MM 19(January 1976):97.

23. Kriegstagebuch manuscript, October 29, 1916. Angress, "Das deutsche Militär und die Juden im ersten Weltkrieg," 99.

24. Julius Marx, *Kriegs-Tagebuch eines Juden* (Zurich, 1939), 139.

25. Memorandum of police president of Frankfurt am Main, January 16, 1917. Angress, "Das deutsche Militär und die Juden im ersten Weltkrieg," 119.

26. "Hauptversammlung des Centralvereins deutscher Staatsbürger jüdischen Glaubens," February 4, 1917, IdR 23/2(February 1917):57; Dr. Felix Goldmann, "Zukunftsarbeit," IdR 23/7–8(July-August 1917):299.

27. Werner Becker, "Die Rolle der liberalen Presse," Mosse/Paucker, 87.

28. Eduard Bernstein, "Vom Mittlerberuf der Juden," NJM 1(April 25, 1917):397 ff.

29. Konstantin Freiherr von Gebsattel, "Alldeutsch—vielleicht alljüdisch?" *Deutsche Zeitung*, June 18, 1917.

30. Die deutsche Vaterlandspartei und der Antisemitismus," IdR, 24/3(March 1918):104–6.

31. Cited in Moses Wiesenfeld, "Begegnung mit Ostjuden," in F. Weltsch, ed.,

Dichter, Denker, Helfer: Max Brod zum fünfzigsten Geburtstag (Mährisch-Ostrau, 1934), 55.

32. Max Marcuse, cited in George Fritz, *Die Ostjudenfrage, Zionismus und Grenzschluss* (Munich, 1915), 42.

33. M. J. Bodenheimer, "Einwanderungsbeschränkung der Ostjuden," *Süddeutsche Monatshefte* 13/5(February 1916):731.

34. Kurt Alexander, "Deutschland und die Ostjudenfrage," IdR 22/1–2 (January-February 1917):25.

35. Trude Maurer, "Medizinalpolizei und Antisemitismus. Die deutsche Politik der Grenzsperre gegen Ostjuden im Ersten Weltkrieg," *Jahrbücher für Geschichte Osteuropas* 33/2(1985):210.

36. "Grenzschluss gegen Juden in Deutschland," JR, July 26, 1918, p. 229.

37. Heinrich Margulies, "Der Krieg der Zurückbleibenden," JR, February 5, 1915, p. 41.

38. Jacob H. Schiff to Dr. Arthur Zimmermann, October 19, 1914. Angress, "Das deutsche Militär und die Juden im ersten Weltkrieg," 106.

39. Max M. Warburg, "Die Judenfrage im Rahmen der deutschen Gesamtpolitik," November 1916. Angress, ibid., 106.

40. MVA 26/6(March 23, 1916):48.

41. "Umschau," IdR 24/9(September 1918):331.

42. "Sein oder Nichtsein—IV," *Ost und West* 17/7(July 1918):199.

43. Stefan von Licht to the president of the Jewish community, December 11, 1916. CAHJP A/W 15.

44. Amitai, "Chronik," *Der Jude* 3(1919):450.

45. Stölzl, *Kafkas böses Böhmen*, 97.

Bibliographical Essay

There are a number of standard works that provide an excellent overview of the whole period covered by this volume, or, at any rate, the greater part of it. For Germany these are Werner E. Mosse, ed., with the assistance of Arnold Paucker, *Juden im Wilhelminischen Deutschland, 1890–1914* (1976), which also covers events before 1890; Peter Pulzer, *Jews and the German State: The Political History of a Minority, 1848–1933* (1992); Shulamit Volkov, *Die Juden in Deutschland, 1780–1918* (1994); Trude Maurer, *Die Entwicklung der jüdischen Minderheit in Deutschland (1780–1933)* (1992); and Alfred D. Low, *Jews in the Eyes of Germans: From the Enlightenment to Imperial Germany* (1979). A number of eminent scholars have published relevant collections of essays, including Eva G. Reichmann, *Grösse und Verhängnis deutsch-jüdischer Existenz* (1973); and Fritz Stern, *Dreams and Delusions: The Drama of German History* (1987). The specific problem of Jewish assimilation is addressed in B. Vago, ed., *Jewish Assimilation in Modern Times* (1981), with chapters by Leni Yahil on Germany and William O. McCagg, Jr., on Austria. The daily life of German Jewry in this period is reflected in M. Richarz, ed., *Jüdisches Leben in Deutschland. Selbstzeugnisse zur Sozialgeschichte im Kaiserreich* (1979).

There is a growing literature on Jewish life and politics on a regional and local level. Some of the most important works are Paul Arnsberg, *Die Geschichte der Frankfurter Juden seit der französischen Revolution* (3 vols., 1983); J. Bohnke-Kollwitz et al., eds., *Köln und das rheinische Judentum* (1984); M. Treml and W. Weigand, eds., *Geschichte und Kultur der Juden in Bayern* (1988); C. Heinemann, ed., *Neunhundert Jahre Geschichte der Juden in Hessen* (1983); J. B. Paulus, ed., *Juden in Baden, 1809–1984. 150 Jahre Oberrat der Israeliten Badens* (1984); Helga Krohn, *Die Juden in Hamburg. Die politische, soziale und kulturelle Entwicklung einer jüdischen Grossstadtgemeinde nach der Emanzipation,*

1848–1918 (1974); H. Lamm, ed., *Von Juden in München* (1958); G. Rhode, ed., *Juden in Ostmitteleuropa von der Emanzipation bis zum Ersten Weltkrieg* (1989), containing chapters on Pomerania, Poznania, and Silesia as well as Galicia and Hungary; R. Rürup, ed., *Jüdische Geschichte in Berlin. Essays und Studien* (1995); and Stefanie Schüler-Springorum, *Die jüdische Minderheit in Königsberg/ Preussen 1871–1945* (1996). For a detailed account of the situation of Jews in the ethnically mixed areas of the German Empire, see William H. Hagen, *Germans, Poles, and Jews: The Nationality Conflict in the Prussian East, 1772–1914* (1980); and Vicki Caron, *Between France and Germany: The Jews of Alsace-Lorraine, 1871–1918* (1988).

For Austria-Hungary the best introduction is William O. McCagg, Jr., *A History of Habsburg Jews, 1670–1918* (1989). More detailed accounts will be found in A. Wandruszka and P. Urbanitsch, eds., *Die Habsburgermonarchie 1848–1918*, especially, volume 3.2 (1980) for the chapter by Wolfdieter Bihl, and volume 4 (1985) for the chapter by Wolfgang Häusler. On Vienna see especially Robert S. Wistrich, *The Jews of Vienna in the Age of Franz Joseph* (1987); and the older, but still informative, Hans Tietze, *Die Juden Wiens. Geschichte-Wirtschaft-Kultur* (1933).

1. Demographic Developments

Census reports provide us with statistical information that is available in numerous official publications but what is still lacking is an up-to-date general assessment of this material. Usiel Schmelz, who had planned such a broad assessment, produced a concise overview within the framework of an essay and a detailed manuscript dealing with Hesse, both of which set standards for this kind of work: "Die demographische Entwicklung der Juden in Deutschland von der Mitte des 19. Jahrhunderts bis 1933," *Zeitschrift für Bevölkerungswissenschaft* 1(1982): 31–72 (repr. BLBI 83[1989]:15–62) and *Die jüdische Bevölkerung Hessens. Von der Mitte des 19. Jahrhunderts bis 1933* (1996). Fortunately, we are able to reach back to the remarkable *Zeitschrift für Demographie und Statistik der Juden*, published by the Office of Jewish Statistics in Berlin, 1905–1931. The ZDSJ also addressed Jewish demographics in Austria, for which there is no recent general treatment either. A statistical reference that continues to be of value is *Die Juden in Österreich* (1908).

Arthur Ruppin was the first to take up the subject of the decline in Jewish population, a disquieting trend to Jewish statisticians. He approached the topic from the Zionist perspective and offered extensive criticism of assimilation in a study translated into English from the second edition as *The Jews of To-Day* (1913). This was followed by Felix Theilhaber's intensely emotional polemic, *Der Untergang der deutschen Juden* (1911; 2d ed., 1921). More current methodologies and material for comparison are found in the collective volume edited by Paul Ritterband, *Modern Jewish Fertility* (1981).

Studies of demographic change on the regional and local level are available for some German states and cities. Aside from the just mentioned work on Hesse by Schmelz, an indispensable study of the largest individual state, Prussia, although it draws primarily on the census of 1925, is Heinrich Silbergleit, *Die Bevölkerungs- und Berufsverhältnisse der Juden im Deutschen Reich*, vol. 1: *Prussia* (1930). Among the studies of individual cities, worth noting is Jan Herman, "The Evolution of the Jewish Population of Prague: 1769–1931," in U. Schmelz et al., eds., *Papers in Jewish Demography* (1980). An older work worthy of recommendation for Vienna is Leo Goldhammer, *Die Juden Wiens. Eine statistische Studie* (1927), which includes tables. Marsha Rozenblit's study, *The Jews of Vienna, 1867–1914: Assimilation and Identity* (1983), provides extensive statistical interpretations pertaining to mobility, occupational distribution, mixed marriages, baptisms, etc. Ivar Oxaal responds to this work, at times critically, in his essay, "The Jews of Young Hitler's Vienna: Historical and Sociological Aspects," in I. Oxaal, M. Pollak, and G. Botz, eds., *Jews, Antisemitism, and Culture in Vienna* (1987), 11–38. Some material for our period is contained in Gabriel Alexander, "Die Entwicklung der jüdischen Bevölkerung in Berlin zwischen 1871 und 1945," JIDG 10(1991):287–314. An older study that deserves mention is Jakob Segall, *Die Entwicklung der jüdischen Bevölkerung in München, 1875–1905* (1910). Interesting also from the methodological perspective with regard to the use of census data for a middle-sized Jewish community is Shulamit Volkov, "Die jüdische Gemeinde in Altona, 1867–1890: Ein demographisches Profil," in *Von der Arbeiterbewegung zum modernen Sozialstaat. Festschrift für Gerhard A. Ritter* (1994), 601–17.

More extensive research has been done on immigration and emigration of Jews than on the internal migration of Jews from rural to urban areas. Shalom Adler-Rudel's *Ostjuden in Deutschland, 1880–1940. Zugleich eine Geschichte der Organisationen die sie betreuten* (1959), contains the first brief account of the immigration of East European Jews before and during World War I. Jack Wertheimer's comprehensive study, *Unwelcome Strangers: East European Jews in Imperial Germany* (1987), takes a more detailed look at the sociohistorical context and the relationship of the *Ostjuden* to the German Jews. Trude Maurer's study of East European Jews during the Weimar Republic, *Ostjuden in Deutschland: 1918–1933* (1986), begins with the World-War-I period; Avraham Barkai, *Branching Out: German-Jewish Immigration to the United States, 1820–1914* (1994) is useful for emigration, although it concentrates more on Jewish entry and integration into America. Two essays by Steven M. Lowenstein examine the urbanization process and the concentration of Jews in several urban residential areas: "The Rural Community and the Urbanization of German Jewry," CEH 13(1980):218–36, and "Jewish Residential Concentration in Postemancipation Germany," LBIYB 28 (1983): 471–95.

In addition to the already mentioned work of Marsha Rozenblit on Vienna and the statistics found in the ZDSJ, which deal with baptism and mixed marriage, there is an important work by Peter Honigmann on Jews who left the Jewish community: *Die Austritte aus der Jüdischen Gemeinde Berlin, 1873–1941: Statistische Auswertung und historische Interpretation* (1988). The reasons for conversion are spelled out in the essay by Alan Levenson, "The Conversionary Impulse in Fin-de-Siècle Germany," LBIYB 40(1995):107–22.

2. Occupational Distribution and Social Structure

To some extent, the literature mentioned for chapter 1 also contains statistics on occupation (e.g., Schmelz), but they are more commonly to be found in economic studies. An older work of importance that deals with occupational distribution is Jakob Segall, *Die beruflichen und sozialen Verhältnisse der Juden in Deutschland* (1912). Another work grounded in statistics is Jakob Lestschinsky, *Das wirtschaftliche Schicksal des deutschen Judentums* (1932), which sets out to show that, despite appearances, the share of Jews in the economy was declining. Arthur Prinz, *Juden im deutschen Wirtschaftsleben: Soziale und wirtschaftliche Struktur im Wandel, 1850–1914* (revised by Avraham Barkai, 1984), is the first modern study to take German economic history into account as a significant context. Barkai published his own separate study, likewise of interest for its methodology, that also considers income and tax payments: *Jüdische Minderheit und Industrialisierung: Demographie, Berufe und Einkommen der Juden in Westdeutschland, 1850–1914* (1988). There is as yet no standard treatment of Jewish economic history in Austria, although reference can be made to Michael John, "Zur wirtschaftlichen Bedeutung des Judentums in Österreich, 1848–1938," in *Österreichisch-Jüdisches Geistes- und Kulturleben* (1990), 3:39–85.

The collective volume edited by Werner Mosse and Hans Pohl, *Jüdische Unternehmer in Deutschland im 19. und 20. Jahrhundert* (1992), provides an interesting overview of Jewish entrepreneurs on all levels. Albert Lichtblau, *Antisemitismus und soziale Spannung in Berlin und Wien 1867–1914* (1994), contains an informative comparison of Jewish economic activity in these two cities, especially with regard to the ready-to-wear clothing industry. On the topic of Jewish entrepreneurs in the latter area, see also Uwe Westphal, *Berliner Konfektion und Mode, 1836–1939. Die Zerstörung einer Tradition* (exp. ed., 1992). The Jewish upper class of millionaires and their social profile receive attention in the two-volume work by Werner E. Mosse, *Jews in the German Economy: The German-Jewish Economic Elite, 1820–1935* (1987) and *The German-Jewish Economic Elite, 1820–1935: A Sociocultural Profile* (1989). Especially noteworthy among works that deal with individual large-scale entrepreneurs are Fritz Stern, *Gold and Iron: Bismarck, Bleichröder, and the Building of the German Empire* (1977); and Lamar Cecil, *Albert Ballin: Business and Politics in Imperial Germany, 1888–1918* (1967).

On Jewish students see pages 77–99 of Norbert Kampe's important study, *Studenten und "Judenfrage" im Deutschen Kaiserreich. Die Entstehung einer akademischen Trägerschicht des Antisemitismus* (1988). Ernst Hamburger, *Juden im öffentlichen Leben Deutschlands. Regierungsmitglieder, Beamte und Parlamentarier 1848–1918* (1968) is a comprehensive study of discrimination against Jews as civil servants, judges, teachers, and professors. We also have the more recent detailed monograph by Barbara Strenge, *Juden im Preussischen Justizdienst, 1812–1918. Der Zugang zu den juristischen Berufen als Indikator der gesellschaftlichen Entwicklung* (1996).

3. Jewish Women in the Family and Public Sphere

The most extensive and important work on the topic of Jewish women in Imperial Germany is Marion Kaplan, *The Making of the Jewish Middle Class: Women, Family, and Identity in Imperial Germany* (1991). Whereas Kaplan accentuates the central role women played in the process of attaining middle-class status, Shulamit Volkov lays more emphasis on the family's role in her "Erfolgreiche Assimilation oder Erfolg und Assimilation. Die deutsch-jüdische Familie im Kaiserreich," in *Wissenschaftskolleg zu Berlin, Jahrbuch 1982/83*, 373–87.

Jewish female students and academics are discussed at length in the broad study by Claudia Huerkamp, *Bildungsbürgerinnen. Frauen im Studium und in akademischen Berufen 1900–1945* (1996), esp. 24–31; for Vienna see the article by Waltraud Heindl and Rudolf Wytek, "Die jüdischen Studentinnen an der Universität Wien, 1897–1938," in *Der Wiener Stadttempel—Die Wiener Juden* (1988), 137–50.

Marion Kaplan has likewise written the definitive monograph on the topic of the Jewish women's movement: *The Jewish Feminist Movement in Germany: The Campaigns of the Jüdischer Frauenbund, 1904–1938* (1979). That the middle-class character of this movement is especially apparent on the local level is clear from Sabine Knappe, "The Role of Women's Associations in the Jewish Community: The Example of the Israelitisch-Humanitärer Frauenverein in Hamburg at the Turn of the Century," LBIYB 39(1994):153–78. To date there is only one work that treats Jewish women who were active in the general women's movement, namely, Irmgard Fassmann, *Jüdinnen in der deutschen Frauenbewegung 1865–1919* (1996). Brief biographies of many German-Jewish women are contained in J. Dick and M. Sassenberg, eds., *Jüdische Frauen im 19. und 20. Jahrhundert, Lexikon zu Leben und Werk* (1993).

4. Religious Life

No systematic study exists on the geographic spread of the opposing religious movements. Much raw material can be gleaned from the numerous local histories of individual German-Jewish communities (some of them mentioned above) and from the statistical reports of the Deutsch-Israelitischer Gemeindebund and Büro fur Statistik der Juden, especially the *Handbuch der Jüdischen Gemeindeverwaltung und Wohlfahrtspflege*. Also valuable are the individual listings in the *Statistisches Jahrbuch des Deutsch-Israelitischen Gemeindebundes* for 1911 and 1913.

The most comprehensive narrative on Liberal Judaism in the period is found in chapter 5 of Michael A. Meyer, *Response to Modernity: A History of the Reform Movement in Judaism* (1988). Jakob Petuchowski's *Prayerbook Reform in Europe: The Liturgy of European Liberal and Reform Judaism* (1968) analyzes liturgical change and ideological controversies over liturgy within German Liberal Judaism. On the *Richtlinien* controversy see Michael A. Meyer, "Caesar Seligmann and the Development of Liberal Judaism in Germany at the Beginning of the Twentieth Century," HUCA 40–41(1969/70):529–54. On Austria see Marsha Rozenblit, "The Struggle over Religious Reform in Nineteenth Century Vienna," *AJS Review* 14(1989):179–221.

Mordechai Breuer, *Modernity Within Tradition: The Social History of Orthodox Jewry in Imperial Germany* (1992), describes and analyzes many aspects of Orthodox life, especially in the cities, including religious ideology and practice, education, and economic and social life. More emphasis on rural traditionalists is present in Yeshayahu Wolfsberg's programmatic article, "Popular Orthodoxy," LBIYB 1(1956):237–54. David Ellenson's sociologically influenced work on German Orthodoxy includes both his *Rabbi Esriel Hildesheimer and the Creation of a Modern Jewish Orthodoxy* (1990) and his analyses of German Orthodox responsa literature, much of it collected in the volume *Tradition in Transition: Orthodoxy, Halakhah, and the Boundaries of Modern Jewish Identity* (1989). On the commonalities between the various movements see Alexander Altmann, "The German Rabbi: 1910–1939," LBIYB 19(1974):31–49.

The secession controversy has been the subject of a considerable literature, a good deal of it polemical. An invaluable, though not entirely neutral, memoir is Saemy Japhet, "The Secession from the Frankfurt Jewish Community Under Samson Raphael Hirsch," *Historia Judaica* 10(1948):99–122. A detailed analysis of the controversy emphasizing the social forces within the Frankfurt community is Robert Liberles, *Religious Conflict in Social Context: The Resurgence of Orthodox Judaism in Frankfurt am Main, 1838–1877* (1985). Jacob Katz's comparative study on secession in Hungary and Germany, *Ha-kera shelo nitaḥah: perishat ha-ortodoksim mikelal hakehilot be-hungaryah ve-germanyah* (The Tear That Was Not Repaired: The Secession of the Orthodox from the General Community in Hungary and Germany, 1995) appeared only after this chapter was completed.

Alhough literature on Wissenschaft des Judentums often concentrates on its pre-1870 practitioners, there are a considerable number of studies on scholars of the *Kaiserreich* period, including articles in the LBIYB on Eugen Tauebler, 3(1958):40–59, Benno Jacob, 7(1962):75–94, Moritz Güdemann, 11(1966):42–66, and Arthur Ruppin, 17(1972):117–41.

5. The Community

An excellent summary of Jewish communal structure in Germany is Kurt Wilhelm, "The Jewish Community in the Post-Emancipation Era," LBIYB 2(1957): 47–75. On the suffrage system in communal elections and its relationship to Jewish party politics there are two monographs by Shmuel Ma'ayan, *Ha-beḥirot bi-kehilat Berlin ba-shanim 1901–1920* (The Elections in the Berlin Jewish Community, 1901–1920, 1977) and *Ha-beḥirot bi-kehilat Köln ba-shanim 1900– 1921* (The Elections in the Cologne Jewish Community, 1900–1921, 1979); as well as Jack Wertheimer, "The Duisburg Affair: A Test Case in the Struggle for 'Conquest' of the Communities," *AJS Review* 6(1981):185–206. For an extended discussion of issues of suffrage and communal elections in Vienna see Harriet Pass Freidenreich, *Jewish Politics in Vienna, 1918–1938* (1991), which also contains material on the prewar period.

Surveys on Jewish publications from the early nineteenth century until 1938 that list many communal periodicals include Margaret T. Edelheim-Muehsam, "The Jewish Press in Germany," LBIYB 1(1956):163–76, and the more recent survey of Barbara Suchy, "Die jüdische Presse im Kaiserreich und in der Weimarer Republik," in J. H. Schoeps, ed., *Juden als Träger bürgerlicher Kultur in Deutschland* (1989), 167–92.

Derek Penslar's article, "Philanthropy, the 'Social Question,' and Jewish Identity in Imperial Germany," LBIYB 38(1993):51–74, discusses the context of the modernization of Jewish charity. Ahron Bornstein's monograph, *Ha-kabtsanim* (The Beggars, 1992), deals with the transformation of Jewish responses to Jewish poverty in Imperial Germany. For the role of women in Jewish communal charity and social welfare see the two books by Marion Kaplan mentioned for chapter 3 above and for gender roles within a Jewish organization see Claudia Prestel, "Weibliche Rollenzuweisung in jüdischen Organisationen. Das Beispiel des Bnei Briss," BLBI 85(1990):51–80.

Jewish education in this period has generally been treated in the context of other institutional issues within the Jewish community. There is considerable attention to the matter both in Breuer's abovementioned history of Orthodox Judaism and in Marjorie Lamberti, *Jewish Activism in Imperial Germany* (1978). Claudia Prestel's monograph, *Jüdisches Schul- und Erziehungswesen in Bayern 1804–1933* (1989), gives a detailed picture of Jewish educational institutions and teacher training in Bavaria. On Jewish youth organizations the basic work is Chaim Schatzker, *Jüdische Jugend im zweiten Kaiserreich. Sozialisations- und Erziehungsprozesse der jüdischen Jugend in Deutschland, 1870–1917* (1988). On one national youth organization see Herbert Strauss, "The Jugendverband: A Social and Intellectual History," LBIYB 6(1961):206–35.

By now Ismar Schorsch, *Jewish Reactions to German Anti-Semitism, 1870–1914* (1972); and Jehuda Reinharz, *Fatherland or Promised Land: The Dilemma of the German Jew, 1893–1914* (1975) have become classic narratives of the rise, respectively, of the Centralverein deutscher Staatsbürger jüdischen

Glaubens (and other defense organizations) and of the Zionist movement. Sanford Ragins, *Jewish Responses to Anti-Semitism in Germany, 1870–1914: A Study in the History of Ideas* (1980) covers much the same territory as Schorsch with a somewhat different emphasis.

Yehuda Eloni in "Die umkämpfte nationaljüdische Idee," in Mosse, 633–88, and in his more recent book, *Zionismus in Deutschland. Von den Anfängen bis 1914* (1987), gives a detailed account of German Zionism. For a descriptive rather than analytic organizational history of Zionism in the Austrian half of the Austro-Hungarian Empire see Adolf Gaisbauer, *Davidstern und Doppeladler: Zionismus und jüdischer Nationalismus in Österreich 1882–1918* (1988).

Evyatar Friesel, "The Political and Ideological Development of the Central-verein before 1914," LBIYB 31(1986):121–46, discusses both changes in CV orientation and in its internal organization. The Hebrew dissertation by Jacob Borut, " 'A New Spirit Among Our Brethren in Ashkenaz': German Jews Between Antisemitism and Modernity in the Late Nineteenth Century" (Hebrew University, 1991), strengthens the association of the CV with Jewish revival already postulated by Schorsch and also analyzes the role of associations for the study of Jewish literature.

In the absence of a full-length volume on Austrian Jewish organizations the best analyses are to be found in two well-researched articles by Jacob Toury: "Troubled Beginnings: The Emergence of the Österreichisch-Israelitische Union," LBIYB 30(1985):457–75, and "Years of Strife: The Contest of the Österreichisch-Israelitische Union for the Leadership of Austrian Jewry," LBIYB 33(1988):179–99; and in Barbara Suchy, "The Verein zur Abwehr des Antisemitismus (I): From Its Beginnings to the First World War," LBIYB 28(1983):205–39. Finally, Jacob Toury, "Organizational Problems of German Jewry: Steps Toward the Establishment of a Central Organization (1893–1920)," LBIYB 13(1968):57–90, deals with the attempts to create a German-Jewish central organization and the obstacles that such attempts encountered.

6. Legal Equality and Public Life

The best account of the emancipation process is to be found in Reinhard Rürup, *Emanzipation und Antisemitismus. Studien zur "Judenfrage" in der bürgerlichen Gesellschaft* (1975). For our period specifically see his "Emancipation and Crisis: The 'Jewish Question' in Germany, 1850–1890," LBIYB 20(1975):13–25. The outstanding works on Jewish participation in German political life are Ernest Hamburger, *Juden im öffentlichen Leben Deutschlands. Regierungsmitglieder, Beamte und Parlamentarier in der monarchischen Zeit 1848–1918* (1968), also mentioned for chapter 2; and Jacob Toury, *Die politischen Orientierungen der Juden in Deutschland. Von Jena bis Weimar* (1966). See also Peter Pulzer, "Die jüdische Beteiligung an der Politik," in Mosse, 143–239. Studies of Jews in various professions include Helmut Heinrichs et al., *Deutsche Juristen jüdischer*

Herkunft (1993); Tillmann Krach, *Jüdische Rechtsanwälte in Deutschland. Über die Bedeutung der freien Advokatur und ihre Zerstörung durch den National-sozialismus* (1991); Konrad H. Jarausch, "Jewish Lawyers in Germany, 1848–1938: The Disintegration of a Profession," LBIYB 36(1991):171–90; Norbert Kampe, "Jüdische Professoren im Deutschen Kaiserreich," in R. Erb and M. Schmidt, eds., *Antisemitismus und jüdische Geschichte. Studien zu Ehren von Herbert A. Strauss* (1987), 185–214. Of the many biographical studies of prominent political and journalistic figures, the following may be singled out, in addition to the work by Fritz Stern on Bleichröder mentioned for chapter 2: James F. Harris, *A Study in the Theory and Practice of German Liberalism: Eduard Lasker, 1829–1884* (1984) and his "Eduard Lasker: The Jew as National German Politician," LBIYB 20(1975):151–77; and Stanley Zucker, *Ludwig Bamberger: German Liberal Politician and Social Critic, 1823–1899* (1975). Works on Jews who became prominent after the turn of the century are listed for chapter 8.

The constitutional position of Jews in Austria is elucidated by Gerald Stourzh, "Galten die Juden als Nationalität Altösterreichs? Ein Beitrag zur Geschichte des cisleithanischen Nationalitätenrechts," in Gerald Stourzh, *Wege zur Grundrechtsdemokratie. Studien zur Begriffs- und Institutionsgeschichte des liberalen Verfassungsstaates* (1989). J. Fraenkel, ed., *The Jews of Austria* (1967) contains a number of informative essays. On the role of Jews in the Austro-Hungarian army see Erwin A. Schmidl, *Juden in der K. (u.) K. Armee 1788–1918* (1989); and István Deák, *Jewish Soldiers in Austro-Hungarian Society* (1990). On the situation of Jews in the German-Czech borderlands see, above all, Hillel Kieval, *The Making of Czech Jewry. National Conflict and Jewish Society in Bohemia, 1870–1918* (1988); Gary B. Cohen, *The Politics of Ethnic Survival: Germans in Prague, 1861–1914* (1981) and "Jews in German Society: Prague, 1860–1914," CEH 10(1977):28–54.

7. The Return of Old Hatreds

The literature on antisemitism, especially that of Germany, is huge. A good introduction is provided by Jacob Katz, *From Prejudice to Destruction: Anti-Semitism, 1700–1933* (1980); a helpful bibliography of primary and secondary literature is R. R. Auerbach, ed., *The "Jewish Question" in German-Speaking Countries, 1848–1914* (1994). For general surveys of our period see Paul W. Massing, *Vorgeschichte des politischen Antisemitismus* (1959), an older work now partly superseded, and Eva G. Reichmann's influential sociological interpretation, *Die Flucht in den Hass. Die Ursachen der deutschen Judenkatastrophe* (1956). More recent overviews include Hermann Greive, *Geschichte des modernen Anti-semitismus in Deutschland* (1983); Helmut Berding, *Moderner Antisemitismus in Deutschland* (1988); and Peter Pulzer, *The Rise of Political Anti-Semitism in Germany and Austria* (2d ed., 1988). See also the scholarly analysis by Werner Jochmann, "Struktur und Funktion des deutschen Antisemitismus," in Mosse,

389–477; and Shulamit Volkov's seminal essay, "Antisemitism as a Cultural Code," LBIYB 35(1990):279–96. On the Treitschke-Mommsen controversy, see W. Boehlich, ed., *Der Berliner Antisemitismusstreit* (1964). Rather narrower in focus but detailed and informative is Richard S. Levy, *The Downfall of the Anti-Semitic Parties in Imperial Germany* (1975). On continuities in German antisemitic ideology see Paul Lawrence Rose's controversial *Revolutionary Antisemitism in Germany, from Kant to Wagner* (1990).

The religious dimension of antisemitism is covered in Stefan Lehr, *Antisemitismus—Religiöse Motive im sozialen Vorurteil* (1974); Isak Arie Hellwing, *Der konfessionelle Antisemitismus im 19. Jahrhundert in Österreich* (1972); Uwe Mazura, *Zentrumspartei und Judenfrage 1870/71–1933. Verfassungsstaat und Minderheitenschutz* (1994); and the symposium "Christian Religion and Anti-Semitism in Modern German History," in CEH 27(1994):261–353. On Christian-Jewish relations as they affected antisemitism, see Uriel Tal, *Christians and Jews in Germany: Religion, Politics, and Ideology in the Second Reich, 1870–1914* (1975); K. H. Rengstorf and S. von Kortzfleisch, eds., *Kirche und Synagoge. Handbuch zur Geschichte von Christen und Juden* (1970); and Christopher Clark, *The Politics of Conversion: Missionary Protestantism and the Jews in Prussia, 1728–1941* (1995). On the Tisza-Eszlár affair, see Andrew Handler, *Blood Libel at Tiszaeszlar* (1980). Notable works on leading antisemites include Moshe Zimmermann, *Wilhelm Marr. The Patriarch of Anti-Semitism* (1986); Günter Brakelmann et al., *Protestantismus und Politik. Werk und Wirkung Adolf Stöckers* (1987); Andrew G. Whiteside, *The Socialism of Fools: Georg von Schönerer and Austrian Pan-Germanism* (1975); and John W. Boyer, "Karl Lueger and the Viennese Jews," LBIYB 26 (1981):125–41. For antisemitism in academic life, see the already mentioned Norbert Kampe, *Studenten und "Judenfrage" im Deutschen Kaiserreich* (1988); Konrad H. Jarausch, *Students, Society, and Politics in Imperial Germany: The Rise of Academic Illiberalism* (1982); and Tobias Brinkmann, *Duell, Student und Davidstern. Satisfaktion und Antisemitismus in Deutschland 1871–1900* (1996).

8. The Response to Antisemitism

On Jewish organizational reactions to antisemitism, see, in addition to the works by Schorsch, Ragins, and Suchy mentioned for chapter 5, Michael A. Meyer, "Great Debate on Antisemitism: Jewish Reaction to New Hostility in Germany, 1879–1881," LBIYB 11(1966):137–70; Jehuda Reinharz, "The Zionist Response to Antisemitism in Germany," LBIYB 30(1985):105–40; and Arnold Paucker's magisterial survey, "Zur Problematik einer jüdischen Abwehrstrategie in der deutschen Gesellschaft," in Mosse, 479–548. On Austria, see Jacob Toury, "Defense Activities of the Österreichisch-Israelitische Union Before 1914," in J. Reinharz, ed., *Living With Antisemitism* (1987), 167–92; Jacques Kornberg, "Vienna in the 1890s— The Austrian Opposition to Antisemitism: The Verein zur Abwehr des Antisemitismus, LBIYB 41(1996):161–96; and Marsha L. Rozenblit, "The Assertion of Identity: Jewish Student Nationalism at the University of Vienna Before the First World War," LBIYB 27(1982):171–86. On other Jewish political organizations see Marjorie Lamberti's *Jewish Activism in Imperial Germany*, mentioned for chapter 5, and her "The Prussian Government and the Jews: Official Behaviour and Policy Making in the Wilhelminian Era," LBIYB 17(1972):5–17; see also Walter Breslauer, "Der Verband der deutschen Juden (1904–1922)," BLBI 7(1964):349–79.

Biographical studies of politically prominent Jews during this period include Lamar Cecil's work on Albert Ballin, mentioned for chapter 2; Gotthart Schwarz, *Theodor Wolff und das 'Berliner Tageblatt.' Eine liberale Stimme in der deutschen Politik, 1906–1933* (1968); and the essay by Ernst Schulin on Emil and Walther Rathenau in Mosse, 115–42. Much can be learned about the attitudes of the imperial family from John C. G. Röhl, "Kaiser Wilhelm II und der deutsche Antisemitismus," in John C. G. Röhl, *Kaiser, Hof und Staat. Wilhelm II und die deutsche Politik* (4th ed., 1995), 203–22; and from Lamar Cecil, "Wilhelm II und die Juden," in Mosse, 313–47. Relations between Jews and the socialist left are covered comprehensively in Robert S. Wistrich, *Socialism and the Jews: The Dilemmas of Assimilation in Germany and Austria-Hungary* (1982); Edmund Silberner, *Sozialisten zur Judenfrage* (1962); W. Grab, ed., *Juden und jüdische Aspekte in der deutschen Arbeiterbewegung* (1977); L. Heid and A. Paucker, eds., *Juden und deutsche Arbeiterbewegung bis 1933* (1992); and Rosemarie Leuschen-Seppel, *Sozialdemokratie und Antisemitismus im Kaiserreich* (1978). Valuable studies of prominent Jewish socialists include J. P. Nettl, *Rosa Luxemburg* (1966); Kenneth R. Calkins, *Hugo Haase: Democrat and Revolutionary* (1979); Francis Ludwig Carsten, *Eduard Bernstein (1850–1932). Eine politische Biographie* (1993); and Karl Otto Watzinger, *Ludwig Frank. Ein deutscher Politiker jüdischer Herkunft* (1995).

For the political position of Jews in the mixed-language regions of the Habsburg monarchy, see, in addition to the items listed for chapter 6, Christoph Stölzl, *Kafkas böses Böhmen. Zur Sozialgeschichte eines Prager Juden* (1975); E. Rychnovsky et al., eds., *Masaryk and the Jews: A Collection of Essays* (1944); H. Gold, ed., *Geschichte der Juden in der Bukowina* (2 vols., 1958–62); and Martin Broszat, "Von der Kulturnation zur Volksgruppe—Die nationale Stellung der Juden in der Bukowina im 19. und 20. Jahrhundert," *Historische Zeitschrift* 200 (1965).

9. Ideology and Identity

Extensive discussion of the controversies between the CV and the Zionists is to be found in the studies by Schorsch, Reinharz, Ragins, Eloni, and Lamberti mentioned for chapter 5. A valuable collection of documents on the subject is J. Reinharz, ed., *Dokumente zur Geschichte des deutschen Zionismus, 1882–1933* (1981). Unlike most of the preceding literature, Michael Berkowitz, *Zionist*

Culture and West European Jewry Before the First World War (1993) emphasizes
the commonality between the various Zionist factions in the West, centering his
analysis on the creation of symbols of a national movement in the practical work
of the Zionist organization. A discussion of the intellectual and literary aspects of
cultural Zionism is given in Mark Gelber, "The Jungjüdische Bewegung: An
Unexplored Chapter in German-Jewish Literary and Cultural History," LBIYB
31(1986):105–19. George L. Mosse deals with "The Influence of the Volkish Idea
on German Jewry," emphasizing Zionism, the youth movement, and Jewish
thought, in a chapter of his *Germans and Jews: The Right, the Left, and the Search
for a "Third Force" in Pre-Nazi Germany* (1970), 77–115. A more specific study
is Joachim Doron, "Rassebewusstsein und naturwissenschaftliches Denken im
deutschen Zionismus während der wilhelminischen Ära," JIDG 9(1980):389–427.
The influence of racial thinking on Jewish physicians in Germany and elsewhere
is the subject of John M. Efron, *Defenders of the Race: Jewish Doctors and Race
Science in Fin de Siècle Europe* (1994).

A number of studies focus on East European Jews in Germany during the
Kaiserreich. Steven E. Aschheim's *Brothers and Strangers: The East European Jew
in German and German Jewish Consciousness, 1800–1923* (1982) deals primarily
with the image of the *Ostjuden*, while Jack Wertheimer's *Unwelcome Strangers*,
mentioned for chapter 2, concentrates more on social and cultural conditions and
on governmental policies toward the immigrants. Shulamit Volkov's article, "The
Dynamics of Dissimilation: Ostjuden and German Jews," in J. Reinharz and W.
Schatzberg, eds., *The Jewish Response to German Culture: From the Enlightenment to the Second World War* (1985), 195–211, emphasizes the role of East
European Jews in reversing the assimilation process.

On the touchy subject of "Jewish self-negation" see Sander L. Gilman, *Jewish
Self-Hatred: Anti-Semitism and the Hidden Language of the Jews* (1986), especially chapter 5. The original concept of self-hatred was developed by Theodor
Lessing in his *Der jüdische Selbsthass* (1930). This book and the concept itself are
the subject of biting criticism in Allan Janik, "Viennese Culture and the Jewish
Self-Hatred Hypothesis: A Critique," in the volume edited by Ivaar Oxaal et al.
(cited below for chapter 10), 75–88. In addition, see the articles on the identity
dilemmas of Otto Weininger, Fritz Mauthner, and Walther Rathenau in LBIYB
6(1961):152–69, 8(1963):136–48, and 13(1968):120–31.

10. Jewish Participation in German Culture

A very comprehensive though not always fully reliable survey of Jewish participation in German culture is the massive work edited by Siegmund Kaznelson
under the title *Juden im deutschen Kulturbereich*. Originally written in the 1930s,
it was updated after the war and published in 1959. In the area of the sciences a
somewhat more analytical and less encompassing survey is David Nachmansohn,
German-Jewish Pioneers in Science 1900–1933: Highlights in Atomic Physics,

Chemistry, and Biochemistry (1979). Shulamit Volkov sketches a social analysis of the reasons for Jewish success as scientists, based on a sample of forty leading figures, in "Soziale Ursachen des jüdischen Erfolgs in der Wissenschaft" in her *Jüdisches Leben und Antisemitismus* (1990), 146–65.

In the essay "Encounter with Modernism: German Jews in Wilhelminian Culture," in his *Freud, Jews, and Other Germans* (1978) 93–168, Peter Gay forcefully argues against the usual view of German-Jewish cultural activity in the Wilhelminian period as distinctively Jewish and avant-garde. Other essays in the volume echo the same theme.

Apart from the frequent mention of Jewish writers in general surveys of German literature, most works on Jews and German literature deal with the Jewish identity problems and reactions to antisemitism of authors of Jewish origin. Lothar Kahn, *Between Two Worlds: A Cultural History of German-Jewish Writers* (1993) is a broad survey. Klara Pomeranz Carmely, *Das Identitäts-Problem jüdischer Autoren im deutschen Sprachraum. Von der Jahrhundertwende bis zu Hitler* (1981); and H. O. Horch and H. Denkler, eds., *Conditio Judaica. Judentum, Antisemitismus und deutschsprachige Literatur vom 18. Jahrhundert bis zum ersten Weltkrieg* (1989) likewise concentrate on identity issues. A useful introduction to the methodological problem of studying Jewish cultural contributions is Horch's article, "Heimat und Fremde: Jüdische Schriftsteller und deutsche Literatur oder Probleme einer deutsch-jüdischen Literaturgeschichte," in the abovementioned J. H. Schoeps, ed., *Juden als Träger bürgerlicher Kultur in Deutschland*, 41–66.

Much has been written concerning the place of Jews in Viennese cultural life. Although it discusses many Jewish figures, Carl E. Schorske, *Fin de Siècle Vienna: Politics and Cultural Life* (1980), does not stress the distinctiveness of the Jewish contribution. Jewish distinctiveness within Viennese culture is, however, dealt with directly and incisively in Steven Beller, *Vienna and the Jews, 1867–1938: A Cultural History* (1989); I. Oxaal, M. Pollak, and G. Botz, eds., *Jews, Antisemitism, and Culture in Vienna* (1987); and most comprehensively in the previously noted Robert S. Wistrich, *The Jews of Vienna in the Age of Franz Joseph*.

On the cultural identity of Jews in Bohemia-Moravia, caught between their Jewishness and pressures to identify with the rival Germans and Czechs, see Hillel Kieval, *The Making of Czech Jewry*, mentioned also for chapter 6, as well as the collection of documents edited by Wilma Iggers, *Die Juden in Böhmen und Mähren* (1986).

In discussing Jewish patronage of culture, Peter Gay, in the article mentioned above, uses Aby Warburg as one of his prime examples. Wilhelm Treue analyzes the important role of Jewish patrons in various fields of scholarship in his article "Jüdisches Mäzenatentum für die Wissenschaft in Deutschland," in W. Mosse and H. Pohl, eds., *Jüdische Unternehmer in Deutschland im 19. und 20. Jahrhundert* (1992). Especially in section 3 of chapter 10 Werner Mosse, in his earlier mentioned *The German-Jewish Economic Elite 1820–1935*, analyzes the role of cultural activities and patronage in the lives of Jewish multimillionaires. There are also individual articles on such notable patrons as James Simon and Aby Warburg in LBIYB 10(1965):3–23 and 16(1971):225–36.

11. New Trends in Jewish Thought

The catalogue for an exhibition held at the Jewish Museum in Berlin, I. Bertz, ed., *"Eine neue Kunst für ein altes Volk." Die Jüdische Renaissance in Berlin. 1900 bis 1924* (1991), contains a comprehensive survey by the editor of the varied expressions of the Jewish renaissance in the arts and literature and considers the significance for the "movement" of East European Jewry as well as of East European Jewish artists who settled in Berlin.

Uriel Tal, *Christians and Jews in Germany*, already mentioned for chapter 7, is a magisterial study of the relations between Jews and Christians in Wilhelminian Germany that reconstructs the ramified and highly charged debate between Jewish and Christian scholars following the publication in 1900 of Adolf Harnack's immensely popular *Das Wesen des Christentums*, with its incidental but stinging criticism of Judaism. It provides a comprehensive bibliography of the debate (see pp. 205–6). See also Tal's essay, "Theologische Debatte um das 'Wesen' des Judentums," in Mosse, 599–632. Leo Baeck's seminal contribution to the debate is learnedly reviewed in Albert H. Friedlander's intellectual biography, *Leo Baeck: Teacher of Theresienstadt* (1968), chapter 3. The concept of "ethical monotheism" and its role in German-Jewish self-understanding is discussed by Max Wiener, "The Concept of Mission in Traditional and Modern Judaism," *YIVO Annual of Social Science* 2–3(1947–48):9–24; and also Max Wiener, *Jüdische Religion im Zeitalter der Emanzipation* (1933), passim.

The debate between Moritz Lazarus and Hermann Cohen regarding the nature and sources of the ethics of Judaism is discussed in detail in Heinz M. Graupe, *The Rise of Modern Judaism* (1978), chapter 19. In the same volume Graupe also provides a comprehensive review of the development of Cohen's general and Jewish philosophy, as does Hans Liebeschütz, "Hermann Cohen and His Historical Background," LBIYB 13(1968):3–33. Liebeschütz further illuminates the historical context of Cohen's thought in his study, *Von Georg Simmel zu Franz Rosenzweig* (1970), chapter 1.

Steven S. Schwarzschild, in his " 'Germanism and Judaism'—Hermann Cohen's Normative Paradigm of German-Jewish Symbiosis," in D. Bronsen, ed., *Jews and Germans from 1860 to 1933: The Problematic Symbiosis* (1979), 129–72, has shown Cohen's two essays on "Deutschtum und Judentum" to be a subtle form of social criticism, calling upon Germany to repudiate antisemitism and affirm its humanistic traditions. The most thorough and nuanced exposition of Cohen's Jewish writings remains Franz Rosenzweig's introduction to the three-volume collection of Hermann Cohen, *Jüdische Schriften*, ed. B. Strauss (1924), 1:xiii–lxiv. A comprehensive bibliography of secondary literature on Cohen and a convenient listing of his writings appear in Helmut Holzhey, *Cohen und Natorp* (1986), 1:353–407.

Martin Buber's evolving role in the shaping of a new Jewish self-understanding is examined in detail, and with perspicacious attention to the zeitgeist, by Hans Kohn, *Martin Buber. Sein Werk and Seine Zeit, Ein Beitrag zur Geistesgeschichte Mitteleuropas 1880–1930*, 2d ed. (1961), 59–210. For a respectful but critical assessment of Buber's early conception of Jewish religiosity, see Gershom Scholem, "Martin Bubers Auffassung des Judentums," in Scholem, *Judaica* 2(1970):133–92.

The varied issues of the *Kunstwart* debate are reviewed in an autobiographical essay by the principal protagonist, Moritz Goldstein, "German Jewry's Dilemma: The Story of a Provocative Essay," LBIYB 2(1957):236–54, and in his *Berliner Jahre. Erinnerungen 1880–1933* (1977).

12. The First World War

The two major works on the situation of Jews in Germany between 1914 and 1918 are W. E. Mosse, ed., with the assistance of A. Paucker, *Deutsches Judentum in Krieg und Revolution, 1916–1923* (1971), with detailed chapters on, inter alia, changes in Jewish identity, Jewish political participation, and the development of antisemitism; and Egmont Zechlin, *Die deutsche Politik und die Juden im Ersten Weltkrieg* (1969). Important studies of individual topics include Steven E. Aschheim, "Eastern Jews, German Jews, and Germany's Ostpolitik in the First World War," LBIYB 28(1983):351–65; two essays by Werner T. Angress, "The German Army's 'Judenzählung' of 1916: Genesis—Consequences—Significance," LBIYB 23(1978):117–37 and "Dokumentation. Das deutsche Militär und die Juden im Ersten Weltkrieg," MM (1976), vol. 19; David Engel, "Patriotism as a Shield: The Liberal Jewish Defense Against Antisemitism in Germany During the First World War," LBIYB 31(1986):147–71; Jürgen Matthäus, "Deutschtum and Judentum Under Fire: The Impact of the First World War on the Strategies of the Centralverein and the Zionistische Vereinigung," LBIYB 33(1988):129–47; and Rivka Horwitz, "Voices of Opposition to the First World War Among Jewish Thinkers," LBIYB 33(1988):233–59. Surprisingly little has been published in either English or German on the situation of Jews in the Habsburg Monarchy during the First World War. There is, however, the excellent doctoral dissertation by David Rechter, "Neither East nor West: Viennese Jewish Politics in World War I" (Hebrew University, Jerusalem, 1995).

Chronology

1867   Austrian constitution guarantees equal rights for all
         religious groups
1869   Jewish synod held in Leipzig and establishment of the German-
         Jewish Communities Alliance (DIGB)
1869   Reichstag of the North German Confederation makes rights and
         duties independent of religious affiliation
1871   Constitution of the German Reich marks conclusion of the eman-
         cipation process
1871   August Rohling's antisemitic pamphlet *Der Talmudjude*
1872   The Liberal Seminary, Hochschule für die Wissenschaft des
         Judentums, opens in Berlin
1873   The Orthodox Seminary, Orthodoxes Rabbinerseminar, is estab-
         lished in Berlin
1876   The Prussian Parliament passes the Secession Law
1876   Karl Emil Franzos's book *Aus Halb-Asien* (From Semi-Asia)
1878   Bismarck's banker, Gerson von Bleichröder, intervenes at the Berlin
         Congress on behalf of the Romanian Jews
1879   Wilhelm Marr's antisemitic *Der Sieg des Judenthums über das
         Germanenthum* (The Victory of Jewry Over Germandom)
1879   The Berlin Antisemitism Controversy
1882   First international "Anti-Jewish Congress" in Chemnitz
1882   The Zionist student fraternity Kadima is founded in Vienna
1886   The Österreichisch-Israelitische Union is established
1891   The defense organization Verein zur Abwehr des Antisemitismus
1892   Ritual murder trial in Xanten

1892	The Tivoli Program of the Conservative Party contains an antisemitic clause
1893	In elections to the Reichstag the antisemitic parties win sixteen seats
1893	Establishment of the Centralverein deutscher Staatsbürger jüdischen Glaubens (Central Association of German Citizens of the Jewish Faith)
1893	A modern rabbinical seminary, the Israelitisch-Theologische Lehranstalt, is established in Vienna
1896	Establishment of a non-Zionist association of Jewish fraternities, the Kartell-Convent deutscher Studenten jüdischen Glaubens
1896	Theodor Herzl's *Judenstaat* (The Jewish State)
1897	First Zionist Congress held in Basel
1897	Establishment of a German Zionist association, the Zionistische Vereinigung für Deutschland
1897	The antisemite Karl Lueger sworn in as mayor of Vienna
1897	Walther Rathenau's essay "Höre Israel" (Hear O Israel)
1899	Houston Stewart Chamberlain's antisemitic work *The Foundations of the Nineteenth Century*
1899	Karl Kraus establishes his literary periodical *Die Fackel*
1900	Sigmund Freud's *The Interpretation of Dreams*
1901	Hilfsverein der deutschen Juden established to aid East European and Asian Jews
1901	The periodical *Ost und West*
1902	The Gesellschaft zur Förderung der Wissenschaft des Judentums established to reinvigorate Jewish scholarship
1904	The Office of Jewish Statistics
1904	The Verband der deutschen Juden established to represent Jewish interests
1904	Bertha Pappenheim founds the Jüdischer Frauenbund (The League of Jewish Women)
1905	The Gesamtarchiv der deutschen Juden founded to collect the documents of German-Jewish communities
1905	Leo Baeck's *The Essence of Judaism*
1906	Martin Buber's *Tales of Rabbi Nachman*
1906	Georg Hermann's novel *Jettchen Gebert*
1908	Arthur Schnitzler's novel *Der Weg ins Freie* (The Road Into the Open)
1912	The Liberal Vereinigung für das liberale Judentum passes a set of religious guidelines
1912	The Jewish youth organization Jüdischer Wanderbund Blau-Weiss
1913	Else Lasker-Schüler's volume of poetry *Hebräische Balladen* (Hebrew Ballads)

1914	Establishment of a Zionist association of Jewish fraternities, the Kartell jüdischer Verbindungen
1914	Komitee für den Osten (Committee for the East) established to assist East European Jews
1915	Hermann Cohen's first essay on the subject "Deutschtum und Judentum"
1916	A census is taken of Jewish participation in the army
1916	Martin Buber founds the periodical *Der Jude*
1917	Establishment of a centralized Jewish welfare organization, the Zentralwohlfahrtsstelle der deutschen Juden
1918	German borders closed to East European Jewish immigrants
1919	Posthumous publication of Hermann Cohen's *Religion of Reason from the Sources of Judaism*

Sources of Illustrations

Berlin, AEG-Archiv 6
Berlin, Bildarchiv Preussischer Kulturbesitz 3, 12, 16, 22
Berlin, Ullstein Bilderdienst 45
Cincinnati, Hebrew Union College (photos: Druce Reilly and Denny Landwehr) 25, 26, 30, 32, 34, 44
Duisburg, Gidal-Bildarchiv im Steinheim-Institut 9, 27, 37, 38
Essen, Stadtarchiv 17
Frankfurt am Main, Jüdisches Museum 29, 35, 46, 47, 48, 49, 50
Frankfurt am Main, Stadtarchiv 24
Hamburg, Institut für die Geschichte der deutschen Juden 11, 21
Jerusalem, Israel Museum 33
Los Angeles, Hebrew Union College Skirball Museum 18
Marburg, Bildarchiv Foto 5
New York, Leo Baeck Institute (photos: Jim Strong) 1, 7, 8, 10, 13, 14, 15, 20, 31, 41, 42, 43
Tel Aviv, Beth Hatefutsoth 23
Vienna, Österreichische Nationalbibliothek 2, 19, 28, 36, 39, 40
Windecken, Bildarchiv Monica Kingreen 4

Maps by John Hollingsworth, Indiana University

Index

Aachen, 61

Abrahamson, Otto, *see* Brahm, Otto

Abwehr-Verein, 144, 254–56, 257, 258, 382; in Austria, 259, 270

Academic antisemitism, 15, 16, 56, 57, 60, 157–58, 159, 177, 239–40, 245, 253, 310, 327–28

Actors, immigrants as, 42

Adler, Alfred, 312

Adler, Friedrich, 277, 377

Adler, Max, 312

Adler, Siegmund, 187

Adler, Victor, 187, 271, 276, 280, 377

Administrators, Jews as, 60

Adult education, 101

ADV, *see* Pan-German League

Advertising, entrepreneurs using, 44

AEG, SEE General Electrical Works

Agrarian League (Bund der Landwirte, BdL), 139–40, 166, 224, 235, 244–45, 256, 272

Agricultural communes, antisemitism in, 242

Agriculture, Jews involved in, 2, 36, 37, 38, 39, 40–44, 46–47, 48, 143

Agudat Israel, 120, 296

Ahad Ha'Am, 348–49

Ahlem, 143

Ahlwardt, Hermann, 222–23, 224, 225, 235, 252

Aid Society of German Jews, *see* Hilfsverein der deutschen Juden

AIU, SEE Alliance Israélite Universelle

Alcohol industry, Jews involved in, 48, 53

Alexander, Kurt, 380

Allgemeine Elektrizitätsgesellschaft (AEG), *see* General Electrical Works

Allgemeiner Deutscher Frauenverein (General German Women's Association), 85, 101

Allgemeiner Deutscher Schulverein (General German Schools Association), 249

Allgemeiner Rabbinerverband (General Association of Rabbis), 116

Allgemeine Zeitung des Judentums

(AZJ), 130, 163, 177, 181, 182, 209,
252, 256, 264, 266, 274; anti-
semitism and, 202, 216–18;
Centralverein deutscher
Staatsbürger jüdischen Glaubens
and, 257
Alliance Israélite Universelle (AIU),
131, 150, 151, 295
Alsace-Lorraine, 24; immigration
and, 13, 27, 28; nationalism in,
166–67
Alsergrund, 33
Altenberg, Peter, 289, 312
Anti-Chancellor League (Anti-
Kanzler-Liga), 201, 208
Anti-Jewish Congresses, 209, 215, 216
Antique stores, Jews involved in, 48
Antisemiten-Liga (Antisemites'
League), 196–97
Antisemiten-Spiegel, 254
Antisemitic Petition, 207
Antisemitische Correspondenz, 209
Antisemitism, 4, 196–251, 385; acade-
mic, 15, 16, 56, 57, 60, 157–58, 159,
177, 239–40, 245, 253, 310, 327–28;
agricultural trade and, 47; in
Alsace-Lorraine, 166–67; in
Austria, 160, 198, 199, 204, 209–13,
215–16, 218–19, 221, 222, 225–31,
236–37, 245, 247–48, 249–50, 361;
baptisms and, 15; blurring of categories of, 220–21; Catholicism
and, 200–1, 209–10, 220, 221, 222,
227, 236–37; class structure and, 7;
cultural, 76, 238–41, 281, 310, 313,
315, 320, 334, 388; dowry and, 84;
East European Jews and, 19; economic, 199, 200, 201, 208, 220, 225,
230; education and, 55, 73, 75–76;
1848 revolutions and, 196, 197–98;
1860s and 1870s and, 198–204;
family and, 83; German youth

movement and, 148; Habsburg
Monarchy and, 209–16, 220,
225–31; in Hungary, 210, 214–15,
227, 231; as ideology, 237–42;
Jewish journalists and, 58; Jewish
pacifism and, 183; Jewish press
and, 58, 200, 204; Jewish white
slave trade and, 97; Jüdischer
Frauenbund and, 98; kosher hotel
establishment and, 45; lawyers
defending Jews against, 59; legal
equality and, 197, 198, 202–3, 205,
206–7, 208, 215, 216, 224, 225, 252;
middle class and, 66–67; mixed
marriages and, 15; as movement,
204–9; nationalistic, 187, 208,
211–12, 219, 220, 238–41, 245; organizations and, 138, 139–40, 141,
143–44, 148, 252–53; Poles and,
165–66; political, 198, 201, 203, 204,
209, 215, 221–25, 234–37, 290; in
public life, 177–79, 180–81; race
and, 196–97, 203–4, 211, 212,
220–21, 227, 238, 241, 242–51; religious, 202–3, 220; self-employment and, 38–39; shortage of academically trained professionals
and, 60; Slavs and, 231–34, 262;
Social Democratic Party and,
278–80; Socialism and, 378;
Stoecker and, 193; upper class
and, 65, 66; in Vienna, 16–17,
210–13, 226–31, 247–48, 262, 265,
292, 313; withdrawal from community and, 16; women's movement and, 102; women teachers
facing, 88–89; World War I and,
360–61, 366, 370, 371–75, 378–84;
youth organizations and, 146; *see
also* Zionism
Antisemitism, response to, 252–80;
achievements and frustrations

of, 263–66; capitalism and socialism and, 271–80; counterattack, 252–63; initial, 206–7, 216–20; politics and, 267–71; *see also* Identity

Antitalmudic writings, 202, 218, 253, 286

Anti-Verein, 259

Anti-Zionist Committee, 300, 302

Arbeiter-Zeitung, 277, 378

Argentina, agricultural colonies in, 151

Arnhold, Eduard, 45, 49

Arnswalde-Friedeberg, 222

Aronsohn, Louis, 268

Art dealers, Jews as, 48

Artisan Congresses (Gewerbekongresse), 212

Artisan movement, in Vienna, 210, 212–13, 225, 226

Artisans, Jews as, 243, 244

Arts/artists, *see* Visual arts

"Aryan paragraphs," 143

Assimilation, 4, 303

Association for International Conciliation, 274

Association for Trade Treaties of 1900, 273

Association of Berlin Specialist Shops, 273

Association of German Chemists, 51

Association of German Department Stores, 273

Association of German Engineers, 51

Association of German Jews, *see* Verband der deutschen Juden

Association of German Jews in the Reich, *see* Reichsverein der deutschen Juden

Association of German Students (VDST), *see* Verein Deutscher Studenten

Association of Ladies' and Girls' Coat Manufacturers, 273

Association of Lower Austrian Farmers, 228

Association of Orthodox Rabbis, *see* Verband orthodoxer Rabbiner

Association of Traditionally Observant Rabbis, *see* Verband traditionell-gesetzestreuer Rabbiner

Athletic associations, 143–44, 145

Auerbach, Berthold, 216, 264, 309

Auersperg, Prince Adolf, 175, 184, 186

Auf Vorposten, 378

Austerlitz, Friedrich, 277, 378

Austria: antisemitism in, 160, 198, 199, 204, 209–13, 215–16, 218–19, 221, 222, 225–31, 236–37, 245, 247–48, 249–50, 361, 383–84; baptisms in, 16–17; class structure in, 65; Deutschnationaler Handlungsgehilfen-Verband and, 244; education in, 55, 57; finance policy in, 189; healthcare facilities in, 133; immigration and, 9, 10, 17, 22, 28–29, 42, 52–53, 379, 380; internal migration in, 28–29; Jewish participation in culture of, 307, 311–13, 314; Jewish population in, 9–10; Jewish press in, 131, 192; Jews as judges in, 156; legal equality in, 2, 153; legal system of, 175, 176, 189; Liberalism in, 183–88, 210, 214, 216, 218, 221, 225, 229, 230, 236, 263, 270–71; Liberal Judaism in, 129; middle class in, 9, 160; mixed marriages in, 14, 17; Nazi parties in, 211, 232, 237; nobility to professing Jews in, 193; occupations in, 42–43, 52–54, 162; organizations in, 140, 151; public life in, 156, 160–61, 194–95; religious life

in, 3; response to antisemitism in, 259, 261–63; Social Democratic Party in, 274, 276–78, 279, 280; Socialism in, 271; social welfare in, 52; university positions in, 157; World War I and, 42, 361, 363–65, 366, 368, 377, 379, 380, 383–84; youth organizations in, 146, 147; Zionism and, 142, 299; see also Galicia; Prague; Vienna
Austria-Hungary, Jews as politicians in, 174, 175–76; see also Austria; Habsburg Monarchy
Austrian-Hungarian Compromise, 227
Austrian-Jewish Union, see Österreichisch-Israelitische Union
Avenarius, Ferdinand, 359
AZJ, see ALLGEMEINE ZEITUNG DES JUDENTUMS

Bab, Julius, 58
Bacher, Eduard, 191
Baden, 24; community life in, 126; education in, 58, 134; immigration to, 27; Jewish population in, 28; Jewish press in, 131; Jews as judges in, 155; legal equality in, 1; occupations in, 51; public life in, 159, 180, 268; religious practice in, 104, 118
Badeni government, 228; language decrees, 230, 232, 262
Badische Anilin- und Sodafabriken, 51
Baeck, Leo, Rabbi, 4, 105, 341–44, 342, 347, 348, 367, 387
Baeyer, Adolf von, 308
Bahr, Hermann, 250
Bakers, Jews as, 36, 44
Balfour Declaration, 370
Ballin, Albert, 19, 45–46, 66, 266, 273, 274, 366, 368, 375, 376

Bamberg, Hermann, 273
Bamberger, Fritz, 343
Bamberger, Ludwig, 163, 176, 177, 178, 179, 181, 182, 183, 188–89, 193, 194, 195, 201, 206, 256, 267, 268
Bamberger, Seligmann Baer, Rabbi, 115
Bamberger family, 138
Bambus, Willy, 291
Bánffy, Baron, 227
Bank(s): central, 180, 189; corporate, 50, 54
Bankers, Jews as, 43, 44, 46, 50, 51, 52, 65; nationalism and, 163–64; in public life, 154, 180, 182–83, 188–89, 190–91, 192–93
Baptisms, 15–17; among university graduates, 56–57; for attending universities, 15; culture and, 312, 334; for ennoblement, 193; gender differences in, 80, 84; for judgeships, 59, 159; for mixed marriages, 14; for occupations, 15, 17, 56–57, 59, 157–58, 159; for political participation, 175, 176, 256, 270; for university positions, 16, 57, 157–58, 159, 310, 327–28; upper class and, 65; in Vienna, 52
Bardewisch, 72
Barissia (dueling fraternity), 147
Bar Kochba Jewish Student Association, 145, 147, 295, 349, 350
Barth, Theodor, 253, 254, 255
Basel: immigration to, 28; Zionist Congress in, 293
Basel Program, 302
Basic Rights of the German People, 1
Bauer, Otto, 277, 278, 279, 312, 329
Bavaria, 25; community life in, 125, 126; immigration to, 21, 27; Jewish population in, 28; Jewish schools in, 135; Jews as judges in, 155, 156;

Matrikelgesetz (Registration Law) in, 23; military service in, 159; Orthodox secession and, 115; public life in, 194; religious practice in, 104

Baxa, Karel, 233

Bayreuth, 246, 248

BdL, SEE Agrarian League

Beauticians, women as, 91

Bebel, August, 203, 276, 280

Beer-Hofmann, Richard, 311–12, 314–15

Beggars (*Schnorrer*), 131–34

Behrend, Friedrich Jakob, 161, 208

Behrend, Jakob Friedrich, 156, 208

Beilis trial, 166

Bendiener, Ludwig, 169

Benedikt, Moritz, 160, 191

Benjamin, Walter, 336

Bergmann, Hugo, 147, 313, 350

Berlin, 386; antisemitism in, 196, 204, 206, 208, 215; athletic association in, 145; baptisms in, 17; Chamber of Commerce in, 272, 273; charitable organizations in, 134; class structure in, 63–64, 65; Congress of, 193; as cultural center, 313–14; education in, 55, 56, 58, 74–75, 86, 88; elections in, 129–30; expulsions from, 20; garment industry in, 36; Greater, 33; gymnastic society in, 144; hospital in, 59, 132–33; Hotel Cassel in, *107*; immigration and, 13, 19–20, 21, 22, 26, 27, 28, 31, 41, 42, 127; Jewish population in, 29, 30, 31–32, *32*; Jewish press in, 73, 131, 191–92, 309, 374–75; mixed marriages in, 15; naturalization in, 20; newspapers in, 191–92; occupations in, 41–42, *43*, 45, 47, 48, 49, *49*, 50, 51, 52, *53*, 58, 59–60; public life in, 194,

267, 268, 269; rabbinical seminaries in, 49, 58, 59, 112, 113, 300; Reform Congregation in, 103, 300; religious life in, 109, 119, 128; residential districts for Jews in, 32–33; University of, 56, 57, 157, 158, 344; withdrawals from Jewish community in, 16; women working in, 94; World Zionist Congress in, 142

Berliner Handelsgesellschaft, 50, 180

Berliner Illustrierte Zeitung, 192

Berliner Morgenpost, 192

Berliner Morgenzeitung, 191–92

Berliner Tageblatt, 73, 191, 309, 374–75

Berliner Volkszeitung, 191

Berlin Merchant Corporation (Kaufmannschaft), 165, 272

Berlin Secession, 324

Bernays, Isaac, Rabbi, granddaughter of, 82

Bernhard, Georg, 375

Bernstein, Eduard, 177, 203, 274, 277, 278, 279, 329, 376, 377

Bernstorff, Count, 367

Bethmann-Hollweg, Theobald von, Chancellor, 249, 370–71, 373, 375, 379

Beuthen, 268

Bildung, 307; *see also* Culture

Billroth, Theodor, 211

Biochemistry, Jews involved in, 327

Birnbaum, Nathan, 147, 173, 174, 291, 296, 368

Birth control, 10

Birthrate: decline in, 10; immigrants and, 22

Bismarck, Otto von, 50, 164, 165, 175, 176, 177, *179*, 180, 182, 183, 189, 201, 202, 204, 207–8, 211, 217, 221, 223, 224, 322

"Black International," 236–37
Blau-Weiss, *see* Jüdischer
    Wanderbund Blau-Weiss
Bleichröder, Gerson, 50, 183, 192–93,
    201, 208, 222, 264, 273
Bleichröder family, 50
Bloch, Joseph, Rabbi, 131, 184, 218–19,
    227, 259, 260, 261, 277, 299, 365, 378
Blumenfeld, Kurt, 296, 369
B'nai B'rith, 97, 133, 140, 141–42, 150,
    268, 328, 368
Boarding schools, antisemitism and,
    240
Böckel, Otto, 47, 209, 215, 222, 225,
    235, 240, 248
Bodenheimer, Max, 291, 296, 368, 380
Bohemia, 3, 386; agriculture in, 2;
    antisemitism in, 210, 231–34, 236,
    237, 262; East European Jews in,
    379; education in, 55, 170; emigra-
    tion from, 9, 18, 22, 29, 31; German
    and Czech languages for official
    business in, 230, 232; healthcare
    facilities in, 133; Jewish popula-
    tion in, 9; nationalism in, 168, 171;
    occupations in, 52, 53; Realist
    Party and, 361; religious life in,
    104, 109; World War I and, 365;
    Zionism and, 142, 143; *see also*
    Prague
Bondy, Serafin, 187
Bonifatius-Verein, 202
Bookkeepers, women as, 90
Book shops, Jews involved in, 48, 49
Borchardt, Georg Hermann, *see*
    Hermann, Georg
Born, Max, 329
Born, Stephan, 177
Börne, Ludwig, 309
Bötticher, Paul, *see* Lagarde, Paul de
Brahm, Otto, 322, 329
Braun, Heinrich, 276, 278

Bremen, 18, 19
Brentano, Lujo, 374
Breslau: expulsions from, 21; hospi-
    tal in, 59; immigrants in, 21;
    income and taxation in, 62;
    Jewish population in, 30; occupa-
    tions in, 48, 272; public life in, 194;
    rabbinical seminary in, 56, 58,
    111–12, 113; University of, 56, 57,
    89, 146–47, 253
Breslauer, Bernhard, 140
Bresslau, Harry, 206
Breuer, Isaac, 121, 336, 364
Breuer, Joseph, 95
Breuer, Solomon, 112
Breznovsky, Václav, 232
Brigittenau, 33
Brod, Max, 147, 313, 350
Brody (Eastern Galicia), 172, 185
Bruckner, Anton, 322
Brünn, 29, 279; Technical University
    of, 171
Brunner, Sebastian, 199
Brunswick, 155
Buber, Martin, 4, 131, 147, 295, 298,
    314, 337, 338, 343, 348–53, 357, 364,
    368, 383–84, 387
Buber, Solomon, 348
Budapest, 160; Landesrabbinerschule
    in, 112–13
Büdinger, Max, 157
Bukovina: immigration and, 22, 29,
    31; Jewish population in, 9, 10;
    nationalism in, 173–74; occupa-
    tions in, 42; Zionism and, 142
Bülow, Chancellor, 270, 273, 275, 375
Bund der Landwirte, *see* Agrarian
    League
Bundesrat, legal unity and, 190
Burckhardt, Jakob, 238
Bureau for Jewish Statistics, 122–23
Bürgerliches Gesetzbuch, 189–90

Burial societies, 132

Burschenschaften, 207, 211, 239, 249

Busch, Moritz, 208

Business, Jews in, 271–73; *see also* Commerce and trade; Entrepreueurs; Occupations; Trade and industry

Butchers, Jews as, 36, 41, 44, 50

Buttenhausen, 24

B.Z. am Mittag, 192

Cantors, 42, 58

Capitalism, Jews and, 271–73

Caprivi, Count Leo, 224, 243

Caro, Heinrich, 51

Carvallo-Schülein, Suzanne, *317*

Cas, 365

Cassel, Oskar, 269

Cassirer, Eduard, 274

Cassirer, Ernst, 329

Cassirer, Paul, 325

Catholicism: antisemitism and, 200–201, 209–10, 220, 221, 222, 227, 236–37; Austria and, 184; Kulturkampf and, 181–82, 201–2; organizations and, 140; Schönerer and, 230; in Vienna, 212, 213, 214; women's movement and, 98; *see also* Center (Zentrum) Party

Cattle trading, Jews involved in, 25, 40, 44, 46, 47, 48

Center (Zentrum) Party, 140, 177, 180, 182, 200, 202; Abwehr-Verein and, 255; antisemitism and, 225, 235, 243, 268; Jews and, 269, 360; World War I and, 370, 372, 373

Central Association of German Citizens of the Jewish Faith, *see* Centralverein deutscher Staatsbürger jüdischen Glaubens

Central Association of German Industrialists, 272

Centralverein deutscher Staatsbürger jüdischen Glaubens (Central Association of German Citizens of the Jewish Faith, cv), 4, 99, 102, 130, 140, 141, 143, 146, 150, 163, 167, 235, 262, 263, 264, 267, 360, 382, 388; antisemtism and, 256–58; immigration and, 380; Jewish identity and, 282–87, 302, 303; Jewish lawyers creating, 58–59; public life and, 268; World War I and, 360, 361, 368, 373; Zionism and, 300–4

Central Welfare Office of German Jewry, 134, *see* Zentralwohlfahrtsstelle der deutschen Juden

Chamberlain, Houston Stewart, 246–47, 248–49, 266, 289, 375

Charitable activity, 125, 131–34; *see also* Organizations

Charles I, Emperor, 233

Charles University, 169, 170

Charlottenburg, 33

Chemical industry, Jews involved in, 51–52, 53

Chemistry, Jews involved in study of, 308, 309, 327

Children: convalescent homes for, 95, 97, 100, 133; in family, 69, *70,* 72, 76, 77, *77,* 106; illegitimate, 11, 95, 97, 98, 99, 100; number of in family, 10, 385; orphanages for, 95–96, 132

Cholera, in Hamburg, 19

Christianity: "essence of Judaism" debate and, 338–47; Jewish doctors and, 57; Jewish lawyers and, 58; occupations and, 38; privileged status and, 1; relationship with Jews and, 83, 101; women's movement and, 98; *see also* Baptisms;

Catholicism; Mixed marriages;
Protestantism
Christian Social Party, 224; antisemitism and, 226, 227–28, 229,
231, 237, 250; in Austria, 214, 228,
237; in Czech lands, 232
Christian Social Workers' Party, 204,
237
Christmas, family observance of, 69,
80, 82–83
Cisleithania, 2, 3, 4
Cities, 2, 11, 386; birthrate and, 10;
challenges of, 127–30; doctors and
lawyers in, 59; elections in,
128–30; immigration to, 21, 25–34,
30, 32, 33, 34, 42, 127; Jewish population in, 3, 7, 24, 127; Jewish
schools in, 135; lower class in,
63–64; middle class in, 7, 10, 15, 24,
32, 34, 61–64; mixed marriages
and, 15; religious life in, 103,
107–8, 109, 127–28, *128;* social welfare institutions in, 64
Citizenship, *see* Naturalization
Civic participation, *see* Public life
Civic truce *(Burgfrieden),* 361–66,
370–78, 388
Civil marriage, 14
Civil service: Jews involved in, 37, 38,
43, 58, 60; *see also* Judges;
Professors; Teachers
Class, Heinrich, 248
Class structure, 2–3, 386; family and,
76–77; immigrants and, 41; mobility and, 7, 23–24; poverty, 62;
social welfare institutions and,
64; *see also* Lower class; Middle
class; Poor; Upper class
Clerical personnel, Jews as, 39, 60
Clothing industry, *see* Garment
industry
Coachmen, Jews as, 45

Coal industry, Jews involved in, 45,
48, 49, 51, 53
Cohen, Hermann, 158, 206, 274, 310,
329, 336–37, 344–47, 353–58, *354,*
367, 387
Cohen-Reuss, Max, 378
Cohn, Emil, Rabbi, 300, 301
Cohn, Hermann, 275
Colmar, 167
Cologne, 291; class structure in, 66;
elections in, 129; hospital in, 59;
immigration and, 21, 29; Jewish
population in, 30; occupations in,
272; religious life in, 118–19, 126;
teacher training institute in, 138;
women working in, 94; World
Zionist Congress in, 142
Commerce and trade, Jews involved
in, 35, 36–37, 38, 39, 40, 42, 43–50,
49, 52, 53; education for careers
outside of, 54–60; *see also* Trade
and industry
"Committeee of December 1 [1880],"
139
Committee for Defense Against
Antisemitic Attacks, 256
Committee for the East, *see*
Komitee für den Osten
Communes, *see* Agricultural com-
munes
Communist Party, 377
Communities, 2, 3, 125–27, *126;* num-
ber of, 127; rabbis in, 125, 126, 127;
religious life in, 127; *see also*
Cities; Education; Jewish press;
Organizations; Social welfare
Community (conservative)
Orthodoxy, 116, 117, 121
Compromise of 1867 *(Ausgleich),* 2,
193
Concordat of 1855, 184, 201, 210
Congress of Berlin, 193

Congress Poland, antisemitism in, 233, 234
Conservative (community) Orthodoxy, 116, 117, 121
Conservative Party, 176, 177, 180, 181, 184, 198; antisemitism and, 199, 200–1, 204, 222–24, 235, 243, 252, 255, 268; nationalism and, 166
Constitutional Party (Verfassungspartei), 176, 184, 186, 187, 210, 211
Constitutional Union of Germans in Bohemia (Verfassungsverein der Deutschen in Böhmen), 185
Constitution of 1867, 210
Convalescent homes, for children, 95, 97, 100, 133
Conversions to Christianity, *see* Baptisms
Copenhagen, World Zionist Congress in, 142
Corporate banks, 50, 54
Corps, 239
Cracow, 29, 156
Credit associations, 47
Criminal law, 258, 262
Criminal statistics, class structure determined from, 65
Cultural criticism, *see* Literary criticism
Cultural Zionism, 294–96, 298–99, 313, 314, 324, 326, 328, 348–49
Culture, 4, 305–59, 387; antisemitism and, 76, 238–41, 281, 310, 313, 315, 320, 334, 388; Austrian, 307; baptisms and, 312, 334; centers of, 311–14; chronology of Jewish participation in, 308–10, 334; explanations for creativity of Jews and, 331–35; family and, 73, 74, 76–78, 307; Jewish participation in German, 305–35; Jews as patrons of, 330–31; literary criticism, 309, 312, 314, 320–22; literature, 42, 73, 307–8, 309–10, 311–12, 313, 314–20; middle-class striving for, 66; organizations and, 144, 147; philosophy, 310, 312, 313, 329; psychoanalysis, 312, 313, 328, 329; sociology, 328; visual arts, 4, 37, 42, 43, 309–10, 314, 324–26, 330; Zionism and, 324, 326, 328; *see also* Education; Jewish thought; Journalism; Music; Sciences
CV, SEE Centralverein deutscher Staatsbürger jüdischen Glaubens
Czech Klub, 184
Czechoslovakia: after World War I, 383; antisemitism and, 231–34; Nazi parties in, 211, 232, 237; Schönerer and, 230; World War I and, 365; Zionism and, 313; *see also* Bohemia; Galicia
Czech Party, 169
Czernowitz: education in, 88; immigration to, 29; nationalism in, 173; public life in, 185; university at, 56; Yiddish language conference in, 296

Danzig, 272
DAP, SEE German Workers' Party
Darmstadt, 268
Darmstädter Bank, 273
Darwin, Charles, 247
Deckert, Joseph, Father, 227, 230
Declaration of the Notables of 1880, 217, 238, 250, 255
Defense organizations, 133, 144, 284–87
Delbrück, Hans, 374
Delbrück, Rudolf von, 189
Delitzsch, Franz, 217, 253
Democrats, in Austria, 212–13, 229

Demographics, 7–34; *see also*
Baptisms; Cities; Expulsions;
Immigration; Mixed marriages;
Mobility; Population; Rural areas
Dentists, Jews as, 59
Department Store of the West
(Kaufhaus des Westens, Kadewe),
48
Department stores, Jews involved in,
44–45, 47, 48, 49, 53, 273
Dernburg, Bernhard, 270
Dernburg, Friedrich, 176
Deutschbund, 246
Deutsche Bank, 180, 189
Deutsche Israelitische Zeitung, 130
Deutsche Nationalsozialistische
Arbeiterpartei (DNSAP), 237
Deutscher, Isaac, 334
Deutscher Klub, 185, 187, 214
Deutscher Nationalverein, 164–65
Deutscher Schulverein für die Juden
des Orients, 151, 249
Deutsche Rundschau, 309
Deutsches Theater, 322
Deutsche Turnerschaft, 249–50
Deutsche Vaterlandspartei, 378
Deutsche Volkspartei, 179, 187–88,
212, 213, 218, 229
Deutsche Wacht, 253
Deutsche Wochenschrift, 187, 214
Deutsche Zeitung, 187, 214, 378
Deutsch-Freisinnige Partei, 177, 221,
255–56
Deutsch-Israelitischer
Gemeindebund (German-Jewish
Communities Alliance, DIGB), 132,
138–39, 140, 141, 150, 180, 194, 216,
217, 252–53, 257, 258, 368
"Deutsch-jüdischer Parnass"
(German-Jewish Parnassus)
(Goldstein), 358
Deutschlands Erneuerung, 378

Deutschnationaler
Handlungsgehilfen-Verband
(DHV), 242–45, 248, 251, 256
Deutschnationale Vereinigung
(German National Union), 214
Deutschösterrichischer Klub, 185, 187
Deutschradikale, 236
"Deutschtum und Judentum"
(Cohen), 356–57
Deutschtum und Judentum
(Germanness and Jewishness),
282, 284, 338, 355–59; *see also*
Identity
DHV, SEE Deutschnationaler
Handlungsgehilfen-Verband
Diederichs, Eugen, 351
Dietary laws, observance of, 69, 78,
79, 80, 81, 82, 107
DIGB, SEE Deutsch-Israelitischer
Gemeindebund
Dilthey, Wilhelm, 349
Diplomatic service, Jews in, 159
Discount stores, Jews opening, 44
Discrimination, 4; *see also*
Antisemitism
Dissimilation, 337–38; *see also*
Jewish thought
Dmowski, Roman, 166, 233
DNSAP, SEE Deutsche
Nationalsozialistische
Arbeiterpartei
Doctors, Jews as, 16, 35, 37, 40, 55, 57,
59–60, 66, 154, 162, 263, 272, 327; in
Austria, 160–61; women as, 40, 89,
92–93
Dohm, Christian Wilhelm, 217, 255
Domestic service: Christians
involved in, 38; housekeeping
schools and, 95, 97; Jewish
women involved in, 37, 38, 39, 40,
42
Donnershag (commune), 242

Dowry, marriage and, 75, 83–84

Dresden, 218; culture in, 313; immigrants in, 21; Jewish population in, 28, 30

Dresdener Bank, 50

Dreyfus, Alfred, 167

Dreyfus Affair, 167, 231, 234, 289, 292

Dual Monarchy, *see* Habsburg Monarchy

Dueling corporations, 207, 212, 283, 291

Dühring, Eugen, 203–4, 207, 212, 220, 222, 236, 240, 242

Duisburg, 61, 302

Düsseldorf: income and taxation in, 62; migration to, 29; teacher training institute in, 138

Eastern Hungary, Yiddish spoken in, 168, 172

East European Jewry (*Ostjuden*), 282, 337; antisemitism and, 19; charitable activities aiding, 99, 131–34, 152; culture and, 307; education for girls and, 90; family and, 71, 76; German Jews distinct from, 123; Hasidism and, 295, 296, 349, 351, 352; identity as Jews and, 282; immigration of, 17–23, 379–81, 386; Jewish thought and, 337; Liberal Jews and, 286; lower class and, 62, 63–65; naturalization of, 20; occupations for women and, 90–91; religious life and, 110, 128; in Social Democratic Party, 279; traditionalists and, 119; in United States, 152; women as doctors and, 89; World War I and, 368, 379–81; Zionism and, 143, 290, 291, 293, 294–96; *see also* Galicia; Poland; Romania; Russia

East Friesland, 104, 105

Eberswald, 49

Ebert, Friedrich, 276

Ebner-Eschenbach, Marie von, 259

Economic antisemitism, 199, 200, 201, 208, 220, 225, 230

Economic life, 2, 3, 13; *see also* Occupations

Edison, Thomas, 52, *53*

Education, 2, 54–60, 74–76, 182; adult, 101; antisemitism and, 55, 73, 75–76; in Austria, 55–57; boarding schools, 240; boys and, 75; elementary school, 55, 90; in Habsburg Monarchy, 170–71, 172, 173; immigrants and, 23; middle class and, 54–60, 66, 307; migration to cities for, 26; mother's role regarding, 72–73; organizations and, 151, 152; public schools, 58; religious instruction and, 136–37; in rural areas, 24–25, 26, 41, 90, 135, 240; secondary, 54, 55; of women, 4, 74–75, 76, 79, 85–91, *87*, 98, 101; *see also* Gymnasium; Kindergarten; Schools, Jewish; Teachers; Technical colleges; University(ies)

Ehrlich, Paul, 59, 161, 309, 327, 363

1848 revolutions, 165, 169, 180, 182, 184, 187; antisemitism and, 196, 197–98, 252

Einstein, Albert, 309, 327, 328, 329, 363, 364

Eisenmenger, Andreas, 202

Eisner, Kurt, 276, 376

Elderly: family and, 69, 74; homes for, 133; population decline and, 11, 12; unemployed, 39

Elections, in cities, 128–30; *see also* Voting

Electrical industry, Jews involved in, 50, 51, 52, *53*

Elementary schools, 55; girls attending, 90; Jewish, 58, 134–35

Ellenbogen, Wilhelm, 276–77

Elstätter, Moritz, 174–75

Emancipation, see Legal equality

Emigration, see Immigration

Engels, Friedrich, 203, 278

England: immigration to, 13; influence of German Judaism in, 123

Engländer, Richard, see Altenberg, Peter

Ennoblements, 193

Entrepreneurs, Jews as, 37, 38, 44, 51, 263; see also Business

"Er is doch e Jud" (He's a Jew After All) (Kraus), 289

Erwartung (Expectation) (Schoenberg), 324

Erzberger, Matthias, 372, 373

Eschelbacher, Joseph, Rabbi, 340

Essen, synagogue in, 110

"Essence of Judaism" debate, 338–47

Ethical Culture Movement, 257

Ethical monotheism, Cohen and, 347

Ettlinger, Anna, 86

Export-import trade, Jews involved in, 45, 48, 52

Expressionism, 325, 351

Expulsions, 23; from Prussia, 19–20

Fackel, Die (The Torch), 309, 364

Falk, Adalbert, 158

Falkowicz, Philip, 169

Family, 3, 4, 68–85, 387; antisemitism and, 83; birth control and, 10; children in, 69, 70, 72, 76, 77, 77, 106; culture and, 73, 74, 76–78, 307; elderly in, 69, 74; husband's role in, 69–71, 78, 79, 106; immigrants and, 22; middle-class status and, 68–78, 82–84, 85; number of children in, 10, 385; religious life in,

68, 69–70, 71, 72, 77–85, 105–7; social gatherings and, 73, 83; tradition and, 76–85; vacations and, 73, 75; wife's role in, 70, 71–74, 76–78, 77, 79–80, 81, 91, 99, 106, 307; see also Marriage

Family business, Jews involved in, 35–54, 60; women and, 74–95

Farben, I. G., conglomerate, 52

Farming, see Agriculture

Federation for Jewish Welfare Work, 134

Federation of Jewish Youth Associations in Germany, see Verband der jüdischen Jugendvereine Deutschlands

Federation of Societies for Jewish History and Literature (Verband der Vereine für jüdische Geschichte und Literatur), 144

Feder, Ernst, 58

Feiwel, Berthold, 295, 298

Fertility: decline in, 10; immigrants and, 22; of mixed marriages, 15

Finance, Jews involved in, 188–89, 190–91, 192–93, 263; see also Bankers

First World War, see World War I

Fischer, Karl, 241

Fischer, Samuel, 51

Fischer, S., Verlag, 51

Fischhof, Adolf, 183, 187–88, 194–95, 212, 213, 218

Fontane, Theodor, 307–8

Food industry, Jews involved in, 41, 42, 44, 48; see also Bakers; Butchers

Forchheimer, Otto, 169, 185

Forckenbeck, Max von, 206, 265

Foreign-born Jews, see Immigration

Förster, Bernhard, 207, 240

Fortschrittliche Volkspartei, 255, 269

Foundation School, 135
France: Dreyfus Affair and, 167, 231, 234, 289, 292; Franco-Prussian War, 183, 278; influence of German Judaism in, 123; *see also* Alsace-Lorraine
Francis Ferdinand, Archduke, 361
Francis Joseph, Emperor, 65, 201, 225, 228, 265, 361, 383
Franck, James, 329
Franconia, 24, 29, 46
Franco-Prussian War, 183, 278
Frank, Ludwig, 278, 279, 377
Frankel, Zacharias, 111
Frankenburger, Wolf, 194
Frankenthal, Käte, 89
Frankfurt am Main, 330–31; antisemitism in, 239; Basic Rights and, 1; class structure in, 66; education in, 55, 88, 112, 135, 136; healthcare facilities in, 133; illegitimate births in, 11; immigrants in, 21; income and taxation in, 62, 63; Jewish population in, 30; migration to, 29; occupations in, 48–49, 51; Orthodox secession and, 115–17; public life in, 179; religious life in, 109; synagogues in, 116; Treaty of, 167; University of, 330–31; women's movement in, 95–97
Frankfurter Handelszeitung, 191
Frankfurter Zeitung, 156, 191, 309, 375
Frankfurt Metal Company, 48–49
Fränkische Tagespost, 276
Frantz, Constantin, 199–200, 201, 238
Franzos, Karl Emil, 294–95, 309, 351
Fraternities, 145–47, 149, 207, 283, 284; dueling and, 212, 283, 291
Frederick, Prince, 265
Free Association for the Interests of Orthodox Judaism, *see* Freie Vereinigung für die Interessen des Orthodoxen Judentums
Free Conservative Party, 164, 176
Free Masonry, 141
Free Pan-German Party, 236; *see also* Deutschradikale
Free professions, Jews involved in, 37, 38, 40, 43, 56, 58–60; *see also* Doctors; Journalism; Lawyers
Freie Blatt, Das, 259
Freie Bühne (Free Stage), 322
Freie Vereinigung für die Interessen des Orthodoxen Judentums (Free Association for the Interests of Orthodox Judaism), 116, 118, 140
Freisinnige Vereinigung, 224, 255
Freisinnige Volkspartei, 255
Freistatt, Die (The Sanctuary), 296
Freud, Sigmund, 17, 33, 82, 160, 312, 313, 315, 328, 332, 364
Freund, Wilhelm Salomon, 194
"Friday Evening" (antisemitic caricature), 306
Fried, Alfred, 273, 274
Friedberg, Heinrich von, 175, 176, 190, 265
Friedberg, Robert, 270
Friedell, Egon, 312
Friedemann, Adolf, 368
Friedemann, Edmund, 256
Friedenthal, Karl Rudolf, 175–76, 181
Friedjung, Heinrich, 187, 188, 211, 214, 271
Friedländer-Fuld, Fritz von, 49, 65
Friedmann, Adolf, 296
Fritsch, Theodor, 167, 209, 218, 244, 251
Froebel, Friedrich, 73, 100–101
Fuchs, Eugen, 294, 302, 303, 373
Furriers, Jews as, 42, 45, 48, 101
Fürstenberg, Carl, 50, 65, 180, 192, 266, 273, 375

Fürth, 135
Fürth, Henriette, 96–97, 99, 102

Gailingen, 24
Galicia, 3, 386; antisemitism in, 210,
    231–32, 233–34, 262; education in,
    172; emigration from, 3, 9, 10, 18,
    22, 29, 31, 33, 42, 52–53, 64, 115, 282,
    379, 380; Hasidism and, 296;
    Jewish population in, 9, 10; Jewish
    schools for immigrants from, 136;
    nationalism in, 171, 172–73; occu-
    pations in, 42; public life in, 184,
    185, 194; religious life in, 3; tailors
    from, 36; World War I and, 365;
    Yiddish spoken in, 168, 172;
    Zionism and, 142, 297
Gans family, 331
Garment industry, Jews involved in,
    25, 36, 37, 40, 40, 42, 43, 44, 45, 47,
    48, 49–50, 51, 52–53, 273
Gartenlaube, Die, 200
Gebsattel, Konstantin von, General,
    249
Geheimer Kommerzienrat, 272
Geiger, Abraham, Rabbi, 110, 111, 112,
    300
Geiger, Ludwig, 300
Gemeinde, 152; see also
    Communities
Gender differences: in baptisms, 17;
    in mixed marriages, 14, 80, 84; in
    withdrawals from community, 16;
    see also Women
General Archives of German Jewry,
    122–23
General Association of Rabbis, see
    Allgemeiner Rabbinerverband
General Electrical Works
    (Allgemeine
    Elektrizitätsgesellschaft, AEG), 50,
    52, 53

General German Schools
    Association, see Allgemeiner
    Deutscher Schulverein
General German Women's
    Association, see Allgemeiner
    Deutscher Frauenverein
George, Stefan, 314, 319, 329
Gera, 48
German Association for the
    Interests of East European Jews,
    368
German Casino, 169, 185
German Committee for the
    Liberation of Russian Jews, 368
German General Association of
    Artisans, 244
Germania, 200, 202
Germania Judaica, 122
Germanization, see Nationalism
German-Jewish Communities
    Alliance, see Deutsch-
    Israelitischer Gemeindebund
German Merchants' Club, 169
German Nationalism, see
    Nationalism
German National Party: anti-
    semitism and, 226; in Austria,
    214, 229
German National Union, see
    Deutsch-nationale Vereinigung
German Oriental Society, 330
German Peace Society, 273–74
German Workers' Party (DAP),
    236–37, 251
German youth movement, see
    Youth movement, German
Gerngross firm, 53
Gerson's, Hermann, Fashion House,
    49, 50
Ginsberg, Asher, see Ahad Ha'Am
Glagau, Otto, 200
Glasenapp, Conrad Friedrich, 248

Glaser, Julius (Joshua), 156, 175, 176, 189
Glückel of Hameln, 100
Gneist, Rudolf von, 206, 255
Gobineau, Count Arthur de, 246
Gobineau-Vereinigung, 246
Goethe, 307
Goitein, Rahel, *see* Straus
Goldberger, Ludwig Max, 180
Golden international, antisemitism and, 199
Goldmann, Felix, 373
Goldmann, Max, *see* Reinhardt, Max
Goldmark, Karl, 309
Goldschmidt, Abraham, Rabbi, 101
Goldschmidt, Henriette, 101
Goldschmidt, Levin, 156, 158, 176, 180, 181, 182, 189, 190, 194
Goldschmidt, Moritz Ritter von, 183
Goldschmidt, Robert, 180
Goldstein, Moritz, 358–59
Goldziher, Ignaz, 328
Gothein, George, 255
Göttingen: culture in, 313; University of, 158
Gradnauer, Georg, 377–78
Graetz, Heinrich, 4, 122, 206
Granville, Lord, 183
Gronemann, Sammy, 26
Grossmann, Stefan, 364
Gründer, 202
Gründerzeit, antisemitism and, 198–99
Grünfeld, Falk Valentin, 180
Grünfeld, Heinrich, 273
Grünfeld, Josef, 261
Grünfeld linen firm, 47
Güdemann, Moritz, Rabbi, 271, 293
Guidelines Toward a Program for Liberal Judaism, 119–20
Guido von List Society, 248, 251

Gundolf, Friedrich, 319
Gustav-Adolf-Verein, 249
Gutmann, Wilhelm, 53–54
Guttmacher, Elijah, Rabbi, 111
Gymnasium (high school), 54, 55, 75; women in, 86–88
Gymnastic societies, 143–44, *145*; antisemitism and, 249–50

Haas, Ludwig, 274, 368
Haase, Hugo, 274, 276, 278, 279, 364, 376, 377
Haber, Fritz, 309, 327, 363
Habsburg Monarchy, 55; antisemitism and, 209–16, 220, 225–31; cities in, 386; Compromise (*Ausgleich*) of 1867 and, 2, 193; economic life in, 2; education of women in, 87; Galician Jews in, 9; immigration and, 8, 17–18, 22, 29, 42; Jewish population in, 9; Jews' loyalty to, 265–66; legal equality in, 2; Liberalism in, 183–88; nationality in, 160–61, 162, 168–74; public life in, 160–61, 162, 168–74; university positions in, 158; *see also* Austria
Haeckel, Ernst, 247
Hahn, Diederich, 243
Haifa, technical school in, 152, 302, 369
Hainisch, Michael, 271
Hajn brothers, 232
Halberstadt, 49, 104
Halle, 207
Hallgarten, Charles, 254
Hamburg, *74*; cholera in, 19; class structure in, 66; culture in, 313; education in, 55, *87*, 135, *136*; hospital in, 59; immigration and, 18, 19, 21, 127; income and taxation in, 62, 63; Jewish population in, 28,

30; Jews as judges in, 155; legal
equality in, 1; mixed marriages
in, 14, 15; occupations for women
in, 91, 94; occupations in, 41–42,
47, 91, 272; as port, 19, 45–56, 266;
public life in, 159, 194; religious
life in, 107–8; residential districts
for Jews in, 32; women's move-
ment in, 95, 97
Hamburg-America Line (HAPAG), 19,
45–46, 266
Hammer, Der, 251
Hammer-Gemeinden, 251
Hammer publishing house, 218
Hammerstein, Wilhelm Freiherr
von, 222
Handbuch der Judenfrage (Manual
on the Jewish Question), 209
Handbuch des Handelsrechts
(Manual of Commercial Law), 190
Handicrafts, Jews involved in, 143
Hanover, teacher training institutes
in, 137
Hanover, Rabbi, *367*
Hansa-Bund, 244, 273
Hanslick, Eduard, 191
Hantke, Arthur, 296–97, 361
Harden, Maximilian, 58, 266, 309,
321–22, 375
Harnack, Adolf von, 338–39, 340,
341–42, 343
Harvestehude, 32
Hasidism, 295, 296, 349, 351, 352
Hasse, Ernst, 248, 250
Hassgesang gegen England (Song of
Hate Against England)
(Lissauer), 363
Haubinda (school), 240, 242
Hauptmann, Gerhart, 307, 322, 329
Healthcare facilities, 134; convales-
cent homes, 95, 97, 100, 133; hospi-
tals, 59, 132–33

Hebrew Union College, 124
Hebrew University, 350
Heidelberg, 313
Heilberg, Adolf, 274
Heim, Georg, 156
Heine, Heinrich, 307, 309, 310
Heisenberg, Werner, 329
Helphand, Alexander Israel, 277
Henrici, Ernst, 215
Herben, Jan, 365
Hermann, Georg, 320, 377
Hertling, Count, 381
Hertz, Heinrich, 308–9
Hertzka, Theodor, 187–88, 191, 218,
242
Herz, Wilhelm, 165, 272, 273
Herzfeld, Joseph, 376
Herzl, Theodor, 82–83, 142, 174, 188,
191, 231, 242, 259, 287–88, 291–93,
292, 296, 348, 368
Herzl, Theodor, Society, 147
Hess, Moses, 177, 290
Hesse, 24, 25, 29; community life in,
126; immigration to, 27; Jewish
population in, 12, 28; Jews as
judges in, 155, 156; occupations in,
46; Orthodox secession and, 115;
public life in, 268; religious life
in, 104
Hesse-Darmstadt, 180
Hesse-Nassau, 24; immigration to,
27, 28; Jewish schools in, 135
Hevrahs, 132; *see also* Charitable
activity
Hibat Tsiyon (Love of Zion), 291, 293
Higher education, *see* High schools;
University(ies)
High schools: Gymnasium, 54, 55, 75,
86–88; Jewish, 135–36
Hikers, *see* Wandervögel
Hildesheimer, Esriel, Rabbi, 112, *113*,
291; seminary of, 49

Hildesheimer, Hirsch, 257
Hildesheimer family, 130, 139
Hilferding, Rudolf, 278
Hilfsverein der deutschen Juden
    (Aid Society of German Jews), *18*,
    49, 151–52, 268, 301, 302, 330
Hilsner, Leopold, 233, 234
Hindenburg, 373
Hinrichsen, Marcus Wolf, 194
Hirsch, Aron, Company
    (Halberstadt), 49
Hirsch, Baron, Foundation, 151
Hirsch, Julius, 366
Hirsch, Maurice de, Baron, 151
Hirsch, Max, 194, 274
Hirsch, Rahel, 89, *90*
Hirsch, Samson Raphael, Rabbi, 89,
    111, 112, 114, 115–16, 120–21, 136, 257
Hirsch-Duncker trade unions, 194
Hirsch family, 49
Hirschfeld Brothers, 47
Hirsch-Realschule, 135, 136
Historiography, Jews involved in,
    328–29
*Historisch-Politische Blätter für das
    Katholische Deutschland*, 201
Hitler, Adolf, 229, 248; *see also*
    National Socialism
Hochschule für die Wissenschaft des
    Judentums, 112, 113, 341
Hoffmann, David, 112
Hofmannsthal, Hugo von, 312, 314–15
Hohenlohe-Schillingfürst, Prince
    Chlodwig von, 224
Hohensalza, 268
Holidays, family observance of, 69,
    71, 80, 83, 105, 107
Holubek, Franz, 218
Holy See, antisemitism and, 227
Horovitz, Marcus, Rabbi, 116, 121
Hospitals, 59, 132–33
Hotels, Jews involved in, 45, *107*

Housekeeping schools, 95, 97; *see
    also* Domestic service
Hruza, Jan, 233
Hruzová, Anezka, 233
Humanities: Jews involved in, 307,
    309–10; universities and, 57, 58,
    89, 157–58, 160; *see also* Culture;
    Literature
Humboldt, Wilhelm von, 255
Hungary, 386; after World War I,
    383; antisemitism in, 210, 214–15,
    227, 231; emigration from, 18, 22,
    31; influence of German Judaism
    in, 123; Jewish population in, 9;
    legal equality in, 2; nationalism
    in, 171–72; nobility to professing
    Jews in, 193; Orthodox Jews from
    in Vienna, 115; Orthodox seces-
    sion and, 114; rabbis from, 112–13,
    116; self-government and, 2; *see
    also* Habsburg Monarchy
Husserl, Edmund, 310, 329

Ibsen, Henrik, 322
Identity, 281–304, 385; secularized
    Jews and, 281–82; self-definition
    as Germans of the Jewish faith
    and, 281, 282–87, 302, 303; self-
    hatred and self-rejection and, 282,
    287–90; *see also* Jewish thought;
    Zionism
IKG, SEE Vienna Organized Jewish
    Community
Illegitimate children, 11, 95, 97, 98,
    99, 100
Im Deutschen Reich,, 130, 131, 257
Immigration, 3, 8, 9, 11, 12–13, 17–23;
    Austria and, 9, 10, 17, 22, 28–29,
    42, 52–53, 379, 380; to cities, 25–34,
    28, *30*, *32*, *33*, *34*, 42; culture and,
    307; decline in, 3; of East
    European Jewry, 17–23, 379–81,

386; emigration offset by, 11–12; Galicia and, 3, 9, 10, 18, 22, 29, 31, 33, 42, 52–53, 64, 115, 282, 379, 380; Habsburg Monarchy and, 8, 17–18, 22, 29, 42; Jewish schools and, 136; lower class and, 62, 63–65; occupations and, 25–26, 41–42, 50, 52–53; Russia and, 8, 17–18, 19–20, 22, 23, 42, 282, 379, 380; shipping lines and, 46; United States and, 12–13, 18, *18*, 19, 46; in Vienna, 312–13; World War I and, 371, 378–81; young men and, 11

Imperial Civil Code, 175

Imperial Constitution of 1871, 7, 385

Imperial Loan Consortium, 50

Imperial Supreme Court, 156, 176

Impressionism, 324–25, 326

Income, class structure determined from, 60–63, 64

Independent Order of B'nai B'rith (Unabhängige Orden Bne Briss, UOBB), *see* B'nai B'rith

Independent Social Democratic Party (USPD), 377

Industrialists, nationalism and, 163–65

Industry, *see* Trade and industry

Infant mortality rate, 12

Inner Austria, Zionism and, 142, 143

Institute for Public Welfare (Institut für Gemeinwohl), 331

Insurance, Jews involved in, 45

Intellectuals, 3, 4, 37, 43; careers for, 54–60; immigrants as, 41, 42; political involvement of, 269; *see also* Culture; Jewish thought

Interest groups, 144; antisemitism and, 242–45

International Arbitration and Peace Association, 183

International Council of Women, 97

Internationale Bank, 180

International reconciliation and arbitration, Jews involved in, 274

Iro, Karl, 365

Iron trade, Jews involved in, 37

Isaac, Julius, 257

Israel, James, *381*

Israel, Nathan, companies, 49

Israelit, Der, 130

Israelite Religious Association, *see* Israelitische Religionsgesellschaft

Israelitische Allianz, 151

Israelitische Familienblatt, 130

Israelitische Freischule (Jewish Free School), 135

Israelitische Gartenbauschule, 143

Israelitische Kultusgemeinde, *see* Vienna Organized Jewish Community

Israelitische Religionsgesellschaft (Israelite Religious Association), 116–17

Israelitische Rundschau, 130; *see also Jüdische Rundschau*

Israelitisches Familienblatt, 73, 79

Israelitische Volksschule, 136

Israelitisch-Humanitärer Frauenverein (Jewish Humanitarian Women's Association), 97

Israelitisch-Theologische Lehranstalt, 113

Istóczy, Gyözö, 214–15

Jacobsonschule (Seesen), 135

Jacoby, Johann, 177

Jacques, Heinrich, 162, 194–95

Jakobsleiter, Die (Jacob's Ladder) (Schoenberg), 324

Jandorf, Adolf, 48

Japhet, Israel Meyer, 109

Jellinek, Adolf, 186
Jesuits, 181
Jewish Citizens' Union (Jüdischer Bürgerverein), 261
Jewish Colonization Association, 151
Jewish Humanitarian Women's Association, *see* Israelitisch-Humanitärer Frauenverein
Jewish National Fund, 298
Jewish press, 58, 130–31, 190, 191–92, 272; advertisements for marriage partners in, 84; antisemitism and, 54, 200, 204; dowry and, 84; expectations of wives discussed in, 79; Socialism and, 182; *see also* Journalism; Newspapers
Jewish Theological Seminary (Breslau), *see* Jüdisch-Theologisches Seminar
Jewish thought, 282, 284, 336–59; *Deutschtum and Judentum* and, 282, 284, 338, 355–59; East European Jews and, 337; "essence of Judaism" debate and, 338–47; on Jewish religiosity, 338, 348–55; Zionism and, 336–37; *see also* Culture
Joachim, Joseph, 309
Jodl, Friedrich, 169
Jogiches, Leo, 277
Josaphat, Israel Beer, 192
Joseph II, 168
Journalism, Jews involved in, 37, 58, 59–60, 263, 309, 313; immigrants and, 42; for Social Democratic Party, 276; *see also* Jewish press; Newspapers; Publishing
Jude, Der, 131, 383–84
Judentag, 140
Judges, Jews as, 37, 56, 57, 59, 60, 155–57, 159, 167
Jüdische Nationalpartei, 173

Jüdische Presse, 130, 182, 257
Jüdischer Almanach (Jewish Almanac), 295, 337
Jüdischer Frauenbund (League of Jewish Women), 91, 97–100, 102, 140, 141, 142
Jüdische Rundschau, 130, 350
Jüdischer Verlag, 295, 326, 337
Jüdischer Wanderbund Blau-Weiss (Jewish Hikers Association Blue and White), 148–49
Jüdisches Comité von 1. Dezember 1880, 218
Jüdische Turnzeitung, 144
Judische Volkspartei, 299
Jüdisch-Theologisches Seminar (Jewish Theological Seminary), 111, 113
Jugendstil, 326, 351
Jung, Carl, 328

Kadima, 147, 291
Kafka, Franz, 147, 174, 296, 313, 319–20, 332, 350
Kaiserjuden, 46, 151, 266
Kaiser Wilhelm Gesellschaft, 331
Kaiser Wilhelm Institute for the Sciences, 160–61, 266, 313, 331, 363
Kalischer, Zevi Hirsch, Rabbi, 111, 290
Kant, Immanuel, 344, 345, 346, 353, 356
Kapp, Friedrich, 264
Karlsruhe, 86, 268
Kartell Convent deutscher Studenten jüdischen Glaubens (Syndicate of German Students of the Jewish Faith, KC), 146–47, 283
Kartell Jüdischer Verbindungen (Syndicate of Jewish Fraternities, KJV), 147

Kassel, 137
Kästner, Martha, 92
Kattowitz, 268, 291
Katz brothers store, 40
Kaufmann, Fritz Mordechai, 296
Kaufmannschaft, see Berlin
  Merchant Corporation
Kautsky, Karl, 276, 278, 377
KC, SEE Kartell Convent deutscher
  Studenten jüdischen Glaubens
Kehillah, 125, 126; see also
  Communities
Kempinski Wine Restaurant, 45
Kempner, Alfred, see Kerr, Alfred
Kerr, Alfred, 58, 320–21
Ketteler, Bishop, 201
Kindergartens, 73; Froebel and,
  100–101; teachers of, 91, 101;
  women's movement and, 95
Kinsky, Franz Joseph Count, Field
  Marshal, 259
Kisch, Enoch, 160
KJV, SEE Kartell Jüdischer
  Verbindungen
Kladderadatsch, 179
Klinger, Heinrich, 126
Klubs, 184, 185, 187, 214
Kohn, Hans, 147, 350, 364
Kokoschka, Oskar, 87
Kolberg, 133
Kollenscher, Max, 166
Kölner Hof hotel (Frankfurt), 239
Komitee für den Osten (Committee
  for the East), 368
Komlóssy, Ferenc, 214
Königgrätz, battle of, 2, 176, 208
Königsberg, 345; expulsions in, 21;
  immigrants in, 21; Jews in busi-
  ness in, 272; University of, 156
Königswarter, Jonas, 52
Königswarter family, 52
Konitz, 235, 258

Kornwestheim, 47
Kosch, Raphael, 153
Kosher laws, see Dietary laws
Krafft-Ebbing, Richard von, 259
Kraus, Karl, 288–89, 309, 312, 320, 321,
  321, 364
Kreuz-Zeitung, 157, 200, 222
Kristeller, Samuel, 257
Krojanker, Gustav, 149
Krojanker, Wilhelm, 47
Kronawetter, Ferdinand, 188, 212, 213,
  229
Krösell, Karl, Pastor, 235
Kulturkampf, 114, 165, 181–82, 191,
  201–2, 253
Kultusgemeinde, 125; see also
  Communities
Kunschak, Leopold, 237
Kunstmann, Wilhelm, 45
Kunstwart, Der, 358, 359

Laborers, Jews as, 60
Labor movement, 165, 198; see also
  Socialism
Ladenburg, Carl, 180
Lagarde, Paul de, 238–39, 240, 245, 246
Landauer, Gustav, 242, 364
Landesrabbinerschule, 112–13
Landmann, Edith, 319
Landsberg, Otto, 377–78
Landtage, 176
Langbehn, Julius, 240–41, 245, 246
Lange, Friedrich, 246
Langer, Jiri Georg, 296
Language, nationalism and, 168–74
Lanz, Adolf Josef (Jörg Lanz von
  Liebenfels), 247, 248, 250
Lasker, Eduard, 114, 163, 176, 177, 178,
  179, 179, 181, 182, 189, 190, 194, 195,
  201, 268
Lasker-Schüler, Else, 289, 310, 316–19,
  318, 329

Lassalle, Ferdinand, 165, 177, 198
Laubhütte, Die, 130
Lawyers, Jews as, 16, 35, 37, 55, 57, 58–60, 66, 154, 156, 162, 189–90, 263, 272
Lazarus, Moritz, 4, 112, 139, 180, 181, 218, 219, 264, 274, 310, 344
League Against Jewish Arrogance (Verband gegen die Überhebung des Judentums), 250–51, 378
League of German Women's Associations, 99, 102
League of Industrialists, 272
League of Jewish Women, *see* Jüdischer Frauenbund
League to Combat Antisemitism, *see* Abwehr-Verein
Leather industry, Jews involved in, 42, 45, 47, 50
Lecturers, Jews as, 57
Left Liberals, 276; Abwehr-Verein and, 255; antisemitism and, 253–54; Jews and, 179–80, 267, 269; uprisings after World War I and, 383; World War I and, 373, 376
Legal equality, 1–2, 7, 153–54, 155, 160, 161–62, 185, 385; Alsace-Lorraine and, 166–67; antisemitism and, 197, 198, 202–3, 205, 206–7, 208, 215, 216, 224, 225, 252; culture achieved for, 307; emancipation and, 217; occupations and, 143; residency rights and, 23; World War I and, 360; *see also* Public life
Legal unity: Austria and, 175, 176, 189; Germany and, 189–90
Lehmann, Emil, 139, 216, 217
Lehmann, J. F., 378
Lehmann, Markus, 130
Lehranstalt für die Wissenschaft des Judentums, *see* Hochschule

Leipzig: antisemitism in, 209; education in, 101, 135; immigrants in, 21; Jewish population in, 28, 30; Jews as judges in, 156; occupations in, 42, 48, 101; synod of Liberal Jews at, 139
Leipziger Volkszeitung, 276
Lemberg, 29
Leopoldstadt, 33, *33*
Leo XIII, Pope, 227
Leseverein der deutschen Studenten Wiens, 211
Lessing, Gotthold Ephraim, 86
Lessing, Theodor, 274, 287
Levi, Hermann, 246
Levi, Paul, 377
Levy, Arthur, Rabbi, *367*
Levy-Lawson family, 266
Levy, Sali, Rabbi, *367*
Lewandowski, Louis, 109
Liberales Judentum, 119
Liberale Vereinigung, *see* Liberal Union
Liberalism, 275, 280; Abwehr-Verein and, 255; antisemitism and, 4, 198, 199, 200–201, 202, 204, 205–6, 208, 209–10, 216, 219, 220, 221, 222, 231, 235, 237, 244, 250, 254, 256, 257, 262, 263; in Austria, 183–88, 210, 214, 216, 218, 221, 225, 229, 230, 236, 263, 270–71; business and, 273–74; East European Jews and, 286; Jewish press and, 191; Jews and, 360–61; middle class and, 66; Polish, 165; public life and, 154, 157–58, 161, 162, 174–88, *178*, *179*, 193, 267, 269, 270; World War I and, 376
Liberal Judaism, 100, 103, 387; antisemitism and, 216; Centralverein deutsche Staatsbürger jüdischen Glaubens and, 257; in cities,

127–28, 129; "essence of Judaism" debate and, 338–47; families observing, 82; geographic distribution of, 104, *105*, 107, 108; in Hungary, 123; identity as Jews and, 281; influence of, 123; institutions and style of, 108–9, 110–11, 114; Jewish schools and, 135, 138; liturgical innovations and, 117–19; middle class and, 66; nationalism and, 163; organizations and, 139, 140, 141, 150; Orthodoxy and, 116, 117–19, 120, 121; rabbinical seminary for, 111, 112, 113; religious significance of women and, 79; residential patterns and, 32; rise of, 103–4, 114; synagogues of, 103; teacher training institutes of, 137–38; traditionalists and, 119; Vereinigung für das liberale Judentum and, 119–20; Zionism and, 117, 299–300

Liberal Temple Association, 108

Liberal Union (Liberale Vereinigung), 178, 179

Libertas of Vienna, 211–12

Librarians, women as, 89

Libraries, 144

Licht, Stefan von, 383

Lichtheim, Richard, 271, 296

Liebermann, Max, 37, 324, *325*, 363

Liebknecht, Karl, 377

Liebknecht, Wilhelm, 276

Liechtenstein, Prince Alois, 212

Lietz, Hermann, 240

Life expectancy, 10, 12, 385

Lilien, Ephraim Moses, *295*, 326

Link, Samuel, *366*

Linz Program of 1882, 187, 211

Lippmann, Leo, 159

Lissauer, Ernst, 363

Lissauer, Hugo, 244

List, Guido von, 247, 248

Literary criticism, Jews involved in, 309, 312, 314, 320–22

Literature, Jews involved in, 42, 73, 307–8, 309–10, 311–12, 313, 314–20

Lodges, Jews excluded from, 141; *see also* B'nai B'rith

Loeser and Wolff, 48

Loewe, Isidor, 180, 222

Loewe, Ludwig, 165, 180, 181–82, 194, 219

Loewenfeld, Raphael, 257, 286

Loos, Adolf, 87

Lower Austria, 230; agriculture in, 2; Jewish population in, 9; Lueger and, 227–28

Lower class, 60–61, 62, 63–65; immigrants as, 50, 64; *see also* Lower middle class; Poor

Lower Franconia, 104

Lower middle class, 62, 64–65, 66; education for girls and, 90; family and, 76–77; occupations for women and, 90–91, 94; religious life of, 71, 76–78

Ludendorff, Erich, 372, 373, 379

Ludwig, Emil, 320

Lueger, Karl, 188, 212, 213–14, 220, 226–31, 228, 237, 248, 259, 262, 265, 270, 271, 292

Lukács, György, 174

Luxemburg, Rosa, 277, 329, 364, 377

Luxury shops, Jews opening, 44

Magnus, Meyer, 265

Magnus, Philip, 219

Magyars: antisemitism and, 231; nationalism and, 171–72

Mahler, Gustav, 310, 312, 322, *323*

Mail order business, Jews involved in, 44, 47, 94

Managers, Jews as, 60

"Manchester doctrine," 200

Mandl, Ignaz, 229

Mandl, Julius, 187

"Manifesto of the Ninety-Three, The," 363

Mannheim: occupations in, 48, 272; public life in, 268

Mannheimer Brothers, 49, 273

Manufacturers, Jews as, 66, 154, 160

Marburg, 209; culture in, 313; University of, 158, 345, 354, 355

Marginality theory, Jewish cultural creativity and, 334

Marks-Hainsdorf Foundation, 137–38

Marriage: brokers and, 84; civil, 14; decline in, 10–11; dowry for, 75, 83–84; economics and, 44; endogamy and, 13–14, 69, 85; girls waiting for, 75, 90; matchmakers and, 84; parental role in, 80, 84; personal choice of partners and, 85; secular Judaism and, 82; social gatherings introducing partners for, 73; women ending employ- ment for, 92; women ending uni- versity education for, 89; *see also* Mixed marriages

Marr, Wilhelm, 196–97, 198, 199, 203, 204, 209, 214, 215, 235, 253

Marx, Julius, 372

Marx, Karl and Marxism, 177, 198, 203, 277, 329, 332

Masaryk, Tomás G., 232, 233, 234, 271, 361, 365

Matchmakers, 84

Maurois, André, 167

Maurras, Charles, 224

Mauthner, Fritz, 170, 310, 329

Mauthner, Siegmund, 169

Max of Baden, Prince, 383

Max-Planck-Gesellschaft, 160

May, Henriette, 100

Mayer, David Hugo, 159

Mayer, Emil, 180

Mayer, Rudolf, 199

Mayer, Sigmund, 271

Mecklenburg, Jakob, Rabbi, 111

Mecklenburg-Schwerin, 126

Medicine, *see* Doctors

Meidner, Ludwig, 325, *326*

Melchior, Carl, 366, 372

Memel, 291, 300

Memmingen, *128*

Mendelssohn, Felix, 309

Mendelssohn, Franz von, 272, 273

Mendelssohn family, 50, 192

Merchants, Jews as, 16, 37, 38, 40–41, 66; education and, 54; migration of to cities, 25; nationalism and, 164–65; in public life, 154, 180; *see also* Commerce and trade; Trade and industry

Merton, Wilhelm, 331

Metal industry, Jews involved in, 48–49, 53

Metz, grand rabbi of, 167

Meyer, Georg, 372

Meyer, Rudolf, 201

Meyerbeer, Giacomo, 309

Meyer family, 72

Meyer spirits company (Berlin), 48

Middle class, 7, 11, 37, 61–65, 66–67, 385, 387; antisemitism and, 264; in Austria, 9, 160; baptisms and, 159; birthrate and, 10; central layer of, 66; charitable activity of, 133; in cities, 7, 10, 15, 24, 32, 34, 61–64; culture and, 307; decline in mar- riages and, 10–11; East European Jews and, 23; education and, 54–60, 66, 307; employment of women and, 39, 91–94; family and attainment of, 68–78, 82–84, 85; legal equality and, 160; life

expectancy and, 12; mixed marriages and, 15; in public life, 154; women's education and, 88; women's movement and, 4, 86, 91, 95–102; *see also* Lower middle class; Upper middle class
Migration, *see* Immigration
Milieufrömmigkeit, 105
Military service, Jews in: in Habsburg Monarchy, 161; Jews stand on, 182–83, 273–74; *see also* War; World War I
Ministerial office, Jews holding, 175–76
Miquel, Johannes, 189–90
Mises, Ludwig von, 160
Mitteilungen aus dem Verein zur Abwehr des Antisemitismus, 254
Mitteilungen der Österreichisch-Israelitischen Union, 262
Mittelstand organizations, antisemitism and, 244
Mixed marriages, 8, 9, 11, 13–15, 17; avoidance of mixed social gatherings and, 83; gender differences in, 14, 80, 84; personal choice of partners and, 85; upper class and, 65
Mobility, 23–24, 27–28; occupational, 25–26, 45; social structure and, 7
Mocatta, F. D., 219
Mommsen, Theodor, 206, 217, 250, 255
Monatsschrift für Geschichte und Wissenschaft des Judentums, 122, 341
Moravia, 3, 386; antisemitism in, 210, 233, 236; East European Jews in, 379; education and, 55; emigration from, 9, 18, 22, 29, 31; healthcare facilities in, 133; Jewish population in, 9; nationalism in, 168–71;

Nikolsburg, *106*; occupations in, 52, 53; Realist Party and, 361; religious life in, 104, 109; World War I and, 365; Zionism and, 142, 143
Morgenpost, 218
Morgenstern, Lina, 101
Mortality, 12
Mosse, Felicia, *70*
Mosse, Rudolf, 51, *70*, 191–92, 274
Mosse family, children of, *70*
Mosse publishing house, 58, 362
Mugdan, Otto, 302
Mühsam, Erich, 242
Münchener Post, 276
Munich: culture in, 313; immigration and, 21, 28; Jewish population in, 10, 30; Orthodox secession and, 115; University of, 158, 327–28
Münster, 137–38
Museums, 144
Music, Jews involved in, 307, 309–10, 312, 314, 322–24; immigrants and, 42; in synagogues, 109, 112, 116, 117, 118–19
Music lessons, women giving, 94

Nachod, Jacob, 180
Nathan, Helene, 89
Nathan, Paul, 151, 254, 256, 302, 368
Nation, Die, 253, 254, 255
National Antisemitic Party, 215
National Democratic Party, 166; in Galicia, 233
Nationalism, 124, 158, 162–67; antisemitism and, 187, 208, 211–12, 219, 220, 238–41, 245; East European Jews and, 123; 1880s and, 187; in Habsburg Monarchy, 162, 168–74; Jewish press and, 130; public life and, 158, 162–67; scholarship related to, 122; Social Democratic Party and, 279; *see also* Zionism

National Liberal Party, 163, 165, 175, 176, 177–78, *178*, 180, 182, 189, 190, 194, 207, 208, 210, 221; Abwehr-Verein and, 255; antisemitism and, 225, 243, 268; Jews and, 267, 269–70
National Socialism, 251; in Austria and Czechoslovakia, 211, 232, 237; *see also* Nazis
National Social Union (National-soziale Vereinigung), 224
National Women's Service, 102
National-Zeitung, 176
Naturalization, for immigrants, 20
Naumann, Friedrich, 224
Nazis, 107, 247; antisemitism and, 204, 209; Nationalsozialistische Arbeiterpartei and, 237; *see also* National Socialism
Neuda, Fanny, 79–80
Neue Freie Presse, 191, 289, 292, 309, 320, 364
Neue Gemeinschaft, 242
Neues Leben, 242
Neues Wiener Tagblatt, 191, 213, 242
Neue Zeit, 276
Neuhof, Karl, Sergeant, *374*
Neu-Isenburg, 100
Neurath, Otto, 160
Neustadt, 32
New Romanticism, 348, 351
News agency, 192
Newspapers, 58; family reading, 73; Jews involved in, 51, 190, 191–92; *see also* Jewish press; Journalism
New Yorker Staatszeitung, 367
Niederösterreichischer Bauernbund, 228
Nietzsche, Friedrich, 207, 240, 316, 352
Nobel, Nehemiah, 121
Northern Baden, 104

Northern Bohemia, 230
Northern Railway, 213
North German Confederation, 176, 189–90, 192; legal equality and, 1, 153, 155; penal code of, 175
North German Lloyd, 19
Nothnagel, Hermann, 259
Nuremberg: immigrants in, 21; Jewish population in, 30; migration to, 29; occupations in, 48; Orthodox secession and, 115; public life in, 194

Oberkirchenbehörde, 104, 126
Oberrat, 104, 118, 126
Obstbau-Kolonie Eden, 242
Occupations, 3, 35–54, 161–62, 386; Austria and, 42–43; baptisms for, 15, 17, 56–57, 59, 157–58, 159; Christians and, 38; cities and, 25–26; class structure and, 60–67; immigrants and, 25–26, 41–42, 50, 52–53; organizations and, 143; in rural areas, 25, 40–41, 44, 46; university degree required for, 37, 40, 54–60; withdrawals from community and, 16; women in, 4, 11, 38, 39–40, *40*, 42, 43, 51, 60, 70, 71, 75, 76, 88–89, 90–95, 96–97, 98, 100, 102; World War I and, 42; *see also* Agriculture; Doctors; Lawyers
Odd Fellows lodges, 141
Offenbach, 42
Office occupations, Jews involved in, 39, 60
Office of Jewish Statistics, 8
Ofner, Julius, 271
ÖIU, SEE Österreichisch-Israelitische Union
Ollendorf, Paula, 100
Önody, Geza, 215

Oppeln, 24
Oppenheim, Abraham, 183, 193
Oppenheim, Franz, 273
Oppenheim, Heinrich Bernhard, 176,
    194, 206
Oppenheim family, 50, 66, 192
Oppenheimer, Franz, 162, 242, 296,
    297, 368
Organizations, 4, 127, 138–52, 386–87;
    antisemitism and, 138, 139–40, 141,
    143–44, 148, 252–53; charitable
    activities and, 131–34; defense, 133,
    144, 284–87; international ties of,
    150–52; lawyers as legal advisers
    for, 58–59; women's movement
    and, 4, 86, 91, 95–101; World War I
    and, 367–68; Zionism and,
    299–304; see also Social welfare;
    Youth organizations
Orient, Der, 168
Orlik, Emil, 323
Orphanages, 95–96, 132
Orthodox Synagogue Association,
    108
Orthodoxy, 3, 123, 387; Agudat Israel
    and, 120, 296; antisemitism and,
    216, 263; Isaac Breuer and, 121;
    Center Party and, 269;
    Centralverein deutscher
    Staatsbürger jüdischen Glaubens
    and, 257; in cities, 127–28; commu-
    nity (conservative), 116, 117, 121;
    culture and, 307; decline in, 103–4;
    defense organizations and, 286;
    East European Jews and, 295;
    family and, 69, 71, 78; geographic
    distribution of, 104, 105, 107–8; in
    Hungary, 123; identity as Jews
    and, 281; institutions and style of,
    109–11; Jewish press and, 130;
    Jewish schools and, 135–36, 136,
    137–38; Liberal Judaism and, 116,

117–19, 120, 121; marriage and, 84;
    middle class and, 66; nationalism
    and, 163; organizations and, 139,
    140, 141, 149–50; rabbinical semi-
    nary for, 112, 113; residential pat-
    terns and, 32; separatist, 109, 112,
    113–17, 118, 119, 120–21, 130, 133, 144,
    263; synagogues of, 103; teacher
    training institutes of, 137, 138; tra-
    ditionalist, 119; upper middle class
    and, 66; women and, 79; World
    War I and, 361, 364; Zionism and,
    117, 120, 121, 299
Ostara, 247–48
Österreichischer Reformverein
    (Austrian Reform Association),
    212–13
Österreichische Wochenschrift, 131,
    219, 259, 261, 365
Österreichisch-Israelitische Union
    (Austrian-Jewish Union, öiu),
    140, 219, 259, 261–63, 270, 283, 290,
    299
Ostjuden, 282; see also East
    European Jewry
Ostmarkenverein, 166
Ostrau, 29
Ost und West, 131, 295, 382
Otto, Rudolf, 347

Painters, see Visual arts
Palacky, 232
Palestine, 152, 291; see also Zionism
Pan-German League (ADV), 248–49,
    250, 251, 378, 383
Pappenheim, Bertha, 91, 95–97, 96,
    99–100
Pasternak, Leonid, 354
Paulsen, Friedrich, 240
Peace Resolution, World War I and,
    373, 375, 376, 378
Peddlers, Jews as, 43

Peltasohn, Martin, 156
Periodicals, *see* Jewish press
Perrot, Franz F., 200
Phenomenology, Jews involved in, 329
Philanthropin, 135
Philanthropists, Jews as, 330–31; *see also* Charitable activity; Organizations
Philippovich, Eugen von, 271
Philippson, Ludwig, 111, 130, 217
Philippson, Martin, 140
Philosophy, Jews involved in, 4, 310, 312, 313, 329
Physicians, *see* Doctors
Physics, Jews involved in, 308–9, 327
Pinkert, Alexander, 218
Pinsker, Leo, 291
Pius IX, Pope, 227
Planck, Max, 329
Poland: antisemitism in, 233–34; immigration and, 17–18, 20, 23, 42, 380; nationalism and, 165–66; tailors in, 36; World War I and, 42, 366–67, 368–69; *see also* Galicia
Polgar, Alfred, 312
Policy lobby, Jews involved in, 272–73
Polish Klub, 184
Polish National Committee, 165
Polish Peasant Party, 233
Political antisemitism, 198, 201, 203, 204, 209, 215, 221–25, 234–37, 290; *see also* Zionism
Political life, *see* Public life
Political Zionism, 291–93, 296, 348
Polná ritual murder trial, 232, 233, 262
Pomerania, 222; emigration from, 27–28; religious life in, 104
Poor, 3; charitable activity aiding, 95, 101, 131–34; Galician Jews and, 9; immigration and, 3; Jewish white

slave trade and, 97, 98, 99, 100; Russian Jews and, 62; *see also* Lower class
Population, 3; in Austria, 9–10; in cities, 127; in German Empire, 2, 7–9; Jews as minority and, 7–13; *see also* Demographics
Posen, 25, 234; immigration and, 13, 27–28; nationalism in, 165–66; public life in, 194, 267, 268; religious life in, 104; Zionistische Vereinigung for Deutschland resolution and, 297, 300, 301
Prague, 170, 232; Buber in, 349–50, 351–53; as cultural center, 313; education in, 87, 169, 170; immigration and, 29, 127; nationalism in, 169, 170; public life in, 160, 185, 194; University of, 56, 160; youth organizations in, 147
Prayer books, for women, 79–80
Prayer houses, 110, 114
Preen, Friedrich von, 238
Preuss, Hugo, 274
Preussische Jahrbücher, 183, 204, 205–6, 339
Printing houses, Jews involved in, 51, 94; *see also* Publishing
Professors, Jews as, 37, 56–57
Progressive Party, 165, 176, 177, 178, 180, 210, 223, 233, 270; old established, 179, 181–82; post-1884 (*Freisinn*), 179
Prostitution, Jüdischer Frauenbund and, 98
Protestantism, 339; Abwehr-Verein and, 254–56, 258, 259; antisemitism and, 200, 202, 220, 221, 249; conversions to, 15–16; Judaism and, 339–40, 345–46; Schönerer and, 230; women's movement and, 98

Protocols of the Elders of Zion, 378
Proto-Zionist movement, 290–91, 296
Prussia: antisemitism and, 207; cities
    in, 25, 27–28; civil marriage in, 14;
    class structure in, 63–64; commu-
    nity life in, 125, 126; criminal sta-
    tistics in, 65; education in, 55, 56,
    57, 88, 135; expulsions from, 19–20;
    family size in, 10; Franco-
    Prussian War, 183; immigration
    and, 19–20, 21, 27–28, 31; income
    and taxation in, 61, 62; Jews as
    judges in, 157; Kulturkampf and,
    114–15, 181–82; lawyers in, 57, 162;
    legal equality in, 1, 155; military
    service in, 159–60; mixed mar-
    riages and, 14; mortality rate in,
    12; naturalization in, 20; nobility
    to professing Jews in, 193; occupa-
    tions in, 45, 59, 162, 272; organiza-
    tions in, 140; Orthodox secession
    and, 114–15; public life in, 155, 156,
    159–60, 164, 164, 175, 178, 179–80,
    194, 267–68, 270; rural areas in, 25;
    universities in, 158; university
    positions in, 158; withdrawals
    from Jewish community and, 15;
    World War I and, 370; see also
    Berlin
Prussian Academy of the Arts, 324
Prussian Schools Bill of 1905, 269
Psychoanalysis, Jews involved in,
    312, 313, 328, 329
Public life, 81, 153–95, 267–71, 309,
    388; antisemitism in, 177–79,
    180–81; baptisms for, 175, 176, 256,
    270; in finance, 188–89, 190–91,
    192–93, 263; German Empire
    structure and, 2; German nation-
    alism and, 158, 162–67; in
    Habsburg Monarchy, 160–61, 162,
    168–74; as judges, 155–57, 159; in

law, 189–90; legal equality and,
    1–2, 7; in Liberal era, 154, 157–58,
    161, 162, 174–88, 178, 179, 193; in
    military, 159–60; in newspapers,
    190, 191–92; policy areas and,
    188–93; in politics, 267–71; reli-
    gious life and, 193–95; restrictions
    on, 154–62, 269–70, 271–72; state
    bureaucracy and, 159, 188; in uni-
    versities, 157–58, 159; World War I
    and, 365–66, 372, 375–76, 380–81,
    382, 383
Public schools, see Education
Publishing, Jews involved in, 51;
    public life and, 154, 190, 191–92;
    see also Jewish press; Journalism;
    Newspapers
Pückler, Count, 235, 258

Rabbinerseminar, 112, 113
Rabbinical seminaries: in Berlin, 49,
    58, 112, 113, 300; in Breslau, 56, 58,
    111–12, 113; denominational, 111–13
Rabbis and rabbinate: in cities, 128;
    education for, 58; from Hungary,
    112–13, 116; immigrants as, 42;
    Liberal Judaism and, 117, 119–20;
    liturgical innovations and, 117–19;
    in small-town communities, 125,
    126, 127; social status of, 55; split
    within Orthodoxy and, 113–17;
    Zionism and, 293; see also
    Rabbinical seminaries
Race, antisemitism and, 196–97,
    203–4, 211, 212, 220–21, 227, 238,
    241, 242–51
Radek, Karl, 277
Radical Progressives, in Czech lands,
    232
Ranzenhofer, Emil, 126
Rathenau, Emil, 50, 52, 53, 65, 273,
    372, 376

Rathenau, Walther, 52, 266, 271, 288, 366
RDMV, SEE Reichsdeutsche Mittelstandsvereinigung
Realist Party, 361
Rebbert, Joseph, 220
Rechtsstaat, 200
Redlich, Josef, 271
"Reform Associations" (Reformvereine), 208–9
Reformgemeinde, 103
Reform Judaism, 103, 111; Jewish press and, 130; Orthodoxy versus, 115, 116; in the United States, 123–24; see also Liberal Judaism; Reformgemeinde
Reformverein, 218, 220–21, 229
Reichenheim, Leonor, 164–65, 194
Reichsdeutsche Mittelstandsvereinigung (RDMV), 244
Reichsgericht, 175
Reichshammerbund, 251, 371
Reichsmark, 188, 189
Reichspartei, 176, 181, 268, 269
Reichsrat, 186, 210, 212, 214, 228, 229–30; antisemitism and, 211, 213, 226, 230, 236, 250, 261, 383; Jews elected to, 184–85
Reichstag, 226, 275; antisemitism and, 207, 222–24, 234–35, 241, 248, 250, 253, 254, 256; Bismarck dissolving, 180; finance policy, 189; Jews elected to, 176–77, 178, 182, 193–94, 267, 268, 274, 275, 276, 278, 279; Kulturkampf and, 181–82; legal unity and, 189–90; Nazis in, 209; Social Democratic Party in, 275, 276, 278, 279; World War I and, 370, 371, 372, 373, 376, 377
Reichsverein der deutschen Juden (Association of German Jews in the Reich), 302, 361

Reinhardt, Max, 322, 363
Religion of Reason (Cohen), 354–55
Religious antisemitism, 202–3, 220
Religious instruction, supplemental, 136–37
Religious leaders, elementary school teachers as, 58; see also Rabbis and rabbinate
Religious life, 103–24; in cities, 103, 107–8, 109, 127–28, 128; family and, 68, 69–70, 71, 72, 77–85, 105–7; gender differences in, 81; German Empire structure and, 2; influence abroad and, 123–24; institutions and style of factions, 108–14; Jüdischer Frauenbund and, 98–99; men and, 69–71, 79, 81, 82; public life and, 193–95; in rural areas, 24–25, 26; scholarship and, 121–23; scientists and, 327–28; strife among factions and, 117–21; withdrawals from Jewish community and, 15, 16; women and, 3, 79–80, 81, 98–99; see also Baptisms; Liberal Judaism; Orthodoxy; Rabbis and rabbinate; Rural traditionalists; Secular Judaism; Synagogues
Relocations, Matrikelgesetz (Registration Law) and, 23
Renan, Ernest, 264
Residency, rights of, 23
Restaurants, Jews involved in, 45
Retail stores, Jews involved in, 41–42, 44, 46, 47, 53, 273
Reuter, Paul Julius, 192
Revolutions of 1848, see 1848 revolutions
Rexingen, 24
Rhina, 24
Rhineland, 24; antisemtism and, 255; immigration and, 27, 29; religious

life in, 104, 118; teacher training
institute in, 138
Rhine Palatinate, 104
Rickert, Heinrich, 253–54, 255, 259
Rieger, Ladislav, 169, 232
Riesser, Gabriel, 155, 217, 273
Riesser, Jakob, 273
Ritual murder accusations, 215, 218,
231, 232, 233, 235, 252, 253, 255, 258
Ritual murder trials, 262, 271
Rodenberg, Julius, 309
Rohling, August, 167, 202, 203, 215,
217, 218, 227, 259, 260
Romania, 22, 193, 194; immigration
and, 18, 282; see also East
European Jewry
Rosegger, Peter, 259
Rosenack, Rabbi, 367
Rosenzweig, Franz, 4, 338, 348, 353
Rosin, Heinrich, 158
Roth, Alfred, 251
Roth, Joseph, 174
Rothenbaum residential area, 32
Rothschild, Guy, 264
Rothschild, Meyer Carl von, 163–64,
164, 176, 182, 264
Rothschild family, 50, 52, 66, 151,
163–64, 164, 192, 213
Rozvoj, 380
Rudolf, Crown Prince, 191
Ruhr, 51
Rülf, Isaac, 291, 300
Ruppin, Arthur, 8, 122, 298–99
Rural areas, 24–25; class structure in,
64; communities in, 127; culture
and, 307; education in, 24–25, 26,
41, 90, 135, 240; family in, 71, 72,
76–78, 105–7; immigration and,
25–26, 27, 29, 127; Jewish press
and, 130; mixed marriages and,
14–15; occupations for women
and, 39, 40, 90–91, 94; occupations

in, 25, 40–41, 44, 46; religious life
in, 24–25, 26, 103, 137; social gatherings in, 83; see also Agriculture;
Communities
Rural traditionalists, 76–78, 80–81,
103, 104–7
Russia: immigration and, 8, 17–18,
19–20, 22, 23, 42, 282, 379, 380;
pogroms and, 291; World War I
and, 42, 364, 368–69; see also East
European Jewry
Russian-Jewish Scholarly
Association (Russisch-jüdischer
wissenschaftliche Verein), 147
Russian Jews: in Argentina, 151; edu-
cation and, 56; Jewish schools for,
136; poverty and, 62; as tailors, 36;
youth organizations and, 147;
Zionism and, 291, 297
Russian Students Association, 147
Russisch-jüdischer wis-
senschaftliche Verein, see
Russian-Jewish Scholarly
Association
Russo-Turkish War, 193

Sabbath, family observance of, 69,
71, 77–78, 79, 80, 81, 82, 83, 105–7
Salamander Company, 47
Sales clerks, Jews as, 43, 60; women
as, 90, 94
Salomon, Alice, 102
Salten, Felix, 312, 364
Samsonschule, 135
Sanitoria, 133
Sare, Dr., 156
Saxony, 244; immigration and, 20,
21, 27; Jewish population in, 28;
Jews as judges in, 155; Orthodox
secession and, 115
Schemann, Ludwig, 246
Schenklengsfeld, 25

Schiff, Jacob, 382
Schiffer, Eugen, 270
Schiller, Friedrich, 307
Schindler, Franz, Prelate, 227, 229
Schlachtensee, 242
Schlemiel, 288
Schleswig-Holstein, 100
Schneider, Ernst, 220–21
Schnitzler, Arthur, 310, 311, 312, 313,
    314, 315, *316,* 364
Schocken, Salman, 48
Schoenberg, Arnold, 87, 310, 312, 322,
    324
Schoenlank, Bruno, 276
Scholarship, Jewish, 121–23; *see also*
    Intellectuals
Scholem, Betty, 94–95
Scholem, Gershom, 83, 94, 148, 350,
    358, 364
Schönborn, Count, 156
Schöneberg, 33
Schönerer, Georg von, 210–11, 212,
    213, 214, 216, 220, 221, 229–30, 236,
    245, 247, 249, 365
Schools, Jewish, 58, 89, 125, 134–38;
    elementary, 58, 134–35; high
    schools, 135–36; Hilfsverein and,
    152; for religious instruction,
    136–37; teachers for, 88–89, 135,
    137–38; yeshivot, 112; *see also*
    Rabbinical seminaries
Schrattenholz, Josef, 253
Schröder, Domvikar, Paderborn, 253
Schrödinger, Erwin, 329
Schultheiss brewery, 165
Schulverein für Deutsche, 249–50
Schwabach, Paul von, 192, 273, 375
Schwarzwald, Eugenie, 87
Schweitzer, Eduard Ritter von, 161
Schwerin, Jeanette, 101–2
Sciences: Jews as scientists and, 3,
    51–52, 162, 308–9, 314, 327–28, 385;

universities and, 57, 157, 158,
    160–61; *see also* Doctors
Seamstresses, women as, 91
Secession, 178, 179; *see also* Liberal
    Union
Secondary schools, *see* High schools
Second-hand stores, Jews involved
    in, 41–42, 48, 94
Secular Judaism, 69, 81–83, 284, 287,
    387; identity as Jews and, 281–82;
    Jewish cultural creativity and,
    333; Zionism and, 300–1
Secular traditionalists, in cities, 108
Seeberg, Reinhold, 373–74
Seesen, 135
Segall, Jacob, 93
Selbstwehr (Self-Defense), 131, 350,
    363
Self-defense organizations, 133, 144,
    284–87
Self-employed, Jews as, 38–39, 43, 56,
    59–61
Self-hatred, as response to anti-
    semitism, *280,* 282, 287–90
Self-improvement, as response to
    antisemitism, 263–64, 283, 287
Seligmann, Caesar, 112
Seminaries, *see* Rabbinical seminar-
    ies
Settlement houses, 142
Ship owners, Jews as, 19, 45–46, 266
Shipping agents, Jews as, 45
Shop employees' trade union, *see*
    Deutschnationaler
    Handlungsgehilfen-Verband
Siemens, Werner von, 206
Sigle, J., and Company, 47
Silesia: antisemitism and, 237; edu-
    cation and, 55; Jewish population
    in, 9; Jews as judges in, 157;
    nationalism in, 170, 171; occupa-
    tions in, 47; public life in, 194, 268

Simmel, Georg, 328
Simon, F., 256, 259
Simon, Gustav, 230
Simon, James, 49, 151, 257, 266, 273,
    302, 330
Simon, Josef, 232
Simon, Moritz, 143
Simon Brothers, 49
Simson, Eduard von, 156, 176, 265
Simultanschule, 134, 138
Singer, Paul, 177, 276, 279
Single people, increase in, 11
Sisterhoods (*Schwesternschaften*),
    141
Slave trade, Jewish white, 97, 98, 99,
    100
Slavs, antisemitism and, 231–34, 262
Small Business Law of 1883, 213
Small business organizations, anti-
    semitism and, 243, 244
Small-town communities, *see*
    Communities; Rural areas
Social Democratic Party (SPD), 75,
    102, 174, 176–77, 182, 204, 221, 223,
    267; Abwehr-Verein and, 255;
    antisemitism and, 230, 235, 256,
    278–80; in Austria, 187, 225, 228,
    230, 236, 274, 276–78, 279, 280, 377;
    in Czech lands, 232, 234;
    Deutschnationaler
    Handlungsgehilfen-Verband and,
    243; Jews and, 16, 272, 274–80, 360,
    361, 377–78; uprisings after World
    War I and, 383; World War I and,
    364, 370, 373, 376–77
Social gatherings, 73, 83
Socialism, 4, 81, 176–77, 182, 243, 250,
    377–78; antisemitism and, 237,
    256, 378; in Austria, 221, 271; Jews
    involved in, 274–80
Socialist press, 58
Socialist theoreticians, Jews as, 329

Social life, 2–3; social gatherings, 73,
    83; upper class and, 65
Social structure, *see* Class structure
Social welfare: in Austria, 52; B'nai
    B'rith and, 142; in cities, 64; com-
    munities and, 3; women's move-
    ment and, 4, 86, 91, 95–102, *see*
    Charitable activity;
    Organizations
Social workers, women as, 35, 39, 91,
    97, 98–99, 101, 102, 131, 134
Societäts Publishing House, 51
Society for the Protection of the
    Religious Interests of Judaism in
    Westphalia, 118
Society to Further Jewish
    Scholarship, 122
Sociology, Jews involved in, 328
Solymosi, Eszter, 215
Sombart, Werner, 302, 305
Sonderling, Rabbi, *367*
Sonnemann, Leopold, 51, 176, 191,
    194, 195, 274
Soup kitchens, women's movement
    and, 101
South Slav lands, after World War I,
    383
Sozialistische Monatshefte, 277, 378
Sozialpolitische Partei, 262, 271
Spartacus League, 377, 383
SPD, *see* Social Democratic Party
Speyer, Georg and Franziska,
    Educational Foundation, 331
Spiritual Judaism, 4
Spiro, Samuel, 25
Sports clubs, 143, 144, *145*
Stampfer, Friedrich, 276, 378
Stapinski, Jan, 233
State bureaucracy, Jews and, 159, 188
Steglitz, German youth movement
    in, 241
Steinbach, Emil, 189

Steinthal, Heymann, 264, 310, 344
Steinthal, Max, 180
Steinwender, Otto, 214, 229
Stoecker, Adolf, 193, 204–5, *205*, 206, 207, 208, 209, 215, 220, 222, 223–24, 225, 235, 244, 265, 266, 279
Stolberg-Wernigerode, Count Otto von, 207
Straucher, Benno, 173, 174
Straus, Rahel, 86, 89, 92
Strauss, Johann, the Younger, 259
Stravinsky, Igor, 324
Struck, Hermann, 326
Student organizations, 145–47, *149*
Stürgkh, Count, 377
Sturmann, Manfred, 80
Stuttgart, 29
Suess, Eduard, 259
Sulzer, Salomon, 109
Susman, Margarete, 319
Suttner, Arthur, Baron Gundaccar von, 259
Suttner, Bertha Gundaccar von, 259, 274
Switzerland, 28
Sybel, Heinrich von, 206
Synagogues, *110*; in cities, 127–28, *128*; of East European Jewry, 110; for Hirsch brassworks, 49; in Jewish residential areas, 32; of Liberal Judaism, 103, 108–9, 114, 116; music in, 109, 112, 116, 117, 118–19; of Orthodoxy, 103, 114, 116; in rural areas, 24, 107; in small-town communities, 127; women and, 117
Syndicate of German Students of the Jewish Faith, *see* Kartell Convent deutscher Studenten jüdischen Glaubens
Syndicate of Jewish Fraternities, *see* Kartell Jüdischer Verbindungen

Szeps, Moritz, 191

Taaffe, Count, 213, 218, 265
Tack and Company, 47
Tailors, Jews as, 36, 39, 44, 50, 91
Talmud, writings against, 202, 218, 253, 286
Talmud-Thoraschule (Hamburg), 135, *136*
Tänzer, Rabbi, *367*
Tavern keepers, Jews as, 45
Taxation, 3; class structure determined from, 61–63, 64, 65; communities and, 127; German Empire structure and, 2
Teachers, Jews as, 37, 39, 41, 56–57, 58, 60; families of, 76–77; for Jewish schools, 88–89, 135, 137–38; for kindergarten, 91, 101; in public life, 154; for religious instruction, 137–38; in rural areas, 24–25; in small-town communities, 127; women as, 88–89, 100
Teamsters, Jews as, 45
Technical colleges, 54, 55; of Brünn, 171; of Prague, 170
Technikum (Technion), 302, 369
Telephones, entrepreneurs using, 44
Teplitz, 29
Textile industry, *see* Garment industry
Theilhaber, Felix, 8–9, 10, 122
Theology, 4
Third Reich, 251; *see also* National Socialism
Tietz, Hermann, 48
Tietz, Leonhard, 48
Tietz, Oskar, 273, 375
Tietz department stores, 48, 49, 273
Tirpitz, Grand Admiral, 191, 376, 378
Tisza-Eszlár ritual murder accusation, 215, 218, 231, 233

Tivoli conference of 1892, 223, 225, 252

Tobacco industry, Jews involved in, 45, 46, 48, 50

Toller, Ernst, 371

Torah, Jewish cultural creativity explained by, 332–33

Toynbee Hallen, 142

Trade and industry, Jews involved in, 35, 36, 37, 38, 39, 40–41, 43–50, 49, 52, 53, 263; see also Commerce and trade

Trade associations, Jews involved in, 273

Trade fairs, Jews involved in, 44

Trade policy, Jews involved in, 272–73

Traditionalists, see Orthodoxy; Rural traditionalists

Transportation, Jews involved in, 45–46

Traube, Ludwig, 157

Traveling salesmen, Jews as, 43, 46, 94

Trebitsch, Siegfried, 364

Treitschke, Heinrich von, 204, 205–6, 208, 209, 217, 218, 219, 239, 248, 253, 265, 355

Trotzjudentum, 284, 338

Tsenah ure'enah, 100

Turkey, World War I and, 369, 370

Uhry, Adolph, 167

Ukraine, World War I and, 365

Ullstein, Hans, 274

Ullstein, Leopold, 51, 95, 191–92

Ullstein publishing house, 58

Ultramontanes, 180, 181

Unabhängige Orden Bne Briss, see B'nai B'rith

Unger, Josef, 175, 176, 189

Union for Liberal Judaism, see

Vereinigung für das liberale Judentum

Union of German-Jewish Organizations for Protecting the Rights of the Jews of the East, 381

Union of Liberal Rabbis, 113

Union of Synagogue Associations, 128

United Christians, 214, 225, 226, 229

United States: East European Jews in, 152; immigration to, 12–13, 18, 18, 19, 46; influence of German Judaism in, 123–24; World War I and, 367, 369–70, 376; Zionism and, 369, 370

University(ies), 75; antisemitism and, 15, 16, 57, 157–58, 159, 177, 207, 239–40, 245, 253, 310, 327–28; in Austria, 160–61; baptisms among graduates of, 56–57; baptisms needed for attending, 15; baptisms required for positions in, 16, 57, 157–58, 159, 310, 327–28; of Berlin, 56, 57, 157, 158, 344; of Breslau, 56, 57, 89, 146, 253; of Brünn, 171; Charles, 169, 170; of Czernowitz, 56; dueling corporations and, 121, 207, 283, 291; of Frankfurt, 330–31; fraternities in, 145–47, 149, 283, 284, 291; of Göttingen, 158; in Habsburg Monarchy, 170–71; Hebrew University, 350; humanities studied in, 57, 58, 89, 157–58, 160; Jewish studies and, 121–22; Jews as professors in, 37, 56–57; Jews as unsalaried lecturers (Privatdozenten) in, 57; Jews denied positions in, 16, 57, 157–58, 159, 310, 327–28; of Königsberg, 156; law studied in, 57, 58–59; in Leipzig, 101; of Marburg, 158, 345, 354, 355; marriage to graduates of,

84; medicine studied in, 57, 89; middle class and, 66; of Munich, 158, 327–28; occupations requiring degree from, 37, 40, 54–60; of Prague, 56, 160, 170; in Prussia, 158; rural Jews in, 25; sciences studied in, 57, 157, 158, 160–61; of Vienna, 56, 89, 157, 160, 175, 299; women in, 86, 87, 88–90; Zionism and, 291; of Zurich, 87; *see also* Doctors; Lawyers; Technical colleges

Unwed mothers, 11, 95, 97, 98, 99, 100

UOBB, SEE B'nai B'rith

Upper class, 3, 62, 63, 64, 65–66; antisemitism and, 264; in Berlin, 33; as patrons of culture, 330–31; in Vienna, 16

Upper Hesse, 104

Upper middle class, 62, 66; family and, 76; immigrants and, 41; public life and, 269

Upper Silesia, 51

Ury, Lesser, 324–25

USPC, *see* Independent Social Democratic Party

vdJ, *see* Verband der deutschen Juden

vDST, *see* Association of German Students

vDST, *see* Verein Deutscher Studenten

Veit-Simon, Hermann, 300

Verband der deutschen Juden (Association of German Jews, vdJ), 140–41, 269, 302, 360; World War I and, 360, 361, 368

Verband der jüdischen Jugendvereine Deutschlands (Federation of Jewish Youth Associations in Germany), 150

Verband der Vereine für jüdische Geschichte und Literatur, *see* Federation of Societies for Jewish History and Literature

Verband orthodoxer Rabbiner (Association of Orthodox Rabbis), 116

Verband traditionell-gesetzestreuer Rabbiner (Association of Traditionally Observant Rabbis), 116

Verein Deutscher Studenten (Association of German Students, vDST), 207, 208, 239–40, 243, 249

Verein für Sozialpolitik, 201

Vereinigung für das liberale Judentum (Union for Liberal Judaism), 119–20, 300

Verein zur Abwehr des Antisemitismus, *see* Abwehr-Verein

Verfassungspartei, *see* Constitutional Party

Viadrina fraternity, 146, 253

Victoria Lyceum, 86

Vienna, 3, 386; antisemitism in, 16–17, 210–13, 226–31, 247–48, 262, 265, 292, 313; artisan movement in, 210, 212–13, 225, 226; baptisms in, 16–17, 52; class structure in, 64, 65; as cultural center, 311–13, 314; East European Jews in, 379; education in, 55, 56, 74–75, 87, 89, 312; elections in, 130; immigration and, 9, 22, 29, 31, 33, 64, 115, 312–13; Jewish community leadership of, *126*, 383; Jewish population in, 10, 31; Jewish residential area of, *33*, 33–34, *34*; Liberalism in, 270–71; occupations in, 36, 43, 52, 59–60, 162; Orthodox secession and, 115; public life in, 160, 194; rabbinical

seminary in, 113; religious life in, 82–83, 104, 109, 110, 115; University of, 56, 89, 157, 160, 175, 299; uprisings after World War I and, 383; World Zionist Congress in, 142; youth organizations in, 147
Vienna Circle, 160
Vienna Organized Jewish Community (Israelitische Kultusgemeinde, IKG), 261
Virchow, Rudolf, 265
Visual arts, Jews involved in, 4, 37, 42, 43, 309–10, 314, 324–26, 330
Vogelsang, Karl Freiherr von, 199, 200, 209, 212, 213, 229
Vogelstein, Heinemann, Rabbi, 112, 117–18
Völkerpsychologie, 344
Volunteer work: charitable activities as, 125, 131–34; women's movement and, 4, 86, 91, 95–102
Vorwärts, 276, 378
Vossische Zeitung, 192, 375
Voting: in Austria, 212, 226, 228, 236, 237; in cities, 128–30; elegibility and, 129, 130; Jüdischer Frauenbund and, 98, 99, 100; women and, 99, 129

Wachenheim, Hedwig, 75
Wagner, Adolf, 199
Wagner, Richard, 198, 239, 240, 246, 307, 359
Wahnschaffe, Arnold von, 382
Wahrmund, Adolf, 222
Waldersee, Alfred von, Field Marshal, 265, 266
Wallach, Oscar, 158
Wallich, Hermann, 189
Wandervögel (Hikers), 148, 241, 242
War, Jews' views on, 182–83, 273–74; *see also* Military service

Warburg, Aby, 37, 330
Warburg, Max, 266, 273, 368, 376, 382
Warburg, Otto, 142
Warburg Bank, 366
Warburg family, 50, 66, *74*
Wassermann, Jakob, 310, 315–16, *317*
Weber, Max, 253
Weibliche Fürsorge (Women's Relief), 96–97
Weininger, Otto, 288, 289–90
Welfare, *see* Charitable activity; Organizations; Social welfare
Welt, Die, 130
Weltsch, Felix, 350
Weltsch, Robert, 147, 313, 346, 350
Werner, Sidonie, 97, 100
Wertheim Brothers, 48
Wertheimer, Joseph von, 151
Westarp, Count Kuno von, 160, 166
Westphalia, 24; immigration to, 27; occupations in, 46; religious life in, 104, 107, 117–18
West Prussia, immigration and, 13, 27–28
White slave trade, Jewish, 97, 98, 99, 100
Wholesalers, Jews as, 43, 46, 48, 52
Wiener Allgemeine Zeitung, 187, 191, 218
Wiener Fabier Gesellschaft, 270–71
Wiener Kirchenzeitung, 199
Wiesinger, Albert, 199
William I, Emperor, 193, 265
William II, Emperor, 46, 65, 151, 223, 224, 247, 265–66, 307, 322, 330, 373, 374
Willstätter, Richard, 158, 309, 327
Wilmanns, C., 199
Wilmersdorf, 33
Winter, Georg, 255
Wissenschaft des Judentums, 112, 121–22, 131; in Hungary, 123

Withdrawals from Jewish community, 15, 16
Witkowski, Felix Ernst, *see* Harden, Maximilian
Witkowsky, Gustav, 269
Wittgenstein, Ludwig, 312, 329
Wolf, Karl Hermann, 236
Wolfenbüttel, 135
Wolff, Bernhard, 192
Wolff, Theodor, 58, 374–75, 376
Wolffsohn, David, 142, 291
Wolffson, Isaac, 190
Wolfskehl, Karl, 319
Wolfskehl, Otto, 180
Women, 85–102; baptisms among, 14, 17; charitable activities of, 132; culture and, 73, 74, 76–78, 307; education of, 4, 74–75, 76, 79, 85–91, *87*, 98, 101; education of children and, 72–73; in family, 70, 71–74, 76–78, *77*, 79–80, 81, 91, 99, 106, 307; Jüdischer Frauenbund and, 91, 97–100, 102, 140, 141, 142; kindergartens and, 100–101; occupations and, 4, 11, 37, 38, 39–40, *40*, 42, 43, 51, 60, 70, 71, 75, 76, 88–89, 90–95, 96–97, 98, 100, 102; religious life and, 3, 79–80, 81, 98–99; sisterhoods and, 141; in synagogue, 117; as unwed mothers, 11, 95, 97, 98, 99, 100; voting rights and, 99, 129; withdrawals from community among, 16; World War II and, 91–92, 102
Women's movement, 4, 86, 91, 95–102
Women's Relief, *see* Weibliche Fürsorge
Women's School of Social Work, 102
World League, 181
World War I, 276, 302, 322, 327, 337, 360–84, 388; antisemitism and, 360–61, 366, 370, 371–75, 378–84; Austria and, 361, 363–65, *366*, 368, 377, 379, 380, 383–84; civic truce and, 361–66, 370–78, 388; constitutional crisis of 1917 and, 373; immigration and, 20–21, 371, 378, 381; Jewish thought and, 336; Jews and German war aims policy and, 366–70, 375–76; Jews serving in, 22, 42, 361, *363*, *366*, *367*, 371–73; occupations and, 42; pacifism and, 373–77; patriotism of Jews and, 360–66, *363*, *366*, *367*, 371–73, 375–76; Peace Resolution and, 373, 375, 376, 378; poverty among East European Jews and, 64–65; women and, 91–92, 102; World Zionist Congress and, 142
World Zionist Organization (WZO), 142, 336
Worms, 81
Wurm, Emanuel, 276
Württemberg, 24, 25; community life in, 126; education in, 134–35; Jewish population in, 28; Jews as judges in, 155; legal equality in, 1; migration from, 29; religious practice in, 104; women working in, 94
Würzburg, 136, 138
WZO, SEE World Zionist Organization

Xanten ritual murder trial, 252, 255

Yeshiva, in Frankfurt, 112; *see also* Schools, Jewish
Yiddish: East European Jews and, 295, 296; in Habsburg Monarchy, 168, 172, 173
Young Czechs, 232
Young Vienna movement, 311, 312, 314, 315

Youth movement, 142, 147–50; *see also* Fraternities; Youth movement, German
Youth movement, German, 147, 148; antisemitism and, 241; Wandervögel (Hikers) and, 148, 241, 242
Youth organizations, student organizations and, 145–47, *149; see also* Youth movement

Zadoc-Kahn, Grand Rabbi, 219
Zeitschrift für das gesamte Handelsrecht, 190
Zeitschrift für Demographie und Statistik der Juden (Journal for Jewish Demographics and Statistics), 8
Zentralwohlfahrtsstelle der deutschen Juden (Central Welfare Office of German Jewry), 100
Zentrum Party, *see* Center (Zentrum) Party
Zionism, 3, 4, 117, 124, 282, 287, 289, 290–304, 348, 387–88; Abwehr-Verein and, 255; Austrian, 299; Martin Buber and, 348–49, 357–58; Centralverein deutscher Staatsbürger jüdischen Glaubens and, 258, 300–4; in cities, 129; Hermann Cohen and, 357–58; cultural, 294–96, 298–99, 313, 314, 324, 326, 328, 348–49; Czechs and, 313; East European Jews and, 123; Hilfsverein and, 152; immigration and, 380;

Jewish press and, 130; Jewish thought and, 336–37; Liberal Judaism and, 117; liturgical innovations and, 118, 119; mixed marriages stopped by, 8; organizations and, 140, 141, 142–44, 148, 149, 258, 300–304; Orthodoxy and, 117, 120, 121; political, 291–93, 296, 348; Posen and, 166; proto-, 290–91, 293; scholarship and, 122; Social Democratic Party and, 277, 279; traditionalist and, 119; United States and, 369, 370; World War I and, 361, 364, 368, 369, 373; youth organizations and, 146, 147; *see also* Herzl, Theodor
Zionist Congresses, 142, 293
Zionistische Vereinigung für Deutschland (Zionist Union for Germany, zvfD), 142, 143, 296–97, 299, 368
Zionist Organization (zvfD), World War I and, 361
Zionist Union for Germany, *see* Zionistische Vereinigung für Deutschland
Zucker, Alois, 170
Zuckerkandl, Emil, 160
Zurich: immigration to, 28; University of, 87
zvfD, *see* Zionistische Vereinigung für Deutschland
Zweig, Arnold, 377
Zweig, Stefan, 364
Zwickau, 48